The Prosecution of Heresy

Collected Studies
on the Inquisition in Early Modern Italy

medieval & renaissance texts & studies

VOLUME 78

The Prosecution of Heresy

Collected Studies
on the Inquisition in Early Modern Italy

John Tedeschi

medieval & renaissance texts & studies
Binghamton, New York
1991

© Copyright 1991
Center for Medieval and Early Renaissance Studies
State University of New York at Binghamton

Library of Congress Cataloging-in-Publication Data

Tedeschi, John, 1931–
  The prosecution of heresy : collected studies on the Inquisition in early
  modern Italy / John Tedeschi.
      p. cm. — (Medieval & Renaissance texts & studies ; v. 78)
  Includes bibliographical references and index.
  ISBN 0-86698-089-X
  1. Inquisition—Italy. 2. Italy—Church history—Modern period.
  1559–   I. Title.   II. Series.
  BX1723.T43   1991
  272′.2′0945—dc20
                                                        90–41103
                                                           CIP

This book is made to last.
It is set in Bembo, smythe-sewn,
and printed on acid-free paper
to library specifications.

Printed in the United States of America

For Anne, Martha and Michael, Philip, Sara and David

With Love and Admiration

Contents

Illustrations

Introduction

The present collection of papers deals with the organization of the Roman Inquisition and the procedures that it followed after its reconstitution in mid-sixteenth century in the struggle to preserve the faith and eradicate heresy. The principal focus, on the operation of the institution itself, overturns some long-standing assumptions that generally have been associated with it. I argue that the Inquisition was not a drumhead court, a chamber of horrors, or a judicial labyrinth from which escape was impossible. The Supreme Congregation in Rome watched over the provincial tribunals, enforced the observance of what was for the times an essentially moderate code of law, and maintained uniformity of practice. While moral justice was impossible, given the presupposition of the Church that it had the right, even the duty, to prosecute those who differed in their religious beliefs, legal justice in terms of the jurisprudence of early modern Europe was indeed dispensed by the Roman Inquisition.

In trials conducted under its jurisdiction loose allegations were not permitted and accusers made their depositions under oath. To forestall charges stemming from personal animosities, since the names of prosecution witnesses were concealed, defendants were asked in advance to provide the names of individuals whom they considered their enemies. The records of the trial proceedings were provided to prisoners and to their lawyers in writing (with the names of deponents deleted) and an appropriate interval, varying from several days to a few weeks, allowed for the preparation of counter arguments and the summoning of friendly witnesses. Judicial torture, which was carefully circumscribed, might be applied only after the defense had made its case and where the *indicia*, the evidence, was compelling. No properly conducted inquisitorial trial commenced with the *rigoroso esamine*. The local bishop or his vicar, duly constituted members of a provincial inquisitorial court, had to concur in the decision and be present during the questioning.

Particularly in witchcraft proceedings, these and many other safeguards were in effect. Physicians were consulted to establish the *corpus delicti*, specifically to determine whether an illness or death might have had a natural cause before jumping to the assumption that a *maleficium* had been perpetrated. The search for the Devil's mark was unknown in the inquisitorial process, and the failure on the part of the accused to evince emotion or shed tears during the interrogation was considered of scant significance. Alleged participants at Sabbats were not allowed to implicate their accomplices, and the testimony of witnesses who suffered from poor reputations could not lead to the torture of the defendant. In serious cases, sentences pronounced by provincial tribunals were scrutinized by the Congregation of the Inquisition in Rome and implausible confessions which contradicted the defendant's testimony during the trial were deemed invalid. No witch was ever sent to the stake as a first offender if she showed the signs of repentance. Even in the extreme case of witches convicted of having caused a fatal injury, it was only Gregory XV, in 1623, in opposition to the prevailing tradition, who attempted to have the death sentence invoked. Relatively few encounters with the Inquisition ended at the stake. This was a fate reserved for the relapsed, the impenitent, and those convicted of attempting to overturn a few central doctrines of the Church. But even in these cases lesser forms of punishment often prevailed.

I suggest further that many aspects of modern criminal law were already in place in rudimentary form or were being introduced in the tribunals of the Roman Inquisition in the sixteenth century. The arraigned had the benefit of a defense attorney, including "public defenders" appointed by the court for the indigent, at a time when this figure did not exist in English law and was being relegated to a secondary role in civil French and imperial codes; confessions obtained extrajudicially were invalid; appeals could be and regularly were made to a higher court, namely the Supreme Congregation in Rome itself; first offenders were dealt with infinitely more leniently than recidivists. Imprisonment as a punishment, rather than merely for the purpose of custody during the trial, was introduced by the Inquisition, a consequence of the canonical prohibition against shedding blood, long before it was adopted by civil authorities at the close of the sixteenth century. Before that time, when pronouncing final judgment, secular courts could only choose from among several extreme alternatives. A sentence to life imprisonment (*carcere perpetuo*) by the Holy Office meant, as it does today, parole after a few years, generally three, subject to good behavior; but commutations after even briefer periods are frequently encountered. And house arrest, joined to work release programs and community service, was a common form of penal practice pursued by the Inquisition in its day.[1] Although abuses occurred at the level of the provincial courts, where the local officials were often overworked, undertrained, and even, occasionally, poorly motivated and unsuited for the task at hand, Rome intervened time and again to enforce acceptable procedure and punish negligent and ignorant judges. The flagrant abuses which beset even the supreme tribunal when Cardinal Carafa, the future Paul IV, was its dominant member, and during his reign as pope, 1555–1559, present a notable aberration in the history of the institution.[2]

This volume leaves unanswered many questions that will have to be confronted by future research. It represents only a modest first step toward the goal of explaining inquisitorial law. It does not attempt to make any serious comparisons with contemporary secular criminal justice, although Alfred Soman's exemplary studies of French criminal trials point to parallels by the seventeenth century with the situation described in these pages. Nor does it venture to examine side by side the Italian and the more famous Spanish Inquisition. Here too the results of recent scholarship suggest that similarities may outweigh the differences. Nevertheless, until a systematic comparative study of these institutions and laws is made, no truly definitive evaluation of the performance of the Holy Office will be possible. Except in the first essay where I do so in passing, I have not seriously touched upon the historiographical problem. I have not asked how the Inquisition came by its reputation for ruthlessness and arbitrary repression if indeed, for much of its existence, it pursued the standards of jurisprudence for which I have argued. The answer is undoubtedly complex.[3] In "Preliminary Observations" I suggest a number of factors that have played a role in perpetuating ancient stereotypes and misconceptions. Recently, I examined documents of inquisitorial provenance which had been used and published in an older study dealing with heresy in Mantua. The author, willfully or not, had incorrectly substituted *abbruciare* (to burn) for *abiurare* (to abjure) every time the word appeared in the text. And when a later writer felt compelled to speak of the "excesses" of the Mantuan Inquisition his source was this philologically garbled account. Clearly, self-perpetuating scholarship of this sort has not contributed to an objective analysis of the question.[4]

The papers that comprise this volume were written between 1971 and 1988 and have all been published before with the exception of "Inquisitorial Sources and Their Uses," which makes its first appearance here; they have been considerably revised and updated bibliographically. "The Organization and Procedures of the Roman Inquisition" has doubled in length. "Preliminary Observations on Writing a History of the Roman Inquisition," however, has been left in its original form, outside of minor corrections, the omission of the first note, and a few additions indicated in brackets. The paper is intended to show the state of scholarship on the Roman Inquisition some two decades ago when my research on the subject began, the considerations that led me to it, and the general directions that I envisioned future research ought to take. The progress that has been made in the ensuing period is discussed perceptively by Agostino Borromeo and Adriano Prosperi in the two surveys noted below.[5] Further testimony is provided by the abundant citations and references which fill the pages that follow. Nevertheless, despite the specific research on individual aspects of Italian inquisitorial organization and practice by such scholars as Albano Biondi, Agostino Borromeo, Andrea Del Col, Massimo Firpo, Adriano Prosperi, Giovanni Romeo, Luciano Osbat, and others, and the useful recent book-length surveys of selected major tribunals by a magistrate, Romano Canosa, all cited in the Select Bibliography, the critical, comprehensive *History* augured in "Preliminary Observations" remains to be written.

In the present volume I have attempted to minimize duplication among the papers by frequent recourse to cross-references. Data dealing with Italian archival repositories has been transferred from "Dispersed Archives of the Roman Inquisition" to "Toward a Statistical Profile." This does away with considerable repetition and brings greater coherence to the two pieces since the primary focus of the former is intended to be the inquisitorial records that have ended up in various European collections. However, some overlapping remains, intentionally, so that each of the eleven essays retains its autonomous quality and can be read independently of the others. The papers published here have generally met with a favorable reception and have been credited with clearing the air of some long-standing misconceptions and helping to inaugurate the new perspective in inquisitorial studies which characterizes much of the recent scholarship. One paper in the volume, the collaborative "Toward a Statistical Profile of the Italian Inquisitions" has gained a certain notoriety. It was the object of special discussion at a conference in Trieste in May, 1988 and received friendly criticism from Andrea Del Col on that occasion and in the pages of *Critica storica*.[6] He argues that the study is based not on the trials themselves, but on inventories of the trials, which are not uniform documents and were compiled by different hands at different historical moments without regard to a common set of criteria. Thus, the terminology differs from inventory to inventory. In the Venetian index, the work of two late nineteenth-century archivists, "Luteranismo" is the equivalent of "religious heresy," while in the Udine catalogues which are based on the judgments of a seventeenth-century inquisitor, the term indicates true Lutherans. As for the statistics themselves, the absolute figures are unreliable since they include not only trials but also denunciations which in many instances never led to formal criminal proceedings. My co-author and I fully accept the validity of these observations. Nevertheless, we remain convinced that our findings stand up in their general configurations, a fact conceded by Del Col and confirmed by other recent investigations, and are useful as far as they go. We were at the time of original writing and are still fully aware of the risks we incurred by basing our study on secondhand materials. But as a preliminary survey of the typology of crimes, as a measure of the relative intensity and rhythms of inquisitorial prosecution, and as a rough comparison of the respective preoccupations in given periods of the Spanish and Italian inquisitors, we feel that "Toward a Statistical Profile" retains its value.

It is a pleasure to acknowledge my debts to the many close friends and colleagues who provided invaluable assistance over the years and made possible the contributions gathered here. I especially wish to recognize the support, in the form of encouragement, references to materials that might otherwise have eluded me, or drafts of their own work received from Albano Biondi, Agostino Borromeo, J. M. De Bujanda, Jaime Contreras, Luigi De Biasio, Andrea Del Col, Robert Evans, Stefania Ferlin Malavasi, Massimo Firpo, Paul F. Grendler, Carlo Ginzburg, Richard Helmholz, Gustav Henningsen, Pier Cesare Ioly Zorattini, Patricia Jobe, William Monter, Mary O'Neil, Sergio Pagano, Adriano Prosperi, Antonio Rotondò, Anne J. Schutte, Lech Szczucki, and Manfred Welti. Other debts are acknowledged at appropriate places in the text.

The several conferences devoted to aspects of inquisitorial studies in which I have participated since 1978, the anniversary of the founding of the Spanish Inquisition, have provided fertile encounters and the opportunities for informal exchanges of information and insights. I am happy to be able to thank the organizers for making these fruitful meetings possible: Copenhagen-Skjoldenaesholm, 1978 (Gustav and Marisa Rey Henningsen); Rome-Naples, 1981 (Armando Saitta); New York City, 1983 (Angel Alcalá); Rome, 1983 (Fabio Troncarelli, Armando Petrucci); Stockholm, 1984 (Bengt Ankarloo, Gustav Henningsen); Madison, 1985 (Henry Kamen, Robert M. Kingdon); Chicago and DeKalb, 1985 (Stephen Haliczer); Ferrara, 1986 (Albano Biondi, Adriano Prosperi, Amedeo Quondam); Trieste, 1988 (Andrea Del Col, Giovanna Paolin); Wolfenbüttel, 1989 (Hans R. Guggisberg, Bernd Moeller, Silvana Seidel Menchi).

The Newberry Library in Chicago, my academic home for two decades, encouraged me to pursue my research and writing, provided me with the congenial atmosphere of its community of scholars, and placed its incomparable collections freely at my disposal. The Institute for Research in the Humanities at the University of Wisconsin-Madison awarded me a fellowship in 1976–1977 and research and travel funds in 1984–1985. A month-long grant-in-aid at the Huntington Library (1984) provided the opportunity for a startling discovery (which tied in directly to my then current research project on inquisitorial manuals, and which I describe in "Literary Piracy in Seventeenth-Century Florence"), in a collection that has always proclaimed itself almost exclusively a repository of English and American history and culture. The indomitable staff in the Department of Special Collections in the Memorial Library of the University of Wisconsin-Madison shielded me from the day-to-day duties of the Department, shouldered many of my responsibilities during this year of revisions, and saved me time and again from tragedy when I seemed permanently to have lost the entire production from the computer screen. The volume benefited greatly from a meticulous reading of the entire manuscript by Judith Sumner, Assistant Editor at MRTS.

Finally, my greatest pleasure comes in acknowledging what I owe to my wife Anne Christian Tedeschi. She stirred to action this otherwise diffident author, and read, criticized, and thereby immeasurably improved every essay when it appeared in its first incarnation.

Notes

1. C. Reviglio della Veneria compares inquisitorial judicial procedures with their modern counterparts in the Italian penal code in his "L'Inquisizione medioevale e la legislazione penale moderna," in *L'Inquisizione medioevale ed il processo inquisitorio*, 2nd ed. (Turin, 1951), Appendix 1, 163–98. The section first appeared in the *Revue internationale de doctrine et de législation pénale comparée* (1940). For a scholarly vindication of the medieval inquisitorial process, as opposed to the performance of papal inquisitors themselves, see now H. A. Kelly, "Inquisition and the Prosecution of Heresy: Misconceptions and Abuses," *Church History* 58 (1989): 439–51.

2. The imprisonment and prosecution of Cardinal Giovanni Morone is the most dramatic example of the Inquisition's disregard for due process in this period. M. Firpo and D. Marcatto are currently preparing a critical edition of the voluminous trial records (see Select Bibliography). The career of Paul IV has received attention recently from A. Aubert, "Alle origini della Controriforma: Studi e problemi su Paolo IV," *RSLR* 22 (1986): 303–55 and P. Simoncelli, "Inquisizione romana e Riforma in Italia," *RSI* 100 (1988): 5–125.

3. Both history and myth are dealt with brilliantly in E. Peters, *Inquisition* (New York and London, 1988).

4. The erroneous reading occurs in S. Davari, "Cenni storici intorno al tribunale della Inquisizione in Mantova," *ASL* 6 (1879): 547–65, 773–800, at p. 790, and is exposed by L. von Pastor, *The History of the Popes from the Close of the Middle Ages*, 40 vols. (St. Louis, 1898–1953), 17:322. E. Verga is the later writer who perpetuated Davari's error. See his "Il municipio di Milano e l'Inquisizione di Spagna, 1563," *ASL* ser. 3, 8 (1897): 86–127, at p. 88.

5. A. Borromeo, "The Inquisition and Inquisitorial Censorship," in *Catholicism in Early Modern History 1500–1700: A Guide to Research*, J. W. O'Malley, S.J, ed. (St. Louis, 1988), 253–72; A. Prosperi, "L'Inquisizione: verso una nuova immagine?," *Critica storica* 25 (1988): 119–45.

6. A. Del Col, "Problemi per la catalogazione e repertoriazione unificata degli atti processuali dell'Inquisizione romana," *Critica storica* 25 (1988): 155–63, with an appendix (163–67) by Mariangela Sarra Di Bert.

Bibliographical Note

"Preliminary Observations on Writing a History of the Roman Inquisition" originally appeared in *Continuity and Discontinuity in Church History, Essays Presented to George Huntston Williams on the Occasion of his 65th Birthday*, ed. F. F. Church and T. George (Leiden, 1979), 232–49. "The Dispersed Archives of the Roman Inquisition" was first published in Italian in the *Rivista di storia e letteratura religiosa* 9 (1973): 298–312, and in English in *The Inquisition in Early Modern Europe: Studies on Sources and Methods*, ed. G. Henningsen and J. Tedeschi in association with C. Amiel (De Kalb, 1986), 13–32. "Inquisitorial Sources and Their Uses" is unpublished. An abridged Italian version was prepared for the proceedings of the conference, "Gli Archivi dell'Inquisizione in Italia," Trieste, 18–20 May 1988, ed. Andrea Del Col and Giovanna Paolin. "Toward a Statistical Profile of the Italian Inquisitions" originally appeared in *The Inquisition in Early Modern Europe*, 130–57 in collaboration with William Monter and in Monter's *Enforcing Morality in Early Modern Europe* (London [Variorum Reprints], 1987) (the present revision is my work). "The Organization and Procedures of the Roman Inquisition" is a thoroughly revised and greatly expanded version of a piece that first appeared with the same title in French in the pages of *Commentaire* 8 (1985), no. 31: 845–55; in Spanish in *Inquisición española y mentalidad inquisitorial*, ed. A. Alcalá (Barcelona, 1984), 185–206; and in the English version of the same work, *The*

Spanish Inquisition and the Inquisitorial Mind (Boulder, 1987), pp. 187–215. An expanded version, with a different focus, entitled "Inquisitorial Law and the Witch," was published in *Early Modern European Witchcraft: Centres and Peripheries*, ed. B. Ankarloo and G. Henningsen (Oxford, 1990), pp. 83–118. It appeared earlier in the Swedish version of these conference proceedings, *Häxornas Europa 1400–1700. Historiska och antropologiska studier* (Lund, 1987), 83–108. "The Roman Inquisition and Witchcraft" was published first in English in the *Revue de l'Histoire des Religions* 200 (1983): 163–88 and in a corrected Italian version in the *Annuario dell'Istituto Storico Italiano per l'Età Moderna e Contemporanea* 37–38 (1985–86): 219–41. "The Question of Magic and Witchcraft" appeared in *The Proceedings of the American Philosophical Society* 131 (1987): 92–111. It was preceded by an Italian version in *La città dei segreti: Magia, astrologia e cultura esoterica a Roma (XV–XVIII)*, a cura di F. Troncarelli (Milan, 1985), 78–95. "Literary Piracy in Seventeenth-Century Florence" was published first in *The Huntington Library Quarterly* 50 (1987): 107–18. "Florentine Documents for a History of the *Index of Prohibited Books*" originally appeared in *Renaissance Studies in Honor of Hans Baron*, ed. A. Molho and J. Tedeschi (Florence and DeKalb, 1971), pp. 577–605. "A Sixteenth-Century Italian Erasmian and the *Index*" was published in *Essays Presented to Myron P. Gilmore*, ed. S. Bertelli and G. Ramakus, 2 vols. (Florence, 1978), 1:305–15. "Northern Books and Counter-Reformation Italy" appeared in *I Valdesi in Europa*, Collana della Società di Studi Valdesi, 9 (Torre Pellice, 1982), 151–64.

Abbreviations

ACAU	Udine, Archivio della Curia Arcivescovile
AFP	Archivum Fratrum Praedicatorum
ASL	Achivio Storico Lombardo
ASRSP	Archivio della Società Romana di Storia Patria
ASV	Venice, Archivio di Stato
BA	Bologna, Biblioteca dell'Archiginnasio
BAV	Biblioteca Apostolica Vaticana
BN	Bibliothèque Nationale
BODL	Oxford University, Bodleian Library
BRB	Brussels, Bibliothèque Royale
BSSV	Bollettino della Società di Studi Valdesi
DBI	Dizionario Biografico degli Italiani
NRS	Nuova Rivista Storica
RSCI	Rivista di Storia della Chiesa in Italia
RSI	Rivista Storica Italiana
TCD	Dublin, Trinity College Library
Ill.mi	Illustrissimi
N.ro	Nostro
N.S.	Nostro Signore
R. mo	Reverendissimo

R.tia	Reverenza
Sig.ri	Signori
S.re	Signore
SS.ri	Signori
S. S.tà	Sua Santità
S.to	Santo
V.P.M.R.	Vostra Paternità Molto Reverenda
V.ra	Vostra
V.R.	Vostra Reverenza
V.S.	Vostra Signoria

The Prosecution of Heresy

ONE

༄

Preliminary Observations
on Writing a History of the Roman Inquisition*

The idea of the "History" probably dates to my first serious encounter with great quantities of inquisitorial documents at Trinity College, Dublin in the summer of 1967.[1] My original intention, as I began to forage through this important manuscript collection, was to calendar the sixteenth- and early seventeenth-century materials, consisting of sentences pronounced by the Roman and provincial Italian tribunals of the Holy Office. At this time I was interested in the suspects: who they were, the heresies they had espoused, the books they had possessed or read. I was pursuing a scholarly interest in the Italian Protestant reformers first kindled by George Williams during my years in graduate school.

My attention began to wander to other things: monastic or house arrest as the prevailing forms of imprisonment, the weight given to extenuating circumstances and the opinions of learned legal advisers, the relative mildness of witchcraft proceedings, the large number of cases that terminated with abjurations on cathedral steps, and the infrequency of capital punishment. I became sidetracked. A picture of Inquisitorial justice began to form in my mind which differed from the traditional view I had always naturally accepted and which is commonly associated with Henry Charles Lea's *A History of the Inquisition of the Middle Ages*. Although Lea's monumental study is addressed to the workings of the institution in a period earlier than my own, it enters a sweeping indictment which was intended to apply also to the sixteenth century: "A few words will suffice to summarize the career of the medieval Inquisition. It introduced a system of jurisprudence which infected the criminal law of lands subjected to its influence, and rendered the administration of penal justice a cruel mockery for centuries."[2]

A change in my thinking occurred very gradually. I can still remember my reaction toward the beginning of my work on the Dublin documents upon encountering this sentence pronounced at the conclusion of a trial: ". . .and because you have conducted yourself more openly and sincerely than the others in confessing your errors, it seems proper for us to proceed against you with greater mercy. . . ."[3] The offender was condemned to a *carcere perpetuo.* I was appalled. If this was mild treatment what did inquisitors do when they were severe? Later, I discovered why the judges in this case thought they were dealing mercifully by sentencing this individual to what seemed to be life imprisonment. Inquisitorial manuals are unanimous in their opinion that this sentence should be commuted, when the convicted heretic had shown signs of real contrition, after a lapse of three years.[4] The failure to understand inquisitorial terminology has misled more than one well-intentioned scholar and has contributed to the ill-fame of the institution.[5]

If a tentative new perspective was one factor that helped to persuade me of the importance of studying the Inquisition, the second was the fact that, despite the current active interest in the Catholic Reformation and Counter-Reformation, the Roman Inquisition has been generally ignored by modern scholarship. No one, to the best of my knowledge, has approached the organization and procedures of this institution as subjects worthy of critical study on their own account. Of the fifty-four articles which comprise the first *Festschrift* for Hubert Jedin, not one deals with the Inquisition.[6] The two volumes which cover the Counter-Reformation in the authoritative Fliche and Martin, *Histoire de l'Eglise* devote a grand total of six and one half lines to it,[7] and there are only a few words on the subject in the apposite volume of Jedin's otherwise comprehensive manual of church history.[8] The Inquisition fares no better in the distinguished histories of this period by Dickens and O'Connell.[9] The ample historiographical survey by Eric Cochrane fails to turn up a single work on this subject or a single reference to research in progress.[10] The Inquisition apparently was not deemed sufficiently controversial to warrant discussion in a recent symposium volume devoted to religious "problems" in sixteenth-century Italy.[11] Not one recent title is listed in Van der Vekene's admittedly lacunous bibliography[12] or in Bell's survey of current research in legal history.[13] One can also search in vain the published proceedings of recent congresses devoted to the history of law[14] or such publications on ecclesiastical law in particular as *Studia Gratiana* or the *Bulletin of Canon Law*. Enormous erudition is brought to bear in the pages of these scholarly journals to explicate minute points of legal doctrine, and yet the Inquisition, which immediately comes to mind when one thinks of the administration of justice by the Catholic Church in the medieval and early modern periods, is studiously ignored. One would also never guess leafing through such volumes interested in Dominican and Franciscan history as the *Archivum Fratrum Praedicatorum* and the *Archivum Franciscanum Historicum* that staffing the tribunals of the Holy Office had been the exclusive responsibility of these two mendicant orders. When a recent study mentions "a field of scholarship as well-tilled as the Inquisition under the pontificate of Paul IV"[15] it is not able to support this statement by referring to a single work published since 1959; and in all the writings cited, the diffusion of Protestantism in Italy, and not the Inquisition, is the real subject of investigation.

For the moment our knowledge of the organization and procedures of the Roman Holy Office is still largely based on the general chapters devoted to it in Pastor's *History of the Popes*;[16] on the old and diffuse studies of provincial tribunals by Battistella,[17] Fumi[18] and Amabile;[19] on the brief sketch in Niccolò del Re's survey of the Roman Congregations;[20] on the somewhat apologetic observations in Angelo Mercati's editions of the trials of Giordano Bruno and Niccolò Franco;[21] and, above all, on the precious information that can be gleaned from almost every page in several writings by Luigi Firpo, especially in his important reconstruction of the trial of Giordano Bruno.[22] Inquisitorial sources have been relied upon heavily by students of Italian heresy, witchcraft, popular religion, and censorship of the press. Extremely useful insights into the administration of inquisitorial courts are furnished *indirectly* by the exemplary studies and documents published recently by such scholars as Aldo Stella,[23] Antonio Rotondò,[24] Carlo Ginzburg,[25] Valerio Marchetti,[26] Paul Grendler,[27] and Pasquale Lopez,[28] among others.

In the light of the many modern works devoted to the Jesuits and other religious orders, to the Council of Trent, to the reforming measures of the episcopacy, and to the nunciatures,[29] the neglect which surrounds the

Roman Inquisition is indeed curious. This cannot be explained in terms of its relative unimportance. On the contrary, in the sixteenth century it held a place of honor among the various bodies and programs which were called into being or revitalized by the Catholic Church as bulwarks against the spread of heresy and as agents of reform. Cardinals vied with one another to secure appointments as members of the Holy Office,[30] quite understandably when one thinks of the succession of sixteenth- and early seventeenth-century popes who served apprenticeships as inquisitors.[31] The construction of St. Peter's was brought to a standstill and its workforce diverted to speed the completion of the new palace of the Holy Office begun by Pius V in 1566.[32] This position of pre-eminence received formal recognition in 1588 when Sixtus V elevated the Inquisition to the first position among the fifteen departments or congregations into which papal government was divided.[33]

Nor can this neglect by current scholarship be explained in terms of the relative inactivity of the institution. On the contrary, the full involvement of the Roman tribunal and its provincial chapters in the conflicts and controversies of the age is attested by the voluminous nature of the surviving records. Despite the fact that the archive in the palace of the Holy Office remains, with isolated exceptions, barred to scholars, we possess in abundance the sources necessary to undertake the study of the Roman Inquisition. A full discussion of the many different types of primary materials which may be considered pertinent occupies a central place in my ongoing investigations. For the moment I should like only to call attention to the obvious sources of direct inquisitorial provenance: the thousands of trials surviving in the libraries and archives of Bologna, Modena, Naples, Udine, Venice, and elsewhere; the hundreds of sixteenth- and seventeenth-century sentences in Trinity College, Dublin; the correspondence between the Roman Congregation and several provincial inquisitors preserved in a number of repositories (virtually intact from the year 1571 onward in the case of Bologna); the many memoranda, *pratiche*, summaries of proceedings, and decrees copied for the personal use of high officials of the Holy Office which, with the rest of their papers, found their way into various public libraries and archives in Italy and abroad; newly discovered inquisitorial archives, such as in Siena and Pisa; or those finally made accessible, such as the *fondo Inquisizione* in the Curia Arcivescovile, Naples.[34]

Studies on the medieval phase of the Inquisition seem to have been more plentiful;[35] but this does not justify, and cannot be used to explain, the absence of attention to the restructuring of that body which Paul III set in motion in 1542. The Inquisition, far from being a monolithic structure, was an institution which experienced development and change in terms of organization, procedures, and definitions of the law throughout its long history. The two stages, medieval and modern, must not be understood as a single phenomenon.[36]

Though the Roman Inquisition has never been studied for its own sake, numerous writers have discussed "the Inquisition" and have used sources connected with its activity in their research. Although several were dealing with the medieval Inquisition, they made sweeping generalizations, as did Lea, intended to encompass also the later history of the institution.[37] The results are confusing. Serious scholars—I am excluding from consideration sensationalist writers and apologists—[38] can be found taking diametrically opposed positions on almost every imaginable issue. Their disagreement ranges from such specific and readily verifiable questions as whether defense counsel was permitted in trial proceedings,[39] to broader ones such as whether the Spanish and Italian inquisitors of the sixteenth and seventeenth centuries were agents fueling the witch persecutions or were among the few not sharing in the excesses;[40] whether, in fact, the administration of law by the Inquisition was a mockery and perversion of justice or, by contemporary standards at least, a painstaking and honest effort to reach a correct verdict.[41] The confusion is compounded when we encounter contradictory points of view in the works of single individuals.[42] The issue is complicated further because some of these writings do not always meet the critical standards one expects in serious works of history. They misuse sources,[43] fail to substantiate claims,[44] and, on rare occasions, even seem to be perpetrating willful distortions.[45] It is difficult to imagine a situation in modern scholarship where greater uncertainty prevails, where the sure and fixed guidelines are so few. The unresolved disputes which continue over these questions also must be counted among the reasons which led me to undertake the specific study of the phenomenon known to history as the Roman Inquisition, in its sixteenth- and seventeenth-century form.

One of the principal assignments of my research, then, has been to analyze the surviving evidence, as it exemplifies both theory and practice, at first hand, and to examine step by step, from the initial summons to its final disposition, the unfolding of a trial before an inquisitorial court.

I have come to the conclusion that, while *moral* justice was impossible in a context where the Catholic Church felt, together with virtually all other secular and religious authorities on both sides of the Alps, that it had the right, even the duty to persecute those who differed in their religious beliefs, *legal* justice in sixteenth-century terms was dispensed by the Roman Inquisition. It was not a drumhead court, a chamber of horrors, or a judicial labyrinth from which escape was impossible. Capricious and arbitrary decisions, misuse of authority, and wanton abuse of human rights were not tolerated.[46] Rome watched over the provincial tribunals, enforced the observance of what was for the times an essentially moderate code of law,[47] and maintained, to the extent that a consensus existed, uniformity of practice.

It may not be an exaggeration to claim, in fact, that in several respects the Holy Office was a pioneer in judicial reform. The defense attorney was an integral part of Roman trial procedure[48] at a time when he played only a ceremonial role in the great imperial legal code, the *Constitutio Criminalis Carolina* (1532)[49] and was being deliberately excluded by the French Ordinance of Villers-Cotterets (1539).[50] In England felons were denied the right to counsel until 1836.[51] Whereas in inquisitorial courts the defendant received a notarized copy of the entire trial (with the names of the prosecution witnesses deleted) and was given a reasonable period of time to prepare his reply to the charges,[52] in secular courts the evidence against him was read and he had to make his defense on the spot.[53] Skepticism in regard to witchcraft invaded Roman legal circles at a time when other parts of Europe remained in the grip of a witchhunting mania. Not least among the reasons which spared Italy the epidemics of bloody persecutions which ravaged northern Europe from the late sixteenth through much of the seventeenth century, was the insistence by the Inquisition that the testimony of a suspected witch was of extremely limited validity as a basis for prosecution against others. Judges were instructed, for example, to discount testimony of a witch against persons whom she named as participants at Sabbats since it was assumed that frequently they were transported to these nocturnal reunions not physically but in illusions inspired by the Devil.[54] And, if it is true, as John Langbein asserts in his book, *Prosecuting Crime in the Renaissance*, that the beginning of imprisonment for punishment, rather than for the purpose of custody during the trial, can be traced back on the continent only to the closing decades of the sixteenth century, then the Inquisition, through its centuries-long practice of incarcerating *ad poenam*, must be regarded also as a pioneer in the field of penology, at a time when secular judges, in pronouncing sentence, had as alternatives only the stake, mutilation, the galleys, and banishment.[55]

The Roman Inquisition needs to be studied as a legal system, in its organizational and judicio-procedural aspects. The composition of the central tribunal in Rome and of its provincial branches, and the qualifications and backgrounds of the officials who staffed them should be examined, together with the establishments which housed them and their means of support. Attention should be given to the crucial jurisdictional issues and resulting tensions, as they manifested themselves in several different ways: in the relationship of the Inquisition to the episcopal courts, with whom the former enjoyed an ancient but uneasy association;[56] to the secular tribunals who were, at least in theory, relegated to a position of inferiority but who disputed the jurisdiction of the Holy Office in such cases as witchcraft, sorcery, blasphemy, and bigamy where the heretical implications of the crime frequently were difficult to establish;[57] to secular rulers at whose pleasure the Inquisition functioned, if it was permitted to function at all, outside the papal states;[58] to the Franciscans and Dominicans who controlled the convents where the local Inquisitions had their quarters and to whose officials inquisitors remained bound by the rules of their order;[59] and, finally, in the relationship between Rome and the local inquisitorial courts. The extent of the authority possessed by the latter to act independently of the supreme tribunal, at least in so-called routine matters, was the subject of recurring discussion and recrimination.[60]

Examination of the judicial side of the inquisitorial system needs to focus especially on those issues, connected with the definition of heresy as a public, capital, or "excepted" crime, which introduced important procedural disabilities (of which one of the most famous perhaps was the concealment of the names of prosecution witnesses), intended to favor the prosecution in support of the interests of the faith.[61] Whether these exceptions had this effect in reality, when offset by compensating safeguards,[62] whether they were consistently employed in the Roman courts, is not so certain. Even Lea spoke of "theoretical severity and practical moderation."[63] Moreover, jurists were unanimous that in view of the seriousness of the crime of heresy, the gravity of the consequences, and the exceptions in the legal procedure, proof of guilt had to be without question, clearer than the light of mid-day.[64] There were some who did not hesitate to assert that it was preferable to allow the guilty to go unpunished rather than to see an innocent person condemned.[65] In no case should the disabilities be permitted to impair the conduct of proper and legitimate proceedings.[66]

The attempts of succeeding generations of lawyers to accommodate theories, hammered into being under the stress and violent conditions of the thirteenth century, to a more rational and equitable system of law,[67] as well as their attempts to reconcile contradictory opinions are, in my opinion, among the more interesting findings emerging from this research. Inquisitorial law was not always uniform and its manuals not necessarily unswerving procedural guides. I have encountered many issues where a precise definition was not attained, over which jurists of equally great reputation disagreed,[68] where the practice of Rome differed in some instances, but not in others, from the opinions of such revered authorities as Iacobo Simancas (d. 1583), resulting in predictable uncertainty and confusion for the practicing judge.[69]

Above all, it must be recognized that there was development and change in the interpretation of legal procedure. Those modern scholars are in error, for example, who assume that the notorious *Malleus Maleficarum*, the work of two German Dominicans first published in 1486, remained "the standard manual for the persecutors of the next two centuries, not only in Catholic but in Protestant countries as well."[70] On the contrary, a philosophy entirely opposed to that of the *Malleus* was gaining ascendancy in the tribunals of the Holy Office throughout the second half of the sixteenth century and was made normative thanks to the *Instructio pro formandid processibus in causis strigum, sortilegiorum & maleficiorum* which began to circulate in manuscript at least as early as 1624 and was incorporated into the *Sacro Arsenale* (beginning with the edition of 1625), the most widely followed Italian inquisitorial handbook of the age.[71] At the close of the sixteenth century, even Martinus Del Rio, an unquestioning enemy of witchcraft, had separated himself from many of the teachings pronounced by the *Malleus Maleficarum* a hundred years before.[72]

A reappraisal of the Inquisition should not gloss over its many weaknesses and deficiencies, the chief of which, perhaps, was the fact that the entire legal fabric patiently constructed over several centuries, in practice, if not in theory, was at the mercy of one man, the pope. During the pontificate of that zealous persecutor, Paul IV (1555–1559), due process was placed under an almost unbearable strain, and the Church during his reign did fall into the grip of a witchhunting mentality. Paul gladly would have departed from strict judicial procedure and would have exchanged the seemingly endless deliberations for more summary forms of justice.[73] Although many of his excesses disappeared with him there is no doubt that they must be counted among the factors contributing to the unfavorable reputation which the Holy Office has endured for centuries.

The results of a careful examination of inquisitorial procedure and law should be useful not only to legal historians, but also to those seeking to bridge the gap between seemingly irreconcilable views of the Roman Church in the sixteenth century.[74] Our understanding of the Counter-Reformation necessarily must be affected by any new light cast on one of its most controversial institutions.

Notes

*Except for a few minor corrections and changes the present text is an unrevised version of the paper originally published in the *Festschrift* honoring George Huntston Williams. No attempt has been made to update the notes and bibliography. Occasional cross-references to materials in this volume are placed in square brackets. It is my intention here to describe the state of inquisitorial studies when I began my research over twenty years ago and the factors which led me to it. See p. xii of the Introduction.

1. The Dublin documents (henceforth abbreviated TCD) are part of the valuable materials removed by the French in the early nineteenth century from Roman archives. [For a full account of their provenance and contents, see "The Dispersed Archives of the Roman Inquisition," pp. 25 ff. in this volume.]

2. *A History of the Inquisition of the Middle Ages*, 3 vols. (New York, 1888; reprint, 1955), 3:650.

3. TCD, vol. 1224, fol. 201: "Et perchè tu sei proceduto più liberamente et sinceramente de gli altri nel confessare gli errori tuoi, ci pare ancora conveniente usarti magiore misericordia. . . ." The sentence is against the Bolognese Antonio de' Ludovisi and is dated Rome, 21 September 1567.

4. See, among many others, I. Simancas, *De Catholicis Institutionibus* (Rome, 1575), 113: "Solet praeterea poena perpetui carceris post lapsum triennii plerumque remitti, si eo tempore vincti humiles et veri poenitentes fuerint." I was fortunate to find Ludovisi mentioned in letters (28 August and 25 September 1574) addressed by the Roman tribunal to the Bolognese inquisitor asking about his behavior and

ordering his release from monastic confinement. In Ludovisi's case the "life sentence" lasted six years: BA, MS. B–1860, fol. clxlv, clxxxxviiii.

5. See, for example, F. Gaeta, "Documenti da codici vaticani per la storia della Riforma in Venezia," *Annuario dell'Istituto storico italiano per l'età moderna e contemporanea* 7 (1955): 5–53, at p. 7, discussing a carpenter arrested in Venice in 1533: ". . .il 9 e il 10 maggio egli è arrestato e le porte della prigione non gli si apriranno mai più, perchè il 6 giugno dell'anno seguente verrà condannato *ad perpetuos carceres.*"

6. E. Iserloh & K. Repgen, eds., *Reformata Reformanda: Festgabe für Hubert Jedin zum 17. Juni 1965*, 2 vols. (Münster, 1965).

7. L. Cristiani, *L'Église à l'époque du Concile de Trente* (Paris, 1948); L. Willaert, *Après le Concile de Trente: La Restauration Catholique, 1563–1648* (Paris, 1960), 56.

8. *Handbuch der Kirchengeschichte: IV. Reformation, Katholische Reform und Gegenreformation* (Freiburg, Basel, Vienna, 1967), 509.

9. A. G. Dickens, *The Counter Reformation* (London, 1968), 106; it contains only a few sentences based on the account in B. J. Kidd, *The Counter-Reformation, 1550–1600* (London, 1933), 42 ff.; M. R. O'Connell, *The Counter-Reformation, 1559–1610* (New York, 1974) where the Inquisition is mentioned in passing but nothing is said about its activities. Other agencies of the Roman Church (Jesuits, Council of Trent, Nunciatures) are discussed in the bibliographical essay, but not the Holy Office.

10. "New Light on Post-Tridentine Italy: A Note on Recent Counter-Reformation Scholarship," *Catholic Historical Review* 56 (1970): 291–319. Cochrane laments that "the Italian phase of the Counter-Reformation is barely mentioned in most of the recent literature in English" (p. 292).

11. *Problemi di vita religiosa in Italia nel Cinquecento* (Padua, 1960) where the Inquisition does not even appear in the index.

12. E. Van der Vekene, *Bibliographie der Inquisition: Ein Versuch* (Hildesheim, 1963). [An expanded edition in two volumes appeared in 1982–83. See bibliography.]

13. H. F. Bell, "Research in Progress in Legal History," *American Journal of Legal History* 17 (1973): 66–84.

14. For example, the massive *La formazione storica nel diritto moderno in Europa*. Atti del Terzo Congresso Internazionale della Società Italiana di Storia del Diritto (Florence, 1977).

15. C. Cairns, *Domenico Bollani, Bishop of Brescia: Devotion to Church and State in the Republic of Venice in the Sixteenth Century* (Nieuwkoop, 1976), 121.

16. L. von Pastor, *The History of the Popes from the Close of the Middle Ages*, 40 vols. (St. Louis, 1898–1953), 12:503–13; 13:210–24; 14:259–318; 16:305–52, 478–82; 17:288–343, 400–404; 19:296–322; 21:192–97; 24:198–219. Pastor deals with the external history of the institution, not its judicial procedures. More useful, perhaps, is his edition of *Decreta*, decrees issued by the Inquisition in Rome during its weekly meetings, where the pope himself generally presided: *Allgemeine Dekrete der römischen Inquisition aus den Jahren 1555–1597: Nach dem Notariatsprotokoll des S. Uffizio zum*

ersten Male veröffentlicht (Freiburg i. Br., 1912) (originally published in the *Historisches Jahrbuch der Görres-Gesellschaft* 33 [1912]: 479–549).

17. A. Battistella, "Alcuni documenti sul S. Officio in Lombardia nei secoli XVI e XVII," *ASL*, ser. 3, 3, a. 22 (1895): 116–32; idem, *Il S. Officio e la Riforma religiosa in Friuli* (Udine, 1895); idem, *Processi d'eresia nel Collegio di Spagna (1533–1554): Episodio di storia della Riforma in Bologna* (Bologna, 1901); idem, "Notizie sparse sul Sant'Officio in Lombardia durante i secoli XVI e XVII," *ASL*, ser. 3, 17, a. 29 (1902): 121–38; idem, *Il S. Officio e la Riforma religiosa in Bologna* (Bologna, 1905).

18. L. Fumi, "L'Inquisizione romana e lo stato di Milano. Saggio di ricerche nell'Archivio di Stato," *ASL*, ser. 4, 13, a. 37 (1910): 5–124, 285–414; 14 (1910): 145–220.

19. L. Amabile, *Il Santo Officio della Inquisizione in Napoli: Narrazione con molti documenti inediti*, 2 vols. (Città di Castello, 1892).

20. *La Curia romana: Lineamenti storico-giuridici*, 3rd ed. (Rome, 1970), 89–100 (the account is taken from the beginnings to the reign of Paul VI).

21. A. Mercati, *Il sommario del processo di Giordano Bruno, con appendice di documenti sull'eresia e l'Inquisizione a Modena nel secolo XVI* (Vatican City, 1942); *I costituti di Niccolò Franco (1568–1570) dinanzi l'Inquisizione di Roma esistenti nell'Archivio Segreto Vaticano* (Vatican City, 1955).

22. "Il processo di Giordano Bruno," *RSI* 60 (1948): 542–97; 61 (1949): 5–59; reprinted separately with an index of names (Naples, 1949). In "Una relazione inedita sull'Inquisizione romana," *Rinascimento* 9 (1958): 97–102, Firpo published an account from an early seventeenth-century manuscript describing the composition and routines of the Supreme Congregation in Rome. A recent unpublished paper by him ("Due esecuzioni capitali di eretici a Roma nel 1595") presented at a historical meeting in Torre Pellice is described as "uno studio dei metodi inquisitoriali e delle procedure del Sant'Uffizio alla fine del Cinquecento": A. Olivieri, "Permanenze nella storiografia religiosa italiana: il XV Convegno di studi sulla Riforma e i movimenti religiosi in Italia (Torre Pellice, 1–3 settembre 1975)," *BSSV*, a. 96, no. 138 (1975): 131–48, at p. 144.

23. A. Stella's two monographs, *Dall'Anabattismo al Socinianesimo nel Cinquecento veneto* (Padua, 1967) and *Anabattismo e Antitrinitarismo in Italia nel XVI secolo* (Padua, 1969) are based on Venetian inquisitorial documents, as are his "Ricerche sul Socinianesimo: Il processo di Cornelio Sozzini e Claudio Textor (Banière)," *Bollettino dell'Istituto di Storia della Società e dello Stato veneziano* 3 (1961): 77–120; "Il processo veneziano di Guglielmo Postel," *RSCI* 22 (1968): 425–66. Disappointingly general is Stella's "L'Inquisizione romana e i movimenti ereticali al tempo di San Pio V," in *San Pio V e la problematica del suo tempo* (Alessandria, 1972), 65–82.

24. A. Rotondò, "Per la storia dell'eresia a Bologna nel secolo XVI," *Rinascimento*, ser. 2, 2 (1962): 107–54; "Nuovi documenti per la storia dell' 'Indice dei Libri Proibiti' (1572–1638)," ibid., ser. 2, 3 (1963): 145–211; *Camillo Renato, Opere, documenti e testimonianze*, Corpus Reformatorum Italicorum (Florence and Chicago, 1968), are

based primarily on documents preserved in the Archivio di Stato, Modena and the Biblioteca dell'Archiginnasio, Bologna.

25. Carlo Ginzburg has made effective use of inquisitorial sources preserved in the Archivio di Stato, Venice and in the Archivio della Curia Arcivescovile, Udine in his studies of sixteenth-century religious heresy and in his more recent pioneering work on Italian popular culture. About him see A. J. Schutte, "Carlo Ginzburg," *Journal of Modern History* 48 (1976): 296–315.

26. A part of Valerio Marchetti's important research on early Socinianism is now conveniently gathered in his *Gruppi ereticali senesi del Cinquecento* (Florence, 1975), based heavily on Sienese inquisitorial documents, a long lost *fondo* which he personally rediscovered. See his "L'Archivio dell'Inquisizione senese," *BSSV*, a. 93, no. 132 (1972): 77–83.

27. P. Grendler, *The Roman Inquisition and the Venetian Press, 1540–1605* (Princeton, 1977), based on inquisitorial materials in Venice, the Vatican, and other Italian and foreign archives. The judicial procedures of the Holy Office are not a central concern of the book and occupy only a few pages (42–62).

28. Ample use of inquisitorial documents, preserved primarily in the Archivio Storico Diocesano of Naples, *fondo* "Sant'Ufficio," is made by P. Lopez, *Inquisizione, stampa e censura nel Regno di Napoli tra '500 e '600* (Naples, 1974), a book which would be interesting to compare with Grendler's (see note above) in regard to sources, methods, and conclusions.

29. See Cochrane, "New Light on Post-Tridentine Italy," passim.

30. See the autobiography of Giulio Antonio Santorio, cardinal of Santa Severina, a senior member of the Holy Office: "Gli diedi [to Pope Urban VII] una nota dei Signori Cardinali e Consultori del Sant'Ufficio acciò non aggiungesse, ne mutasse senza saputa della Congregazione le persone, poichè molti pretendevano quel loco, si de' cardinali, come de' prelati . . .": cited from Newberry Library MS. Case 6A 35, fol. 862. [See also p. 84, n. 118 in this volume].

31. Pastor, *Popes*, passim: Marcello Cervini, Marcellus II (1555); Gianpietro Carafa, Paul IV (1555–59); Michele Ghislieri, Pius V (1566–72); Felice Peretti, Sixtus V (1585–90); Giovanni Battista Castagna, Urban VII (1590); Giovanni Antonio Facchinetti, Innocent IX (1591); Camillo Borghese, Paul V (1605–21). Adrian VI (1522–23) had served as Grand Inquisitor of Spain in 1516. [Ibid., 19: 626–28 for a list of the Cardinals of the Inquisition, 1566–1621, from the reigns of Pius V to Paul V inclusive.]

32. Pastor, *Popes* 17:289, quoting from a Roman *Avviso* dated 5 October 1566: "La fabrica della Inquisizione tuttavia si sollicita, et per formarla presto, hanno levato li muratori et scarpellini di S. Pietro, nel qual hora si fa niente."

33. By virtue of the Bull "Immensa Aeterni Dei," dated 22 January 1588. It is published in many collections. See C. Cocquelines, *Bullarum, Privilegiorum ac Diplomatum Pontificum Amplissima Collectio* (Rome, 1747), 4, pt. 4: 392–93.

34. [For a preliminary brief description, see "Toward a Statistical Profile of the Italian Inquisitions," pp. 109–10 in this volume.] On the Neapolitan documents, see

the articles by L. Osbat, "Sulle fonti per la storia del Sant' Ufficio a Napoli alla fine del Seicento," *Ricerche di storia sociale e religiosa* 1 (1972): 419–27; "I processi del Sant'Ufficio a Napoli: Alcuni problemi di metodo," in *La società religiosa nell'età moderna* (Naples, 1973), 941–61; "Un importante centro di documentazione per la storia del Mezzogiorno d'Italia nell'età moderna: L'archivio storico diocesano di Napoli," *Mélanges de l'École Française de Rome* 85 (1973): 311–59.

35. See, for example, the useful anthology of documents by K.-V. Selge, *Texte zur Inquisition* (Gütersloh, 1967) and the excellent editions of legal handbooks by A. Patschovsky, *Die Anfänge einer ständigen Inquisition in Böhmen: Ein Prager Inquisitoren-Handbuch aus der ersten Hälfte des 14. Jahrhunderts* (Berlin, 1975); and by L. Paolini, *Il "De Officio Inquisitionis": La procedura inquisitoriale a Bologna e a Ferrara nel Trecento* (Bologna, 1976).

36. One of the best ways I know to get at the differences between medieval and modern inquisitorial practices and teachings is to study closely the commentary by the noted curial jurist Francisco Peña (d. 1612), to his editions of the authoritative manual, the *Directorium Inquisitorum* by the fourteenth-century inquisitor of Aragon, Nicolau Eymeric. Peña never missed an opportunity to indicate the development and change from Eymeric's day to his own. For the various editions of this famous work, see E. Van der Vekene, *Zur Bibliographie des Directorium Inquisitorum des Nicolaus Eymerich* (Luxembourg, 1961); idem, "Die gedruckten Ausgaben des *Directorium Inquisitorum* des Nicolaus Eymerich," *Gutenberg Jahrbuch* (1973): 286–97. The recent French abridgment by L. Sala-Molins, *Le manuel des Inquisiteurs* (Paris, 1973) should be used with caution. On Peña see E. M. Peters, "Editing Inquisitors' Manuals in the Sixteenth Century: Francisco Peña and the *Directorium Inquisitorum* of Nicholas Eymeric," *The Library Chronicle* 40 (1974): 95–107 [see also pp. 53–56 in this volume].

37. J. B. Russell, *Witchcraft in the Middle Ages* (Ithaca, 1972), 158: "The principles by which the Inquisition would operate for centuries were established in the thirteenth." See also E. M. Peters, introduction to H. C. Lea, *Torture* (Philadelphia, 1973), xvii.

38. They are frequently, unwittingly, one and the same. See, most recently, J. A. O'Brien, *The Inquisition* (New York, 1973), a work which accepts uncritically the tales of horror associated with the Inquisition but tries to explain them in "the special context of medieval society, culture and tradition" (p. 3).

39. The denial of counsel to the defendant in Inquisitorial proceedings is asserted by Russell, *Witchcraft*, 158; Peters, introduction to Lea, *Torture*, xii, and many other writers. See W. Ullmann, "The Defense of the Accused in the Medieval Inquisition," *The Irish Ecclesiastical Record*, ser. 5, 73 (1950): 481–89, at p. 481: "Canonistic scholarship was unanimous in its demand that the accused must not be deprived of legal aid ... the inquisitor was bound to grant him legal aid in the person of a qualified advocate." See also below at nn. 48 and 67.

40. R. H. Robbins, introduction to *Catalogue of the Witchcraft Collection in Cornell University Library* (Millwood, 1977), xxvii: "The Inquisition continued to pro-

vide the intellectual and religious sanction for judicial murder, and issued many manuals on witch hunting throughout the seventeenth century." Cf. H. C. Lea, *Minor Historical Writings*, edited by Arthur C. Howland (Philadelphia, 1942), 3 (a letter from Lea to George Lincoln Burr): "It is a very curious fact which I have nowhere seen recognized, that in both Spain and Italy the Holy Office took a decidedly sceptical attitude with regard to the Sabbat and the *Cap. Episcopi.*, that preserved those lands from the madness prevailing elsewhere."

41. As spokesmen for the negative view, considered applicable also to the later Inquisition, see Peters, introduction to Lea, *Torture*, xvii; Russell, *Witchcraft*, 158; L. W. Levy, "Accusatorial and Inquisitorial Systems of Criminal Justice: The Beginnings," in *Freedom and Reform: Essays in Honor of Henry Steele Commager*, H. M. Hyman and L. W. Levy, eds. (New York, 1967), 16–54. For the opposite point of view, on the painstaking efforts made by sixteenth-century Spanish and Italian inquisitors to separate the innocent from the guilty, on their methods which were "honest, simple, and straightforward," see H. Kamen, *The Spanish Inquisition* (London, 1965), 173. In basic agreement are C. Roth, "The Inquisitional Archives as a Source of English History," *Transactions of the Royal Historical Society*, ser. 4, 18 (1935): 107–22, at p. 107; R. E. Greenleaf, *The Mexican Inquisition of the Sixteenth Century* (Albuquerque, 1969), 4; P. Grendler, *The Roman Inquisition*, 56.

42. See W. Ullmann, "The Defence," 486: "For the innocence of the accused was always taken for granted, so long as the prosecutor did not bring forth convincing proof of the defendant's guilt"; and see the contrary view by the same author in his introduction to H. C. Lea, *The Inquisition of the Middle Ages, Its Organization and Operation* (London, 1963), 29: "There is hardly one item in the whole inquisitorial procedure that could be squared with the demands of justice; on the contrary, every one of its items was a denial of justice or a hideous caricature of it."

43. There is a tendency on the part of several writers to see the aberrations as the rule. They hold up abuses on the part of provincial officials, against which Rome was reacting, as the normal and accepted *modus operandi*. For example, an investigatory commission sent out by Clement V in 1306 had discovered inhuman conditions in the prison of Carcassonne. Lea generalized from this: "Starvation, in fact, was reckoned as one of the regular and most efficient methods to subdue unwilling witnesses or defendants" (*History of the Inquisition of the Middle Ages* 1:142).

44. See, for example, H. C. Erik Midelfort, *Witchhunting in Southwestern Germany, 1562–1684: The Social and Intellectual Foundations* (Stanford, 1972), 19: "In fact, the Inquisition conducted trials in secret, used torture frequently, denied counsel or defense to the accused and demanded the names of accomplices." When one turns to the accompanying note (p. 234 n. 50) for the supporting documentation one finds only: "Actually, the sixteenth-century Italian and Spanish Inquisitions did conduct moderate witchcraft trials, since they forbade the use of torture to discover accomplices."

45. A recent glaring example of this occurs in R. H. Robbins, *Encyclopedia of Witchcraft and Demonology* (New York, 1974) which at pp. 267, 268, 270 reproduces

a series of torture scenes labeled "Horrors of the Inquisition," "Tortures of the Inquisition," and "More Tortures of the Inquisition," all "according to Samuel Clarke, *Martyrology* (1651)." The reader who troubles himself to actually consult Clarke's *Martyrology* will be surprised to find that there the illustrations are intended to depict something quite different. The subjects are, in turn, "The Tenth Primitive Persecution which began anno Christi 308"; "The Persecution of the Albigenses" (i.e., of the seventeenth-century Waldensians by the Dukes of Savoy); "The Persecution of the Church in France."

46. When abuses or inconsistencies in trial procedures were discovered the Supreme Congregation rarely failed to take corrective action. I can cite, among many other cases, a letter from Cardinal Pompeo Arrigoni, a member of the Roman tribunal, to the inquisitor of Bologna (29 July 1606; BA, MS. B–1863, fol. 34) which discusses the case of a certain Bartolomeo Betti. Betti had been tried in Ferrara but his case was ordered reopened and transferred to Bologna because the Roman officials, after a careful study of the proceedings, were "not satisfied with the confession made by Betti before the inquisitor of Ferrara and feared that it had been extorted from him *con mali modi.*"

47. To cite one example, in the procedure of the Holy Office witchcraft was treated as a category of heresy. This meant that the penitent first offender (one who had not formally abjured on a previous occasion) was permitted to be reconciled with the Church and generally punished with a prison sentence of short duration. And it was not until the decree *Omnipotentis Dei* issued by Gregory XV on 20 March 1623 that consignment to the secular arm (*debitis poenis puniendus*) was prescribed for the witch who had apostatized to the Devil and had caused injury or death through his or her *maleficii*. See *S.mi D.N.D. Gregorii Papae XV: Constitutio adversus Maleficia, seu Sortilegia Committentes* (Rome, 1623).

48. See, for example, Eymeric's *Directorium Inquisitorum*, 446: "Et sic concedentur sibi [to the suspect] advocatus, probus tamen, et de legalitate non suspectus, vir utriusque iuris peritus, et fidei zelator. . . ." And in the case of an indigent defendant, counsel had to be provided by the court. See the letter from a cardinal of the Roman Congregation to the inquisitor of Florence (16 August 1603; BRB MS. II 290, cod. 1, fol. 118): "Se per la povertà loro non haveranno il modo di fare la spesa dell'avvocato et procuratore, V. R. gliene proveda ex officio acciochè non restino indifesi." The inquisitor's obligation to the indigent extended to providing travel expenses for defense witnesses who might have to be summoned from distant parts. See E. Masini, *Sacro Arsenale, overo prattica dell'officio della Santa Inquisitione* (Genoa, 1621), 268.

49. See J. H. Langbein, *Prosecuting Crime in the Renaissance: England, Germany, France* (Cambridge, Mass., 1974), 189: An "orator" for the accused did not appear on the scene until the judgment day, "Rechttag," after the offender had been convicted.

50. Ibid., 313, Article 163 of the Ordinance: "In criminal matters the parties shall in no wise be heard through counsel or the agency of any one else, but they shall answer the charges of which they are accused through their own mouths. . . ."

51. D. Melinkoff, "Right to Counsel: The Message from America," in F. Chiappelli, ed., *First Images of America*, 2 vols. (Berkeley, 1976), 1:405–13, at p. 406, by provision of the "Prisoners' Counsel Bill." Until 1695 the same rule had applied to indictments for high treason.

52. On the defense phase of the trial (known as the *processo repetitivo*) as opposed to the prosecution phase (the *processo informativo*), see, among others, Masini, *Sacro Arsenale*, 85 ff., who emphasized the care with which the judge should govern the proceedings: "E perchè tal repetitione è molto difficile, dee con somma isquisitezza e diligenza maneggiare; perciochè da essa pende l'honore, la vita & i beni de' rei."

53. Langbein, *Prosecuting Crime*, 247. See also G. Cozzi, "Note su tribunali e procedure penali a Venezia nel '700," *RSI* 77 (1965): 931–52, at p. 945.

54. See, for example, the chapter "De Sortileghi" in the widely diffused inquisitorial manual, "Prattica per le cause del Sant'Officio," usually attributed to Cardinal Desiderio Scaglia (d. 1639), for many years one of the most influential members of the Roman Congregation: "Si procede contro li complici, eccetto contro quelli che esse dicono haver veduto nel giuoco ò tripudio. Sopra di che vi è decreto speciale del Supremo Tribunale che non si proceda contro essi potendo le deponenti ingannarsi circa le persone nominate per illusione del Demonio." BAV, Borg. lat., 660, pp. 29–42, at p. 39. [On the "Prattica" see pp. 229–58 in this volume.]

55. *Prosecuting Crime in the Renaissance*, 195. In a later work (*Torture and the Law of Proof: Europe and England in the Ancien Régime* [Chicago, 1976], 29), the earlier use of incarceration by the Church to punish crime is recognized.

56. Despite centuries of collaboration in the pursuit of heresy between bishop and inquisitor and thousands of pages written attempting to work out the rights and spheres of jurisdiction of each, doubts and confusion on the subject persisted to the end. See, for example, the interesting letter from the cardinal inquisitor d'Ascoli to the inquisitor of Bologna reprimanding him for his excessive cooperation with the officials of the episcopal court: ". . . essendo senza essempio che gl'Inquisitori dipendono da gl'ordinarii, o, faccin con essi un sol tribunale nelle cose della fede. . . ." (4 June 1588; BA, MS. B–1861, fol. 64).

57. See, for example, the compendium of inquisitorial procedure, BAV, Barb. lat. 1370, fol. 24: "Carcerati in S.to Officio non sunt interim pro aliis causis molestandi. . . .Causa S.ti Officii prius terminanda quam aliae." Individuals in a secular prison denounced to the Inquisition as suspected heretics had to be consigned to the latter immediately "aliorum criminum cognitione suspensa" (Bull of Pius V, undated but 1566, in Cocquelines, *Bullarum*, 4, pt. 2: 276). Secular judges were obliged to carry out sentences pronounced by the Holy Office without access to the trial records. See Peña's commentary in Eymeric, *Directorium Inquisitorum*, 563.

58. For instance, the Holy Office was never admitted into the Republic of Lucca and in Naples had to operate under the cloak of the episcopal courts. In Genoa, Savoy, Venice, and later in Tuscany lay officials either were members of the court, contrary to customary procedure, or interfered freely in given cases. In these states any serious action contemplated by an ecclesiastical judge, such as arrest, extradi-

tion of a suspect to Rome, and confiscation of property depended on the assent of secular authorities. There is no comprehensive modern study dealing specifically with these questions. For individual states, see G. Bertora, "Il tribunale inquisitorio di Genova e l'Inquisizione romana nel '500 (alla luce di documenti inediti)," *La civiltà cattolica* a. 104, 2 (1953): 173–87; M. Berengo, *Nobili e mercanti nella Lucca del Cinquecento* (Turin, 1965), chap. 6 "La vita religiosa"; V. Marchetti, *Gruppi ereticali*, passim; N. Rodolico, *Stato e chiesa in Toscana durante la reggenza lorenese (1737–1765)* (Florence, 1910), 182–266. For the vicissitudes of the Holy Office in Naples, Savoy, and Venice, see the apposite volumes of the *Nunziature d'Italia* in the course of being published by the Istituto Storico Italiano per l'Età Moderna e Contemporanea in Rome.

59. Inquisitors frequently complained that the heads of convents interfered with their duties. Priors accused inquisitors of needlessly taking advantage of their special positions to escape from the common discipline. Some of the problems and abuses existing in their relationship are discussed in an interesting letter from the Roman Congregation to the General of the Dominicans (4 September 1580; Pastor, *Allgemeine Dekrete*, 68–69). From a letter written to the inquisitor of Bologna by the *Commissario Generale* of the Roman Holy Office (28 July 1623; BA, MS. B–1866, fol. 119) one gains the impression that disaffection between provincial inquisitors and the rulers of convents was a general problem: "Sono molto pregiuditiali le liti e dissentioni non convenevoli che vertono fra gli Inquisitori e Priori alla riputatione della Religione, al buon governo de' conventi, et agli interessi proprii di essi." In the present case he ordered "che si dovesse correggere il P. Inquisitore di Modena, e cassare il Priore. . ." [See also p. 64 in this volume.]

60. Much ink was spilled by Rome trying to help its lower officials to distinguish what was ordinary from critical business. But the issue was never resolved satisfactorily. See the patient letter from Antonio Balduzzi, Commissioner of the Roman Congregation, to the inquisitor of Bologna (11 March 1573; BA, MS. B–1860, fol. 120) who had written asking to be instructed on the question. Balduzzi replied that it was impossible to make general rules and that the inquisitor's own judgment should be able to tell him how to regulate himself. [For the text see p. 69 n. 20 in this volume.]

61. O. Ruffino ("Ricerche sulla condizione giuridica degli eretici nel pensiero dei Glossatori," *Rivista di storia del diritto italiano* 46 [1973]: 30–190) describes the appropriation by canon law, beginning with the decretal *Vergentis in senium* (1199), of the Roman concept of *crimen maiestatis*.

62. See, for example, Masini, *Sacro Arsenale*, 283: "Essendo la facoltà che si dà al reo di difendersi in causa d'heresia in un certo modo manchevole, posciache non se gli fanno sapere i nomi de' testimoni, è necessario che le prove per convincerlo siano chiarissime e certissime."

63. *Materials Toward a History of Witchcraft*, arranged and edited by Arthur C. Howland, 3 vols. (Philadelphia, 1939; reprint New York, 1957), 2:952.

64. See, among many other authorities, C. Carena, *Tractatus de Officio Sanctissimae Inquisitionis et Modo Procedendi in Causis Fidei* (Cremona, 1642), 338: "Criminalistae

omnes clamant in criminalibus iuditiis probationes debere esse luce meridiana clariores . . . [when] de vita hominis agatur probationes clarissimae esse debent. . .''; *Repertorium Inquisitorum Pravitatis Haereticae* (Venice, 1575), 635: ''Quanto magis crimen est grave, maiores praesumptiones & evidentiora indicia requiruntur.''

65. ''. . .ad nullius vero condempnationem sine lucidis et apertis probationibus vel confessione propria procedatis. Sanctius enim est facinus impunitum relinquere, quam innocentem condempnare'' (from the fourteenth-century manual *De Officio Inquisitionis*, p. 139, cited above at n. 35, [quoting the Council of Narbonne (1243?)].)

66. Peña, in his commentary to Eymeric's *Directorium*, 583: ''Ordinem et solemnitates à iure alias requisitas non esse necessario observandas [in heresy trials]: ille tamen ommitendae non sunt quae ad substantiam causae spectant, hoc est illae, sine quibus nec iuste, nec recte aut commode negotium tractari posset.'' Among the essentials which could not be eliminated were those ''sine quibus aut vere delictum probari non posset, aut reus non posset se iure defendere.''

67. Jurists, for example, had to contend with the pronouncement of successive medieval popes: ''Concedimus, quod in Inquisitionis haereticae pravitatis negotio, procedi possit simpliciter et de plano, et absque advocatorum ac iudiciorum strepitu et figura'' (in Eymeric, *Directorium*, 111). Inquisitors circumvented the apparent prohibition of the defense attorney by distinguishing between the pertinacious ''haereticus'' who wanted to defend the validity of his heresy and the ''causa haeresis.'' See, for example, the *Repertorium Inquisitorum*, 35: ''Advocatus dandus est imputato de haeresi, nisi constet illum esse haereticum & in haeresi persistere. . . .''

68. Symptomatic of this uncertainty are the several briefing books, *pratiche*, listing precedents on questions of inquisitorial procedure, compiled from various sources, but usually from Rome's correspondence with provincial Inquisitors. One such is cited at n. 57.

69. For example, the teaching of the great Spanish jurist denying to the defense in trial proceedings the possibility of cross-examining the testimony of prosecution witnesses was in direct conflict with the practice of the Holy Office where ''sine dubio totum contrarium observetur'' (Carena, *De Officio Sanctissimae Inquisitionis*, 372). And yet, in a letter from the supreme tribunal in Rome to the inquisitor of Bologna (7 November 1573; BA MS. B–1860, fol. 160) the latter is reminded not to let himself be persuaded by anyone to ''fare cose nuove,'' that he should be cautious about proceeding to arrest a suspect ''come ben insegna il Simanca.''

70. G. Henningsen, *The European Witch-Persecutions*, DFS Translations 1 (Copenhagen, 1973), p. 12; also Russell, *Witchcraft*, 231.

71. The earliest evidence for its diffusion is a letter from Cardinal Millino of the Roman Congregation to the bishop and inquisitor of Lodi (9 May 1624; BAV, Borg. lat. 660, no. 130) accompanying a copy of the Instructions. The letter, itself a remarkable document, begins ''La materia de' maleficii è qui sempre stata stimata fallace, et incerta assai, come è in effetto . . .'' [On the *Instructio* see pp. 205–27 in this volume].

72. Del Rio, *Disquisitionum Magicarum Libri Sex* (Lyons, 1612), 323: ''Praxis vero

illa, quam Sprengerus ponit (p. 3 *Mallei* q. 14) ut damnetur non ad torturam iterandam, sed ad eandem alio die continuandam, & hoc posse fieri non ortis novis indiciis; mihi callidior, quam verior; et crudelior, quam aequior videtur."

73. Pastor, *Popes*, 14:306 n., quoting from Bernardino Pia's report on Paul's attitude toward the trial of Cardinal Giovanni Morone: "Dice [it is not clear to whom this refers] che el papa quattro dì sono bravò gagliardamente saper i casi suoi, che non occorrevano tanti processi, scritture ne giustificationi, ne servar termini, che saveva benissimo come si stesse il fatto, che esso era il giudice vero che senza altro poteva et doveva dar la sentenza et altri simili et terribili parole. . . ."

74. The leading Catholic scholarly spokesman for a negative assessment of Counter-Reformation religion is Romeo De Maio, for example in his *Riforme e miti nella Chiesa del Cinquecento* (Naples, 1973), whose views, John W. O'Malley justly observed (*Catholic Historical Review* 62 [1976]: 113–15), appear irreconcilable with the much more benign interpretation by another distinguished Catholic authority, H. O. Evennett (*The Spirit of the Counter-Reformation . . . Edited with a Postscript by John Bossy* [Cambridge, 1968]).

TWO

❧

The Dispersed Archives
of the Roman Inquisition

I t is well known and frequently lamented that the Archive of the Holy
Office in Rome is inaccessible even to serious scholars. Behind this obstruction of legitimate research there is nothing more sinister than
bureaucratic obstinacy and inertia, which time may overcome. Actually,
if the doors of the Congregation for the Doctrine of the Faith (formerly
the Inquisition) were to be thrown open tomorrow we probably would
not find terrible secrets; in fact, we would find relatively few documents,
mainly doctrinal decrees and the papers of the now defunct Congregation
of the Index, which were transferred to the palace of the Inquisition when
it discontinued its censorship activities in 1917.[1] The Archive of the
Holy Office was impoverished by several terrible depredations. The first
occurred on 18 August 1559, when a Roman mob celebrated the death
of Pope Paul IV by sacking the headquarters of his most cherished institution, liberating its prisoners and burning its records.[2] A second took
place more than two and a half centuries later when, to fulfill Napoleon's
dream of a central archive for the empire and a supra-national center of
learning in Paris, valuable books and manuscripts were removed from
libraries and archives of conquered Europe, including the Vatican.[3] More
than three thousand crates were distributed over several convoys; the first
set out from Rome in the dead of winter, February 1810, and attempted
the long and laborious journey over the Alps.[4] The convoys were accom-

panied by archivists of the Church, whose feelings we can imagine when they watched two wagons disappear into the rushing waters of a torrent at Borgo San Donnino, near Parma, or when eight cases slid into a canal on the road between Turin and Susa.[5]

An inventory of the foreign material which had ended up in Paris from the four corners of the empire was compiled in 1813 by Pierre Claude Daunou, Napoleon's archivist.[6] It is an incredible list. Roman depositories, for example, had been stripped of the contents of the Nunciatures, Dataria, Propaganda Fide, Penitenzieria, the entire series of acts and registers pertaining to the Council of Trent, and, of course, the trials, sentences, decrees, correspondence, dispensations, petitions, and doctrinal pronouncements that made up the archive of the Roman Inquisition.

Immediately after Napoleon's fall, Marino Marini, the archivist and papal commissioner who had accompanied these collections to Paris, began to arrange for their return to Rome. He was hampered by the lack of funds to pay for their transport. "We are not a spending ministry," he was summarily informed by the French minister of the interior who repeatedly refused financial assistance and eventually disbursed a sum sufficient to cover only a fraction of the total expenses.[7] Napoleon's brief restoration to power for the famous Hundred Days brought Marini's efforts to a standstill, and he obtained permission from his superiors to return to Rome. On 23 March 1816, Ercole Consalvi, the cardinal secretary of state, wrote to Count Giulio Ginnasi in Paris to resume Marini's work. To reduce the expenses of the transport as much as possible, Consalvi instructed him to forego the shipment of certain useless papers ("alcune carte che sono inutili"). And to assist the count in separating the valuable from the useless he included a list ("foglio di notizie") prepared by a Roman abbot, Domenico Sala.[8] On 9 June the secretariat of state circulated a memorandum to the various Congregations requesting them to specify what material formerly in their custody might be abandoned in Paris and, presumably, destroyed.[9]

The archivists of the Inquisition replied to Consalvi on 12 July and explained that although a large quantity of material had been recovered, the large codex that was the index to the Holy Office decrees on doctrine was still missing. Many other volumes that comprised this series were also still in Paris. These had to be returned at all costs. As for the rest, the trials and related papers which made up, in their estimation, roughly two-thirds of the transported material, these could be disposed of as His

Holiness saw fit.[10] Despite the guidelines that had been provided for him, Count Ginnasi's efforts left much to be desired. His sale of inquisitorial trials to the delicatessen shops of the city as wrapping paper for anchovies and sardines may have fallen within the purview of his instructions. But his failure to tear them up first proved to be a cause for embarrassment when a number of volumes fell into hostile hands; and his sale of hundreds of registers of papal Bulls belonging to the Dataria clearly was contrary to Consalvi's intentions. By the spring of 1817, roughly one year from Ginnasi's assumption of his duties, two convoys of archival material reached Rome. As their contents gradually came to light, great cries went up on all sides from the archivists of the Congregations. They complained, in the words of Consalvi's written rebuke to Ginnasi (18 May 1817), "that they had received the useless papers, and not those which were useful and necessary."[11]

There was nothing for the cardinal secretary of state to do but replace the hapless count. Marini was dispatched to Paris to organize the shipment of the remaining material. He succeeded in reclaiming a considerable portion of the archive of the Dataria alienated by Ginnasi, but he also sold another 2,600 volumes of inquisitorial trials as scrap to paper manufacturers. To guard against the kind of embarrassment suffered by Ginnasi, he had them shredded before they left their depository.[12] From Rome, Consalvi expressed his enthusiastic approval.[13] Later, Marini would inform Consalvi that his travel and maintenance were costing nothing to the Holy See. The sale of the Holy Office records more than covered the expenses.[14] Among the untold treasures that perished in Paris were the youthful writings of Tommaso Campanella and the defense testimony in the trials before the Inquisition of Giordano Bruno.[15]

Somehow, by ways that no one has as yet succeeded in explaining, a considerable body of this material became separated and was saved. Thirty-seven volumes containing trial proceedings fell into the hands of a group of French bankers who promptly offered them back for sale to the Church, threatening otherwise to turn them over to the liberal newspaper, *Mercure de France*. Rome, having little choice, made the purchase in 1819 and immediately eliminated the documents from public view.[16]

The largest portion of material, which first passed through the hands of the viscount Mandeville, later duke of Manchester, was acquired by Dublin's Trinity College in 1854.[17] The Dublin documents consist of nineteen volumes of sentences issued by the Roman or provincial Inquisi-

tions between 1564 and 1659.[18] Unfortunately, only four volumes deal
with the sixteenth century, spanning the years 1564–1568 and 1580–1582,
and containing approximately five hundred sentences.[19] They are almost
equally divided between documents resulting from proceedings before the
central tribunal in Rome and certified copies of sentences and recantations
pronounced in the outlying Inquisitions that had been forwarded to Rome
for the consideration of the Supreme Congregation. Sentences do more
than declare a defendant's guilt or innocence; they summarize in detail
the charges and sometimes even the responses to them. They frequently
run to many pages and, consequently, are often satisfactory substitutes
for the records of the complete trials, which, for the most part, perished
in Paris. Another thirty-five volumes at Trinity College contain progress
reports on litigation before provincial tribunals, which had been sent to
the Holy Office for its decision. They range in date from 1625 to 1789.[20]

Four volumes of criminal proceedings which originally belonged to the
archive of the Florentine Inquisition were purchased in 1878 by the Royal Library of Brussels from a painter, J. de Meerts, whom I have been
unable to identify. Recently they were transferred to the Archive of State
in Brussels.[21] The first two volumes contain exclusively letters directed
to the inquisitor of Florence by the cardinals of the Roman Congregation, dating roughly from 1580 to 1610.[22] They are grouped by subject
rather than by date, but I am uncertain whether this was their original
arrangement since they were rebound during the nineteenth century. Because the description of the contents of each section is furnished in Latin
on a covering sheet, it is likely that the scheme of grouping the documents by subject antedates their rebinding. I suspect that the letters, edicts,
and assorted documents were arranged thematically for handy reference
when a precedent on a given question might be needed.[23]

The pursuit of native Italian evangelicals had given way by the closing
years of the sixteenth century to vigilance against blasphemy, magic arts,
the relapse of *conversos*, and the circulation of suspended or prohibited books.
The Florentine documents reflect, as do those at Trinity College, the increasing dependence of the provincial courts on instructions from Rome.
By the end of the century, for example, interrogations under torture,
hedged in by many restrictions and precautions even in earlier periods,
rarely were conducted without the prior authorization of the central
tribunal. And this authorization was not granted until the cardinal inquisitors, assisted by their staff of canon lawyers and theologians, felt that
they were in full possession of all the facts in a given case.

The final two Florentine volumes contain trials and printed edicts of the seventeenth and eighteenth centuries, circulars prepared in Rome for the edification of the outlying officials.[24] The seats of the local tribunals were usually Dominican houses, but inquisitors were not necessarily their superiors. A theme of these documents is the insistence that the work of the inquisitor must not interfere with the good discipline and efficient operation of the convent and that under no pretext should an inquisitor use his office to avoid his duties and responsibilities as a brother.[25] A second theme is the demand for an accurate and scrupulous recording of even the most minute items of income and expenditure. The fierce "black and white watchdogs" of the faith (as inquisitors liked to refer to themselves, from the colors of their Dominican garb) were in peril of being transformed into a class of bookkeepers and accountants.[26]

A single miscellaneous volume of correspondence and trial records was acquired at an unspecified date, late in the nineteenth century, for the Bibliothèque Nationale in Paris by Léopold Delisle, curator of manuscripts in the library.[27] France and Frenchmen abroad are the exclusive subject of the several otherwise disparate documents gathered in B. N. *Codex latinus* 8994. The dates covered are, roughly, the last fifteen years of the sixteenth century. It is too much of a coincidence that this should have been the only inquisitorial volume, of the many that escaped destruction in Paris, to have turned up in a French library. It makes me suspect that still others may have been offered to Delisle but that such practical considerations as cost or space dictated their refusal. We know, for example, that the Trinity documents eventually purchased by the Duke of Manchester were first rejected by the Trustees of the British Museum because of what they considered an exorbitant price.[28]

In addition to the material dispersed in Ireland, Belgium, France, and many other European and American libraries,[29] inquisitorial documents are also preserved in several Italian repositories. The reforms that led to the suppression of the Inquisition in the second half of the eighteenth century and the early years of the nineteenth, resulted in the eventual transfer of documents connected with the activities of the Bolognese, Modenese, Venetian, and other tribunals either to public institutions or to ecclesiastical archives.[30] In contrast to the material preserved in Italy, the dispersed archives outside Italy have received scant attention. The Paris codex, to the best of my knowledge, has never been studied; at least, I do not know of a single publication even partly based on it. Inquisitorial sources have been the backbone of research into strictly Italian problems: the spread of Reformation currents in the peninsula, witchcraft, and the censorship practices of post-Tridentine Rome. I would like to mention a few of the contributions that these records can make to areas of historical investigation more European in scope.

The several documents gathered in the Paris codex, as I noted, deal with various aspects of sixteenth-century French religious history, including thick dossiers compiled in the course of investigating French bishops suspected of favoring the Huguenots.[31] In my opinion, however, the most tantalizing material that it contains concerns the propaganda campaign that was being waged in Italy during the early 1590s on behalf of Henry of Navarre, already king of France but not yet recognized as such by the Holy See. Henry, born and reared a Protestant, had permitted himself to be converted to Catholicism to secure his succession to the throne at the death in 1589 of Henry III, the last Valois. Rome questioned the sincerity of his Catholic convictions. The legitimacy of Henry's claims was being advanced in Italy by means of a curious form of propaganda. On 22 May 1590, a member of the household of the cardinal of Santa Severina appeared before the Holy Office in Rome to denounce the chamberlain of a highly placed Roman ecclesiastic, Monsignor Ferratino, accusing him of keeping a portrait of the still young and handsome king folded and concealed in a footstool in the antechamber of his master's residence, and of producing it on occasion for the benefit of visitors and petitioners.[32] The portrait bore a sub-title declaring that Henry IV was the rightful king of France. The same witness informed the Inquisition that gentlemen were exhibiting such portraits from the windows or while standing on the running boards of the elegant carriages belonging to the entourage of the French ambassador as they paraded in the Piazza Navona and other populous places in the city.[33] On the basis of this information, the Holy Office began an investigation directed principally against the bookshops and artists' studios of the city. An engraver testified that an unknown person had brought two portraits to him with the request that he inscribe upon them in Latin the legend "Henry IV by Grace of God King of France and of Navarre."[34] A search of one bookshop led to the discovery of numerous other such portraits and the tradesman's admission that he had been selling them openly. He had purchased them over a year before from an Italian merchant, who also had sold him many other portraits which he said came from Flanders. The bookseller claimed that he did not know the identity of the subject on the portrait under investigation. He was under the impression that it was of a great military figure, but he knew nothing more.[35]

While officials were confiscating and burning the image of Henry in Rome, reports began to stream in from the outlying tribunals. On 21 June 1591, the inquisitor of Genoa wrote to his superiors that he had apprehended a painter in that city who had been producing and publicly selling large portraits of the French king.[36] They had been commissioned by prominent gentlemen, and a few of the portraits already adorned the walls of their residences. The original had been provided by a certain Paolo Spinola, who testified that he had obtained it in Venice where the portraits were being sold with enormous success.[37] This information was confirmed by the inquisitor of Vicenza, one of the principal cities under Venetian jurisdiction, in a letter addressed to Rome, 1 January 1592, stating that street vendors were hawking a portrait bearing the inscription in Italian: "Henry IV, King of France and of Navarre, with the extinction of the Valois upon the death of Henry III, King of France and of Poland, descended in a direct line from Robert Count of Clairmont, son of St. Louis, forty-fourth King of France."[38]

Did the idea of the portrait as an instrument of propaganda originate in the needs of French diplomacy, or in Italy itself where much of the country was under Spanish domination and the Huguenot party from the days of the great Condé was seen as an instrument to restore ancient liberties?[39] On the basis of several names gathered by the Inquisition in the course of its investigation, it should be possible to answer the many questions that arise from this curious footnote to the history of the wars of religion.

Ottoman expansion northward in eastern Europe, lightning raids by Barbary corsairs on the coasts of southern Italy, the endemic piracy of the Mediterranean, all resulted in the enslavement of thousands of Christians during the late sixteenth century. Many of these unfortunates did eventually return to their homes. Some were ransomed, while others escaped or were rescued when the Muslim galleys on which they served were defeated in combat with Christian vessels.[40] It was customary for the Inquisition to examine these returnees to Christendom who washed ashore in Italy. An analysis of the Trinity sentences dating from 1580 to 1582 and 1603 (the year of the next volume and the only one for the seventeenth century that I have examined personally) indicates that the investigation of apostasy to Islam was now an important item of inquisitorial business.[41]

Suspects who confessed having fallen away from Catholicism invariably claimed that they had been reduced to this extremity to escape the beatings of their masters who desired their conversion (claims that the Inquisition was cautious in accepting);[42] and they insisted that their adherence to the law of Mohammed had been purely external, that in their hearts they had never separated from the teachings of the Roman Church. The Inquisition generally dealt lightly with these apostates, and a simple abjuration, the performance of salutary penances, and a brief refresher course on Catholic fundamentals sufficed for their reconciliation. Inquisitors maintained that individuals who had fled voluntarily from the lands of Islam, who had apostatized at a very young age, or who had been converted by force could be reconciled to the Church and be pardoned. The Holy Office considered intention to be the crucial point in this, as in other cases which came before it, namely, whether an individual had accepted the Muslim faith in his very heart or only externally. Depending on how this question was settled, the defendant would have to abjure either as an apostate or as one suspected of apostasy. The penances imposed would be considerably lighter in the second case.[43]

The question became more complicated in the case of the many renegade Christians captured on Barbary corsairs who were not serving as oarsmen chained to the benches of galleys but in positions of responsibility, as gunners, navigators, and even, on occasion, as masters of vessels.[44] The Inquisition handled these men with circumspection and did not accept unreservedly their statements that they had apostatized so that they could sign aboard the pirate craft and hopefully find an opportunity to escape. Too many complaints had been received from the Knights of Malta that renegades who had been absolved and released were returning voluntarily to the lucrative life of piracy.[45] One interesting case of this type concerns a Frenchman, Jean Fabre, tried by the Holy Office in 1593. He had come ashore at Civitavecchia on a Christian grain ship which his Turkish master had captured off Sardinia. Fabre claimed before the inquisitors that he had seized control of the prize from the handful of Turks who had been assigned to man her and sail her home. He had done this by means of a fiery wine ("vino focoso") that he had discovered on board which kept the crew happily drunk ("et così gli tenevamo allegramente mezzo inbriachi").[46] Unfortunately, the records of these inquisitorial proceedings remain neglected sources for the study of Mediterranean culture and of European relations with North Africa and the Ottoman Empire in the last quarter of the sixteenth century.[47]

By the end of the century, the Inquisition in Rome was occupied with the reconciliation of still another class of religious deviant, not apostates or suspected apostates, such as the Christians who had bowed to Islam, but foreign heretics who traveled to the Holy See to reembrace the faith which they or their fathers had abandoned. They came, a few dozen each year, from every corner of Europe, Arians from Transylvania and Calvinists from Scotland, by devious and dangerous routes to be received as prodigal children of the Catholic Church. Many of them attributed their change of heart to the effectiveness and purity of Catholic preaching. A certain Thomas Busbridge, for example, a man of twenty-seven from the diocese of Canterbury, who abjured in Rome on 20 April 1582, claimed that the impulse to conversion had been provided by the eloquence and fortitude in martyrdom displayed by Edmund Campion during his clandestine mission to England in 1581. The English College in Rome, over which Cardinal William Allen presided for many years, assisted the Inquisition in its work of reconciliation. The names of its priests and seminarians appear in the trial records as interpreters, and among the salutary penances imposed on the English converts, a period of instruction in the College is occasionally encountered.[48]

How many of these conversions were sincere? It is difficult to give a definite answer because a majority of the names encountered in the Trinity sentences belong to obscure individuals of modest birth, and to trace their steps is probably next to impossible. It is legitimate to entertain doubts, however, because travel in Italy by citizens of Protestant countries was an enterprise filled with uncertainties and dangers; it seems natural to assume that a foreigner who had aroused suspicion might try to explain that he was there for the good of his soul. This was the apparent stratagem of a man from Normandy who was thrust into prison in Naples in 1589 for having been heard to exclaim that there was more charity in Elizabethan England than in papist Italy. He tried to justify his outburst by saying that at the time of his apprehension he had been engaged on a pious errand, visiting the religious shrines of southern Italy, attempting to support himself along the way by begging—but with poor results. One of the peculiar features of this trial is the disclosure of the presence in Naples of a sizable colony of indigent French families, from whom the Inquisition sought information about the background and behavior of this prisoner.[49]

The longing to travel to Italy, whether it was to admire the antiquities of Rome, perfect courtly skills in the Florence of the Medici, or pursue

legal studies at the great universities in Bologna and Padua, was shared
by the educated classes of northern Europe.[50] In spite of knowing this,
we are still surprisingly ignorant about the rights and the status of foreigners
visiting this Catholic country in the late sixteenth and early seventeenth
centuries. The central tribunal of the Holy Office, with its network of
provincial courts, was kept well informed on the movements of suspi-
cious individuals; and it regularly communicated what it knew to the appropriate outlying officials. In most cases, the correspondence was
accompanied by *contrassegni*, amazingly detailed and up-to-date physical
descriptions of the persons in question.[51] The evidence suggests that suspected foreign heretics were not tolerated, in theory at least, although
in actual practice absolute prohibitions were impractical to enforce. One
also gains the impression from a small sample of instructions received by
the inquisitor of Florence that occasionally such individuals were to be
kept under close surveillance but not molested unless they caused scandal
by openly practicing or proselytizing for their faith.[52] Fynes Moryson,
who has left us a colorful account of his Italian travels in his *Itinerary* published in London in 1617, makes it clear that the mere presence of the
foreign heretic was unlawful. He describes his uneasiness in Rome during
the Lenten season of 1594 when priests descended in droves upon the inns
of the city to record the names of the guests for the purpose of verifying
who had received Communion at that holy time of year.[53] During his
Italian travels, Moryson alternated passing himself off as a Frenchman and
as a Dutchman.[54] In the course of his masquerade he acquired habits that
proved difficult to shake off. He was in Geneva the following year — 1595.
Entering a church in the company of Theodore Beza and intent on the
great reformer's words, Moryson's fingers instinctively reached up for the
holy water, only to find the poor box. This little scene was not lost on
Beza, who lowered Moryson's hand and admonished him gently "to es-
chew these ill customes, which were so hardly forgotten."[55]

I do not think that the seeming discrepancy in policies toward non-
Catholic foreigners between Florence and Rome is simply attributable to
the fact that the former was an independent secular state. There is evidence, for example, that even in papal Bologna, with its large population
of ultramontane students, Germans were prosecuted not for the mere fact
of being heretics but when they were suspected of publicly flaunting their
faith.[56] In all likelihood, Rome itself had not worked out a consistent
policy concerning the legal status of the non-Catholic visitor.[57] Or if it

had, political realities prevented it from being applied in a uniform way. Everywhere in Italy, outside the states of the Church, the movements of the Inquisition took place at the pleasure of the secular ruler; and the cooperation that it could expect from him varied from state to state and from crisis to crisis. As a rule, the Holy Office was not free to proceed to the arrest of suspects without the permission of the secular authorities, who, in fact, frequently provided the personnel without whom it could rarely be effected. Obviously, the princes and republics of Italy would be reluctant to interfere with the lives of foreigners in their dominions if this invited reprisals against their subjects abroad. Even Rome, whose nuncios and Jesuit missions were penetrating the farthest reaches of Europe, could not be insensitive to this danger.[58]

Thousands of Italians, for a variety of political, commercial, or religious motives, traveled to and frequently settled in Protestant lands during the sixteenth century. Other Italians, their ears filled with rumors about the religious revolution in the north, ventured forth briefly to observe it with their own eyes. Geneva was the object of special curiosity. Many of the inquisitorial trials of individuals returning to Italy after visits to the north record how travel to the birthplace of Calvinism had been undertaken simply to observe how the "Lutherans" were living. The interrogations or trials to which the Holy Office subjected these returning travelers—suspected of harboring heretical leanings—are sources that have been ignored by students of the Protestant Reformation.[59] The importance of the information which these documents furnish naturally varies depending on the powers of observation of the individual and the length of the sojourn abroad. It could be as trifling as a peep at Geneva's blue laws provided by one disenchanted visitor who lamented that the inns of the city refused to serve food and drink during the hours of religious services.[60] Or the information furnished by these trials can be as substantial as that provided by a Genoese merchant who had resided in Lyons for much of his adult life. His description of events under the short-lived Huguenot regime (May 1562–June 1563) is as valuable for the historian as are his insights into the unwitting erosion worked on his Catholic beliefs and practices by the many years he spent in a milieu where Catholicism and Calvinism enjoyed an uneasy coexistence. His statements attest that he increasingly ignored fast days, that social concerns might occasionally conduct him to hear the sermons of heretical preachers, and that his scriptural readings came to be based on readily available vernacular texts rather than the prescribed Vulgate.[61]

These are some of the research possibilities that occurred to me in examining the dispersed archives of the Roman Inquisition. I mention them because they struck me both as neglected aspects of sixteenth-century life and as problems of history that one might not ordinarily think of pursuing through these relatively obscure sources.

Notes

1. A suggestion of its contents can be gleaned from various articles by Luigi Firpo, one of the few scholars to have gained access to the archive of the Inquisition: "Una relazione inedita su l'Inquisizione romana," *Rinascimento* 9 (1958): 97–102; "Filosofia italiana e Controriforma," *Rivista di filosofia* 41 (1950): 150–73, 390–401; 42 (1951): 30–47; "Il processo di Giordano Bruno," *RSI* 60 (1948): 542–97, and esp. 544–47; 61 (1949): 5–59. Monsignor Giuseppe De Luca was admitted to the Holy Office at the behest of Pope John XXIII but was not allowed to take notes. See P. Simoncelli, *Il caso Reginald Pole: Eresia e santità nelle polemiche religiose del Cinquecento* (Rome, 1977), p. 15, n. 11. Father Sergio Mario Pagano was permitted access for the purpose of preparing a new edition of Galileo's trial: see *I documenti del processo di Galileo Galilei* (Vatican City, 1984), 4 ff. for Pagano's description of the archive. Another recent study by the same author (in collaboration with C. Ranieri) is also based on access to Roman Holy Office documents: *Nuovi documenti su Vittoria Colonna e Reginald Pole.* Collectanea Archivi Vaticani, 24 (Vatican City, 1989). J. I. Tellechea Idigoras gained entrance for his monumental investigation of the Roman trial of Archbishop Carranza (personal communication to this writer). These scholars were preceded early in the century by Antonio Favaro (*Galileo e l'Inquisizione* [Florence, 1907], 7 ff). E. Carusi ("Nuovi documenti del processo di Giordano Bruno," *Giornale critico della filosofia italiana* 6 [1925]: 121–39, and "Nuovi documenti sui processi di Tommaso Campanella," ibid., 8 [1927]: 321–59) provides a cursory description of the Holy Office archive and publishes several of its documents. Firpo doubts that Carusi actually personally penetrated the archive: see "I primi processi Campanelliani in una ricostruzione unitaria," ibid., 20 (1939): 27. Ludwig von Pastor describes his futile attempts to gain access to the inquisitorial papers in his *Allgemeine Dekrete der Römischen Inquisition aus den Jahren 1555–1597* (Freiburg i. Br., 1912), 4 f. The great Catholic historian of the Jesuit order, P. Tacchi Venturi, fared no better (ibid., 5). Cf. O. Chadwick, *Catholicism and History: The Opening of the Vatican Archives* (Cambridge, 1978), 139 on the Pastor episode. The Inquisition also disregarded Leo XIII's desire that Cardinal Gasquet be permitted to enter the Holy Office. Eventually the documents Gasquet needed were "brought out for his use" (140). Carlo Ginzburg describes his own frustrations in this regard (which included an appeal to Pope John Paul II in 1979) in "The Dovecote Has Opened Its Eyes:

Popular Conspiracy in Seventeenth-Century Italy," in *The Inquisition in Early Modern Europe: Studies on Sources and Methods*, edited by G. Henningsen and J. Tedeschi in association with C. Amiel (De Kalb, 1986), 190–98, at 198. See also M. Firpo, whose appeal was turned down in January 1983 with the response that ". . . la prassi vigente non ammette alla consultazione diretta persone estranee alla Congregazione": V. Ferrone and M. Firpo, "Galileo tra inquisitori e microstorici," *RSI* 97 (1985): 177–238, at p. 179. In the case of another noted scholar access to the Holy Office collection was granted in the form of a microfilm, collated against the original. See P. O. Kristeller, "Francesco Patrizi da Cherso, 'Emendatio in libros suos Novae Philosophiae,'" *Rinascimento*, ser. 2, 10 (1970): 215–18.

On the transfer of the archive of the Congregation of the Index to the Palace of the Holy Office, see A. Villien, "Le Sainte-Office et la suppression de la Congregation de l'Index," *Le canoniste contemporain* 40 (1917): 98–111; and R. De Maio, *Riforme e miti nella Chiesa del Cinquecento* (Naples, 1973), 366 f.

The closed door policy of the Holy Office is based on an internal bureaucratic decision and does not represent the official position of the Catholic Church in regard to access to inquisitorial documents. Provincial ecclesiastical repositories rich in materials of this kind, in Naples, Pisa, Udine, Florence, and elsewhere, are increasingly being opened for serious research; and countless inquisitorial codices preserved in the Biblioteca Vaticana and the Archivio Segreto Vaticano have been made available even on microfilm to scholars around the world.

2. See L. von Pastor, *The History of the Popes* (St. Louis, 1924), 14:414 ff. A rare German newsletter, which provides a vivid eyewitness account of the turbulence in the streets of Rome after the death of the pope, was recently acquired by The Newberry Library: *Warhafftige Newe Zeittung, was sich für Empörung nach des Bapsts Pauli des IIII Todt, welcher den 18 Augusti dises 1559 Jars verschiden, zu Rom zugetragen hat . . . Von Rom geschriben an einen guten Freundt in Deudtschlandt* (N.p., n.d). The text is dated, Rome, 19 August. For other descriptions of the attack on the Holy Office, see the letter of the same date from Fra Vincenzo Ercolani to the Dominicans of S. Marco in Florence, published in B. Aquarone, *Vita di Fra Jeronimo Savonarola*, 2 vols. (Alessandria, 1857–58), 2:xxii–li; and the summary of the diary kept by G. F. Firmano, master of ceremonies of the papal chapel under six popes, published by M. De Bréquigny in *Notices et extraits des manuscrits de la Bibliothèque du Roi* (Paris, 1789), 2:626–68, esp. 638 ff.

3. The most complete account of the entire affair and of the ensuing efforts to recover the material is R. Ritzler's "Die Verschleppung der paepstlichen Archive nach Paris unter Napoleon I und deren Rückführung nach Rom in den Jahren 1815 bis 1817," *Römische Historische Mitteilungen* 6–7 (1962–64): 144–90, which is based largely on correspondence in the Vatican Secretariat of State. Fundamental sources for the entire episode are the "Memorie storiche" by Marino Marini, papal archivist in Paris, written to justify his actions in the recovery of the transported material. They were published as an appendix to the *Regestum Clementis Papae V* (Rome, 1885), 1:ccxxviii–cccxxv. Much important additional information is contained in

Léopold Delisle's review of Marini's work that appeared in the *Journal des Savants*, 1892: 429–41, 489–501. G. Bourgin ("Fonti per la storia dei Dipartimenti romani negli Archivi Nazionali di Parigi," *ASRSP* 29 [1906]: 97–144, esp. 109) indicates a series of French archival sources directly pertinent to the study of the transport and recovery of the Roman documents: *Archives étrangères*: "Envoi des archives romaines à Paris (1810–1811)"; "Frais d'envoi de ces archives; leur restitution (1811–1817)." See also Bourgin's "Les archives pontificales et l'histoire moderne de la France," *Bibliographe moderne* 9 (1905): 251–362. See, most recently, M. Giusti, "Materiale documentario d'archivio degli archivi papali rimasto nell'Archivio Nazionale di Parigi dopo il loro ritorno a Roma negli anni 1814–1817," in *Roemische Kurie, Kirchliche Finanzen, Vatikanisches Archiv: Studien zu Ehren von Hermann Hoberg*, ed. E. Gatz, 2 vols. (Rome, 1979), 1:263–74. I owe this reference to the kindness of Bruno Neveu.

4. Ritzler, "Verschleppung," 145. It is important to remember that the flow of treasures to Paris commenced before these events and that Napoleon was continuing, in a much intensified form, an older policy. A list of manuscripts brought to the Bibliothèque Nationale, beginning with the removal of numerous documents from the Biblioteca Ambrosiana in 1796, is contained in Delisle's *Le Cabinet des Manuscrits de la Bibliothèque Nationale* (Paris, 1874), 2:33–36. See also the contemporary descriptions: *Recensio manuscriptorum codicum qui ex universa Bibliotheca Vaticana selecti iussu Dni Nri. Pii VI . . . procuratoribus Gallorum jure belli . . . et initiae pacis traditi fuere* (Leipzig, 1803), a catalogue of the five hundred and one manuscripts taken by the French from the Vatican under the terms of the 1798 armistice; and the *Catalogo de' capi d'opera di pittura, scultura, antichità, libri, storia naturale ed altre curiosità trasportati dall'Italia in Francia: Seconda edizione, fatta su quella di Venezia del 1799* (Milan, n.d.), listing works of art and books confiscated on the same occasion from major Italian centers.

5. Delisle, in *Journal des Savants*, 1892: 438.

6. It is published in H. Bordier, *Les archives de la France, ou histoire des archives de l'empire* (Paris, 1855), 396–407.

7. Marini, "Memorie," ccliii.

8. Ritzler, "Verschleppung," 163 f. Marini himself may have fathered the idea of destroying so-called useless material to reduce expenses. Writing to Consalvi, "Di casa," i.e., Rome, on 7 March he claimed that this had occurred to him when he was still in Paris, but he had held back for fear that "l'abbruciar le carte della Inquisizione potesse provocare i motti satirici de' Parigini contro la Santa Sede." Among other documents that could have been destroyed without serious consequences, in Marini's opinion, were "I Vescovi e Regolari, molte della Penitenzieria, della Rota, del Buongoverno, etc., etc.," ibid., 163. On the secretary of state, Consalvi, see J. M. Robinson, *Cardinal Consalvi, 1757–1824* (New York, 1987). The work makes no specific mention of either the transport or destruction of the inquisitorial materials, but confines itself to a few general remarks about Marini's efforts to return to Rome the Vatican archives and art treasures.

9. Ritzler, "Verschleppung," 164–65.

10. Ibid., 165: ". . . potendo poi di tutti gli altri volumi e filze criminali, civili ed economiche, che formano forse li due terzi delle carte al S. Offizio involate, e colà rimaste, disporne, come meglio l'E.V. crederà più espediente, in conformità degli ordini del S. Padre."

11. Ibid., 182.

12. Ibid., 158, letter of Marini to Consalvi dated at Paris, 3 July 1817: "Il rimanente dei processi del S. Offizio è stato da me fatto lacerare in minuti pezzi e venduto per due mila e settecento franchi . . . Se vi sono altre carte inutili saranno vendute alla cartiera." This brought the number of inquisitorial volumes destroyed in Paris to 4,158.

13. Ibid., letter of Consalvi to Marini, 25 July 1817: "Ha fatto benissimo di ridurre in minuti pezzi li processi del S. Offizio, vendendoli con altre cartaccie, ed è tutto guadagnato con quello che mi accenna di averne ritratto."

14. Ibid., letter of Marini to Consalvi, 5 September 1818: ". . . il mio invio colà non fu di alcun aggravio alla Santa Sede, e per l'utile ch'io le procurai di quattro e più mila scudi, e per aver supplito alle spese del mio mantenimento colla vendita dei processi del Santo Offizio."

15. L. Firpo, "Il processo di Galileo," in *Nel quarto centenario della nascita di Galileo Galilei* (Milan, 1966), 86.

16. There is a full account of the blackmail in A. Mercati, *Il sommario del processo di Giordano Bruno* (Vatican City, 1942), 3n.

17. In the library at Trinity College, Dublin (TCD), a box marked MS. 3216 contains a letter (published by U. Balzani, see n. 18 below) describing the purchase, written by the Reverend Richard Gibbings, an Anglican clergyman with strong anti-Roman sentiments, who engineered the transfer of the documents from the duke of Manchester to Dublin. The dossier also contains several brief notes between the two men regarding the transaction. See J. Tedeschi, "A 'Queer Story': The Inquisitorial Manuscripts," in *Treasures of the Library, Trinity College, Dublin*, ed. Peter Fox (Dublin, 1986), 67–74.

Gibbings, who served as the Regius Professor of Divinity at Trinity from 1863 to 1878, began to publish sentences from the collection while they were still in the duke's hands: *Were "Heretics" ever burned alive in Rome? A report of the proceedings in the Roman Inquisition against Fulgentio Manfredi; taken from the original manuscript brought from Italy by a French officer, and edited, with a parallel English version, and illustrative additions* (London, 1852); *Records of the Roman Inquisition; case of a Minorite friar, who was sentenced by St. Charles Borromeo to be walled up, and who having escaped was burned in effigy, edited with an English translation and notes* (Dublin, 1853); *Report of the trial and martyrdom of Pietro Carnesecchi, sometime secretary to Pope Clement VII and apostolic protonotary, transcribed from the original manuscript* (London, 1856). See also the sentence pronounced 31 July 1580 against a school teacher in the south of Italy, pp. 321–34 in this volume.

In addition to the inquisitorial materials described below, many Lateran registers (also survivals from materials sold in Paris as waste paper) came to Trinity College. For a recent description of this collection, see L. E. Boyle, *A Survey of the Vatican Archives and of Its Medieval Holdings* (Toronto, 1972), 145–48. On Gibbings, see R. B. McDowell and D. A. Webb, *Trinity College Dublin, 1592–1952: An Academic History* (Cambridge, 1982), ad indicem.

George Montagu, sixth duke of Manchester (Viscount Mandeville until 1843) died 18 August 1855 at the age of 56. He had served as a commander in the Royal Navy and as an M.P. He is described as "a zealous Protestant" in *The Complete Peerage* (London, 1932), 8:376. Several pamphlets from his pen, comments on biblical passages and on the Second Advent (none even faintly related to Trinity College materials) are listed in *The British Library General Catalogue of Printed Books to 1975* (London, 1984), 225: 91–92.

18. A partial calendar of the collection is provided by T. K. Abbott, *Catalogue of the Manuscripts in the Library of Trinity College, Dublin* (Dublin and London, 1900; reprint 1980), 241–84, MSS. 1224–1277. K. Benrath, who examined the documents personally, was the first foreign scholar to make critical use of them: *Über die Quellen der italienischen Reformationsgeschichte* (Bonn, 1876), esp. 23–25, and "Akten aus römischen Archiven in Trinity College Library, Dublin," *Historische Zeitschrift* 41 (1879): 249–62. This article was translated into Italian, with an appendix of the most important sentences from the first volume (a total of 111 documents), covering the period 16 December 1564 to 21 September 1567: "Atti dagli archivi romani della Biblioteca del Collegio della Trinità in Dublino," *La rivista cristiana* 7 (1879): 457–72, 497–505; 8 (1880): 10–13, 55–58, 94–97, 137–43. See also H. Gaidoz, "De quelques registres de l'Inquisition soustraits aux archives romains," *Revue de l'instruction publique* (May 1867), nos. 16 and 23: 102–4, 114–17; S. Gherardi, "Il processo Galileo riveduto sopra documenti di nuova fonte," *Rivista europea*, a.1, vol. 3 (1870): 3–37, 398–419; U. Balzani, "Di alcuni documenti dell'archivio del Santo Uffizio di Roma relativi al ritrovamento del cadavere di Paolo Sarpi," *Rendiconti della reale Accademia dei Lincei, classe di scienze morali, storiche e filologiche*, ser. 5, 4 (1895): 595–617 (which provides a good overview of the collection and focuses on a fascicle of Venetian materials entitled "Circa la reperizione del supposto cadavere di Fr. Paolo Sarpi"; the letter by Gibbings cited in n. 17 appears at pp. 597–98 in the article. See also L. Salazar, "Documenti del Santo Officio nella Biblioteca del Trinity College," *Archivio storico per le province napoletane* 33 (1908): 466–73 (identifies documents that concern Neapolitan subjects). The claim that the Trinity documents were removed from Rome only during the French occupation of the city in the mid-nineteenth century (and not during the Napoleonic period) is refuted by C. Corvisieri, "Compendio dei processi del Santo Uffizio di Roma (da Paolo III a Paolo IV)," *ASRSP* 3 (1880): 264.

19. TCD, MSS. 1224–1227; Abbott, *Catalogue*, 243–53.

20. TCD, MSS. 1243–1277; Abbott, *Catalogue*, 253–84. C. Ginzburg ("Una testimonianza inedita su Ludovico Zuccolo," *RSI* 79 [1967]: 1122–28) publishes the deposition of a "sponte comparente" dated 1625 contained in MS. 1244. The collection, widely available on microfilm, remains basically underused.

21. For a rudimentary calendar, see J. Van Den Gheyn, *Catalogue des Manuscrits de la Bibliothèque Royale de Belgique* (Brussels, 1903), 4:84–86 (MS. II 290). Brief surveys of the collection are contained in G. Biagi, "Le carte dell'Inquisizione fiorentina a Bruxelles," *Rivista delle biblioteche e degli archivi* 19 (1908): 161–68; M. Battistini, "Per la storia dell'Inquisizione fiorentina (documenti inediti della Biblioteca reale di Bruxelles)," *Bilychnis* 18 (1929): 425–48; A. D'Addario, *Aspetti della Controriforma a Firenze* (Rome, 1972), 37–38. The Brussels manuscripts are not assumed to be materials removed from Vatican and Italian archives at the order of Napoleon, and they are not mentioned by A. Panella, *Gli archivi fiorentini durante il dominio francese, 1808–1814* (Florence, 1911).

The papers of the Florentine Inquisition were transferred to the archiepiscopal archives in Florence in compliance with the Leopoldine reforms which suppressed the Holy Office in Tuscany at the end of the eighteenth century. The Brussels documents were removed from this depository at an unknown date and under mysterious circumstances. The disappearance is discussed by A. Favaro in the *Archivio storico italiano*, ser. 5, 42 (1908): 451–69, a critical review of M. Cioni, *I documenti galileiani del S. Uffizio di Firenze* (Florence, 1908). Favaro (p. 452) attacks Cioni's contention that the archive of the Florentine Holy Office first passed to the state archives (where the collection could have been plundered) before moving to the archiepiscopal archives. Favaro quotes the edict of Pietro Leopoldo, dated 5 July 1782, abolishing the Holy Office in Tuscany. Article 4 expressly specified that all documents be transferred directly to the appropriate episcopal archives in Florence, Pisa, and Siena. We now know with certainty that the basic *fondo* of the Florentine Inquisition rests undisturbed in the archiepiscopal archive in Florence, the contents of which have been described by Monsignor Celso Calzolai in the *Rassegna storica toscana* 3 (1957): 127–81. The first modern studies based on this collection, by Adriano Prosperi, are cited at p. 110 in this volume. Eight thick codices from this archive are preserved in the Archivio di Stato, Florence, I, XI, vols. 1271–1278. The documents, which range in date roughly from 1500 to 1784, are almost exclusively of economic interest, *Contratti, Ricevute, Bilanci di Entrata e Uscita*, and so forth, pertaining to the Holy Office in Florence.

22. See pp. 273–319 in this volume where I have published twenty-eight letters from the cardinals of the Congregation of the Index to the inquisitor of Florence, ranging in date from March 1592 to September 1606.

23. For example, BRB, MS. II 290, vol. 1, fol. 1, "Decreta ab anno 1583 ad an. 1609"; vol. 2, fol. 1, "Decreta torturae"; fol. 23, "Decreta contra Anglos, Germanos et omnes Protestantes"; fol. 63, "Decreta contra Haebreos"; fol. 114, "Decreta contra libros."

24. Vol. 3 contains the trial of Ascanio Capponi, procurator of the convent of San Martino, suspected of heretical dealings with the nuns, and of Suor Caterina Teresa Antinori, suspected of apostasy to Judaism (1726–33). Vol. 4 contains numerous seventeenth- and eighteenth-century printed edicts issued by the Roman Inquisition and, in addition, the "Risposta del Fisco all'informazione del Sig. Ottavio Castelli

nella causa d'Inquisizione formata contro di lui, Andrea Fanetti, e Francesco Cappelli" (fols. 6–29).

25. For example, vol. 4, fol. 1, edict of 1611, reissued in 1656, quoted at length at p. 81, n. 104 in this volume.

26. Ibid.: "Quando haveranno carcerati poveri, che viveranno alle spese del Sant' Officio, le metteranno ne' conti, quali mandino a Roma col nome proprio di quel povero carcerato, & il numero anco de' giorni che ha havute le spese, facendovi mettere sotto la propria mano, overo la mano de' vicarii de' vescovi, in testimonio che non le ha pagate. Et l'istesso osservino nelle catture, tormenti, & altre spese straordinarie, che non potranno pagar i poveri rei. Non si faccino pagar da rei per le spese occorse, se non doppo, che saranno determinate le cause, dando a lor la lista sincera a parte di quanto sarà speso, & haveranno da pagare, acciochè conoscano, che non sono aggravati fuora di ragione nel pagarle." See also the records of income and expenditure for the Florentine Inquisition preserved in the Archivio di Stato, Florence (cited at n. 21 above).

27. Mentioned by Delisle in *Journal des Savants* (1892): 492, and in *Manuscrits latins et français ajoutés aux fonds des nouvelles acquisitions pendant les années 1875–1891* (Paris, 1891), xlix.

28. See J. Tedeschi, "A 'Queer Story'," 69.

29. To mention only one example, among the many which could be cited, see the MSS in the Henry C. Lea Library described in N. P. Zacour and R. Hirsch, *Catalogue of Manuscripts in the Libraries of the University of Pennsylvania to 1800* (Philadelphia, 1965), 146–230, containing a number of items of Italian provenance including the "Prattica" by Desiderio Scaglia discussed at pp. 229–58 in this volume.

30. See the detailed listings in "Toward a Statistical Profile," passim, in this volume. Even a cursory examination of some early volumes in the still incomplete *Inventari dei manoscritti delle biblioteche d'Italia* reveals the existence of inquisitorial documents in the following: Ambrosini, Archiginnasio, Universitaria, Breventani (Bologna); Marciana (Venice); Forteguerri (Pistoia); Bertoliana (Vicenza); Accademia dei Concordi (Rovigo); Classense (Ravenna); Comunale (Perugia); Civica (Novara); Nazionale (Florence); Comunale and Accademia Etrusca (Cortona); Universitaria (Sassari); Raccolta di Ca d'Orsolino (Benedello); Comunale (Trento); Comunale (Fano); Giovardiana (Veroli); Oliveriana (Pesaro); Comunale (Faenza); Comunale (Argenta).

The closing of the monasteries was not always accompanied by the orderly transfer of documents. In Milan, for example, the abolition of the Inquisition in 1775 resulted in the wholesale destruction of its records: see L. Fumi, "L'Inquisizione romana e lo stato di Milano," *ASL*, ser. 4, 13 (1910): 5–124, 285–414; 14 (1910): 145–220, esp. the last installment. On the Napoleonic legislation in regard to the religious orders, see C. A. Naselli, *La soppressione napoleonica delle corporazioni religiose: Contributo alla storia religiosa del primo Ottocento italiano, 1808–1814*. Miscellanea Historiae Pontificiae, vol. 52 (Rome, 1986).

31. B.N. Paris, Cod. lat. 8994, fols. 126–221.

32. Ibid., fols. 308–61. The proceedings are entitled "Pro Fisco Sancti Officii

contra retinentes imaginem pretensi Regis Navarrae." The testimony is at fol. 310: ". . . viddi in casa di Mons.r Ferratino in mano di Ms. Riccio cameriero di detto Mon.re nell'anticamera un ritratto in stampa del pretenso Re di Navarra." Riccio produced it from a "scabello da sedere qual'egli havea nella detta anticamera."

33. Ibid., fol. 311: ". . . io essendo in Piazza Navona e passando di la l'Ambasciador Lusemburg con 19 o 20 cocchi, appresso nel secondo o terzo cocchio, e credo fusse più presto il terzo che il secondo, ci era uno che stava in porta di detto cocchio, e portava spiegato detto ritratto verso le persone che passavano per la strada . . . pareva Francese."

34. Ibid., fol. 317, deposition of 2 June 1590.

35. Ibid., fol. 333, deposition of 30 January 1591.

36. Ibid., fol. 338.

37. One wonders if he was related to the poet Publio Francesco Spinola, executed by the Inquisition in January 1567, who also appears to have been implicated in Huguenot attempts to proselytize in Italy. See E. Pommier, "Notes sur la propagande protestante dans la République de Venise au milieu du XVIe siècle," *Aspects de la propagande religieuse* (Geneva, 1957), 244.

38. B.N. Paris, Cod. lat. 8994, fol. 342.

39. Pommier, "Notes," 245.

40. There is a vast literature on this fascinating subject. Good, recent, if somewhat popular, accounts are S. Bono, *I corsari barbareschi* (Turin, 1964); R. Panetta, *Pirati e corsari turchi e barbareschi nel mare nostrum, XVI secolo* (Milan, 1981). From among A. Tenenti's numerous contributions on the subject, see his "Gli schiavi di Venezia alla fine del Cinquecento," *RSI* 67 (1955): 52–69, for a discussion of ransoming procedures.

41. Of the eighty-one sentences pronounced in Rome between 19 January 1582 and 30 December 1583 (recorded in TCD, MS. 1227), twenty-two are for apostasy or suspected apostasy to Islam. The number decreased to fifteen in 1603, in addition to the reconciliation of six Spanish "Christiani novi" (TCD, MS. 1228). The various motives that might have led Christians in the sixteenth century to embrace the Muslim faith voluntarily are suggested by C. De Frede, "Il proselitismo musulmano," chap. 4 in *La prima traduzione italiana del Corano sullo sfondo dei rapporti tra Cristianità e Islam nel Cinquecento* (Naples, 1967). See also L. Rostagno, "Apostasia all'Islam e Santo Ufficio in un processo dell' Inquisizione veneziana," *Il Veltro* 23 (1979): 293–313 (the case concerns a member of the order of S. Bonaventura, Fra Alfonso da Malta, tried 1690–93); idem, *Mi faccio Turco: Esperienze ed immagini dell'Islam nell'Italia moderna* (Rome, 1983), cases of apostasy to Islam in the Udine inquisitorial records; P. C. Ioly Zorattini, "Processi del S. Uffizio di Aquileia e Concordia contro 'Lapsi' nell'Islamismo tra Sei e Settecento," *Memorie storiche forogiuliesi* 60 (1980): 117–28, and, most recently, B. Bennassar, *Les Chretiens d'Allah: L'histoire extraordinaire des renégats, XVe–XVIIe siècles* (Paris, 1989). Cf., on a related issue, P. Dressendörffer, *Islam unter der Inquisition: Die Morisco-Prozesse in Toledo, 1575–1610.* Veröffentlichungen

der orientalischen Kommission der Akademie der Wissenschaften und der Literatur, vol. 26 (Wiesbaden, 1971).

42. It was generally not Ottoman policy to coerce conversions. See, for example, the *Relazione* read before the Venetian senate in 1594 by Matteo Zane at the completion of his embassy to Constantinople: "Onde [the Turks] usano di permettere nei loro stati, sino ai Luterani, il libero esercizio di qualsivoglia religione senza timore di essere contaminati," in E. Albèri, *Le relazioni degli ambasciatori veneti al Senato*, ser. 3 (Florence, 1855), 3:405. G. Georgiades Arnakis ("The Greek Church of Constantinople and the Ottoman Empire," *Journal of Modern History* 24 [1952]: 235–50) describes the guarantees and safeguards obtained by Christian establishments. L. Santini ("A proposito di una traduzione italiana del 'Piccolo Catechismo' di M. Lutero," *NRS* 49 [1965]: 627–35) discovered that the Italian translation of Luther's *Catechism* (1585) was actually prepared to bring religious comfort to Christian slaves in Constantinople. See also S. Bono, *Corsari*, 243 f., 252; E. G. Friedman, "The Exercise of Religion by Spanish Captives in North Africa," *The Sixteenth Century Journal* 6 (1975), fasc. 1: 19–34; idem, "Christian Captives at 'Hard Labor' in Algiers, 16th–18th Centuries," *International Journal of African Historical Studies* 13 (1980): 616–32; idem, *Spanish Captives in North Africa in the Early Modern Age* (Madison, 1983); B. Bennassar, "Conversion ou reniement? Modalités d'une adhésion ambiguë des chrétiens à Islam (XVIe–XVIIe s.," *Annales: E.S.C.* 43 (1988): 1349–66. Specifically on the ransoming of Christian slaves, see A. Riggio, "Schiavi calabresi in Tunisia barbaresca (1583–1701)," *Archivio storico per la Calabria e la Lucania* 5 (1935): 131–77 (fewer than a hundred names from incomplete records preserved in the old French consulate in Tunisia (1582–1705); M. Lenci, "Riscatti di schiavi cristiani dal Maghreb. La Compagnia della SS. Pietà di Lucca (secoli XVII–XIX)," *Società e storia* 9 (1986): 53–80; W. H. Rudt de Collenberg, *Esclavage et rançons des chrétiens en Méditerranée (1570–1600), d'après les 'Litterae Hortatoriae' de l'Archivio Segreto Vaticano* (Paris, 1987).

43. The theory is outlined in a disquisition on the Holy Office of Malta preserved in BAV, Borg. lat. 558, fol. 79. Cf. BAV, Barb. lat. 1370, fols. 347–56, "De apostatis existentibus in triremibus."

44. See, for example, the *Relazione* of Paolo Contarini returning from an embassy to Constantinople in 1583: "Ha il capitano [of the Turkish fleet] al suo servizio molti rinnegati italiani, a quali ha dato il carico di capitani di galera," in Albèri, *Relazioni*, ser. 3, 3:223. The capture of these renegades at sea raised an interesting jurisdictional question: should these suspected apostates to Islam seized on infidel ships practicing piracy be permitted to remain as prizes of their captors? The Inquisition replied negatively, claiming the right to institute a trial against them. The issue is discussed in BAV, Borg. lat. 558, f. 79.

45. S. Bono, *Corsari*, 265 ff.

46. See B.N. Paris, Cod. lat. 8994, fol. 271.

47. These sources could have been used profitably, for example, by F. Braudel in his monumental *La Méditerranée et le monde méditeranéen à l'époque de Philippe II*, 2nd ed., 2 vols. (Paris, 1966).

48. Busbridge's sentence and abjurations are in TCD, MS. 1227, fol. 57. Twenty-seven reconciliations of foreign heretics are included among the eighty Roman sentences recorded between 19 January and 30 December 1582 in TCD, MS. 1227. The figure skyrockets to 58 (out of 107 sentences) in 1603. See TCD, MS. 1228.

49. Extracts from the trial of Franciscus Moriscus, held first before the episcopal court of Avellino and later before the Inquisition in Rome, are contained in B. N. Paris, Cod. lat. 8994, fols. 3–49. In general, see E. G. Léonard, "Protestants français poursuivis par l'Inquisition dans l'Italie meridionale au XVIe siècle," *Bulletin de la Société de l'histoire du protestantisme français* 83 (1934): 470–74.

50. Many firsthand travel accounts are recorded in E. Cox, *A Reference Guide to the Literature of Travel*, 2 vols. (Seattle, 1935) and L. Tresoldi, *Viaggiatori tedeschi in Italia, 1452–1870. Saggio bibliografico*, 2 vols., (Rome, 1975–77). Neither J. Stoye (*English Travellers Abroad, 1604–1667* [London, 1952]) nor J. R. Hale (*England and the Italian Renaissance* [London, 1954]) used inquisitorial documents in their descriptions of the difficulties and uncertainties of Italian travel.

51. A number of these papers are included among the "Decreta contra Anglos, Germanos et omnes Protestantes," in BRB, MS. II 290, vol. 2, fols. 23–62. They range in date from 1591 to 1607. For a sample, see the instructions sent to the Florentine inquisitor by the cardinal of Santa Severina on 26 January 1591 (fol. 24): "Si è inteso che alli 19 del presente era in Roma uno che si crede sia spia della già regina d'Inghilterra, et perchè potrebbe forse capitar costì, Vostra Reverentia facci ogni possibil diligenza, se si ritrovasse; et ritrovandolo lo facci carcerare con dar avviso di quel ch'esseguirà. Costui è huomo di 40 anni incirca, grasso, et pien di vita, di statura mediocre, di pelo rosso, la faccia con molte lenticchie, con capelli lunghi a mezz'orecchia, barba tagliata . . . altiero et superbo. Portava cappello di feltro nero alquanto elevato, ferraiolo negro lungo, col collare foderato di velluto, giubbone di peli di fiandra di color di piombo, calzette bianche, et ha nome Roberto Hauffeld Gloustiense, ma si potrebbe haver mutato il nome."

52. Ibid., fol. 52. See the letter addressed to him by cardinal inquisitor Pompeo Arrigoni (dated 18 February 1606) communicating that three Germans, a nobleman, his tutor, and a servant had taken up lodgings near the hospital where the tutor was studying medicine: ". . . per quanto s'intende sono heretici . . . li faccia osservare come vivono costì, se ragionano, o trattano d'heresie, o fanno atti alcuni contro la fede cattolica."

53. Fynes Moryson, *An Itinerary* (Glasgow, 1907), 1:303.

54. Ibid., 304, 334.

55. Ibid., 390.

56. See the letter (dated 25 February 1589) from the cardinal of Santa Severina to the inquisitor of Bologna: ". . . non si procede contra gli Alemanni e Tedeschi per essere Alemanni e Tedeschi, ma per quanto sono stati conosciuti e scoperti per Lutherani, Calvinisti, o altrimenti heretici, *et che habbiano trattato di tali errori o heresie in Italia*" (italics mine): BA, MS. B–1861, fol. 92. See also H. Kellenbenz ("I rapporti tedeschi con l'Italia nel XVI e all'inizio del XVII secolo e la questione religio-

sa," in *Città italiane del '500 tra Riforma e Controriforma: Atti del convegno internazionale di studi, Lucca, 13–15 ottobre 1983* [Lucca, 1988], 111–25), who discusses episodes of German Protestant merchants before the Inquisition, and the efforts of the international commercial community to obtain their release.

57. That there was quite a diversity of opinion on the status of the English merchant in the Grand Duchy of Tuscany emerges from the discourse on the Florentine Holy Office in BAV, Borg. lat. 558, fols. 30–35. See also, among many other such handbooks where precedents on topics of current interest were collected, BAV, Borg. lat. 548, "Haeretici volentes accedere in Italiam, ibique degentes," 359–61, and "Haeretici in locis Italiae commorantes seu petentes ad ea accedere," 363–65. Even the traditional privileges and immunities of the ultramontane students were occasionally called into question by ecclesiastical authorities. See A. Stella, "Tentativi controriformistici nell'Università di Padova e il rettorato di Andrea Gostynski," *Relazioni tra Padova e la Polonia* (Padua, 1964), 75–87. P. Simoncelli ("Clemente VIII e alcuni provvedimenti del Sant'Uffizio. ['De italis habitantibus in partibus haereticorum']," *Critica storica* 13 [1976]: 129–72, esp. 142 ff.) discusses the conditions and restrictions placed by the Inquisition on Italian Catholics living in "heretical parts."

58. In a letter dated 5 December 1567 to the Doge of Genoa, the cardinal of San Clemente recalled the cases of certain Germans, favorites of the duke of Saxony, who had intentionally been permitted to flee from a Roman prison during the reign of Pius IV "per paura che quel duca non facesse amazzare li nostri nuntii che andavano per Germania intimando il concilio." The letter is published in M. Rosi, "La Riforma religiosa in Liguria e l'eretico umbro Bartolomeo Bartoccio," *Atti della società ligure di storia patria* 24 (1892): 555–726 at p. 696.

59. TCD, MS. 1224, fol. 5, sentence against Giovanni Micro, a Neapolitan: "Sei stato a Geneva et hai udito una volta come dici le prediche de li heretici" (16 December 1564); fol. 65, sentence against Antonio Mercugliano of Castelpoti who confessed to "esser stato a Genevra per sei mesi in circa per servitore con Galeazzo Caracciolo" (8 June 1566); fol. 163, sentence against mastro Giovanni Zerbino. Among various accusations against him he had "laudato gl'heretici con dire ch'a Ginevra è il paradiso, et a Roma il purgatorio" (31 May 1567); MS. 1226, fol. 29, sentence against Christophoro Guzeno di Zamberi, who claimed that the year he spent in Geneva during which he attended the "prediche de' lutherani" was without malicious intent, since he had gone to that heretical capital simply "per imparar qualche arte mechanica" (13 January 1581). These data support findings about the predominantly transient nature of Geneva's Italian colony: E. W. Monter, "The Italians in Geneva, 1550–1600: A New Look," in *Genève et l'Italie*, ed. L. Monnier (Geneva, 1969), 53–77.

60. See the trial in Novara of a Frenchman, Bertrand de Santré (1590), preserved in B.N. Paris, Cod. lat. 8994, fol. 74: "Et quando fanno la Cena, o predicano, gl'hosti non danno da mangiare ai forestieri, finchè non hanno finito."

61. The trial of Agostino Centurione is not an inquisitorial document. Instead of responding to the summons of the Genoese Holy Office, he appealed his case to the Council of Trent, which absolved him of heretical charges on 7 April 1563.

The proceedings are preserved in the Archivio Segreto Vaticano, *Concilio di Trento*, 12: fols. 129–49. Excerpts have been published by L. Carcereri, "Agostino Centurione mercante genovese processato per eresia e assolto dal Concilio di Trento (1563)," *Archivio trentino* 21 (1906): 65–99.

SACRO
ARSENALE
Ouero
PRATTICA
DELL'OFFICIO
Della
SANTA INQVISITIONE.

Di nuouo corretto, & ampliato.

IN BOLOGNA, M. DC.LXV.

Ad instanza del Baglioni.

Con Licenza de' Superiori.

Eliseo Masini, *Sacro Arsenale*. Bologna, 1665. [From the author's collection.]

THREE

◈

Inquisitorial Sources and Their Uses

In the preceding chapter I drew attention to the far-flung availability of inquisitorial sources, despite the great losses suffered by the archives, and the closed door policy that still prevents access to the palace of the Holy Office in Rome.[1] We have come a long way from the time when scholars were lamenting that the scarcity of trials and other appropriate documents made the serious study of the Inquisition an impossible task.[2]

I should like now to survey briefly the range of materials available, identify supplementary sources which also serve the task at hand, and consider a few problems and questions of method connected with their use. Some sources are obvious — trials, sentences, manuals — others perhaps less so. We recently have been given an excellent overview of the types of documents one might encounter in the archive of a local tribunal in Albano Biondi's rich study of Modena after it was elevated in 1598 from vicariate to full inquisitorial status.[3]

Let us begin with trial records. Andrea Del Col, in his important paper entitled "I Processi dell' Inquisizione come fonte,"[4] observed that most scholars in the field read trial dossiers in isolation, rarely making use of the available remaining pertinent documentation. Not only would this extra effort help place the trial in question in proper context, but it might prevent factual errors and misinterpretations to which unpracticed readers of inquisitorial records have often succumbed. Holy Office proceed-

ings are highly technical and specialized in nature, and the jargon of canon law can be a serious obstacle to correct interpretation.[5] The many
scholars in related disciplines—social and economic historians, historical
ethnographers, art historians—who have turned increasingly to inquisitorial
sources in pursuit of specific research goals, particularly need to be aware
of the complexity of the subject matter.

Del Col also adds his voice to those who in recent years have weighed
the reliability of inquisitorial trials as historical documents. Carlo Ginzburg, beginning with his early essay, "Stregoneria e pietà popolare,"[6]
pointed to the distance in background, education, and language that often
separated judge and defendant, and speculated on the consequences, asking if these sources, filtered down to us through representatives of learned
culture, could faithfully reproduce the ideas and words of the accused and
of witnesses under such circumstances. There is no easy answer to these
doubts. It is my impression, however, that at least the more responsible
officials of the Holy Office were themselves well aware of the dilemma
and worked to close the gap and avert possible abuses. Suggestive questioning, the authorities of the time unceasingly reiterated, which might
lead the interrogation down a preconceived path was to be scrupulously
avoided. We find this admonition repeated not only in the manuals, which
express the theory behind inquisitorial procedure,[7] but also in the correspondence between Rome and the provincial courts—documents intended
to oversee that the theory became translated into practice. To take one
among many examples, a letter dated 7 March 1626 addressed by the Roman Congregation of the Inquisition to its official in Saluzzo reminded
him that in the future "the summaries that you send should not be in
Latin but in the vernacular, and, on the important points, in the very
words of the witnesses and of the defendant. . . ."[8] Testimony, thus, was
to be reported verbatim, not transmitted through a notary's shorthand
version of the proceedings.

That inquisitors were prone to twist testimony to fit predetermined
mental schema, especially in the case of alleged witchcraft, underlies an
indictment against inexperienced and unrigorous judges pronounced by
the *Instructio pro formandis processibus in causis strigum, sortilegiorum, et maleficiorum*, an "Instruction" on correct trial procedure in witchcraft cases by
an anonymous author, a man who was certainly a high official of the Roman Congregation, perhaps Cardinal Desiderio Scaglia.[9] We know from
the numerous surviving manuscript copies that the *Instructio* circulated wide-

ly among the peripheral tribunals, especially to those involved in intense witchcraft prosecution. Scaglia, or whoever the author may have been, pilloried those judges who falsely believed, "because they had read some book or other discussing magic and witches," that women accused of various magical practices must have made formal apostasy to the Devil, and who, consequently, found ways of persuading them to confess what had never been in their minds.[10] And he urged these same officials, when women began to confess their apostasy, to forget everything that the Doctors had written on this subject, since on the basis of these authorities great injustices were often perpetrated against ignorant defendants.[11]

It has become customary to speak of the inquisitor as the representative of high culture and thus, often incapable of grasping the moral and intellectual world of socially and culturally subaltern defendants. (The possibility of a reverse situation is generally not raised.) Yet, among these officials there must have been many of modest, rural background who had been raised in a milieu of folk traditions. Moreover, there seems to be evidence, again provided by the *Instructio*, that jailers, certainly not typical representatives of high culture, who had more intimate proximity to the imprisoned women than did the judges, were often guilty themselves of suggesting what they should confess at the interrogations.[12]

In the absence of trials, and we know how many were destroyed in Paris after the fall of Napoleon, denunciations and sentences can sometimes fill the void. There is no need to dwell at length over the first because this type of document has been thoroughly described by, among others, Luciano Osbat and his team in their catalogue of the archive of the archiepiscopal see of Naples.[13] Denunciations are of two principal types: they may be simple accusations, not leading to further judicial proceedings, or be the preliminaries to actual trials. They become extremely useful in the latter case in the event that the trial dossier itself no longer exists.

The same is true in the case of sentences which, along with abjurations, are the crucial concluding appendages to judicial proceedings. Since they summarize in detail the charges raised against the defendant and frequently run to many pages, they are often satisfactory substitutes for the lost records of the trials. Sentences and abjurations, a supreme form of public humiliation, were recited in the provincial centers on cathedral steps, or during religious services before the throngs of assembled churchgoers in the town where the offense had been committed.[14] In Rome, the scene of these ceremonies was the Church of Santa Maria Sopra Minerva; for members of orders it might be their next provincial chapter.[15] But in some instances, for a variety of motives, the reading was conducted privately. This could occur when the recitation of certain crimes risked embarrassing the Church, as in the case of priests who had solicited sexual favors in the confessional. A public reading, many authorities argued, would frighten the faithful into staying away from the sacrament of penance, cast disrepute upon it, and provide ammunition to its Protestant critics.[16] In the instance of certain occult crimes, the Roman Congregation warned the provincial officials that in preparing the sentence they were not to describe the magical practices involved in the case for fear of contaminating bystanders.[17] Finally, people of rank and quality, and women with nubile daughters, were frequently spared the shame of public ceremonies,[18] at least when the nature of their crime permitted a milder form of abjuration, *de levi*, rather than *de vehementi*. Offenders convicted under the second designation, in the event of a repeated fall, would be liable to the extreme penalties reserved for the *relapsus*.[19]

In the course of the sixteenth century it became the practice increasingly for Rome to be kept minutely informed about developments in the outlying inquisitions, and it was customary for the latter to send detailed reports of trials in progress or completed — and then await instructions before passing sentence. The central tribunal's quest for uniformity resulted in a series of measures which assigned the final disposition of all but the most ordinary cases to Rome. There are many letters, almost sarcastic in tone, in which members of the Congregation attempt to differentiate for the benefit of the local officials what is ordinary from what is not. An example is the letter to the inquisitor of Bologna from Antonio Balduzzi, Commissioner of the Holy Office in Rome, dated 11 March 1573:

I don't believe that I have anything special to tell you besides responding to two questions of yours. The first, concerns the small things which you should work out on your own without disturbing these illustrious lordships. What I meant was that I do not want you to take as a decision or law anything that I write to you as brother Antonio, but rather as friendly and fraternal bits of information and advice. Now let me tell you, that the things which pass through your hands will of themselves show if they are small or great, and if they deserve or not to be brought to the attention of this holy tribunal; and from here I would not know how to give you a fixed rule, but your own good sense must guide you. Certainly you do not need to write about every minutia, or about every bit of testimony. But when the cases are serious or you are ready to come to some important decision such as sentencing or the like, it is wise to inform us, also stating the opinions of your consultors, and any accomplices who were named.[20]

Later it was deemed, as we know from a letter dated 21 March 1594 to the inquisitor of Florence from the cardinal of Santa Severina, that "cause ordinarie" were those that were not "serious either because of the quality of the persons or of the crimes."[21]

One of the largest collections of sentences is preserved today at Trinity College, Dublin and is discussed in more detail elsewhere in this volume.[22] Of these Trinity documents only a few have been published — the most sensational — by the Anglican clergyman Richard Gibbings, who engineered their acquisition by the College in mid-nineteenth century.[23] Karl Benrath produced a calendar of the first volume covering the years 1564–1567, but not in toto, and not without errors in transcription.[24] A very incomplete listing, but one that attempts to encompass the entire collection, is included in the *Catalogue* of Trinity manuscripts prepared by the College Librarian, T. K. Abbott.[25]

Certainly, a critical inventory, a calendar of all the material which would fully identify the accused, their "crimes," their religious affiliations if members of orders, their occupations and social class, their geographical distribution, the books they read or possessed, their punishments, and other noteworthy facts would seem to be greatly desirable. Such a project, first announced on the dustjacket of an early volume of the *Corpus Reformatorum Italicorum*, failed to materialize. It should be accorded high priority in any future discussion concerned with the computerized cataloguing of large inquisitorial collections, especially since the documents have ramifications that go well beyond the study of Italian heresy and have important European ramifications.[26]

One of the principal tools at our disposal for the deciphering of inquisitorial law is the manual or handbook intended as a working guide for the inquisitor. It is, ideally, a distillation of the teachings of canon law, ancient tradition, and current practice. With this category of literature, we are not faced with the problem of devising ambitious cataloguing strategies, as with trials, sentences, and correspondence. Rather, we need to attempt to answer certain questions connected with their production and use. Too often, I am afraid, scholars have picked up a manual at random and, without further scrutiny, assumed that they held in their hands the sacrosanct key to inquisitorial law and practice. Instead, I believe that the authority and currency of each work and, in fact, of each edition needs to be thoroughly verified.

The publishing history of Eliseo Masini's *Sacro Arsenale* (1st ed. 1621) offers a case in point and alerts us to the care we must exert when we select our guides through the inquisitorial maze. Our author waited until the second edition of his work, in 1625, four years after its first appearance, to include any discussion of witchcraft. This is certainly a strange omission, since the issue was one of great moment in the courts of the time and had been discussed at length by all previous writers. A reader who prided himself in ferreting out the first appearance of a work would in this case come away with a very serious distortion of the real situation. When Masini finally did add a chapter on occult crimes to his manual, he at least had the good sense to do so by appropriating the enlightened teachings of the *Instructio*, which had just begun to circulate in manuscript among the outlying tribunals. He translated a long section from Latin into the vernacular and incorporated it (without acknowledging its provenance) as part seven of his *Arsenale*.[27]

The earliest treatises have been meticulously described by Antoine Dondaine.[28] Succinct biographical sketches of their authors can be read in von Schulte's *Die Geschichte der Quellen und Literatur des Canonischen Rechts*[29] and in bio-bibliographies of the Franciscan and Dominican orders, discussed in a later section. A large, but still incomplete survey of their publishing history is furnished by Van der Vekene's bibliography;[30] a great many texts were collected by the Spanish jurist Francisco Peña and reprinted conveniently in 1584, with his commentaries, in one massive volume;[31] and substantial fragments, virtually from the entire known corpus, secular and ecclesiastical compositions alike, published and unpublished, are included in two massive anthologies by Henry Charles Lea and Joseph Hansen.[32]

Our concern here is with the texts which were in actual use during the sixteenth and seventeenth centuries. It is remarkable that several works of Spanish origin were printed in Italy in this period, two of which are of medieval provenance. One is the *Repertorium Inquisitorum*, in diction-

ary form, written by an anonymous fifteenth-century inquisitor of Valencia, first published in that city in 1484, and then again in Venice in 1575
and 1588 with the learned commentaries of two Italian jurists.[33] The second manual is the infinitely more famous and elaborate *Directorium Inquisitorum* by the fourteenth-century inquisitor of Aragon, Nicolau Eymeric.
It was republished in Rome in 1578 and on several other occasions in
the closing decades of the sixteenth century and in the early seventeenth
century. The latter editions, prepared by Francisco Peña, are models of
philology, enriched by his lengthy commentary and appendix of pertinent canon law documents, the so-called *Litterae Apostolicae*, collected at
the behest of the Roman Congregation.[34] Juan de Rojas, Jacobo de
Simancas (d. 1583) and Sébastian Salelles (d. 1666) are other Spanish authors
whose inquisitorial guides were published in Italy on more than one occasion, Simancas as late as 1690.[35]

Setting aside the case of Peña, whose long career in the curia and close
links to the Supreme Congregation qualify him as an unquestioned authority
on Roman inquisitorial doctrine, and whose extensive commentary to Eymeric's *Directorium* constituted a total adaptation of this older Spanish writer
to Roman usage, how do we explain this phenomenon? Despite the common underpinning of both Spanish and Italian tribunals in canon law,
there were serious doctrinal and judicial discrepancies between them, in
addition to the well-known organizational differences. In Spanish practice, sequestration of property occurred at the moment of arrest, followed
by confiscation in the event of conviction;[36] in Italy property of defendants usually survived even the admission of guilt in the case of penitent
heretics, with the exception of funds exacted to sustain them in prison
during the trial. In Spanish law, consultors attached to the courts saw
trial proceedings in their entirety, including the names of the prosecution
witnesses, before delivering their opinions; these names were withheld
in the Italian tribunals.[37] Under the Spanish, the confession of a minor
was null and void without the presence of a special defense official, the
curatore, but this figure seems to have been absent from Italian practice.[38]
In Italian usage a defense attorney was mandatory, if requested, even to
an offender who had admitted his crime, but was withheld in such a case
in Spanish courts.[39] The Inquisition in the Roman system regularly
prosecuted polygamy, viewing this as a heresy against the sacrament of
matrimony. Spanish inquisitors, on the other hand, questioned their jurisdiction over bigamists, tending to conceive the offense as carnally moti-

vated, rather than heretical. They felt, consequently, that it fell to the authority of the secular courts.[40] The list could be extended.

Were these Spanish manuals actually used in the Italian courts, or could it simply be a matter of Italian printers serving a Spanish market? Given the relative underdevelopment of Spanish printing and the trade connections enjoyed by Italian publishers with Spain, there is probably some truth in both assumptions. The *Repertorium* would not have been critically edited by two Italian jurists if it had not been intended for distribution in Italy. Peña's editions of Eymeric were in fact used widely and frequently reprinted. In the case of the works by Simancas, they were highly esteemed in Rome, although we lack direct evidence about their actual circulation.

There can be several criteria for determining the popularity of a given work: repeated editions, abundant and widely dispersed surviving manuscript copies, external testimonies by users, and evidence of borrowing by one writer from another, whether acknowledged or not. It is curious that while some manuals of questionable applicability were produced in Italy, writings by unimpeachable authorities remained in manuscript despite seeming popularity in their day. The "Prattica" of Cardinal Desiderio Scaglia (d. 1639), and the "Praxis" of Francisco Peña (d. 1612), both high functionaries of the Roman Holy Office, circulated among the provincial inquisitions, but were not published in their authors' lifetimes.[41] Writers whose works are most frequently cited by contemporaries for their popularity are Peña, Carena, and, surprisingly perhaps, a secular jurist, Prospero Farinacci, one of the more flamboyant and trouble-prone figures of turn-of-the-century Roman society.[42] On the basis of repeated republication, Peña's edition of the *Directorium*, Masini's *Sacro Arsenale*, and Carena's *Tractatus* (more about the second two below) would have to be considered widely accepted in the seventeenth century.[43] None, however, was elevated to the rank of "official" or exclusive guide to inquisitorial law, a point to which we shall return.[44]

The case of Masini described above is not the only instance of free borrowing from one writer by another. Deodato Scaglia, in his own "Prattica" plunders, without citing them, from both the homonymous work by his uncle, Desiderio, and Masini's *Arsenale*;[45] while later in the seventeenth century, Giovanni Battista Neri, a Florentine writer who had chanced upon a manuscript copy of Desiderio's vernacular work, translated it into Latin, embellishing generously as he did so, and published it as his own, after taking many bows for his labors, with the totally altered title, *De iudice S. Inquisitionis opusculum* (Florence, 1685).[46]

Inquisitorial manuals are generally thought to represent the theoretical side of judicial procedure, and it would be a mistake, of course, to rely on them exclusively for our understanding of inquisitorial justice. But they can also provide us with important practical insights based on actual eyewitness observation of the events transpired. Umberto Locati, to whom we shall return, inquisitor first in Pavia and then in Piacenza, appended to his manual, *Opus quod iudiciale inquisitorum dicitur* (Rome, 1570), a number of actual cases (under fictitious names) which had been tried before the Piacenza tribunal, together with the opinions of jurists who had been consulted about them.[47] Cesare Carena (d. 1659), who served both secular and ecclesiastical courts in Cremona, in his weighty *Tractatus de Officio Sanctissimae Inquisitionis* (1st ed. 1631), draws from his own courtroom experiences, beginning his recollections, "I will tell you what happened to me in my inquisition of Cremona" ("dicam quod mihi accidit in inquisitione mea Cremonae").[48] His is one of the most useful of all the texts for the comparison of secular with inquisitorial procedure, especially in regard to the handling of witchcraft prosecution, the crime over which the two jurisdictions competed most fiercely.

Similarly, Francisco Peña's extensive late-sixteenth-century commentary to Eymeric's *Directorium* is a highly reliable and comprehensive guide to distinguish the differences between medieval and modern inquisitorial teachings and practices. Peña rarely missed an opportunity to indicate the development and change that had occurred from Eymeric's day to his own. The Spanish-born and -trained Peña, whose entire mature career was spent engrossed in curial duties in Rome, is also one of our surest authorities in pointing out the differences between Iberian and Italian doctrine and practice.[49]

Although of all inquisitorial sources, with the exception of the canonical legislation on which they are based, manuals are those closest to pure theory, it is doubtful that they could be "scrupulously observed in all trials,"[50] as one recent writer observed. Too many unreconciled, even contradictory opinions existed. Inquisitorial law was not always uniform and its manuals not necessarily unswerving procedural guides. Issues are frequently encountered where a precise definition was not attained, over which jurists of equally great reputation disagreed, where the practice of Rome might on one occasion differ from the opinion of Iacobo de Simancas, while on another it held him up as a model to be followed because of the excellence of his teachings.[51] All this resulted in predictable confusion for the practicing judge.

Symptomatic of this uncertainty are the many surviving briefing books, further discussed below, where the law and precedent were searched to resolve such questions as, "Can the case of the person who presents himself to the court without having been summoned be decided by the inquisitor alone, without the bishop?"; "Are discussions between Catholics and heretics permissible?"; "Is a secular magistrate obliged to carry out sentences of the Holy Office if he has not seen the trial records?";[52] or even such life and death issues as whether penitent witches in their first lapsus were to be treated as any other first-time offender or consigned to the secular arm. Cardinal Francesco Albizzi, one of the most influential members of the Congregation of the Inquisition, in his *De Inconstantia in Iure*, cites a long list of authorities who had argued that penitent witches in their first fall under no circumstances were to be handed over to the secular arm. But Gregory XV opposed this view in his constitution *Omnipotentis Dei*, issued in 1623.[53]

The manuals abound with one writer's criticism of another, as when Peña, analyzing Camillo Campeggi's discussion of the comparative authority of bishop and inquisitor, remarks that it is so confusing, "one hardly knows what he wants" ("ut vix saepe intelligas quid velit";[54] or, elsewhere, when he rejects outright the opinion expressed in the *Repertorium*, "which for many reasons I do not approve" ("quod multis rationibus non probo") that corporal punishment could be substituted for a fine when the offender was unable to pay.[55] And he often concludes that if he had been the judge in a given situation, he would have imposed a "truer and milder sentence" than the one which was actually applied.[56] This repugnance was shared by Carena in regard to another seriously controverted point of law, namely the position upheld by Antoninus Diana, as well as other jurists, that a witness could be compelled to testify against himself, a doctrine against natural law that filled Carena with "maxima trepidatione."[57]

Despite the Supreme Congregation's endorsement of Peña's edition of the *Directorium*, the respect it voiced for Simancas, the countenancing in the next century of repeated reprintings of manuals by Masini and Carena, and the widespread circulation in manuscript of Desiderio Scaglia's "Prattica," no single compilation, as we have already had occasion to say, achieved the status of official and authoritative compendium of inquisitorial law. It would appear that provincial inquisitors possessed a certain latitude in selecting the texts by which they wished to be guided. In view of the discordant opinions these manuals contained on a variety of issues, the result could indeed have been rampant confusion.

With another type of source we enter squarely and incontrovertibly into the realm of inquisitorial practice. Correspondence, the letters exchanged by the Roman Congregation with its provincial tribunals, as well as by inquisitors themselves with their vicars in villages and hamlets, helps us penetrate behind theoretical treatises to chronicle the day-to-day affairs of these outlying courts, enabling us to peer behind the cold and austere formulations of trials, sentences, and legal treatises.

The surviving correspondence consists of two principal types: letters sent from the twin Congregations of the Inquisition and the Index to individual inquisitors, discussing business specific to each local tribunal, and circular letters directed to all of them at once. We have long surviving series for Bologna, Modena, Udine, Malta, and Florence, and others will undoubtedly come to light.[58] It was incumbent on each new inquisitor when taking up his office to familiarize himself with the previous history of his post and the manner in which he was expected to conduct its affairs through the correspondence in the archive of his tribunal. We can cite as an example the instructions to Monsignor Ricciulo taking up his assignment as minister to the Holy Office in Naples in 1633: "You will examine the letters that have been written by this Sacred Congregation to your predecessors so that you can be fully informed about how affairs were handled in the past and which can serve as your guide when similar matters arise in the future."[59]

Rome itself, which kept copies of all its outgoing correspondence, made extensive extracts from it searching for precedents on a wide variety of current legal questions where doubts and uncertainties still seemed to prevail, or where points of doctrine and practice which had been the subject of recent abuse or misunderstanding on the part of provincial officials were involved. These handy-reference problem books were sometimes arranged by subject in dictionary form (alphabetically, from "Abiuratio" to "Votum"), or sometimes geographically, for problems that had arisen in specific tribunals. They are an eloquent illustration of the doubts and uncertainties that still remained, at least at the grass-roots level, where the law was actually applied in the outlying courts, even a half century and more after the reconstitution of the Inquisition with *Licet ab initio* (1542).[60]

The importance of correspondence as an intimate source to penetrate the public facade of the Inquisition cannot be overemphasized. Insights about actual practices can be gained from documents of this sort that may elude us if we confine ourselves to legal documents alone. For example, although the entire juridical literature devotes cumulatively thousands of pages to the subject of interrogation, it is in a snippet from a letter addressed by Antonio Balduzzi, the *Commissario* of the Roman Congregation, to the inquisitor of Bologna (13 June 1573) that I learned the precise lengths to which secrecy was carried. In Rome the chamber of torture was customarily cleared even of the officials who administered the torments. The letter, regarding the interrogation of Constanza Guaina, whom we met earlier, reads: ". . . have the cord administered to her, and in the records write the length of time which it was applied. I also want to advise you not to permit the jailers or anyone else to remain in the torture chamber for greater secrecy; this is the custom in our Holy Office, that when offenders have been raised [off the ground] they [the guards] are asked to leave."[61] This certainly evokes a different scene from the usual iconographic evidence depicting sinister figures lurking in dark corners of the interrogation room. Another letter reveals the preferred Roman procedure for the selection of the defense attorney: writing to the inquisitor of Modena on 7 March 1626, the Supreme Congregation informed him that "the custom of the tribunal is to have defendants name at least three lawyers, one of whom is then selected by the inquisitor."[62]

The legal manuals are unswerving in their insistence that the office of inquisitor was infallible.[63] A less flattering and quite different reality recurs in the correspondence, these sources behind the sources. Disappointment and reproaches for frequently indifferent performance are common features in Rome's instructions to its local officials. With thinly veiled irony, Antonio Balduzzi, the Congregation's *Commissario*, expressed his condolences to the Bolognese inquisitor who had attempted to excuse his desultory correspondence as an unfortunate consequence of a physical ailment. Balduzzi writes, "I am sorry about the hurt finger which prevented you from writing, especially if it was bed warmer sickness that kept you, as I suspect; oh well, patience."[64] A succession of letters from Rome in the 1570s urge the Bolognese official to show more zeal and take a little more interest in his work, and scold him for abandoning his post without permission and for having appointed as *procuratore* someone who himself had once been indicted. Other letters encourage him to "a bit of exertion and diligence" ("un puoco di fatica e diligenza") and the avoidance of petty intrigues, and firmly remind the inquisitor that he should be writing his own letters and not passing the responsibility on to a lesser official. Rome was evenhanded in the distribution of reprimands, and other inquisitors whose performance was found wanting did not go unscathed. Thus, the inquisitor of Florence might be taken to task for appointing as his vicar in Pietrasanta a man who was both illiterate and of poor reputation ("non solo idiota, ma di poco buona fama"); and the inquisitor in Udine shamed with a letter reminding him that he had not written for many months "just as if there was no Inquisition in that city and diocese and no business to transact."[65]

In the next century an extremely interesting and revealing panorama of the conduct of inquisitorial affairs from the perspective of Rome for the triennium 1626–1628 is afforded by the three fat volumes of *copialettere* preserved in the *fondo* Barberini of the Vatican Library, "Registr(i) delle Lettere della Sacra Congregatione Scritte a Diversi."[66] Some are individual communications, others are circular letters addressed to all the outlying tribunals jointly. They too supply evidence of the irregularities, ignorance, and confusion that still prevailed at the level of the provincial courts and their vicariates several decades into the seventeenth century. The Supreme Congregation was compelled to express its disbelief over miscarriages of justice occurring at every stage of the legal process, from the initial indictment to the imposition of the sentence,[67] or over erratic procedures during trials flouting century-old traditions for the protection of the anonymity of witnesses.[68]

It is not possible, for the moment, to do more than mention other forms of epistolary exchanges. Nunciatures[69] and other forms of diplomatic documents,[70] as well as correspondence exchanged by Rome with secular rulers,[71] can be of great importance in reconstructing the activities of the Inquisition even if they are not exclusively inquisitorial sources. From the reports of secular ambassadors we glean such precious pertinent information as the judicial shortcuts Paul IV would gladly have followed to obtain a hasty conviction of Cardinal Morone,[72] the eyewitness account of the sack of the palace of the Holy Office in 1559,[73] and a perceptive character sketch of a senior official of the Inquisition, the cardinal of Santa Severina—a difficult man, in the envoy's opinion, who would go to any lengths to aggrandize the authority of the institution he served so intensely.[74] These sources are especially valuable for the study of events outside the states of the Church where the Inquisition functioned in large measure at the discretion of the secular authorities. The cardinals of the Roman Congregation frequently felt compelled in arduous cases to come to the assistance of their provincial officials, interceding directly with the rulers in question, or through the nuncio, who outranked the local inquisitor, spoke with greater authority, and enjoyed easier access to governing circles. In March 1626 an uncontrollable witch panic in Florence had led secular magistrates to intervene, resulting in the gross miscarriage of justice. The nuncio to that city was asked by the Roman Congregation to use his office to persuade "cotesti principi" that the voice suggesting the presence of many witches in Florence and in the *contado* had been produced by the imagination of men and had no basis in fact.[75]

A discussion of this type of material would be incomplete without mention of the massive correspondence of Charles Borromeo, totaling approximately 60,000 pieces according to a recent estimate, principally conserved in the Biblioteca Ambrosiana. Although not all the letters are relevant to our subject, a large number of them are, and several of the more pertinent codices have been identified. After the destruction of the archive in the Chiesa delle Grazie in 1788, the correspondence between Borromeo and the Congregation in Rome has become one of the principal sources for the reconstruction of inquisitorial activity in Milan.[76] Since a bishop (or his vicar) was a duly constituted member of the provincial tribunal in his see, episcopal correspondence has a rich potential for yielding pertinent data, as a recently published series from the diocese of Aquileia shows.[77]

Among the more valuable and yet underused categories of sources are the many varied types of documents, both printed and in manuscript, connected with the Dominican and Franciscan orders, and especially the former, since it bore the chief burden of inquisitorial activity.[78] The list is long, containing bio-bibliographies, of which the best known and most comprehensive is Quétif and Echard's *Scriptores Ordinis Praedicatorum*, (published between 1719 and 1723);[79] the correspondence of high officials, including the general and cardinal protector of the order;[80] the *Acta* of the general chapters, the proceedings of the meetings occurring every three years, which have been critically edited and are readily available in the series of Dominican *Monumenta*;[81] the *Registers* of the master general, an important source for the appointment and dismissal of the inquisitors from 1508 until about 1553, when that responsibility was assumed by the reconstituted Congregation of the Inquisition in Rome;[82] histories of the orders[83] and of the single convents which housed the provincial tribunals;[84] and the collections of Bulls and edicts compiled from time to time which were intended to regulate the life of the orders.[85]

Materials of this type are crucial for the reconstruction of the careers and literary activity of the inquisitors, their appointments and transfers from one seat to another, their assignment to educational establishments, and in general, their rise and fall on the hierarchical ladder. Also interesting are their descriptions of convent life and especially of the tensions that might be experienced by inquisitors attempting to fulfill their juridical duties while abiding by their calling as religious and by the communal rules of the establishments within which they had to operate.

Bio-bibliographies are important tools for reconstructing the external careers of the members of orders. Despite their formal, stylized nature, they also unexpectedly occasionally allow us to perceive occurrences from daily life, as we noted earlier in the instance of the manuals, which have been similarly treated as merely theoretical formulations. A dramatic instance of this is provided by Serafino Razzi's *Istoria* of illustrious Dominicans published at Lucca in 1596. In the entry devoted to Nicolò de Alessi, who died in 1585 "septuagenarian," theologian, poet, distinguished Latin orator — and inquisitor of Perugia for a term — Razzi provides us with this brief personal reminiscence: ". . . [Alessi] was not overly severe (as some are today) but he did everything with mildness and gentleness. And it is told that he often cried out of mercy and compassion when, in the course of his duties, he had to employ torture and the cord on defendants."[86]

This statement highlights what must have been a dilemma for many individuals in the religious life, who found themselves obliged to take their turns administering a judicial and penal system involving them in activities alien to the life of meditation, prayer, scholarship, and charity which they had chosen. For some, the duties and responsibilities of inquisitor, as in the case of Alessi, must have been burdensome and foreign to their personalities and aspirations. Yet it was a service that fell to many and which not all could fulfill with the required zeal, as we saw from the letters sent by the Congregation in Rome to its provincial officials.[87]

Other documents cast light on still other aspects of the tension inherent in the dichotomy of religious-inquisitor. Inquisitors were also members of their convents, obliged to follow a common discipline, and were frequently burdened with duties and responsibilities imposed by their order which interfered with their function as ecclesiastical prosecutor and judge.

A letter of 1549 informs us that a prisoner needed to be transferred to Bologna because the inquisitor "has a lectureship in the convent, and for this reason cannot absent himself to come and judge him in Ferrara without great inconvenience to himself. . . ."[88] Another, dated 1572, from the *Commissario* of the Roman Congregation to the inquisitor of Bologna, who was also prior of his convent, ordered him not to mix the affairs of his two jurisdictions in the same letter, "so that if the need arises I can show them and have them read in our meetings . . . ."[89] A 1584 decree of the Roman Congregation attempted to end the endemic delays in trial proceedings caused by the frequent long absences of inquisitors by restricting their travels, even to provincial and general chapters of their order, without special license;[90] and a letter of 1613 from Cardinal Millino to the inquisitor of Bologna forbade him from hearing the confessions of nuns in neighboring convents, a service he was continuing from the days when he had been prior, but which now constituted a real conflict of interest.[91]

Further attempts at legislation to relieve the office of inquisitor from duties as a religious are recorded by the *Acta* of the general chapters. The proceedings of these triennial reunions reveal that if an inquisitor was elected prior of a convent, confirmation should await consultation with the general of the order, "lest the office of inquisitor be seriously hindered";[92] when an inquisitor from the Lombard Province, Eliseo Capi, was assigned as *reggente* of the Dominican *Studium* in Bologna, a proviso was added that if he could not fulfill the charge because of his duties as inquisitor, then the new responsibility should devolve to another brother, a certain Fra Battista da Genova.[93]

These documents also assist in reconstructing the organization and daily life within the convents of the orders and the place of the inquisitors within them. The *Acta* record the consequent jurisdictional and disciplinary tensions, the formalities for travel and residence outside the convent, from which even inquisitors were not wholly spared,[94] the creation and maintenance within these establishments of infirmaries,[95] prisons[96] and libraries,[97] the arrangements for communal sleeping, from which the prior and a few senior brothers were exempted,[98] the prohibitions against the display of profane images in cells,[99] and, repeatedly, injunctions against staging plays because it meant donning secular garb, as well as against ridiculing their bishop in the impersonations which the brothers regularly mounted in the convents on various feast days throughout the year.[100]

The strains provoked by the presence in Dominican convents of the local tribunals of the Inquisition were long enduring. The religious houses were usually poor and overcrowded, and the residents tended to view inquisitors, with their hangers-on and prisoners in their midst, as unwelcome additional burdens.[101] Inquisitors were reminded not to employ outsiders ("forastieri"), and thereby add to the mouths needing feeding, when the regular brothers of the house could perform the desired services.[102] The fact that the inquisitor was an agent of the central papal government and not to be interfered with by the superior of the house was repeated in numerous communications from the cardinals of the Roman Congregation. On the other hand, inquisitors were reminded that they were bound by the rules of their order and that they were expected to participate in the regular routines of their house and not use their office as a pretext to escape the common discipline, an accusation that was frequently made against them. Both sides of the question are discussed in a letter from the Roman Congregation to the general of the Dominicans, dated 4 September 1580:

> His Holiness has learned that inquisitors of the order of St. Dominic, under the pretext of the Holy Office, pretend to be wholly exempt from obedience to their superiors and do not want, like the others, to obey or observe the Rule, going out of monasteries at will without revealing their whereabouts; and their companions, the vicars, notaries and other agents are doing the same, from which arises laxness in observance of the Rule with disservice to God and scandal toward their neighbors. On the other side, inquisitors complain that because of the contrariness of their superiors in the order, or out of some fear of giving displeasure to princes and noblemen, and of generating hatred for the convent, they are prevented from performing their duties and many difficulties are created for them by the superiors themselves.[103]

A later attempt to implement reform is contained in the *Ordini da Osservarsi da gl'Inquisitori, per Decreto della Sacra Congregatione del Sant'Officio di Roma*, dated 1611. This is one of the most detailed and comprehensive single statements on the regulation of inquisitorial establishments within the convents of the orders:

> ... inquisitors should exercise their office diligently, but with the least possible inconvenience to the discipline of the order, especially

in the observance of enclosure, so that the gates of the convents and the other customary places can remain shut, and that under pretext of the Holy Office no order and law made by superiors should be broken, such as in the number of retainers, absences from the choir, study and rules of all sorts, and in wanting to keep or disguise under the mantle of the Holy Office whomever they please. Therefore, everyone is to remain under the obedience of their superiors, who will be able to dispose of them just like the other brothers at the times when they are not occupied in the service of the Holy Office.[104]

One has the impression that this tension between responsibilities and vocations within the mendicant orders was endemic and could not be legislated away: the disaffection apparent in the two documents cited above was still a reality decades later. A 1623 letter from the *Commissario* of the Roman Congregation to the inquisitor of Bologna, in reference to the situation in Modena, lamented that "the inappropriate quarrels and controversies which go on between inquisitors and priors are very detrimental to the reputation of the order, to the good governance of convents, and to their own proper interests."[105] Shortly after mid-century it was felt necessary to reissue the edict of 1611, evidence that the situation had escaped solution.[106]

Three other types of sources essential for the study of the Italian inquisitorial tribunals are of curial provenance. The first category is papal legislation, Bulls, and constitutions. These range from the pronouncements collected by Peña, the *Litterae Apostolicae* appended to his editions of Eymeric's *Directorium*, which are the basic canonical statements on the question of the extirpation of heresy from the medieval period through 1587,[107] to the landmark sixteenth- and seventeenth-century Bulls, *Licet ab initio*, reconstituting the Inquisition in Rome in 1542; *Immensa Aeterni Dei*, elevating it to a position of preeminence among the congregations into which papal government was divided in 1588; or *Omnipotentis Dei* in 1623, which attempted to overturn existing witchcraft legislation. Fortunately, papal Bulls have been collected and edited progressively in a series of monumental publications;[108] the apposite texts now need to be identified and used appropriately.

Another pertinent type of document is the vast assortment of "instructions," both printed and in manuscript, issued generally at the behest of the reigning pope himself. They were intended occasionally to introduce new legislation, but more often to reinforce existing statutes and procedures, such as the celebrated *Instructio* for the proper conduct of witchcraft trials, issued before 1624.[109] These slight pamphlets of a few pages were intended to impart the essentials of the law more conveniently to the beleaguered provincial judge than the weightier manuals.

The third source of curial provenance consists of the *decreta* of the Supreme Congregation in Rome, the minutes, decisions, pronouncements of this body emanating from its weekly sessions at which the pontiff himself presided.[110] They are key administrative documents affecting every aspect of inquisitorial activity. Many reflect final measures adopted by the Holy Office after the regular review and discussion of trials in progress and of recently received correspondence from the provincial tribunals. The majority of inquisitorial *decreta*, numbering 250 volumes according to a recent count, and ranging in date from 1546 to 1682, are preserved in the still inaccessible archive in the palace of the Holy Office in Rome, to which only a handful of scholars have had access in this century.[111] Smaller collections have been dispersed to other Roman depositories, the Vatican Library and Archives,[112] the Casanatense Library,[113] and, undoubtedly, farther afield. The search for and systematic inventorying of these documents should have a high priority. The Casanatense codex, for example, which covers only the biennium 1600–1602, is almost eight hundred pages in length and averages about 5–7 entries, that is separate items of business, per page.

So much then, for the principal categories of official inquisitorial sources. But this survey would be incomplete if it did not at least mention some important subsidiary types of documents that have proven to be pertinent to our study. Although not generated by the Inquisition itself, they contribute to our knowledge of it. This class of material includes contemporary histories of the institution,[114] sometimes born in the heat of controversy, as well as polemical works which, even if they do not always provide objective information, at least help us trace such aspects as the developing image of the Inquisition projected to a northern public;[115] accounts of such specific events as a frenzied manhunt conducted in Bologna in the early 1620s against a secret conventicle of gross blasphemers;[116] vivid descriptions of *autos da fé* and the accompanying penitential sermons;[117] biographies, autobiographies, and personal eyewitness accounts about and by some of the principal figures on both sides of the docket;[118]

documents associated with the charitable work of the confraternities which comforted the condemned and accompanied them to their death;[119] and even descriptions of wanted men, the frequently colorful, bizarre, _contrasegni_ circulated by Rome among the provincial authorities, urging them to be on the lookout, as in one case, for an Englishman last seen weeks before wearing "white sox."[120]

There are still other sources, secular in provenance, which similarly make an important contribution to our subject. These include the documentary repositories of magistracies, whose active role in the repression of heresy in the territories they governed brought them into contact (and conflict) with the Holy Office. I am alluding, in Venice, to the Council of Ten which jealously guarded its jurisdiction over all aspects of life within its dominions;[121] or, in Lucca, where the Inquisition was never admitted, despite tremendous pressure, to its surrogate, a lay body founded in 1545, the _Offizio sopra la Religione_.[122] And even where the Inquisition had freer rein, in Siena and in the Grand Duchy of Tuscany, secular intervention in the conduct of its affairs resulted in extensive series of relevant documents finding a resting place in state archives.[123] Diplomatic reports, the correspondence of ambassadors with their princes, have already been mentioned.[124] To these could be added chronicles,[125] diaries,[126] broadsides and early newssheets,[127] and more purely literary works.[128] Finally, the time has undoubtedly come when serious consideration should be given to the identification and inventorying of contemporary iconographic evidence.[129] This too will be an essential step in that process of disentangling fact from fiction which underlies so many of our efforts in the study of the Inquisition.

Notes

1. See "The Dispersed Archives of the Roman Inquisition," p. 23.

2. M[ario] N[iccoli], "Inquisizione," _Enciclopedia italiana_ 19:338: "La pressoché assoluta mancanza di documenti, lo speciale segreto del qual fu circondata l'opera degl'inquisitori non consentono di seguire con precisione l'azione dell' Inquisizione romana."

3. A. Biondi, "Lunga durata e microarticolazione nel territorio di un Ufficio dell'Inquisizione: Il 'Sacro Tribunale' a Modena (1292–1785)," _Annali dell'Istituto storico italo-germanico in Trento_ 8 (1982): 73–90, esp. pp. 89 ff. The inventory is of the documents of the Modena tribunal after its reorganization in 1598 from vicariate to full inquisitorial court. It consists of: (1) letters from the Supreme Congregation in Rome,

1568–1784; (2) correspondence of the Modena Inquisition with various parties, including its branch offices, the vicariates; (3) printed edicts and decrees received from various inquisitorial tribunals; (4) denunciations, pre-trial investigations, trials, sentences, etc. For further use by Biondi of the Modena documents, see his "La 'Nuova Inquisizione' a Modena: Tre inquisitori (1589–1607)," in *Città italiane del '500: Tra Riforma e Controriforma* (Lucca, 1988), 61–76. My examination of the inquisitorial materials in the Archivio della Curia Arcivescovile, Udine revealed these general categories of materials: trials; sentences; correspondence with the Holy Office in Rome and with the Congregation of the Index, Nuncios, and Patriarchs; Bulls, decrees, edicts of the Roman Holy Office; denunciations; financial documents ("Redditus et Introitus S. Officii"); legal handbooks and manuals. It is a pleasure to repeat my thanks to Professor Luigi De Biasio, who has responsibility over this collection, for his extreme courtesy during my visit in May 1988.

4. A. Del Col, "I processi dell'Inquisizione come fonte: considerazioni diplomatiche e storiche," *Annuario dell'Istituto storico italiano per l'età moderna e contemporanea* 35–36 (1983–84): 29–49, esp. pp. 32 ff. The principal manuscript trial repositories are indicated in "The Dispersed Archives," and in "Toward a Statistical Profile of the Italian Inquisitions." See also the interesting analyses of the various components of the trial document by S. Abbiati, "Intorno ad una possibile valutazione giuridico-diplomatica del documento inquisitorio," *Studi di storia medioevale e di diplomatica* 3 (1978): 167–79.

5. I point out an instance of modern scholarly confusion over the term *carcere perpetuo* which, rather than actual imprisonment for life, denotes incarceration for about three years on condition of good behavior, in "Preliminary Observations," p. 12 in this volume.

6. C. Ginzburg, "Witchcraft and Popular Piety: Notes on a Modenese Trial of 1519," in *Clues, Myths, and the Historical Method*, trans. J. and A. C. Tedeschi (Baltimore, 1989), 1–16, 165–70; originally published as "Stregoneria e pietà popolare: Note a proposito di un processo modenese del 1619," *Annali della Scuola Normale Superiore di Pisa: Lettere, storia e filosofia*, ser. 2, 30 (1961): 269–87. This thesis underlies Ginzburg's *The Night Battles: Witchcraft and Agrarian Cults in the Sixteenth and Seventeenth Centuries* (Baltimore, 1983), originally published as *I Benandanti: Stregoneria e culti agrari tra Cinquecento e Seicento* (Turin, 1966). Cf. Del Col, "I processi," 33: "Ci si chiede in che misura i verbali corrispondono agli interrogatori come si svolsero di fatto, quanto in essi rifletta solo il pensiero dei giudici e quanto, almeno parzialmente, le idee e le affermazioni degli imputati e dei testimoni." The question receives this answer from G. Merlo in the context of particular medieval inquisitorial sources: ". . . i verbali degli interrogatori sono assai più pieni di vita e aderenti alla verità di quanto normalmente, ma erroneamente, si creda": "I registri inquisitoriali come fonti per la storia dei gruppi ereticali clandestini: il caso del Piemonte basso medievale," in *Histoire et clandestinité du Moyen-Age à la première guerre mondiale. Colloque de Privas (Mai 1977). Actes recueillis par* M. Tilloy, G. Audisio et J. Chiffoleau (Albi, 1979), 72.

7. See, for example, Bernardo da Como, "Tractatus de Strigibus," in *Lucerna Inquisitorum Haereticae Pravitatis* (Rome, 1584), 150; Francisco Peña, commentary in Nicolau Eymeric, *Directorium Inquisitorum* (Rome, 1587), 422: "Id vero in primis praecavere debent iudices violatae religionis, ne ita reos interrogent, ut suggerere illis potius, ac fugiendi modos praescribere, quam veritatem ab eis indagare videantur," etc.

8. BAV, Barb. lat. 6334, fols. 58v–59r: "... li sommarii che manda, sieno non latini, ma volgari, et con le parole stesse nelle cose sostantiali de' testimonii et del reo. . . ." For other samples from the correspondence, see BRB, MS. II 290 vol. 2, fol. 172, letter of the senior member of the Roman Congregation, Giulio Antonio Santorio, Cardinal of Santa Severina, to the Florentine inquisitor, dated 18 November 1600: "Per ordine della S.tà di N.ro S.re, V.ra R.tia per l'avvenire nello essamine de' testimonii, et constituti de' rei nel S.to Officio faccia scrivere per extensum tutti gli interrogatorii, obiettioni et repliche per ovviare à pregiudicii che si fanno in non scriversi gl'interrogatorii, et per vedere se siano suggestivi o no. . . ."

9. On this celebrated reforming document, see "The Roman Inquisition and Witchcraft," pp. 205–27.

10. I cite from the first version of the text of the *Instructio* to appear in print, in Tommaso Castaldi (or Gastaldi), *De Potestate Angelica*, 3 vols. (Rome, 1650–52), 2:244: "Et ad hoc maxime advertere debeant iudices, quia multi in hoc decipiuntur falso putantes, quod huiusmodi sortilegia fieri non possint sine apostasia formali ad daemonem: et hinc oriuntur maxima praeiudicia mulieribus inquisitis de huiusmodi sortilegiis. Iudices enim minus periti, vel alias nimis faciles (ob lecturam aliquando librorum de sortilegiis, & strigibus tractantium) hoc falso praesupposto decepti nullam viam relinquunt, etiam indebitam, pro extorquenda confessione mulierum, quae saepissime ob diversos malos, & illicitos modo habitos, tandem inducuntur ad fatendum ea, quae nunquam cogitarunt."

11. Ibid., 245: "Et ut facilius iudices possint se abstinere à quaqunque suggestione, quando mulieres incipiunt fateri talem apostasiam; forsan melius esset ut tunc iudices oblivescerentur eorum quae dicunt doctores quidam in ista materia: quia saepe visum est, quod iudices in ordine ad ea, quae praeleguntur penes doctores, multa praeiudicia faciunt his mulieribus."

12. Ibid., 244: "Nullo modo curent, neque permittant iudices, quod custos carceris, aut quivis alius ille sit, mulieribus sic carceratis suggerant, quid fateri debeant cum examinatae fuerint."

13. See the entry "Sant'Uffizio" prepared by Osbat and colleagues in G. Galasso and C. Russo, eds., *L'Archivio storico diocesano di Napoli*, 2 vols. (Naples, 1978), 2:627–914, and Osbat's "La sezione 'Denunce' del fondo 'Sant'Ufficio' nell'archivio storico diocesano di Napoli," *Atti del congresso internazionale di studi sull'età del Viceregno* (Bari, 1977), 2:403–33.

14. For a dramatic case where the reading of the abjuration was transformed into a last, courageous attempt at freedom of expression, see Andrea Del Col, "L'abiura trasformata in propaganda ereticale nel duomo di Udine (15 Aprile 1544)," *Metodi*

e ricerche 2 (1981): 57–73. See Del Col's "I processi dell'Inquisizione come fonte," 34 for the reminder that the abjuration was generally prepared by the judge on the basis of the trial testimony, not by the defendant.

15. BAV, Barb. lat. 6334, fol. 71, letter from the Supreme Congregation to the inquisitor of Genova, 20 March 1626, concerning the case of a Servite, Fra Antonio Aurighi: ". . .la sentenza si leggerà nel primo capitolo generale della sua Religione et nel luogo del delitto."

16. See Giovanni Battista Neri, *De iudice S. Inquisitionis opusculum* (Florence, 1685), 58: "Dicunt tamen DD. quod sententiae latae ab inquisitoribus contra sollicitantes non debent legi in publico actu fidei, sed in secreto coram consultoribus ecclesiasticis, ne, si legerentur in publico actu fidei, multi a receptione sacramenti paenitentiae se abstinerent, & haeretici, qui tale sacramentum detestant omnino sacerdotes nostros irriderent. . . ." To see how Rome construed "public" and "private" in practical terms, cf. n. 67.

17. The relevant texts are cited in "The Question of Magic and Witchcraft," p. 229.

18. BA, MS. B–1860, fol. 149, letter of the *Commissario* of the Supreme Congregation in Rome, Antonio Balduzzi, to the inquisitor of Bologna, 22 August 1573: "Vi mando con questa il decreto della rissolutione fatta nella causa di madonna Constanza Guaina, et così l'espedirete secretamente, dandole però tutte l'altre penitenze consuete a darsi a chi abiura formalmente. La gratia fattale d'abiurare secretamente è stata per rispetto delle figliuole ch'ha da maritare, che altrimenti non s'otteneva, et s'è ottenuta anco con qualche difficoltà."

19. For the different grades of abjuration and their consequences, see Peña's commentary to Eymeric's, *Directorium Inquisitorum*, 488: "Denique ultima, & potissima differentia est, quoniam qui de vehementi abiurat, si relabatur in haeresim, relapsorum poena punitur, & curiae seculari traditur; qui vero de levi abiurat, quamvis relabatur in haeresim sive abiuratam sive aliam: nec putatur relapsus, nec relapsorum poena plectitur, quamvis acrius ob secundum lapsum puniatur."

20. BA, MS. B–1860, fol. 120: "Non mi pare d'havere a dirvi cosa particolare se non sodisfare a due dimande vostre, l'una quello ch'io intendo per le cose piccole ch'havete a trattare da voi senza altrimenti molestarne questi SS.ri Ill.mi, a che vi dico, prima ch'io non voglio ch'in cosa alcuna ch'io vi scriva da me come frate Antonio habbiate come decisione e leggi, ma come avvisi e pareri amichevoli e fraterni. Appresso vi dico, che le cose che vi passarano per le mani da se si mostrarano se sono piccole ò grandi, e se sono degne d'avisarne questo S.to Tribonale, ò no, e che quà io non vi saprei dare regola certa, ma il vostro giudicio v'ha da regolare. Certo è che non ogni minutia, ne d'ogni depositione s'ha da scrivere. Ma quando le cause sono fondate ò volete venire a qualche atto importante come di sentenza, ò simili, è bene d'avisarne, e dire ancho il parere delli vostri consultori, e sempre date aviso delli complici che fossero nominati." The cardinal of Santa Severina wrote in almost identical terms to the inquisitor of Florence on 21 May 1594 (BRB, MS. II 290, vol. 2, fol. 170). Provincial officials were experiencing difficulty defining

their proper sphere of activity. Cf. L. von Pastor, _Allgemeine Dekrete der römischen Inquisition aus den Jahren 1555–1597: Nach dem Notariatsprotokoll des S. Uffizio zum erstenmale veröffentlicht_ (Freiburg.i.Br., 1912), 37, decree of 18 September 1581: ". . . quod inquisitores sententias omnes transmittant ad hoc Sanctum Officium, non autem processus, nisi in arduis causis; sed bene ante expeditionem summarium transmittant et responsum expectent." This provision has to be reaffirmed in a decree of 7 September 1594 (ibid., 54).

21. BRB, MS. II 290, vol. 2, fol. 170.

22. See "The Dispersed Archives," esp. pp. 37–38 and "A Statistical Profile," pp. 123–24 in this volume.

23. They are listed in my "Dispersed Archives," p. 37.

24. K. Benrath, "Atti degli archivi romani della Biblioteca del Collegio della Trinità in Dublino," _La rivista cristiana_ 7 (1879): 457–72, 497–505; 8 (1880): 10–13, 55–58, 94–97, 137–43. This is a translation, with the addition of the calendar of sentences, of "Akten aus römischen Archiven in Trinity College Library, Dublin," _Historische Zeitschrift_ 41 (1879): 249–62.

25. T. K. Abbott, _Catalogue of the Manuscripts in the Library of Trinity College, Dublin_ (Dublin and London, 1900), 241–84, MSS. 1224–1277. This includes another thirty-five volumes at Trinity College which contain progress reports sent to Rome dealing with litigation before provincial tribunals.

26. See "The Dispersed Archives," esp. pp. 23–45 and notes in this volume.

27. _Sacro Arsenale, overo Prattica dell'Officio della S. Inquisitione, ampliata_ (Genova, 1625), "Settima Parte," 175–82. The second edition totaled 438 pp., as opposed to 320 for the first (Genova, 1621). E. Van der Vekene (_Bibliotheca Bibliographica Historiae Sanctae Inquisitionis_, 2 vols. [Vaduz, 1982–83], ad indicem) records ten editions, the last in 1730, of this popular manual which was expanded several times in the course of republication.

28. Antoine Dondaine, "Le manuel de l'inquisiteur (1230–1330)," _AFP_ 17 (1947): 85–194. Dondaine was building on the survey of inquisitorial materials in Italian libraries and archives conducted by Charles Molinier, "Rapport à M. le Ministre de l'Instruction Publique sur une mission exécutée en Italie de février à avril 1885," _Archives des missions scientifiques et littéraires_, ser. 3, t. 14 (1888): 133–336.

29. J. Friedrich von Schulte, _Die Geschichte der Quellen und Literatur des canonischen Rechts_, 3 vols. (Stuttgart, 1875; reprint Graz, 1956), ad indicem.

30. E. van der Vekene, _Bibliotheca Bibliographica Historiae Sanctae Inquisitionis_ (cited at n. 27).

31. _Tractatus illustrium in utroque tum pontificii, tum caesarei iuris facultate iurisconsultorum de iudiciis criminalibus S. Inquisitionis_, 11, pt. 2 (Venice, 1584). On Peña, indefatigable editor of inquisitorial texts, see below at n. 34. The _Tractatus_ includes writings by J. Simancas, J. de Rojas, Z. Ugolini, C. Campeggio, B. da Como, B. Spina, P. Ghirlandi, C. Bruni, F. Ponzinio, and Peña himself.

32. H. C. Lea, _Materials Toward a History of Witchcraft_, arranged and edited by A. C. Howland, 3 vols. (Philadelphia, 1939; reprint New York, 1957). For the

inquisitorial materials, see esp. pp. 942–1038; J. Hansen, *Quellen und Untersuchungen zur Geschichte des Hexenwahns und der Hexenverfolgung im Mittelalter* (Bonn, 1901; reprinted Hildesheim, 1963).

33. I have used the second of the two Venetian editions: *Repertorium inquisitorum pravitatis haereticae, in quo omnia, quae ad haeresum cognitionem, ac S. Inquisitionis forum pertinent, continentur* (Venice, 1588). The editors were Quintilianus Mandosius, "civis romanus," and Petrus Vendramenus, each of whom signed with his initials those "Additiones" for which he was responsible. They supplied references to sources, corrected quotations, and cited a range of authorities from Cicero to F. Hotman (p. 338). There is now a modern French version by L. Sala-Molins, *Le dictionnaire des inquisiteurs: Valence 1494* (Paris, 1981).

34. See also n. 107 below. The standard collection of canon law texts is E. A. Friedberg's *Corpus iuris canonici*, 2nd ed., 2 vols., (Graz, 1955). The principal texts affecting inquisitorial procedure occur in the "Sexti Decretalium Liber Quintus," 2: cols. 1069–78 and "Clementinarum Lib. V. Tit. III, De Haereticis," cols. 1181–84. See now the fundamental guide to these sources and to the ecclesiastical institutions which generated them: *A Catalogue of Canon and Roman Law Manuscripts in the Vatican Library, I: Codices Vaticani latini 541–2299*, compiled under the direction of S. Kuttner and R. Elze, Studi e Testi, 322 (Vatican City, 1986). See also the useful anthology of inquisitorial canonical texts collected in K.-V. Selge, *Texte zur Inquisition*, Texte zur Kirchen-und Theologiegeschichte, 4 (Gütersloh, 1967).

On Peña and his editorial labors, which extended far beyond his re-edition of Eymeric's *Directorium*, see E. M. Peters, "Editing Inquisitors' Manuals in the Sixteenth Century: Francisco Peña and the *Directorium inquisitorum* of Nicholas Eymeric," *The Library Chronicle* 40 (1974): 95–107, and the exhaustive treatment of the subject in A. Borromeo's "A proposito del 'Directorium Inquisitorum' di Nicolas Eymerich e delle sue edizioni cinquecentesche," *Critica storica* 20 (1983): 499–547. Borromeo's essay was elicited by the abridged French translation of the *Directorium*: *Le Manuel des Inquisiteurs* (introduction, translation and notes by L. Sala-Molins [Paris and The Hague, 1973]), of which he is justly critical. Portions of the *Directorium* (Pt. 2, Quaestiones 42, 43) appear in English translation as appendix 2 in Peters's *The Magician, the Witch and the Law* (Philadelphia, 1978), 196–202 and in *Witchcraft in Europe, 1100–1700: A Documentary History*, edited with an introduction by A. C. Kors and E. Peters (Philadelphia, 1972), chap. 3, pt. 14.

35. For Juan de Rojas in Italy, see his *Singularis iuris in favorem fidei, haeresisque detestationem, Tractatus de haereticis*, edited by Peña (Venice, 1583). For the esteem enjoyed by Simancas in the highest councils of the Roman Inquisition, see the letter from Fra Paolo da Ferrara, an official of the Supreme Congregation, to the inquisitor of Bologna, 7 November 1573 (BA, MS. B–1860, fol. 160): "Non mancarò di ricordare a V.R. che non si lassi indurre da chi si voglia, in fare cose nuove et dare penitenze e castighi insoliti a qual sorte di persone si voglia, ma seguiti il costume ordinario, e come ritrova ne i processi essersi fatto in simili casi, o almeno dia prima aviso a questi SS.ri Ill.mi del parere de suoi consultori, e di Mons. re Vicario &

anche suo, ed aspetti la risposta. Ne sia molto facile V.R. in venire alla captura come ben insegna & conseglia il Simanca. . . ." At this date, if we limit ourselves to Italian imprints, the allusion could have been to Simancas's *Praxis Haereseos, sive Enchiridion Iudicum Violatae Religionis* (Venice, 1568; reprinted Venice 1569 and 1573). Another, later, Italian edition of a work by this author was his *De Catholicis Institutionibus Liber, ad praecavendas & extirpandas haereses admodum necessarius* (Rome, 1575; Ferrara, 1692; 1st ed., Valladolid, 1552). Simancas's *Enchiridion*, dedicated to Pius V, was intended as a handy, concise guide for judges who found the *De Catholicis Institutionibus* too bulky (*Enchiridion*, Antwerp, 1573, p. [3]). Cf. also Zanchino Ugolini's *De haereticis . . . tractatus aureus . . . Iacobi Simancae adnotationes . . .* (Rome, 1579). Salelles's magnum opus was his *De materiis Tribunalium S. Inquisitionis, seu de Regulis multiplicibus pro formando quovis eorum ministro, praesertim consultore . . .*, 3 vols. (Rome, 1651–56). The author is described on the titlepage as a Jesuit from Valencia who served for forty years as a consultor in the Holy Office of Malta.

36. See H. Kamen, "Confiscation in the Economy of the Spanish Inquisition," *Economic History Review* 18 (1965): 511–25, and idem, *Inquisition and Society in Spain in the Sixteenth and Seventeenth Centuries* (London, 1985), 146 ff.; E. Masini, *Sacro Arsenale*, 386 (cited in full at n. 27; I use the Bologna 1665 ed.).

37. A. Diana, *Coordinati, seu omnium resolutionum moralium . . . editio novissima* (Venice, 1698), 5:366: "Et tandem pro coronide huius resolut. notandum est hic obiter in ordine ad praxim, quod in aliquibus Inquisitionibus consuetudo obtinuit, ut nomina testium consultoribus non manifestentur. . . . Verum praxis nostrae Inquisitionis Hispanicae contrarium observat, & ideo consultoribus manifestantur nomina testium. . . ." Diana served as inquisitor in Palermo.

38. For the Spanish position, see F. Peña, "Instructio seu Praxis Inquisitorum," in Cesare Carena's *Tractatus de Officio Sanctissimae Inquisitionis* (Bologna, 1668), 393, and Carena's note that the custom was not observed in Italy (p. 394).

39. A. Borromeo, "A proposito del 'Directorium Inquisitorum'," 541; E. Masini, *Sacro Arsenale*, 139 (cited in full at n. 27; I use the Bologna, 1665 ed.).

40. See J. Alberghini, *Manuale Qualificatorum Sanctae Inquisitionis* (Palermo, 1642, etc.); I cite from the Venice, 1754 ed.: "Ratio vero quare Romana Inquisitio observat infectionem haeresis, nostra vero Hispanica, vel libidinem, vel cupiditatem, videtur quaeri posse . . ." (pp. 130 ff.).

41. Scaglia's writing circulated under two titles: "Prattica per procedere nelle cause del S. Officio" and "Relatione copiosa di tutte le materie spettanti al tribunale del S. Officio." I discuss it in "The Question of Magic and Witchcraft," pp. 229–58. Cf. at n. 46 below. Peña's "Instructio seu Praxis Inquisitorum" was printed for the first time as an appendix to the Cremona, 1655 edition of Cesare Carena's *Tractatus de Officio Sanctissimae Inquisitionis*, 433 ff. Peña's habit of quoting at length from Spanish inquisitorial legislation may have been a factor inhibiting its earlier publication and wider distribution. In fact, after each short chapter, Carena felt compelled to add his explanatory "Annotations." Admittedly, both "Prattica" and "Praxis" have a certain informal, unfinished tone and treat their subject somewhat sketchily.

42. The authorities most often cited by Giovanni Alberghini, inquisitor of Palermo, in his *Manuale Qualificatorum*, are Peña, Farinacci, Carena, and Simancas. Desiderio Scaglia, in his widely circulated "Prattica" confirms this, at least in part: "Trattano de' delitti heretricali tutti li autori che scrivano di questa materia [i.e. witchcraft], ma il più frequente che si prattica hoggi di è il Pegna nel *Direttorio*" (Bodleian Library, MS. Mendham 36, fol. 3v). These words are echoed closely by Desiderio's nephew, Deodato, in his "Theorica di procedere tanto in generale, quanto in particolare ne i casi appartenenti alla Santa Fede" (BAV, Borg. lat. 571, fol. 70v), who adds the name Farinacci. He attributes their popularity "poichè questi, oltreche abbracciano tutto quello ch'hanno detto gl'altri, scrivono anche più conforme allo stile, che si usa nel S.to O[fficio]." In the case of Farinacci, the allusion is undoubtedly to his *Tractatus de Haeresi* (Rome, 1616, etc.). On this leading secular jurist, see N. Del Re, "Prospero Farinacci giureconsulto romano (1544–1618)," *ASRSP*, ser. 3, 29 (1975): 135–220. The influence of civil lawyers on the judicial procedures of the Holy Office is still a largely unexplored subject. References to them abound in the writings of Carena, Diana, Peña, etc.

43. See E. Van der Vekene, *Bibliotheca Bibliographica Historiae Sanctae Inquisitionis*, ad indicem.

44. The suggestion that Eymeric's *Directorium* enjoyed this status was made by L. Sala-Molins (*Le Manuel des Inquisiteurs* [Paris, 1973], 17) and convincingly refuted by A. Borromeo, "A proposito del 'Directorium Inquisitorum'," 544 ff.

45. I supply the evidence in "The Question of Magic and Witchcraft," p. 232 and note.

46. See "Literary Piracy in Seventeenth-Century Florence," pp. 259–72. The title page identifies Neri as reader in theology, professor in canon law, and a former provincial of his order for Tuscany, the Minorite friars of San Francesco di Paola. The book is dedicated to Cosimo III, grand duke of Tuscany.

47. *Opus quod iudiciale inquisitorum dicitur . . . Cum additione nonnullarum quaestiuncularum, & decisionum quorundam notabilium casuum tam in Urbe, quam Placentiae discussorum, ac formulis agendorum in fine positis* (Rome, 1568; republished in expanded editions in 1570 and 1583). On Locati, see also n. 128.

48. *Tractatus de Officio Sanctissimae Inquisitionis et Modo Procedendi in Causis Fidei*, 1st ed. (Cremona, 1631). The title varied slightly in some subsequent editions: *Tractatus de Modus Procedendi in Causis S. Officii . . .* (Cremona, 1636). I cite this passage from the Cremona, 1668 edition, 387. On Carena, see Gabriele C. Medici, "Cesare Carena, giurista cremonese del secolo XVII," *ASL*, ser. 6, a. 57 (1930): 297–330. Curiously, there is no entry for Carena in the *DBI*. He was treated exhaustively in a still unpublished paper ("Lettura storica di manuali per inquisitori") presented by A. Rotondò at the symposium *L'Inquisizione nei secoli XVI–XVII: Metodologia delle fonti e prospettive storiografiche*, Rome and Naples, 1–4 October 1981.

49. See A. Borromeo, "A proposito del 'Directorium Inquisitorum'," passim.

50. L. Firpo, "Il processo di Giordano Bruno," *RSI* 60 (1948): 542–97; 61 (1949): 5–59, at p. 547.

51. For example, the teaching of the great Spanish jurist denying to the defense in trial proceedings the possibility of cross-examining the testimony of prosecution witnesses was in direct conflict with the practice of the Holy Office where "sine dubio totum contrarium observetur" (Carena, *Tractatus*, p. 271 of the 1668 ed.). And yet, in a letter from the supreme tribunal in Rome to the inquisitor of Bologna (7 November 1573; BA, MS. B–1860, fol. 160) the latter is reminded, as we have seen at n. 35, not to let himself be persuaded by anyone to "fare cose nuove," that he should be cautious about proceeding to arrest a suspect "come ben insegna il Simanca."

52. "Sponte comparente, an possit expediri a solo Inquisitore sine Ordinario?"; "Disputationes inter Catholicos et Haereticos an admittendae?"; "Iudex secularis debet exequi sententias S.ti Officii non viso processu?" These examples are drawn from BAV, Barb.lat. 1370. Apropos the conditions under which it might be permissible for Catholics to reside in northern Europe, see P. Simoncelli, "Clemente VIII e alcuni provvedimenti del Sant'Uffizio ('De Italis habitantibus in partibus haereticorum')," *Critica storica* 13 (1976): 129–72 (based on a thorough knowledge of the various types of inquisitorial materials preserved in Roman repositories).

53. *De Inconstantia in Iure* (Amsterdam, 1683), 349. For Gregory's decree, dated 20 March 1623, see C. Cocquelines, *Bullarum, Privilegiorum ac Diplomatum Romanorum Pontificum Amplissima Collectio*, 14 vols. (Rome, 1733–62), 5, pt. 5: 97–98. Henceforth, when bodily injury or death ensued from a maleficium, the offense was to be treated as a capital crime.

54. See Peña's commentary in Eymeric's *Directorium* (1587 ed.), 538.

55. Ibid., 649.

56. Ibid., 663: ". . . verior sententia & mitior est (à qua non recederem si iudex in tali lite futurus essem). . . ."

57. See Carena, *Tractatus* (1668 ed.), 271: "Dubia tamen admodum est controversia, num testis teneatur respondere interrogationi criminosae & concernenti suam turpitudinem, vel infamiam. . . . Et cum hac opinione transeo ego pro nunc, favore fidei, sed vere cum maxima trepidatione conscientiae, quia huic sententiae repugnant omnes regulae iuris naturalis, & civilis, secundum quas nemo cogendus est revelare propriam turpitudinem. . . ."

58. For Bologna, see [G. Mazzatinti and A. Sorbelli] *Inventari dei manoscritti delle biblioteche d'Italia, vol. 79. Bologna, Biblioteca Comunale dell' Archiginnasio* (Florence, 1954), MSS. B–1856–1944. For the Modenese correspondence, the reader is referred to A. Biondi's "Lunga durata," esp. 89 ff. and now especially to G. Biondi's "Le lettere della Sacra Congregazione romana del Santo Ufficio all'Inquisizione di Modena: Note in margine a un regesto," *Schifanoia* 4 (1989): 93–108, the most precise analysis to date of this type of material. The letters are distributed in nine *buste* and cover the years 1568–1784, with many lacunae. The article is a preliminary report on a project to inventory Holy Office correspondence being conducted by the Istituto di Studi Rinascimentali, Ferrara. The Modenese *fondo* includes letters between the Modena tribunal and its numerous vicariates, as well as with the

Supreme Congregation in Rome. Long extracts directed by the Congregation of the Index to Modenese and Bolognese inquisitors were published by A. Rotondò, "Nuovi documenti per la storia dell' 'Indice dei Libri Proibiti'(1572–1638)," *Rinascimento*, ser. 2, 3 (1963): 145–211. The Udine correspondence is preserved in the Archivio della Curia Arcivescovile in that city. For Malta, see P. Piccolomini, "Corrispondenza tra la corte di Roma e l'inquisitore di Malta durante la guerra di Candia (1645–69)," *Archivio storico italiano*, ser. 5, t. 41 (1908): 45–127. Andrew P. Vella, *The Tribunal of the Inquisition in Malta* (Malta, 1964), reports that the archive of the Maltese Inquisition, preserved in the Archiepiscopal Seminary, contains thirty-five volumes of correspondence exchanged with the Roman Congregation, 1588–1793. In my "Florentine Documents," pp. 273–319, I publish twenty-eight letters dating 1592–1606 addressed to the inquisitor of Florence. For Naples, Savoy, and Venice much of Rome's business with its outlying officials was handled through the nunciatures. Long series of these dispatches are now published. See n. 69 below.

59. BAV, Borg. lat. 558, fols. 186r–v: "Vedrà le lettere che si sono scritte da questa Sacra Congregatione alli' antecessori suoi, per rendersi pienamente informata del modo tenuto nella speditione de' negotii passati, che le sarà norma occorendole cause simili in avvenire."

60. For a description of the handbooks that have ended up among the Vatican manuscripts in the microfilm collection of St. Louis University, see P. H. Jobe, "Inquisitorial Manuscripts in the Biblioteca Apostolica Vaticana: A Preliminary Handlist," in G. Henningsen and J. Tedeschi, eds., *The Inquisition in Early Modern Europe*, 33–53.

61. BA, MS. B–1860, fol. 139.: ". . . gli facci dare la corda, et nel processo si scriva il tempo che vi sarà stata. L'avvertirò ancho che non lassi stare i sbirri ne altri in loco tormentorum per più secretezza, che così s'usa in questo Sant'Officio, che quando hanno ligati et alzati i rei si fanno partire."

62. BAV, Barb. lat. 6334, fol. 56v: ". . . il solito del tribunal è che gli rei nominino tre avvocati almeno, et uno di essi sia poi eletto dall'inquisitore."

63. See, for example, S. Mazzolini da Prierio, *Modus solennis et authenticus, ad inquirendum & inveniendum & convincendum Luteranos* (Rome, 1553), Tertia Regula: "Necesse est summe, ut inquisitor ipse quoque certus sit, se non posse errare in hoc actu."

64. BA, MS. B–1860, fol. 156, letter of 3 October 1573: "Mi spiace del suo male del deto che l'ha impedito dal poter scrivere, massimamente se fosse stato el male del scalda letto, come credo, pure pacienza." The inquisitor of Bologna in this period was Fra Innocenzo Morandi who held the post 1572–74. See A. Battistella, *Il S. Officio e la Riforma religiosa in Bologna* (Bologna, 1905), 200.

65. For the Bolognese letters, BA, MS. B–1860, fols. 68, 83–85, 107, 109, 130, 137, etc.; the letter to the Florentine inquisitor is from the cardinal of Santa Severina and is dated 11 May 1592 (BRB, MS. II 290, vol. 1, fol. 43); the letter to the Friulian inquisitor, from Cardinal Arrigoni, is in ACAU, Epistolae S. Officii, 1588–1613 and is dated 25 June 1611 (unpaginated).

66. BAV, Barb. lat., MSS. 6334–36.
67. BAV, Barb. lat., 6334, fol. 21v., letter to the inquisitor of Modena, 24 January 1626: "A V.R. poi mi hanno ordinato questi miei SS.ri Ill.mi d'avvertire seriamente de' modi poco giusti et discreti tenuti in questo processo, comminando al reo di trattarlo come heretico negativo, dandoli la corda mentre haveva impedimento nelle braccia, facendolo abiurare in pubblico, che tale è il farlo abiurare in una chiesa alla presenza di 30 o 40 persone, com'ella scrisse con lettera del 18 di Ottobre, quantunque con l'ultima di 27 di Dicembre, dice, che non v'intervenissero più di 10 ò 12, et dandogli maggior grado di abiura di quella che comportasse la qualità delle propositioni dette per burla, et la minorità del reo di 17 anni."
68. Ibid., fol. 133, letter to the inquisitor of Verona, 23 May 1626, concerning the case of a soliciting priest: "Non lascerò d'avvisarla che si sono maravigliati questi miei SS.ri Ill.mi che contra lo stile del Tribunale si siano manifestati al reo li nomi delle denuntianti et de' testimonii, interrogandolo se conosce Francesca, Achillina, Agnese et se mai in confessione ha trattato con loro di cose dishoneste. . . ."
69. The publication of several series of nunciatures is well underway, involving both Italian and foreign missions. Such series as the *Nunziature* for Venice, Naples, and Savoy published by the Istituto Storico Italiano in Rome; the *Acta Nuntiaturae Gallicae*; the *Nuntiaturberichte aus der Schweiz*; the *Nuntiaturberichte aus Deutschland* are all too well known to require further comment here. Their significance has been discussed at length in various review articles. For perceptive recent appraisals, see G. Alberigo, "Diplomazia e vita della Chiesa nel XVI secolo (a proposito di recenti edizioni di nunziature)," *Critica storica* 1 (1962): 49–69; H. Jedin, "Osservazioni sulla pubblicazione delle 'Nunziature d'Italia'," *RSI* 75 (1963): 327–43; H. Lutz, "Nuntiaturberichte aus Deutschland: Vergangenheit und Zukunft einer 'klassischen' Editionsreihe," *Quellen und Forschungen aus italienischen Archiven und Bibliotheken* 45 (1965): 274–324 (with an appendix containing a listing of all the published *Nuntiaturs* and of those in preparation); and the review essays by H. Lutz, G. Müller, H. Jedin, H. Goetz and G. Lutz, ibid., 53 (1973): 152–275. On the establishment and early years of the Italian nunciatures, see P. Villani, "Origine e carattere della nunziatura di Napoli (1523–1569)," *Annuario dell' Istituto storico italiano per l'età moderna e contemporanea* 9–10 (1957–58): 283–539; P. Caiazza, "Nunziatura di Napoli e problemi religiosi nel Viceregno post-tridentino," *RSCI* 42 (1988): 24–69; L. Chevaillier, "Les origines et les premières années de fonctionnement de la 'Nonciature de Savoie' à Turin (1560–1573)," in *Études d'Histoire du Droit Canonique dediées à Gabriel Le Bras* (Paris, 1965), 1:489–512. In addition to the actual series of diplomatic reports themselves, one should also consider the papacy's instructions to its envoys, such as, for example, *Die Hauptinstruktionen Clemens VIII für die Nuntien und Legaten an den europäischen Fürstenhöfen, 1592–1605*, 2 vols. (Tübingen, 1984). Cf. H. Lutz, "Le ricerche internazionali sulle nunziature e l'edizione delle istruzioni generali di Clemente VIII (1592–1605)," in *L'Archivio Segreto Vaticano e le ricerche storiche* (Rome, 1983); S. M. Pagano, "L'edizione delle istruzioni generali di Clemente VIII," *Benedictina* 33 (1986): 183–90.

70. See immediately below.

71. See, as an example, in the Archivio di Stato, Modena, the long series, *Carteggio con principi esteri*, which contains many letters from the Congregation of the Inquisition in Rome. For a useful survey of the principal documentary collections, see V. Ilardi and M. L. Shay, "Italy," in *The New Guide to the Diplomatic Archives of Western Europe*, eds. D. H. Thomas and L. M. Case (Philadelphia, 1975), 165–211.

72. For the report by Bernardino Pia, see L. von Pastor, *The History of the Popes from the Close of the Middle Ages*, 40 vols. (St. Louis, 1898–1953), 14:306n.

73. "Relazione di Roma di Luigi Mocenigo, 1560," in *Le relazioni degli ambasciatori veneti al Senato durante il secolo decimosesto*, edite dal cav. E. Albèri, 15 vols. (Florence, 1839–63), 10:36 f.

74. "Relazione di Giovanni Dolfin tornato da Roma nel 1598," ibid., 481.

75. BAV, Barb. lat. 6334, fol. 67v.

76. Domenico Maselli's several articles on Milanese heresy in the second half of the sixteenth century, heavily based on the Borromeo correspondence, have now been collected as *Saggi di storia ereticale lombarda al tempo di S. Carlo* (Naples, 1979), esp. pp. 16–31, a useful description of the apposite sources. See also G. Alberigo's "Problemi e indirizzi di storia religiosa lombarda, secoli XV–XVII," in *Problemi di storia religiosa lombarda* (Como, 1972), 111–27, esp. pp. 126 f., for a description of two projects from the late 1950s involving editing the Borromeo letters.

77. A rich source of this type is the edition of *Le lettere di Paolo Bisanti, vicario generale del Patriarca di Aquileia (1577–1587)*, by F. Salimbeni (Rome, 1977), ad indicem.

78. See L. Pasztor, *Guida delle fonti per la storia dell'America latina negli archivi della Santa Sede e negli archivi ecclesiastici d'Italia*, Collectanea Archivi Vaticani, 2 (Vatican City, 1970). The usefulness of this guide extends well beyond Latin American research. For the Dominicans, see 446–47, a survey of the *Archivio Generale dei Frati Predicatori*. The description encompasses twenty-one categories of materials. See 7, "Magistri S. Palatii, Commissarii S. Officii, Secretarii Indicis, Inquisitio." Two notable tribunals which were in the hands of Franciscans were the Florentine and the Venetian (until 1560 when it passed to the Dominicans). G. Zarri, "Aspetti dello sviluppo degli Ordini religiosi in Italia tra Quattro e Cinquecento: Studi e problemi," in *Strutture ecclesiastiche in Italia e in Germania prima della Riforma*, edited by P. Prodi and P. Johanek (Bologna, 1983), 207–57, provides a detailed survey of research in progress on the orders, without specific reference, however, to the inquisitorial connection.

79. J. Quétif and J. Echard, *Scriptores Ordinis Praedicatorum recensiti*, 2 vols. (Paris, 1719–23). But one of the most specific to our subject is an earlier work, V. M. Fontana, *Sacrum Theatrum Dominicanum* (Rome, 1666), pt. 3: 497–616, 619–24, "De Ministris S. Inquisitionis," with a detailed index of names.

80. S. L. Forte, "I Domenicani nel carteggio del card. Scipione Borghese, protettore dell' Ordine," *AFP* 30 (1960): 351–416. The correspondence calendared here includes many letters of recommendation for the post of inquisitor which are interesting as illustrations of the patronage system. This particular group is preserved

in the Archivio Segreto Vaticano and the Biblioteca Angelica. See also n. 104 for other instances of involvement in inquisitorial affairs by cardinal protectors. By the same author, see also *The Cardinal-Protector of the Dominican Order* (Rome, 1959); "Le province domenicane in Italia nel 1650, conventi e religiosi," *AFP* 39 (1969): 425–585; "Le province domenicane in Italia nel 1650, conventi e religiosi. V. La 'Provincia utriusque Lombardiae'," ibid., 41 (1971): 325–458; "Le province domenicane in Italia nel 1650, conventi e religiosi. VI. La 'Provincia Santi Dominici Venetiarum'," ibid., 42 (1972): 137–66.

81. *Acta Capitulorum Generalium Ordinis Praedicatorum*, ed. B. M. Reichert (Rome and Stuttgart, 1901–2). The pertinent volumes, chronologically, are 4, 1501–1553; 5, 1558–1600; 6, 1601–1628; 7, 1629–1656. They appear as vols. 8–12 of the *Monumenta Ordinis Fratrum Praedicatorum Historica*.

82. D. A. Mortier, *Histoire des Maîtres Généraux de l'Ordre des Frères Prêcheurs*, 8 vols. (Paris, 1903–30). Vols. 5 and 6 cover the years 1487–1650. See esp. 5:401 ff.

83. V. M. Fontana, *Monumenta dominicana breviter in synopsim collecta* (Rome, 1675), a massive work of over 700 pages arranged chronologically from the founding of the order to 1674. It devotes considerable attention to episodes of inquisitorial history. The appointment of members of the Franciscan order as inquisitors is regularly reported in Lucas Wadding, *Annales Minorum, seu trium Ordinum a S. Francisco institutorum* . . . , 3rd ed., 31 vols. (Ad Claras Aquas, 1931–56). Wadding compiled the entries for the period 1208–1540; other writers carried the labor forward to 1611. See, for example, 21:174, under the year 1578, the appointment in Florence of Dionysius Costacciarius, replacing Franciscus Pisanus. The entry notes that the power to make the selection had passed from the general and provincial of the order to the Supreme Congregation.

84. See, for example, Girolamo Gattico's manuscript history of the convent of Santa Maria delle Grazie, used by L. Fumi, "L'inquisizione romana e lo stato di Milano: Saggio di ricerche nell'Archivio di Stato," *ASL*, ser. 4, vol. 13, a. 37 (1910): 5–124, 285–414; vol. 14 (1910): 145–220, at 13:10.

85. See, for example, *Bullarium Franciscanum*, ed. I. H. Sbaralea (Rome, 1759–68); *Bullarium Ordinis FF. Praedicatorum*, ed. T. Ripoll and A. Bremond, 8 vols. (Rome, 1729–40).

86. S. Razzi, *Istoria degli huomini illustri, così nelle prelature come nelle dottrine, del Sacro Ordine degli Predicatori* (Lucca, 1596), 315–16: ". . . non era egli [Alessi] soverchiamente austero (come tal'hora alcuni sono) ma il tutto facea con clemenza, e mansuetudine. Onde narrano che più volte pianse per pietà e compassione, mentre che, per debito del ufficio, adoperava i tormenti e la fune intorno ai rei." Razzi was "Reggente" of the Dominican convent in Perugia the year Alessi, "charissimo et familiarissimo padre," died.

87. The question of this possible conflict is not raised by A. H. Thomas, "La profession religieuse des Dominicains: Formule, cérémonies, histoire," *AFP* 39 (1969): 5–52.

88. See the letter of Girolamo Papino to Alessandro Guarini, Bologna, 13 March

1549, in F. Valenti, "Il carteggio di padre Girolamo Papino informatore estense dal Concilio di Trento durante il periodo bolognese," *Archivio storico italiano* 124 (1966): 303–417, at p. 408: ". . . l'inquisitore ha qua una lectione ordinaria in convento, et per questo non pò absentarse a venire a iudicarlo in Ferrara senza moltissimo suo incomodo . . ."

89. BA, MS. B–1860, fol. 88. Letter of Antonio Balduzzi to the inquisitor of Bologna, Rome, 4 October 1572: ". . . acciò bisognando le possi mostrare e fare legere nelle congregationi. . . ."

90. Decree of 21 March 1584. See L. von Pastor, *Allgemeine Dekrete*, p. 39: ". . . decreverunt, ut in posterum inquisitores provinciae utriusque Lombardiae, quocunque praetextu seu quaesito colore, extra propriam diaecesim non se transferant, neque ad ullum accedant capitulum generale aut provinciale, etiam si in socios electi fuerint, sine expressa licentia obtenta in scriptis a supradictis ill.mis etc."

91. BA, MS. B–1864, fol. 105, letter dated 6 August 1613 in which Millino informed the inquisitor that the cardinals of the Congregation "desiderano sapere se ella ascolti le confessioni sacramentali delle monache costì, in quali monasterii, e da quanto tempo in quà." The Bolognese official replied on 7 September that he occasionally heard such confessions "mentre è stato priore, et è stato richiesto da i priori pro tempore." On the 21st of the month Millino issued a definitive prohibition (fol. 111).

92. *Acta Capitulorum Generalium*, 5:199, Rome Chapter, 1580: "Admonemus reverendos provinciales, quod, si reverendos inquisitores in priores eligi contigerit, non confirmentur nisi consulto reverendissimo generali magistro ordinis, ne forte sanctum inquisitionis officium impediatur." Combining the responsibility of the two offices had its advantages, as the inquisitor of the newly elevated but impoverished Modena tribunal testified: "Io al presente per essere Priore del convento me la passo bene nella cella del Priorato, ma finito che haverò da qui a un anno questo effetto, bisognerà patire molti incommodi fino a tanto che venghi qualche ventura." (Cited from A. Biondi, "Lunga durata," 81).

93. *Acta Capitulorum Generalium* 5:256, Rome Chapter, 1583: "In provincia utriusque Lombardiae in studio Bononiensi damus in regentem pro annis 1583, 1584 et 1585 patrem magistrum fr. Eliseum Capys inquisitorem, quod munus si ob officium inquisitionis exercere non valebit, damus patrem magistrum fr. Baptistam de Genua."

94. Ibid., 6:19, Rome Chapter, 1601: "Ordinamus et praecipimus omnium conventuum praesidentibus sub poena absolutionis ab officio, ne facile facultatem tribuant etiam de consilio patrum fratribus vagandi extra conventum vel eundi ad alios conventus seu oppida, etiam praetextu alicuius necessitatis, nisi vera sit et urgentissima, cum constet huiusmodi discursus magna parere incommoda et scandala." See also the texts quoted at notes 103–4.

95. Ibid., 7:112–13, Rome Chapter, 1644: "Proinde volumus, ut in singulis conventibus commoda infirmaria habeatur pro fratribus aegrotis atque languentibus, eaque nulli in privatam habitationem sive tota sive ex parte concedatur. Item

deputetur idoneus infirmarius maior, cui pro exigentia officii ac temporis unus aut plures fratres conversi pro ministeriali adiutorio adiungantur; teneanturque prior aut praeses conventus una cum medico et p. infirmario fratres suos infirmos benigne et crebrius invisere ac eorum necessitatibus providere. . . ."

96. Ibid., 5:87, Rome Chapter, 1569: "Admonemus omnes patres priores conventuum, ut ordinationem alias factam in capitulo Avenoniensi et aliis capitulis generalibus de aptandis carceribus in eorum conventibus cum serra et pessulo et clave firmis et fortibus omnino executioni mandent, et qui infra sex menses a notitia praesentium id non praestiterint, a provinciali in visitatione ab officio absolvantur."

97. Ibid., 5:92, Rome Chapter, 1569: "Ordinamus, ut in omnibus conventibus nostris, ubi non sunt constructae librariae communes, quamprimum construantur, et ubi deest locus ad hoc idoneus, ad minus aptetur aliqua camera, in qua libri reponantur, et fratres convenire possint ad studendum; libri vero fratrum decedentium nullo modo vendantur, nisi pro emendis aliis libris magis necessariis, extra ordinem, sed serventur pro fratrum et maxime juvenum commoditate; et si priores reperti fuerint huiusmodi libros distrahere, ab officio absolvantur." On the library of the Dominican convent at Bologna, see G. Zaccagnini, "Le scuole e la libreria del convento di S. Domenico in Bologna dalle origini al secolo XVI," *Atti e Memorie della R. Deputazione di Storia Patria per le Provincie di Romagna*, ser. 4, 17 (1927): 228–37; G. Zucchini, *Le librerie del convento di S. Domenico a Bologna* (Pistoia, 1937) (originally published in *Memorie domenicane*, 1936–37); C. Lucchesi, "L'antica libreria dei padri domenicani di Bologna alla luce del suo inventario," *Atti e memorie della R. Deputazione di Storia Patria per l'Emilia e la Romagna* 5 (1940): 205–51; M.-H. Laurent, *Fabio Vigili et les bibliothèques de Bologne au début du XVIe siècle d'après le ms. Barb. lat. 3185*, Studi e testi, 105 (Vatican City, 1943); V. Alce and A. D'Amato, *La biblioteca di S. Domenico in Bologna* (Florence, 1961). For Rome, see G. Meersseman, "La bibliothèque des Frères Prêcheurs de la Minerve à la fin du XVIe siècle," in *Melanges Auguste Pelzer, Université de Louvain, recueil de travaux d'histoire et de philologie*, ser. 3, 26 (1947): 605–31. In general, see the detailed geographical survey by T. Kaeppeli, "Antiche biblioteche domenicane in Italia," *AFP* 36 (1966): 5–80, which concentrates on the libraries' manuscript holdings; R. De Maio, "I modelli culturali della Controriforma: Le biblioteche dei conventi italiani alla fine del Cinquecento," in the author's *Riforme e miti nella Chiesa del Cinquecento* (Naples, 1973), 365–81, with a rich bibliography. This important study focuses on the inventory made of the monastic libraries at the instigation of the Congregation of the Index between 1598 and 1603. Cf. M. Dykmans ("Les bibliothèques des religieux d'Italie en l'an 1600," *Archivum historiae pontificiae* 24 [1986]: 385–404), who discusses these catalogues and remarks on the absence of Dominican and Jesuit inventories.

98. *Acta Capitulorum Generalium* 5:323, Venice Chapter, 1592: "Ordinamus, ut omnes fratres, cuiuscunque gradus et conditionis sint, in communi dormitorio, non in separatis ediculis vel cameris habitent, unica tantum paupere cella contenti, praelato et graviori aliquo patre exceptis, quibus duae ad summum concedi poterunt, si hactenus tot habuere, absque eo quod noviter accomodentur maxime cum aliorum incomoditate."

99. Ibid.: "Ab his [i.e., cells] vero superfluitates omnes, ornamenta vana, praetiosa quaeque et omnia tandem, quae religiosam paupertatem non sapiunt, omnino auferantur."

100. Ibid., 33, Avignon Chapter, 1561: "Ordinamus et ordinando praecipimus . . . reverendis provincialibus, vicariis, prioribus seu praesidentibus quibuscunque nostri ordinis, ne permittant, quod fratres in conventibus nostris sive sorores in monasteriis deinceps faciant comedias sive repraesentationes cuiuscumque generis . . ."; Ibid., 172–73, Barcelona Chapter, 1574: "Item ordinamus . . . ne de caetero audeant repraesentare per iocum episcopi personam, uti consuevit fieri in festo Innocentium, et festa divi Vincentii et similia omnia praecipue quoad electiones et institutiones priorum similium festorum . . ."

101. See the letter of the cardinal of Pisa to the inquisitor of Bologna, 12 March 1572, concerning the case of a blind prisoner confined in a convent (BA, MS. B–1860, fol. 69): "Fu ragionato in questa ultima congregatione intorno il fatto di quel cieco a chi fu dato per carcere da cotesto S.to Ufficio il Monasterio di S. Proculo; et perchè fu fatta relatione ch'egli haveva il modo di vivere del suo, et che ritornandosene a casa saria stato governato da la moglie assai meglio che non era da quei padri, li quali dall'altro canto si aggravavano di farli più le spese, allegando oltra il danno, ancho l'incomodità che causava ad essi loro. . . ."

102. BAV, Barb. lat. 6334, fol. 238v, letter from Supreme Congregation to inquisitor of Reggio, 22 August 1626: "Si è inteso che il vicario et notaro di cotesto S.to Officio non sono de' frati ordinarii assignati in cotesto convento, ma forastieri chiamati da lei per tale ministero, et anche che poco frequentano il choro, et si esercitono nelle altre funtioni regolari." If changes had to be made in the future, "ch'ella elegga per quegli ufficii alcuno de' frati assignati da suoi superiori in cotesto convento."

103. "Nostro Signore havendo inteso che gl'inquisitori della religione di S. Domenico, sotto il manto del S.to Offizio, pretendono del tutto essere immuni dall'obbedienza de' suoi superiori, non vogliono come gl'altri obedire nè servare la regola, uscendo anco a posta loro da' monasteri, senza sapersi dove vadano, e facendo anco lo stesso li loro compagni, vicarii, notari et altri ministri, donde ne nasce molta rilassazione di obedienza regolare con disservizio di Dio e scandalo del prossimo; e che dall'altra parte gl'inquisitori si dolgono che, non solamente non possono per le straniezze de loro superiori regolari o per dubio di non dispiacere a principi e gentiluomini e generar odio al convento, far l'ufficio suo, ma spesse volte sono impediti e li sono generate di molte difficoltà da suoi superiori stessi. . . ." The letter appears in its entirety in L. von Pastor, *Allgemeine Dekrete*, 68–69.

104. ". . . che [gl'inquisitori] esercitino l'officio loro con diligenza, ma con manco incommodo della disciplina Regolare che sia possibile, particolarmente nell'osservanza della clausura, che possano stare le porte de' conventi serrate, & gl'altri luoghi consueti, & che sotto ombra del Santo Officio non si trasgredisca ogni ordine, e ogni legge, che si suol fare da superiori nell'haver tanti che gli servono, & si esentono dal Choro, da gli studii & da ogni obedientia, nel voler mantenere, o mantellare sotto l'ombra del Santo Officio ciascuno che pare. Però ogn'uno starà sotto l'obe-

dienza de i superiori, i quali ne potranno disporre come degl'altri frati, nel tempo che non saranno occupati nel servitio del Sant'Officio." I have used the 1656 reprint of the 1611 *Ordini*, preserved among the remains of the Florentine Inquisition (BRB, MS. II 290, vol. 4, fol. 1). It circulated among the provincial tribunals in both printed and manuscript versions. In the latter form, I discovered a copy among the correspondence in ACAU, Epistolae S. Officii, 1588–1613 (at the beginning of the codex which is not paginated). See ibid., Epistolae S. Officii, 1614–1646, letter dated 29 July 1620 (unpaginated) from Cardinal Millino of the Supreme Congregation to the inquisitor in Udine ordering him to distribute the edict as follows: copies to hang on the walls of his room and archives, and a third to be filed with the books of the Holy Office. The text is based on the "Ordini stabiliti nella Sacra Congregatione da osservarsi da gl'Inquisitori quali furno mandati sotto li 14 di luglio 1597, a SS.ri Cardinali Alessandrino e Cusano, l'uno protettore de' Padri Predicatori, et l'altro de' Minori Conventuali" (BAV, Barb. lat. 1370, pp. 129–38).

105. BA, MS. B–1866, fol. 119, letter dated 28 July 1623: "Sono molto pregiuditiali le liti e dissentioni non convenevoli che vertono fra gli Inquisitori e Priori alla riputatione della Religione, al buon governo de' conventi, et agli interessi proprii di essi che perciò vi è stato parere che per opportuno rimedio si dovesse correggere il P. Inquisitore di Modena, e cassare il Priore, et per essempio d'altri, et per propria loro istruttione."

106. See n. 104 above.

107. See also n. 34 above. The full title is *Litterae Apostolicae diversorum Romanorum Pontificum pro officio Sanctissimae Inquisitionis ab Innocens III Pont. Max. usque ad haec tempora MDLXXXVII*, with separate title page and numbering. The section closes with an extremely important *Disputatio* by Peña on the question of the authority retained by older papal texts as they are succeeded by new pronouncements (pp. 145–53). A. Diana, in his *Resolutionum Moralium* (cited at n. 37), 5:367–408, supplemented Peña's *Litterae* with "Decreta et Constitutiones Recentiorum Pontificum ad Tribunal S. Officii Spectantes."

108. I have not had access to the modern edition of papal bulls, *Bullarum, diplomatum et privilegiorum sanctorum romanorum pontificum taurinensis editio* (Turin, 1857–72) and have used the magnificent older collection compiled by Carolus Cocquelines: *Bullarum, Privilegiorum ac Diplomatum* (cited in full at n. 53). For *Licet ab initio*, 4, pt. 1: 211–12; for *Immensa Aeterni Dei*, 4, pt. 4: 392 ff.; for *Omnipotentis Dei*, 5, pt. 5: 97–98. Untold numbers of texts concern the affairs of the Inquisition. For a detailed study of the genre over seven centuries of history, see M. Giusti, *Studi sui registri di bolle papali*, Collectanea Archivi Vaticani, 1 (Vatican City, 1968), and the useful clarifications of L. Pasztor, "La Curia romana e i registri di bolle papali," *Studi romani* 17 (1969): 319–23.

109. See above at n. 9. For another example of the genre, see *Instructio particularis circa conficiendos processus inquisitionis ... Iussu D.N. Urbani PP. VIII* (Rome, 1627), 8 pp. (prescribing how to conduct background checks on persons nominated to the governance of cathedrals and monasteries).

110. L. Firpo published an early seventeenth-century text, "Delle Congregazioni di Roma" (Vienna, Nationalbibliothek, MS. 6328, fols. 527–48), which describes, among other matters, the composition and routines of the Supreme Congregation in Rome and its schedule of thrice-weekly meetings: "Una relazione inedita su l'Inquisizione romana," *Rinascimento* 9 (1958): 97–102.

111. See S. M. Pagano, *I documenti del processo di Galileo Galilei* (Vatican City, 1984), 4 ff., for an excellent description of the Roman Archive of the Inquisition and of the surviving *decreta*, which later came to be known as "Acta Congregationum." At 217 ff., Pagano publishes 37 *decreta* concerned with the Galileo case, reprinting, based on an examination of the originals and with some additions, the documents that had been published earlier by A. Favaro, *Galileo e l'Inquisizione: Documenti del processo galileiano esistenti nell'Archivio del S. Uffizio e nell'Archivio Segreto Vaticano* (Florence, 1907), 13–31. E. Carusi published additional decrees from the Holy Office Archive, "Nuovi documenti del processo di Giordano Bruno," *Giornale critico della filosofia italiana* 6 (1925): 121–39 (decrees, sentences, etc. for the period 1593–1600); idem, "Nuovi documenti sul processo di T. Campanella," ibid., 8 (1927): 321–59 (the texts of 100 *decreta*, 1594–1636). Corrections to the above and the addition of 23 unpublished decrees for the years 1593–97 appeared in L. Firpo's "Appunti campanelliani," ibid., 29 (1950): 68–95, on the basis of an inspection of the originals. It is uncertain, instead, whether Carusi actually was permitted access to the archive.

112. An extremely important collection of *decreta* from various Vatican collections, principally Barberini codices, a small sample of what survives, was published by L. von Pastor in his *Allgemeine Dekrete* (cited in full at n. 20). They span the years 1555–97. Pastor was not one of the fortunate scholars to gain access to the Holy Office Archive. P. H. Jobe describes a number of these volumes in her "Inquisitorial Manuscripts in the Biblioteca Apostolica Vaticana," in G. Henningsen and J. Tedeschi, eds., *The Inquisition in Early Modern Europe*, passim.

113. Rome, Biblioteca Casanatense, MS. 3825, containing decrees for the years 1600–1602. The codex was apparently acquired by Count Giuseppe Manzoni, a minister of the Roman Republic, in 1849, after the Holy Office Archive was despoiled during the French occupation. From Manzoni it passed, at an uncertain date, to the Casanatense (see E. Carusi, "Nuovi documenti sui processi di T. Campanella," 324n). (For the restitution of additional inquisitorial documents by Manzoni and by his son Luigi to the Holy See, see V. Ferrone and M. Firpo, "Galileo tra inquisitori e microstorici," *RSI* 97 [1985]: 185.) A few items from this volume have been published by E. Celani, "Processi di Fr. Tommaso Campanella: Note sommarie inedite," *Archivio storico per le provincie napoletane* 25 (1900): 462 ff. Other Casanatense manuscripts concerned with inquisitorial affairs are discussed by P. Simoncelli, "Clemente VIII e alcuni provvedimenti del Sant'Uffizio," esp. pp. 158 ff. They belonged to Cardinal Girolamo Casanate (1620–80), a highly placed member of the Roman Holy Office, who founded the library which bears his name. On him, see the excellent biographical sketch by L. Ceyssens in *DBI* 21: 144–47, and V. De

Gregorio, "Gli 'Indici' della libreria privata del cardinale Girolamo Casanate," *Accademie e biblioteche d'Italia* 52 (1984): 199–211. See now by M. Panetta, *La "libraria"* *di Mattia Casanate* (Rome, 1988), a study based on the inventory of the library of the cardinal's father, who died in 1651.

114. A well known early example is Paolo Sarpi's *Historia della Sacra Inquisitione composta già dal R.P. Paolo servita, ed hora la prima volta posta in luce, opera pia, dotta e curiosa a consiglieri, casuisti e politici molto necessaria*, 1st ed. (Serravalle, 1638). A reply was prepared by Cardinal Francesco Albizzi, a member of the Supreme Congregation: *Risposta all' Historia della Sacra Inquisizione, composta già dal R. P. Paolo Servita ...* (N.p., n.d., but c. 1670).

115. Hieronymus Massarius, *Eusebius captivus, sive modus procedendi in Curia Romana contra Lutheranos* (Basel [1553]). This book purports to describe the Inquisition's proceedings against an imaginary Eusebius Uranius. See also P. P. Vergerio, *A gl'Inquisitori che sono per l'Italia: Del catalogo di libri eretici, stampati in Roma nell'anno presente MDLIX* (N.p., 1559).

116. Ridolfo Campeggi, *Racconto degli heretici iconomiasti giustiziati in Bologna a gloria di Dio, della B. Vergine et per honore della patria ...* (Bologna [1623]). The progress of the case was watched closely by the Supreme Congregation in Rome, which sent detailed instructions to its inquisitor in Bologna.

117. See E. van der Vekene, *Bibliotheca Bibliographica Historiae Sanctae Inquisitionis* 1:151–253 (nos. 608–980). The vast majority of the entries deal with Spanish accounts. Only ten printed "Italian" descriptions are recorded (nos. 948–57), and of these, eight deal with Sicilian *autos*. Van der Vekene's listings do not exhaust the Italian literature. See n. 127 below, as an example, for a ceremony reported in a Roman *Avviso*. And, of course, despite their obvious bias, the Protestant martyrologies should be considered as well. In the eighteenth century especially, highly colored descriptions of *autos* and sentences connected with cases of affected sanctity, containing explicit sexual details, were collected and circulated in numerous manuscript copies (see the texts in Bodleian Library, MS. Mendham 36 and the "Compendio di Varie Abiure," a thick codex now in the Institute of Medieval Canon Law [MS. 121], Boalt Hall, at the University of California, Berkeley).

118. See, from among many examples, Antonio Caracciolo's (d. 1642) manuscript, "Vita del Sommo Pontefice Paolo IIII. ..." I have used a contemporary (early seventeenth-century) copy in The Newberry Library (Case 5A 107). For inquisitorial history, see esp. bks. 3 and 4 (chap. 17 includes a description of the sack of the Holy Office in 1559 and the destruction of the trial records). The autobiography of Giulio Antonio Santorio, cardinal of Santa Severina, a member of the Congregation of the Inquisition, yields occasional insights into the affairs of the institution: "Gli diedi [to Pope Urban VII] una nota dei Signori Cardinali e Consultori del Sant'Ufficio acciò non aggiungesse, ne mutasse senza saputa della Congregazione le persone, poichè molti pretendevano quel loco, si de' cardinali, come de' prelati ..." I cite from Newberry Library MS. Case 6A 35, fol. 862 (an early seventeenth-century copy). The autobiography has been published by G. Cugnoni in the *ASRSP* 12

(1889): 329–72; 13 (1890): 151–205 (an edition based only on two manuscripts in the Biblioteca Corsiniana, Rome) and studied by H. Jedin, *Die Autobiographie des Kardinals Giulio Antonio Santorio*, Akademie der Wissenschaften und der Literatur, Abhandlungen der Geistes-und Sozialwissenschaftlichen Klasse, Jhrg. 1969, no. 2 (Mainz, Wiesbaden, 1969). For an outsider's point of view, see, by the distinguished German historian, Philipp Camerarius, his own firsthand account of the brief imprisonment he endured in 1565 at the hands of the Roman Inquisition, during which he had the opportunity to debate theological questions with Peter Canisius and the cardinal inquisitors: "Relatio vera et solida de captivitate romana, ex falsa delatione orta, et liberatione fere miraculosa Philippi Camerarii et Petri Rieteri," in J. G. Schelhorn, *De vita, fatis ac meritis Philippi Camerarii* (Nuremberg, 1740), 104 pages. Camerarius had been a student in various north Italian universities at the time he was captured. See also the long study and edition of the text by Lech Szczucki, *Philippus Camerarius: Prawdziwa i wierna relacja o uwiezieniu w Rzymie* (Warsaw, 1984); P. Paschini, "Episodi dell'Inquisizione a Roma nei suoi primi decenni," *Studi romani* 5 (1957): 285–301, esp. pp. 294 ff.; and my "Florentine Documents" at p. 311.

119. For Rome see the records of the *Venerabile Arciconfraternità di San Giovanni Decollato* whose function it was to comfort the condemned during the long night before their execution and accompany them to their death. They are published in D. Orano, *Liberi pensatori bruciati in Roma dal XVI al XVIII secolo* (Rome, 1904; reprint Livorno, 1971). On the confraternity, see V. Paglia, *La morte confortata: Riti della paura e mentalità religiosa a Roma nell'età moderna* (Rome, 1982); idem, *"La pietà dei carcerati": Confraternite e società a Roma nei secoli XVI–XVIII* (Rome, 1980); the volumes edited by L. Fiorani, *Le confraternite romane: Esperienza religiosa, società, commitenza artistica* (Rome, 1984) and *Storiografia e archivi delle confraternite romane* (Rome, 1985), respectively vols. 5 and 6 of the *Ricerche per la storia religiosa di Roma*. Cf. the remarks on the current scholarship by R. Grégoire, "Le confraternite romane: Esperienza religiosa, società, commitenza artistica," *Studium* 81 (1985): 367–70, and D. Balestracci, "Le confraternite romane fra tardo medioevo ed età moderna nei contributi della recente storiografia," *Archivio storico italiano* 146 (1988): 321–30. For other areas, see A. Prosperi, "Il sangue e l'anima: Ricerche sulle compagnie di giustizia in Italia," *Quaderni storici* 17 (1982): 959–99; idem, "Mediatori di emozioni: La compagnia ferrarese di giustizia e l'uso delle immagini," in *L'impresa di Alfonso II: Saggi e documenti sulla produzione artistica a Ferrara nel secondo Cinquecento* (Bologna, 1987); C. Parnisetti, "La pena capitale in Alessandria e la confraternità di S. Giovanni Decollato," *Bollettino storico-bibliografico subalpino* 29 (1927): 353–463; for Bologna, see the "Libro de' Morti" in BA, Fondo Ospedali, MS. 53, MS. 54. The persons who were executed are identified by little drawings indicating the means of their death, fire, a noose, etc. Although victims of the Inquisition are not specified, they can be deduced by such entries as one under the date 9 October 1568: "Silvio Lanzoni mantuano fu abbruciato vivo per Lutherano ostinatissimo"; for Milan, see the manuscript "Registro de' giustiziati della nobilissima scuola di S. Gio. Decollato . . . dall'anno MCDLXXI in avanti." It records a total of 3124 executions in 294 years, of which only a hand-

ful pertain to the Inquisition. Fragments are published in Matteo Benvenuti, "Come facevasi giustizia nello stato di Milano dall'anno 1471 al 1763," *ASL* 9 (1882): 442–82; G. Maffani, *Operetta la qual contiene lordine & il modo hanno a tenere quelli de la Compagnia di Giustizia di Perugia quando haveranno a confortare li condannati alla morte* (Perugia, 1545). For contemporary discussions on the subject in general, see *Instruttione per consolar i poveri afflitti condannati a morte* (Bergamo, 1586); M. Mansio, *Documenti per confortare i condannati a morte* (Rome, 1625). See also, C. F. Black's *Italian Confraternities in the Sixteenth Century* (Cambridge, 1989), 217–23, "Imprisoned and Condemned."

120. A number of these papers are included among the "Decreta contra Anglos, Germanos et omnes Protestantes," in BRB, MS. II 290, vol. 2, fols. 23–62. They range in date from 1591 to 1607. I quote at length from these documents in "The Dispersed Archives," p. 43 n. 51 in this volume.

121. The best study to date is A. Del Col, "L'Inquisizione romana e il potere politico nella repubblica di Venezia (1540–1560)," in *La Inquisición y los poderes políticos: Actas del Congreso de Madrid-Alcalá-Sigüenza (Septiembre 1984)* (in press), based on systematic research in the archives of the Council of Ten, preserved in the Archivio di Stato, Venice. I wish to thank the author for graciously sharing his work with me before its publication. A related source of similar importance is the reports to the Council of its outlying agents, the *Rettori*, who were equally involved in defending state interests against presumed ecclesiastical interference. See the *Relazioni dei rettori veneti in Terraferma* (Milan, 1973–). Volumes for Udine, Belluno, Feltre, Treviso, and Padua have appeared. See also the useful anthology of documents covering the entire peninsula, the majority of them governmental provisions for the control of religion and the Inquisition, in *Potestà civile e autorità spirituale in Italia nei secoli della Riforma e Controriforma*, edited by G. Catalano and F. Martino (Milan, 1984).

122. For a thorough study of Lucchese heresy based on the newly reordered archive of the *Offizio sopra la Religione* in the Archivio di Stato, Lucca (and the recently opened inquisitorial repository in the Archivio Arcivescovile, Pisa), see S. Adorni Braccesi, "Il dissenso religioso nel contesto urbano lucchese della Controriforma," in *Città italiane del '500*, 225–39. For an archival overview see G. Tori, "I rapporti tra lo stato e la chiesa a Lucca nei secoli XVI–XVIII: Le istituzioni," *Rassegna degli archivi di stato* 36 (1976): 37–81. The article deals with the two Lucchese government bodies established in mid-sixteenth century for the purpose of pursuing heresy in the Republic, the *Offizio sopra la Religione* and the *Offizio sopra la Giurisdizione*.

123. See, for example, P. Piccolomini, "Documenti del R. Archivio di Stato in Siena sull'eresia in questa città durante il secolo XVI," *Bullettino senese di storia patria* 17 (1910):3–35, and idem, "Documenti fiorentini sull'eresia in Siena durante il secolo XVI (1559–1570)," ibid.: 159–99 (49 documents from the Medici archives, primarily correspondence between members of the ruling family and their governors in Siena, but including a letter between the Holy Office in Rome and Cosimo). There is also the famous example, discussed at p. 109 in this volume, of the trials conducted before the Sienese Inquisition which ended up among the notarial documents in the

Sienese state archives thanks to a bureaucratic decision of the Medici administration.

124. See above at nn. 72 ff.

125. A. Biondi ("Lunga durata," 80) examines the reactions to the elevation of the Modenese Inquisition to full tribunal status reported in G. B. Spaccini's *Cronaca di Modena dal 1588 al 1636*, edited by P. E. Vicini, T. Sandonnini, G. Bertoni (Modena, 1911–1919).

126. For samples, see "The Organization and Procedures of the Roman Inquisition," p. 199 for references to G. Gigli, (*Diario romano, 1608–1670* [Rome, 1958]), who describes how sentences to the galleys were sometimes translated into alternate duties ashore. See also the extracts published by Pastor (*History of the Popes* 17:400–404) from the "Diarium" of Cornelius Firmanus which concern the activities of the Roman Inquisition, 1566–68; or the "Memorie e Ricordi" of the Florentine G. B. Fagiuoli which cover the years 1672–1695 and describe *autos da fé* and abjurations celebrated in the church of Santa Croce in 1679, 1688, and 1695. See S. Tosti, "Descriptio codicum Franciscanorum Bibliothecae Riccardianae Florentinae," *Archivum Franciscanum Historicum* 8 (1915): 625 ff. The article is in many installments over several years.

127. See "The Organization and Procedures of the Roman Inquisition," p. 201 for the vivid description of an *auto da fé* from a Roman *Avviso*. For more comprehensive descriptions of these early newsletters, see S. Bongi, "Le prime gazzette in Italia," *Nuova antologia* 11 (1869): 311–46; T. Bulgarelli, *Gli avvisi a stampa in Roma nel Cinquecento* (Rome, 1967). For related materials, see the collection of *Regesti di bandi, editti, notificazioni e provvedimenti diversi relativi alla città di Roma ed allo stato pontificio*, 7 vols. (Rome, 1920–28) (thirteenth to seventeenth centuries). Late sixteenth-century *Avvisi* reporting condemnations and executions are preserved in BAV, Urb. lat. 1044, 1045, 1047, 1063, 1064, etc., and collections of *Bandi* in the Archivio di Stato, Rome, *Governo di Roma*. My reference to these codices comes from L. von Pastor, *History of the Popes*, 19:301 ff. and P. Simoncelli, "Clemente VIII e alcuni provvedimenti del Sant'Uffizio," passim (cited at n. 52).

128. See, among many examples, G. F. Pico's *Dialogus in tres libros divisus: Titulus est Strix, sive de Ludificatione Daemonum* (Bologna, 1523, etc.), a work inspired by the Mirandola witch trials of 1522–23, in which an inquisitor and a witch are among the interlocutors. Cf. P. Burke, "Witchcraft and Magic in Renaissance Italy: Gianfrancesco Pico and His Strix," in S. Anglo, ed., *The Damned Art: Essays in the Literature of Witchcraft* (London, 1977), 32–52; A. Biondi, "Gianfrancesco Pico e la repressione della stregoneria: Qualche novità sui processi mirandolesi del 1522–23," in *Deputazione di Storia Patria per le Antiche Provincie Modenesi. Biblioteca*, n.s., 76 (1984): 331–49. The dialogue is reprinted, with the publishing history of the work, in S. Abbiati, A. Agnoletto, M. Rosario Lazzati, eds., *La stregoneria: Diavoli, streghe, inquisitori dal Trecento al Settecento* (Milan, n.d.), 231–47. Other literary contributions which touch on the Inquisition are: T. Garzoni, *La piazza universale di tutte le professioni del mondo, e nobili et ignobili* (Venice, 1585), which contains a chapter devoted to "De gli heretici, et degli inquisitori" (pp. 541–49). It is omitted from P. Cherchi's edition of Garzoni's *Opere* (Naples, 1972). Purely literary and histori-

cal works by inquisitors themselves are revealing for what they tell us about their authors' cultural background. Among the best known are the *Historie di Bologna* (1541–43) and *Descrittione di tutta Italia* (1550), among other writings by Leandro Alberti (1479–1553?), who was inquisitor of Bologna, 1550–51. See *DBI* 1:699–702. Another famous literary inquisitor was Umberto Locati, compiler of a procedural manual (see above at n. 47), but also historian of his native Piacenza and author of an *Italia travagliata* (Venice, 1576). See the perceptive analysis by S. Ditchfield, "Alla ricerca di un genere: come leggere la 'cronica dell'origine di Piacenza' dell' inquisitore piacentino Umberto Locati (1503–1587)," *Bollettino storico piacentino* 82 (1987): 145–67.

129. I am thinking of such individual pieces as Ludovico Cardi da Cigoli's *Processione penitenziale*, preserved in the *Gabinetto disegni e stampe* in the Uffizi gallery, Florence, reproduced in A. D'Addario, *Aspetti della Controriforma a Firenze*, Ministero dell'Interno, Pubblicazioni degli Archivi di Stato, 77 (Rome, 1972), facing p. 420; the depictions of the *autos* treated by M. V. González de Caldas, "Nuevas Imagenes del Santo Oficio en Sevilla: El auto de fe," in A. Alcalá, ed., *Inquisición española y mentalidad inquisitorial* (Barcelona, 1984), 237–65, and in English, "New Images of the Holy Office in Seville: The Auto de Fe," in A. Alcalá, ed., *The Spanish Inquisition and the Inquisitorial Mind* (Boulder, 1987), 265–300; the bilingual exhibition catalogue, *Strumenti di tortura, 1400–1800/Torture Instruments, 1400–1800, nella Casermetta di Forte Belvedere, Firenze, May–September, 1983* (Florence, 1983), preponderately devoted to secular instruments; N. Johnston's *The Human Cage: A Brief History of Prison Architecture* (New York, 1973), which includes a brief section on "Religious Imprisonment"; U. Rozzo, "Il rogo dei libri: Appunti per una iconologia," *Libri e documenti* 12 (1986): 7–32; and the graffiti uncovered in prison cells of the Palermo Inquisition in the Palazzo Chiaramonte, discussed by G. Pitré and C. A. Garufi (see at n. 144 in "The Organization and Procedures of the Roman Inquisition"). In general, see also the fine study by Samuel Y. Edgerton, *Pictures and Punishment: Art and Criminal Prosecution during the Florentine Renaissance* (Ithaca, 1985). The polemical inspiration behind many early depictions of inquisitorial activity is treated by E. Peters, *Inquisition* (New York and London, 1988), chap. 7, "The Inquisition in Literature and Art."

❦

FOUR

Toward a Statistical Profile of the Italian Inquisitions, Sixteenth to Eighteenth Centuries
(with William Monter)

Although there has been a recent rer iissance of interest in the Spanish Inquisition, its Roman and Italian counterparts have attracted
considerably less scholarly attention.[1] Historians from Spain, France, and
Denmark have helped bring studies of the Spanish tribunals to a new level of sophistication through a methodical exploration of the long runs
of surviving records from the sixteenth and seventeenth centuries. But
nothing remotely similar has yet been attempted for the other great modern
Inquisition of the Mediterranean basin.

Of course, there are excellent reasons why historians have concentrat-
ed their efforts on the mountains of Hispanic documents. Most important has been the recent discovery of the master file of the Spanish
Inquisition, containing *relaciones de causas*, or résumés, of all cases tried
every year in each of its tribunals between 1540 and 1700, approximately
44,000 of them. Provided with such a comprehensive data bank, scholars
have eagerly classified and measured the overall activities of this institution.[2] But unlike Spain, Rome had no central file, no data bank, no annual summaries of the activities of the provincial courts under its
supervision. On the contrary, the archives of the Roman Inquisition constitute an extremely dispersed source, scattered from Ireland to Belgium,
with only a fraction of the original documents preserved in Rome itself.
As the Roman Holy Office was a victim of Napoleonic looting, so other

important provincial Inquisitions, in Florence, Milan, and Palermo, were victims of Jacobin riots or suppression of the religious establishments which housed them. The consequence was the large-scale destruction or disappearance of their records.[3]

One need not be too pessimistic, however. Abundant documents still exist, not only in Rome but also in several other parts of Italy. Students of Italian dissent in the sixteenth and seventeenth centuries have skillfully exploited inquisitorial records in Bologna, Venice, Modena, Udine, and elsewhere in order to recover the history of heresy in Italy.[4] Occasionally, as at Siena, Pisa, Florence, Reggio and elsewhere, a previously unknown inquisitorial *fondo* is announced.[5] But from the viewpoint of scholars wishing to exploit Italian archives in the exhaustive and systematic fashion so brilliantly attempted for Spain, these records are often discouraging. Sometimes parts of a collection are complete while others are lacking: Bologna, for example, has a superb run of inquisitorial correspondence but almost no trial dossiers; Modena has a rich series of trials but no single readily available index to them.[6]

Fortunately, a few Italian Inquisitions possess surviving archives which are sufficiently complete and sufficiently well indexed to permit tentative comparisons with current work on Spanish materials. Three or four places presently meet these criteria. The largest and perhaps the most important is the Sant'Uffizio of Venice, whose 150 *buste* of trials are supplemented by a manuscript index covering about 3,600 defendants between 1547 and 1794.[7] Among the six Inquisitions of the Venetian Terrafirma, Aquileia and Concordia (covering present-day Friuli) appear to have virtually complete records between 1557 and 1786, involving about 2,100 defendants, supplemented by recently published inventories.[8] For the southern part of the peninsula, the archives of the Holy Office in Naples have been fully opened to scholars since 1970; here a magnificent recent index has catalogued approximately 3,000 cases between 1564 and 1780.[9] Finally, even farther away is Sicily, whose Inquisition was reorganized after the Spanish conquest and attached to the Secretariat of Aragon. From this tribunal an almost complete series of *relaciones de causas* after 1537 has been preserved; in all, they include about 3,200 persons tried or denounced between 1540 and 1700.[10] Taken together, these four Inquisitions offer almost 12,000 cases, spread out over a quarter of a millenium—nowhere near the bulk of the complete Spanish system but a sufficiently large sample to contrast with it. Moreover, these four split easily into two matched pairs—one from the Venetian Republic, the other from the heart of the *Viceregno*: opposite extremes both geographically and politically in early modern Italy. We should not be surprised to uncover important differences between the Alpine Friuli and the *Mezzogiorno*; it is more important to find the similarities between them. It should be noted that many of the records listed in the inventories on which this study is based refer only to denunciations and preliminary inquests that did not necessarily culminate in actual trials. This fact does not affect the significance of the statistics from the point of view of establishing a typology of crimes that preoccupied the Holy Office in this period.

The Sicilian Inquisition was of course not a Roman tribunal at all, but the Venetian also differed from other branches of the Roman system. Its most important peculiarity (not unique to Venice, however) was the requirement that lay representatives of the *Serenissima*, known as the *Savii sopra eresia*, should sit alongside the clerical members of this tribunal. Venice imposed other special rules as well, such as the requirement that all inquisitors must be Venetian citizens, the inadmissibility of denunciations and testimony forwarded by courts outside the dominion, and the prohibition against the confiscation of a convicted heretic's property.[11] Perhaps the most serious Venetian infringement on ordinary inquisitorial procedure was the extent of competition from local secular courts, which claimed jurisdiction in many cases involving such offenses as bigamy, blasphemy, perjury to the Inquisition, and some forms of suspected witchcraft. This influenced the types of cases which the Venetian Holy Office was permitted to prosecute, and consequently affected the statistics of its operations.[12] Other inquisitorial tribunals in Venetian territory, such as in Aquileia-Concordia, were also touched, but perhaps to a lesser degree, by similar restrictions.

But jurisdictional conflicts and curbs on ecclesiastical tribunals were not peculiar to Venice or its territories. Any branch of the Roman Inquisition located in the domains of an aggressive secular ruler labored under some set of special disabilities; and Naples, where Spain kept a careful eye on papal privileges and where the local citizens had rioted in 1547 against the establishment of the Spanish Inquisition, was obviously such a place.[13] Even Sicily witnessed squabbles of comic-opera ferocity between inquisitors and viceroys, particularly in the sixteenth century.[14] Only in the states of the Church — where good statistical series seem difficult to obtain — did the "pure" theory and legal practices of the Roman Inquisition find free expression in the courts.[15] Almost everywhere else its activities took place at the pleasure of secular rulers. Because much of the Italian peninsula was not under papal rule, the statistical configurations from such places as Aquileia-Concordia, Naples, or even Venice are probably broadly representative of other Italian Inquisitions.

Let us now turn to the overall numbers. The most important feature for all four tribunals is their remarkably high level of activity during the late sixteenth and early seventeenth centuries. Each one reached its maximum between 1580 and 1610. At Naples, the busiest decade was the 1590s, with over 400 accused, followed by 1601–1610 with over 300. Aquileia-Concordia reversed this, with its busiest decade in 1601–1610 (381 defendants) and its second busiest in the 1590s (282). The Venetian index is lacunous from 1593 to 1616[16] apart from the single year 1610; the height of its activity was reached in the 1580s, with over 440 defendants, and its fractional totals for 1591–1592 and 1610 are also unusually high. Sicily conformed to the Spanish rhythm by having its busiest decade in the 1580s. Overall, these three examples from the Roman system show numerical fluctuations similar to those of the Spanish Inquisition, whose activity was greatest between 1560 and 1615 and whose peak decade was 1585–1594.[17]

The pace dropped off sharply in all four Italian territories after 1620 or thereabouts. Venice, which had averaged 33 inquisitorial defendants annually from 1547 to 1630, fell to 15 per year from 1631 to 1720. In the Friuli, the drop was equally noticeable, from an average of 25 cases per year (1580–1615) to only 10 (1615–1700). Naples fell from an annual average of 31 defendants (1564–1620) to only 14 (1621–1700), while Sicily fell from 33 defendants per year (1560–1614) to 14 (1615–1700). Once again, as with the extremely high levels of activity from 1580 to 1615, this decline is quite similar to the general picture in Spain, where total annual caseloads fell sharply from 517 (1560–1614) to 170 (1615–1700). In a Braudelien, *longue-durée* perspective, the two great Mediterranean inquisitorial systems followed very similar cycles.

This conclusion is reinforced by our fragmentary figures from the eighteenth century, a time for which the Spanish have no central data bank to chart their inquisitorial business. In Italy the various branches of the Roman Inquisition were somnolent. From 1721 to 1794, the Venetian Holy Office averaged three cases per year, the same as Aquileia-Concordia between 1691 and 1780. Naples, whose records stop by 1780, averaged fewer than four cases per year after 1700. Once again, indirect evidence from Spain suggests an equally abrupt collapse of inquisitorial activity during the eighteenth century, when most of its twenty tribunals passed three or four sentences annually.[18]

During most of the 250 years which separated the creation of the Roman Inquisition from its demise, the degree of congruence between Italian and Spanish statistical fluctuations is significant. But numerical similarities can, and often do, mask even more significant differences in the typology of cases handled by inquisitors in the two areas. In this respect, the differences between Italy and Spain outweigh the similarities.

The Roman Inquisition was reconstituted in 1542 to combat the menace of Protestantism in the Italian peninsula, whereas the Spanish Inquisition had been created more than half a century earlier to deal with massive numbers of converted Jews. The nature of what was considered "heresy" in each system reflects these original concerns. In northern and central Italy, "Lutheranism" overwhelmingly dominated the first generation of inquisitorial activity, lasting until the 1580s.[19] The Venetian records offer a truly remarkable example: over its first thirty-five years (1547–1582) this Holy Office tried more than 700 "Lutherans" among its first 1,200 cases — plus 36 Anabaptists, 68 cases of "heresy in general," 20 of eating meat during Lent, and almost 90 concerned with possession or reading of prohibited books. Approximately 80 percent of these early cases, therefore, concern Protestant or crypto-Protestant behavior. In the Venetian Terrafirma, Aquileia-Concordia showed a similar concentration on such offenses during its first thirty-eight years (1557–1595); of its initial 380 cases, 200 were for suspected Protestant heresies and 74 for consuming meat during Lent (a possible indication of northern influences at work). In this rural area of low literacy there were only 12 cases of prohibited books. Again, over 75 percent of these cases may have involved Protestant sympathies.[20]

In the Spanish portions of southern Italy our statistics suggest a different meaning in the Holy Office's concern with heretics. Although a sizable share of the earliest preserved cases from Naples may be classified as heresy trials, few dealt with Protestants; in fact, through 1620 accused Mohammedans outnumbered reputed Protestants by more than five to one. In Sicily, the imbalance was almost as extreme. The diligent Spanish inquisitors uncovered large numbers of Protestants, but here too these were numerically swamped by the followers of Islam. Before 1560, the Sicilian Holy Office tried more than fifty Protestants (more than any other tribunal in the Spanish system) and only eleven Moslems; but between 1560 and 1615, they judged nearly four Moslems for every Protestant (471 and 138 respectively).[21]

The heavy concentration on Protestants which characterized the Venetian, or Friulian, Inquisitions slackened, as the appendices show, in the late sixteenth century, although these courts became busier than ever and their activities encompassed a remarkable variety of offenses. The misdemeanors of Venetian laymen included exotica ranging from selling bogus indulgences to insulting a converted Jew. Venetian clergy were charged with a broad array of crimes, from the illegal celebration of Mass to painting one's concubine *in atto di adorazione* and displaying her portrait as an image of St. Lucia.[22] On the whole, we are left with the impression that the Inquisition took an extremely broad view of its assignment, the pursuit of heresy. Cases of clerical misconduct and disciplinary infractions which should have fallen to the courts of the bishop or of the religious orders increasingly came under its jurisdiction. What adds interest to this phenomenon is the spectacle of hundreds of priests and monks appearing as defendants before a church tribunal on which secular officials sat alongside ecclesiastical judges.

In this cornucopia of Venetian offenses, illicit magic replaced Protestantism as the most common charge after 1585.[23] In the Friuli we find a similar story, with accused religious heretics dominating until 1595, followed by magicians and witches afterward. At Naples, where Reformation currents apparently had never been a serious problem for the Holy Office,[24] illicit magic became the single most common charge as early as the 1570s and remained so until the 1720s. In Sicily, however, charges of superstitious magic were relatively infrequent; during the peak period (1560–1614) they accounted for only 8 percent of all cases — but this was the second largest total for any branch of the Spanish system before 1615; and before 1575 more necromancers, magicians, and witches were tried in Sicily than in either Venice or the Friuli.[25]

Wherever one turns, therefore, it appears that Italian inquisitors were becoming preoccupied with superstitious magic and witchcraft well before 1600 — unlike their Spanish counterparts, who held barely 2 percent of their pre–1615 trials for such offenses.[26] In the seventeenth century this Italian concern with magicians and witches persisted, while the attention that needed to be devoted to religious deviants continued to diminish. Illicit magic alone constituted over 40 percent of all cases both at Venice and in the Friuli and close to 40 percent in Naples.[27] Even in Sicily, where it accounted for only 25 percent of Holy Office activity after 1615, illicit magic was the largest single category and the 310 trials for this offense were the largest total from any of the twenty Spanish tribunals during this period. After 1600, prosecution of magicians dominated the business of the Italian Inquisitions, far more dramatically than it ever did in any part of the Spanish system: in the nine Castilian tribunals, for example, "superstition" accounted for only 12 percent of the 6,240 trials held between 1615 and 1700.[28] As late as the decade 1701–1710, illicit magic made up 69 percent of all Venetian inquisitorial cases and 61 percent of those at Naples.

The rubric of "illicit magic" obviously covered a great many different practices, just as "Lutheranism" had during the sixteenth century. Because of discrepancies in the nomenclature used by our sources, it is difficult to obtain satisfactory subdivisions within this grouping and thus to uncover the primary concerns of seventeenth-century Italian inquisitors. The most detailed and probably the most reliable subdivison comes from the Friuli, as Table 1 and the literature will show.[29]

TABLE 1. FRIULIAN INQUISITION: "MAGICAL ARTS"[a]

Offense	1596–1610		1611–1670		1671–1785		
	Men	Women	Men	Women	Men	Women	Total
General magic	10	16	12	7	18	7	70
Divination-necromancy	5	6	3	1	4	0	19
Therapeutic magic	50	60	39	48	0	2	199
Benandanti	5	5	26	8	6	0	50
Love magic	14	20	25	18	32	6	115
Spell of *tamiso*[b]	4	6	15	5	12	1	43
Spells *vs.* wolves, storms, etc.	2	1	7	21	0	0	31
Spells *vs.* bullets	0	0	1	0	8	0	9
Other spells	3	8	3	2	8	2	26
Spells to acquire wealth	0	0	0	0	34	1	35
Maleficia-witchcraft	8	39	12	72	20	29	180
Totals	101	161	143	182	142	48	777

[a] For the statistics before 1595 (45 cases of magical activity), see Appendix 2.
[b] The spell of *tamiso* was generally used in love magic and is bracketed with it.

Apart from black magic, where women continued to hold a narrow edge (although several suspected perpetrators of *maleficia* were Freemasons!),[30] the defendants were overwhelmingly male after 1670. Men, it seems, occasionally used magic to win love, though more often they employed it to obtain riches or even to become bulletproof; a group of enterprising youths from one village won a remarkable package deal from the Devil in 1754 promising all three.[31] In the words of a recent writer, "Men declared, without difficulty, that they had tried to give their soul to the Devil in exchange for money; but the Devil, although frequently invoked, never appeared, and so they gave up, more from ineffective magic than from respect for the faith. . . . It all transpired among a disillusioned witch, a reluctant Devil, and an indifferent inquisitor."[32] The world of the Enlightenment had truly arrived.

Magic, as we have seen, was by far the single largest heretical category handled by the Inquisitions of Italy after the first wave of Protestantism had abated. But it was certainly not the only type of offense. Other significant categories showed considerable variation from place to place. Unlike the Spanish Inquisition, for example, where the prosecution of Judaizers continued at a high rate down to 1700, the Italian tribunals were much less preoccupied with this offense.

In our sample, Jews were rarely molested by the Holy Office of Aquileia-Concordia (five cases among more than two thousand, but there were few Jewish settlements in the Friuli).[33] At Naples, Judaism was an even rarer offense than Protestantism, at least during the century after 1590 (about thirty compared to four dozen Protestants).[34] The Sicilian Inquisition was originally highly anti-Semitic: approximately half of its first 160 cases after its 1537 reorganization involved Judaizing. But even Sicily had few such cases after 1560 — only eight, in fact, the lowest total of any tribunal in the Spanish system.[35]

In contrast, the index to the trials of the Venetian Holy Office includes almost eighty Jews and Judaizers — a surprisingly large total since Venice has often been regarded as one of the most tolerant havens in Catholic Europe. However, most of these cases are simple denunciations rather than full-dress trials.[36] The charges seem similar to those levelled elsewhere in Italy: attempting to proselytize Christian servants; attending Mass; sexual relations with Christians. A "Levantine" was denounced for insulting a Greek in 1582. Other Jews sold meat to Christians during Lent or even performed exorcisms for them.[37] However, because evidence from foreign tribunals was inadmissible in any Venetian court, baptized Jews who fled to Venice and relapsed into Judaism escaped the harsh punishments meted out to apostates. Apparently no Judaizers were executed by any of these four tribunals, except for one Jewish woman by the Sicilian in 1549.[38]

Another remarkable difference emerges from a comparison of the treatment of bigamy in north and south. In Venice or in the Friuli, this crime was ordinarily judged by secular courts, as the nuncio complained, and only sporadically did such defendants turn up in inquisitorial records.[39] But in Naples and Sicily it accounted for large numbers of defendants, especially during the seventeenth century—about 14 percent in both places. Bigamy, in fact, was a much more frequently tried offense in the Inquisitions of Spanish Italy than it was in Spain itself. Sicily prosecuted more than twice as many bigamists as any other single Spanish tribunal during the seventeenth century, yet it was outstripped by Naples.[40]

On the other hand, possession of prohibited books continued to be a much rarer offense in the *Mezzogiorno* than in the Venetian Republic. At Venice, this accusation had been prominent between 1570 and 1592: eighty-four cases, or almost 10 percent of the total. But prosecutions apparently dropped off during the Republic's quarrel with the papacy, which culminated in the 1606 Interdict, and *libri proibiti* never regained their relative importance afterward, falling to less than 4 percent.[41] In the rural Friuli, prohibited books remained a minor charge during the great Protestant hunt before 1595 but became more important afterward; from 1601 to 1700—a time when it accounted for less than 1 percent of inquisitorial accusations in the great city of Naples—this rubric comprised 15 percent of the Holy Office's business in the Friuli.[42]

What exactly were these prohibited books? During most of the sixteenth century the inquisitors were presumably interested mainly in Protestant titles; as the pursuit of religious heresy gave way to witch-hunting, the nature of the forbidden literature also shifted. Our most detailed evidence comes from the Friuli, where in a sample of fourteen cases (1596–1610) in which the index of trials identifies the type of literature, all but one were for magical rather than religious books. A later and larger sample of 120 offenders (1641–1670) showed ten of the prohibited titles to be concerned with theological heresy; over twenty were magical or astrological books; and the vast majority, sixty, were "libertine" works.[43]

If statistics for bigamy or prohibited books can help us identify some of the important differences between inquisitorial patterns in northern and southern Italy, other figures can point to similarities. Consider blasphemy, so grave an offense that it could entail the death penalty in extreme cases.[44] To deal with the crime, Venice created a special morals tribunal, the *Esecutori contro la bestemmia*, a full decade before it reorganized the Inquisition. This secular court had jurisdiction over ordinary blasphemy, and soon over such related misdemeanors as gambling or unlicensed printing. Like the Holy Office, it continued to function until the end of the Venetian Republic, separately from the city's other criminal courts. As one might expect, the *Esecutori* had several possible spheres of overlapping jurisdiction with inquisitors. In theory, the competence of the latter extended only over cases of suspected heretical blasphemy. In practice, it was often not possible to determine the type of blasphemy that had been committed until the case was brought to trial, and frequently not even then. It was not the act — an oath against the Virgin, for example — that constituted the heresy, but the intent, the true sentiments about the Virgin Birth harbored by the suspect. Because of the delicate theological issues involved in ferreting out the heretical element in blasphemy cases, some canonists adopted the position that both heretical and ordinary blasphemy pertained to the Inquisition. At any rate, Venetian Holy Office records are filled with instances of alleged usurpation of the ecclesiastical jurisdiction on the part of secular authorities.[45]

When the *Esecutori* were at peak efficiency between 1550 and 1570, they judged 110 cases of blasphemy,[46] in comparison to 4 brought before the Holy Office during those decades. But after 1580, when the secular magistracy began to shift its attention to morals charges and gambling, the instances of accusations for this crime before the ecclesiastical court increased. From 1586 onward trials for this offense accounted for 4 to 5 percent of Venetian inquisitorial activity — exactly the same proportions as blasphemy represented both in the Friuli and at Naples after 1610, although it had occurred infrequently during the first phase of their activity.[47]

Another offense with similar distribution was "solicitation" by priests of penitent women in the confessional. This rarely appeared in sixteenth-century inquisitorial records but became more frequent as Tridentine legislation bit more deeply into daily life. After 1610 it accounted for roughly seventy cases in Venice, sixty-one in Sicily, and seventy in the Friuli —

between 5 and 8 percent of inquisitorial business, at a time when "solicitation" accounted for 2.5 percent of all cases judged by the Spanish Inquisition. This crime continued to concern Italian inquisitors in the eighteenth century, as it did the Spanish.[48]

In the Spanish system, the single largest category of offenses, accounting for about 28 percent of its total activity, was the loosely defined cluster of doctrinal errors which had been labelled as *proposiciones heréticas* (including heretical blasphemy and many other crimes, such as the belief that sexual intercourse between unmarried individuals was not sinful). In each branch of the Roman system some cases were described as *proposizioni ereticali*, although they were never very numerous (during the seventeenth century, they constituted under 10 percent of accusations in each tribunal).[49] However, the Italian indices that we have examined also included many defendants charged with sundry types of irreligious actions or erroneous beliefs, less serious than formal doctrinal error, which logically belong with the *proposizioni* and which the Spanish tabulations have in fact included under this heading. For the two tribunals of the Venetian Republic, we have simply combined such charges as "erroneous preaching" or "disrespect for religion" with *proposizioni*, separating out only blasphemy, "abuse of sacraments" (much of it for magical purposes), and accusations of atheism or materialism. In the Friulian trial inventory, where descriptions are less laconic than in the Venetian index, a plurality of these propositions refers to improper notions about sexual morality. In the Neapolitan catalogue, which is unusually specific and detailed, we have distinguished not only these categories but also such accusations as acts against religious vows and precepts, acts against saints, and sacrilege from simple charges of *proposizioni ereticali*. When these categories are recombined, they amount to a significant share of the activities of the Roman tribunals, as much as the Spanish: between 1621 and 1700, for example, such charges comprised about 20 percent of the business of the Neapolitan Holy Office, or exactly the same share as *proposiciones* held in Sicily between 1615 and 1700.[50]

Three scattered branches of the Roman Inquisition cannot give us a true picture of the entire system, no matter how many similarities and regional differences they suggest. If we seek a general overview of the network of Inquisitions in Italy, preferably at or near peak activity, we can find one small but interesting avenue of approach. The dispersed papers of the Roman Inquisition preserved at Trinity College in Dublin include several volumes of sentences issued by the Roman and provincial tribunals between 1564 and 1659. Four volumes deal with the sixteenth century, covering the years 1564–1568 and 1580–1582, containing approximately 500 sentences.[51] We have selected two of the richest volumes (MS. 1225 and MS. 1226), which contain copies of more than 200 sentences sent to Rome by local branches of the Holy Office for confirmation or revision between 1580 and 1582.[52]

TABLE 2. SENTENCES, 1580–1582 (TCD, MSS 1225–1226)

Region	Protestantism	Magic	Witchcraft	Blasphemy	Materialism	Opposition[a]	Miscellaneous[b]	Total
Venetian Republic	59	9	2	1	6	4	4	85
Duchy of Milan	15	4	10	3	0	1	2	35
Piedmont and Genoa	15	0	7	1	0	1	0	24
Po Duchies[c]	10	16	0	6	1	3	5	41
Tuscany	1	6	0	0	0	0	1	8
Papal States[d]	11	5	1	0	0	1	1	19
Kingdom of Naples[e]	1	7	0	0	1	0	4	13
Totals	112	47	20	11	8	10	17	225

[a]"Opposition" to the Holy Office includes four persons who failed to denounce heretics, three jailbreakers, two offenders who attempted bribery, and a pseudo-inquisitor in Milanese territory.
[b]"Miscellaneous" includes three Judaizers, an apostate to Islam, and three bigamists.
[c]Mantua (26), Ferrara, Modena, Parma-Piacenza.
[d]Bologna (7), Ancona (7), Imola-Faenza (5).
[e]Castro (8), Campagna (3), Mileto, Naples. (The last two have the only Judaizers on the list apart from a woman in Milan).

These sentences represent a fraction of the offenders who actually came to the attention of Italian inquisitors during those years. Only six of the thirteen people in the Friuli inventory appear here and only eleven of the forty Venetian defendants. The Trinity materials serve as a guide to some of the more serious and difficult cases actually judged in those years, which represent fewer than half of those who were denounced or even arrested during 1580 or 1581. Nevertheless, these documents are obviously very valuable for their indication of overall patterns of inquisitorial activity. As Table 2 shows, the geographical differences within Italy were remarkable. Three-eighths of these sentences originated in the lands of the Venetian Republic. Most of the remainder came from northern and north-central

Italy, with a remarkable cluster of twenty-six sentences from the unusually zealous or unusually careful inquisitors at Mantua. Tuscany is poorly represented; the Papal States south of Bologna and Imola, together with the entire Kingdom of Naples, accounted for less than a tenth of the total.

Half of the sentences shown in Table 2 were for various Protestant and crypto-Protestant activities; most of the remainder were for either illicit white magic or black magic, necromancy or witchcraft. The list includes three Judaizers, plus an unbaptized Jew who was banished from Imola for teaching necromancy to Christians. Only one woman was "vehemently suspected" of apostasy to Islam, on the grounds that she had married a Turk many years before. The list also contains three bigamists (sentenced to the galleys) and twenty witches in Novara tried together in 1580 (resulting in only one conviction; TCD MS. 1225, fol. 232).

The geographical patterns revealed by these classifications are important. Protestant heretics accounted for the overwhelming majority of defendants sentenced throughout the Venetian dominions, thus providing valuable confirmation of the patterns already discerned in Venice or in the Friuli. Except for major witch-hunts in the dioceses of Como and Novara and in the Piedmontese Alps, Protestants also dominated the sentences of other tribunals throughout northern and western Italy — regions which, like Venice, bordered on heresy-infested Switzerland or Dauphiné. The witches included two *benandanti* in the Friuli (then a novel problem)[53] and a widow at Imola who had been married to a German and had lived in Nuremberg; but otherwise such cases were confined to the mountains of the north and west. Significantly, materialists, who claimed that the soul died with the body, were generally encountered only at Padua and surrounding Venetian dioceses. In the small independent duchies of the Po basin, principally Mantua, the configurations were different from those in the north and west: here only a fourth of the sentences concerned Protestantism, but blasphemy — and particularly necromancy — formed the most common charge. Apart from Bologna (which tried seven Protestants and saw one of the four executions on this list), Protestants appear rarely in the figures from central and southern Italy: a conventicle of five women who celebrated their own communion at Ancona provided the only significant episode. From Tuscany southward, magic was the most common charge. Naples itself reported only one sentence against a female Judaizer. Taken all in all, these documents add up to a tantalizing snapshot of the general activities of the Roman Inquisition at a moment when the Holy Office of the Venetian Republic resembled those throughout northern Italy in their preoccupation with Protestant heresies, while those in the duchies of the Po valley or Tuscany were already turning to the prosecution of illicit magic as their chief concern.

Finally, subsequent Trinity College records show that Rome was engaged not only in punishing heretics and magicians but also in the happier business of formalizing seemingly voluntary reconciliations of foreigners who had converted (or re-converted) to Catholicism. Two volumes of formal sentences pronounced at Rome, in 1582 and in 1603, contain little else but abjurations of non-Catholics or apostates, made without duress. In the first of these two years there were 49 such instances among 80 sentences; in the second, 78 among 107. In 1582, ex-Protestants outnumbered ex-Moslems 27 to 22; in 1603, this margin increased to 58 to 20 (Englishmen provided the largest group of converts).[54] Similar conversions occurred elsewhere in Italy, although with less éclat than at Rome. In Naples, Holy Office records show 98 between 1564 and 1590, two-thirds of whom were sailors captured during the mid–1580s.[55] In the Friuli, which bordered on Protestant-infested Slovenia, almost 250 such conversions (mainly soldiers in the Palma Nova garrison) were registered after 1596: 111 Lutherans, 62 Calvinists, 36 Moslems, 43 Greek Orthodox, plus a "Hussite," a "Persian," and an "Anabaptist."[56] Such statistics serve to remind us that the Inquisition in Counter-Reformation Italy was concerned with conversion as well as coercion.

By adding our data from the Trinity College records for the years 1580 through 1582 to the long series from northeastern Italy and the *Mezzogiorno*, we can discern some major differences between the Roman and Spanish Inquisitions. To oversimplify: Rome was chiefly concerned with Protestantism in the sixteenth century and much less concerned with Judaizers than was Spain; and Rome had become far more preoccupied with illicit magic by 1590 than the Spanish would ever be.[57] The attention paid by the former to magicians and witches did not, however, imply any very great severity toward them. In Italy (as in Spain), the rubric of "magic" rarely involved witchcraft and apostasy to the Devil; and even when it did, the Italian inquisitors, unlike secular judges, rarely punished the crime with death. The notorious executions of a handful of Basque witches by the Logroño Inquisition in 1611 had no parallel in the ecclesiastical courts of early modern Italy, where witchcraft was treated as any other heresy, and a first offender who expressed a desire to repent was never handed over to the secular arm.[58]

What remains exceptional is the extent of the Roman Inquisition's deal-ings with superstitious practices, far beyond anything in the Spanish sys-tem: the example of seventeenth-century Sicily, with the largest number of accused magicians among the twenty tribunals under the *Suprema*, but the lowest by far in our Italian sample, is decisive.[59] Why Rome moved in this direction, while Spain looked to *proposiciones heréticas* as a replace-ment for heresy trials, seems impossible to determine. Certainly there was no greater credence in the efficacy of magic or greater fear of witches in Rome than in Castile. If we can find the supreme Spanish tribunal warn-ing its provincial officials as early as 1538 that judges must not accept everything printed in the *Malleus maleficarum* even if "he [the author] writes about it as something he himself has seen and investigated,"[60] we can also find the Roman Congregation sentencing a minor judge in the Papal States to ten years in the galleys for judicial improprieties in a witchcraft case a few decades later.[61] Both great Mediterranean Inquisitions, despite occasional aberrations, were remarkably cautious and moderate in these matters, as even H. C. Lea recognized almost a century ago, compared to Europe's secular courts.[62]

What can be said about the relative severity or leniency of inquisitorial justice? What was the outcome in the thousands of trials recorded in the appendices to this essay? Despite popular notions to the contrary, only a very small percentage of cases concluded with capital punishment. Can-on law prescribed that only the obstinate and unrepentant who refused to be reconciled to the Church, those who had suffered previous convic-tions for formal heresy,[63] or those who were convicted of especially heinous crimes[64] were liable to the death penalty. The available figures on the numbers of those handed over by the Inquisition to the secular arm suggest that the executed were relatively few. Only four of the first thousand defendants who appeared before the tribunal of Aquileia-Concordia (1551–1647) were put to death.[65] A tentative calculation for Venice has counted fourteen executions between 1553 and 1588, plus four deaths occurring in prison and four extraditions to deaths in Rome be-tween 1555 and 1593.[66] Only twelve executions for heresy have been counted for Milan during the second half of the sixteenth century (but on the basis of incomplete documentation), and only one, in 1567, for religious heresy in Modena;[67] and of the more than two hundred sen-tences (several involving more than one defendant) contained in the Trinity College manuscripts mentioned above, for parts of the years 1580–1582, only four called for condemnations to the stake.[68] In his studies of the

Friuli witchcraft trials, Carlo Ginzburg encountered neither the use of torture in the proceedings nor a single execution; in fact, only rarely was a case brought to a conclusion.[69] The names of ninety-seven victims of the Holy Office in the city of Rome for the period 1542–1761 have been extracted from the records of the Archconfraternity, whose function it was to accompany the condemned to their deaths.[70] As for Spanish inquisitorial courts, they executed approximately 820 people between roughly 1540 and 1700, out of a total of more than 44,000 cases, for a rate of 1.9 percent.[71]

A comparison between Venice and Sicily suggests a slightly higher execution ratio for the latter. Between 1537 and 1572, the Sicilian Holy Office celebrated nineteen *autos da fé* during which twenty-two prisoners were sentenced to death: seventeen Protestants, a Jewess, and four unrepentant apostates to Islam, captured at Lepanto and burned at Palermo in 1572. Between 1573 and 1618 the Sicilian tribunal executed seven more "Lutherans," two Calvinists, and an unrepentant materialist. Overall, Sicily's branch of the Spanish Inquisition killed almost twice as many heretics as did the Inquisition at Venice, over a longer period of time (1542–1618 vs. 1553–1593). Yet Venice had put more than four times as many suspected Protestants on trial—over 800 before 1593 vs. under 200 by 1620.[72]

The stake, imprisonment "for life,"[73] and the galleys are those dramatic forms of penal practice generally associated with inquisitorial procedures. But a survey of the hundreds of sentences preserved at Trinity College suggests that in actual fact milder forms of punishment prevailed. Most frequently encountered are public humiliation in the form of abjurations read on cathedral steps on Sundays and on feast days before the throngs of churchgoers, and salutary penances, a seemingly endless cycle of prayers and devotions to be performed over many months or years.

Statistics can reveal significant discrepancies between comparable institutions—between the Holy Offices of Venice and Naples, between the Roman and Spanish Inquisitions—but they cannot by themselves explain them. We do not yet know, for example, why Sicily—and even more, Naples—led all other courts in their pursuit of bigamists; nor do we know why more magicians and witches were prosecuted in Sicily than anywhere else in the Spanish system (although Sicily's totals fall far below all other Italian tribunals in this category). But one must discover differences before they can be explained, and a statistical overview of this sort may help to prepare the ground for more sophisticated tasks in comparative history.

APPENDIX 1

VENETIAN INQUISITION

Offense	1547–1585	1586–1630	1631–1720	1721–1794	Total
Lutheranism	717	109	77	2	905
Anabaptism	37	0	1	0	38
Judaizing	34	16	28	0	78
Mohammedanism	10	27	42	1	80
Calvinism	13	18	29	0	60
Greek Orthodoxy	3	8	11	0	22
"Heresy in general"	68	27	6	1	102
Materialism–atheism	1	4	14	7	26
Apostasy	15	17	12	0	44
Proposizioni ereticali	62	26	107	105	300
Prohibited books	93	48	40	0	181
Prohibited meats	23	12	16	5	56
Blasphemy	17	41	61	10	129
Abuse of sacraments	9	12	106	9	136
Bigamy	3	7	12	0	22
Concubinage	7	5	4	0	16
Adultery	3	7	0	0	10
Sodomy	5	5	5	1	16
Solicitation	3	22	72	23	120
Magical arts	59	319	641	22	1041
Offenses against Holy Office	10	8	6	1	25
Pseudo-sainthood	0	1	5	1	7
Illegal celebration of Mass	2	4	14	8	28
False testimony	14	7	4	0	25
Miscellaneous	21	66	31	7	125
Totals	1229	816	1344	203	3592
Annual averages	32	35	15	3	
Multiple defendants	18	5	2	0	25
Secondary charges					
Prohibited books	9	2	1	0	12
Blasphemy	2	4	5	0	11
Lutheranism	5	1	1	0	7
Magical arts	1	2	4	0	7
Abuse of sacraments	2	1	18	0	21
Sodomy	1	0	1	0	2
Solicitation	0	1	2	1	4
Other minor heresy	2	1	1	0	4
Other sex crimes	4	2	0	0	6
Miscellaneous	8	9	4	0	21
Totals	34	23	37	1	95

Note: In this and the following tables, the figures refer to numbers of defendants and not to numbers of trials. Several trials involved more than one individual. The category "Multiple defendants" designates cases with an unspecified number of defendants. "Secondary charges" applies to defendants accused of more than one crime. The years 1593–1615 (except for 1610) are not included in these statistics. See note 7.

APPENDIX 2

FRIULIAN INQUISITION

Offense	1557–1595	1596–1610	1611–1670	1671–1786	Total
Heresy and suspected heresy	200	64	37	33	334
Judaizing	1	0	3	1	5
Proposizioni ereticali	34	45	89	89	257
Abuse of sacraments	1	4	12	12	29
Prohibited meats	66	153	40	10	269
Prohibited books	7	46	127	13	193
Apostasy	0	0	3	7	10
Atheism	0	0	0	3	3
Blasphemy	4	11	31	30	76
Bigamy	1	0	12	1	14
Concubinage	2	1	0	0	3
Solicitation	1	1	47	62	111
Magical arts	45	256	317	196	814
Offenses against Holy Office	1	13	8	6	28
Pseudo-sainthood	0	0	8	1	9
Illegal Mass	0	0	1	1	2
False testimony	0	0	2	0	2
Miscellaneous	11	5	13	10	39
Lutheranism	0	5	56	50	111
Calvinism	0	1	31	30	62
Mohammedanism	0	4	30	2	36
Greek Orthodoxy	0	0	26	17	43
Other religious conversions	0	0	2	1	3
Totals	374	609	895	575	2453
Annual averages	10	43	15	5	—
Multiple defendants	6	3	4	2	15
Secondary charges					
Heresy and suspected heresy	1	1	2	1	5
Proposizioni ereticali	5	1	4	7	17
Prohibited meats	12	7	4	4	27
Prohibited books	9	3	9	8	29
Magical arts	6	15	12	14	47
Blasphemy	1	4	4	4	13
Abuse of sacraments	0	4	15	25	44
Miscellaneous	1	0	8	3	12
Totals	35	35	58	66	194

APPENDIX 3

NEAPOLITAN INQUISITION

Offense	1564–1590	1591–1620	1621–1700	1701–1740	Total
Protestantism	19	18	26	1	64
Judaizing	41	8	20[a]	0	69
Mohammedanism	126	67	13	0	206
Atheism	4	8	11	1	24
Proposizioni ereticali	38	86	50	6	180
Prohibited books	7	9	15	0	31
Blasphemy	15	32	49	6	102
Offenses against sacraments	27	30	39	18	114
Offenses against vows and precepts	50	49	63	16	178
Bigamy	9	73	169	38	289
Concubinage	7	7	2	1	17
Magical arts	178	498	387	64	1127
Sacrilege, offense to saints, images, and holy places	11	6	5	16	38
Offenses against Holy Office	16	39	4	2	61
Commerce in false relics and indulgences	2	12	18[b]	5	37
False testimony	39	43	146	13	241
Reconciliation of foreign Protestants	98	3	8	0	109
Conversion of Muslims to Christianity	0	9	0	0	9
Miscellaneous	48	24	61[c]	9	142
Totals	735	1021	1086	196	3038
Annual averages	28	35	14	5	
Secondary charges					
Protestantism	6	2	0	0	8
Judaizing	0	1	0	0	1
Mohammedanism	3	0	0	0	3
Proposizioni ereticali	4	18	11	3	36
Prohibited books	0	2	4	2	8
Blasphemy	18	20	5	3	46
Offenses against sacraments	8	4	2	0	14
Offenses against vows and precepts	21	10	4	0	35
Bigamy	1	0	1	0	2
Concubinage	4	1	2	0	7
Magical arts	12	24	23	6	65
Sacrilege, offense to saints, images, and holy places	4	8	1	3	16
Offenses against Holy Office	2	8	0	0	10
Miscellaneous	1	13[d]	0	0	14
Totals	84	111	53	17	265

[a]Of which 8 are repeaters.
[b]Includes cases involving an unspecified number of defendants.
[c]Includes many repeaters and cases involving an unspecified number of defendants.
[d]Includes cases involving several defendants.

APPENDIX 4

SICILIAN INQUISITORIAL TRIALS, 1560–1700

Offense	1560–1614	1615–1700
Judaizing	8	0
Mohammedanism	471	261
Lutheranism	138	45
Alumbrados	1	15
Proposiciones[a]	531	230
Bigamy	164	172
Solicitation	53	61
Offenses against Holy Office	157	72
Superstition	146	310
Miscellaneous	88	62
Totals	1757	1228
Annual averages	33	14

Sources: The table has been compiled from statistics assembled by Jaime Contreras and Gustav Henningsen, which appear in *The Inquisition in Early Modern Europe*, pp. 114–19.
[a]Includes blasphemy.

Notes

1. There has been a veritable explosion of Spanish scholarship on the Inquisition, too extensive to be cited here. The major results are highlighted in several collected volumes: J. P. Villanueva, ed., *La Inquisición española: Nueva visión, nuevos horizontes* (Madrid, 1980), containing the proceedings of the international symposium held at Cuenca in September 1978; B. Bennassar, ed., *L'Inquisition espagnole, XVe–XIXe siècle* (Paris, 1979); A. Alcalá, ed., *Inquisición española y mentalidad inquisitorial* (Barcelona, 1984), the acts of an international conference in New York City, 1983, also available in an occasionally unreliable English-language edition: *The Spanish Inquisition and the Inquisitorial Mind* (Boulder, 1987); J. P. Villanueva and B. Escandell Bonet, eds., *Historia de la Inquisición en España y América* (Madrid, 1984–), a work projected in three volumes, limited to Spanish participants. The extraordinary resurgence in activity is noted by B. Bennassar, "Un phénomène historiographique: l'accéleration des recherches sur l'Inquisition espagnole; enjeux et débats," *Histoire, economie et société* 2 (1983): 367–72. See also the following surveys of the recent literature: A. Márquez, "Estado actual de los estudios sobre la Inquisición," *Arbor* 101 (1978): 85–96; G. Parker, "Some Recent Work on the Inquisition in Spain and Italy," *Journal of Modern History* 54 (1982): 519–32; W. Monter, "The New Social History and the Spanish Inquisition," *Journal of Social History* 17 (1984): 705–13; J. L. González Novalín, "L'Inquisizione spagnola: Correnti storiografiche

da Llorente (1817) ai nostri giorni," *RSCI* 39 (1985): 139–59; M. Olivari, "A proposito di Inquisizione spagnola," *Rivista di storia e letteratura religiosa* 24 (1988): 331–46. Cf. the essays by Prosperi and Borromeo cited in the introduction at n. 5.

For the state of the question in regard to Italy, see J. Tedeschi, "Preliminary Observations on Writing a History of the Roman Inquisition" and the surveys by Prosperi and Borromeo. Two magnificent publishing programs call for special notice: the voluminous records of the trial of Cardinal Giovanni Morone edited by M. Firpo and D. Marcatto (cited in full at p. 372) and the proceedings against Venetian Jews and Judaizers being critically edited in many volumes by P. C. Ioly Zorattini (cited at n. 36 below).

2. For statistical studies of the records of the Spanish Inquisition, see G. Henningsen, "El 'Banco de datos' del Santo Oficio: Las relaciones de causas de la Inquisición española (1550–1700)," *Boletín de la Real Academia de la Historia* 174 (1977): 547–70, now incorporated in J. Contreras and G. Henningsen, "Forty-four Thousand Cases of the Spanish Inquisition (1540–1700): Analysis of a Historical Data Bank," in G. Henningsen and J. Tedeschi, eds., *The Inquisition in Early Modern Europe* (De Kalb, 1986), 100–129 (excluding figures from the Madrid and Cuenca tribunals); G. Henningsen, "La elocuencia de los números: Promesas de las 'relaciones de causas' inquisitoriales para la nueva historia social," in A. Alcalá, ed., *Inquisición española y mentalidad inquisitorial*, 207–25; V. González Caldas, "La correspondencia inquisitorial como fuente de estudio del Santo Oficio: Las relaciones de causas," in *Jornadas (II) de metodología y didáctica de la historia. Historia moderna: Letras.* Presentación de Angel Rodríguez Sánchez (Cáceres, 1983), 443–49; J. Contreras, "Las causas de fe de la Inquisición de Galicia: 1560–1700," in J. P. Villanueva, ed., *La Inquisición española*, 355–70; idem, *El Santo Oficio de la Inquisición en Galicia, 1560–1700: Poder, sociedad y cultura* (Madrid, 1982); J.-P. Dedieu, "Les causes de foi de l'Inquisition de Tolède: Essai statistique," *Mélanges de la Casa de Velázquez* 14 (1978): 143–71; J.-P. Dedieu and M. Demonet, "L'activité de l'Inquisition de Tolède: Étude statistique, méthodes et premiers résultats," *Annuario dell' Istituto storico italiano per l'età moderna e contemporanea* 37–38 (1985–86): 11–39. For succinct surveys of the principal Spanish inquisitorial documentary collections, in Madrid and Simancas, see M. Vergara Doncel, "Breves notas sobre la Sección de Inquisición del Archivo Histórico Nacional," in Villanueva, ed., *La Inquisición española*, 839–43; A. Represa Rodríguez, "Documentos sobre Inquisición en el Archivo de Simancas," ibid., 845–54; M. Escamilla-Colin, "L'Inquisition espagnole et ses archives secrètes," *Histoire, economie, et société* 4 (1985): 443–77.

3. See "The Dispersed Archives of the Roman Inquisition."

4. The literature is enormous and growing. Some of the most important recent research is mentioned in the surveys cited in n. 1. See also the references to the principal source collections and their inventories in the notes below.

5. V. Marchetti recently discovered numerous trials conducted before the Sienese tribunal among the notarial registers in the Archivio di Stato, Siena. Medici reforms in the sixteenth century ordered that all "scritture pubbliche di qualsivoglia qualità"

be placed in the state archives ("L'Archivio dell'Inquisizione senese," *BSSV* 93 [1972], no. 132: 77–83). A small *fondo* of inquisitorial documents has recently become accessible in the Archivio della Curia Arcivescovile in Pisa. It has been used by C. Ginzburg in his "Folklore, magia, religione," in *Storia d'Italia* [Einaudi], vol. 1 (Turin, 1972), 655n; and more recently in several studies by S. Adorni Braccesi: "Giuliano da Dezza, caciaiuolo: Nuove prospettive sull'eresia a Lucca nel XVI secolo," *Actum Luce: Rivista di studi lucchesi* 9 (1980), nos. 1–2: 89–138, esp. p. 90, a series of denunciations dated 1576; idem, "Il dissenso religioso nel contesto urbano lucchese della Controriforma," in *Città italiane del '500 tra Riforma e Controriforma: Atti del convegno internazionale di studi, Lucca, 13–15 ottobre 1983* (Lucca, 1988), 225–39, based on the Pisa documents, but also on the recently reorganized archive of the *Offizio sopra la Religione* (the body entrusted with the prosecution of heresy in Lucca) in the city's Archivio di Stato; and G. Romeo, "Una città, due inquisizioni: l'anomalia del Sant' Uffizio a Napoli nel tardo '500," *Rivista di storia e letteratura religiosa* 24 (1988): 42–67, esp. pp. 60 ff. The archive was the subject of a *tesi di laurea* at the Faculty of Letters at the University of Pisa in the academic year 1970–71: Danilo Sbrana, "Il processo di Félix Brouxon davanti al tribunale dell'Inquisizione di Pisa, 1595–1596." We are deeply grateful to Dr. Grazia Tommasi Stussi, who visited the archive on our behalf. She reports that the collection contains twenty-five *filze* ranging in date roughly from 1537 to 1731, and includes a handful of trials. An inventory of the archiepiscopal archive is in progress: L. Carratori, *Inventario dell' Archivio Arcivescovile di Pisa. I. (Secoli VIII–XV)* (Pisa, 1986). Excellent use of the Florentine materials has been made by A. Prosperi in his "Vicari dell' Inquisizione fiorentina alla metà del Seicento: Note d'archivio," *Annali dell' Istituto storico italo-germanico in Trento* 8 (1982): 275–304; and "L'Inquisizione fiorentina al tempo di Galileo," in *Novità celesti e crisi del sapere: Atti del convegno internazionale di studi galileiani*, supplement to the *Annali dell' Istituto e Museo di Storia della Scienza*, Anno 1983, fasc. 2: 315–25. Prosperi's "L'Inquisizione fiorentina dopo il Concilio di Trento," *Annuario dell' Istituto storico italiano per l'età moderna e contemporanea* 37–38 (1985–86): 97–124 notes the lack of sixteenth-century materials in the archive. Documents pertaining to Florentine trials held in the triennium 1565–68 are preserved in the *fondo* of the nuncio since this official participated in the judicial proceedings. For a summary description of the Florentine archive as a whole, see C. C. Calzolai, "L'Archivio arcivescovile fiorentino," *Rassegna storica toscana* 3 (1957): 127–81. Fragmentary materials of inquisitorial interest are preserved in the Archivio Arcivescovile, Sarzana. See A. Landi, "Sfogliando le carte di un tribunale ecclesiastico del Cinquecento," in D. Maselli, ed., *Da Dante a Cosimo I: Ricerche di storia religiosa e culturale toscana nei secoli XIV–XVI* (Pistoia, n.d.), 254–88. S. Seidel Menchi alludes to the new inquisitorial deposits being made accessible to scholars through the cataloguing projects under way in several Italian episcopal archives in her "Lo stato degli studi sulla Riforma in Italia," *Wolfenbütteler Renaissance-Mitteilungen* 5 (1981): 35–42, 89–92 (esp. the latter section), and in "Humanismus und Reformation im Spiegel der italienischen Inquisitionsprozessakten," in *Renaissance-Reformation: Gegensätze und Gemeinsamkeiten*, ed. A. Buck (Wies-

baden, 1984), 47–64. The author's *Erasmo in Italia, 1520–1580* (Turin, 1987) is based
on a firsthand examination of virtually all the then known repositories of inquisitorial
trials, and probably constitutes our most complete listing of this material. Work
on the records preserved in the archiepiscopal archive of Rovigo was reported by
E. Rotelli, "Il XVI convegno di studi sulla Riforma ed i movimenti religiosi in
Italia," *BSSV* 97 (1976), no. 140: 137. Extensive use of the Rovigo documents has
been made by G. Marchi, *La riforma tridentina in diocesi di Adria nel secolo XVI, descritta con il sussidio di fonti inedite* (Cittadella, 1969; 1st ed., 1946), esp. pp. 164–274
for a discussion of the Holy Office; and S. Ferlin Malavasi in her numerous studies
of heresy in the Veneto. See, as examples, her "Sulla diffusione delle teorie ereticali
nel Veneto durante il '500: Anabattisti rodigini e polesani," *Archivio veneto*, a. 103
(1972): 5–24; idem, "Intorno alla figura e all'opera di Domenico Mazzarelli, eterodosso
rodigino del Cinquecento," *BSSV* 94 (1973), no. 134: 28–33; idem, "Il processo
per eresia di Alfonso Ariano," *Archivio veneto*, ser. 5, 114 (1980): 112–19. See also
P. C. Ioly Zorattini, "The Trials of the Holy Office of Adria (Rovigo) against Jews
and Judaizers," in *Ninth World Congress of Jewish Studies: Division B, vol. 1, The History of the Jewish People (from the Second Temple Period until the Middle Ages* (Jerusalem, 1986), 167–74. A remnant of the archive of the Reggio Inquisition, four *buste*
containing correspondence with the Supreme Congregation for the years 1640–1780,
has turned up in the Archivio di Stato, Modena, *Fondo Inquisizione,* bb. 260–63.
See G. Biondi, "Le lettere della Sacra Congregazione romana del Santo Ufficio al-
l'Inquisizione di Modena: Note in margine a un regesto," *Schifanoia* 4 (1989): 106
(information based on a University of Bologna *tesi di laurea* presented by Maria Grazia Cavicchi in the 1986–1987 academic year). An important collection of inquisitorial
trials, chiefly of the seventeenth century, and many of them dealing with witchcraft
and superstitious practices, is presently being catalogued in the Archivio Diocesano
of Gravi (Bari). We are indebted to Professor Giuseppe Coniglio of the University
of Naples for this information.

6. For the Bologna documents, see [G. Mazzatinti and A. Sorbelli], *Inventari
dei manoscritti delle biblioteche d'Italia. 79. Bologna, Biblioteca Comunale dell'Archiginnasio* (Florence, 1954), MSS. B–1856–1944. The material was used recently in a *tesi
di laurea* defended in the 1981–82 academic year at the University of Bologna, Faculty
of Political Science, by Milena Brugnoli, "Superstizione e repressione: Il tribunale
della Santa Inquisizione a Bologna e contado nell'ultimo quarto del XVII secolo."
(We are grateful to Mary O'Neil for a copy of this dissertation.) The activities of
the Holy Office in Imola (province of Bologna) was also the subject of a *tesi* presented in the Faculty of Letters at the University of Bologna in the academic year 1973–74:
Raffaella Rotelli, "Il tribunale del Sant'Uffizio a Imola dalla fondazione al 1578."

The documents concerning Modena are in the Archivio di Stato of that city.
While the trials are in the *fondo Inquisizione,* letters from the Congregation of the
Inquisition in Rome are also in the *Carteggio con principi esteri.* Several 1973 disserta-
tions defended in the Faculty of Letters at the University of Bologna by M. C. As-
senza, M. P. Danieli, F. Fantuzzi, S. Giovanetti, and G. Grillenzoni consist of analyses

and inventories of the Modenese trials, especially of the late sixteenth-and early seventeenth-century materials, with the exception of Grillenzoni's which deals with proceedings against Jews during the period 1599-1670.

Excellent critical use of the sixteenth-century Modenese documents has been made recently for the study of religious heresy by S. Peyronel Rambaldi, *Speranze e crisi nel Cinquecento modenese: Tensioni religiose e vita cittadina ai tempi di Giovanni Morone* (Milan, 1979); C. Bianco, "La comunità di 'fratelli' nel movimento ereticale modenese del '500," *RSI* 92 (1980): 621-79; M. Firpo, "Gli 'Spirituali,' l'Accademia di Modena e il formulario di fede del 1542: Controllo del dissenso religioso e Nicodemismo," *Rivista di storia e letteratura religiosa* 30 (1984): 40-111. A. Rotondò's fundamental study of Bolognese heresy in the decade of the 1540s, "Per la storia dell'eresia a Bologna nel secolo XVI," *Rinascimento*, ser. 2, 2 (1962): 107-54 is based in large measure on Modenese inquisitorial documents. Exploitation of this *fondo* for the study of witchcraft had its modern renaissance with N. Corradini, "I processi delle streghe a Modena nella prima metà del sec. XVI," *Folklore modenese*, Atti e Memorie del I Congresso del Folklore modenese, 1-2 Nov. 1958 (Modena, 1959), 44 ff.; and, especially, with C. Ginzburg, "Stregoneria e pietà popolare: Note a proposito di un processo modenese del 1519," *Annali della Scuola Normale Superiore di Pisa: Lettere, storia e filosofia*, ser. 2, 30 (1961): 269-87 (now translated among the author's collected essays, *Clues, Myths, and the Historical Method*, trans. J. and A. C. Tedeschi [Baltimore, 1989], 1-16, 165-70). See also S. Abbiati, "A proposito di taluni processi inquisitori modenesi del primo Cinquecento," *BSSV*, no. 146 (1979): 101-18, and the excellent studies by A. Biondi and M. O'Neil cited at pp. 66, 258. For the later phase, see C. Righi, "L'Inquisizione ecclesiastica a Modena nel Settecento," in A. Biondi, ed., *Formazione e controllo della opinione pubblica a Modena nel Settecento* (Modena, 1986), 53-95 and G. Orlandi, *La fede al vaglio: Quietismo, satanismo e massoneria nel ducato di Modena tra Sette e Ottocento* (Modena, 1988), based on Modenese inquisitorial trials for solicitation, affected sanctity, and superstitious practices, with a documentary appendix containing excerpts from these records. On the history of the Modenese Inquisition itself, the most useful study remains A. Biondi's "Lunga durata e microarticolazione nel territorio di un Ufficio dell'Inquisizione: Il 'Sacro Tribunale' a Modena (1292-1785)," *Annali dell'Istituto storico italo-germanico in Trento* 8 (1982): 73-90.

7. Archivio di Stato, Venice (henceforth ASV), *Savii all'Eresia (S. Uffizio), Indice* 303, compiled in 1870 by the archivists Luigi Pasini and Giuseppe Giomo. The index has a tripartite arrangement: alphabetical, chronological, and geographical. Not all the Venetian inquisitorial materials are in the Archivio di Stato. Four *buste* of trials are preserved in the Archivio della Curia Patriarcale (Venice), *Criminalia S. Inquisitionis*, comprising, respectively, the years 1461-1558, 1561-1585, 1586-1599, 1586-1622. See the description in P. C. Ioly Zorattini, *Processi del S. Uffizio di Venezia contro Ebrei e giudaizzanti*, 1:61-63 (cited in full at n. 36). Portions of the index were published by E. Comba, "Elenco generale degli accusati di eresia dinanzi il Sant'Ufficio della Inquisizione di Venezia an. 1541-1600," *Rivista cristiana* 3 (1875):

28–34, 71, 100–101, 158, 207, 235, 297, 326, 366–67, 411–12, 447; ibid., 4 (1876): 14, 57, 93, 136, 178 (the "Elenco" is arranged geographically). A. J. Schutte, "Un inquisitore al lavoro: Fra Marino da Venezia e l'Inquisizione veneziana," in *I Francescani in Europa tra Riforma e Controriforma: Atti del XIII Convegno internazionale, Assisi, 17–18–19 ottobre 1985* (Perugia, 1987), 165–96 has an appendix of "heretics" tried in Venice December 1544-July 1550, a total of 35 persons identified by place of origin, occupation, length of proceedings, etc. A. Del Col ("Organizzazione, composizione e giurisdizione dei tribunali dell'Inquisizione romana nella repubblica di Venezia [1500–1550]," *Critica storica* 25 [1988]: 244–94, at p. 277) publishes a table of persons accused and tried during the decade 1541–1550.

8. *1000 Processi dell'Inquisizione in Friuli (1551–1647)* (Udine, 1976); *I Processi dell'Inquisizione in Friuli dal 1648 al 1798* (Udine, 1978). The two catalogues, which were compiled by Luigi De Biasio and Maria Rosa Facile, appear as volumes 4 and 7 in the series *Regione Autonoma Friuli-Venezia Giulia: Quaderni del Centro Regionale di Catalogazione dei Beni Culturali*. We are extremely grateful to Carlo Ginzburg for bringing them to our attention and to Luigi De Biasio for making these rare volumes available to us. For recent studies based on this splendid but largely unexplored collection, see notes 21, 29, 32, and 33. The total number of trials in the inventory by De Biasio and Facile, from which our Appendix 2 was compiled, is about 3 percent higher than the figures in A. Del Col, "La storia religiosa del Friuli nel Cinquecento: Orientamenti e fonti," *Metodi e ricerche*, n.s., 1 (1982): 69–87, at p. 73. See the discussion of the different types of surviving Friulian inquisitorial records at p. 71 of the article. There is a partial breakdown of trials for the two dioceses of Concordia and Aquileia in *Società e cultura del Cinquecento nel Friuli occidentale: Catalogo della mostra*, a cura di P. Goi (Pordenone, 1985), chap. 5, "Inquisizione": p. 185, a list of persons denounced or tried in the diocese of Concordia, 1548–84 on suspicion of heresy (30 cases, some involving several individuals); p. 186, similar data spanning the same period for the diocese of Concordia for formal heresy (20 cases, some involving more than one person). This section of the handsome catalogue was prepared by A. Del Col. The 1583 trial of Domenico Scandella, "Menocchio" was among the items exhibited. Superseding all previous statistical analyses, see M. Sarra, "Distribuzione statistica dei dati processuali dell'inquisizione in Friuli dal 1557 al 1786: Tecniche di ricerca e risultati," *Metodi e ricerche*, n.s., 7 (1988): 5–31, based on a firsthand examination of the trials proper. This rich and detailed study breaks down the data by decade and by place of origin of the accused, as well as by typology of the heresy, identifying twelve major criminal classifications and numerous sub-categories. See also A. Del Col, "Problemi per la catalogazione e repertoriazione unificata degli atti processuali dell'Inquisizione romana," *Critica storica* 25 (1988): 155–67 which contains an "Indice generale dei delitti dell'Inquisizione di Aquileia e Concordia," compiled by Mariangela Sarra Di Bert (pp. 165–67). The most thoroughgoing comprehensive study of the Friulian tribunal remains Del Col's unpublished dissertation, "Il Tribunale del Sant'Ufficio del patriarcato e diocesi di Aquileia nei primi anni di attività (1557–1562)," University of Trieste, Facoltà di Lettere, 1970–71.

It should be noted that the Holy Office did not have jurisdiction throughout the Friuli. It operated only in the diocese of Aquileia, politically under Venetian control. The secular courts prosecuted witchcraft and related crimes in the Habsburg domains. See L. De Biasio, "Esecuzioni capitali contro streghe nel Friuli orientale alla metà del secolo XVII," *Memorie storiche forogiuliesi* 58 (1978): 148.

9. G. Galasso and C. Russo, eds., *L'Archivio storico diocesano di Napoli*, 2 vols. (Naples, 1978), 2:627–914: "Sant'Ufficio," ed. L. Osbat and collaborators (henceforth cited as Osbat). These holdings have been described in more detail by Osbat himself in a series of articles: "Sulle fonti per la storia del Sant'Ufficio a Napoli alla fine del Seicento," *Ricerche di storia sociale e religiosa* 1 (1972): 419–27; "I processi del Sant'Ufficio a Napoli, alcuni problemi di metodo," in *La società religiosa nell'età moderna* (Naples, 1973), 941–61; "Un importante centro di documentazione per la storia del Mezzogiorno d'Italia nell'età moderna: L'Archivio storico diocesano di Napoli," *Mélanges de l'École française de Rome* 85 (1973): 311–59; "La sezione 'denunce' del fondo 'Sant'Ufficio' nell'archivio storico diocesano di Napoli," in *Atti del Congresso internazionale di studi sull'età del Viceregno* (Bari, 1977), 2: 403–33. By the same writer, see also *L'Inquisizione a Napoli: Il processo agli ateisti, 1688–1697* (Rome, 1974). It is important to remember that the Holy Office was barred from openly exercising its functions in Neapolitan territory. Its judicial responsibilities were filled by the episcopal courts under Rome's watchful eyes. For recent studies of this phenomenon, see n. 13 below.

10. The most complete statistical information on the operation of the Inquisition in Sicily is now contained in Contreras's and Henningsen's study cited at n. 2 and in Contreras's "Algunas consideraciones sobre las relaciones de causas de Sicilia y Cerdeña," *Annuario dell' Istituto storico italiano per l'età moderna e contemporanea* 37–38 (1985–86): 181–99. See also n. 14. These studies are based on *relaciones de causas*, trial summaries, since the trial records themselves were destroyed in 1783 after the tribunal of the Inquisition was abolished in Sicily. The *relaciones* are preserved in the Archivo Histórico Nacional, Madrid. For inventories of the inquisitorial documents that have survived in the Archivio di Stato, Palermo, see P. Bulgarella, "I registri contabili del Sant'Uffizio di Sicilia nell'Archivio di Stato di Palermo," *Rassegna degli Archivi di Stato* 31 (1971): 677–89 and the detailed survey "Fonti d'Archivio sull'Inquisizione spagnola in Sicilia," *Annuario dell'Istituto storico italiano per l'età moderna e contemporanea* 37–38 (1985–86): 143–60. On the *relaciones* see also the bibliography cited at n.2.

11. There are a number of excellent recent studies which take up, in greater or lesser degree, the organization and procedures of the Venetian Holy Office. See, among others, P. Grendler, *The Roman Inquisition and the Venetian Press, 1540–1605* (Princeton, 1977), esp. pp. 43–62; B. Pullan, *The Jews of Europe and the Inquisition of Venice, 1550–1670* (Oxford, 1983), esp. pt. 1; N. Davidson, "Rome and the Venetian Inquisition in the Sixteenth Century," *Journal of Ecclesiastical History* 39 (1988): 16–36; idem, "Chiesa di Roma ed Inquisizione veneziana," in *Città italiane del '500*, 283–92; J. Martin, "L'Inquisizione romana e la criminalizzazione del dissenso religioso

a Venezia all'inizio dell'età moderna," *Quaderni storici*, no. 66 (1987): 777–802. A. Del Col's "Organizzazione, composizione e giurisdizione dei tribunali dell'Inquisizione romana nella repubblica di Venezia (1500–1550)" (cited at n. 7) is fundamental for the period treated, one generally neglected in the recent scholarship. See also Del Col's "L'Inquisizione romana e il potere politico nella Repubblica di Venezia (1540–1560)," in press in the volume *La Inquisición y los poderes políticos*, Actas del Congreso de Madrid-Alcalá-Sigüenza, Septiembre 1984 (we are grateful to the author for providing us with a typescript); A. J. Schutte, "Un inquisitore al lavoro: Fra Marino da Venezia e l'Inquisizione veneziana" (cited at n. 7); A. Santosuosso, "The Moderate Inquisitor: Giovanni Della Casa's Venetian Nunciature, 1544–1549," *Studi veneziani*, n.s., 2 (1978): 119–210.

On the exceptions to standard procedures claimed by Venetian secular authorities, see the thirty-nine articles drawn up in Paolo Sarpi's *Historia della Sacra Inquisitione: Composta già dal R.P. Paolo Servita ed hora la prima volta posta in luce* (Serravalle, 1638). A separate chapter is devoted to each of the articles. Some examples: "Che ne i processi non si porranno decreti, o precetti che venghino di fuori dello stato" (chap. 15); "Che l'Inquisitione non farà essecutione contra i beni de i condannati" (chap. 27); "Che non si publicherà Bolla, ned'ordine della Congregatione di Roma, senza licenza del prencipe" (chap. 28). The majority of the articles spell out the jurisdiction and roles of the lay members of the inquisitorial court. Cf. P. Grendler, "The *Tre Savii sopra Eresia*: A prosopographical Study," *Studi veneziani*, n.s., 3 (1979): 283–340; reprinted in Grendler's *Culture and Censorship in Late Renaissance Italy and France* (London: Variorum Reprints, 1981). As we mentioned in passing, a lay presence in the courts of the Inquisition was not unique to Venice or to the Terrafirma. For the situation in another maritime republic, see G. Bertora, "Il tribunale inquisitorio di Genova e l'Inquisizione romana nel '500 (alla luce di documenti inediti)," *La Civiltà cattolica*, vol. 104, t. 2 (1953): 173–87, esp. pp. 175 ff.

12. The most important special Venetian court whose jurisdiction overlapped with that of the Inquisition has been studied by G. Cozzi, *Religione, moralità e giustizia a Venezia: Vicende della magistratura degli Esecutori contro la bestemmia* (Padua, 1969); G. Scarabello, "Figure del popolo veneziano in un processo degli Esecutori contro la bestemmia alla fine del' 700," *Studi veneziani* 17–18 (1975–76): 321–98; and, most recently, in the comprehensive treatment by R. Derosas," Moralità e giustizia a Venezia nel '500-'600: gli Esecutori contro la bestemmia," in *Stato, società e giustizia nella Repubblica veneta (sec. xv–xviii)*, ed. G. Cozzi (Rome, 1980), 431–528. For a fuller discussion of this competing tribunal, see the text at n. 45 below.

For examples of trials which we would expect to encounter among the records of the Holy Office but which, instead, were adjudicated by secular courts, see C. Boccato, "Un processo contro Ebrei di Verona alla fine del Cinquecento," *Rassegna mensile di Israel* 40 (1974): 345–70. The sentence, emitted on 6 April 1592 by the *podestà* of Verona, is against six Jews convicted of having persuaded two *conversos* to return to Judaism. The trial is preserved in the Archivio di Stato, Venice, *Quarantia Criminal, Processi*, b. 109; C. Boccato, "Processi ad Ebrei nell' archivio degli Ufficiali al Cattaver a Venezia," *Rassegna mensile di Israel* 41 (1975): 164–80. See also M. Dell'Acqua, "Una benandante friuliana in un processo di stregoneria a Parma nel 1611," *Archivio storico per le provincie parmensi*, ser. 4, no. 28 (1976): 353–81. The trial is preserved in the Archivio di Stato, Parma.

See also the case of a Brescian who was tried and executed by secular authorities for striking a crucifix and a statuette of the Virgin. Inquisitors were not provided an opportunity to ascertain whether he had been motivated by heretical considerations ("fuit suspensus ac combustus Venetiis absque eo quod fuerit examinatus ab Inquisitore supra intentione . . ." [BAV, Borg. lat. 558, fol. 404r]). The date is 28 March 1592.

13. Study of the underground operations of the Holy Office in Naples under cover of the episcopal courts was long dominated by L. Amabile, *Il Santo Officio della Inquisizione in Napoli*, 2 vols. (Città di Castello, 1892). The recent cataloguing of the *fondo* "Sant' Ufficio" in the Archivio Storico Diocesano in Naples has led to the publication of several excellent studies (see n. 9). For a general orientation, see especially G. Romeo, "Per la storia del Sant'Ufficio a Napoli tra '500 e '600, documenti e problemi," *Campania sacra* 7 (1976): 5–109; idem, "Una città, due inquisizioni: L'anomalia del Sant'Ufficio a Napoli nel tardo '500," (cited at n. 5); A. Borromeo, "Contributo allo studio dell'Inquisizione e dei suoi rapporti con il potere episcopale nell'Italia spagnola del Cinquecento," *Annuario dell'Istituto storico italiano per l'età moderna e contemporanea* 29–30 (1977–78): 219–76; G. Coniglio, "Società e Inquisizione nel Viceregno di Napoli," ibid., 37–38 (1985–86): 127–39. For the situation in Spanish Milan, see by the same author, "Le controversie giurisdizionali tra potere laico e potere ecclesiastico nella Milano spagnola sul finire del Cinquecento," *Atti dell'Accademia di San Carlo: Inaugurazione del IV Anno Accademico* (Milan, 1981), 43–89.

14. See V. La Mantia, "Origine e vicende dell'Inquisizione in Sicilia," *RSI* 3 (1886): 481–598; H. C. Lea, *The Inquisition in the Spanish Dependencies* (New York, 1908), 1–43; C. A. Garufi, *Fatti e personaggi dell'Inquisizione in Sicilia* (Palermo, 1978) (originally published in installments in the *Archivio storico siciliano*, 1914–17). On specific aspects of Sicilian inquisitorial activity, see idem, "Secundo proceso de Jacopo Bruto reconciliado por la Inquisizion del Reyno de Sicilia y relaxado en Palermo al brazo seglar con sentencia de 10 Julio 1590," *Bulletin de la société d'histoire vaudoise*, no. 36 (1916): 68–96; S. Caponetto, "Origini e caratteri della Riforma in Sicilia," *Rinascimento* 7 (1956): 219–341; idem, "Dell'Agostiniano Ambrogio Bolognesi e del suo processo di eresia a Palermo (1552–1554)," *BSSV* 76, no. 102 (1957): 39–49 (reprinted with notes and the text of the trial in the *Bibliothèque d'Humanisme et Renaissance* 20 [1958]: 310–43); idem, "Ginevra e la Riforma in Sicilia," in *Ginevra e l'Italia* (Florence, 1959), 287–306. These essays have now been collected in Caponetto's *Studi sulla Riforma in Italia*. Università degli Studi di Firenze, Dipartimento di Storia (Florence, 1987). On the later period see the general survey by R. Canosa and I. Colonnello, *Storia dell'Inquisizione in Sicilia dal 1600 al 1720*, Biblioteca Siciliana di Storia e Letteratura. Quaderni, 45 (Palermo, 1989). Additional bibliography is cited at n. 10.

15. The repositories of inquisitorial legal doctrine are the manuals discussed in detail elsewhere in this volume, esp. at pp. 51–7 and notes.

16. Materials from these years are preserved in the Archivio della Curia Patriarcale, Venice. See n. 7 above.

17. For the total known activity of the Spanish Inquisition, see Contreras and Henningsen, "Forty-four Thousand Cases of the Spanish Inquisition" (cited at n. 2).

18. J.-P. Dedieu ("Les quattre temps de l'Inquisition," in *L'Inquisition espagnole*, ed. B. Bennassar, 31–33) used the *Alegaciones fiscales* to calculate annual averages of between two and five sentences per year from fourteen Iberian tribunals during the 1700s: the overall total was 4,184; the overall average was three per year. Cf. Contreras and Henningsen, "Forty-four Thousand Cases of the Spanish Inquisition," 101 for a map of all the tribunals that made up the Spanish system, with the dates of their founding, including those situated outside the peninsula.

19. See the tables in Appendices 1–4. It is clear that the designation "Lutheran" in our inquisitorial inventories covered a wide range of Protestant currents, certainly including the Calvinist. Although there are a number of excellent specialized studies dealing with Italian aspects of the Reformation, we still lack a complete, critical, general treatment. For now we must rely on the excellent brief synthesis by M. Welti: *Kleine Geschichte der italienischen Reformation* (Gütersloh, 1985), also in translation as *Breve storia della Riforma italiana* (Casale Monferrato, 1985).

20. There is a vast and growing literature on Protestant activity in Venice and the Veneto in the sixteenth century. The scholarship, in recent years, has been dominated by the important books and articles of Nicholas Davidson, Andrea Del Col, Carlo Ginzburg, Stefania Ferlin Malavasi, John Martin, Achille Olivieri, Anne J. Schutte, and Aldo Stella, among others, listed in the Select Bibliography.

For Reformation currents in the Friuli, see A. Battistella, *Il Sant'Uffizio e la Riforma religiosa in Friuli* (Udine, 1895); idem, "Brevi note sul S. Offizio e la Riforma religiosa in Friuli," *Atti dell'Accademia di Udine*, ser. 3, no. 10 (1902–1903): 265–85; P. Paschini, "Eresia e riforma cattolica al confine orientale d'Italia," *Lateranum*, n.s., 17, nos. 1–4 (Rome, 1951); L. De Biasio, "L'eresia protestante in Friuli nella seconda metà del secolo XVI," *Memorie storiche forogiuliesi* 52 (1972): 71–154; idem, "Fermenti ereticali in Friuli nella seconda metà del sec. XVI," in *La filosofia friulana e giuliana nel contesto della cultura italiana: Atti del primo convegno regionale di filosofia friulana e giuliana . . . Cividale del Friuli, 6–8 dicembre 1970* (Udine, 1972), 145–53; G. Paolin, "Dell'ultimo tentativo compiuto in Friuli di formare una comunità Anabattista: Note e documenti," *NRS* 62 (1978): 3–28; idem, "L'eterodossia nel monastero delle clarisse di Udine nella seconda metà del '500," *Collectanea franciscana* 50 (1980): 107–67 (covers the period 1550–1625 and publishes fragments of trials from the ACAU for the year 1587); G. Zanier, "La nobiltà castellana e l'Inquisizione aquileiese," in T. Miotti, *Castelli del Friuli: La vita nei castelli friulani* (Udine, 1981), 93–124 (not seen); A. Del Col, "Fermenti di novità religiose in alcuni cicli pittorici del Pordenone e dell' Amalteo," in *Società e cultura del Cinquecento nel Friuli occidentale: Studi*, a cura di A. Del Col (Pordenone, 1984), 229–54. On the controverted question of the extent of Protestant inroads in the Friuli, see A. Del Col, "La riforma cattolica nel Friuli vista da Paschini," in *Atti del convegno di studio su Pio Paschini nel centenario della nascita, 1878–1978: Pubblicazioni della Deputazione di Storia Patria per il Friuli,* 10:123–41.

21. Contreras and Henningsen, "Forty-four Thousand Cases of the Spanish Inquisition," 118. A brief but readable survey of the question of "Lutheran" penetration in Spain is contained in J.-P. Dedieu, "Le refus de la Réforme et le contrôle de la pensée," in B. Bennassar, ed., *L'Inquisition espagnole,* 269–311. See, most recently, C. Larquié, "Le Protestantisme en Espagne au XVI siècle," *Bulletin de la Société de l'Histoire du Protestantisme français* 129 (1983): 155–82 and J. L. Gonzalez Novalín, "Luteranismo e Inquisición en España (1519–1561): Bases para la periodización del tema en el siglo de la Reforma," *Annuario dell'Istituto storico italiano per l'età moderna e contemporanea* 37–38 (1985–86): 43–73.

22. ASV, *Savii all'eresia* (*S. Uffizio, Indice* 303, B. 62/6, p. 36 of the index), the case of Fra Dionisio da Verona. See also the trials against Fra Guglielmo da Ravenna in 1588, B. 64/93 (p. 55 of the index) for bearing arms while celebrating Mass; against the priest Girolamo Longo in 1587, B. 59/55 (p. 65 of the index) for burial of a "Lutheran" in a Catholic cemetery; against Fra Pietro Villa in 1631, B. 88/4 (p. 120 of the index) for "vita scandalosa," etc.

23. As long as there were religious heretics to pursue, the overburdened inquisitors clearly gave a lower priority to the prosecution of witchcraft. This is suggested by C. Ginzburg, *The Night Battles: Witchcraft and Agrarian Cults in the Sixteenth and Seventeenth Centuries,* trans. J. and A. C. Tedeschi (Baltimore, 1983), 38, 71. Cf. S. Ferlin Malavasi ("Il processo per eresia di Alfonso Ariano," 112–19), who notes the disappearance of heretical propaganda in the Rovigo area in the 1570s and the subsequent dramatic increase of witchcraft trials. An intensification of prosecutions for the occult arts is noted in another neighboring Venetian city during the years 1573–75. See D. De Antoni, "Processi per stregoneria e magia a Chioggia nel XVI secolo," *Ricerche di storia sociale e religiosa* 4 (1973): 187–228. The most recent contribution to the subject is R. Martin, *Witchcraft and the Inquisition in Venice, 1550–1650* (Oxford, 1989).

24. Heresy in Naples, at least during the first half of the sixteenth century, is generally associated with the circle of Juan de Valdés, which included, at one time or another for short periods, such leading figures in later Italian Protestantism as Bernardino Ochino and Peter Martyr Vermigli. See, most recently, P. Lopez, *Il movimento valdesiano a Napoli, Mario Galeota e le sue vicende col Sant'Uffizio* (Naples, 1976), with bibliography; G. Gonnet, " Le Protestantisme dans l'Italie medidionale à l'epoque moderne," in *Religion et culture dans la cité italienne de l'antiquité à nos jours: Actes du colloque du Centre Interdisciplinaire de Recherches sur l'Italie des 8-9-10 Novembre 1979: Bulletin du CIRI,* ser. 2, Université de Strasbourg, 1981, 117–27. There is a vast literature on Valdés and his relationship to Italian evangelism. Among the most recent literature, see C. Gilly, "Juan de Valdés, traductor y adaptador de escritos de Lutero en su *Diálogo de Doctrina Christiana,*" in *Miscelánea de Estudios Hispáni-*

cos: *Homenaje de los Hispanistas de Suiza, a Ramon Sugranyes de Franch (Se publica al cuidado de Luiz López Molina)* (Montserrat, 1982), 85–106, reprinted in an amplified German translation in the *Archive for Reformation History* 74 (1983): 257–305; C. Ossola, "Lutero e Juan de Valdés: Intorno alla formula 'Beneficio di Cristo,'" in *Lutero e la Riforma, Vicenza, 27/28 Novembre 1983* (Vicenza, n.d.) (I have consulted the reprint); M. Firpo, "Juan de Valdés e l'evangelismo: Appunti e problemi di una ricerca in corso," *Studi storici*, no. 4 (1985): 733–54; idem, "Valdesianesimo ed evangelismo alle origini dell' *Ecclesia Viterbiensis (1541),*" in *Libri, idee e sentimenti religiosi nel Cinquecento italiano* (Ferrara and Modena, 1987), 53–71 and the "Intervento" by G. Fragnito, 73–76.

25. Contreras and Henningsen,"Forty-four Thousand Cases," 118. Sicily's 146 trials for "Superstición" during the period 1560–1614 were second only to the 200 of the Basque tribunal at Logroño, the site, between 1610 and 1613, of the greatest witch panic in the history of the Spanish Inquisition. Only one other Spanish tribunal was close to them—Sardinia, whose 123 cases from 1560 to 1614 accounted for 22 percent of its total, far above the ratios for Sicily or Logroño. Sicily led all other Spanish tribunals in the subsequent period as well, with 310 cases of "Superstición" between 1615 and 1700 (ibid., 119). On the famous panic at Logroño, see G. Henningsen, *The Witches Advocate: Basque Witchcraft and the Spanish Inquisition (1609–1614)* (Reno, 1980) (also in Danish, Italian, Spanish, and Swedish). Cf. the perceptive comparative analysis by R. Garcia Carcel, "El modelo mediterraneo de brujeria," *Annuario dell'Istituto storico italiano per l'età moderna e contemporanea* 37–38 (1985–86): 245–57, with a table at p. 251 based on the compilations of Contreras and Henningsen detailing the distribution of Spanish witchcraft proceedings among nineteen tribunals during the period 1560–1700.

26. Contreras and Henningsen, "Forty-four Thousand Cases," 117–18.

27. For Naples, see P. Lopez, *Inquisizione, stampa, e censura nel Regno di Napoli tra '500 e '600* (Naples, 1974), chap. 13, "Libri e Magia"; G. De Rosa, "Magismo e pietà nel Mezzogiorno d'Italia," in *Società, chiesa e vita religiosa nell'Ancien Regime,* ed. C. Russo (Naples, 1976), 443–98 (and the bibliography cited therein); J.-M. Sallmann, *Chercheurs de trésors et jeteuses de sorts: La quête du surnaturel à Naples au XVIe s.* (Paris, 1986). For the Friuli, see n. 29, below. The question as a whole is discussed in F. Salimbeni's historiographical survey, "La stregoneria nel tardo Rinascimento," *NRS* 60 (1976): 269–334.

28. See n. 25 above. In the ten tribunals which comprised the Secretariat of Aragon (including the Sicilian), "Superstición" accounted for 21.2 percent of the cases from 1615 to 1700 (Contreras and Henningsen, "Forty-four Thousand Cases," 119).

29. The most important recent study on Italian witchcraft (and one which concentrates on the Friuli) remains C. Ginzburg's *The Night Battles* (cited at n. 23 above). More recently, specifically on Friulian witchcraft, see M. Romanello, "Culti magici e stregoneria del clero friulano," *Lares* 36 (1970): 341–72; M. Dell'Acqua, "Una benandante friuliana in un processo di stregoneria a Parma nel 1611," (cited at n. 12); L. De Biasio, "Esecuzioni capitali contro streghe nel Friuli orientale alla metà

del secolo XVII" (cited at n. 8). On spells against wolves, see P. C. Ioly Zorattini, "'Preenti' contro il lupo negli atti del S. Uffizio di Aquileia e Concordia," *Ce fastu?* 52 (1976): 131–46; idem, "Un 'Preento' contro il lupo in un procedimento seicentesco del S. Uffizio di Aquileia e Concordia," *Memorie storiche forogiuliesi* 59 (1979): 163–68. See also by the same author, "Il diavolo del Sant'Uffizio e le tradizioni popolari friulane," *Rassegna di pedagogia* 26 (1968), nos. 2–3: 84–130.

30. De Biasio and Facile (*I processi dell'Inquisizione in Friuli dal 1648 al 1798*, pp. 80–81) record a cluster of *Liberi Muratori* at Buttrio in 1747, charged with "stregoneria con abuso di sacramenti [e] adorazione del demonio."

31. Ibid., 88. Of all the men who made similar pacts, the luckiest one, in 1765, declared that he had received 18,000 ducats from the Devil and even held a receipt for them (p. 93).

32. L. Accati, "Lo spirito della fornicazione: virtù dell'anima e virtù del corpo in Friuli fra '600 e '700," *Quaderni storici* 41 (1979): 669.

33. See De Biasio and Facile, *1000 processi*, pp. 23, 62; and *I processi dell' Inquisizione in Friuli dal 1648 al 1798*, pp. 15, 35, 82. The principal authority on the subject is P. C. Ioly Zorattini. Among his numerous publications, see "Un giudaizzante cividalese del Cinquecento: Gioanbattista Cividin," in *Studi storici e geografici* (Pisa) 1 (1977): 193–208; "Processi contro ebrei e giudaizzanti nell'Archivio del S. Uffizio di Aquileia e Concordia," *Memorie storiche forogiuliesi* 58 (1978): 133–45; "Aspetti e problemi dei nuclei ebraici in Friuli durante la dominazione veneziana," *Atti del Convegno Venezia e la Terraferma attraverso le Relazioni dei Rettori, 23–24 ottobre 1980* (Milan, 1981), 227–36, which underscores the smallness of the Jewish population in the Friuli resulting from the repeated expulsions that it suffered; "Gli Ebrei a Udine dal Trecento ai giorni nostri," *Atti dell'Accademia di scienze, lettere e arti di Udine* 74 (1981): 45–58; "Il prestito ebraico nella fortezza di Palma nel secolo XVII," *Studi storici Luigi Simeoni* 33 (1983): 271–76; "I cimiteri ebraici del Friuli veneto," *Studi veneziani,* n.s., 8 (1984): 375–90; *Leandro Tisanio un giudaizzante sanvitese del Seicento: Tra i nuclei ebraici del Friuli e la diaspora marrana* (Florence, 1984); "The Jews and the Inquisition of Aquileia and Concordia," in Y. Kaplan ed., *Jews and Conversos: Studies in Society and the Inquisition.* Proceedings of the Eighth World Congress of Jewish Studies, Hebrew University of Jerusalem, August 16–21, 1981 (Jerusalem, 1985), 225–36; "Gli insediamenti ebraici nel Friuli veneto," in *Gli Ebrei e Venezia, secoli XIV–XVIII: Atti del Convegno internazionale organizzato dall'Istituto di storia della società e dello stato veneziano della Fondazione Giorgio Cini, Venezia, Isola di San Giorgio Maggiore, 5–10 giugno 1983*, edited by G. Cozzi [Milan, 1987], 261–80.

34. For Naples, see Osbat (cited at n. 9 above), 833 ff.: nine Jews who were tried during the winter of 1627–28 were retried the following winter (nos. 212–541 and 213–543). On the fortunes of the Jews in the *Vicereame,* see now V. Bonazzoli, "Gli Ebrei del Regno di Napoli all'epoca della loro espulsione," *Archivio storico italiano* 137 (1979): 495–559; 139 (1981): 179–287, with excellent bibliography, and V. Giura, "Gli Ebrei nel Regno di Napoli tra Aragona e Spagna," in *Gli Ebrei e Venezia, secoli XIV–XVIII* (cited at n. 33), 771–80.

35. Garufi, *Fatti e personaggi dell'Inquisizione in Sicilia*, chap. 1, provides data on Judaizers from all the early *autos*. See also Contreras and Henningsen, "Forty-four Thousand Cases," 118. It is impossible even to begin citing the vast literature on the Spanish Inquisition and the Jews. One of the best recent contributions is H. Beinart, *Conversos on Trial: The Inquisition in Ciudad Real* (Jerusalem, 1981). Still fundamental for an overview of the entire period, including non-Spanish developments, is S. W. Baron, *A Social and Religious History of the Jews*, vol. 13, *Inquisition, Renaissance and Reformation*, 2nd rev. and enlarged ed. (New York and London, 1969). We have not had the opportunity to consult a new work by J. Blázquez Miguel, *Inquisición e criptojudaismo* (Madrid [1988]) described in the publisher's announcement as "the first thorough and exhaustive study" of the subject.

36. See, in general, C. Roth, *The Jews in Venice* (Philadelphia, 1930). On the background, see the excellent recent article by R. Finlay, "The Foundation of the Ghetto: Venice, the Jews and the War of the League of Cambrai," *Proceedings of the American Philosophical Society* 126 (1982): 14–54. B. Pullan's earlier studies have been superseded by his magisterial *The Jews of Europe and the Inquisition of Venice, 1550–1670* (Oxford, 1983), with a rich bibliography; now available in Italian as *Gli Ebrei d'Europa e l'Inquisizione a Venezia dal 1550 al 1670* (Rome, 1985). The proceedings conducted by the Venetian Inquisition against Jews and Judaizers are being critically edited by P. C. Ioly Zorattini, *Processi del S. Uffizio di Venezia contro Ebrei e giudaizzanti*, 7 vols. (Florence, 1980–). On this monumental project, see A. Antoniazzi Villa, "Per la storia degli Ebrei a Venezia: Pier Cesare Ioly Zorattini ed i 'Processi del Sant'Uffizio di Venezia contro ebrei e giudaizzanti,'" *NRS* 67 (1983): 138–43, K. R. Stow, "Zorattini's 'Processi del S. Uffizio di Venezia'," *Jewish Quarterly Review* 74 (1983/84): 88–90, and J. Schatzmiller, "Processi del Sant'Uffizio di Venezia contro ebrei e giudaizzanti," *Studi storici* 28 (1987): 531–35. By Ioly Zorattini see also "Note e documenti per la storia dei marrani e giudaizzanti nel Veneto del Seicento," in S. Simonsohn, ed., *Michael: On the History of the Jews of the Diaspora* (Tel-Aviv, 1972), 326–41; "Il 'Mif'aloth Elohim' di Isaac Abravanel e il Sant'Offizio di Venezia," in *Italia: Studi e ricerche sulla cultura e sulla letteratura degli Ebrei d'Italia* 1 (1976): 54–69; "The Inquisition and the Jews in Sixteenth-Century Venice," in *Proceedings of the Seventh World Congress of Jewish Studies: History of the Jews in Europe* (Jerusalem, 1981), 83–92 (an Italian version appeared earlier in *RSCI* 33 [1979]: 500–508); *Battesimi di fanciulli ebrei a Venezia nel Settecento* (Udine, 1984); "Gli Ebrei a Venezia, Padova e Verona," in *Storia della cultura veneta* (Vicenza, 1980), vol. 3, pt. 1: 537–76; "Gli Ebrei nel Veneto durante il Settecento," ibid., vol. 5, pt. 2: 459–86; L'emigrazione degli Ebrei dai territori della Repubblica di Venezia verso le contee di Gorizia e Gradisca nel Settecento," in Ioly Zorattini, ed., *Gli Ebrei a Gorizia e a Trieste tra "Ancien Regime" ed Emancipazione*, Atti del Convegno Gorizia, 13 giugno 1983 (Udine, 1984), 111–18; "Ebrei sefarditi e marrani a Ferrara dalla fine del Quattrocento alla devoluzione del Ducato estense," in *Libri, idee e sentimenti religiosi nel Cinquecento italiano*, 117–30, based chiefly su Venetian Holy Office records; "Battesimi 'invitis parentibus' nella Repubblica di Venezia durante l'età moderna:

i casi padovani," in *Ebrei e cristiani nell'Italia medievale e moderna: Conversioni, scambi, contrasti*, Atti de VI Congresso internazionale dell'AISG, S. Miniato, 4–6 novembre 1986, edited by M. Luzzati, M. Olivari, A. Veronese (Rome, 1988), 171–82. See also R. Segre, "Neophytes during the Italian Counter-Reformation: Identities and Bibliographies," in *Proceedings of the Sixth World Congress of Jewish Studies, Held at the Hebrew University of Jerusalem, 13–19 August 1973*, 2 vols. (Jerusalem, 1975–77), 2:131–42. By 1600, Jews accounted for 2 percent of Venice's 100,000 inhabitants. See, also, K. R. Stow, *Catholic Thought and Papal Jewry Policy, 1555-1593* (New York, 1977). On the entire question of Jews in the peninsula, see the bibliography compiled by A. Milano, *Bibliotheca historica italo-judaica* (Florence, 1954), with *Supplemento 1954-1963* (Florence, 1964) and the proceedings of two recent state sponsored congresses: *Italia Judaica: Atti del I Convegno internazionale, Bari 18–22 maggio 1981*, Ministero per i Beni Culturali e Ambientali, Pubblicazioni degli Archivi di Stato, Saggi 2 (Rome, 1983) and *Italia Judaica: "Gli Ebrei in Italia tra Rinascimento ed Età barocca": Atti del II Convegno internazionale, Genova 10–15 giugno 1984*, Ministero per i Beni Culturali e Ambientali, Pubblicazioni degli Archivi di Stato, Saggi 6 (Rome, 1986). In the latter volume, see especially R. Segre, "Il mondo ebraico nei cardinali della Controriforma," 119–38, on the question of forced baptisms of Jews and the attitude of the Inquisition (p. 132).

37. ASV, *Savii all'Eresia (S. Uffizio)*, Index 303.

38. Garufi, *Fatti e personaggi dell'Inquisizione in Sicilia*, 21.

39. Grendler (*Roman Inquisition*, 209–11) counted at least a dozen jurisdictional disputes over the question of bigamy between 1590 and 1625. In the Friuli, for example, we counted only one case, occurring in 1579, for the period 1557–95. See De Biasio and Facile, *1000 Processi*, 24.

40. Contreras and Henningsen, "Forty-four Thousand Cases," 119. For Naples, see Appendix 3.

41. On prosecution for prohibited books in the Veneto, see P. Grendler's *The Roman Inquisition* (with full bibliography of manuscript and printed sources); and, more recently, C. Fahy, "The *Index Librorum Prohibitorum* and the Venetian Printing Industry in the Sixteenth Century," *Italian Studies* 35 (1980): 52–61 and S. Cavazza, "Libri in volgare e propaganda eterodossa: Venezia 1543-1547," in *Libri, idee e sentimenti religiosi nel Cinquecento italiano*, 9–28. The first two Venetian Indices of Prohibited Books have now been critically edited: *Index de Venise 1549, et de Venise et Milan, 1554 par J. M. De Bujanda: Introduction historique de P. F. Grendler*, Index des Livres Interdits, 3 (Sherbrooke and Geneva, 1987) (with bibliography). See also the indispensable studies of A. Del Col, "Il Nuovo Testamento tradotto da Massimo Teofilo e altre opere stampate a Lione nel 1551," *Critica storica* 15 (1978): 642–75 (based heavily on Venetian inquisitorial records); "Il secondo processo veneziano di Antonio Brucioli," *BSSV*, no. 146 (1979): 85–100; "Il controllo della stampa a Venezia e i processi di Antonio Brucioli (1548-1559)," *Critica storica* 17 (1980): 457–510. Ugo Rozzo's exemplary studies on Italian censorship also have strong Venetian connections: "Dieci anni di censura libraria (1596-1605)," *Libri e documenti* 9

(1983): 43–61; "Il rogo dei libri: Appunti per una iconologia," ibid., 12 (1986): 7–32.

42. For the Friuli, see S. Cavazza, "Inquisizione e libri proibiti in Friuli e a Gorizia tra Cinquecento e Seicento," *Studi goriziani* 43 (1976): 29–80. For Naples, see the rich study by P. Lopez, *Inquisizione, stampa e censura nel Regno di Napoli* (cited at n. 27) and, of the various articles by C. De Frede, "Per la storia della stampa nel Cinquecento in rapporto con la diffusione della Riforma in Italia," *Gutenberg Jahrbuch* 39 (1964): 175–84 (the emphasis is Neapolitan); "La stampa nel Cinquecento e la diffusione della Riforma in Italia," *Atti della Accademia Pontaniana*, n.s., 13 (1963/64): 87–91; "Tipografi, editori, librai italiani del Cinquecento coinvolti in processi di eresia," *RSCI* 23 (1969): 21–53.

43. De Biasio and Facile, *1000 Processi*, and *I processi dell'Inquisizione in Friuli dal 1648 al 1798*.

44. On the question, see the controversial study by L. W. Levy, *Treason against God: A History of the Offense of Blasphemy* (New York, 1981).

45. For the bibliography on the *Esecutori*, see above at n. 12. C. Carena (*Tractatus de Officio Sanctissimae Inquisitionis* [Bologna, 1668], 123) asserted that cases of non-heretical blasphemy "sunt mixti fori," that is, could be tried in either secular or ecclesiastical courts. In his commentary to Nicolau Eymeric's *Directorium Inquisitorum* (Rome, 1587), 334–35, Francisco Peña went further and took the position that any blasphemer opened himself to the suspicion of heresy and therefore should come before the Inquisition.

46. *Religione, moralità e giustizia*, 11 (cited at n. 12). Even in clear cases of heretical blasphemy, where the jurisdiction of the Inquisition should not have been in dispute, secular officials claimed that only the administration of the abjuration belonged to the tribunal, whereas setting the penalty belonged to them. See BAV, cod. Borg. lat. 558, fols. 400–402, a discussion of several cases of heretical blasphemy where Rome alleged that lay authorities had intervened improperly.

47. See Appendices 1–4.

48. Ibid. In the Neapolitan inventory (Osbat, see n. 9 above), cases of solicitation are not catalogued separately and may be subsumed under the designation *sospetto d'eresia*.

49. Appendices 1–4. After 1720, *proposizioni ereticali* accounted for almost half of all charges.

50. By combining atheism, *proposizioni*, blasphemy, and offenses against both sacraments and precepts one reaches a total of 217 cases out of 1,086, almost the same ratio as for the Sicilian *proposiciones*.

51. For a rudimentary calendar of this collection, see T. K. Abbott, *Catalogue of the Manuscripts in the Library of Trinity College, Dublin* (Dublin and London, 1900; henceforth abbreviated TCD), 241–84 (MSS. 1224–1242; the sixteenth-century materials are contained in MSS. 1224–1227). For the bibliography on these materials, see "The Dispersed Archives of the Roman Inquisition" in this volume.

52. TCD, MS. 1226 (with a few sentences from 1578 and 1579). Several sentences emitted in 1582 also comprise MS. 1227.

53. TCD, MS. 1226, nos. 93, 94 (fols. 328, 329), dated November 1581. Cf. C. Ginzburg, *The Night Battles*—among the earliest cases of illicit magic here.

54. TCD, MSS. 1227–28.

55. See Osbat (note 9, above), 751, 753–54, 760, 763, 783, 815, 837–39, 855, 880–81. Forty-nine Englishmen were "converted" in this fashion in 1585, twenty-five Germans in 1585 and 1586, and nineteen Swedes in 1588 and 1589, all mariners.

56. De Biasio and Facile, *1000 Processi* and *I Processi dell' Inquisizione in Friuli dal 1648 al 1798*.

57. Throughout the history of the Spanish Inquisition, "Superstición" accounted for 7.5 percent of its caseload (Contreras and Henningsen, "Forty-four Thousand Cases," 114). During the seventeenth century (1615–1700) the incidence was 19.3 percent (ibid., 119), still considerably below the Italian figures (see Appendices).

58. See the discussion of this point at pp. 211, 222 in this volume.

59. The Sicilian led all Spanish tribunals in the prosecution of "Superstición" with 456 cases between 1540 and 1700. (Contreras and Henningsen, "Forty-four Thousand Cases," 114). On the special nature of Sicilian witchcraft, see G. Henningsen, " 'The Ladies from Outside': An Archaic Pattern of the Witches' Sabbath" in B. Ankarloo and G. Henningsen, eds., *Early Modern European Witchcraft: Centres and Peripheries* (Oxford, 1990), pp. 191–215. The volume, the proceedings of a 1984 Stockholm conference, appeared earlier in Swedish as *Häxornas Europa, 1400–1700* (Lund, 1987).

60. Henningsen, *Witches Advocate*, 347.

61. TCD, MS. 1227, fol. 139, sentence dated 31 May 1582 against Joannes Pilutius de Castro Julianelli, who was condemned to seven years of galley service for the unjust prosecution of four women "sub praetextu quod essent striges."

62. See Lea's undated letter to George Lincoln Burr, cited in *Minor Historical Writings and Other Essays by Henry Charles Lea*, ed. A. C. Howland (Philadelphia, 1942), 3: "It is a very curious fact . . . which I have nowhere seen recognized, that in both Spain and Italy the Holy Office took a decidedly sceptical attitude with regard to the Sabbat and the *Cap. Episcopi*, that preserved those lands from the madness prevailing elsewhere. I have a good many original documents that place this in a clear light and I think will prove a surprise to the demonologists." For Rome's position regarding witchcraft prosecution, see "The Roman Inquisition and Witchcraft" and "A Question of Magic and Witchcraft" in this volume.

63. Mandatory execution of the *relapsus* dated to the decretal "Ad Abolendam," 4 November 1184. The relapsed might either be penitent or not. In the first case, he was absolved in respect to his conscience (*in foro interno*); but on the ecclesiastical level (*in foro externo*) he remained a *relapsus*, even though he had repented. This difference did not affect the final outcome, which was in any event the stake. However, the penitent was first beheaded (if he was a gentleman) or hanged (in the case of a commoner), either in the prisons of the Holy Office or by the secular authorities who were responsible for carrying out the execution. See also "The Organization and Procedures of the Roman Inquisition," in this volume, at n. 170.

64. For the decrees of Paul IV establishing in 1556 and 1558 a class of crimes against the central doctrines of the Church which called for the death penalty even when the accused was neither relapsed nor impenitent, see ibid. at n. 171.

65. See De Biasio and Facile, *1000 Processi*, 8.

66. Grendler, *Roman Inquisition*, 57 and n. 92. This provisional list excludes executions carried out elsewhere in Venetian territory by direct orders of the Council of Ten—for example, that of Benedetto del Borgo at Rovigo or of Agostino Tealdo at Vicenza (see A. Stella, *Anabattismo e antitrinitarismo in Italia nel XVI secolo* [Padua, 1969], 109, 198).

67. See D. Maselli, *Saggi di storia ereticale lombarda al tempo di S. Carlo* (Naples, 1979), 28; Cf. M. Bendiscioli ("Penetrazione protestante e repressione controriformistica in Lombardia all'epoca di Carlo e Federico Borromeo," in *Festgabe Joseph Lortz*, ed. E. Iserloh and P. Manns, 2 vols. [Baden-Baden, 1958], 1:404) who counts a lesser number of executions (7) and for a longer period, 1560–1630. The Modena case is cited by A. Prosperi, "L'Inquisizione romana e la morte dell'eretico," in *Glaubensprozesse-Prozesse des Glaubens? Religiöse Minderheiten zwischen Toleranz und Inquisition*, hrsg. T. Heydenreich/P. Blumenthal (Stuttgart, 1989), pp. 43–52, at p. 50.

68. TCD, MS. 1225, fol. 344, dated 11 June 1580, against Augustino Vanzo; MS. 1226, fol. 297, dated 28 October 1581, concerning Aurelio Nanarino of Bologna; fol. 377, dated 29 December 1582, against Battista Pagello of Padua. In addition, the volume contains the sentences against seven persons who were burned in effigy after they were pronounced contumacious because of their refusal to appear before the Holy Office (MS. 1225, fols. 160, 258; MS. 1226, fols. 142, 162, 164, 166, 326).

69. C. Ginzburg, *The Night Battles*.

70. The surviving records of the Venerable Arciconfraternità di San Giovanni Decollato have been published by D. Orano, *Liberi pensatori bruciati in Roma dal XVI al XVIII secolo* (Rome, 1904; reprint Livorno, 1971). To the ninety-seven names encountered in the confraternity's records, Orano suspected fifteen others should be added who are mentioned in the *Archivio del Governatore* (p. xiv) and fifty others who are on the lists of the society but whose certificates of execution are not to be found among the books of the *Provveditore* (pp. 118–19). These figures should now be integrated with L. Firpo, "Esecuzioni capitali in Roma, 1567–1671," in *Eresia e Riforma nell'Italia del Cinquecento*, Biblioteca del Corpus Reformatorum Italicorum (De Kalb and Chicago, 1974), 309–42. Firpo identifies the names on Orano's list, adds to the numbers of executed (the vast majority of whom were the victims of secular justice, not the Inquisition) and subtracts from Orano a handful of names which the latter had mistakenly labelled as heretics sent to their fate by the Holy Office. The older work by A. Bertolotti, *Martiri del libero pensiero e vittime della Santa Inquisizione nei secoli XVI, XVII e XVIII* (Rome, 1902), is uncritical and fragmentary. A. Ademollo's compilation ("Le giustizie a Roma dal 1674 al 1739 e dal 1796 al 1840," *ASRSP* 4 [1880–81]: 429–534) consists primarily of executions for secular

offenses drawn from a manuscript "Diario" kept by an eighteenth-century abbot, Placido Eustachio Ghezzi.

71. This figure includes statistics from tribunals outside the mainland, in Mexico, Sicily, etc. Executions occurred at the rate of 1.83 per 100 persons tried. See Contreras and Henningsen, "Forty-four Thousand Cases," 114. For the penal practices of the other great Iberian tribunal, see C. Amiel, "The Archives of the Portuguese Inquisition: A Brief Survey," in *The Inquisition in Early Modern Europe*, 79–99, at p. 87: a total of 6 percent relaxed to the secular arm (4 percent in person, 2 percent in effigy) out of a rough total of over 31,000 persons tried between 1536 and 1794.

72. For Venice, see n. 66. For Sicily, see Garufi, *Fatti e personaggi dell'Inquisizione in Sicilia*, 10–11, 19, 21–22, 26–27, 30, 33, 35–36, 40, 50–51, 55–56, and 139–43 (on the 1574–1618 cases). Contreras and Henningsen give a smaller total for Sicily: 25 persons "relaxed" in person and an equal number in effigy for the period 1540–1700 (loc. cit.). In a new book (*Frontiers of Heresy: The Spanish Inquisition from the Basque Lands to Sicily* [Cambridge, 1990], 326, 331), William Monter raises the Sicilian totals for the years 1540–1640 to 51 and 38, executions carried out in person and in effigy, respectively.

73. In inquisitorial practice a sentence to a *carcere perpetuo* was commuted after three years of confinement if the prisoner had shown signs of real contrition. See "The Organization and Procedures of the Roman Inquisition" at n. 140.

FIVE

༄

The Organization and Procedures of the Roman Inquisition: A Sketch

The subjects of this essay are the judicial and penal systems of the Roman Inquisition, the institution which was established on ancient foundations in mid-sixteenth-century Italy as a response to the Protestant challenge in that country.[1] It is not to be confused with the medieval Inquisition which came into being early in the thirteenth century (and of which it was a continuation),[2] or with the Spanish tribunal founded in 1478, which had a separate history.[3]

With the Bull *Licet ab Initio*, July 1542, the pope was not creating a brand new institution *ex nihilo*, for inquisitors had, of course, operated in the Middle Ages.[4] Like other sixteenth-century monarchs, he reshaped a previously existing governmental function as part of a program to centralize authority.[5] The defense of the faith was placed in the hands of a commission of cardinals invested with sweeping authority in the pursuit of heresy—the future Congregation of the Inquisition—whose assignment included the appointment of provincial inquisitors (always members of the Dominican and Franciscan orders), and the coordination and supervision of their efforts. Previously this had been a responsibility of the generals and provincials of the two orders, who, however, continued to serve as channels through which recommendations to fill empty positions reached the Congregation, sometimes through appeals to the cardinal protector of the orders.[6] The authority vested in inquisitors was to be understood as emanating directly from the pope.[7]

The uprooting of heresy, previously vested in both bishops and inquisitors, now became principally the burden of the inquisitorial courts. Problems which had been caused by overlapping spheres of activity were greatly reduced, if not totally eliminated, with the bishop retaining responsibility to proceed against heretics in localities without an inquisitorial court.[8] The inquisitorial tribunals gained precedence over all other tribunals, lay and ecclesiastical alike.[9] Privileges exempting clergy and laity from prosecution were annulled, although the jurisdiction of the provincial inquisitor was not extended to cover bishops, nuncios or certain other high members of the hierarchy. Such cases would be reserved to the Supreme Congregation in Rome or to special courts established by it for the purpose.[10] A local inquisitor, beset by an aggressive bishop or by an uncooperative magistrate, could be certain that the most powerful ecclesiastics in Rome stood behind him and his cause. Two future popes were among the first six cardinals appointed to the Holy Office in 1542. And in the reorganization of the Curia achieved in 1588 by Sixtus V, the Holy Office was ranked first among the fifteen Congregations into which papal government was divided.[11]

New tribunals continued to be added and older jurisdictions reapportioned long after the reorganization of 1542. Locations served by vicariates were elevated to full inquisitorial status, such as Parma in 1588, Reggio Emilia and Modena in 1598, previously under the authority of Piacenza and Ferrara respectively (for the latter two cities).[12] The seats of the local inquisitions were usually Dominican or Franciscan convents,[13] and inquisitors themselves were always members of one of these two orders.[14] If the regularly assigned facilities of a tribunal were inadequate, or when a bishop chose to attend a trial personally, the court might, in deference to his superior status, meet in the episcopal palace if he so wished. In the cities of the Veneto the Inquisition regularly met in the episcopal residence, although in Venice proper it was peripatetic, meeting in various churches about the city.[15] Originally, inquisitors had to have reached their fortieth year (although the minimum age for bishops was only thirty), but this limit was waived when the appointment of inquisitors was considered to have devolved to the pope and through him to the Congregation.[16] Ideally, inquisitors would have attained degrees in both theology and law, but since such highly trained individuals were rare, opinion divided on which of the two forms of preparation best suited an inquisitor for his task. In Italy, as it turned out, the majority of appointees had theological backgrounds, and in Spain, legal.[17] The qualities required in an inquisitor, in the opinion of Francisco Peña, were first of all prudence, followed by knowledge of dogma and of heresies, both ancient and modern, without which it would be practically impossible to properly fulfill the duties of the office.[18]

The fact that the inquisitor was an agent of the central papal government and not to be interfered with by the superior of the house is repeated in numerous official communications from the cardinals of the Roman Congregation. On the other hand, inquisitors were reminded that they were bound by the rules of their order and that they were expected to participate in the regular routines of their house, seeking no special dispensation from the communal discipline beyond what was strictly necessary.[19]

The inquisitor's principal task was, of course, the pursuit of heresy, throughout the large geographical area under his jurisdiction. Of this responsibility he had to give a back-breaking detailed accounting to Rome—one that must have been extremely onerous to compile—describing the status of every trial in progress, of every denunciation received in the course of a year, whether each one had led to formal proceedings being instituted, and if not, the reason why.[20] In the course of time, inquisitors would be called upon to fulfill a broad range of miscellaneous duties that were only indirectly related to the active pursuit of heresy, in addition to their obligations as members of orders, which ran the gamut from occupying the priorates of their convents to readerships in theology.[21] Nothing more time-consuming fell to the inquisitor's lot than the scrupulous reporting of every item of income and expenditure. Although a tribunal's property was usually of modest proportions, some knowledge of investment strategies was required of each holder of the office. The Roman Congregation exerted a close surveillance over finances, and when the inquisitor of Aquileia and Concordia felt the need to keep a horse for his frequent travels, even this expense had to be justified to the cardinals of the Holy Office.[22]

In addition, inquisitors were called upon to maintain surveillance over foreign visitors, including the food prepared in the hospice kitchens that fed them, and grant licenses to Italians "who asked permission to travel to Protestant lands."[23] They were also involved in the control of illicit trade—from customs duties inspecting bales of merchandise suspected of containing heretical books, to the thwarting of the clandestine exportation of Christian boys on Turkish vessels.[24] It fell to inquisitors to regulate the lives of Jews, ruling on their petitions to employ Christians as wet nurses or to tend their hearths on the Sabbath; to intervene to prevent the construction of new synagogues or order their removal from locations where they constituted a nuisance for Catholic services; and to prevent Christian attendance at such Jewish rites as circumcisions and weddings.[25] If these duties could be interpreted as playing a preventative role in the battle against heresy, the same cannot be said for unspecified duties required of the inquisitor of Pavia (necessitating absence from his post) connected with the construction of fortifications by the Republic of Genoa and the duchy of Parma in winter-spring 1626;[26] or the peace-keeping functions in domestic disputes requested of the inquisitor of Cremona in August of the same year.[27] It may be this myriad of duties which inspired Guillaume Postel's lament during his trial before the Venetian Inquisition that "since judges are so busy and full of concerns, they have but little time to think about what is told or written to them."[28]

A vicar assisted the inquisitor in discharging his many responsibilities, substituted for him in his absence, and was authorized to fulfill some of the judicial functions of his superior. Although he was nominated to his office by the inquisitor, he was considered an apostolic legatee since it was the Supreme Congregation which confirmed his appointment. A network of lesser officials, *vicari foranei*, selected from the ranks of the regular clergy and parish priests, represented the parent tribunal in the small towns and hamlets under its jurisdiction. They were selected directly by the inquisitor and required no further ratification on the part of Rome (although the Congregation kept a watchful eye even over these choices). Their judicial role was generally limited to conducting preliminary inquiries and receiving depositions.[29]

The present study is based on evidence drawn from a wide assortment of printed and manuscript sources. Despite the inaccessibility of the archives in the palace of the Holy Office in Rome, we do not suffer from a shortage of original inquisitorial documents. Among our most important printed materials are legal manuals composed between the early fourteenth and mid-seventeenth centuries by such lawyers or practicing inquisitors as Nicolau Eymeric, Zanchino Ugolini, Iacobo de Simancas, Juan de Rojas, Umberto Locati, Eliseo Masini, Francisco Peña, Prospero Farinacci, and Cesare Carena, among others. As I have noted elsewhere, a significant number of these manuals printed in Italy and used in the Italian courts were of Spanish origin.[30]

Surprisingly large quantities of manuscript records are also available. Thousands of trials have survived intact in Italian public or ecclesiastical archives and libraries—in Udine, Venice, Modena, Rovigo, Naples, and elsewhere; extensive series of correspondence exist between the Supreme Congregation of the Inquisition in Rome and some of its provincial tribunals in Bologna, Modena, and Udine; a large body of sentences spanning a century and a half (1556–1700) found their way in the mid-nineteenth century to Trinity College, Dublin (a part of the Napoleonic loot that was not returned to Rome after the collapse of the empire).[31] And in the Vatican Library and Archives one encounters correspondence, decrees, and manuscript inquisitorial manuals, handbooks, and memoranda, materials which had been copied for the use of cardinals who sat on the Holy Office and which were transferred to these repositories along with their other papers at their deaths.[32]

Granted that such documents are available, what about their trustworthiness as historical sources? Could not inquisitors have attempted to suppress or distort information so that their activity would remain hidden from contemporaries and posterity alike? On the contrary, it was strict Holy Office practice to preserve detailed records of all its proceedings from the first summons to the final sentencing. The insistence on the meticulous recording of every word uttered during a trial was intended to discourage the inclination to ask leading questions which would suggest to the accused how they should reply. A permanent member of every inquisitorial court was the notary, who took down in writing every question and every answer, including the exclamations of pain emitted by the victims of torture.[33] Inquisitors did not feel that they had anything to hide. By bringing renegade Christians to punishment—but above all to reconciliation with the Church—they were redeeming offenses committed against God and saving souls for eternal life. A frequent preamble to final sentencing is the biblical story of the prodigal son, a popular paradigm for the inquisitors, who compared themselves to the loving and forgiving father.[34] Moreover, in the fulfillment of his office, the inquisitor was considered to be standing in a direct line of succession that went back to God the Father, "Inquisitore maraviglioso" when he punished Adam, passed through all the Old Testament kings and patriarchs, to Jesus Christ "first and supreme inquisitor under the evangelical law"; and Peter Martyr was their protector saint.[35]

What serious modern scholarly discussion exists concerning the trustworthiness of inquisitorial sources has focused on the possible distortions in the evidence ensuing from the cultural and linguistic gaps that often separated judges and defendants. The scrupulous recording of every word and gesture transpiring in the trial chamber has not been questioned, except, that is, by the Supreme Congregation itself, critically watchful of trials as they unfolded in the lower courts. No better example of this attention to every procedural detail is offered than a letter dated 12 December 1609 from Cardinal Millino to the inquisitor of Aquileia and Concordia, concerning the case of a certain Fra Angelo Alpino da Marostica: "In reading the summary [of the trial] we have noted that Your Reverence has not put into writing the friar's replies in the second session under the pretext that he did not understand the terms. To the witnesses, moreover, you directed certain leading questions, and in referring to the testimony of some of them in your summary, you report it with these words 'I have heard the above. . . .' I bring these deficiencies to your attention so that you will refrain from them in the future. You must write down and not leave out the replies of the accused, and make your summaries fuller, clearer and more specific so that we may be able to discuss better how to decide on the cases."[36]

This is not to say that inquisitors worked in public; far from it. Each official took a solemn vow of secrecy, conducted interrogations in strict privacy, and jealously guarded the records of trial proceedings.[37] There were several reasons for this. Witnesses for the prosecution remained anonymous, since they had to be protected from possible retaliation by the family and friends of the accused, not an unknown occurrence.[38] Moreover, once a defendant named his accomplices, the Holy Office might have to move swiftly to bring them into custody. Its effectiveness would have been seriously impaired if word of their incrimination leaked out to them before they could be apprehended.[39] And, finally, a reason which may seem unexpected, the reputation of the accused had to be protected.

It was an often reiterated principle that inquisitors should act cautiously when making an arrest. "Great prudence must be exercised in the jailing of suspects," wrote Eliseo Masini, inquisitor of Genoa, in his popular manual, the *Sacro Arsenale*, "because the mere fact of incarceration for the crime of heresy brings notable infamy to the person. Thus it will be necessary to study carefully the nature of the evidence, the quality of the witnesses, and the condition of the accused."[40] And in a letter written in 1573 by an official of the Roman Congregation to the inquisitor of Bologna: "Let not your reverence be hasty in proceeding to make an arrest

because the mere capture, or even the rumor of it causes serious harm."[41]
Again, in a letter dated 4 March of the same year from Antonio Balduzzi,
commissioner general of the Roman Inquisition, to the Bolognese official:
"Concerning that Carmelite friar . . . they [meaning the cardinals of the
Holy Office] have ordered that unless your reverence possesses more evidence against him than what has been sent to us, he is not to be disturbed
in any way, and he is to be left in peace and to his prayers."[42] The case
of a suspected witch arrested by the Bolognese inquisitor in violation of
accepted procedure elicited a reprimand from the cardinal of Santa Severina, one of the senior members of the Congregation, writing on 18 May
1591: "And even if Antonia [a principal accuser of the defendant] was
indisposed and anguished by the death of her son and for this reason you
did not question her, I have been asked to remind you that in the future
you must cross-examine witnesses under oath before making an arrest."
Anonymous denunciations and unsworn testimony were unacceptable.[43]
The Roman Congregation, which required a close accounting of the cases
before its provincial tribunals, intervened time and again, ordering the
lower court to drop an unfounded case and free its prisoner.[44] Evidence
originating in the violation of the secrecy of the confessional, even if requested by the defendant, would be similarly invalid and inadmissible,
and inquisitors as well as other officials attached to their tribunals were
rigorously prohibited from hearing confessions, an article of procedure
that must have been difficult to enforce since we have occasional, late evidence of its infringement.[45]

Outside papal territory, in secular states where the Inquisition experienced limitations on its activities, permission to arrest a suspect, especially if his extradition to Rome was at issue, required the approval of
the governing authorities.[46] Interestingly, entire trials might be conducted without the formal incarceration of the suspect. This seems to have
been the fortunate situation of Lisia Fileno (alias Camillo Renato) who
was probably housed in a Ferrarese convent, perhaps the establishment
that served as the seat of the Holy Office, the Dominican convent "degli
Angeli." This permitted him access to a rich library and the works of
Scotus, St. Thomas, Lombard, and the many other theological and legal
authorities he cited to advantage in his *Apologia*, his principal defense
statement.[47]

There was little fear of prosecution for the *sponte comparente*, the offender
who freely presented himself unsummoned to the Inquisition before the

tribunal had received evidence against him. All the manuals prescribed benign treatment. Salutary penances, a private abjuration, and perhaps a fine would be the extent of the punishment.[48]

The rules prescribed by Masini for the investigation of witchcraft show a high regard for due process:

> In prosecuting suspected witches the inquisitor must not reach the point of incarceration, inquisition or torture until the *corpus delicti* is judicially established. Sickness in a person or the presence of a corpse in themselves do not constitute adequate evidence, since infirmity and death do not need to be connected to acts of witchcraft but can result from a large number of natural causes. The first step, therefore, is to question the physician who attended the patient.

In examining the house of the suspected witch the notary was to list everything—items which would serve the prosecution as well as such things as religious icons and devotional books which would be to the advantage of the defendant. If such dubious objects as powders and ointments were discovered, they were to be examined by experts "to determine if they could have been used for ends other than sorcery." Inquisitors were not to permit themselves to be troubled over the discovery of large quantities of pins and needles, natural items for women to possess.[49]

There is abundant evidence that these theoretical safeguards were actually enforced in practice by the Roman Congregation and imposed upon the provincial tribunals where the procedural abuses were most likely to occur. In a series of letters to the nuncio, archbishop, and inquisitor of Florence written in March 1626 the Holy Office attempted to quell a witch panic in that city that had led secular authorities to intervene, resulting in gross miscarriages of justice. Summing up the evidence that it had received, the Congregation wrote, "these matters are extremely fallacious, and, as daily experience demonstrates, much more real in the imagination of men than in the reality of events; too often every illness whose cause is not immediately discernible, or whose remedy is not readily available is attributed to malefice." The nuncio was then asked to inform the secular authorities that the voice suggesting the presence of many witches in Florence and the *contado* had no basis in fact.[50]

In addition to such growing skepticism in Roman legal circles in regard to witchcraft, two crucial procedural points spared Italy the epidemics of bloody witch persecutions that ravaged northern Europe from the late sixteenth to the end of the seventeenth century. The first was the insistence by the Inquisition that the testimony of a suspected witch was of extremely limited validity as a basis for prosecution against others. Judges were instructed, for example, to discount the testimony of a witch against persons whom she named as participants at sabbats, since witches were frequently transported to these nocturnal reunions not physically but only in their fancy and in illusions inspired by the Devil.[51]

The second point consists in the fact that the notorious Devil's mark, which if discovered on the body of the defendant in secular trials was treated as a piece of evidence almost as conclusive as a confession, played no part in inquisitorial procedure.[52] Unlike lay courts, which invariably administered the death penalty for witchcraft when the offender admitted participation in the sabbat, apostasy to the Devil, or perpetration of a *maleficium*,[53] the Inquisition treated witchcraft as any other heresy, and the first-time offender who expressed a desire to repent was reconciled to the Church.[54]

Various legal safeguards for the rights of the accused were part of the trial procedure.[55] First of all, the defendant could petition for a change of venue and to have the inquisitor removed in his case, a procedure known as *De recusatione iudicum*. Needless to say, these must have been rare occurrences, granted only when the judge's gross lack of objectivity could be demonstrated. Knowledge of a few such instances has come down to us.[56] But in the pages of this volume we encounter many more where the Supreme Congregation of the Inquisition felt compelled to intervene itself on behalf of defendants when it perceived lapses or conscious miscarriages of justice on the part of its provincial officials.[57]

If, after the presentation of evidence through the prosecution witnesses and the completion of the interrogation of the accused, the latter had neither cleared himself nor confessed to the charges, he was permitted to prepare his defense, receiving a notarized copy made at his expense — gratis in the case of those who could not afford it — of the entire trial conducted up to that point, with the charges (*articuli*) against him in the vernacular so that they might be more easily understood.[58] He was then allowed a determinate period to study the evidence against him; he was permitted to prepare a series of questions intended to rebut the testimony of his accusers — questions which would be put to the witnesses by the inquisitor himself since face-to-face confrontations between deponents and defendant were not allowed; and he could call friendly witnesses to testify in his behalf, close relatives excluded.[59] In the case of the indigent, the inquisitor was obliged to provide travel expenses for defense witnesses who might have to be summoned from distant parts, arrange to have them make their depositions before a court or an official closer to their domiciles, or simply gather evidence needed by the defendant for the preparation of his case. When the inquisitor himself had to travel to interview witnesses for the defendant, he would be reimbursed by him for his expenses at a fixed rate while he was on the road, and at half that amount during the time spent at his destination. He was to dispatch his business as promptly as possible and be accompanied only by essential companions so as to minimize the financial burden on the payer.[60]

If the accused failed to take advantage of his right to legal defense, to rebut the testimony of the prosecution witnesses, their testimony was considered as *ipso facto* accepted by him, and he threw himself on the mercy of the court. And in many cases, where the evidence against the accused was overwhelming, this was thought to be the best strategy.[61] But by no means was the possibility for a defense to be denied even when a confession had been obtained, if the accused requested it. In fact, writers urged the judge to be solicitous about offering it, and to insist that it be accepted, even when guilt was assumed and the prisoner failed to ask for it himself. They argued on two levels, one moral, the other pragmatic. First, the right to a defense was sanctioned by natural law ("defensiones sint de iure naturae") and should be denied to no one. But second, from a practical point of view, the due observance of the provisions for defense, even if the accused did not take advantage of them, would silence later cries and appeals that the trial had not been allowed to run its regular course.[62] Jurists agreed, however, that the pertinacious heretic was never to be permitted to use this opportunity to attempt to vindicate his error or prove that teachings condemned by the Church were not heretical.[63]

Despite such provisions, it would have been difficult for anyone unpracticed in the law to mount an effective defense, a fact recognized by the Inquisition.[64] When the accused declared that he lacked experience in such matters and required the assistance of a lawyer, this information had to be duly entered in the trial records, and his wishes heeded.[65] It appears to have been the prescribed usage of the Holy Office in Rome, at least in the seventeenth century, to allow the prisoner to suggest the names of three lawyers, of whom one was assigned by the court to serve him. It is more likely, however, that in the majority of cases before the

The interrogation of a witness or a suspect from Limborch's *Historia Inquisitionis*. Amsterdam, 1692.
[Courtesy of the University of Wisconsin-Madison Library.]

hæreſes credit & docuit, ſpeciatim auté
hanc & illam. Quibus enumeratis,
concludit promotor fiſcalis, petens vt
Bucerus tanquam hæreticus pertinax
puniatur: & pœnas grauiſsimas hæreſis
expoſcit. Aliam prolixiorem formu-
lam alij tradunt, nos tamen hac vtimur
[vide Specul. titul. de hæreti. Brunum
lib. 4. cap. 7.]

12 Promotor fiſcalis præſente eo quem
accuſat, in ſcriptis iudici accuſationem
offerre debet, & propria voce literas
ſuæ accuſationis legere, vt Calixtus Papa conſtituit : & ſtatim iurare ſolet, accuſationem illam a ſe non malitioſe edi
tam eſſe, ſed vt ſuum officium faciat,
quia obiecta crimina probare intendit.
[c. vlti. 2. quæſt. 8.]

De Aduocatis   Titulus V.

SVMMARIVM.

1 A Duocati hæreticos nequeunt deſen-
dere, niſi id eis ab inquiſitoribus p-
miſſum fuerit.
2 Aduocati quando hæreticis concedendi.
3 Aduocati in hæreſis iudicium qui ſint ad
hibendi, & quid ab eis exigendum ſit.
4 Aduocatorum in cauſa hæreſeos officiū.
5 Hæretici patrocinium qui ſuſcepit, non
debet rogari de eadem cauſa ſentētiam

dicere.
6 Aduocatis vnde dandum ſit ſtipēdium,
vt pauperum cauſas defendant.
7 Aduocatis, ex bonis reorum qui pauperes non ſunt, merces tribuenda eſt.
8 Aduocatorum verba, quæ ipſi reo præſente allegant, quando tanquam ab ipſo
reo prolata, & quando non ita ſunt ac-
cipienda.

De Aduocatis.

 ONIFACIVS octauus
iam olim cōſtituit, vt
in inquiſitione praui-
tatis hæreticæ proce-
datur ſimpliciter, de
plano, & abſque ad-
uocatoruin ac iudiciorum ſtrepitu & fi
gura. Sed nonnunquam opus eſt aduocatis, vt reus ſe defendere poſsit. Mul
tæ enim ſunt exceptiones ac defenſio-
nes, quibus accuſati de hæreſi vti poterunt, vt alio loco dixero Cæterum aduocati defendere reos nequeunt, niſi id
eis ab inquiſitoribus permiſſum ſuerit.
[c. vltim. de hæreti. lib. 6. Laudu. in
Clementin. 1. de exceſsib. prælator.
Matthæus in conſtitut. Sicilię titu. 1.
Ponziñibius, de lamijs. nume. 78. Ca-

rerius de hæreti. num. 114. vide Go-
dofred. in. l. curiales. 7. C. de hæreti.]
2 Nam cum reus fatetur obiecta crimina, nullo aduocato eget. Cum autem
poſt tres monitiones reus negat, ſe vn-
quam hæreticum fuiſſe: tunc aduocatus
ei dandus eſt, etiam non petenti. Nam
& ſi quadam inſtructione caueatur, vt
reo petenti detur aduocatus: mea tamen
ſententia, vbi id expedire videbitur,
iudices prouidere debent, vt aduocatus adſit, ne reus defenſore careat: in-
quiſitores enim non iudices modo, ſed
& patres reorū eſſe debent. [prima in-
ſtruct. Hiſpalen. cap. 16.]
3 Non quilibet aduocatus adhibendus
eſt in hoc iudicium : ſed is tantum, qui
ſit idoneus ad reorum cauſas defenden-
                                    C   das:

The provision for a defense attorney from Simancas's *De Catholicis Institutionibus Liber.*
[From the author's collection]

outlying tribunals where the accused lacked either the means or the contacts to seek assistance on their own, it was the inquisitor who appointed counsel in the form of the "public defenders" attached to the tribunal.[66] Legal aid was not reserved for those who could afford it, as we learn from a letter dated 16 August 1603 from Cardinal Borghese of the Roman Congregation to the inquisitor of Florence: "If due to their poverty they [the accused in a given case] do not have funds for a lawyer . . . your reverence must provide one so that they do not remain undefended."[67]

The qualities required of lawyers permitted to practice before the Holy Office were easily stated, but probably not always attainable: they must be men themselves above the suspicion of heresy, zealous supporters of the faith and upright, versed in both laws (canon and civil), and especially in the type of litigation which pertained to the inquisitorial tribunals. They had to swear an oath of secrecy, undertake to protect diligently the interests of the accused, which included persuading them to confess the truth, be brief in their defense, and guarantee to restore the trial records to the tribunal at the termination of the proceedings. The fact that these court attorneys occasionally were appointed on the basis of patronage must have served to introduce some mediocrities into the system.[68]

The assignment of a *curator* to offer special legal assistance to the minor under twenty-five years of age at the inception of proceedings against him (and not just at the defense phase, the usual practice) was a beneficent practice restricted to the courts of the Spanish Inquisition, according to Peña and Carena; but there is evidence that Rome was itself adopting this safeguard for the rights of minors towards the end of the sixteenth century.[69] The defendant's right to the services of a *procurator*[70] or *advocatus* — the difference between them is roughly analogous to that between solicitor and barrister in English legal practice — was an ancient feature of inquisitorial procedure, despite continuing confusion on the subject and contradictory statements by modern scholars on the question of whether the assistance of counsel was permissible in the inquisitorial courts.[71] Those who have argued that it was not, may have been misled by the famous pronouncements of such medieval popes as Innocent III (d. 1216) and Boniface VIII (d. 1303) that inquisitorial proceedings must be conducted "simply and plainly, and without the turmoil and figures of lawyers and judges."[72] This prohibition was not accepted at face value by the jurists charged with interpreting and applying the law, who distinguished between the pertinacious heretic, not eligible for legal assistance, and cases where heretical intent had not been established, thus making counsel permissible.[73] At any rate, whatever the frequency of the appearance of the defense attorney in medieval times, his role was well established by the early modern period that concerns us here.[74]

By today's standards of jurisprudence the lawyer-client relationship was a curious one, for, as we have just noted, if the lawyer became convinced that his client was indeed guilty and could not be persuaded to abandon his error, he was obliged to discontinue the defense or fall under suspicion himself. In other words, the fall into heresy could be defended, but pertinacity in adhering to it could not. In a real sense, much more so than today, defense attorneys were officers of the court.[75] Nevertheless, even with this limitation, the discovery of inconsistencies and contradictions in the arguments of deponents for the prosecution and the strategic use of friendly witnesses to corroborate the Christian morals and behavior of the defendant were obviously enhanced by the attorney's presence. He could present extenuating circumstances—from drunkenness and anger to insanity—seek postponements and delays in the proceedings, bring to light perjured and inconsistent testimony by the accusers, assist the client to prepare an "apology" for his actions, argue against a sentence to proceed to interrogation with torture, and persuade the court to milder sentencing.[76]

Many inquisitorial handbooks are generous with their suggestions for possible defense strategies. Peña, Simancas, and Carena went to great lengths outlining the steps which should be included in a sound and diligent defense. It should begin with a denial of the charge, proceed to discredit the testimony of the hostile witnesses, and produce evidence of the upright and Catholic character of the client. Peña underscored the obvious—that the articles presented for the defendant should not inadvertently bring new evidence to bear against him.[77] Simancas urged the defense to compel the prosecution to specify the time and place of the alleged misdeed, so that it then could be demonstrated, through deponents superior in standing to the prosecution's, that the accused had been elsewhere at that particular moment. In addition to undermining the credibility of the hostile witnesses (which Simancas concurred was the linchpin of the defense) and building up the accused's reputation as a faithful, practicing Catholic, an equal effort needed to be directed to establishing that the sin, the crime—if its occurrence was beyond refutation—had not been committed voluntarily, that the intellect had not participated in it. And the writer adduces the several extenuating factors that could be marshalled for consideration, a lapse of the tongue, inebriation, temporary insanity, rusticity, simplicity, and even sleep-walking.[78] Scanaroli's guidelines for the *procurator pauperum* included advising his charges among the indigent in Rome's civil prisons not to aggravate their situations with unruly behavior and instructing them in how to act appropriately when they finally appeared before a busy magistrate, refraining from irritating him with irrelevancies and long, bumbling discourses.[79]

The right to counsel and other safeguards in the inquisitorial system of law were impaired, but by no means rendered ineffectual, by the anonymity of informers or prosecution witnesses. The defendant could know the evidence against him, but not the names of his accusers, a provision difficult to maintain consistently in practice, established centuries before to preserve witnesses from possible reprisals. Originally intended as a temporary measure during a period of turbulence, it became institutionalized and a regular feature of inquisitorial proceedings.[80] Only in the rarest exceptions, where identities were clearly in question, under rigidly controlled conditions and after having obtained the consent of the bishop and of the consultors, might a form of direct confrontation be permitted. And then only when the witnesses were themselves accomplices in the alleged crime, and were *vilissimi* or "infamous."[81] This was the theory. However, the repeated reminders to provincial inquisitors that "testium nomina publicari non debent"; the oaths required of defendants at the conclusion of their trials not to molest witnesses who had testified against them;[82] the imposition of heavy penalties for offenses against witnesses contained in Pius V's Bull *Si de Protegendis*;[83] and the numerous cases that have come to our attention where secrecy was violated, including that of Giordano Bruno who threw a suspected accuser into the Tiber, offer clear evidence of both the need to shield witnesses and the difficulty of maintaining anonymity in practice.[84]

The many instances of serious intimidation of witnesses by defendants, their families, and cohorts clearly suggests that the provision for the anonymity of witnesses was not a mere pretext to obtain an advantage for the cause of the faith. The harassment might take a mean and petty form, such as occurred in the case of a poor Franciscan, a certain Fra Calisto da Napoli, who had testified in the Holy Office—undoubtedly against members of his own order—and was now suffering retaliation from his provincial, who buffeted him about from one convent to another without cease.[85] The wheels of the entire judicial process ran the risk of grinding to a halt when the inquisitor of Aquileia and Concordia had to query the Supreme Congregation whether he should proceed in cases where there was a mortal danger to the deponents and witnesses. When the cardinals of the Holy Office in Rome asked the inquisitor of Modena, in a letter dated 11 July 1626, to confirm the report that a mother and son who had testified in a trial against a certain Turri had indeed been murdered, the provincial official had to admit that it was so.[86] But the danger, of course, was twofold, not directed at witnesses alone. It was also experienced by prisoners of the Holy Office upon release, fearful of the anger of those who had joined in their prosecution. While the good behavior of a defendant or convict returning to society was hopefully guaranteed by the heavy security he had to put up, no such restraint existed to control the actions of his enemies who awaited him on the outside.[87] Further confirmation of the fear that stalked the inquisitorial courtroom — even for those working for the cause of the faith — was the shortage of notaries to fill what, in the words of Pius IV, was perceived as an "odious office."[88]

The Inquisition acknowledged that the concealment from the defendant of the identities of witnesses placed him at a serious disadvantage. "Because," wrote Masini, "the capacity for defending himself which we grant to the accused is somewhat deficient, since we do not inform him who the accusers are, it is necessary that the evidence for conviction be absolutely clear and beyond doubt."[89] It was incumbent on the inquisitor, in view of this hindrance to a fair defense, to investigate with the greatest care the reputation, faithfulness, and customs of deponents before the tribunal, as well as the motives which had led them to come forward to testify.[90] At the commencement of the defense the accused was required to name any persons whom he suspected bore him malice. If these coincided with the prosecution witnesses, the inquisitor was obliged to investigate their motives and credibility, and the nature and gravity of the quarrel between the parties, proceeding with special care where mortal enmity was alleged.[91] If the results were positive, their testimony was examined for possible perjury. Moreover, as we have mentioned, the Holy Office did not permit unsworn testimony or denunciations. The many sentences delivered against false witnesses indicate that the duty of verification was taken seriously.[92] Parenthetically, one wonders why the writers on the subject did not perceive the danger to be present in trials other than heresy proceedings. Certainly, papal legislation for secular criminal cases conducted in the states of the Church called for the full disclosure of accusers' names to defendants.[93]

Judicial torture, interrogation under torment, the *Quaestio*,[94] began to be adopted by lay courts as an extreme measure for obtaining confessions early in the thirteenth century, making its first reappearance in a medieval legislative text in the *Liber iuris civilis* of Verona in 1228, followed in rapid succession by other Italian civic statutes. It was introduced into the inquisitorial process in the Bull *Ad Extirpanda* issued by Innocent IV on 15 May 1252, although the application of torture even in heresy cases remained in secular hands for a few more years, until Alexander IV authorized ecclesiastics to absolve one another from the canonical penalties incurred with these activities. The document expressed the view that if it was proper to employ coercion in cases involving the simple theft of worldly goods, how much more justification was there in applying it against heretics, whose offense, the theft of souls, was so much greater.[95] Masini, in his *Sacro Arsenale*, did not consider torture an unfitting instrument in the hands of the Church, because its chief beneficiaries were the victims themselves: "Heretics," he wrote, "by confessing their crimes become converted to God, and through reconciliation save their souls"; Peña justified its necessity in "the dangerous times" in which he was living, finding it an especially appropriate device in occult crimes where proof was difficult to establish,[96] while Simancas described its use as "ancient and hallowed," recommended by just laws and wise men through the ages.[97]

Interrogation with torture might be employed in two general situations: first, where the burden of evidence against the defendant clearly indicated a guilt which he or she denied but had been incapable of disproving, and second, where it was suspected on reasonable grounds that the confession had not been full and sincere and all the accomplices had not been named.[98] The evidence to justify torture generally had to be supported by the testimony of two witnesses of good standing ("omni tamen exceptione maiores"), although in some instances a single deponent of sound reputation who did not suffer from any disabilities or exceptions and was an eyewitness to the fact might suffice, but not, however, against a defendant who was himself of unblemished reputation.[99] Certain social groups — academics, knights, noblemen, clerics — which were exempted from being subjected to torture in the civil law enjoyed no special protection in heresy cases.[100] Pregnant women or women who had given birth within a forty-day period, the aged, children under fourteen years of age and the physically impaired enjoyed immunity and were spared the ordeal.[101]

Torture was rigidly controlled and various restrictions were enforced in Roman practice. In the first place, the judge could not proceed to the *rigoroso esamine*, interrogation under torture, unless the evidence against the accused was compelling and until the defense had presented its case. "Never commence with the torture but with the evidence," was Masini's formula. "It would be iniquitous and against all human and divine law to expose anyone to torment without weighty evidence."[102] Nor did the inquisitor alone determine whether torture was justified. He was obliged to seek the opinion of the *consultori*, the half-dozen or so lawyers and theologians who formed a permanent advisory council for every inquisitorial court. This body composed of both laymen and clerics (who served without pay, but enjoyed certain privileges in return, such as licenses to read prohibited books) had as its chief function the counseling of the inquisitor on any difficult question, from the feasibility of making an arrest to sentencing at the conclusion of a trial.[103] In the cynical opinion of Zanchino Ugolini, an early fourteenth-century inquisitor in Romagna, these *periti* (experts) were there to save inquisitors, who were often ignorant of the law, from making grievous mistakes that might lead to the acquittal of the guilty and the execution of the innocent.[104] The legal status of the board of *consultori* and its prerogatives were the subject of long controversy, but it became the generally accepted position that judges, namely inquisitors and bishops, were not under obligation to follow its opinions. Although consultors were entitled to examine the full trial records, the names of witnesses had to be withheld even from them, except in a few special cases, such as when the veracity and objectivity of deponents had been called into question.[105] However, the inquisitor was required to furnish some particulars about them to assist the consultors in their deliberations.[106] As we have seen, there is evidence that members of this group, familiar figures to the inquisitor, and versed in the appropriate law, might be called upon to serve as defense attorneys.[107]

When the question to be resolved was especially difficult, it was laid before the supreme tribunal in Rome, with the testimony of the defendants and witnesses reported in their own words, in the vernacular, not in Latin summaries or translations prepared by the notary.[108] In the course of the sixteenth century it became increasingly the practice for Rome, minutely informed on the progress of all trials conducted in the provincial courts, to issue the instructions for torture, instructions which even the cardinal inquisitors felt needed the sanction of their own advisers and legal experts. The administration of torture at the local level was scrutinized scrupulously, as we note, for example, in a letter from the cardinal of Pisa to the inquisitor of Bologna, asking him to produce a copy of his authorization to torture in a given case, as well as from the disciplinary action taken against abusive judges.[109] Correspondence reveals that generally it was the pope himself, who personally presided over the weekly meetings of the Congregation of the Inquisition where the disposition of cases was discussed, who acquiesced in the measure.[110]

Deviations from accepted procedure—and many occurred in the provincial tribunals—were not tolerated by Rome, as we observe in the letter written on 18 November 1589 from the cardinal of Santa Severina to the inquisitor of Florence because the latter's vicar and the episcopal court of Pistoia had mistreated three women suspected of sorcery and sacrilegious acts. The confessions, which had been obtained from them under torture, were to be thrown out of court on the following grounds: first, the evidence against them had not been of sufficient weight to justify such an extreme form of interrogation, since it was based primarily on the testimony of a witness who had a poor reputation; and, second, the torments had been administered before the women had been given the opportunity to respond to the charges, and the confessions elicited under duress had been inconsistent and contradictory. The Florentine inquisitor was then ordered to proceed immediately to Pistoia and assume personal direction of the trial.[111]

Another important provision serving to inhibit the use of torture was the ancient requirement contained in the decretal *Multorum Querela* dating to the pontificate of Clement V (1305–1314) that both inquisitor and bishop (or their vicars) agree to, and be present during, its application.[112] A further restricting factor was the physical condition and age of the defendant. There are numerous instances where Rome is informed, after it has instructed the provincial inquisitor to proceed to interrogation under torture, that the examining physician has declared the defendant incapable of supporting it.[113]

From Eymeric on, jurists resurrected the ancient teachings of the Roman legist Ulpian that "torture is a fragile and dangerous thing and the truth frequently is not obtained by it. For, many defendants because of their patience and strength are able to spurn the torments, while others would rather lie than bear them, unfairly incriminating themselves and also others."[114] Nevertheless, well into the seventeenth century the Inquisition, as well as every other European court system, continued to rely on this device to reach its decisions in situations where it was felt that essential evidence was being held back.

For inquisitors the most crucial information that they required consisted in determining the intention behind the offender's criminal act.[115] Heresy, in the eyes of the Church, was a sin of the intellect, and a heretic was a person who consciously espoused and clung to a doctrinal error. Following St. Augustine, the Spanish jurist Simancas declared: "A heretic is not one who lives badly, but who believes badly" ("non est hereticus, qui male vivit, sed qui male credit").[116] Thus, for example, in the case of a convicted bigamist it would have to be determined whether his transgression revealed conscious disbelief in the sacrament of marriage. A person who had been apprehended in the act of hurling excrement against a statuette of the Virgin would be interrogated to determine whether he had acted in a fit of anger or he indeed did not believe in the Virginity of the Mother of God.

One of the most pressing questions concerned the effect on the outcome of the proceedings when the defendant sustained torture without changing his testimony and confessing a heretical intention behind a criminal act or word. In many instances the evidence was indeed considered purged, and absolution ensued.[117] Inquisitors attempted to protect themselves from this eventuality, where the indications of guilt were overwhelming, by recommending scrutiny of all the particulars in the case in question — the nature of the evidence, the quality of the witnesses and, especially, the duration of the torture and the rigor with which it had been applied.[118] Even if heretical intention behind a proven crime could not be verified, thus sparing the defendant from the full sanctions of the law, the *pena ordinaria*, a lesser form of abjuration and punishment could be recommended.[119] The formula in the decree invoking torture thus carried the clause that the questioning was only being conducted *pro ulteriori veritate et super intentione*. What had already been confessed and proved in full could not be purged through victory over torture. Resistance to the torment could not be allowed to prejudice what had been judicially achieved up to that point.[120] First offenders who wished to be reconciled to the Church were usually spared capital punishment regardless of the category of their abjuration. However, in the event of a second fall, if the offender had abjured as a formal heretic at the conclusion of the first trial, he would be liable to the extreme penalties reserved for the relapsed.[121]

When torture was employed in inquisitorial tribunals, in cases where more than one defendant was involved, the recommended practice was to begin with the most suspect; but if they seemed equally implicated, a start should be made with the seemingly weakest and most tremulous. Where both men and women were involved, the torment should begin with the latter since they were felt to be "more timid and inconstant." This was a teaching contradicted by the medico-legal evidence that women, at least anatomically, were better equipped than men to resist the pain of the strappado.[122] Before the onset of the torment, an interval of six to ten hours after meals had to elapse to prevent nausea and vomiting.[123] Torture customarily consisted in the elevation of the victim by means of a rope and pulley, with his arms bound behind his back.[124] In this position, after the room had been cleared even of the jailers, and only the inquisitor, the episcopal delegate, and the notary remained, the accused was interrogated.[125] The ordeal generally did not go beyond thirty minutes, and an hour was the maximum permitted.[126] According to Masini, the addition of weights to the feet of the defendant, and dropping him in sudden jerks (*squassi*) stopping just short of the floor, widely practiced in secular courts, was strictly prohibited in his day.[127] Torture, he prescribed, should be moderate in such a way that the victim is preserved, if innocent, to enjoy his freedom, and if guilty, to receive his just punishment.[128]

It is hard to imagine more than one conclusion in any trial in which torture was used. And yet, in an astonishing number of cases involving both men and women, it did not produce admissions of guilt or revisions of the original testimony.[129] The effectiveness of torture might depend on such factors as the thickness of the rope, the physique and stamina of the victim,[130] and perhaps even his or her access to amulets or other presumed magical devices thought capable of dulling the sensations of pain either because they possessed narcotic properties or, even if innocuous, for their psychological effects as placebos.[131]

Confessions obtained by this means were not considered valid until their ratification by the defendant twenty-four hours later outside the chamber of torments, and the Congregation of the Inquisition in Rome scrutinized trial records sent to it by the provincial tribunals for fulfillment of this provision.[132] Sentences were ordinarily reviewed in Rome before they were pronounced, and the circumstances surrounding confessions obtained under duress, especially if retracted during the twenty-four hour interval, received special attention. I can cite the case of a certain Maria de' Gentili, a Bolognese woman suspected of being a witch, who had confessed to a homicide. After a thorough review of the proceedings by the Roman Congregation, the cardinal of Santa Severina wrote to the inquisitor of Bologna on 18 May 1591: "There are too many contradictory elements in her confession which do not agree with the evidence presented in the trial." Her punishment was temporary banishment from the city of Bologna.[133] A case in which Rome ordered a trial to be reopened and transferred to another court concerned Bartolomeo Betti. His confessions made before the inquisitor of Ferrara were overturned by the Congregation because it suspected that they had been extorted "con mali modi." The trial was transferred to Bologna and ended with Betti's release.[134] The case of alleged Milanese witches was thrown out, after review in Rome, because of their vacillating, contradictory confessions, revoked by them more than once in the course of their trial, and the weakness of the evidence against them. Their fate was not the stake but assignment to "a good and prudent confessor."[135] Finally, there are numerous examples of requests to Rome appealing the decisions of the provincial tribunals, cases in which both trial records and defendants were transferred to the higher court, and the investigation reopened. In 1593 a certain Giovanni Paolo delle Agocchie, who had been sent by the Bolognese court to the papal galleys for five years and had already begun to serve his term, received a commutation of his sentence by the Holy Office in Rome to a fine of 200 *scudi* to be applied for the sustenance of indigent prisoners.[136] The cardinal of Santa Severina, despite the skepticism of his colleagues on the Roman Congregation concerning the case of a prisoner who had been transferred to Rome and was now alleging that he had made an invalid confession, ordered the inquisitor of Florence to put to certain witnesses in that city questions which the defendant had prepared, even after the conclusion of his trial in which he had freely acknowledged his alleged errors. He now argued that he had confessed out of fear that he would be tortured and in the hope of being quickly freed.[137] And when a priest of Verona, similarly condemned to a harsh galley sentence, claimed that he had not been permitted a full defense, it was ordered that his case should be reopened and every possibility to present his case provided.[138] Although torture, as we have seen, was an integral component in inquisitorial judicial proceedings, and not designed as a penal measure, the *tratto di corda* commonly served this purpose in secular law and might even be invoked in cases of infraction of discipline in the Roman prisons of the Inquisition, as well as on other, probably rare, occasions.[139]

In the area of penal practices as well, a close examination of the sources may dispel some lingering misconceptions. The solemn words pronounced in countless sentences have misled modern scholars to form an incorrect impression of inquisitorial justice. Condemnation to a *carcere perpetuo* (life imprisonment) was actually intended by the canonists to suggest a confinement of roughly three years, provided, of course, that the accused demonstrated sincere signs of contrition;[140] *carcere perpetuo irremissibile* indicated eight years;[141] and true imprisonment for life, *immuratio* (which itself might be commuted to a lesser term), denoted confinement in a cell surrounded by four walls, and not literally a walling in, as some writers have supposed.[142] I have encountered instances of pardons granted, even within six months of sentencing, to individuals condemned to so-called perpetual imprisonment, although it was more customary to allow a few years to elapse. Two examples are offered by the cases of Antonio de Ludovisi and Hieronimo Guastavillani who were among a group of Bolognese gentlemen found guilty of heretical activities and sentenced on 20 September 1567—Ludovisi to *carcere perpetuo* and Guastavillani to *immuratio*. During the years 1573–1574 a number of letters were exchanged between the Roman Congregation and the inquisitor of Bologna concerning their conduct in confinement, in which the pope himself had taken interest. It was concluded that their behavior had earned them a reduction of their sentences. Both men were permitted to doff that mark of shame, the *habitello*, the penitential garment worn by the convicted heretic, and to leave their monastic prisons. Guastavillani, however, was limited in his movements to the *contado* of Bologna and prohibited from entering the city proper.[143]

In the sixteenth century, outside Rome, the Inquisition possessed very few actual prisons.[144] Convicted offenders, both lay and clerical, might be sentenced to monastic confinement which could be of two kinds, varying in severity, as we see from the case of a Don Flavio Uberti, a Celestine, who was condemned in March 1603 to spend one year "in carcere formali" in a monastery, followed by four more years in a house of his order "in loco di prigione." The first form of imprisonment involved formal confinement in a cell. The second permitted circulation about the grounds of the convent, subject, however, to the performance of salutary penances as prescribed by the inquisitors. Thus, in the case of Fra Angelo da Casale, sentenced at Mantua 30 June 1581 as a necromancer, he was condemned ". . . three times in the public refectory where the brothers eat to sit on the ground with the bread and water of the family and make your prostrations." In the case of members of orders, their prison expenses were to be defrayed by their former convents.[145] According to one knowledgeable seventeenth-century authority, Cesare Carena, the influential official in the Cremona Inquisition, this form of incarceration had fallen into disuse in his day and monasteries and convents were returning to their intended function as "ports of safety from the tempest of life." Monastic confinement, however, was still being employed occasionally for women sentenced to perform charitable work gratis in convent hospitals.[146] House arrest,[147] or the restriction of movement to a geographical area which might range in size from one's village, to the city of Rome, or even to an entire *contado*[148] were other possibilities generally available to the sentencing judges. The elderly, modest wage earners with large families to support or nubile daughters to marry off, and witches whose husbands would have them back, were frequently assigned to their homes and to their shops,[149] especially since monks tended to view prisoners in their midst as unwelcome burdens on their usually poor and overcrowded convents.[150] Faithful fulfillment of the terms of home confinement was reasonably assured by the depositing of an adequate monetary security. In the case of poor prisoners this might be waived and an oath substituted for it. A poor German of Milan with a large family to maintain received this grace and the added concession of being able to roam the whole city and eke out a living.[151] In secular practice, imprisonment *ad poenam* (as punishment) rather than simply *ad custodiam* (for the purpose of custody during the trial phase of the judicial process) did not make its appearance until late in the sixteenth century.[152]

Based on various records, including the trial of Giordano Bruno, and a personal visit, Luigi Firpo reconstructed conditions in the Roman prisons of the Holy Office housed in the Palazzo Pucci, debunking legendary assertions made by older writers: cells were commodious and well lit, and could be furnished by prisoners at their own cost with a bed, table, sheets, and towels. The Inquisition itself was only expected to provide a straw pallet, a single sheet, and a long cloak or blanket. Prisoners

*Vestitus pœnitentis
qui vocatur Sambenito.*

The garment imposed on the penitent heretic from Limborch's *Historia Inquisitionis.*
Amsterdam, 1692. [Courtesy of the University of Wisconsin-Madison Library.]

Veſtitus relapſi vel impœnitentis comburendi
qui vocatur Samarra.

The garment worn by the obdurate and relapsed heretic
from Limborch's *Historia Inquisitionis.* Amsterdam, 1692.
[Courtesy of the University of Wisconsin-Madison Library.]

had access to a barber, bathing facilities, laundry service, and mending, and were permitted a change of clothing twice weekly. All this was at their expense, if they could afford it. In the case of the indigent, public charity would be expected to support them (more modestly), while religious were considered the burdens of their orders. Prisoners appeared periodically before the Congregation to testify concerning their material needs; and the cardinals, in turn, were obliged to inspect conditions in the prisons. As for prohibitions, prisoners could not converse with their fellows in other cells; they could not attempt to read or write about matters that did not immediately concern their cases; nor could they converse privately with their jailers or use them to communicate with the outside world.[153] These optimum conditions were clearly not met in the provincial tribunals. There, facilities were frequently inferior, when they existed at all, as we learn from prisoners' appeals and from the repeated attempts by Rome to remedy the situations.[154] When not in use, cells might serve for storage purposes, as in San Domenico in Bologna where confiscated books were housed pending a decision about how to dispose of them.[155]

There is little that can be said in mitigation of that living hell that was the world of the galleys. The Church, together with every other Mediterranean sea power, reserved this fate for many of its offenders.[156] The evidence suggests that the galleys were considered appropriate punishment for individuals convicted of especially serious and perverse crimes: gross blasphemers who had vilified the cardinal dogmas of the Church, archheretics, necromancers who had grossly defiled the altar and sacraments, prison breakers, false witnesses and perjurers, defendants who had been deliberately obstructive and evasive during their trials, and abusive judges, including a certain Fra Constanzo da Sala, O.P. sentenced at Pavia on 25 June 1580 to three years of service. He had falsely claimed the title of inquisitorial vicar in the town of Valenza so as "to be held in greater honor," and had perpetrated many crimes under his fraudulent cloak of office, which included attempting illicit sexual congress, the incarceration of a child for swearing, and the indiscriminate licensing of booksellers.[157] The fact that the accused had attempted flight on one occasion or another is mentioned in many sentences to the galleys, a form of punishment which served the purpose roughly of maximum security prisons in our day.[158]

The Church claimed a higher standard of behavior from ecclesiastics than from laymen. Consequently, the former incurred heavier penalties, which frequently took the form of galley sentences.[159] The hardships endured by the convict at sea were well-known, and officials pondered the proper uses of this form of penal servitude. This concern even touched that unflinching persecutor of heretics, Michele Ghislieri (the future Pius V), while he served in Rome as commissioner general of the Holy Office. Replying on 20 June 1556 to an inquiry from the inquisitor of Genoa, he described the reluctance of the Roman Congregation to assign its prisoners to the galleys, which it considered a form of penance fit only for the desperate and the damned.[160] Again, writing on 29 September 1563, Ghislieri reassured the Jesuit Cristoforo Rodriguez (on a mission to the Waldensians in the Puglie and Calabria) in regard to the fate of the local inhabitants: "Concerning those that have been sent to the galleys, your reverence should give us an account of each one individually, mentioning if they are burdened by families, because if they should persevere in their repentance — and if it is not feigned — their sentences will certainly be commuted."[161] Members of the nobility and academics (but not ecclesiastics) were generally spared galley service, but the question of eligibility seems not to have been settled juridically if it could still be raised by the inquisitor of Malta early in the seventeenth century. In this, as in other instances, Rome advised that a general rule could not be formulated and that each case should be settled on its merits.[162]

Expiration dates of sentences were observed, although justice might be thwarted when prisoners were not serving directly on papal vessels. The nuncio to Naples, Antonio Sauli, had to make strenuous efforts to free several convicts, citizens of the papal states, who had been sentenced during the reign of Pius IV. The galleys on which they were serving had subsequently been sold to Spain and their officers refused to recognize that the prisoners' terms had expired. The pope himself, Gregory XIII, took a keen interest in the affair, and demanded that justice be done.[163]

Many of those condemned to the galleys survived and returned to their homes, although for churchmen the stigma attached to galley service would bar them from again officiating at the altar.[164] Those who could demonstrate medically that they had become physically unfit for the oar had their sentences commuted to a lesser punishment.[165] Even short-term hardship leaves to attend to family problems at home seem not to have been unheard of events.[166] There is a shred of evidence, if we accept it at face value, that the way was open for prisoners to purchase the services of substitutes more apt for the life than themselves, or at least this is what seems to be suggested by the curious case of Carlo Chiavello, a spice merchant of Savona sentenced to twenty years in the galleys by the inquisitor of Genoa on 8 January 1581. At the conclusion of his trial an appeal had been addressed to the pope on his behalf which alleged that "the poor man is old, sick, paralyzed in his lower body, useless for fulfilling the punishment . . . laden down with seven children . . . of whom four are girls, who, without their father's help, will fall into ruin with danger to their souls." In a letter to Cardinal Savello of the Roman Congregation, written on 9 June, the inquisitor of Genoa disputed many of these facts: ". . . Chiavello does indeed have many children but he is well off because he is a successful tradesman and now on the galley he is conducting a lively wine business and is not going without. He is very industrious, old he is not, concerning which he stated a falsehood. He is a man forty years of age, more or less . . . and for all this there is a remedy. Let him buy a Muslim slave to row for him. He has the means to do it."[167] And some individuals destined to the galleys actually may never have set foot aboard one, although their alternative duties ashore, such as transporting the bodies of plague victims, were probably no less harsh or no less filled with peril.[168]

The stake, incarceration, and the triremes are those dramatic forms of penal procedure which are generally associated with inquisitorial practice. But a survey of the thousands of surviving sentences suggests that in actual fact milder forms of punishment prevailed. Most frequently encountered are public humiliation in the form of abjurations read on the cathedral steps on Sundays and feast days before the throngs of churchgoers, and salutary penances, fines or service for the benefit of charitable establishments, and a seemingly endless cycle of prayers and devotions to be performed over many months or years.[169]

Despite popular notions to the contrary, only a small percentage of cases concluded with capital punishment. The penalty of death by burning at the stake was reserved for three principal categories of offenders: the obstinate and unrepentant who refused to be reconciled to the Church; the relapsed, those who had suffered a previous sentence for formal heresy;[170] and individuals convicted of attempting to overturn such central doctrines of the Church as the Virgin Birth and the full divinity of Christ. With two Bulls, *Cum Quorundam Hominum* (22 July 1556) and *Cum Ex Apostolatus Officio* (15 February 1558) Paul IV established a class of crimes against the central doctrines of the Church which called for the death penalty even when the accused was neither relapsed nor impenitent. Relaxation to the secular arm for execution was also prescribed by the pontiff for individuals not in holy orders who celebrated Mass or heard confessions.[171] In actual practice, however, I have encountered an extraordinary number of cases of individuals convicted of the heresies specified in the Pauline decrees who received lesser penalties.[172]

Some of the known, but still tentative, figures for executions are presented in the statistical study elsewhere in this volume.[173] If this is still not a pleasant picture, it is also not the unfettered violence which we may have been led to assume. To the very end every attempt was made to persuade impenitent heretics to reflect, to admit the errors of their acts and teachings and seek reconciliation with the Church. From Giordano Bruno to the most modest prisoner in a provincial cell, it was the policy of the Holy Office to assail the condemned with the exhortations of "learned, religious and pious" men hoping to extract a last-minute conversion. Even family members were enlisted in the cause. In the opinion of the cardinal of Santa Severina, these good works were necessary, not only in the hope that one more soul might be snatched from the Devil's grasp, but also possibly to allow more time for evidence to surface which would preserve innocent victims from an atrocious fate.[174]

The final act in the inquisitorial process was the *auto da fé*, the public ceremony where, after sentencing, penitent heretics abjured and were reconciled to the Church, and the obdurate and relapsed went to their fate. Abjurations were performed *de levi, de vehementi*, and *de formali*. The first took place privately in the episcopal residence or in the seats of the various inquisitions, the second two publicly in churches, on cathedral steps, and during the *autos*. Because of the stigma attached to the ceremony, before ordering a public abjuration inquisitors were expected to consider whether an offender was a family head with nubile daughters. The latter category of abjuration was infinitely more serious because in the case of relapse the offender was liable to suffer the ultimate penalty. However, minors under twenty-five years of age who abjured as formal heretics were exempted from the punishment of the relapsed in case of a second conviction.[175]

The *autos da fé*, "acts of faith," were held in the presence of great throngs and before assembled dignitaries of church and state ensconced on specially erected platforms. These ceremonies could attain dramatic levels which evoked visions of the Last Judgment in at least one spectator of such an event in Spain. He could imagine no scene more apt to inspire terror than what he was witnessing. And this impression was corroborated by another, anonymous, description of such an event, a Madrid *auto* carried out amidst the roar of a frenzied crowd screaming "burn them alive," against a background of rolling drums, the crack of musket fire and clashing metal, the barking of dogs, themselves being hurled on the flames with a woman accused of bestiality.[176] A newssheet of the day has left us an equally vivid account of the martyrdom of Giovanni Luigi Pascale, a Calvinist missionary to his homeland, executed in Rome on 15 September 1560. When he saw the platform intended to seat the cardinals of the Holy Office collapse under their weight when one more member tried to mount it, he was heard to cry out, "Behold the Judgment of God."[177]

In Rome, the scenes of these macabre affairs were generally the misnamed Campo dei Fiori or the square adjacent to the bridge by the Castel Sant'Angelo. The condemned were accompanied by official comforters belonging to the charitable confraternity assigned to this purpose.[178] Before being bound to the stake, gentlemen were beheaded, lesser mortals hung. And even those who were condemned to the agony of being burned alive because they refused to the bitter end to recant their errors and be reconciled to the Church, might have, in later usage at least, the moment of final release hastened with small sacks of gunpowder dangled around their necks.[179]

In conclusion, although capricious and arbitrary decisions, misuse of authority, and wanton abuse of human rights occurred, they were not an integral part of inquisitorial procedure, nor tolerated by the Holy Office. There is a scrupulous, almost pedantic reverence for tradition, which Fra Paolo da Ferrara, a high functionary in the Roman Congregation, sums up in a letter dated 7 November 1573 to the inquisitor of Bologna: "Your reverence should not allow himself to be persuaded by anyone to innovate or give unusual penances and punishments, regardless who is involved, but should follow common practice, and the sound teachings of Simancas."[180] And when the same provincial official, who had suspected Protestant sympathies behind the failure to observe a day of fasting, exceeded proper limits of investigation, Antonio Balduzzi, commissioner of the Roman Inquisition, wrote a sad letter of reproach:

Concerning that poor man who ate meat, it seems to me that you acted much too harshly against him. I know well that I [and Balduzzi had himself once served as inquisitor of Bologna] would not have done half of what was done by you. A man who, as soon as he was corrected, admitted his mistake and explained that he had forgotten that it was a fast day and a Saturday, a man almost unknown to other men, to have put him in prison and tortured him to me seems too much.[181]

And Cesare Carena, who discussed the question of forbidden foods at length, would have agreed. Unless the act was consciously and admittedly committed in contempt of the Church, it did not in itself render the offender suspect of heresy; and torture *super intentione* was never to be applied in any case before the tribunal, unless the suspicion against the accused was of a vehement or serious nature.[182]

As we have seen, the central tribunal's quest for correct procedure and uniformity throughout its vast system of provincial courts resulted in a series of measures which assigned the final disposition of all but the most ordinary cases to Rome.[183] And the cardinal inquisitors hesitated to pass judgment until they were genuinely convinced that they were in full possession of all the facts, including extenuating circumstances.[184] In the case of a grocer of Legnago who had denied the immortality of the soul, they determined that he had come to his erroneous opinion "through ignorance and passion and that he had not learned it consciously from others";[185] and before proceeding to a decision against a monk of the order of San Salvador who had run away from his monastery, they wanted to know at what age he had entered his religious vocation.[186] In the case of a blasphemer from Bologna who had desecrated a crucifix, they needed to be informed whether his sacrilege had been committed while in a state of reason or during a fit of anger, and whether he had been an offender before, "because these circumstances diminish the seriousness of the crime." Madness and anger were admissible as extenuating factors, but only after thorough investigation.[187]

It is impossible to condone coercion, the stake, and the other horrors perpetrated in the name of religion during the Reformation era. They were employed not only by the Inquisition but by virtually all other judicial bodies in Europe. In the sixteenth century they were an unquestioned part of legal proceedings. But I believe that future research will show that they were used less frequently, with greater moderation, and with a higher regard for human rights and life in the tribunals of the Holy Office than elsewhere. Skepticism and incredulity in regard to witchcraft invaded Roman legal circles between the end of the sixteenth and the beginning of the seventeenth centuries at a time when the lands north of the Pyrenees and the Alps remained in the grip of a witch-hunting mania. It was a modest step toward sanity, and a glimmer of hope at the end of a dark tunnel.

Notes

1. For an orientation and the appropriate general bibliography on the history and organization of the institution, see my "Preliminary Observations" at pp. 12–14, esp. notes 16–22. I should like to add the following older titles which were inadvertently omitted: P. Hinschius, *System des katholischen Kirchenrechts, mit besonderer Rücksicht auf Deutschland*, 6 vols. (Berlin, 1869–97), esp. 1:448–51 for the reorganization of 1542; 6:420–25 for the inquisitorial trial; and 5:449–92 on the medieval origins and the underlying legal theory and practice; C. Henner, *Beiträge zur Organisation und Competenz der päpstlichen Ketzergerichte* (Leipzig, 1890). Although the work concentrates on the medieval foundations, later developments are discussed. It is worth noting that the University of Pennsylvania Library copy of the *Beiträge* which came to me on inter-library loan was personally inscribed by Henner to Hinschius and is profusely annotated by the recipient. Despite its title, M. Heimbucher, *Die Orden und Kongregationen der katholischen Kirche*, 3 vols. (Paderborn, 1907–8) devotes only one page to the medieval Inquisition (2:118) and deals exclusively with the religious orders. The Congregations founded in the sixteenth century, into which papal government was divided, are ignored.

2. There is an abundant literature on the medieval phase of the Inquisition. One of the single best general treatments remains H. Maisonneuve, *Études sur les origines de l'inquisition*, 2nd ed. (Paris, 1960). The background is sketched objectively by M. Bévenot, "The Inquisition and its Antecedents," *The Heythrop Journal* 7 (1966): 257–68, 381–93; 8 (1967): 52–69, 152–68. See now the richly documented essay by J. Given, "The Inquisitors of Languedoc and the Medieval Technology of Power," *American Historical Review* 94 (1989): 336–59. See also the survey of the literature by G. Gonnet, "Recent European Historiography on the Medieval Inquisition," in *The Inquisition in Early Modern Europe: Studies on Sources and Methods*, edited by G. Henningsen and J. Tedeschi in association with C. Amiel (De Kalb, 1986), 199–223, and the bibliographical essay in E. Peters, *Inquisition* (New York and London, 1988), esp. pp. 317–19. Specifically on the underlying legal theory, in addition to the works cited above, see O. Ruffino, "Ricerche sulla condizione giuridica degli eretici nel pensiero dei glossatori," *Rivista di storia del diritto italiano* 46 (1973): 30–190, and W. Trusen, "Der Inquisitionsprozess: Seine historischen Grundlagen und frühen Formen," *Zeitschrift der Savigny-Stiftung für Rechtsgeschichte: Kanonistische Abteilung*

105 (1988): 168–230. For a rather general comparison with the modern form of the institution (primarily the Spanish), see T. R. Ruiz, "La Inquisición medieval y la moderna: Paralelos y contrastes," in A. Alcalá, ed., *Inquisición española y mentalidad inquisitorial* (Barcelona, 1984), 45–66, and in English, with a misleading title, "The Holy Office in Medieval France and in Late Medieval Castile: Origins and Contrasts," in A. Alcalá, ed., *The Spanish Inquisition and the Inquisitorial Mind* (Boulder, 1987), 33–51.

3. On the Spanish Inquisition see the Bibliography to this volume and the notes in "Toward a Statistical Profile of the Italian Inquisitions," esp. notes 1 and 2. For a comparison of the Spanish and Italian tribunals, the recent studies by A. Borromeo cited in the Bibliography are useful. Eagerly awaited is his "Spanische und römische Inquisition" announced for the *Vorträge* of the Institut für Europäische Geschichte, Mainz. Two inquisitorial manuals offer special insights: the Spaniard Francisco Peña, who spent much of his career in Holy Office circles in Rome, remarked on differences between Spanish and Roman procedures in his extensive commentary to Nicolau Eymeric's *Directorium Inquisitorum* (Rome, 1578, etc.; I cite from the Rome, 1587 edition) and in his *Instructio seu Praxis Inquisitorum* published posthumously in Cesare Carena's *Tractatus de Officio Sanctissimae Inquisitionis* (Bologna, 1668), 348–434. The *Tractatus* itself is an important source because it is based on Carena's long service as *consultore* and Fiscal Advocate in the tribunal of Cremona, in Spanish Lombardy. See 9 ff.: "De Supremo Tribunali Inquisitionis in Regnis Hispaniarum." Descriptions of the workings of the Spanish Inquisition began to be compiled in Rome itself. Among the handbooks drawn up at the order of the Congregation of the Holy Office containing sections "De S.to Officio Hispaniarum," see BAV, Borg. lat. 558, fols. 1r–9v. Immediately subsequent entries deal with Aragon, Catalonia, Evora, Granada, Portugal ("Lusitaniae"), Sardinia, and Sicily. For an excellent, detailed analysis of the components of the Spanish inquisitorial trial, see now J.-P. Dedieu, "L'Inquisition et le droit: Analyse formelle de la procedure inquisitoriale en cause de foi," *Melanges de la Casa de Velazquez* 23 (1987): 227–51.

4. See L. von Pastor, *The History of the Popes from the Close of the Middle Ages*, 40 vols. (St. Louis, 1898–1953), 12:503. The Bull, dated 21 July 1542, is published in C. Cocquelines, *Bullarum, privilegiorum ac diplomatum pontificum amplissima collectio*, 14 vols. (Rome, 1733–62), 4, pt. 1: 211–12, and summarized in B. J. Kidd, *The Counter-Reformation, 1550–1600* (London, 1933; reprinted 1937, 1958), 43. The way for *Licet ab Initio* was paved by an earlier Bull *In Apostolici Culminis* (14 January 1542) (see n. 10 below).

5. See J. Delumeau, "Les progrès de la centralisation dans l'état pontifical au XVIe siècle," *Revue historique* 226 (1961): 399–410; P. Prodi, *La crisi religiosa del XVI secolo* (Bologna, 1964), 112 ff.; idem, *Lo sviluppo dell'assolutismo nello stato pontificio, secoli XV–XVI. 1. La monarchia papale e gli organi centrali di governo* (Bologna, 1968); idem, *Il sovrano pontefice* (Bologna, 1982), now in English translation, *The Papal Prince, One Body and Two Souls: The Papal Monarchy in Early Modern Europe*, trans. S. Haskins (Cambridge, 1987). For a testing of the thesis of a "reformed"

sixteenth-century cardinalate, see A. V. Antonovics, "Counter-Reformation Cardinals: 1534–90," *European Studies Review* 2 (1972): 301–28.

6. See C. Carena, *Tractatus*, 15: "Hodie tamen a dictis Generalibus et Provincialibus non eliguntur Inquisitores, sed immediate a Sanctissimo Domino nostro, vel per breve, quomodo eligi solent Inquisitor Mediolani & Genuae, vel per literas patentes . . . a Sacra Congregatione . . . emanatas." The authority to remove an inquisitor from office also had passed from the orders to Rome. See Peña's commentary to Eymeric's *Directorium Inquisitorum*, 541: "Hodie nullae sunt horum praelatorum partes in removendis inquisitoribus, nam reverendiss. domini cardinales inquisitores generales. . ., ex causa, re mature cognita (ut decet) inquisitores removent, mutant, ac de uno, cum expedit, ad alium locum transferunt." Requests for appointments and recommendations flooded the correspondence of the cardinal protector of the Dominican order. See the calendar in S. L. Forte, "I Domenicani nel carteggio del card. Scipione Borghese, protettore dell'Ordine (1606–1633)," *AFP* 30 (1960): 351–416.

Principally, Franciscans were inquisitors in Venice (until 1560) and in Tuscany. By 1645 the fourteen inquisitors assigned to the entire Venetian dominion were evenly divided between Franciscans and Dominicans. See P. F. Grendler, *The Roman Inquisition and the Venetian Press, 1540–1605* (Princeton, 1977), 48n. There seems to have been a general sentiment that Franciscans—considered more prone to leniency, of greater independence of spirit, even susceptible to Reformation currents—were less suited for the office than Dominicans. See the harsh estimate in the letter to Duke Ercole II d'Este written by Girolamo Papino, his observer at the Council of Trent, dated Bologna, 25 February 1549: "Et quantunque li frati de San Francesco habiano la inquisitione de Romagna, non sono a proposito per castigar costui . . . et credetemi che quelli che procurano che sia datto in mane a frati de San Francesco lo fano per liberarlo, sapendo che ditti frati mai castigano heretici." In a subsequent letter to his superior, Papino actually asserted that "frati minori favoriscono li heretici." See F. Valenti, "Il carteggio di padre Girolamo Papino informatore estense dal Concilio di Trento durante il periodo bolognese," *Archivio storico italiano* 124, T. 451 (1966): 303–417, at pp. 403, 406. (It is well to remember that Papino was himself a Dominican.) There is evidence that both Paul IV and Pius V also had a low opinion of the Franciscans' capacity to serve as inquisitors. In 1567 Pius transferred responsibility for the Inquisition of Romagna from the very conventuals excoriated by Papino, to the Dominicans of San Andrea in Faenza. See F. Lanzoni, *La controriforma nella città e diocesi di Faenza* (Faenza, 1925), 156 f. On Pius's displeasure with the work of the Franciscan inquisitors in Verona and Vicenza, see A. Righi, "Eretici a Verona nella seconda metà del secolo XVI," *Nuovo archivio veneto*, ser. 3, 20 (1910): 305–13 at p. 305. Cf. "The Roman Inquisition and Witchcraft" at n. 51 for a reference to the trial of the Franciscan inquisitor of Venice, Fra Marino, on suspicion of harboring Protestant sympathies.

For an example of the selection process to replace an inquisitor who had asked to be relieved because of his "indisposition," see the letter of Cardinal Arrigoni to the inquisitor of Bologna, 25 (?) February 1606 (BA, MS. B-1863, fol. 14): "Si sono lette le sue de' 15 con le quali dimanda licenza d'esser liberata dal carico di cotesta Inquisitione per l'infirmità che patisce de gl'occhi . . . [the cardinals of the Congregation] hanno ordinato che si facciano le liste de' soggetti atti ad essercitare cotesto offitio per fare elettione del nuovo inquisitore, come a suo tempo ne sarà avvisata."

7. See Peña's annotations to Eymeric's *Directorium Inquisitorum*, 539: "Certissima est autem haec Eymerici doctrina, inquisitores enim haereticae pravitatis a quocunque eligantur, seu nominentur, semper sunt papae delegati, & ab eo accipiunt iurisdictionem & potestatem. . . ."

8. Every inquisitorial manual contains a lengthy discussion of the respective roles of bishop and inquisitor. See, for example, Umberto Locati's *Opus quod iudiciale inquisitorum dicitur ex diversis theologis et I.U.D. . . . nuper extractum . . . nunc auctum et correctum* (Rome, 1570), 168 f. Locati (d. 1587) had served as commissioner general of the Holy Office in Rome. The precedence of the inquisitor over the bishop in the pursuit of heresy stemmed from the fact that the former was delegated to his office by the pope and could cite witnesses and pursue suspects even outside his area of jurisdiction. In hierarchical terms a bishop outranked an inquisitor, but an inquisitor preceded an episcopal vicar. On the bishop's competence in heresy cases, see Peña's *Instructio seu Praxis Inquisitorum*, in Carena's *Tractatus*, 434: "Soli episcopi procedere solent, & possunt contra haereticos, & suspectos de haeresi in omnibus provinciis, & locis, ubi non sunt apostolici inquisitores. . . ." See also n. 112 below.

9. For an actual example, see the case of Rainero Manzella, a Neapolitan, who in 1564 was transferred from the prison of the governor of Rome, the Torre di Nona, to the Holy Office for trial when heretical activity on his part came to light. This information is taken from his sentence, dated 8 February 1567, now preserved in TCD, MS. 1224, fol. 116. The principle is reaffirmed in a decree of the Roman Congregation dated 24 October 1584: L. von Pastor, *Allgemeine Dekrete der römischen Inquisition* (Freiburg i. Br., 1912), 39. Naturally, it would be difficult for the Inquisition to apply this provision outside the papal states. Everywhere else its activities were conducted at the pleasure of the lay authorities.

10. The lifting of exemptions from inquisitorial prosecution for members of orders was accomplished by Paul III (and renewed by successive pontiffs) with the Bull *In Apostolici Culminis*, dated 14 January 1542 (Cocquelines, *Bullarum*, 4, pt. 1: 194–95). Before this a religious was under the exclusive jurisdiction of his superior. This was emphasized, for example, in various decrees concerning Franciscans: B. Fontana, "Documenti vaticani contro l'eresia luterana in Italia," *ASRSP* 15 (1892): 71–165, 365–474, at pp. 140, 158 (memorials dated 23 June 1534 and 15 December 1537). See also Simancas, *De Catholicis Institutionibus Liber* (Rome, 1575), 263: "Demum procedere possunt contra quoscunque apostatas, haereticos & suspectos, etiam si multis magnisque privilegiis, dignitatibus, aut exemptionibus illi muniti sint. Nulla enim praerogativa cuiquam prodesse potest, ut a iurisdictione inquisitorum eximatur. . . ." See also at p. 264: "Sunt autem aliqua inquisitoribus prohibita . . . pri-

mum, ne in episcopos, vel superiores praelatos inquirant, nisi hoc fuerit illis expresse commissum. Deinde prohibetur eis, ne adversus nuntios, vel alios officiales apostolicae sedis procedant insciente papa, sed possunt examinare testes, ut papam consulant. . . ." The Supreme Roman Congregation expressed its disbelief to the inquisitor of Modena that his vicar in Camporeggiano had been gathering evidence against the bishop of Sarzana "senza partecipazione di questa S. Congregatione." See BAV, Barb. lat. 6334, fol. 75v (letter dated 28 March 1626).

11. See "Preliminary Observations," at p. 6.

12. See BAV, Borg. lat. 558, fols. 44r, 46r, 48r. An idea of the network in the seventeenth century is provided by a list of provincial inquisitors who were decreed by the pope on 30 June 1633 to receive notification of Galileo's sentence. See A. Favaro, *Galileo e l'Inquisizione: Documenti del processo Galileiano esistenti nell' Archivio del S. Uffizio e nell' Archivio Segreto Vaticano per la prima volta integralmente pubblicati* (Florence, 1907), 103 ff.

13. Descriptions of the Milanese, Bolognese, and Modenese establishments are contained respectively in L. Fumi, "L'Inquisizione romana e lo stato di Milano," *ASL*, ser. 4, 13 (1910): 5–124, 285–414; 14 (1910): 145–220, esp. pp. 8 ff. in the first installment; A. Battistella, *Il S. Officio e la riforma religiosa in Bologna* (Bologna, 1905), passim; A. Biondi, "Lunga durata e microarticolazione nel territorio di un ufficio dell' Inquisizione: Il 'Sacro Tribunale' a Modena (1292–1785)," *Annali dell' Istituto storico italo-germanico in Trento* 8 (1982): 73–90, esp. pp. 81 ff. The inquisitorial tribunals in Modena, the Veneto, Turin, Genoa, Lombardy and Tuscany are surveyed in R. Canosa, *Storia dell'Inquisizione in Italia dalla metà del Cinquecento alla fine del Settecento*, 5 vols. to date (Rome, 1986–).

For the various officials who comprised a tribunal—inquisitors, bishops, vicars, consultors, "public defenders," notaries, jailers, "familiars," see Carena, *Tractatus*, pt. 1, pp. 10–42. One of the most elusive is the so-called "Fiscal Advocate," (ibid., 31–35) even though he is described by the author as "minister intimus & necessarius S. Officii & sine quo causae S. Officii non expediuntur." His role, roughly, was that of prosecutor, without incurring any of the liabilities attached to the accuser in the medieval period. "Munus Advocati Fiscalis consistit in porrigenda accusatione contra haereticos, post assumptas in summario iud. contra eos informationes. . . . Fiscales accusare non possunt, nisi inquisitione, vel delatione praecedente. . . . Debet etiam dicta testium exquirere, libros denunciationum revolvere, ut quos reos cognoverit, possit coram inquisitoribus instare, ut carceribus mancipentur & debitis poenis mulctentur . . ." (ibid., 33). On the positions of vicar and notary, see below at notes 29, 33. The medieval origins of the lay confraternity which assisted the inquisitor in various aspects of his work are traced by L. Paolini, "Le origini della 'Societas Crucis,'" *Rivista di storia e letteratura religiosa* 15 (1979): 173–229.

14. Although he was an Augustinian, Fra Adeodato da Siena served as provisional inquisitor of Siena in 1559. See V. Marchetti, *Gruppi ereticali senesi del Cinquecento* (Florence, 1975), 176 and *DBI* 1 (1960): 274. Adeodato was himself

investigated and absolved by the Inquisition in Rome in 1544 over doctrines expressed in a sermon delivered in Treviso.

15. See the letter from the Roman Congregation to the bishop of Como, 4 July 1626 (BAV, Barb. lat. 6334, fol. 179r). In reply to a question from the provincial official the Congregation stated that the custom varied, but the tribunal could very well be held in the episcopal palace when the bishop was present. See also the letter from the Congregation to the inquisitor of Vicenza, written two weeks later (18 July; ibid, fol. 196r): "Si è fatto col S.re Car.le Cornaro nuovo vescovo di Vicenza l'uffitio perchè assegni per gli esami nelle cause del S.to Officio una stanza nel suo palazzo episcopale, et se n'è riportata buona intentione. . . ." On the Venetian situation see the long late sixteenth-century report by the nuncio Alberto Bolognetti in A. Stella, ed., *Chiesa e stato nelle relazioni dei nunzi pontifici a Venezia: Ricerche sul giurisdizionalismo veneziano dal XVI al XVIII secolo*, Studi e Testi, 239 (Vatican City, 1964), 293: "Il Tribunal di Venetia non ha ancora luogo dove si faccino le congregationi chè, se bene nell'altre città del Dominio si fanno . . . nel palazzo del vescovato, non si fanno però in Venetia nel palazzo del patriarcato" for reasons of distance, etc. "Di presente [in Venice] le congregationi dell' Inquisitione non si fanno sempre nell' istesso luogo, ma la estate in una chiesetta contigua a S. Marco et il verno in una stanza della canonica . . ." (ibid., 294).

16. The limit in age was established by the Clementine *Nolentes* at the Council of Vienne in 1311–12. See *Repertorium Inquisitorum Pravitatis Haereticae* (Venice, 1588), 306. See also Eymeric's *Directorium Inquisitorum* and Peña's commentary (p. 536): ". . . nam et experientia docet, in tam iuvenili aetate non facile contingere tam acre adesse iudicium, & tantam prudentiam, quanta ad hoc gravissimum officium exercendum requiruntur." As for the lower minimum age for bishops, Peña subscribed to the view of the famous jurist Panormitanus (Niccolò de Tudeschi) that they were chosen with more care than inquisitors: ". . . sed officium Inquisitionis non committitur cum tanta indagatione. . . ." Thirty years sufficed for the inquisitor's vicar (ibid., 548). Cf. Carena, *Tractatus*, 15: "Nam hodie, quoniam eliguntur, vel immediate a Papa, vel a Sacra Congregatione, nec Papa, nec Sacra Congregatione ligatur dispositione dictae Clementinae. . . ." And Carena recalls that Giovanni Battista Martinengo had scarcely passed thirty years of age when he was appointed inquisitor in Carena's own tribunal of Cremona (p. 16). Ippolito-Maria Beccaria, within a period of 7 years, 1582–89, was twice prior, once provincial, inquisitor of Milan (1588), *Commissario* of the Holy Office in Rome, and general of his order before reaching the age of forty. See D. A. Mortier, *Histoire des Maîtres Généraux de l'Ordre des Frères Prêcheurs*, 8 vols. (Paris, 1903–30), 6:2–3.

17. See Peña's commentary in Eymeric's *Directorium Inquisitorum*, 534 f. Eymeric favored the election of a theologian as inquisitor, Simancas a jurist (*De Catholicis Institutionibus*, 535). Peña himself was a master in theology and doctor in both canon and civil law. On the differing usages between Italy and Spain, see Carena, *Tractatus*, 18. R. Creytens ("Il Registro dei maestri degli studenti di Bologna [1576–1604]," *AFP* 46 [1976]: 25–114) records the promotion of inquisitors in Bologna to the

grade of master in theology in the period 1589–1604, a total of twelve names.

18. See Peña's annotations to Eymeric's *Directorium Inquisitorum*, 429: "Primum est prudentia, quae in iudice violatae religionis debet esse maxima . . . alterum est peritia, & notitia non mediocris dogmatum, sectarum, errorum, vitae, & morum ipsorum haereticorum, tam veterum quam recentiorum: sine his enim ferme impossibile est Inquisitorem recte suo munere fungi posse."

19. See the documents cited at length in "Inquisitorial Sources and Their Uses," at notes 103 ff. The tension between inquisitors and their superiors in the orders went back to the early years of their relationship, as we see from Alexander IV's *Catholicae Fidei* pronounced in 1260 to protect the freedom of action of inquisitors against possible interference on the part of "magister & minister generales aliique priores, & ministri provinciales, ac custodes, seu guardiani aliquorum locorum vestrorum ordinum, praetextu quorumqumque . . ." (published in the *Litterae Apostolicae* appended to Eymeric, *Directorium Inquisitorum*, 40).

20. It is safe to assume that the letter addressed by the Supreme Congregation to the inquisitor of Aquileia and Concordia went to all the tribunals. See ACAU, Epistolae S. Officii, 1614–46 (4 November 1623; unpaginated): "Reverendo Padre. Desiderando questi miei SS.ri Ill.mi essere informati di quello che si è fatto et si fa in cotesta inquisitione, hanno ordinato che V.R. al ricevere di questa mandi una nota distinta delle denuntie date costì dal principio di questo anno sino al giorno di oggi, tanto di quelle che non si sono proseguite, significandone la causa, perchè si sono lasciate in sospeso, quanto delle proseguite, con avvisare, se il processo che vi si è formato sopra, è terminato, o no, et essendo terminato, in che modo si sia venuto alla speditione, et in caso, che tuttavia penda, in che stato si trovi. Il che ella eseguirà subito, con mandare quì la relatione tanto distinta e chiara, che i sudetti miei S.ri Ill.mi veggano la sua diligenza, et sufficienza in far l'ufficio suo. . . ."

21. See "Inquisitorial Sources and Their Uses," at notes 91 f.

22. A letter, requiring a careful accounting of all property and transactions was addressed to all provincial tribunals. I quote from the copy in BRB, MS. II 290, vol. 2, fol. 177, letter, dated 5 December 1603, from Cardinal Borghese to the Florentine inquisitor: "Per degni et ragionevoli rispetti questi Ill.mi et R.mi SS.ri Cardinali miei colleghi hanno risoluto, che nell'archivio di questo S.to Officio si tenga un libro dove si annotino tutte le intrate et rendite delle Inquisitioni particolari et si registrino le scritture de' titoli et acquisti fatti di esse, acciochè in ogni tempo, et in ogni occorrenza se ne possa havere notitia qui commodamente . . . ch'ella mandi copia autentica di tutte le bolle di unioni di beneficii, o riservatione di pensioni . . . con gl'inventarii de' beni delle chiese unite, et anco la copia autentica di tutti gli acquisti per via di contratti, donationi, ultime volontà, o che in altra maniera si siano fatti sin qui a cotesta inquisitione con la copia dell'inventario de' beni stabili, o rendite non vacabili che'l S.to Officio gode, et possiede in qualsivoglia modo . . ." (I have seen a copy of this letter also among the correspondence of the inquisitors of Bologna and of Aquileia and Concordia). See also the earlier letters from the cardinal of Santa Severina, 1 August 1598, requesting a detailed listing of what prisoners

were being charged for the various inquisitorial services. This too is a circular letter. I cite from the Udine copy addressed to the inquisitor of Aquileia and Concordia (ACAU, Epistolae S. Officii, 1588–1613, unpaginated): ". . . mandi quanto prima copia delle tasse delle mercedi, che si pagano da processati in cotesta inquisitione, così per le spese del vitto, scritture de' notarii, et altri officiali, come anco a lei medesima in qual si voglia modo, con dare anco avviso di tutto quello che si paga per stile et consuetudine, ancora che non sia scritto nelle tasse. . . ." For the cardinal's advice to seek investments at 7 percent interest, see ibid., letter of 3 October 1598. Permission to keep a horse followed a month or so later, on 28 November: "Si sono ricevuti i conti di cotesta inquisitione, et quanto al tenere il cavallo per i bisogni occorrenti di fare spesso viaggi per le cause et altri negotii del Santo Uffizio, i detti SS.ri Cardinali si contentano ch'ella possa tenerlo." For the study of an individual tribunal, see A. Prosperi, "Il 'budget' di un inquisitore: Ferrara, 1567–1572," *Schifanoia* 2 (1987): 31–40.

23. See "The Dispersed Archives of the Roman Inquisition" at notes 23 ff. With a letter dated 19 September 1580 the cardinal of Santa Severina instructed the inquisitor of Florence (BRB, MS. II 290, fol. 58) to inform himself about the Florentine merchant Filippo Corsini, who had been residing in London for several years, to determine the contacts he was maintaining at home, the attempts he might be making to lure others abroad, etc. For the surveillance of foreign merchants in Milan, see M. Bendiscioli, "Penetrazione protestante e repressione controriformistica in Lombardia all' epoca di Carlo e Federico Borromeo," in E. Iserloh and P. Manns, eds., *Festgabe Joseph Lortz*, 2 vols. (Baden-Baden, 1958), 1:369–404, at pp. 394 ff. For the inspection of "hospitii dove alloggiano oltramontani . . . per vedere alla cucina se trova cibi prohibiti," see A. Stella, ed., *Chiesa e stato*, 385.

24. On the inspection of bales of merchandise for contraband books, see Grendler, *The Roman Inquisition and the Venetian Press, 1540–1605*, 185 ff. and passim; on measures to prevent the disappearance of Christian children, see BAV, Barb. lat. 1370, p. 291, summary of a letter to the inquisitor of Venice (18 July 1592) from the Roman Congregation: "Commendatur Inquisitor Venetiarum qui obtinuit . . . fieri posse [?] perquisitionem in navibus Turcarum, ne pueros Christianorum ad Turcos conducant pro fidem abneganda."

25. On the synagogue restrictions, see BAV, Barb. lat. 1370, pp. 314–16, excerpts of letters from the Roman Congregation to various bishops and inquisitors, ranging in date from 1597 to 1601. The petition for Christian domestics is contained in BAV, Borg. lat. 558, fols. 69r–v.

26. BAV, Barb. lat. 6334, fols. 36v, 77r, 164r. See, as an example, the letter dated 14 February: "Per urgente bisogno della fortificatione che la Republica di Genova fa fare nella Piazza di Gavi è stata supplicata la S.tà di N.S.re a concederli la persona di V. R. per 15 giorni. . . ."

27. Ibid., letter from the Roman Congregation to the inquisitor of Cremona, 22 August 1626: ". . . ma più di tutto si preme in che si reintegri l'amore fra lui, la moglie, socero et socera, però saranno le parti di V.R. di fargli in questa parte

una buona esortatione et procurare anche con l'auttorità del S.re Cardinale che segua fra loro intiera reconciliatione."

28. See A. Stella, "Il processo veneziano di Guglielmo Postel," *RSCI* 22 (1968): 425–66, at p. 454.

29. On the qualifications and prerogatives pertaining to the office of vicar general, see Eymeric, *Directorium Inquisitorum* and Peña's accompanying commentary, pp. 545 ff. The vicar had to have reached thirty years of age and possess qualities resembling the inquisitor's, for whom he had to substitute. Confirmation of the appointment by Rome was reiterated in the *Ordini Generali* of 1611 (cited in full at n. 58): ". . . e nell' elettione de' vicarii non si risolveranno senza participatione de gl'illustrissimi & reverendissimi Signori Cardinali Generali Inquisitori." The provincial inquisitor was expected to nominate several prospects from which the Congregation chose one. See BAV, Barb. lat. 6334, fol. 160v, letter to the inquisitor in Turin: "Approvano questi miei SS.ri Ill.mi la persona di fra Gio. Battista Balbi proposto da V.R. per vicario di cotesta inquisitione, essendosi havute buone relationi della sua integrità et sufficienza. Potrà V. R. deputarlo a suo beneplacito avvertendo in altre simili occasioni di nominare alla S. Congregatione conforme al solito più d'un soggetto. . . ." On the inferior grade of vicar, see Peña's annotations to Eymeric's *Directorium Inquisitorum*, 538 and the instructions prepared for their rural officials by successive inquisitors of Modena: Arcangelo Calbetti, *Sommaria instruttione a' suoi RR. vicarii nella Inquisitione sodetta intorno alla maniera di trattar alla giornata i negotii del Sant' Ufficio per quello che a loro s'appartiene* (Modena, 1604); and Michelangelo Lerri, *Breve informatione del modo di trattare le cause del S. Officio per li molto reverendi vicarii della Sancta Inquisitione, instituiti nelle diocesi di Modena, di Carpi, di Nonantola e della Garfagnana* (Modena, 1608). See also P. M. Festa, *Breve informatione del modo di trattare le cause del S. Officio per li molto R.R. vicarii della Santa Inquisitione istituiti nella diocesi di Bologna* (Bologna, 1604); Pierantonio Gherardi, *Breve istruzione . . . per i novelli vicari foranei del S. Uffizio* (Rome, 1752). The best modern study on the office and functions of the vicariate is A. Prosperi's suggestive study, "Vicari dell' Inquisizione fiorentina alla metà del Seicento: Note d'Archivio," *Annali dell'Istituto storico italo-germanico in Trento* 8 (1982): 275–304 which, in appendix, lists the names of all the officials serving the inquisitor of Florence in 1657, almost 150 names of vicars, consultors, censors of books, physicians, notaries, etc.

30. See "Inquisitorial Sources and Their Uses," notes 33 ff.

31. See "The Dispersed Archives of the Roman Inquisition" and "Toward a Statistical Profile of the Italian Inquisitions."

32. See P. H. Jobe, "Inquisitorial Manuscripts in the Biblioteca Apostolica Vaticana: A Preliminary Handlist," in *The Inquisition in Early Modern Europe*, 33–53.

33. See BRB, MS. II 290, vol. 2, fol. 172, letter of the cardinal of Santa Severina to the inquisitor of Florence, dated Rome, 18 November 1600: "Per ordine della S.tà di N.ro S.re, V.ra R.tia per l'avvenire nello essamine de' testimonii, et costituti de'rei nel S.to Officio faccia scrivere per extensum tutti gli interrogatorii, obiettioni et repliche per ovviare à pregiudicii che si fanno in non scriversi gl'interrogatorii,

et per vedere se siano suggestivi o no." This was a circular letter addressed to all inquisitors. Cf. E. Masini, *Sacro Arsenale ovvero prattica dell' officio della Santa Inquisitione* (Bologna, 1665), 157: "Et procureranno i giudici, che il notaro scriva non solamente tutte le risposte del reo, ma anco tutti i ragionamenti e moti che farà, e tutte le parole ch' egli proferirà ne' tormenti, anzi tutti i sospiri, tutte le grida, tutti i lamenti e le lagrime che manderà." Masini served as inquisitor of Genoa, 1609–27. The first edition of the *Arsenale* was published in 1621.

On legislation regulating the appointment of the notary, see S. Abbiati, "Intorno ad una possibile valutazione giuridico-diplomatica del documento inquisitorio," *Studi di storia medioevale e di diplomatica* 3 (1978): 167–79, at p. 175 n. and C. Henner, *Beiträge*, 115–37. Permission for the inquisitor or his vicar to select their own notaries was granted by Pius IV only in 1561 with his privilege *Pastoralis Officii Cura*. On the general question of the reliability of trial records, see also "Inquisitorial Sources and Their Uses," note 6.

34. See Simancas, *De Catholicis Institutionibus*, 266: "Et ut iam ante dixi, inquisitores non tantum iudices, sed etiam curatores & patres reorum esse debent. Plus erga corrigendos agat benevolentia, quam severitas . . . plus exhortatio, quam comminatio, plus charitas, quam potestas. . . ."

35. Masini, *Sacro Arsenale*, 15. See S. Razzi (*Istoria degli uomini illustri così nelle prelature, come nelle dottrine, del sacro Ordine degli Predicatori* [Lucca, 1596], 314), who claims the saint as "singolare advocato e patrone de i nostri padri inquisitori."

36. See ACAU, Epistolae S. Officii, 1588–1613 (unpaginated), letter of Cardinal Millino to the inquisitor of Aquileia and Concordia, dated 12 December 1609 (the Supreme Congregation had received a summary of a trial against Fra Angelo Alpino da Marostica): "Nel leggere detto sommario si è considerato che V.R. non ha fatto scrivere le risposte di detto frate nel secondo constituto sotto pretesto che non intendeva i termini. Di più a i testimonii ha fatto alcuni interrogatorii suggestivi, et nel riferire i detti di alcuni testimonii nel sommario, pone il loro detto con queste parole, 'Ho sentito quanto di sopra,' onde l'avertisco de i sudetti difetti acciò per l'avvenire se ne astenga, dovendo far scrivere et non tralasciare le risposte de i rei, et far i sommarii più pieni, chiari et distinti per deliberar meglio intorno alle speditioni delle cause." See especially the discussion in "Inquisitorial Sources and Their Uses," at notes 7 ff.

37. For the vow of absolute secrecy which even the cardinals of the Roman Congregation had to take, see their decree dated 25 January 1560 in Pastor, *Allgemeine Dekrete*, 24. Witnesses too had to take an oath of silence, and incurred heavy penalties if they revealed their testimony outside the trial chamber. See Carena, *Tractatus*, 229. Secrecy must have been difficult to obtain, and officials needed to be reminded of this obligation. See, for example, the circular letter of Cardinal Arrigoni of the Roman Congregation addressed to all provincial tribunals. I cite from the copy to the inquisitor of Bologna, 24 December 1611 (BA, MS. B–1864, fol. 43) accompanying a papal edict requiring that the inquisitor take a solemn oath of secrecy in the presence of his consultors. The fact had to be authenticated by a notary and

the act forwarded to Rome, as well as registered in the books of the local Holy Office.
38. See below at notes 80 ff.
39. See BA, MS. B–1860, fol. 109 dated 10 January 1573, letter from the assistant of the cardinal of Pisa, a member of the Roman Congregation, to the inquisitor of Bologna: "Gli dico solo che per mio conseglio, farà bene di mai lassare partire alcuno inditiato doppo l'esamine perchè è cosa molto pericolosa, o della fuga, o dell'andare a consultarsi, o d'avisare complici. Questo dico per conto di quel giovene ch'ha carcerato doppo il 2o esamine."
40. Masini, *Sacro Arsenale*, 360.
41. BA, MS. B–1860, fol. 160, letter from Fra Paolo da Ferrara, dated 7 November 1573.
42. Ibid., fol. 119. On the *Commissario*, who functioned as a sort of chief administrative officer for the Congregation of the Inquisition, see I. Taurisano, "Series Chronologica Commissariorum S. Romanae Inquisitionis ab Anno 1542 ad annum 1916," *Analecta Sacri Ordinis Fratrum Praedicatorum* (1916): 495–506. On Balduzzi (d. 1580), who served in this post from 1572 to 1576, see p. 499. He hailed from Forlì, himself served as inquisitor of Bologna, 1560–1572, as well as prior of San Domenico, before being appointed inquisitor of Milan, a position which regularly served as the stepping stone to promotion to *Commissario*. Cf. A. Battistella, *Il S. Officio e la riforma religiosa in Bologna*, 199.
43. BA, MS. B–1861, fol. 133. See also the *Editto del Maest.[ro] F. Francesco Galassini Generale Inquisitore di Perugia, Umbria, e dell'altre città annesse* (Perugia, 1626), reminding the faithful to denounce heretics to the Holy Office, with the warning, however, that anonymous accusations would be held in no account: ". . . avvertendo, che a questi nostri precetti non sodisfaranno, ne s'intendano sodisfare quelli, che con bollettini, o lettere senza nome, & cognome delli autori, o in altra maniera incerti (delle quali niun conto si tiene nel Sant'Offitio) pretendessero revelare i delinquenti." Cf. F. Peña, *Instructio seu Praxis Inquisitorum*, in Carena's *Tractatus*, 361: "Denunciator non recipitur, nisi praestito per eum iuramento de veritate dicenda."
44. See BAV, Barb. lat. 6334, fol. 166r, letter of the Roman Congregation to the inquisitor of Florence, dated 20 June 1626: "Dal processo mandato da V. R. contra Caterina Ballarini et Maria di Prato, è parso a questi miei SS.ri Ill.mi che non risulti cosa per la quale si possa con fondamento procedere contra di loro. Però V. R. dovrà farle scarcerare, ammonendo l'esorcista, che senza giurisdittione con modi indebiti, et con carcere privato ha proceduto contra di loro."
45. See Peña's commentary to Eymeric's *Directorium Inquisitorum*, 228: "An si sacerdos, aut per imprudentiam, aut per malitiam, aut alia quamvis de causa confessionem revelaverit, ea faciat indicium, aut probabilitatem aliquam, ita ut iudices virtute talis revelationis, seu confessionis possint procedere ad torturam, aut alios actus iudiciales contra reum. Omissis multis, breviter respondeo, hanc confessionem factam de delicto manifestato in confessione sacramentali, nullum penitus effectum operari, nec facere aliquod indicium ad torturam." See also the decree of the Supreme Congregation, 24 April 1593, banning inquisitors and their official families from hear-

ing confessions (Pastor, *Allgemeine Dekrete*, 62): ". . . quod non expediat duos poeniten-
tiarios esse consultores S. Officii ob suspicionem, quae multis oriri potest causa confessionis sacramentalis, ob quam rationem inquisitores prohibentur audire confessiones
sacramentales." As late as 1632 the inquisitor of Turin and his vicar were ordered
to refrain from this practice (BAV, Borg. lat. 558, fol. 105v). See the letter of the
cardinal of Santa Severina to the inquisitor of Aquileia and Concordia, 25 February
1595, refusing permission to a certain Fabio Borcato (or Boreato) "che vorrebbe
essaminare *ad defensam* il suo proprio confessore, et dargli licenza di revelare la confessione. . . ."

46. See the letter of the cardinal of Santa Severina to the inquisitor of Florence,
19 September 1598 (BRB, MS. II 290, vol. 1, fol. 87): "Reverendo padre. Con
l'alligata scrivo al Serenissimo Gran Duca, pregando Sua Altezza a voler commet-
tere la carceratione di Oratio Scarabello orefice, che fa bottega costì a Pontevecchio,
essendo necessaria la sua persona per una causa di molta importanza che pende in
questa S.ta Inquisitione et che sia condotto a Roma alle carceri della medesima Inquisitione. Però V. R.tia la presentarà di persona a Sua Altezza, facendo anco a bocca l'officio."

47. The *Apologia* is critically edited in A. Rotondò, *Camillo Renato, opere, documenti
e testimonianze*, Corpus Reformatorum Italicorum (Florence and Chicago, 1968),
30–89. See p. 289 for Rotondò's conjecture that Fileno was not imprisoned.

48. Masini, *Sacro Arsenale*, 106: ". . . non dovrà esser dal giudice fuorche benig-
namente ricevuto, piacevolmente trattato, e paternamente spedito, senza alcun rigore
di carceri, e senza spese, tormenti, o pene di qualsivoglia sorte. E spontaneo comparente s'intende essere solamente quello, che non prevenuto d'indicii, ne citato,
o ammonito in particolare, viene ad accusare se stesso"; Carena, *Tractatus*, 235:
"Haeretici sponte comparentes, mitissime sunt tractandi." The benevolent treatment
afforded to this class of individual is confirmed by such a hostile critic as Hieronimo
Piazza, an apostate from the Roman Church, who had once served as vicar of the
inquisitor in Osimo (Ancona): ". . . for the Inquisition (as it is true) never punishes
nor treats them with severity, that go and voluntarily accuse themselves of what
sins soever they have committed . . . on the contrary, they are kindly receiv'd, and
privately and secretly dispatch'd only with some salutary penance. . . ." H. B. Piazza, *A Short and True Account of the Inquisition and Its Proceedings . . . in Italy . . .* (London, 1722), 54.

49. *Sacro Arsenale*, 202–11. The quotation is at p. 203. There is no discussion
of witchcraft prosecution in the first edition. The apposite section made its first
appearance in the Genoa, 1625 edition, pp. 175–82. The text borrows heavily from
the Latin Roman *Instructio* which circulated in manuscript for several decades before
it was finally printed at mid-century. See "The Roman Inquisition and Witchcraft."

50. BAV, Barb. lat. 6334, fol. 67v: ". . . dalli processi fatti dal canonico non
consta cosa concludente de' maleficii, se bene egli vi habbi usato isquisita diligenza,
che simili materie sono fallacissime, et come l'esperienza cotidiana mostra assai maggiori nell'apprensione degli huomini che nella realtà de' successi, riducendosi troppo

facilmente a maleficio ogni malattia della quale non sia conosciuta subito la causa, o trovato efficace il rimedio . . . la voce levata, che in Fiorenza et nel contado sieno molte streghe non ha fondamento reale. . . ." On this episode, see also at p. 60 and p. 219.

51. See the authorities cited in "The Question of Magic and Witchcraft," at note 48, and in "The Roman Inquisition and Witchcraft," note 64.

52. See "The Question of Magic and Witchcraft," p. 239.

53. For sixteenth-century restatements of the attitude toward witchcraft in the civil law, see P. Grillando, "Tractatus de sortilegiis," (1st ed. 1536) in the miscellaneous volume edited by F. Peña, *Tractatus illustrium in utraque tum pontificii, tum Caesarei iuris facultate iurisconsultorum de iudiciis criminalibus S. Inquisitionis* (Venice, 1584), 11, pt. 2: fol. 394r: "De iure autem civili haec sortilegia gravius puniuntur, quia iura ipsa multum abhorrent artem maleficam . . . & ideo omnes isti malefici puniuntur ultimo supplicio. . . ."

54. See "The Roman Inquisition and Witchcraft," note 6.

55. See the discussion in "Preliminary Observations," at pp. 8 f.

56. Simancas, *De Catholicis Institutionibus*, 125: "Magna reorum defensio esse poterit, si forte inquisitor suspectus sit, ut reiiciatur, propositis in eum justis reiectionis sive recusationis causis. Veluti si inimicus sit, si coniuravit in reos, aut si tale quippiam probari possit, nec enim ob causas leviores recusatio admittenda est. . . ." Cf. Peña's commentary in Eymeric's *Directorium Inquisitorum*, 452; Carena, *Tractatus*, 285; *Repertorium Inquisitorum*, 453, which advises the judge to proceed cautiously because many, by acting like enemies of the defendants, make themselves liable to rejection. In a case asking for the recusation of the Modenese inquisitor, the Supreme Congregation acquiesced and ordered the trial to be transferred to Bologna. See the letter of Cardinal Millino to the inquisitor of Bologna, 2 May 1614 (BA, MS. B–1864, fol. 132): ". . . ne confidando egli [the accused] nel P. Inquisitore di Modena per alcune cause. . . ." In another instance the Congregation transferred the long, drawn-out trial (1606) of Bartolomeo Betti from the jurisdiction of the inquisitor of Ferrara to Bologna when it suspected that the confessions had been extorted through irregular means (ibid., MS. B–1863, fol. 34). When a Giuseppe Cappa, who was contesting his sentence, asked for his appeal to be heard by a different judge than the inquisitor who had tried him, the Supreme Congregation agreed to take on his case itself. See BAV, Barb. lat. 6334, fol. 277r, letter of the Congregation to the inquisitor of Genoa, 30 October 1626: "Ha supplicato Gioseppe Cappa a N. S.re che la causa d'appellatione da lui interposta da una sentenza di V. R. sia commessa ad un altro giudice in partibus, a che non havendo S. Beat.ne voluto condescendere, ha deliberato che la causa sia revista in questa S. Cong.ne. Piacerà per tanto a V. R. di mandare quantoprima un sommario del suo processo con la copia della sentenza." Other cases are cited by G. Biondi, "Le lettere della Sacra Congregazione romana del Santo Uffizio all'Inquisizione di Modena: Note in margine a un regesto," *Schifanoia* 4 (1989) 98 f. On the classical and medieval origins of the doctrine of removal of the suspect judge, see R. Helmholz, "Canonists and Stan-

dards of Impartiality for Papal Judges Delegate," *Traditio* 25 (1969): 386–404 and L. Fowler, "Recusatio iudicis in Civilian and Canonist Thought," *Studia Gratiana* 15 (1972): 719–85.

57. See at notes 111, 113, 135, etc.

58. See as an example of this procedure, the instructions in the letter of the Commissioner of the Roman Holy Office, Antonio Balduzzi, to the inquisitor of Bologna, 20 September 1572 (BA, MS. B–1860, fol. 85): "V. R. farà giuridicamente offerire le difese al P. F. Ambrosio da Milano nella causa soa, con la copia del processo, ec., et se l'accetta, diteli che deponga quatro o cinque scudi almeno *ad bonum computum* per la copia, perchè la mandarò di quà perchè non voglio mandare tutto'l di nanzi e indrieto quel processo. . . ." On the requirement that the accusations should be in the vernacular, see Peña's *Instructio seu Praxis Inquisitorum* in Carena's *Tractatus*, 418. The printed edict, *Ordini da osservarsi da gl'Inquisitori, per decreto della Sacra Congregatione del Sant'Officio di Roma* (Rome, 1611) specified that "quando li notarii danno le copie del processo alli rei debbano gl'inquisitori avvertire, che le carte siano piene di linee, & parole competentemente, di modo che li rei non siano defraudati." Various manuscript versions of this document were circulated to the provincial tribunals. See "Inquisitorial Sources and Their Uses" at note 104.

59. The fullest and best modern discussions of the defense phase of the trial (the *processo ripetitivo*), as opposed to the prosecution phase (the *processo informativo*), are now contained in M. Firpo's "La fase [difensiva] del processo inquisitoriale del cardinal Morone: documenti e problemi," *Critica storica* 33 (1986): 121–48 and his edition of the records of the Morone trial, especially the defense dossier: M. Firpo and D. Marcatto, *Il processo inquisitoriale del cardinal Giovanni Morone: Edizione critica. III. I documenti difensivi* (Rome, 1985). For the description of the defense documents in a late trial for Lutheranism, see S. Prete, "Le 'Difese' del Capitano Paolino Paolini da Offida al Santo Ufficio (1627)," *RSCI* 15 (1961): 491–97. The manuscript, totaling 30 leaves, is preserved in the Biblioteca Comunale, Fermo (MS. 128, Miscellanea sec. XVII–XVIII). See also Masini, *Sacro Arsenale*, 114 ff., "Del modo di formare il processo ripetitivo e difensivo." See p. 351 on the exclusion as defense witnesses of relatives "sino al quarto grado inclusivamente." The right of the accused to see and rebut the testimony of the prosecution witnesses was emphasized in a decree of the Roman Congregation dated 20 October 1562. See Pastor, *Allgemeine Dekrete*, 25. This right is reaffirmed in a long discussion by Cesare Carena in his *Tractatus* (p. 271) directed against Iacopo de Simancas, who denies to each party the right to interrogate the witnesses of the other. Carena suggests that the Spanish writer may be discussing the usage in his own country, but nowhere is this restriction observed in an Italian inquisitorial court: "Et ratio istius praxis Supremi Tribunalis duplex est. Prima, quia de iure testes ab una parte producti, examinari debent super interrogatoriis partis adversae. . . . Altera est, quod ex non editione nominum testium, & denunciantium satis trunca, & manca redditur defensio reorum in hoc tribunali, absque eo, quod aliud novum speciale inducendo, magis adhuc trunca, & manca eadem defensio raddatur, ex omissione interrogatorium istorum,

ex parte rei, & ita passim observatur contra Symancham in omnibus Inquisitionibus Italiae." See also Peña's step-by-step outline of a typical defense proceeding in his *Instructio seu Praxis Inquisitorum* in Carena, *Tractatus*, 414 ff. But the interrogation of the prosecution witnesses, with questions and challenges prepared by the defendant or his lawyer, was conducted by the inquisitor. One of the most complete treatments of the possibilities for the defense available in secular, as well as in ecclesiastical, proceedings is provided by the Roman jurist Sebastiano Guazzini, *Tractatus ad defensam inquisitorum, carceratorum, reorum et condemnatorum super quocunque crimine*, 2 vols. (Rome, 1614).

The period of time allotted for the preparation of the defense varied from case to case. Don Domenico Morando was allowed five days in 1558; Cardinal Morone was granted one month a year later in an infinitely more complicated trial (M. Firpo, "La fase [difensiva]," 127 f.); Bartolomeo Nelli was permitted ten days in his Sienese trial of 1560 and assigned the services of a lawyer (see V. Marchetti, *Gruppi ereticali senesi*, 192 f.); the *benandante* Maria Panzona received eight days at her Friulian trial in 1619, as well as legal assistance (see C. Ginzburg, *The Night Battles: Witchcraft and Agrarian Cults in the Sixteenth and Seventeenth Centuries*, trans. J. and A. Tedeschi [Baltimore, 1983], 104).

60. Masini, *Sacro Arsenale*, 351: "Se un reo nel Santo Officio allegherà per sua difesa qualche cosa da provarsi, anco in parti assai lontane, e non potrà egli per la sua povertà farla provare, è obligato il giudice in ogni meglior modo a ricercarla, & investigarla, acciò senza difese non si rimanga alcuno in così santo tribunale, & in cosa di tanta importanza." See, as an example, the letter of Cardinal Arrigoni of the Roman Congregation to the inquisitor of Bologna, 26 July 1614, (BA, MS. B-1864, fol. 149): "Per servitio della causa di un carcerato in questo Santo Offitio è necessario che V. R. facci fare diligenza nella Terra di Bagno alla Poretta di cotesto stato di Bologna, se si trova nel libro de' Battesimi un tal Pellegrino figliolo del quondam Sante di Malversi. . . ." Cf. M. Firpo, "La fase [difensiva]," 133. On reimbursement for inquisitors' travel expenses, see the 1611 *Ordini da osservarsi da gl'Inquisitori*: "Quando sarà necessario a gl'inquisitori, o loro vicarii, fiscali e notarii cavalcare fuori della città & terre, per essaminare testimonii *ad defensam*, si possino far pagare le spese del vitto, & per se & per i cavalli . . . avvertendo gl'inquisitori, che in questi casi debbano spedirsi quanto prima acciochè li rei non siano gravati per soverchia lunghezza, & di condur seco le persone necessarie solamente. . . ."

61. Masini, *Sacro Arsenale*, 129. The case of Carnesecchi, mentioned at n. 76, in the eyes of contemporaries, was an extremely misguided defense for this very reason. Commissioner Antonio Balduzzi, in ordering the inquisitor of Bologna to offer to make a copy of the trial records for Fra Ambrosio da Milano — a service for which he would be charged — if the latter chose to rebut the evidence against him, adds that he should advise the prisoner he would probably be throwing his money away since "le sue confessioni sono troppo chiare, e troppo frequentate e ratificate, pur faccia egli."

62. See Carena, *Tractatus*, 286: "Omnes DD. clamant reum in causa criminali,

maxime ubi ageretur de poena corporis afflictiva, non posse renunciare defensionibus.... In nostro tribunali S. Officii consulo inquisitoribus, ut non obstantibus
renunciationibus defensionibus, quae fiunt a reis, semper sinant labi terminum, seu
terminos reis ad defensiones faciendas assignatos, antequam eorum causas expedi-
ant, ut, et in cautela abundent, & calumniantium reorum ora claudant." See also
Peña's comment to Eymeric's *Directorium Inquisitorum*, 447: "... quonian iusta defensio
est de iure naturae, & propterea nullo modo potest, aut debet denegari ..."; Simancas, *De Catholicis Institutionibus*, 125: "Quid autem si reus defensionibus suis renun-
tiet, dicatque se habere rata testimonia, nec velle ut repetantur testes? Et communi
sententia receptum est, hanc renuntiationem nullius esse momenti, quia non est au-
diendus reus perire festinans ..."; Masini, *Sacro Arsenale*, 139 f.: "E finiremo ...
col dire che, essendo le difese di ragione naturale, devono non pure al reo non convinto, ne confesso, avanti la tortura, e sentenza, ma anco al reo convinto, e confesso
darsi le difese, & a favor di lui ascoltarsi per ogni modo l'avvocato, percioche possono sempre & alla confessione, & a i testimoni, & a i loro detti opporsi di cose assai."
For an instance of this doctrine at work see the case of Jean Dupuy (cited at n.
76 below), who was offered his defenses and a lawyer even though he remained
obstinate in his beliefs (see B. N. Paris, MS. Lat. 8994, fol. 389).

63. See Carena, *Tractatus*, 279: "Vel haereticus est notorie talis, & notorie pertinax, et in hoc casu utique ei sunt denegandae defensiones ... & hinc est, quod
defensiones non sunt dandae haeretico, qui vellet probare haeresim, uti talem ab ecclesia damnatum, non esse haeresim."

64. Masini, *Sacro Arsenale*, 115: "E perchè tal repetitione è molto difficile, deve
con somma esquisitezza & diligenza maneggiarsi, perciochè da essa pende l'honore,
la vita, & i beni de' rei. Laonde convien si faccia dall'inquisitore istesso, & con gran
cautela, e sollecitudine, per impedire ogni frode, e schifare ogni cavillatione...."

65. Ibid.: "E dicendo il reo, di non intendersi di tal cosa, e non sapere quello
che si habbia a fare, & che volentieri parlerà col Signor Procuratore, o avvocato,
& poi si risolverà intorno alla detta repetitione, dovrà cotal sua risposta registrarsi...."

66. BAV, Barb. lat. 6334, fol. 56v, letter, dated 7 March 1626, from the Roman Congregation to the inquisitor of Modena: "... il solito del tribunale è che
gli rei nominino tre avvocati almeno, et uno di essi sia poi eletto dall'inquisitore."
In his commentary to Eymeric's *Directorium Inquisitorum* Peña vigorously supports
the older writer's statement that "et concedo sibi talem quem petit in advocatum,
& talem in procuratorem." Writes Peña: "Haec verba diligenter sunt observanda,
quoniam saepe vidimus dubitari, an inquisitor debeat reo petenti hunc vel illum advocatum concedere alium ab eis qui sunt ordinarii advocati constituti in officio inquisitionis ..." (ibid., 453).

67. See BRB, MS. II 290, vol. 1, fol. 118. In the Biblioteca Nazionale, Naples,
MS. XI. B. 34 consists of a collection of briefs prepared by defense lawyers for Holy
Office prisoners during the years 1673–80, the majority prepared by Clemente Fer-
relli, "avvocato de' poveri." It is cited in L. Amabile, *Fra Tommaso Campanella*,
2:165 (cited in full at n. 76).

68. See Carena, *Tractatus*, 35 ff., "De Advocato et Procuratore Reorum in Sancto Officio." Lawyers had to be "viri de haeresi non suspecti, fidei zelatores, probi, legales & in utroque iure (maxime vero in materiis ad hoc tribunal spectantibus) non mediocriter versati" (ibid., 36). This high ideal was not fulfilled in a blasphemy case tried before the Inquisition in Venice where a defense lawyer procrastinated bestirring himself for his clients. See BAV, Vat. lat. 10249, fol. 24r: ". . . gli furono intimate le difese sino ai 13 del passato, e benche dal loro avocato sia stato veduto il processo informativo non gli è però [illegible word] l'animo di portar cosa alcuna a loro difesa." For an instance of pressure from high places to fill the position of *procuratore* in Bologna, recently made vacant by the death of its incumbent, Gian Francesco Grati, see the various recommendations gathered in BA, MS. B–1862, including one from Cardinal Domenico Pinelli of the Roman Congregation to the local inquisitor, 27 February 1602 (ibid., fol. 61), which states that he had been approached in the matter "da persona alla quale desidero fare servitio."

69. On the question "De curatore dando in hoc foro minoribus 25 annis," see Peña's *Instructio seu Praxis Inquisitorum*, 394: "Tamen in Inquisitione Universali Romana, & in aliis inquisitionibus Italiae constitutio haec curatoris non servatur. . . ." For evidence seeming to qualify this statement, see BAV, Barb. lat. 1370, p. 45, excerpts from several letters to the inquisitors of Mantua, Brescia, Reggio, and Pavia, written between 1593 and 1598 inquiring whether it was the usage in their tribunals to assign just such an official to minors "in causis criminalibus delictorum attrocium . . ." (letter to inquisitor of Mantua, 21 August 1593). The order to actually employ a *curator* is communicated to the inquisitor of Bologna by Cardinal Arrigoni on 6 January 1607 (BA, MS. B–1863, fol. 55) in the case of a certain "Carlo Magliere di Nant in Bertagna": "Appresso gl'assegni il termine a far le difese con deputarli il curatore stante la sua minorità d'anni 18. . . ."

70. I. de Simancas, *Enchiridion Iudicum Violatae Religionis* (Antwerp, 1573), 201: "Ad graviora crimina defendenda non admittitur procurator, nisi reus sit in carcerem coniectus . . ."; *Repertorium Inquisitorum*, 643–45; Carena (*Tractatus*, 36, 279), who does not distinguish their functions.

71. See, most recently, W. L. Wakefield, "Inquisition," in *Dictionary of the Middle Ages*, ed. J. R. Strayer (New York, 1985), 6:485: "No lawyer acted for the defense, for to do so would risk the charge of protecting a heretic." On the other hand, see W. Ullmann, "The Defense of the Accused in the Medieval Inquisition," *The Irish Ecclesiastical Record*, ser. 5, 73 (1950): 481–89, at p. 481: "Canonistic scholarship was unanimous in its demand that the accused must not be deprived of legal aid . . . the inquisitor was bound to grant him legal aid in the person of a qualified advocate." See also "Preliminary Observations," at p. 15.

72. The papal pronouncement is quoted by Eymeric, *Directorium Inquisitorum*, 111: ". . . concedimus quod in inquisitionis haereticae pravitatis negotio procedi possit simpliciter et de plano, et absque advocatorum ac iudiciorum strepitu et figura." For further references to the sources and modern discussions, see A. P. Evans, "Hunting Subversion in the Middle Ages," *Speculum* 33 (1958): 1–22, esp. pp. 11 ff.

73. See *Repertorium Inquisitorum*, 35: "Advocatus dandus est imputato de haeresi, nisi constet illum esse haereticum & in haeresi persistere. . . ." Eymeric, *Directorium Inquisitorum*, 446: "Et sic concedentur sibi advocatus, probus tamen, & de legalitate non suspectus, vir utriusque iuris peritus, & fidei zelator. . . ." See also Simancas (*De Catholicis Institutionibus*, 17), who quotes Boniface's Bull and offers several exceptions to it.

74. See A. P. Evans, "Hunting Subversion," 11: "In the actual records of the Inquisition, however, no evidence of the presence of advocates before the court, either to advise the accused or actually to argue the cases, appears prior to the third decade of the fourteenth century."

75. Masini, *Sacro Arsenale*, 418: "Quell' avvocato, il quale, conoscendo apertamente il reo esser veramente heretico, ad ogni modo lo difende, è infame, e degno di grave punitione. . . ." And if, in the course of his duties, the attorney learned the names of the defendant's accomplices he was to reveal them to the court. See Pastor, *Allgemeine Dekrete*, 26: ". . . et si in prosecutione causae alicuius complicis vel alterius culpabilis notitiam habere continget, quam citius revelare teneatur sub poena arbitrio cardinalium" (decree of the Congregation of the Inquisition, 18 June 1564).

76. It is difficult to say how frequently defendants availed themselves of legal aid, since the majority of trials are no longer extant. But for those that have survived, several reveal evidence of the employment of an attorney, although only in a handful of cases has the full defense apparatus survived. What follows is merely a sampling, drawn with an exception or two, from printed sources. Lisia Fileno (Camillo Renato) enjoyed an attorney's services at his Ferrarese trial in 1540 (see n. 107 below). The presence of several defense lawyers is attested in the celebrated trials of P. P. Vergerio, the reforming bishop of Capodistria, in 1546. See L. A. Ferrai, "Il processo di Pier Paolo Vergerio," *Archivio storico italiano*, ser. 4, 15 (1885): 201–20, 333–44; 16 (1885): 25–46, 153–69; and A. J. Schutte, *Pier Paolo Vergerio: The Making of an Italian Reformer* (Geneva, 1977), 222–23. Also note the trial of Pietro Carnesecchi, which culminated with his execution in 1567. See G. Manzoni, ed., "Estratto del processo di Pietro Carnesecchi," *Miscellanea di storia italiana* 10 (1870): 187–573, at p. 569; O. Ortolani, *Per la storia della vita religiosa italiana nel Cinquecento: Pietro Carnesecchi. Con estratti dagli atti del processo del Santo Officio* (Florence, 1963), esp. pp. 171–260 for the long extracts from the trial; T. Bozza, "Introduzione al processo del Carnesecchi," *Annuario dell'Istituto storico italiano per l'età moderna e contemporanea* 35–36 (1983–84): 81–94, and the excellent entry for Carnesecchi by A. Rotondò in *DBI* 20 (1977): 466–76. In the face of the overwhelming evidence against him, Carnesecchi's decision to mount a full-scale defense, rather than throw himself on the mercy of the court, was judged by all observers of the case a disastrous decision which would preclude a papal pardon (see Ortolani, 147 f.). A team of jurists led by Marcantonio Borghese and Antonio Massa, "i due principi del foro romano" (see Firpo, "La fase [difensiva]," 131) defended Cardinal Morone. Ser Marsilio Seghizzo, the advocate of Cataldo Bozzale, a Modenese prisoner

of the Inquisition, petitioned the city authorities to indemnify his client for the costly expenses of his confinement (see T. Sandonnini, *Lodovico Castelvetro e la sua famiglia: Note biografiche* [Bologna, 1882], 341). The doctor in both laws, Benedetto Bariselli, "extended his protection" to the Venetian Jew Righetto in 1572 (see B. Pullan, " 'A Ship with Two Rudders': 'Righetto Marrano' and the Inquisition in Venice," *The Historical Journal* 20 [1977]: 25–58). Counsel was offered to the Frenchman Jean Dupuy at his trial in Turin in 1595. The lawyer's only request was for a doctor to visit his client "a veder se per sorte havesse qualche insania o pazzia come havea prima negli atti detto haver altre volte patito" (see B. N., Paris, MS. Lat. 8994, fol. 389). Counsel was offered also to the wife of the duke of Savoy, known as "L'Ammiraglia," charged with casting spells on her daughter and other sortileges. At her husband's strenuous request an "assistant" was granted who would be involved from the inception of the trial, not just during the defense phase. In acquiescing, the Holy Office specified that this was not to be construed as a precedent (see BAV, Barb. lat. 1370, pp. 318 ff.). Counsel was provided to Bartolomeo Nelli at his Sienese trial in 1560 (see V. Marchetti, *Gruppi ereticali senesi*, 193 f.). The lawyer assigned to Tommaso Campanella in Naples in 1601, G. B. del Grugno, was a distinguished jurist and a professor in the Naples *Studio* (see L. Amabile, *Fra Tommaso Campanella: La sua congiura, i suoi processi e la sua pazzia*, 3 vols. [Naples, 1882], 2:167 and G. di Napoli, "L'eresia e i processi campanelliani," in *Tommaso Campanella [1568–1639]: Miscellanea di studi nel 4o centenario della sua nascita* [Naples, 1969], 171–258, at p. 225). Flaminio Rinaldini, whose case was moved from Bologna to Rome, asked the Congregation to obtain for him the defense dossier which his lawyer had prepared in his favor before transfer of the trial. See the letter of Cardinal Arrigoni to the inquisitor of Bologna, 24 May 1608 (BA, MS. B–1863, fol. 119). Requested in the prisoner's favor were "le allegationi et considerationi fatte dal D. Domenico Medici avvocato a suo [Rinaldini's] favore, et la copia de gl'articoli da provare a sua difesa, et dice che dette scritture sono costì nell' officio."

For instances of legal aid to the indigent or lower classes in society, see the case recalled at n. 67 and that of Domenico Scandella ("Menocchio"), who had the advantage of attorneys at his two trials in 1584 and 1599: see C. Ginzburg, *The Cheese and the Worms: The Cosmos of a Sixteenth-Century Miller*, trans. J. and A. Tedeschi (Baltimore, 1980), 7 ff., 110; and now for the texts of the entire proceedings, including documents not used by Ginzburg, the edition *Domenico Scandella, detto Menocchio: I processi dell'Inquisizione (1583–1599)*, ed. A. Del Col (Pordenone, 1990). Legal counsel was offered also to the *benandanti* Maria Panzona at her Friulian trial in 1619 and Michele Soppe in 1650, despite the fact that the latter had already confessed (see C. Ginzburg, *The Night Battles*, 104, 128); Fra Ludovico Alberti served as a lawyer for a suspected witch tried in Triora (province of Genoa) in 1588 (see G. Bonomo, *Caccia alle streghe: La credenza nelle streghe dal sec. XIII al XIX con particolare riferimento all'Italia* [Palermo, 1971], 260). Even these bits of scattered evidence disprove the modern scholars who continue to state that defense counsels were barred from operating in inquisitorial courts (see "Preliminary Observations" at n. 39).

On the defense lawyer's right to dispute the interim sentence for questioning of his client under torture, see the *Repertorium Inquisitorum*, 33, 771. Carena, *Tractatus*, 56 concedes that the accused had the privilege to appeal the decree to torture, but that the appeal was rarely heeded because the decision was based on the duly pondered opinion of the consultors. And, as we have seen, in the course of the sixteenth century it was the Roman Congregation itself that granted the authorization. Appeals were successful, however, when they could adduce a physical handicap on the part of the accused or one of the other disqualifying factors mentioned at n. 113.

77. See Peña, *Instructio seu Praxis Inquisitorum* in Carena, *Tractatus*, 416 ff. See p. 418: "Articuli ad deffensionem rei inquisiti pro crimine haeresis debent excludere, vel minuere delictum"; "Articuli ad deffensionem reorum producendi sunt primo super negando facto, secundo super exceptionibus contra testes, tertio super bona vita, & moribus reorum." Cf. Carena's *Annotationes* (ibid., 419): "Circa modum formandi articulos ad reorum deffensionem debet advocatus ipsorum diligenter perquirere omnes fere fontes, ex quibus eorum deffensio hauriri possit, & sic legere poterit totum titulum de deffensionibus reorum." Cf. Carena's long discussion in the main body of the *Tractatus*, 278 ff., "De Defensionibus Reorum," where more good practical advice is offered. The greatest victory for the defense is acknowledged to be the repudiation of the testimony offered by the prosecution witnesses.

78. Simancas, *De Catholicis Institutionibus*, 118 f.: "Reus ergo absolvendus est, cum probaverit pluribus testibus & melioribus, quod eo loco & tempore, nihil eorum ab eo dictum est, aut factum, de quibus testes accusatoris testimonium dixerint: addita ratione, quia id nec dici, nec fieri potuit, quin ipsi testes audissent, aud vidissent"; "Magna item defensio erit, si reus testes refutaverit: nam si probare potuerit, accusatoris testes inimicos esse, aut ab inimicis pecunia subornatos, aut contra reum coniurasse, nulla eis fides habenda est. . . ."; "Hinc est, quod haeresis a furioso dicta, impunita esse debet: idemque erit, si ab insano, amente, fanatico, & furiis seu demonibus agitato, dicatur ii enim omnes & id genus alii, nec errorem intellectus habent, nec pertinaciam voluntatis. . . ."

79. See G. B. Scanaroli, *De Visitatione Carceratorum Libri Tres* (Rome, 1655), 106: "Procurator pauperum moneat carceratos, ut ita se in carcere gerant, ne intemperantia, vel immodestia causam suam deteriorem reddant." Other advice includes shunning the dishonest coaching of witnesses, modesty "in sermone," avoidance of building up false hopes in capital cases (in one such instance the condemned man could be persuaded to receive the last sacrament only with the greatest difficulty). In cases of absolution, vigilance was to be exerted for fulfillment of the sentence. Where exile had been ordered, the procurator was to obtain time for the defendant to make his arrangements, gather the necessities for his journey, etc.

80. See A. C. Shannon, "The Secrecy of Witnesses in Inquisitorial Tribunals and in Contemporary Secular Trials," in J. Mundy, ed., *Essays in Medieval Life and Thought Presented in Honor of Austin Patterson Evans* (New York, 1955), 59–69; A. P. Evans, "Hunting Subversion," 14 f.: "Experience has shown that witnesses ran grave danger of injury or death from attack by relatives or friends of those against

whom they testified." That numerous guilty persons were evading justice because of the reluctance of witnesses to step forward where their identities were known, is also attested by R. Van Caenegem, "La preuve dans le droit du Moyen Age occidental," *Recueils de la société Jean Bodin pour l'histoire comparative des institutions. XVII. La preuve. Deuxième partie. Moyen age et temps modernes* (Brussels, 1965), 691–753, at p. 733. There is a diffuse and generally uncritical discussion of the subject in F. Darwin, "The Holy Inquisition: Suppression of Witnesses' Names," *Church Quarterly Review* 125 (1938): 226–46; 126 (1938): 19–43. The formal pronouncement for the anonymity of witnesses dates to the decree of Innocent IV, 9 March 1254, *Cum Negotium* (Cocquelines, *Bullarum*, 3, pt. 1: 342): "Sane volumus, ut nomina tam accusantium pravitatem haereticam, quam testificantium super ea, nullatenus publicentur, propter scandalum, vel periculum, quod ex publicatione huiusmodi sequi posset. Et adhibeatur dictis huiusmodi testium nihilominus plena fides." Innocent was confirming a practice that had been developing for several decades. (See also Evans, "Hunting Subversion," 14 f.) There is an excellent analysis of the several issues discussed here and in the notes below in M. O'Neil's "Witness for the Inquisition: Non-Defendant Testimony in the Holy Office of Modena," presented originally at the conference "Inquisition as Court and Bureaucracy," sponsored by The Newberry Library Center for Renaissance Studies and Northern Illinois University, October 1985. The paper is scheduled to appear in O'Neil's forthcoming monograph "Healing and Harming: Inquisition Trials for Magical and Superstitious Offenses in Sixteenth–Seventeenth-Century Modena" (preliminary title).

81. See Peña's commentary in Eymeric's *Directorium Inquisitorum*, 526, where Peña states that confrontation could occur "quando testes complices sunt eiusdem criminis cum reo . . ." or "cum vilissimi sunt testes & rei qui parum curant bonam vel malam habere famam, quales sunt vilissimae meretices [sic], & vilissimi homines . . ."; and Masini, *Sacro Arsenale*, 73–83, "Modo di fare giudicialmente da i testimoni riconoscere un reo, che nega d'esser desso," etc. Masini recommends a form of police line-up with the accused standing in a group of persons. If the inquisitor has reason to suspect that the confrontation carries heavy risks, the witness remains hidden or masked. But open face-to-face encounters under inquisitorial auspices of accuser and accused also were arranged with predictably dramatic results. See the case of the *benandante* Giovanni Sion described by C. Ginzburg, *The Night Battles*, 110 f. A face-to-face confrontation between defendant and witness occurred in the case of the suspected witch Chiara Signorini. See C. Ginzburg, "Witchcraft and Popular Piety: Notes on a Modenese Trial of 1519," in Ginzburg's *Clues, Myths and the Historical Method*, trans. J. and A. C. Tedeschi (Baltimore, 1989), 4, 170. See also n. 84 below for a confrontation which occurred through an inquisitor's blunder.

82. For instances of oaths by released prisoners not to avenge themselves on witnesses, see the letter from Cardinal Savello of the Roman Congregation to the inquisitor of Florence, July 1583 (BRB, MS. II 290, vol. 1, fol. 5) authorizing him to release a certain Cosimo Tornabuoni from his house arrest and allow him to cir-

culate throughout the city and district on condition of his offering new surety and a guarantee "di non offendere li testimonii conforme al decreto che si manda quì incluso." This is a procedure the inquisitor was asked to follow in future cases. (The decree may have been the Bull *Si de Protegendis* discussed in the next note.) See also the letter of Cardinal Arrigoni to the inquisitor of Bologna, 29 June 1607 (BA, MS. B-1863, fol. 76) ordering him to sentence a certain Bartolomeo Betti to some form of light incarceration after reading to him Pius's Bull and obtaining security (a sum left to the discretion of the inquisitor) "di non offendere li testimonii." The evidence could be multiplied many times.

83. Pius V's *Si de Protegendis*, published on 2 May 1569, invoked the most severe penalties against any persons obstructing the work of inquisitors and their associates, including witnesses. The text is printed in the *Litterae Apostolicae* appended to Eymeric's *Directorium Inquisitorum*, 135–37. The danger to witnesses came not only from the powerful but also from the poor and the lowly. See C. Campeggi's "Additions" to Zanchino Ugolini's "Tractatus de Haereticis," in *Tractatus illustrium*, fol. 242v: ". . . nullo modo testium nomina publicentur. Compertum quippe est, varia pericula semper testibus huiusmodi imminere, quia non solum divites & nobiles, sed etiam pauperrimi & ignobilissimi plerunque potentiores sunt ad nocendum." Cf. T. Garzoni, *La piazza universale di tutte le professioni del mondo* (Venice, 1565), *discorso* 63, "De gli Heretici et de gl'Inquisitori," 398: "Sopra tutto in questo ufficio si ricerca al tempo nostro tremore, & horrore per causa della moltiplicatione de gli heretici, & dell' orgoglio, c'hanno molti insultatori aperti d'esso ufficio, non si vergognando (com'io stesso ho provato in me medesimo) d'impedire con la violenza, e travagliare indegnamente le persone, che per qualche legitima causa facciano ricorso a quello. . . ."

84. For the Bruno episode, see n. 86 below. For cases where, contrary to correct procedure, the names of accusers and witnesses were intentionally communicated to the defendant—a priest charged with solicitation of sexual favors in the confessional—see the letter from the Roman Congregation of the Holy Office to the inquisitor of Verona, 23 May 1626 (BAV, Barb. lat. 6334, fol. 133): "Non lascerò d'avvisarla che si sono maravigliati questi miei SS.ri Ill.mi che contra lo stile del tribunale si siano manifestati al reo li nomi delle denuntianti et di testimonii, interrogandolo se conosce Francesca, Achillina, Agnese et se mai in confessione ha trattato con loro di cose dishoneste. . . ." See also the letter to the inquisitor of Florence (1603) cited at n. 67: "Appresso ella ripeta li testimonii del Fisco con la diligenza che si conviene per trovare la verità; et finita la repetitione offerisca a principali la copia del processo, con cassare li nomi et altre circonstanze de' testimonii, per le quali possa venire in notitia di essi, benche alcuni siano stati confrontati con li principali stessi contra lo stile del S.to Officio che non suole fare confrontationi se non rarissime volte, et all'hora tra i complici istessi per trovare meglio la verità. . . ." A shrewd and perceptive defendant might very well be able on his own to reconstruct at least partial identities from the copy of the indictment made available to him so that he might prepare his case, even when witnesses' names and other iden-

tifying attributes were, in theory, suppressed. Thus Lisia Fileno (Camillo Renato) in his *Apologia* identified one "quae est foemina" or another as being Modenese "Mutinensis," etc. See A. Rotondò, ed. *Camillo Renato, Opere*, 65 f. It would have been practically impossible to conceal the identity of the accusers when they belonged to the family of the defendant and resided under the same roof. A letter from the Holy Office in Rome to the inquisitor of Cremona (22 August 1626) discusses the case of a certain Giovanni Paolo Resta who had aggravated his situation by threatening the life of his father-in-law, who had denounced him as a blasphemer to the court (BAV, Barb. lat. 6334, fol. 240v). Cf. J.-P. Dedieu ("The Archives of the Holy Office of Toledo as a Source for Historical Ethnology," in *The Inquisition in Early Modern Europe*, 158–89, at p. 189) who similarly questions the extent to which prosecution witnesses remained concealed from the defendant in Spanish trials.

85. See BAV, Barb. lat. 6334, fol. 235v, letter dated 22 August 1626 from the Supreme Congregation to the bishop of Molfetta: "Alla lettera di V.S. che accompagna il memoriale di Fra Calisto da Napoli, Min. Oss.te, quale si duole di essere dal Commissario della Provincia trabalzato in questo et in quello convento per havere, come egli si crede denuntiato al S.to Officio, questi miei SS.ri Ill.mi mi hanno ordinato di rispondere che dal suddetto commissario intenda la causa di queste frequenti mutationi . . . et lo ricerchi a provedere che Fra Calisto suddetto non habbi alcuna giusta occasione di dolersi."

86. See ACAU, Epistolae S. Officii, 1588–1613 (unpaginated), letter, dated 5 June 1599, of the cardinal of Santa Severina to the inquisitor of Aquileia and Concordia: "Quanto al particolare che ricerca se deve procedere contra le persone denuntiate quando vi è pericolo della vita a testimonii, che hanno deposto, o denuntiato, Sua S.tà ordina che V. R.tia mandi copia delle denuntie per farvi la debita deliberatione sopra." For a similar scholarly assessment of the situation in the medieval period, see the remarks quoted at n. 80. On the murdered witnesses, see BAV, Barb. lat. 6334, fols. 192r, 215v–216r. The Congregation received a reply in the affirmative to the query "se sia vero che la donna et il figlio che denuntiarono contra di lui [Turri] siano stati ammazzati. . . ."

For cases involving harassment of witnesses, see, for example, the violence worked by a powerful landowner of Imola, Roderico Alidosio, upon a vassal who had testified against him. The information is contained in a letter from Cardinal Millino of the Roman Congregation to the inquisitor of Florence, 7 November 1609 (BRB, MS. II 290, vol. 1, fol. 183): "È venuto a notitia di questa Sacra Congregatione che detto Alidosio sotto vari pretesti ha fatto ritener carcerato per cinque mesi Anibale delle Vigne da Castel del Dio in vendetta di essersi essaminato contro di lui nel Sant'Officio, et che hora l'astringe a pagare 155 lire . . . per le spese mentre è stato ritenuto prigione. . . ." See also C. Ginzburg, *The Cheese and the Worms*, 139, and A. Del Col, ed. *Domenico Scandella, detto Menocchio*, pp. LXXXI ff.: The priest Don Odorico Vorai, whose denunciation began all Menocchio's troubles, was harassed and threatened by the latter's relatives and villagers. The witnesses in an aborted trial against an abbot were "molestati," as we learn in an angry letter from Cardinal Millino to the inquisitor of Bologna, 14 October 1623 (BA, MS. B-1866, fol. 123). The charge against Giordano Bruno was made at his Venetian trial on 23 March 1592 by Zuane Mocenigo. See A. Mercati, *Il sommario del processo di Giordano Bruno: Con appendice di documenti sull'eresia e l'Inquisizione a Modena nel secolo XVI*, Studi e Testi, 101 (Vatican City, 1942), 107. For a Milanese case (1597) of a witness beaten by the husband of an accused woman, see L. Fumi, "L'Inquisizione romana," 37. See Carena (*Tractatus*, 205) who recalls ". . . hic Cremonae fuit executum [a long galley sentence] in persona unius, qui baculo percusserat quedam testem qui in S. Officio deposuerat contra eius fratrem. . . ." Giovanni Battista Spinello, prince of Scalea, while in prison during his trial, corrupted a notary and thus obtained the names of the witnesses who were testifying against him. See E. G. Léonard, "Il principe di Scalea Giovanni Battista Spinelli processato per libertinaggio dall'Inquisizione," *Archivio storico per le province napoletane*, n.s., 19 (1933): 397–400 at p. 400. In a similar case, occurring in Milan, Niccolò Cid, incarcerated between 1565 and 1571, corrupted his jailers and came to know everything that was being testified in the courtroom against him. See D. Maselli, *Saggi di storia ereticale lombarda al tempo di S. Carlo* (Naples, 1979), 123. The *podestà* of Castelnuovo, Girolamo Canossa, attempted to prevent his sister and cousin from testifying against him for blasphemies uttered. See the letter of the Supreme Congregation to the inquisitor of Reggio Emilia, dated 13 June 1626 (BAV, Barb. lat. 6334, fol. 157v): ". . . il quale li giorni passati diede qualche impedimento alla citatione di sua sorella et cugina, testimonii, che si dovevano esaminare contra di lui per conto d'alcune bestemmie. . . ."

87. Ibid., fols. 158r–v, letter dated 13 June 1626 from the Congregation to the bishop of Conversano: "È stato caro l'avviso dato da V. S. con due lettere de' 22 et 29 di Maggio della scarceratione degli inquisiti nella causa di Rutigliano, legati con sicurtà di non offendere li denuntianti, e testimonii . . . Al giusto timore secondo ella scrive degli inquisiti di non essere irritati da testimonii et denuntianti, che non hanno com'essi il freno delle sicurtà, è parso a questi mie SS.ri Ill.mi che possa la prudenza di V. S. provedere con far secretamente chiamar li suddetti denuntianti et testimonii, et avvertirli a non inquietare . . . in modo alcuno gli inquisiti, che altrimente si procederà severamente contra di loro. . . ."

88. See Pius's *Pastoralis Officii Cura* (27 August 1561) among the *Litterae Apostolicae* in Eymeric's *Directorium Inquisitorum*, 125 and in Cocquelines, *Bullarum*, vol. 4, pt. 2: 87. It had been reported to Pius by inquisitors everywhere that there was a serious lack of upright and qualified notaries, "unde officio ipsius Inquisitionis, tum propter ipsorum notariorum penuriam, tum quia plerique officium huiusmodi tamquam odiosum exercere recusant, ne illud suscipiendo quemquam offendere videantur, magnum incommodum, & detrimentum generatur." The pope thereby authorized inquisitors to recruit notaries even from the orders and the secular clergy. Priests in Lombard cities who were not able to authenticate, due to the shortage of notaries, that they had published and circulated edicts from the Holy Office, could perform the verification with the aid of two proper witnesses. See BAV, Borg. lat. 558, fol. 55r (document dated 28 April 1610).

V.R.tia et per la fede che ne fanno gli altri reverendi consultori, che al detto Don Matteo non se gli possa dar nessuna sorte di tormento. . . ." See also Masini, *Sacro Arsenale*, 155: ". . . fa di bisogno [where the application of torture is in question] per caminare sicuramente, che l'inquisitore proponga prima nella congregatione de' Consultori del Santo Officio il processo offensivo e difensivo, e col dotto e maturo consiglio d'essi (ancorche il loro voto non sia decisivo, ma solamente consultivo) si governi, & adopri sempre. O pure, essendo la causa grave, e difficultosa, ne dia parte al sacro, e supremo Tribunale della Santa & Universale Inquisitione Romana, e di là n'attenda la risolutione." BA, MS. B–1859 is composed entirely of "Consilia et Vota in Materia S. Officii," Bolognese documents of the fifteenth and sixteenth centuries. See also Locati, *Opus quod iudiciale inquisitorum dicitur*, 482 for the text of the usual "Forma sententiae interlocutoriae ad supponendum aliquem quaestionibus, seu tormentis."

For the legislation establishing the consultors, see Abbiati, "Intorno ad una possibile valutazione," 177n, and, especially, C. Henner, *Beiträge*, 138–53. Cf. Eymeric, *Directorium Inquisitorum*, 629 ff. and especially Peña's accompanying commentary. In the words of the latter, "in causa haeresis nullam habent iurisdictionem ordinariam, aut delegatam" (ibid., 630). On the anonymity of witnesses, see above at nn. 80 ff. and the note below. The consultors in the trial of Lisia Fileno (Camillo Renato) were two jurists and three theologians, men of rank and distinction. They are fully identified by A. Rotondò, ed., *Camillo Renato, Opere*, 33, n. 2.

106. See Peña's commentary to Eymeric's *Directorium Inquisitorum*, 632: "Inquisitorum tamen partes erunt notare testium qualitates, ut si religiosi, si periti, si graves fuerint & probati: aut contra, si minus probati, si plebei, et pauperes, si iuvenes, si imperiti, aut similes. . . ."

107. The defense counsel assigned by the court to Lisia Fileno during his Ferrarese trial in 1540 was Ludovicus de Silvestris, doctor in both laws, who also served as one of the *consultori* pronouncing an opinion in his case (see A. Rotondò, ed., *Camillo Renato, Opere*, 188). Later decrees of the Holy Office in Rome (1564, 1602) logically specified that "Consultores in Congregationis S.ti Officii non possint esse advocati reorum" (see BAV, Barb. lat. 1370, p. 124). But this malpractice could not be stamped out entirely, and we see a consultor appearing as advocate in the case of Flaminio Rinaldini. See the reprimand to the inquisitor of Bologna, who had permitted it, from Cardinal Arrigoni, 4 February 1607 (BA, MS. B–1863, fol. 60): ". . . li consultori del S.to Officio non devono pigliar carico di difendere li rei processati nella S.ta Inquisitione. Onde ella averta di non far per l'avenire simile deputatione nelle cause del S.to Officio." Carena informs us (*Tractatus*, 36) that in his own tribunal of Cremona, consultors were frequently called upon to serve as defense lawyers, but then they abstained from deliberating and voting in the cases in question.

108. BAV, Barb. lat. 6334, fol. 56v, letter from the Roman Congregation to the inquisitor of Saluzzo, 7 March 1626: "In tanto avverto a V.R. che non deve venire, come ha fatto, alla tortura de' rei in quelle cause nelle quali vuole consultare

la S. Congregazione prima di haverne l'ordine di qui, et insieme che li sommarii che manda, sieno non latini, ma volgari, et con le parole stesse nelle cose sostantiali de' testimonii et del reo. . . ."

109. See the letter from the cardinal of Pisa to the inquisitor of Bologna, 29 September 1576 (BA, MS. B–1860, fol. 241): "Questa S.ta Congregatione ha inteso l'escusatione di vostra paternità circa la tortura data a Don Claudio da Bologna, et è stato ordinato ch'ella ci mandi il decreto, o vero ordine fatto su questa causa. . . ." See also J. Sambuc, "Le procès de Jean de Roma, inquisiteur, Apt 1532," *BSSV*, a. 97, no. 139 (1976): 45–55. In the trial against the inquisitor Jean de Roma, the use of fire as an instrument of torture was considered an abuse of power.

110. See, from the many cases which could be cited, the letter of the cardinal of Pisa, a member of the Roman Holy Office, to the inquisitor of Bologna, 26 July 1572: "Si è proposto in Congregatione et fatto vedere da consultori il caso di M.ro Pavolo Vasellaro, et di comun parere si è concluso che se gli habbia a dare di buona corda per chiarirsi se è veramente relapso, et se le cose che se li oppongono sono state dette da lui con mala intentione . . ." (BA, MS. B–1860, fol. 79). On papal participation in the decision-making process, see, as an example, the case of a Neapolitan bigamist, Antonio Frezza, whose trial was transferred to Rome. On 20 September 1607 "S.mus decrevit ut torqueatur supra intentione et si nihil superveniat, abiuret de vehementi, et damnetur ad triremes per quinquennium" (BAV, Borg. lat. 558, fol. 162r). The reigning pope would have been Paul V. The composition and routines of the Congregation of the Holy Office in Rome are described in an early seventeenth-century manuscript published by L. Firpo, "Una relazione inedita su l'Inquisizione romana," *Rinascimento* 9 (1958): 97–102.

111. BRB, MS. II 290, vol. 2, fols. 6r–9r: ". . . Circa il qual processo due cose primieramente si sono havute in consideratione. La prima è che gl'indicii per quello risultanti contra le predette donne sono assai leggieri e deboli, per esser fondati nella depositione di Menichina parimente meretrice, la quale oltra che per la sua confessione si scuopre di esser inimica delle dette Spinetta e Calochina. . . . La seconda è che le dette meretrici e Zino. . . non hanno havute le loro defensioni, et essendo stati posti nel tormento, e più di una volta ciascuno in se stesso, e con gli altri ha variato assai nelle sue confessioni. Onde si è venuto in parere, che per le confessioni loro fatte de' detti delitti non si possa realmente venire ad alcuna salda e fondata risolutione, e se bene per le cose predette si può dubitare, che quelle siano fatte, et estorte per tormenti, o per timore di essi. . . ."

112. "Duro tamen tradere carceri sive arcto, qui magis ad poenam quam ad custodiam videatur, vel tormentis exponere illos [the defendants], aut ad sententiam procedere contra eos, episcopus sine inquisitore, aut inquisitor sine episcopo dioecesano aut eius officiali. . . ." Cited from Fiorelli, *Tortura* 2:54; B. da Como, *Lucerna Inquisitorum Haereticae Pravitatis* (Venice, 1596), 124; Masini, *Sacro Arsenale*, 407. Failure to share authority on the part of the inquisitor of Siena brought a reprimand from Cardinal Giovanni Ricci of the Roman Congregation (letter of 12 February 1568): "Si lamentano anchora quelli del vescovo che voi non lasciate essere presente al dare

della corda il vicario di esso monsignore, il che noi non credemmo che voi usiate di fare, et però datici aviso come passa questo facto": P. Piccolomini, "Documenti fiorentini sull'eresia in Siena durante il secolo XVI (1559–1570)," *Bullettino senese di storia patria* 17 (1910): 159–99 at p. 175. See also the letter of the cardinal of Santa Severina to the inquisitor of Florence, dated 29 January 1594 (BRB, MS. II 290, vol. 1, fols. 63r–v) in which the issue arises in the context of territorial jurisdiction: "Et si come ella riferisce per il passato havere permesso che l'Inquisitore di Faenza faccia l'ufficio suo in quelle terre, così ancora potrà contentarsi per l'avvenire, massime stante così lunga distantia, come è da Fiorenza a quelle terre, et l'incommodità del trattare le cause, poichè in caso di tortura, o di condannatione hanno da convenire insieme l'Ordinario, et l'Inquisitore il che sarebbe impossibile, o difficilissimo, perchè il Vescovo di Faenza ne il suo Vicario possano essercitare giurisdittione *extra diocesim*, ne V.R.tia per la lunga distanza potrebbe andare a Faenza." The possibilities of action for bishop and inquisitor are spelled out in chap. 24, "Delli avvertimenti generali" in Desiderio Scaglia's "Prattica." I cite from the edition published by A. Mirto, "Un inedito del Seicento sull'Inquisizione," *Nouvelles de la Republique des Lettres* 1 (1986): 136: ". . . alcuni ordinarii et inquisitori poco prattici si lamentano alle volte che gli uni faccino quello che non possano fare senza gli altri, ancor che lo possino fare, et alle volte pretendano di poter fare soli quelli che realmente fare no[n] possano se no[n] insieme. Le cose che possano fare gli inquisitori senza gli ordinarii, e gli ordinarii senza inquisitori sono cinque: citare, prendere, carcerare, formare processo informativo, e far decreto assolutorio. Quelle che non possano fare gli uni senza gli altri sono tre: dar pena, tormentare, e sententiare." The exclusion of the episcopal vicar from all inquisitorial business in Pisa, with the exception of the application of torture and sentencing, strained relations and tempers to a boiling point, resulting in the assault and beating of the inquisitor, Francesco Pratello, by the vicar and his allies in a church crowded with parishioners in July 1581. The outlandish episode is described by G. Romeo, "Una città, due inquisizioni: L'anomalia del Sant'Ufficio a Napoli nel tardo '500," *Rivista di storia e letteratura religiosa* 24 (1988): 60 ff.

113. See, as an example, the letter of the cardinal of Santa Severina to the inquisitor of Bologna, 1 May 1593 (BA, MS. B–1861, fol. 175): "Ho data parte à questi Ill.mi et Rev.mi SS.ri Cardinali Generali Inquisitori miei colleghi di quanto V.R.tia scriveva circa Fabio Locatelli, al quale secondo l'attestatione dei medici mandatemi con la sua de' XVII ricevuta a 30 di Marzo non si poteva dar corda ne stanghetta; et le loro Ill.me et R.me Signorie hanno ordinato che s'el detto Fabio è capace di qualche altra sorte di tormento, V.R.tia glielo facci dare ad arbitrio di lei, havendo rigguardo a tutte le debite circonstanze. Et quando non sia habile a sostenere alcuna sorte di tormento, proceda all'espeditione della sua causa con consiglio di theologi et canonisti della sua congregatione per giustitia"; see also the sentence against Francesco Vidua of Verona, 25 April 1580: ". . . non si potendo per via dei tormenti levare le presuntioni et suspitioni le quali sono contra di te, et questo per la indispositione del tuo corpo, habbiamo determinato di venire alla . . . sententia" (TCD, MS. 1225,

fol. 184). This provision, like so many others, would be ignored occasionally in practice at the provincial level. For a trial marred by several procedural lapses, see Barb. lat. 6334, fol. 212v, letter from the Roman Congregation to the inquisitor of Modena, 24 January 1626: "A V. R. poi mi hanno ordinato questi miei SS.ri Ill.mi d'avvertire seriamente de' modi poco giusti et discreti tenuti in questo proces-so, comminando al reo di trattarlo come heretico negativo, dandoli la corda mentre haveva impedimento nelle braccia, facendolo abiurare in publico . . . et dandogli mag-gior grado di abiura di quello che comportasse la qualità delle propositioni dette per burla, et la minorità del reo di 17 anni. . . ."

114. Eymeric, *Directorium Inquisitorum*, 483: "Questioni fidem non semper, nec tamen nunquam habendam . . . etenim res est fragilis & periculosa & quae veritatem fallat: nam plerique patientia sive duritia tormentorum, ita tormenta contemnunt, ut exprimi ab eis veritas nullo modo possit. Alii tanta sunt impatientia, ut quodvis mentiri quam pati tormenta velint." This statement is repeated virtually verbatim in Locati, *Opus quod iudiciale inquisitorum dicitur*, 377 and in I. Simancas, *De Catholi-cis Institutionibus*, 494. Peña, in Eymeric's *Directorium Inquisitorum*, 483 describes it as a "locus communis."

115. I. Simancas, *De Catholicis Institutionibus*, 506: "Ille quoque torqueri poterit, qui confessus fuerit, se dixisse, aut fecisse aliquid haereticum, sed negat intentionem haereticam. Nam cum eo ipso sit plane convictus, aut certe vehementer suspectus, iure quam optimo torqueri potest, ut intentionem declaret. . . ."

116. Ibid., 228 and 119: "Is etiam haereticus non est, qui errat sine pertinacia contra aliquam veritatem catholicae fidei, quam explicite scire non tenebatur, & eo magis, si ab aliquo deceptus fuit. . . ." For a discussion of the appropriation by Ey-meric in his *Directorium Inquisitorum* of the Thomistic doctrine that heresy consists of the intellectual choice of a mistaken doctrine and attachment with one's heart to that doctrine, see L. Sala-Molins, "Utilisation d'Aristote en droit inquisitorial," in *XVI Colloque International de Tours: Platon et Aristote à la Renaissance* (Paris, 1976), 191–99.

117. I. Simancas, *De Catholicis Institutionibus*, 510: "Si vero reus in quaestionibus pernegaverit, ac tormenta vicerit, hoc ipso obiecta crimina diluit & purgat, ut aiunt, omnia praecedentia indicia." See also the following letters of the Roman Congrega-tion: to the inquisitor of Alessandria (29 August 1626): ". . . havendo fra Pompeo Bianco Carmelita purgati con la tortura quasi del tutto gli inditii che contra di lui resultano . . ." (BAV, Borg. lat. 6334, fol. 247v); to the inquisitor of Perugia (9 October 1626): ". . . Questi miei SS.ri Ill.mi hanno approvato il parere di V.R. di spedire il sud.o fra Gio. Salice giachè ha sostenuto la corda con relegarlo in un convento della sua Religione . . . (ibid., fol. 280v); letter of Fra Domenico da Imo-la, episcopal vicar in Modena, to Cardinal Giovanni Morone, bishop of Modena, dated "il giorno di S. Francesco 1567": "Questa settimana è stato il vicario dell' inquisitore a Modena . . . li dui soldati con tutti li tormenti che li sono stati datti, corda et fuoco a piedi, non hano confessato et così havendo sodisfatti si lassarono con sicurtà come voliano le leggi" (quoted from A. Mercati, *Il sommario del processo*

di Giordano Bruno, 142). One of the most dramatic cases of this type concerns Tommaso Campanella, who successfully sustained the pretense of madness through the long torture of the *veglia*, thus avoiding the death penalty. See n. 124.

118. Eymeric, *Directorium Inquisitorum*, 485: "Ubi autem decenter quaestionatus, & tormentis expositus noluerit detegere veritatem, amplius non vexetur, sed abire libere dimittatur." In his comment Peña attempts to define the point at which the defendant can be said to have been sufficiently questioned: "Tunc autem dicitur reus tortus sufficienter, quando ita rigida inflicta est sibi tortura, ut iudicio prudentum considerata indiciorum qualitate ea ipsa indicia purgaverit, et nihil fuit confessus, sed in tortura semper mansit in negativa, ut ergo intelligatur quando per torturam indicia sint purgata, commensuranda est qualitas rigiditatis inflictae torturae, cum qualitate gravitatis indiciorum" (ibid.).

119. See Peña's annotations in Eymeric, *Directorium Inquisitorum*, 620: ". . . si nihil confiteatur, quia hoc casu non potest videri purgasse indicia per torturam, cum sint multa & urgentissima ac vehementissima contra eum, ad abiurationem saltem de vehementi . . . iustissime compelletur."

120. See Carena, *Tractatus*, 299: the formula reads: ". . . citra praeiuditium probatorum, vel confessi & convicti . . . quod plene probata non elidantur per torturam, dummodo super eis specifice reus non interrogetur . . ."; Masini, *Sacro Arsenale*, 160: ". . . i giudici facciano la protesta, che non gli si dà la tortura, se non *pro ulteriori veritate* & *super intentione*, senza alcun pregiuditio delle cose da lui già confessate, e delle quali è convinto . . . perchè, se il reo, ancorche confesso, e pienamente convinto, senza detta protesta negasse in tortura il fatto, come pur talvolta occorre, & in detta sua negativa persistesse, dovrebbe andarsene assoluto."

121. On the various stages of abjuration and their consequences, see pp. 49–50, 152, 201, n. 175.

122. See the letter of the cardinal of Santa Severina to the inquisitor of Florence, 26 March 1594 (BRB, MS. II 290, vol. 2, fol. 1), the case of several monks accused of having desecrated holy images in the church of their monastery. The evidence against them was grave enough to justify torture, which was to be applied "cominciando a dar la corda a quello di essi che giudicarà sia più facile a scoprire la verità. . . ." Cf. *Repertorium Inquisitorum*, 767: "Quando sunt plures rei unius facinoris, ita audiendi sunt, ut ab eo primum incipiatur tortura, qui timidior est, vel tenerae aetatis videtur . . ."; Masini, *Sacro Arsenale*, 381. These judicial tactics are already stated by Ulpian (see E. Peters, *Torture*, 168). On women's greater resistance see G. B. Scanaroli, *De Visitatione Carceratorum*, 292. He explains it "quia habent maiorem pectoris latitudinem" and because "carent certis partibus quae maxime dolorem augent." This opinion is repeated by P. Zacchia (*Quaestionum medico-legalium tomi tres*, 2: 491), who adds the common opinion that women "in confitenda veritate sint pertinaciores, sed quae summa animi pertinacia dotantur."

123. Masini (*Sacro Arsenale*, 360) recommends waiting nine or ten hours after eating.

124. This was the most common form of torment practiced in both secular and ecclesiastical courts. See J. Döpler (*Theatrum poenarum, suppliciorum et executionum*

criminalium [Sondershausen, 1693], 295–301), who provides a graphic description of this form of interrogation being applied to a robust victim whose dislocated limbs had to be readjusted at the conclusion of his ordeal. When the *strappado* was inapplicable other methods of torture were available. See Masini, *Sacro Arsenale*, 167: "E perchè il reo alle volte, o per notorii difetti del corpo, o per evidente minorità degli anni, si rende incapace del tormento della corda, & conviene perciò dargli altro tormento, o di fuoco (se bene questo, per esser molto pericoloso, hormai poco si usa), o di stanghetta, o di cannette, che altri chiamano suffoli, o di bacchetta. . . ." Torture by fire was accomplished "nudatis pedibus, illisque lardo porcino iniunctis, & in cippis iuxta ignem validum retentis" (ibid.; this was applied in a case mentioned in n. 117). Masini's statement that interrogation with fire had fallen into disuse by his day is confirmed by the reprimand sent to the inquisitor of Vicenza by the Roman Congregation in 1635, "ut in futurum se abstineat" from that particular torment (BAV, Borg. lat. 558, fol. 407r); by the *stanghetta*, "in terra prostratus, talo pedis dextri denudato inter duos ferreos taxillos concavos posito, & ministro eos stanghetta comprimente . . ." (Masini, p. 169); by the *cannette*, ". . . manibus ante iunctis, & inter binos earum singulos digitos sibilis accommodatis, & ministro fortiter praemente . . ." (ibid.). For the description of the application of the *stanghetta* to Pietro Antonio da Cervia during his Bolognese trial in June 1567, see the records of these proceedings, available in English translation: J. Tedeschi and J. von Henneberg, "Contra Petrum Antonium a Cervia relapsum et Bononiae concrematum," in J. Tedeschi, ed., *Italian Reformation Studies in Honor of Laelius Socinus* (Florence, 1965), 243–68, at pp. 266–68. Earlier in the proceedings Cervia is described as being "infermo" and thus unable to support the customary *strappado*. In the case of two Augustinian nuns, Suor Herminia and Suor Chiara of Piacenza, sentenced 10 December 1578, a form of rigid fasting seems to have been the torture imposed on them: see TCD, MS. 1226, fols. 337v, 343: ". . . quali cose hai rattificato, et dopo la tortura dattoti in degiuni per alchuni giorni astretta sei perseverata nella prima confessione" (sentence of Suor Herminia); ". . . dandoti penitenza de degiuni et abstinenza in loco di tortura tu hai prima confessato spontaneamente . . ." (sentence of Suor Chiara). For further detailed descriptions, see P. Zacchia, *Quaestionum medico-legalium tomi tres*, 2: 477–95, "De Tormentis et poenis." On the atrocious torture of the *veglia*, endured over a period of thirty-six hours (4–5 June 1601) by Tommaso Campanella during his Neapolitan trial, see L. Firpo, *Il supplizio di Tommaso Campanella: Narrazioni, documenti, verbali delle torture* (Rome, 1985). Firpo reprints with corrections, together with an Italian translation and a new apparatus, texts originally published by L. Amabile, *Fra Tommaso Campanella* (vol. 3). Campanella's torture was interrupted briefly to permit him to urinate and defecate, to have his nose blown, and to "drink" three raw eggs and imbibe a little wine. For a description of the *veglia*, see Scanaroli, *De Visitatione Carceratorum*, 290–93 and appendix, pp. 43–45; Zachia, *Quaestionum medico-legalium tomi tres*, 2: 479–81, 491–92. The torture combined features of the strappado, the *equuleus*, a form of triangular wooden sawhorse with sharpened point, and sleeplessness. This torture was employed sparingly and almost exclusively in secular courts in cases involving *delictis atrocissimis* in which the evidence was *urgentissima*. Its use in Campanella's case by Neapolitan ecclesiastical judges is explained by Amabile, *Fra Tommaso Campanella* 2:220, in terms of the Roman practice of applying severe torture in cases of alleged madness, especially since it was held that there was less danger of death ensuing from the ordeal in these instances. The entire question, including the ways to determine if the madness was feigned, is discussed in Peña's commentary to Eymeric's *Directorium Inquisitorum*, 432.

125. For this provision that the chamber of torture should be cleared of all superfluous officials, see "Inquisitorial Sources and Their Uses," at n. 61. One wonders how rigorously it could be adhered to in actual practice.

126. See C. Carena, *Tractatus*, 446: "Quoniam tortura inventa est ad veritatem eruendam, non ad homines enecandos, ideo D.D. volunt eam omnino debere esse moderatam, & quod non possit tormentum funis excedere horam." These limits were exceeded in the Roman trial of Niccolò Franco (1569–70), accused of having written a libelous work against Paul IV and his family, who was tortured near the beginning of his trial (on 5 September 1569) and again toward its conclusion on 1, 2, 4, and 25 February 1570 for close to or over an hour on each occasion. See A. Mercati, ed., *I costituti di Niccolò Franco (1568–1570) dinanzi l'Inquisizione di Roma esistenti nell' Archivio Segreto Vaticano*, Studi e Testi, 178 (Vatican City, 1955), 6.

127. Masini, *Sacro Arsenale*, 189.

128. Ibid., 412. Masini was simply echoing a doctrine already enunciated a century earlier by B. da Como, *Lucerna Inquisitorum*, 127: "Tortura debet esse moderata, & debet iudex animadverte ad indicia & ad qualitatem personae, an sit fortis in resistendo, an ne; et debet ita torquere, ut tortum servet incolumem innocentiae vel supplicio, ut sic si deliquit possit pati supplicium debitum, si vero est innocens, non patiatur corporis defectum." The first posthumous edition of this work was published in 1566. On the author, see J. Quétif and J. Echard, *Scriptores Ordinis Praedicatorum*, 2 vols. (Paris, 1719–23; reprint New York, 1959), vol. 2, pt. 1: 22–23.

129. See, for example, TCD, MS. 1226, fol. 184, sentence emitted at Novara, 2 June 1581, against a certain Margarita "dicta la Mora de Casale," who had been denounced to the inquisitor as a "lamia": "Quae in carceribus detenta et examinata, omnia semper negavit, quare de consilio peritorum sufficienter torta, nihil amplius confessa est sed semper in negatione persistit, et de eodem consilio relevata fuit et dimissa." Other cases are cited at n. 117 above. A recent study conducted on a thorough examination of the criminal law proceedings of the *Parlement* of Paris for the late sixteenth and early seventeenth centuries reveals that torture produced a confession rate of only 1 percent. See A. Soman, "Deviance and Criminal Justice in Western Europe, 1300–1800: An Essay in Structure," *Criminal Justice History* 1 (1980): 1–28, at p. 24. See also J. Langbein, *Torture*, 185: "We must bear in mind that no aspect of the human condition has changed so greatly in the twentieth century as our tolerance of pain. The common pain-killers and anesthesia have largely eliminated the experience

of pain from our lives. In disease, childbirth, surgery, and dentistry, our ancestors were acclimated to levels of suffering we find incomprehensible."

130. See Fiorelli, *Tortura* 1:215: "Molti tirati sù colla fune, resistevano grazie alla robustezza delle braccia; altri resistevano per la loro leggerezza, talché le braccia non restavano oppresse dal peso del corpo; altri ancora per l'agilità delle membra, che riuscivano a snodare e a piegare di dietro in avanti senza pericolo di slogature."

131. On this illegal remedy, dubbed *maleficium taciturnitatis* by the jurists, see the discussion in "The Question of Magic and Witchcraft," at notes 62–66.

132. Masini, *Sacro Arsenale*, 183 f. See also for an example from the practice, the letter of the cardinal of Pisa to the inquisitor of Bologna, 27 October 1571 (BA, MS. B–1860, fol. 53): "Si sono havute le due vostre di XIII e XVII del presente . . . et l'essamine che ci havete mandato, fatto da voi a quel Mro Agostino nella tortura. Si aspettarà che lo facciate ratificare extra tormenta, dandoci poi aviso di tutto quello che haverà detto."

133. BA, MS. B–1861, fol. 133: ". . . non sopravenendo altro, essendosi venuto in parere ch'ella non si debba rilasciar alla corte secolare . . . perchè le sue confessioni quanto all'homicidio sono parse assai inverisimili per molte circonstanze che si raccogliono dal suo processo." This case is discussed also in "The Roman Inquisition and Witchcraft," at n. 71.

134. See the letter of Cardinal Arrigoni to the inquisitor of Bologna, 29 July 1606 (BA, MS. B–1863, fol. 34). This case is discussed also at notes 56, 82.

135. See BAV, Barb. lat. 6334, fol. 239v, letter from the Supreme Congregation to the inquisitor of Milan, 22 August 1626: "Si sono considerate le informationi da V. R. mandate contra Caterina alias [?] Catina, Giovannina et Lucretia pretese streghe, et viste le contrarietà delle loro confessioni più d'una volta rivocate et la debolezza degli inditii, che le precedono, si è giudicato ch'alle revocationi si habbi a dar fede, et però V.R. farà scarcerare le suddette tre donne, le assignerà un buono et prudente confessore, le farà un precetto penale di non partire dalla città. . . ."

136. BA, MS. B–1861, fol. 171, letter from the cardinal of Santa Severina to the inquisitor of Bologna, 13 March 1593.

137. See Santa Severina's letter to the inquisitor of Florence, 6 January 1590 (BRB, MS. II 290, vol. 2, fol. 15): "Fra Pietr' Antonio da Montemignaio dell'Ordine de' Minori Osservanti, che V.Rtia per ordine di questo S.to Officio mandò a queste carceri, ne'primi suoi essamini fattili da questi officiali confessò liberamente li suoi errori, et ratificò pienamente quanto haveva confessato in cotesta S.ta Inquisitione. Nondimeno, dopo ha rivocato le dette sue confessioni e ratificationi, alligando di haver confessato per timore di non esser tormentato, e con speranza di esser presto liberato. Et per questo fa instanza che siano essaminati alcuni testimonii nominati in piede di alcuni articoli ch'egli ha prodotti."

138. BAV, Barb. lat. 6334, fol. 66r, letter dated 21 March 1626, from the Roman Congregation to the inquisitor of Verona: "Se Don Bernardino Anderlini condannato alla galera per 10 anni non ha potuto, com'egli suppone intieramente difendersi, gli miei SS.ri Ill.mi ordinano, che se gli dia di nuovo le difese, et si proceda anco

ex officio d'avvocato che lo difenda, et però trattandosi di pena molto grave, et di persona per il sacerdotio qualificata, V.R. non mancherà di darli ogni giusta commodità di giustificarsi. . . ."

139. See Pastor, *Allgemeine Dekrete*, 53, decree of the Roman Congregation of the Inquisition, 23 June 1593: ". . . decreverunt quod quotiescunque reverendus pater commissarius generalis S.ti Officii compererit aliquem ex carceratis in S.to Officio committere in eisdem carceribus aliquod facinus, idem commissarius puniat dictos carceratos illatione trium ictuum funis, et postea referat." Cf. BAV, Barb. lat. 6334, fol. 272v, letter from the Roman Congregation to the inquisitor of Ancona (1626) ordering that a false witness, a certain Domenico Franceschini, should receive as punishment "tre tratti di corda," as well as a prison term left to the discretion of the inquisitor. See Fiorelli, *Tortura* 1:226 f. for evidence that in secular law the *tratto di corda* was used as a punishment for relatively insignificant offenses, for example in Ferrara and in Rome for masquerading in a religious habit during carnival; at Mantua for throwing a cabbage or a snowball; in Rome for disturbing the competition of the *palio*; in Florence for loud games and disturbances in the vicinity of churches, etc. This Italian usage made its way to Saxony as a special punishment for fish poaching. See H. C. Lea, *Materials Toward a History of Witchcraft*, arranged and edited by A. C. Howland, 3 vols. (Philadelphia, 1939; reprint New York, 1957), 2:831, referring to the legal manual by Benedict Carpzov, *Practica Rerum Criminalium* (Wittenberg, 1670).

140. Simancas, *Enchiridion*, 293: ". . . haec poena perpetui carceris post lapsum triennii remitti solet" (following Plato, *Laws*, bk. 10); idem, *De Catholicis Institutionibus*, 113: "Solet praeterea poena perpetui carceris post lapsum triennii plerumque remitti, si eo tempore vincti humiles et veri poenitentes fuerint." Peña's commentary on Eymeric (*Directorium*, 590) follows this opinion. See also T. Del Bene, *De Officio S. Inquisitionis circa Haeresim* (Lyons, 1666), 467: "Regulariter cum condemnato ad carcerem perpetuum dispensatur post annos tres" (cited from N. Paulus, *Hexenwahn und Hexenprozess vornehmlich im 16. Jahrhundert* [Freiburg i. Br., 1910], 252).

141. I. Simancas, *De Catholicis Institutionibus*, 113: "Ubi autem poenitenti[a] imposita est poena carceris irremissibilis, remitti solet post octo annos."

142. A. Battistella (*Il S. Officio e la riforma religiosa in Bologna*, 77) fell into this error. Paulus, *Hexenwahn*, demonstrated conclusively that in inquisitorial speech *muros* designated the walls of a prison. See chap. 12, "Die Einmauerung der Hexen in Rom." The first trial of Domenico Scandella, "Menocchio," concluded with the following judgment: "Te sententialiter condemnamus ut inter duos parietes immureris, ut ibi semper et toto tempore vitae tuae maneas." Within two years (18 January 1586) he presented a supplication to be released and was granted his village of Montereale as a perpetual prison: Ginzburg, *The Cheese and the Worms*, 95, 165.

143. Their sentences are in TCD, MS. 1224, fols. 201, 203. For the correspondence between Rome and Bologna, see BA, MS. B–1860, fols. 132, 136, 186, 195, 199. See, for example, the letter from Antonio Balduzzi to the Bolognese official,

16 May 1573 (fol. 132): "Mons.re Ill.mo di Pisa credo gli scriverà domandandogli relatione dei portamenti di Ms. Hieronimo Guastavillani, penitentiato dal S.to Officio, et sta a un luogo de' frati di San Francesco fuori di Bologna che si chiama i Ronchi. La R.V. gli usi diligenza et ne dia informatione chiara perchè si legerà avanti di N. S.re et l'avvertisco che dove con verità et giusta conscienza gli puo giovare non manchi di farlo perchè farà opera buona." Guastavillani's release was ordered on 6 June.

For a case where release from prison occurred only a few months after sentencing, see the letter of Cardinal Arrigoni of the Holy Office to the inquisitor of Bologna, 22 October 1611, granting "gratia della pena del carcere" to a certain Baldassar Soprani "abiurato costì a mesi passati a ciò possa haver cura de' suoi figlioli piccioli, et della moglie ben spesso inferma" (ibid., MS. B–1864, fol. 38).

144. The fullest account of the Roman prison system (together with the apposite legislation) is in the monumental work by G. B. Scanaroli, *De Visitatione Carceratorum* (cited in full at n. 79). On the author, see P. Cirillo da Leguigno, "Giambattista Scanaroli (1579–1665) apostolo modenese nelle carceri romane," *Italia francescana* 45 (1970): 318–40. See also A. Bertolotti, *Le prigioni di Roma nei secoli XVI, XVII e XVIII* (Rome, 1890); *Avventure di Giuseppe Pignata, fuggito dalle carceri dell'Inquisizione di Roma*, ed. O. Guerrini (Città di Castello, 1887); P. Barrera, ed., *Una fuga dalle prigioni del Sant'Uffizio (1693)* (Milan, 1934), with useful historical introduction. Pignata's highly colored account of Roman prison life and of his escape first appeared as *Les aventures de Joseph Pignata echappé des prisons de l'Inquisition de Rome* (Cologne, 1725; a doubtful place of publication); V. Paglia, *"La pietà dei carcerati": Confraternite e società a Roma nei secoli XVI–XVIII* (Rome, 1980); K. R. Stow, "Delitto e castigo nello stato della chiesa: Gli Ebrei nelle carceri romane dal 1572 al 1659," in *Italia Judaica: "Gli Ebrei in Italia tra Rinascimento ed Età barocca": Atti del II Convegno internazionale, Genova, 10–15 giugno 1984*, Ministero per i Beni Culturali e Ambientali, Pubblicazioni degli Archivi di Stato, Saggi 6 (Rome, 1986), pp. 173–92. For other localities, see S. Biffi, *Sulle antiche carceri di Milano e del ducato milanese e sui sodalizi che vi assistevano i prigionieri ed i condannati a morte* (Milan, 1884); M. Olivieri Baldissarri, *I "poveri prigioni": La confraternità della Santa Croce e della Pietà dei carcerati a Milano nei secc. XVI–XVIII* (Milan, 1985); G. Scarabello, *Carcerati e carceri a Venezia nell'età moderna* (Rome, 1979); idem, "La pena del carcere: Aspetti della condizione carceraria a Venezia nei secoli XVI–XVIII," in G. Cozzi, ed., *Stato, società e giustizia nella repubblica veneta (sec. XV–XVIII)* (Rome, 1980), 317–76; M. Scaduto, "Le carceri della Vicaria di Napoli agli inizi del Seicento," *Redenzione umana* 6 (1968): 393–412; G. Pitré, *Del Sant'Uffizio a Palermo e di un carcere di esso* (Rome, 1940); C. A. Garufi, *Graffiti e disegni dei prigionieri dell' Inquisizione* (Palermo, 1978) (archeological "digs" in the prisons of the Inquisition in the Palazzo Chiaramonte, Palermo).

The development of the legal doctrine of incarceration is discussed in R. Grand, "La prison et la notion d'emprisonement dans l'ancien droit," *Revue de l'histoire du droit français et étranger* 19–20 (1940–41): 58–87; A. Porteau-Bitker, "L'emprisonnement dans le droit laïque du Moyen-âge," *Revue historique de droit français et étranger*

46 (1968): 211–45, 389–428; N. Sarti, "Appunti su carcere-custodia e carcere-pena nella dottrina civilistica dei secoli XII–XVI," *Rivista di storia del diritto italiano* 53–54 (1980–81): 67–110.

145. See TCD, MS. 1228, fol. 111; TCD, MS. 1226, fol. 178, and the letter of the cardinal of Pisa to the inquisitor of Bologna, 9 July 1575, BA, MS. B–1860, fol. 210: ". . . Si è ricevuta la sua di XXVIIII del passato con la confessione et ratificatione di fra Concetto et letto il tutto nella S.ta Congregatione. È stato risoluto che se le scriva come si fà, che lo condanni a stare carcerato nelle carceri di cotesto S.to Officio di Bologna per anni cinque continui et lo privi di voce attiva et passiva in perpetuo. Et che per il tempo che starà in dette carceri faccia pagare le spese del vitto suo al convento de' frati di San Francesco."

146. C. Carena, *Tractatus*, 318. Carena was writing in the third decade of the century.

147. See n. 149 below.

148. TCD, MS. 1225, fol. 224, sentence dated 16 June 1580 against Giannina Caravello, suspected of witchcraft: confinement in "la tua terra di Croda"; ibid., MS. 1224, fol. 139, sentence dated 29 March 1567 against Jacobum Aemilium Laodicensem Germanum: "Tibi pro carcere assignamus urbem, quam non exitis sine nostri licentia . . ."; ibid., fol. 142, sentence dated 1 April 1567 against Hugo Villeti: "Ti assignamo la città di Roma ed li suoi borghi e distretto per priggione. . . ."

149. Ibid., MS. 1226, fol. 314, sentence pronounced at Vicenza, 13 October 1581, against Antonio Bonente of Cittadella: "Te condaniamo al carcere perpetuo et usando con te misericordia et compatendo alla tua senile età, et havendo riguardo al stretto carcere qual hai patito, et alla tua povertà con la gravezza de' molti tuoi figlioli, ti assegnamo al presente pro carcere la casa tua in Cittadella. . ."; ibid., MS. 1225, fol. 118, sentence pronounced at Bergamo, 26 February 1580 against Ludovicus de Moianonibus. The term of his *carcere perpetuo* was to be served in "domum et apothecam propriam." The opening section of BRB, MS. II 290, vol. 1, entitled "Decreta ab anno 1583 ad an. 1609," contains numerous "habilitations" to house arrest by the inquisitor of Florence.

150. BA, MS. B–1860, fol. 69, letter of the cardinal of Pisa to the inquisitor of Bologna, 12 March 1572: "Fu ragionato in questa ultima congregatione intorno il fatto di quel cieco, a chi fu dato per carcere da cotesto S.to Ufficio il monasterio di S. Proculo; et perchè fu fatta relatione ch'egli haveva il modo di vivere del suo, et che ritornandosene a casa saria stato governato da la moglie assai meglio che non era da quei padri, li quali dall'altro canto si aggravavano di farli più le spese, allegando oltra il danno ancho l'incomodità che causava ad essi loro. . . ." A subsequent letter from Rome to Bologna (ibid., fol. 105; 19 December 1572) improved the prisoner's lot once again: he was to be assigned the entire city of Bologna as a prison and freed from the obligation of wearing the penitential garment, the *habitello*, "acciò possi procurarsi da vivere."

151. See BAV, Barb. lat. 6334, letter from the Roman Congregation, dated 25 July 1626, to the inquisitor of Milan: "Giachè Giacomo Heber tedesco non puo per

la sua povera conditione ritrovar chi li faccia sicurtà d'haver la casa per carcere, si contentano questi miei SS.ri Ill.mi dell'obligo suo giuratorio et di un precetto penale di non partire. . . ." Less than two weeks later, on 8 August, he is assigned the entire city "per carcere" since he cannot support his numerous family remaining at home (ibid., fol. 227r).

152. Locati, *Opus quod iudiciale inquisitorum dicitur*, 37: "Carcer regulariter est ad custodiam, non autem ad poenam . . . sed hoc intellige de iure civili, non de iure canonico." See also Langbein, *Prosecuting Crime in the Renaissance*, 195: "It must be remembered that the Carolina [1532] dates from half a century before the advent in Europe of the sentence of imprisonment as a regular mode of punishment"; idem, "The Historical Origins of the Sanction of Imprisonment for Serious Crime," *Journal of Legal Studies* 5 (1976): 35–60. Cf. N. Z. Davis, *The Return of Martin Guerre* (Cambridge, Mass., 1983), 87, who remarks that "a term in prison was not one of the possibilities for Arnaud du Tilh, of course, for prisons were only for people awaiting trial and convicted debtors." On early experimentation with the use of imprisonment as a form of punishment even by secular authorities in the medieval period, see J. Given ("The Inquisitors of Languedoc," 343) who concludes, however, that "it may have been rarely applied."

153. See L. Firpo, "Il processo di Giordano Bruno," *RSI* 60 (1948): 542–97; 61 (1949): 5–59, at p. 577; idem, "In margine al processo di Giordano Bruno: Francesco Maria Vialardi," ibid., 68 (1956): 325–64, at p. 345 for Vialardi's own account of his transfer to the prison of the Holy Office in Rome (1592): "Uscito di galera, menato sciolto a Roma e benissimo trattato di stanze, commodità di studiare e di ogni cosa, non negatimi i sagramenti santi, né compagnia, né visite, né scrivere; accarezzato da' cardinali. . . ." The provision for the regular inspection of prisons was an ancient one. See Eymeric, *Directorium Inquisitorum*, 590: "Inquisitores autem aliquotiens in anno perpetuum carcerem visitabunt, ut videant qualiter vivant, quomodo tractentur, & quam vitam degant. . . ." It was reinforced through numerous decrees issued by the Roman Congregation during the sixteenth century. See, among others, one dated 18 June 1564, in Pastor, *Allgemeine Dekrete*, 25. The decree, dated 12 April 1593, was intended to prevent protracted judicial proceedings. Every month the names of the prisoners and the status of their trials were to be presented to the Congregation of the Inquisition for its review (ibid., 52). On the change of laundry for inmates, see the decree of 14 March 1595 (ibid., 55 f.). On the obligations concerning cell furnishings, see the 1611 *Ordini da osservarsi da gl'Inquisitori*: "Non tenghano presso di se lenzola, tovaglie, mantelli, ne cose simili, per accomodar in affitto a carcerati, ma gli provedano d'un pagliariccio, d'un lenzolo solo, e di una schiavina [a long outer garment or cloak], o una coperta, e chi vorrà star più commodamente, se li trovarà a loro spese a pigione." On the expenses incurred in the Holy Office for the maintenance of prisoners in Rome during a single month (November 1596), see A. Mercati, *Il sommario del processo di Giordano Bruno*, 121–26. As an example of what was incurred by a single prisoner over a one month period, see the itemized account for a certain Don Scipione Mesita: "Deve

il Santo Officio per le spese cibarie di detto Scipione dal primo di Agosto 1593 per tutto li 20 di Maggio 1595 a scudi quattro il mese: scudi 86.61. Per un giuppone, giuli 16: 1.60; per un paro di calzette, giuli cinque: .50; per un paro di scarpe et un paro di pianelle [slippers], giuli sette e mezzo: .75; per un paro di calzoni, giuli dicidotto: 1.80; per carta straccia, baiochi dui: .2; al barbiero, giuli undici: 1.10; panni lavati, giuli quattro: .40. In tutto, scudi 92.84." In general, see A. Bertolotti, *Le prigioni di Roma*, and especially Scanaroli, *De Visitatione Carceratorum*, passim.

In April 1986 I was permitted to visit the ancient apartments of the Holy Office in the convent of San Domenico in Bologna. The interrogation room on the top floor is an elegant, airy, richly frescoed (eighteenth-century?) chamber. Down the hall from it were the tribunal's offices and cells. On a lower floor is a comfortable bedroom once used by the inquisitor (it too beautifully frescoed), equipped with a large bed and desk. Today it accommodates the convent's distinguished overnight visitors. The hall outside the bedroom is adorned with a long series of inquisitors' portraits. At one end of it another bedroom serves as quarters for the provincial.

154. BAV, Barb. lat. 6334, fol. 38r, letter of the Roman Congregation to the inquisitor of Rimini, 14 February 1626: "Gasparo Giurza [?] già fiscale di cotesto S.to Officio si duole della lunga prigionia in carcere humido et cattivo con evidente pericolo della salute sua in età già grave et valetudinaria, facendo istanza di essere quantoprima spedito et in tanto habilitato. Questi miei SS.ri Ill.mi mi hanno commesso di scrivere a V.R. che subito mandi quello che ha contro di lui . . . et in tanto con sicurtà de tutto carcere lo habiliti a miglior stanza"; ibid., fol. 42v., letter from the Roman Congregation to the bishop of Lucca, 21 February 1626, ordering more comfortable prisons for two women "sortileghe" accused of attempted murder: ". . . si sono dolute [the women] di essere già molti mesi ritenute in pessime prigioni con evidente pericolo della vita . . ."; see also the letter to the Roman Congregation from a provincial official: ". . . quà non sono prigioni sicure secrete": *Istruzioni ed atti relativi ad un procedimento inquisitoriale di stregoneria nella terra di Sermoneta, l'anno 1575: Lettere delli cardinali di Pisa e Sermoneta al vicario Gio. Francesco Bonamici Commissario dell' Inquisitione di Roma a Sermoneta* (Florence [1920], 7). The problem of the lack of adequate prisons fills the correspondence of the cardinal of Santa Severina with the inquisitor of Aquileia and Concordia. The pope himself had to intervene to order the patriarch to construct prisons in that city for Holy Office use. See, among several letters of the cardinal, one dated 7 December 1591, inquiring whether the patriarch had kept his word (see ACAU, Epistolae S. Officii, 1588–1613, unpaginated).

155. See BA, MS. B–1860, fol. 110, letter of Antonio Balduzzi, commissioner of the Roman Congregation, to the inquisitor of Bologna (21 January 1573): "Occorrendo che da V.R. comparessero alcuni Hebrei, o altri per loro, et domandassero una, o due copie d'un indice de' suoi libri, che furono posti lì nel S.to Ufficio, et anco vi si trovano, sarà contenta dargliela facendogli pagare, o per dire meglio, fare cortesia al nuotaro che la scriverà per le sue fatiche. Il detto indice si trova tra le scritture del S.to Ufficio, o nel primo armariolo, entrando nello studio o in una

di quelle cassette. Di più se vorano vedere detti libri, V.R. gli lasciarà vedere, che sono là in quelle priggioni da basso, non però permetta che se ne porti via alcuno senza nostr'ordine." Balduzzi is well informed because the books must have been consigned to the Bolognese Holy Office when he served there as inquisitor.

156. In general, see M. Bourdet-Pléville, *Justice in Chains: From the Galleys to Devil's Island*, trans. from the French by A. Rippon (London, 1960); P. W. Bamford, *Fighting Ships and Prisons: The Mediterranean Galleys of France in the Age of Louis XIV* (Minneapolis, 1973); R. Pike, *Penal Servitude in Early Modern Spain* (Madison, 1983) and "Penal Servitude in Early Modern Spain: The Galleys," *Journal of European Economic History* 2 (1982): 197–217; P. M. Conlon, *Jean-François Bion et sa relation des torments soufferts par les forçats protestants* (Geneva, 1966) (the first ed. of Bion's *Relation* dates to 1708). His account served as the basis of André Chamson's remarkable and moving "roman dans l'histoire," *La Superbe* (Paris, 1967). For Italy in particular, see A. Vecchi, "Le memorie di un uomo da remo (1565–1576)," *Rivista marittima* 16 (1884): 51–80, 209–58 (the recollections of a Florentine musician, Aurelio Scetti); B. C. [i.e., Benedetto Croce], "La vita infernale delle galere," *Quaderni della critica* 3 (1948), no. 10: 84–91 (publishes the "Suma de la vida infernal de galera," the anonymous verses of a Spaniard residing in Naples sentenced to the galleys. One can consult with great profit the numerous studies on sixteenth-century seafaring by A. Tenenti, such as his "Gli schiavi di Venezia alla fine del Cinquecento," *RSI* 67 (1955): 52–69 and *Piracy and the Decline of Venice* (London, 1967), esp. chap. 6, "The Light Galleys." An extremely important source for galley life in the sixteenth century is Cristoforo Canale's *Della milizia marittima*, ed. M. N. Mocenigo (Rome, 1930), written c. 1540, a year or two before Venice changed from voluntary to largely convict labor on its galleys. This departure was conceived by Canale (*Provveditore Generale dell'Armata*), who died in combat with Barbary corsairs on 18 June 1562. On this brilliant naval theoretician, see Tenenti's *Cristoforo da Canal: La marine vénitienne avant Lépante* (Paris, 1972). For the papal navy, see A. Guglielmotti's *Storia della marina pontificia*, 10 vols. (Rome, 1886), esp. 7:195 ff. for regulations of convict life on the galleys, wardrobe, alimentation, dockside duties, etc. On the Turkish slaves who comprised a large percentage of the crews of the Christian vessels in the sixteenth and seventeenth centuries and on the possibilities open to them of purchasing their freedom, see A. Bertolotti, "La schiavitù in Roma dal secolo XVI al XIX," *Rivista di discipline carcerarie* 17 (1887): 3–41; J. Mathieux, "Trafic et prix de l'homme en Méditerranée aux XVIIe et XVIIIe siècles," *Annales: ESC* 9 (1954): 157–64. The best recent treatment is A. Viario, "La pena della galera," in G. Cozzi, ed., *Stato, società e giustizia nella repubblica veneta (sec. XV–XVIII)*, 377–480. See also, by the same author, "I forzati sulle galere veneziane (1760–1797)," *Studi veneziani*, n.s., 2 (1978): 225–50; F. C. Lane, "Wages and Recruitment of Venetian Galeotti, 1470–1580," ibid., n.s., 6 (1982): 15–44; R. Bernardini, "Un convegno sulla vita a bordo delle navi nel Mediterraneo nel Cinquecento e nel Seicento," *Archivio storico italiano*, a. 145, no. 534 (1987): 677–86 (the papers from this symposium have been published in *Quaderni stefaniani* 6 (1987): 1–198; A. Olivieri, "Un

'modello' Mediterraneo: La città nave in Cristoforo da Canal," *Il Veltro* 23 (1979): 229–40 and "Ordine e fortuna: Lo spazio della galea veneziana del '500," ibid., 27 (1983): 469–76. Olivieri's two somewhat elusive but interesting studies focus on da Canal's utopian conceptions of the possibilities offered by galley life. M. Aymard ("Chiourmes et galères dans la Méditerranée du XVIe siècle," in *Histoire économique du monde méditerranéen, 1450–1650,* Melanges en l'Honneur de Fernand Braudel [Toulouse, 1973], 1:49–64) is indispensable for the recruitment of the crews, as is G. Alessi Palazzolo ("Pene e 'remieri' a Napoli tra Cinque e Seicento: Un' aspetto singolare dell'illegalismo d'ancien régime," *Archivio storico per le province napoletane,* ser. 3, 15 [1976]: 235–51), which concentrates on judicial short-cuts and illegalities practiced in Neapolitan civil courts to guarantee a sufficient number of oarsmen, always in short supply.

157. TCD, MS. 1225, fol. 232. He had been convicted "dell' esserti nominato falsamente inquisitore et vicario et come tale fatto molte cose, et sotto pretesto dell'officio cercato haver pratica disonesta con donne . . . hai fatto carcerare un putto per la bestemmia . . . davi licentia a librari di vender libri in Valenza."

158. TCD, MS. 1226, fol. 316, sentence to three years in the galleys pronounced in Milan (13 October 1581) against Giovanni Francesco Castiglione for blasphemy and sacrilege: ". . . che biastemando hai tagliato li piedi a una imagine d'uno crocifixo depinto . . . che hai gettato delli danari in faccia di detto crocifixo depinto, dicendo 'piglia traditore'. . . che hai detto che non volevi più Iddio dalla tua parte, ma il demonio." Persons liable to the death penalty for heresies proscribed in the special decrees of Paul IV (see n. 171) frequently had their sentences reduced to terms of service on the galleys or imprisonment. See also TCD, MS. 1228, fol. 218, sentence to seven years at the oar "remigando nel pane del dolore" imposed in Rome against Guido Ricci da Monte Alcino for bigamy and the use of false witnesses; TCD, MS. 1224, fol. 217, sentence against Jammone de Mina of Faenza, "hortulano" (20 September 1567): he had repeatedly denied his heresies and finally confessed under torture; so that he might be an "essempio alli ostinati et renitenti al confessare la verità, ti condenniamo alla galera per cinque anni"; ibid., fol. 211, sentence against Don Hieronymo del Pozzo, a priest of Faenza (20 September 1567) who avoided being sent to the galleys because of a physical disability: ". . . meritando tu grandissima pena per esser sacerdote . . . attesa l'infirmità tua ti condenniamo ad essere immurato perpetuamente"; TCD, MS. 1225, fol. 294, sentence to seven years in the Venetian galleys pronounced at Verona on 11 September 1580 against Giacomo dell'Amingella da Brenzon, a bigamist, who "più volte [hai] tentato di fugire rompendo le carcere"; TCD, MS. 1227, fol. 139, sentence dated 31 May 1582 against Joannes Pilutius de Castro Julianelli, condemned to seven years of galley service for the unjust prosecution of four women "sub praetextu quod essent striges." See also the severe legislation enacted by the Roman Congregation against members of orders convicted of practicing occult arts: "Ill.mi etc. decreverunt et declaraverunt quod decretum alias die 19 septembris 1591 habitum quod fratres ordinis Minorum de Observantia reperti culpabiles in materia nicromantiae condemnentur ad triremes

per decennium, stare et intelligi debeat ita, ut usque ad talem poenam inclusive damnari possint plus et minus iuxta delictorum, personarum, locorum et temporum scandalique resultantis et aliarum circumstantiarum qualitatem, dummodo talis poena non excedatur" (Pastor, *Allgemeine Dekrete*, 53; decree of 25 May 1593 confirming the earlier pronouncement).

159. See, for example, the sentence against Hieronymo del Pozzo in the note above.

160. Letter printed by Pastor, *History of the Popes* 14:459, in which Ghislieri referred to galley sentences as "penitentia da disperati o da dimonii et di poco frutto."

161. M. Scaduto, "Tra inquisitori e riformati: Le missioni dei Gesuiti tra Valdesi della Calabria e delle Puglie, con un carteggio inedito del card. Alessandrino (S. Pio V), 1561–1566," *Archivum Historicum Societatis Iesu* 15 (1946): 1–76, at p. 47.

162. The inquiry of the Holy Office of Malta (12 May 1604) is preserved in BAV, Borg. lat. 558, fol. 52. The same advice was also received by the inquisitor of Milan: Fumi, "L'inquisizione Romana," 31. According to Döpler (*Theatrum Poenarum*, 793), practices in Italy varied: "Nobiles et minores in Regno Neapolitano loco ejusdem poenae triremium relegantur in aliquam insulam . . . sed in statu ecclesiastico hoc male servatur, quia etiam nobiles transmittuntur ad triremes . . . sed doctores ad triremes de facili condemnari non debent. . . ."

163. See the letter dated 1 March 1572 to Sauli from the cardinal secretary of state, Tolomeo Galli: "De li forzati vedo che V.S. si piglia quel travaglio et usa quella diligenza che conviene per obedir al commandamento di N.S. et meritar insieme col far opera di charità tanto degna. Così son certo che lei supererà tutte le difficultà et subterfugii di quelli che li hanno in potere." See P. Villani, ed., *Nunziature di Napoli, 26 Luglio 1570–24 Maggio 1577* (Rome, 1962), 1:397.

164. See Bodl. MS. Mendham 36, a volume of miscellaneous writings of inquisitorial interest, chapter entitled "Delli Avvertimenti Generali," fol. 75r: "Quelli sacerdoti che sono condannati alla galera del S. Officio, et in effetto vi sono mandati a remigare, se o per haver compiuto il tempo della loro condannatione, o per gratia che ottengono dalla benignità del S. Officio ne vengono liberati, gl'inquisitori et ordinarii non sogliono habilitargli più a celebrare la S.ta messa essendosi indecentissimo e scandaloso il veder passare huomini dal remo all'altare." On the degradation of clerics sentenced to the galleys or to perpetual imprisonment, carried out "verbaliter" only, see Peña's commentary to Eymeric's *Directorium Inquisitorum*, 518.

165. In two sentences to the galleys pronounced by the Inquisition of Verona in August and September 1580 (TCD, MS. 1225, fols. 265 and 294) it was specified that if the prisoners at any time became *inhabili* their sentences were to be commuted to banishment. See also BAV, Barb. lat. 6334, fol. 168r, letter dated 20 June 1626, from the Supreme Congregation to the inquisitor of Pisa: "A Stefano Fiorini da Pescia già che per la relatione che V. R. ne da col parere de' medici si trova affatto inhabile a continuare la pena della galera, si contentano questi miei SS.ri Ill.mi di commutargliela in che tenga la casa per carcere et dia sicurtà idonea di non uscire senza licenza di V. R." Further evidence of medical inspections is offered by a slightly later communication to the same inquisitor of Pisa (25 July; ibid., fol. 208v): "Frate

Ubertino della Badia di S. Salvatore Min. Oss.te condannato dal S.to Officio alla galera ha supplicato per la gratia, dando fede del Bellati et Chiappini, fisico et chirurgo dell'hospedale de' schiavi et forzati delle galere, di essere per alcune indispositioni poco habile alla fatica del remo." The Congregation asks for confirmation of this condition. Scanaroli (*De Visitatione Carceratorum*, 353) describes the heartrending sight of a group of prisoners being returned to the Torre di Nona in Rome, a civil prison, after having been deemed unable to support further the life of the galley slave: "Quam miserum de se spectaculum praebent! exangues, pallidi, toto corpore immanes plagarum vibices, & tergum crudelissimis verberibus laceratum ostentant."

166. See the letter from the Roman Congregation to the bishop of Todi, 13 January 1626 (BAV, Barb. lat. 6334, fol. 3v) concerning a certain Prospero Rubino, assigned to the vigilance of the bishop during the month Rubino would be at home. The prisoner had been granted permission "di poter venire costà et trattenervisi un mese per dare in quel tempo rassetto alle cose sue famigliari; vogliono però che egli stia in casa, e non esca se non rarissime volte, et con licenza di V. S., la quale sarà parca in concedergliela, et alla fine del mese gli incaricherà il ritorno a Roma. . . ." See also the letter to the inquisitor of Milan written on the same day (ibid., fol. 6v) concerning a Giovanni Battista Cattaneo, a priest who had been sent to the galleys in July 1620 for seven years. He now alleged that his family—an aged mother and three sisters, one of them unmarried—was in need. Since he had served much of his term, his sentence was commuted and he was returned to his home, with the obligation to fulfill the salutary penances which had been imposed on him.

167. See TCD, MS. 1226, fols. 10 ff. for the dossier containing the case of Carlo Chiavello. The appeal addressed to the pope alleged that "il povero huomo si ritrova vecchio, infermo, crepato dalle parti da basso, inutile a essercitare tal pena . . . trovandosi carico di sette figlioli . . . tra quali quattro femmine, che senza l'aiuto paterno andaranno in ruina con pericolo anco dell'anime loro. . . ." The letter to Cardinal Savello from the inquisitor of Genoa disputed many of these facts: ". . . ha [Chiavello] molti figlioli costui ma è molto accomodato di robba perchè trafica bene et adesso in galera fa mercantia di vino et non si lascia mancar. È molto industrioso, vecchio non è, nel che ha supplicato il falso. È huomo d'anni 40 in circa più et meno . . . et a questo v'è il rimedio, compri uno schiavo Mahumettano et lo facci vogar per lui. Ha il modo di poter farlo."

168. See G. Gigli, *Diario romano, 1608–1670* (Rome, 1958), 191, which describes the reading of a sentence in St. Peter's in Rome (19 March 1640) against a Capuchin who had apostatized from his order and married: ". . . questo fu condannato in galera, o per dir meglio, nel loco destinato per i Religiosi delinquenti a Civitavecchia"; and ibid., 481, where Gigli reports services performed in the city during a plague in July 1656: "Li ammalati erano portati al Lazzaretto dentro una bara coperta da doi schiavi, cioè huomini condannati alla galera. . . ."

169. This conclusion is based especially on a close analysis of the sentences preserved in Trinity College Library, Dublin.

170. Mandatory execution of the *relapsus* dated to the decretal "Ad Abolendam" issued by Pope Lucius III, 4 November 1184. See H. Maisonneuve, *Études sur les origines de l'inquisition*, 153: "Illos autem qui post abjurationem erroris vel postquam se, ut diximus, proprii antistitis examinatione purgaverunt, deprehensi fuerint in abjuratam haeresim recidisse, saeculari judicio sine ulla penitus audientia decernimus relinquendos, bonis damnatorum ecclesiis quibus deserviebant secundum sanctiones legitimas applicandis." On the punishment of the relapsed and of the pertinacious heretic who, even though convicted, tenaciously clung to his error, see, among many other authorities, the discussion in C. Carena, *Tractatus*, 314 ff: "De poena mortis naturalis." Burning as a means of execution had its origins in the Old Testament (2 Kings 23). Only the obdurate and pertinacious were burned alive (Carena, ibid.). For surveys of the question, see C. Moeller, "Les buchers et les auto-da-fé de l'Inquisition depuis le Moyen Age," *Revue d'histoire ecclésiastique* 14 (1913): 720–51; 15 (1914): 50–69, G. G. Coulton, *The Death Penalty for Heresy*, Medieval Studies 18 (London, 1924), and now especially L. Milva, "Violenza, guerra, pena di morte: Le proposte degli eretici medievali," *RSCI* 43 (1989): 123–44.

171. The Bulls are printed in the appendix to Eymeric's *Directorium Inquisitorum*, 121–25. See also chap. 16, "Di quelli che negano la Trinità, la Divinità di Christo, la sua Concettione di Spirito Santo, la sua Morte per nostra Redentione, o la Verginità di Maria Nostra Signora," in Cardinal Desiderio Scaglia's "Prattica" discussed at pp. 229–58. An example of the pertinent offenses is contained in a letter from the cardinal of Santa Severina to the inquisitor of Florence, dated 2 March 1591 (BRB, MS. II 290, vol. 2, fol. 19r): "V.R.tia avvertisca, che per la Bolla di Papa Paolo 4 di felice memoria promulgata contro quelli che negano, o non credano la S.ma Trinità, la perpetua virginità della Beatissima sempre Vergine Maria, o la Divinità di Christo N.ro Sig.re, ancorchè siano nel primo lapso, et siano penitenti, nondimeno si rilasciano al braccio secolare. Il che potrà dire a cotesti reverendi consultori, aciochè non habbino da dubitare dell'intelletto della predetta Bolla." The decree punishing unqualified celebrants is published in Locati, *Opus quod iudiciale inquisitorum dicitur*, 476.

172. A long galley sentence might be substituted. See, for instance, the case of Don Ottavio Piamontesi, who was sentenced at Reggio on 21 April 1581 to ten years of service at the oar for blasphemies in which he had denied the Virgin Birth, etc. (TCD, MS. 1226, fol. 126).

173. See "Toward a Statistical Profile," at pp. 103 f.

174. See, for an example of the practice, the letter of the cardinal of Santa Severina to the inquisitor of Aquileia and Concordia, 10 September 1588 (ACAU, Epistolae S. Officii, 1588–1613; unpaginated) concerning the case of a Daniele Cargniello, "heretico ostinato": the inquisitor is ordered "di far condurre il detto Daniele in alcuna terra o luogo della sua diocesi dove le carceri siano sicure in modo che non possa fuggire, et quivi sia ritenuto per alcun mese, et tra tanto sia instrutto et spesse volte visitato et essortato da persone dotte, religiose et pie . . . usi et facci ogni diligenza possibile per liberare quell'anima dalle mani del Demonio. . . ." Almost a month

later, on 8 October, a second letter from the cardinal acknowledged that caution in rushing to judgment might forestall gross miscarriages of justice: ". . . si procede con termini più lunghi *ad resipiscendum*, et si danno e concedono . . . più volte per il pericolo che porta tal giudicio ch'egli sia innocente et i testimonii non veri . . ." The cardinal urges the custom of sending pious people to win over the pertinacious heretic "conforme all' instruttione del *Direttorio*. . .," undoubtedly a reference to one of several possible passages in Eymeric's *Directorium Inquisitorum*. See, for example, Peña's commentary at p. 331: "In his pertinacibus haec regula est observanda: diu sunt detinendi & saepius monendi ut convertantur, quod si noluerint poenitere, tradendi sunt absque misericordia curiae saeculari." On the supplication of family members, brought to Rome from Piedmont in the case of G. L. Pascale, see n. 177.

175. See Carena, *Tractatus*, 317; F. Peña, commentary to Eymeric's *Directorium Inquisitorum*, 488. See also the letter from the Roman Congregation to the inquisitor of Milan, 21 March 1626: ". . . se egli [a certain Albertino accused of occult practices] ha col cuore apostatato abiuri de formali, essendo l'età sua d'anni 16 molto bene capace d'abiura, nella quale però attesa la minorità dovrà mettersi la clausola 'citra poenam relapsi'" (BAV, Barb. lat. 6334, fol. 69v). See also "Inquisitorial Sources and Their Uses," notes 14 ff.

176. Peña in Eymeric's *Directorium Inquisitorum*, 512: ". . . licet enim cum ita res haec celebratur in Hispania, videre, horrendum, ac tremendum spectaculum, & quasi imaginem futuri iudicii, quo nihil esse potest ad terrorem incutiendum in hac causa aptius et accomodatius." The second account is in Bodl. MS. Mendham 36, fols. 235–36, an undated description of a Madrid *auto*. On the iconography of these ceremonies, see M. V. González de Caldas, "Nuevas imagenes del Santo Oficio en Sevila: El auto de fe," in A. Alcalá, ed., *Inquisición española y mentalidad inquisitorial*, 237–65.

177. See especially the vivid contemporary account in a Roman *Avviso* (BAV, Cod. Urbin. 1039, fol. 205v) cited by P. Paschini, "Episodi dell'Inquisizione a Roma nei suoi primi decenni," *Studi romani* 5 (1957): 285–301, at pp. 292 f.: "È stato brusciato questi dì un gentilhuomo piemontese di Cunio, il quale è stato lungamente in Calabria, ove ha seminato la heresia lutherana, et è stato fatt'ogni possibile per farlo rivocare, d'un suo fratello ed d'altri suoi parenti venuti a posta di Piemonte per questo, ma non ha mai voluto moversi della sua opinione, et così è morto costantissimamente, et inanti la morte sua essendosi fatto un palco, sopra il quale erano i R.mi Alessandrino, Carpi, Araceli, Reumano, et volendovi anche montare il R.mo Queva, cadette il palco, pur nisuno si fece male, et allora vedendo quello il condannato, cominciò a cridar che questo era giudicio di Idio." J. R. Reinhard ("Burning at the Stake in Medieval Law and Literature," *Speculum* 16 [1941]: 186–209) deals with purely literary treatments of sanctions for adultery.

178. For the bibliography on the Roman confraternity of San Giovanni Decollato and similar associations elsewhere, see the bibliography cited in "Inquisitorial Sources and Their Uses," at n. 119.

179. See H. C. Lea, *Materials Toward a History of Witchcraft* 2:674, 808; O. Aureggi, "La stregoneria nelle Alpi centrali. Ricerche di diritto e procedura penale," *Bolletti-*

no della Società Storica Valtellinese, no. 15 (1961): 114–60, at p. 128n. See also Deodato Scaglia's unpublished "La Theorica di procedere tanto in generale, quanto in particolare ne' casi appartenenti alla Sante Fede": "La prattica però, che per questa equità hoggidi [the work is dated 1637] s'usa è di far prima stroncar questi rei innanzi che si accenda il fuoco" (Bodl., MS. Add. C. 31, p. 78).

Peña, in his commentary to the *Directorium Inquisitorum*, disagreed with Eymeric on the question of whether last minute conversions and abjurations were acceptable, even if the victim was already bound to the stake. The latter had written that they were, and that the sentence could be commuted to perpetual imprisonment (p. 514); but Peña objected, ". . . tutius est, ut nullo modo recipiatur, etiamsi millies promittat veram conversionem . . . tum quoniam experientia docuit, hos ita receptos, raro bonos evasisse: ergo nullo modo recipiantur . . ." (p. 518).

180. BA, MS. B–1860, fol. 160.

181. Ibid., fol. 193 (21 August 1574).

182. *Tractatus*, 214, 216: "Ex quibus colligitur, quod comedens carnes in die Ieiunii, etiam sine licentia superioris, si id non faciat in Ecclesiae contemptum, sed ex iusta causa, maxime per medicum approbata non est de haeresi suspectus . . ."; "Quo ad torturam super intentione, illa non videtur danda regulariter, nisi vehementer suspectis."

183. See "Inquisitorial Sources and Their Uses," at n. 20. This development has counterparts in other European court systems. See J. Langbein (*Torture*, 57), who describes the German process of centralization and professionalization. In Hesse as early as 1540 the government was requiring local courts to forward to it trial dossiers on every case involving capital crimes; in Saxony by 1620 such cases were being assigned to one of four superior courts. In France, for the institutionalization of an obligatory appeal to the *Parlement* of Paris from the lower jurisdictions, see, among A. Soman's many exemplary studies, "La decriminalisation de la sorcellerie en France," *Histoire, économie et société* 4 (1985), no. 4: 179–203; idem, "La justice criminelle aux XVIe–XVIIe siècles: le Parlement de Paris et les sièges subalternes," in *Actes du 107e Congrès national des Sociétés savantes, Brest, 1982. . .1. La faute, la répression et le pardon* (Paris, 1984), 15–52.

184. BA, MS. B–1860, fol. 165, letter of Antonio Balduzzi to the inquisitor of Bologna, 26 December 1573: "Il sfrattato ch'ha preso moglie desiderarei mandassi il caso in forma continente, e quello che s'ha contra di lui, e quello che confessa perchè di queste materie che tanto importano, non è bene parlarne così in aere ma con la verità ben fondata."

185. TCD, MS. 1225, fol. 194, sentence pronounced 26 April 1580 against Giovanni Francesco Pegorari of Legnago, *speciale*.

186. BA, MS. B–1860, fol. 171, Balduzzi to the inquisitor of Bologna, 23 January 1574.

187. Ibid., fol. 163, Balduzzi to the inquisitor of Bologna, 3 December 1573: "Quant' al fatto di quello ch'ha ferito e mal trattato l'imagine del crocifisso, a volere buona rissolutione bisogna che V. R. mi scriva, se l'ha fatto in disprezzo, et ad

animo quieto *vel calore iracundiae*, et s'ha altri indicii di mala vita di questo tale circa la santa fede perchè queste circonstanze aggravano e sgravano assai il delitto. . . ." See Carena's cautioning words in his *Tractatus*, 281: ". . . Inquisitor non debet esse admodum facilis ad credendum excusationem desumptam ex ira. . . ." On the release by the inquisitor of Venice of a certain Antonio da Bassano "in preda d'humor melanconico," see the letter of the nuncio, F. G. A. Facchinetti to M. Bonelli, dated 8 June 1566, in *Nunziature di Venezia*, ed. A. Stella (Rome, 1963), 8:59.

SIX

≈

The Roman Inquisition and Witchcraft: An Early Seventeenth-Century "Instruction" on Correct Trial Procedure

A s had been his custom on numerous other occasions,[1] Cardinal Giovanni Garcia Millino, one of the senior members of the Congregation of the Holy Office, took pen in hand on 9 May 1624 to respond to queries raised by a provincial official in regard to the prosecution of suspected witches. On this particular day, addressing himself to the bishop of Lodi, Millino introduced a significant new element into his reply:

> The question of witchcraft has always been considered fallacious and uncertain here, as it is, in fact; and, often, even experienced and knowledgeable persons have exceeded proper bounds, and quickly encountered difficulties, which occasioned errors prejudicial to the Holy Office, to inquisitors, and also to those instituting trials, since it is a crime difficult to verify, and in which a great role is played by the frivolity and flightiness of women, and the treachery of the Devil who is the teacher and father of lies. Therefore, in regard to what your lordship writes about the witches, I must tell you, by order of my most illustrious colleagues, that you and the father inquisitor should take careful note of the enclosed Instructions, which I send to you, Rome, 9 May 1624.[2]

This is the first mention known to me of the celebrated *Instructio pro formandis processibus in causis strigum, sortilegiorum, et maleficiorum*. This document, addressed to bishops, their vicars, and inquisitors, which opens with the solemn words, "Experientia rerum magistra," contains a thorough-going condemnation of the abuses practiced in the pursuit of witches, and enunciates a number of moderating, reforming principles to guide judges in their search for an equitable resolution in cases of this type.[3]

The *Instructio*, despite the claims that have been made for it as a revolutionary statement introducing "the changed and changing attitudes of the Curia,"[4] and marking an abrupt "break with traditional inquisitorial practice in the matter of witchcraft prosecution,"[5] remains basically little known and has not received the detailed critical study that it deserves. The present brief discussion is intended to stimulate a more complete investigation of the *Instructio*, one based on significant new archival research.

I should like to raise here several questions which touch on virtually every aspect of the *Instructio*, from the historical circumstances that produced it, connected to the issue of its authorship, to the question of its ultimate significance and importance as an innovative document. The uncertainties and confusion which surround our text (or rather texts, because there are many variants among them, as we shall see in a moment) are connected both to the irregular means chosen by Rome for the early circulation and publication of the document, as well as to our ignorance of the development of inquisitorial law, including, of course, its application in witchcraft cases.

What was the original impulse for the writing of the *Instructio*? Was it called forth by a specific event—to mitigate the severity of Gregory XVth Bull "Omnipotentis Dei" (20 March 1623), which imposed the death sentence on persons convicted of having apostatized to the Devil and having committed a *maleficium* resulting in a fatal injury, even though a first offense?[6] Or was it written, as has also been suggested, as a sequel to a celebrated case of two Milanese witches sentenced to death by secular authorities on 28 November 1619 over the protests of the Holy Office in Rome?[7] There are other viable explanations to be considered as well, including the possibility of influence from foreign sources. The German Jesuit Adam Tanner's *Disputationes Theologicae*, a work which breathed moderation into the vexed question of the credence which should be afforded to the testimony of alleged witches,[8] had appeared at Ingolstadt in 1617. Even more fertile terrain for exploration, perhaps, is offered by the possibility that Roman inquisitors, consciously or not, were following the good example of Spanish colleagues on the *Suprema* who, on 29 Au-

Virtually on the heels of its appearance in the *De Potestate Angelica*, the *Instructio* was introduced as an appendix in Cesare Carena's *Tractatus*, beginning with the Cremona edition of 1655, and curiously, it is attributed to him on the title page. This is the text (with Castaldi's reference to meddling secular magistrates omitted), which has been cited by the few modern students of our subject. In this appendix Carena also provides the *editio princeps* of what purport to be books one and two of an *Instructio seu Praxis Inquisitorum* by Francisco Peña, the scholarly Spanish theologian, doctor of both laws, dean of the Rota, and eminent inquisitorial authority. Carena claimed that he had not been able to find the third book which rounded out Peña's work, despite his assiduous efforts to discover it, and he had thus resolved to attach the *Instructio* to it since it dealt with the same matter, witchcraft, as the missing portion of Peña's *Praxis*. It seemed to Carena a convenient way to fill this gap.[22]

The possibility that Peña, editor of inquisitorial texts and perhaps the leading Roman expert on Holy Office procedures in the decades at the turn of the century, was, in fact, himself the author of our text is unlikely if we consider Castaldi's declaration that the mysterious compiler of the *Instructio* was a close friend of his. The discrepancy in dates—Peña died in 1612, Castaldi in 1655—would seem to rule out Peña's direct hand, if not the lingering influence of his learning, in the final preparation of the text.[23]

Two years after its appearance in Carena's *Tractatus*, and more than thirty years after it first circulated in manuscript, the *Instructio* was finally published in Rome, in 1657, as an official pronouncement of the Church in a thin pamphlet of eight closely printed pages, bearing the imprint in the colophon of the *Reverenda Camera Apostolica*. But the document is still clothed in anonymity. It lacks a title page, does not claim to have been issued under the sponsorship of the Holy Office, and curiously survives in only one copy, which bears the signature of the German inquisitor Leonhard Messen, preserved at the Cornell University Library.[24] It is uncertain why Rome chose to openly publish the directive at this time, but certainly the persecution of witches was rampant throughout northern Europe to the enormous detriment of due legal process.

The 1657 edition introduced further textual variants to previous versions. There is now no mention at all of bungling ecclesiastical judges, nor even of meddling secular magistrates, but only of judges, *iudices*, guilty of excesses in the administration of the law; and two sentences critical of the practices of exorcists have also been dropped.[25] Rome, at approximately mid-century, seemed less willing than a generation before to accept blame in the matter of witchcraft prosecution.

The circulation of the *Instructio* in manuscript as well as in new printed editions, both at home and abroad, continued well into the second half of the eighteenth century and testifies to the direct impact of the 1657 Roman printing. In 1661, a German translation was produced by the Benedictine Konrad Hunger, pastor at Einsiedeln, which he dedicated to the *Landrat* of the Canton of Schwyz.[26] In April 1669, Casimir Florian Czartoryski, bishop of Cujavia and Pomerania, issued a pastoral letter which vividly described judicial abuses practiced in the area under his jurisdiction and promulgated a series of reforms, suggested, he said, by an "Instructione Romana—1657 edita" which had come to his attention.[27]

There is evidence of an edition of the *Instructio* at Gdynia (Gedani), based on Czartoryski's pastoral letter;[28] and the work also reappeared in several late and posthumous editions of Carena's *Tractatus*.[29] In 1683 the work was reprinted in the exceedingly rare *De Inconstantia in Iure Admittenda vel non* (Amsterdam, 1683) by Cardinal Francesco Albizzi, an influential member of the Holy Office.[30] Albizzi basically published the version of 1657, but he also took liberties with the text and deleted an entire long paragraph especially devoted to the status of women ("genus est maxime superstitiosum"), which contained the crucial admonition that sortilege was not necessarily accompanied by formal apostasy to the Devil.[31] In a prefatory note to the text, Albizzi offered the interesting observation that the *Instructio* was circulated by the Holy Office to "iudices fidei," accompanied by encyclical letters to ensure that it would be put into effect without fail.[32] The *Instructio* made its final appearance in print in the seventeenth century at Florence in 1685, tucked away as chapter twenty-six of G. B. Neri's *De iudice S. Inquisitionis opusculum*.[33]

The diffusion of the *Instructio* in print continued unabated in the eighteenth century. Editions were brought out in Rome in 1704[34] and, under Jesuit auspices, at Braunsberg in 1705;[35] in versions which differed strikingly from one another and from previous editions by Giacopo Pignatelli in various printings of his *Novissimae Consultationes Canonicae*;[36] and, finally, as an appendix to a late edition of Spee's *Cautio Criminalis* (Augsburg, 1731), a work which, as was noted, has frequently and improperly been given chronological precedence over the *Instructio*. Finally, it was praised for its moderate tone and quoted at length by the celebrated social reformer Girolamo Tartarotti in his manifesto against the continuing witch persecution, *Del congresso notturno delle lammie libri tre* (Rovere-to, 1749).

This brief survey leads to the question: what was the reason for Rome's private circulation of the text in manuscript form and its delay in printing it, a step which would have clearly afforded a greater impact for its reforming message?[37] I have no certain reply, but one strong possibility may be curial hesitation to exacerbate its conflict with secular authorities who were, even before the *Instructio*, accusing the Holy Office of softness in the prosecution of witchcraft, contesting its jurisdiction, and increasing the severity of their own procedures. The lay courts of Italy were making strenuous efforts to appropriate the right of meting out deserved punishment for what was considered a heinous crime.[38] The inquisitorial tribunals, which treated witchcraft as any other heresy and dealt mildly with the first-time offender who expressed a desire to repent, were not thought to be doing their duty in eradicating the scourge. A striking example of this is offered by the case of twenty witches tried together by the inquisitor of Novara in 1580. Their sentence, issued on 3 September, dispensed justice as follows: two were to be retained in prison for further examination, ten were to be released after offering security, seven were totally acquitted, and only one was convicted of the crime. She was sentenced to perpetual imprisonment, tantamount to a confinement of six months to three years, probably to be served in her own home under her husband's watchful eye.[39] Paolo Sarpi's rebuke of the Inquisition's treatment of this offense is well known: "Concerning maleficent witchcraft, the most excellent Grand Council ordered that it be punished by the magistrates, because the ecclesiastical penalties are not adequate chastisement for so great a crime."[40] There is an abundance of evidence that the harsh policy of the secular judges reflected popular hatred of witches. The Congregation of the Inquisition frequently had to remind its ministers to shield from the violence and fury of the people convicted women being led in procession to their abjuration and sentencing or being ceremonially whipped about the town.[41]

The question of identifying the author of the document remains. The most solid clue in our possession, as we may remember, is Castaldi's elusive mention that the compiler of the *Instructio* was a highly placed member of the Holy Office who had been a close friend.[42] There is evidence pointing to Desiderio Scaglia, a senior official of the Roman Congregation who would have been well known to Castaldi. Scaglia, a native of

Brescia,[43] studied theology at the Dominican faculty in Bologna,[44] served as inquisitor successively at Pavia, Cremona, and Milan,[45] and was appointed *Commissario* of the Holy Office by Paul V and cardinal in 1621. He was also twice elected to episcopal sees, Melfi and Como, resigning from the latter responsibility in 1626.[46] During his long Roman career he was at the center of the principal litigation of the day, including the prosecution of Tommaso Campanella,[47] and was a signatory to the sentences of the apostate archbishop of Spalato, Marc'Antonio De Dominis (whom he had prosecuted personally) in 1624,[48] and Galileo in 1633.[49] These are some of the events in an illustrious life that brought Scaglia to the very threshhold of the papacy before his death in July or August 1639.[50]

There is one obscure episode from Scaglia's formative years that has not been mentioned in any of the biographical sketches of him that have come down to us. In the series of letters addressed from the Congregation of the Holy Office in Rome to the inquisitor of Bologna, there is one that defies explanation and whets our appetite to know more about Scaglia's early career. The letter in question, from one of the cardinal inquisitors, Pompeo Arrigoni, dated 1 September 1607, invites the local official to forward a document: "Reverend father. By order of these illustrious cardinals, my colleagues, I should like to ask your reverence to search in the archive of the monastery of St. Dominic there the records of the trial against fra Desiderio Scaglia of Brescia, presently inquisitor in Pavia, along with the sentence emitted against him, and send copies as quickly as possible."[51]

It was this laconic and baffling passage reporting the trial suffered by a young inquisitor who one day would rise to the highest ranks in the hierarchy, which led me, as much as anything else, to wish to know more about the *Instructio*, attributed to Scaglia by a number of sources. I must indeed confess that I succumbed to the romantic notion that Scaglia's youthful offense, perhaps involving the espousal of radical and subversive views, was connected somehow to his later authorship of a text that itself went against the temper of the times. This is pure, unfounded conjecture, of course, but it does help to explain the genesis of my interest in the present research.

Two principal pieces of evidence have led to the attribution of the *Instructio* to Desiderio Scaglia. The first is an entry in one of the earliest bio-bibliographies of the Dominican order, Andreas Rovetta's *Bibliotheca chronologica* (Bologna, 1691). Among the writings listed under Scaglia's name we find an *Instructionem, de modo formandi...*, the very title of our document.[52] We know that Rovetta used his sources negligently, was frequently inexact in his references, multiplied the number of writers to the greater glory of his order (listing the same person, for example, under three headings), introduced an arbitrary chronology, and failed to distinguish between manuscript and printed works.[53] Despite these deficiencies, the entry for Scaglia was basically accepted by the principal bibliographers of the Dominicans, Quétif and Echard, in their famous *Scriptores Ordinis Praedicatorum*.[54] They omitted, however, the word "Instruction" from the title and listed it simply as *De modo formandi processus in causis strigum atque maleficorum*.

The second piece of evidence is tied to the existence of a "Relatione copiosa di tutte le materie spettanti al tribunale del S. Offizio fatta dal Eccellentissimo Signor Cardinal Scaglia" ("Copious relation of every subject pertaining to the tribunal of the Holy Office prepared by the most excellent Cardinal Scaglia"). Chapter eight of this work, which is devoted to the subject of "De Sortileghi," bears a strong resemblance to the *Instructio*.[55] It exudes the same skeptical and cautious tone in regard to the evaluation of evidence, urges reliance on the opinions of physicians, and voices reservations about the honesty of many practicing exorcists.[56] The affinity between the two pieces has suggested that if Desiderio Scaglia was the author of the "Copious relation," he must also have had a hand in the *Instructio*. A plausible conjecture.

What is the true significance of the *Instructio pro formandis processibus in causis strigum et maleficiorum*? What was its real contribution toward the regulation of the prosecution of witches[57] or its true place in the long history of the growth and development of inquisitorial law? We saw at the beginning of this chapter that modern scholars have answered these questions differently. There have been those who, misled by the late publication date of the text, have tended to downplay its importance compared to the allegedly earlier contributions by Spanish inquisitors and German Jesuits, principally Friedrich von Spee.[58] On the other side, Carlo Ginzburg in his *The Night Battles* and Ralph Brown in a 1964 article in *The Jurist* devoted entirely to the *Instructio*, have argued that the document marked a revolution in inquisitorial procedure, a true break with previous practices and abuses.[59]

I respectfully beg to differ with both points of view, with both assessments of the *Instructio*'s importance. As for the first, I believe I have shown that the text was in circulation and even printed earlier than usually assumed and well before such other reforming writings as the *Cautio Criminalis*. As for the school that sees in the document a break on the part of the Holy Office with its previous handling of witchcraft cases, I should like to reiterate what I said earlier: The *Instructio*, by and large, was *not* enunciating new legal doctrines and proposing new safeguards for the rights of the accused, but rather, restating longstanding Roman theory and practice. Significantly, in his *De Potestate Angelica*, Castaldi referred to the *Instructio* as a work that had been "collected," in other words gathered from existing materials, not written.[60] The *Instructio* insisted that provincial judges abide by existing standards for correct procedure which had been set forth at an earlier time. As Cesare Carena admitted in his *Tractatus*, in dealing with witchcraft, a capital crime, judges frequently thought that they could dispense with accepted legal norms and take judicial short cuts.[61] Just as there is much evidence of courtroom abuses, we find vigorous Roman efforts to redress the wrongs, and severe punishments for offending judges.[62]

Only the serious study of the development of inquisitorial doctrine and practices, and a careful comparison with our document, can fully answer the questions regarding the innovative qualities of the *Instructio*. There seems to me little doubt, however, that the insistence on consultation with the physician and care in establishing the *corpus delicti*;[63] caution in proceeding to arrest, and the nullification of the testimony of a witch against an accomplice;[64] the prohibition against suggestive questioning[65] and against such indignities as the shaving of defendants' bodies;[66] the careful verification of confessions;[67] and so many other, for those times, enlightened provisions laid down by the *Instructio* existed long before, even in the pursuit of witchcraft, an excepted crime. The elements are already in place in a letter of Cardinal Millino to a French prelate, dated 1613, offering guidance on the question of witches.[68] But we can go back still further. Let me offer a concrete example.

On 12 March 1650, Cardinal Francesco Barberini, one of the senior members of the Holy Office, wrote to the inquisitor of Aquileia to inform him that the trial of the confessed *benandante* Michele Soppe had been examined in Rome and had been found to be "very defective because almost nothing confessed by him was actually verified in it."[69] The provincial official was then ordered to reopen the case and begin anew with a more

scrupulous examination of all the witnesses concerned. Rome's intervention in this trial and its insistence on a renewed investigation has been
explained in terms of influence exercised by the *Instructio*, which Barberini
actually quoted to the Aquileia inquisitor. It is described as an innovation
in the Inquisition's approach to the prosecution of witchcraft.[70]
   But we find a similar scene being enacted more than a half century before (precisely in 1592), in another provincial tribunal, Bologna, where
the local official was reprimanded in a letter from a cardinal of the Holy
Office for his conduct of a trial against a suspected witch, a certain Maria
de' Gentili. The judge had accepted unsworn testimony, contrary to accepted practice, from the principal accuser, and the defendant had confessed to a homicide.[71] But the cardinal of Santa Severina and his Roman
colleagues performed as diligent an examination of the Bolognese trial
records as Barberini's, decades later, in the case of the Friulian *benandante*;
and they were just as skeptical about the results. Here too the confession
was deemed to be deficient: ". . . her [Maria de' Gentili's] statements concerning the homicide appear highly improbable in light of the facts that
can be gathered from her trial."[72]
   For the closing decades of the sixteenth century this was not an isolated incident. Unfortunately, the general scarcity of inquisitorial records
of earlier provenance prevents us from assigning a precise turning point
in the prosecution of witchcraft as practiced by the Congregation of the
Holy Office in Rome. Regardless when it came, there is no doubt that
it found its fullest and most eloquent expression in the *Instructio pro formandis processibus in causis strigum, sortilegiorum, et maleficiorum.*

Notes

   1. See, for example, Millino's letter to the inquisitor of Bologna, dated 17 October 1609 (BA, MS. B–1863, fol. 183); M. Battistini, "Una lettera del Cardinale
Mellini riguardo un processo di stregoneria," *RSCI* 10 (1956): 269–70 (letter to
a French prelate, dated 6 September 1613); G. Bonomo, *Caccia alle streghe* (Palermo,
1971), 298 (letter to nuncio in Florence, dated 21 March 1626).
   2. BAV, Borg. lat. 660, fol. 103 (modern numbering): "La materia de' malefici
è qui sempre stata stimata fallace, et incerta assai, come è in effetto; et alle volte
anche da persone prattiche et intendenti si è voluto passar troppo oltre, e si sono
più presto incontrate delle difficoltà, ch'hanno dato occasione a errori pregiudiciali
al S. Officio, a gli Inquisitori, et anco a chi ne formava processo, essendo delitto

difficile a verificarsi, e nel quale ha gran parte la leggierezza e facilità delle donne, e l'inganno del demonio che è tuttore e padre delle bugie. Onde a quel che Vostra Signoria scrive intorno alle malefiche, d'ordine di questi miei Signori Illustrissimi devo dirgli, che considerino, e lei et il padre inquisitore l'incluse Instruzioni, che le mando, di Roma, 9 Maggio 1624." I have used the copy in microfilm no. 4463 in the Knights of Columbus Vatican Film Library, St. Louis University. At this date Michelangelo Seghizzi was bishop of Lodi. He reigned from 1616 to 1625. See P. B. Gams, *Series Episcoporum, Ecclesiae Catholicae,* 2nd ed. (Leipzig, 1931), 794. For recent general surveys of the witchcraft literature, see P. C. Ioly Zorattini, "Per lo studio della stregoneria in Italia nell'età moderna," *RSCI* 25 (1971): 231–37; E. W. Monter, "The Historiography of European Witchcraft: Progress and Prospects," *Journal of Interdisciplinary History* 2 (1972): 435–51; idem, "European Witchcraft: A Moment of Synthesis?" *The Historical Journal* 31 (1988): 183–85; F. Salimbeni, "La stregoneria nel tardo Rinascimento," *NRS* 60 (1976): 269–334; A. G. Hess, "Hunting Witches: a Survey of some Recent Literature," *Criminal Justice History* 3 (1982): 47–79. The most comprehensive bibliography remains H. C. Erik Midelfort, "Recent Witch Hunting Research, or Where Do We Go from Here?" *Papers of the Bibliographical Society of America* 62 (1968): 373–420 (509 titles, principally of works published 1940–67).

3. The text begins, "Experience, the mistress of things, openly teaches us that serious errors are committed daily by numerous bishops, vicars and inquisitors in instituting trials against witches, sorceresses and perpetrators of malefices to the notable prejudice of justice, as well as of the women being tried. So that in this General Congregation of the Holy Roman and Universal Inquisition against heretical pravity it has long been observed that hardly a single trial can be discovered in this matter that has been correctly and legally instituted." I quote from the translation by J. and A. Tedeschi in C. Ginzburg's *The Night Battles: Witchcraft and Agrarian Cults in the Sixteenth and Seventeenth Centuries* (Baltimore, 1983), 126. The text of the *Instructio* is summarized in P. Hinschius, *System des Katholischen Kirchenrechts mit besonderer Rucksicht auf Deutschland* (Berlin, 1897), 6, pt. 1: 421–25 and (in English translation) in H. C. Lea, *Materials Toward a History of Witchcraft,* arranged and edited by Arthur C. Howland, 3 vols. (Philadelphia, 1939; reprint New York, 1957), 2:950–63. The bibliography on the *Instructio* is cited below.

4. George Lincoln Burr, manuscript note on a flyleaf of the Cornell University Library copy of the 1657 edition of the *Instructio.*

5. C. Ginzburg, *The Night Battles,* 126.

6. For the text of Gregory's decree, see C. Cocquelines, ed., *Bullarum, Privilegiorum ac Diplomatum Romanorum Pontificum Amplissima Collectio,* 14 vols. (Rome, 1733–62), 5, pt. 5: 97–98 and also printed separately: *S.mi D.N.D. Gregorii Papae XV: Constitutio adversus Maleficia, seu Sortilegia Committentes* (Rome, 1623). (There is an English translation in M. Summers, *The Geography of Witchcraft* [New Hyde Park, 1965], 544–46.) Symptomatic of our uncertainty about the finer points of inquisitorial legal doctrine is the fact that scholars have taken diametrically opposed positions in

their interpretation of the *Omnipotentis Dei*. H. C. Lea suggested, for example, that the *Instructio* was intended to mitigate the severity of Gregory's decree and was issued at some point after his death on 8 July 1623: *Materials* 2:951. On the contrary, A. Panizza ("I processi contro le streghe nel Trentino," *Archivio trentino* 7 [1888]: 1–95, at p. 84) saw the Bull as a moderating document; and recently G. Bonomo (*Caccia alle streghe*, 298) went further and suggested that the *Instructio* may actually have been inspired by it. In fact, the *Omnipotentis Dei* represented a step backward, not forward, and violated the tradition that no repentant offender was handed over to the secular arm on a first conviction. See F. Albizzi's *De Inconstantia in Iure* (Amsterdam, 1683), 349 for a long list of authorities who argued that penitent witches in their first fall were to be spared from execution even where death or injury had ensued from an alleged *maleficium*. Among the names are Iacobo Simancas, Camillo Campeggio, Nicolau Eymeric, and Prospero Farinacci.

7. G. Bonomo (*Caccia alle streghe*, 292) suggests this and speaks of the *Instructio* as "emanata quell'anno medesimo," namely, 1620. For a fuller discussion of the Milanese incident, see L. Fumi, "L'Inquisizione romana e lo stato di Milano," *ASL*, ser. 4, 13 (1910): 116 ff.

8. A. Panizza, "I processi," 84: "La Congregazione del S. Uffizio, messa probabilmente sull'avviso dai libri dello Tanner e dello Spee. . . ." Tanner was an early northern advocate of the view that the accusations made by witches against their alleged companions at the sabbat were not acceptable in courts of law because they might have been inspired by delusions planted by the Devil. On Tanner and the publishing history of his work, see Lea, *Materials* 2:647 ff. and n. 11 below.

9. G. Henningsen, *The Witches' Advocate: Basque Witchcraft and the Spanish Inquisition (1609–1614)* (Reno, 1980). An English translation of the *Instrucción* is at pp. 370–76. The final version follows closely a draft prepared by the inquisitor Alonso de Salazar Frías who had been sent out by the *Suprema* to investigate the situation. In both the Spanish and Italian documents great emphasis is placed on establishing whether suspected acts of witchcraft could have followed from natural causes; otherwise the two texts bear little resemblance. Nevertheless, G. L. Burr suggests Italian indebtedness to the Spanish "Instructions" in his review of H. C. Lea, *A History of the Inquisition of Spain*, 4 vols. (New York, 1906–7) appearing in the *American Historical Review* 13 (1908): 338. The correspondence preserved in the Archivo Histórico Nacional, Madrid, exchanged between the *Suprema* and its agent in Rome, may yield up information on relations between the Italian and Spanish Inquisitions. These documents are discussed by P. Huerga Criado, "Los agentes de la Inquisición española en Roma durante el siglo XVII," in J. P. Villanueva, ed., *La Inquisición española: Nueva visión, nuevos horizontes* (Madrid, 1980), 243–56.

10. See, for example, *Instructio particularis circa conficiendos processus Inquisitionis . . . Iussu D.N. Urbani PP. VIII* (Rome, 1627), and numerous other cases. Even the words "Experientia rerum magistra," with which the *Instructio* opens, served similar functions on other occasions. See Pius V, *Inter multiplices curas* (21 December 1566) in Cocquelines, *Bullarum*, 4, pt. 2: 325, an account of the pontiff's experiences as a provincial inquisitor.

11. The majority of writers credit the *Instructio* to the influence of the German Jesuits Tanner, Paul Laymann, and especially Spee. One of the last authorities to derive the teachings of our document from the *Cautio* is E. Segatti, "La *Cautio Criminalis* di Friedrich von Spee fra precedenti e contemporanei," in *Studi di letteratura religiosa tedesca in memoria di Sergio Lupi* (Florence, 1972), 375–441, at p. 439: "Gli esiti corrosivi della *Cautio* sono visibili in un paragrafo della *Instructio romana*," which Segatti dates to the "prima metà del Seicento" (p. 401). For the most recent work on Spee, see J. F. Ritter, *Friedrich von Spee, 1591–1635: Ein Edelmann, Mahner und Dichter* (Trier, 1977); the handy pocket anthology, *Friedrich Spee von Langenfeld, zur Wiederauffindung seines Grabes im Jahre 1980*, ed. A. Arens (Trier, 1981); K.-J. Miesen, *Friedrich Spee: Pater, Dichter, Hexen-Anwalt* (Düsseldorf, 1987); and now *Friedrich von Spee: Dichter, Theologe und Bekaempfer der Hexenprozesse*, ed. I. M. Battafarano, Apollo: Studi e testi di Germanistica e Comparatistica, 1 (Gardolo di Trento, 1988). There is now an excellent Italian rendering of this work, with critical apparatus and a useful introduction: F. von Spee, *Cautio criminalis, ovvero dei processi contro le streghe*. Edizione italiana ed. A. Foa, trans. N. Timi (Rome, 1986). The translation is based on the Augsburg 1731 edition of the *Cautio*, omitting, however, the *Instructio*, which is appended to it. The many scholars who assume a tardy date for the introduction of the *Instructio* into the European witchcraft debate include A. Panizza, "I Processi," 84; G. L. Burr, "The Literature of Witchcraft," *Papers of the American Historical Association* 4, pt. 3 (1890): 37–66, at p. 62, reprinted in R. H. Bainton and L. O. Gibbons, eds., *George Lincoln Burr, His Life . . . Selections from His Writings* (Ithaca, 1943), 166–89; P. Fiorelli, *La tortura giudiziaria nel diritto comune*, 2 vols. (Milan, 1953–54), 2:232n; O. Aureggi, "La stregoneria nelle Alpi centrali: Ricerche di diritto e procedura penale," *Bollettino della Società storica valtellinese*, no. 15 (1961): 114–60 at p. 121; idem, "Stregoneria retica e tortura giudiziaria," ibid., no. 17 (1963–64): 46–88, at p. 48; E. W. Monter, *Witchcraft in France and Switzerland: The Borderlands during the Reformation* (Ithaca, 1976), 85.

12. G. Bonomo, *Caccia alle streghe*, 294; C. Ginzburg, *The Night Battles*, 126. The document was already considered "old" in 1626. A letter from the Supreme Roman Congregation to the inquisitor of Siena, preoccupied with witchcraft trials in Pitigliano, suggested that he consult the "istruttione antica fatta in questo tribunale in simile materia." The letter is dated 3 October 1626 (BAV, Barb. lat. 6334, fol. 280).

13. I have not encountered either the mention or a copy of the *Instructio* among the letters sent by the Holy Office to Bolognese inquisitors. I have systematically examined these records, preserved in the Biblioteca Comunale dell'Archiginnasio, Bologna, for the dates c. 1570–1635. Significantly, crimes of witchcraft do not appear to have been a central concern of the Bologna tribunal. The *Instructio* seems to have turned up especially in problem areas. For example, a copy dated 25 November 1635 was discovered in the archive of the papal nuncio in Lucerne; this was a frantic period of witch persecution in that canton. See J. Stutz, "Eine kirchliche Instruktion über die Führung von Hexenprocessen," *Katholische Schweizerblätter für Wissenschaft, Kunst und Leben* (1888): 601–25 (605 ff. for the German text of the *Verordnung*).

According to E. W. Monter (*Witchcraft in France*, 49) 505 persons were tried and 254 executed in that canton between 1550 and 1675. Cardinal Millino's letter to the nuncio in Florence (cited in n. 1) accompanied a copy of the *Instructio*, and was in response to actual litigation in progress. The episode is referred to also in "Inquisitorial Sources and Their Uses" at n. 75 and "The Organization and Procedures of the Roman Inquisition" at n. 50 in this volume. It is now the subject of an interesting paper by Adriano Prosperi, entitled "Inquisitori e streghe nel Seicento fiorentino," in *Gostanza, la strega di San Miniato, processo a una guaritrice nella Toscana medicea*, ed. F. Cardini (Bari, 1989), 217–50. I am grateful to the author for allowing me to read it first in typescript. Cardinal Millino's letter to the bishop of Lodi, with which this chapter opens, also was elicited by the practical concerns of prosecution. For additional evidence see below.

14. I have not attempted a systematic search for manuscript copies. They have been located in BAV, Vat. lat. 8193, fols. 730r–748v; Borg. lat., 660, fols. 103 ff.; Barb. lat. 1370, pp. 361–75; Bodl. MS. Mendham 36, fols. 45r–58r; L. Fumi ("L'Inquisizione romana," 13:119) saw a copy in Pavia. The Florentine copy located by G. Bonomo (*Caccia alle streghe*, 298) is noted in *Le carte strozziane del R. Archivio di Stato di Firenze* (Florence, 1891), ser. 1, 2: 148–50. Another Florentine copy, sent by the Supreme Congregation to the inquisitor of the city on 24 September 1658, has been located by A. Prosperi in the Archivio della Curia Arcivescovile, Florence (oral communication to this writer). It is interesting that manuscript copies of the *Instructio* were being circulated to the provincial tribunals even after the official publication of the document in 1657 (see below at n. 24). O. Aureggi ("Stregoneria retica," 48) speaks of vernacular translations of the *Instructio* preserved in manuscript "presso gli uffici giudiziari delle comunità retiche." For a statement that copies of the *Instructio* were circulating in manuscript among the tribunals of the Inquisition in Italy, see the reference to Carena's *Tractatus* cited at n. 17 below. For a copy directed to the Swiss, see J. Stutz in the note above. R. Mandrou (*Magistrats et sorciers en France au XVIIe siècle: Une analyse de psychologie historique* [Paris, 1968], 427n) speaks of various copies preserved in Parisian libraries. He himself cites Bibliothèque Nationale, MSS. fds.–fs. 13055, fols. 353–57. It should also be noted that the *Instructio* appears as chapter 26 in occasional copies of the "Relatione copiosa" or "Prattica" attributed to Cardinal Desiderio Scaglia, discussed below and in "The Question of Magic and Witchcraft" at pp. 229–58 in this volume.

15. See L. De Biasio and M. R. Facile, *I processi dell'Inquisizione in Friuli dal 1648 al 1798* (Udine, 1978), 123: "È un decreto pontificio pubblicato nel 1657 e destinato ai giudici dei singoli tribunali inquisitoriali. Ebbe una diffusione limitatissima, circoscritta praticamente all'ambito del S. Officio. . . ."

16. *Sacro Arsenale, overo Prattica dell'Officio della S. Inquisitione, ampliata* (Genoa, 1625), "Settima Parte," 175–82. I have used the Harvard Law School and University of Pennsylvania copies of this rare imprint. N. Paulus (*Hexenwahn und Hexenprozess vornehmlich im 16. Jahrhundert* [Freiburg i.Br., 1910], 274), followed by C. Ginzburg (*The Night Battles*, 200), asserts that the *Instructio* made its first appear-

ance in the 1639 edition of the *Sacro Arsenale*. Masini's rendering of the text, from a late (1716) version of the *Arsenale*, has now been reprinted in *La stregoneria: Diavoli, streghe, inquisitori dal Trecento al Settecento*, ed. S. Abbiati, A. Agnoletto, M. Rosario Lazzati (Milan, 1984), 346–49.

17. "... desumpsit ex quodam manuscripto, quod in Inquisitionibus Italiae circumfertur cui titulus est ..." (p. 246 of the Cremona, 1642 edition). As has been noted ("Inquisitorial Sources and Their Uses," p. 52 in this volume) in the first, 1621 edition of the *Sacro Arsenale*, witchcraft was not treated in a special section.

18. On Castaldi, see M. Giustiniani, *Gli scrittori liguri* (Rome, 1667), 401; A. Oldoino, *Athenaeum Ligusticum* (Perugia, 1680), 386; J. Quétif and J. Echard, *Scriptores Ordinis Praedicatorum recensiti* (Paris, 1719–23), 2, pt. 2: 582–83. Castaldi was appointed to the Holy Office in Rome by Innocent X.

19. *De Potestate Angelica, sive de potentia motrice, ac mirandis operibus angelorum atque daemonum*, 3 vols. (Rome, 1650–52), 2: 242–46. I have used the Cornell University Library copy.

20. Ibid., 242: "... a diversis ordinariis, vicariis, & inquisitoribus; sed praecipue a saecularibus iudicibus se in huiusmodi extra ius intromittentibus. ..."

21. Ibid.: "Accipe lector instructionem brevissimam sed nervosam, de construendis processibus contra maleficas, & similes, quae annis elapsis fuit a quodam patre officiali supremae Inquisitionis Romanae peritissimo, mihique charissimo collecta."

22. *Tractatus de Officio Sanctissimae Inquisitionis, et Modo Procedendi in Causis Fidei ... Hac novissima editione addita fuit Praxis Inquisitorum Francisci Pegnae ... cum additionibus Carenae, & Tractatus de Strigibus eiusdem Carenae ...* (Cremona, 1655). Carena introduces the *Instructio* at 536 ff.: "Proposuerunt Pegna materiam hanc per tractare in tertio huius suae Instructionis libro, & quoniam hic non fuit inter eius opera repertus, pro debilitate ingenii mei aliqua de hac re scribere quam brevissime decrevi. Inveni in nostris Inquisitionibus Italiae per reverendissimorum Inquisitorum manus circumferri scripturam quandam brevem huiusce argumenti. Animadverti eam doctissimam religiosissimam, & verissimis Iuris nostri principiis ac verae pietatis Christianae fundamentis innixam."

23. On Peña, see E. M. Peters, "Editing Inquisitors' Manuals in the Sixteenth Century: Francisco Pegna and the *Directorium Inquisitorum* of Nicholas Eymeric," *Library Chronicle* 40 (1974): 95–107 and A. Borromeo, "A proposito del 'Directorium Inquisitorum' di Nicolas Eymerich e delle sue edizioni cinquecentesche," *Critica storica* 20 (1983): 499–547.

24. The text of the 1657 edition was slavishly reproduced (it includes original typographical errors) by G. Horst, *Zauberbibliothek*, 6 vols. (Mainz, 1821–26), 3:115–27, using the copy that eventually ended up at Cornell. He had obtained it from the Trier historian Wyttenbach (see H. C. Lea, *Materials* 2:951n). A photocopy of the first page of this edition is in R. H. Robbins, *The Encyclopedia of Witchcraft and Demonology* (New York, 1974), 272.

25. "Et utinam non reperirentur aliqui exorcistae, qui parum fideliter officium tam pium exercentes multas imposturas confingant. Hinc est ut quandoque plures

fuerint privati munere exorcizandi." I quote the passage from Castaldi, *De Potestate Angelica*, 244. This passage had already been omitted in the version of the *Instructio* printed in Carena's *Tractatus*.

26. A. Dettling (*Die Hexenprozesse im Kanton Schwyz* [Schwyz, 1907], 42–54) prints the German translation. For the alleged impact of the *Instructio* (fewer witchcraft trials after 1660), see Dettling p. 54. Cf. O. Kingholz, *Die Kulturarbeit des Stiften Einsiedeln* (Munich, 1909), 16 and N. Paulus, *Hexenwahn*, 275. The 1661 German manuscript translation is preserved in the cantonal archive of Schwyz.

27. H. C. Lea, *Materials* 3:1054–55, 1273–79. According to Lea, it was originally printed as *Instructio circa Judicia Sagarum* (Cracow, 1670) and again in a *Festschrift* of the Albertine University of Königsberg at the Pentecost Feast of 1821 (Lea, *Materials* 3:1279). See also K. Estreicher, *Bibliografia Polska* (Cracow, 1895), 14, pt. 3:543.

28. See J. A. Lilienthal, *Die Hexenprozesse der beiden Städte Braunsberg* (Königsberg, 1861), 62. Cf. B. Duhr, *Die Stellung der Jesuiten in den deutschen Hexenprozessen* (Cologne, 1900), 87–88.

29. See E. Van der Vekene, *Bibliotheca Bibliographica Historiae Sanctae Inquisitionis*, 2 vols. (Vaduz, 1982–83), ad indicem.

30. The *Instructio* is actually contained in the *De Inconstantia in Fide* published within the *De Inconstantia in Iure*. The Amsterdam imprint is doubtful. See G. Moroni, *Dizionario di erudizione storico-ecclesiastica da San Pietro ai nostri giorni*, 103 vols. (Venice, 1840–61), 16:228. On Albizzi see the *voce* in the *DBI* 2 (1960): 23–26 and L. Ceyssens, *Le cardinal François Albizzi (1593–1684): Un cas important dans l'histoire du jansénisme* (Rome, 1977). Albizzi was appointed Assessor of the Holy Office in 1635 and cardinal in 1654. He replied to Paolo Sarpi's *History* of the Inquisition and was the leading Roman opponent of Jansen. Ceyssens (*Le cardinal*, 95) suggests that Albizzi could have collaborated in the writing of the *Instructio*, an assumption based on its late publication date. But the document, as we know, was already circulating in manuscript more than a decade before Albizzi joined the Holy Office.

31. The paragraph runs "ulterius advertendum est . . . quae nunquam cogitarunt." See Castaldi *De Potestate Angelica*, 244.

32. "Suprema, etc., ad instruendos iudices fidei mandavit imprimi Instructionem infrascriptam, illamque litteris encyclicis transmitti ad eosdem, prout executum fuit" (*De Inconstantia in Iure*, 350).

33. This work is discussed in full at pp. 259–72 in this volume.

34. I have seen only the version printed in facsimile by De Biasio and Facile, *I processi dell'Inquisizione in Friuli dal 1648 al 1798*, 129–36. It is the 1657 Rome edition, with typographical errors corrected.

35. B. Duhr, *Die Stellung*, 87.

36. Pignatelli published two strikingly different versions of the text even in the same edition of his work. In the Cosmopoli, 1711 imprint, the *Instructio* appeared at 1:505–7 and at 2:537–39. The two versions of the text were reprinted in the Venice, 1723 edition of the *Novissimae Consultationes Canonicae*, 1:386–90; 2:418–20. In the first volume of each of the two editions the text generally follows the version

of Castaldi and contains the opening phrase "sed praecipue a secularibus iudicibus." The second volume contains the earlier form of the text limiting the blame for past errors simply to bishops, their vicars and inquisitors.

37. There seem to be some points in common with the appearance of the Spanish "Instructions" of 1614. They too were published anonymously without identifying typographical information and have survived in a few copies containing variants in the texts. See G. Henningsen, "The Papers of Alonso de Salazar Frias: A Spanish Witchcraft Polemic, 1610–1614," *Temenos* 5 (1969): 85–106, at p. 103, and *Witches' Advocate*, p. 546, n. 57.

38. On the reluctance of the Inquisition to return to the secular court for punishment witches that had been tried in both tribunals, see the laments of the Milanese governor Velasco on the mildness of the Holy Office procedures, in M. Bendiscioli, "Penetrazione protestante e repressione controriformistica in Lombardia all'epoca di Carlo e Federico Borromeo," in *Festgabe Joseph Lortz*, ed. E. Iserloh and P. Manns, 2 vols. (Baden-Baden, 1958), 1:403; G. Bonomo, *Caccia alle streghe*, 292 ff. For an episode involving several suspected witches transferred to the Inquisition of Genoa after they had been condemned to death in 1588 by a secular tribunal in Triora, see P. F. Ferraironi (*Le streghe e l'Inquisizione* [Rome, 1955]; based on documents unearthed by M. Rosi), who published the protests of a magistrate: "Questi populi sono restati molto attoniti di questo fatto, poichè per essempio haveriano havuto grandissimo piacere si fusse esseguita la sentenza, contro loro data" (p. 80). These cases of conflict on this issue between the two jurisdictions could be multiplied many times.

39. The sentence of Novara is preserved in TCD, MS. 1225, fol. 282. See, for example, P. Farinacci, *Tractatus de Haeresi: Editio novissima* (Lyon, 1650), q. 181, no. 48, p. 61: "Bene verum est, quod si lamiae poenitentes veniam petunt, et ad Ecclesiam ex corde redire volunt, sunt admittendae ad poenitentiam, ac etiam reconciliandae, nec ullo pacto curiae saeculari tradendae; etiam quod infantes occiderint, seu alia atrociora et nefanda crimina perpetraverint"; I. Simancas, *De Catholicis Institutionibus Liber, ad praecavendas & extirpandas haereses* (Rome, 1575), Tit. 37, no. 16, p. 282: "Posthaec, de poenis lamiarum videndum est, quas si constiterit haereticas fuisse, punire debent inquisitores, perinde atque alios quoscunque haereticos . . . si veram poenitentiam agere voluerint, recipiendae sunt benigne iuxta canonicas sanctiones . . ." (see also n. 6 above). "Striges & sortilegi quomodo puniri possint . . ." is the subject excerpted from a group of letters written by officials of the Holy Office, dating from the 1580s and 1590s (BAV, Barb. lat. 1370, fols. 377–80). See also the group of sentences preserved in TCD, MS. 1225, fol. 61 ff. for the years 1579–80 (in addition to the Novara sentence cited above). Confinement to their own homes, banishment, public whipping, and, of course, salutary penances are the most frequently encountered punishments meted out by the inquisitorial courts to convicted witches.

40. P. Sarpi, *Historia della Sacra Inquisitione* (Serravalle, 1638), 63: "Intorno alle stregherie malefiche, l'eccellentissimo Maggior Consiglio ordinò che fussero punite

dal magistrato perchè le pene ecclesiastiche non sono sofficiente castigo di così gran sceleratezza."

41. See, for example, the letter of Cardinal Camillo Borghese of the Holy Office to the inquisitor of Florence (1604) enjoining him to be watchful of the populace on the day assigned for the public whipping of a converted witch: ". . . avvertendo di provedere in maniera, che nell'atto della frusta non le sia fatta violenza dal popolo, come suole spesso accadere per l'odio che si porta alle streghe" (BRB, MS. II 290, vol. 2, fol. 4r). For instances of public violence against witches during the act of imposing the sentence of ceremonial whipping, in Gubbio (1633) and Mantua (1641), see H. C. Lea, *A History of the Inquisition of Spain*, 4:243. Cf. C. Ginzburg, *The Night Battles*, 116 and L. De Biasio and M. R. Facile, *I processi dell' Inquisizione in Friuli dal 1648 al 1798*, p. 392, a reference to two suspected witches killed extrajudicially in 1663 "a furor di popolo." For a contemporary description of the ceremonial procession, see "The Question of Magic and Witchcraft," p. 237 in this volume.

42. See above n. 21.

43. There is no separate study, ancient or modern, devoted to Scaglia. His biography must be reconstructed principally from short sketches in older sources. On Scaglia's alleged repudiation of his modest Brescian origins ("figlio d'un barbiere e d'una levatrice") and pretensions to noble birth in Cremona, see A. Zanelli, "Di alcune controversie tra la Repubblica di Venezia e il Sant'Officio nei primi anni del pontificato di Urbano VIII (1624–1626)," *Archivio veneto*, ser. 5, 6 (1929): 186–235, at p. 197.

44. See R. Creytens, "Il registro dei maestri degli studenti dello Studio domenicano di Bologna (1576–1604)," *AFP* 46 (1976): 25–114, at pp. 55, 78 for the successful examination of "Desiderius de Brixia."

45. For letters by or involving Scaglia which illustrate his career as provincial inquisitor, see A. Favaro, *Galileo e l'Inquisizione* (Florence, 1907), 53 ff. (24 June 1615); BA, MS. B–1865, fol. 68 (16 December 1616); ibid., fol. 173 (7 September 1619); S. L. Forte, "I Domenicani nel carteggio del card. Scipione Borghese, protettore dell'Ordine (1606–1633)," *AFP* 30 (1960): 351–416, at p. 403 (6 February 1618). See also V. M. Fontana, *Sacrum Theatrum Dominicanum* (Rome, 1666), pt. 3, "De ministris S. Inquisitionis," 545, 566, 605. See also n. 51 below.

46. In general, on Scaglia, see A. Ciaconius and A. Oldoino, *Vitae et res gestae Pontificum Romanorum et S.R.E. cardinalium . . .*, 4 vols. (Rome, 1677), 4: col. 460; V. M. Fontana, *Monumenta dominicana breviter in synopsim collecta* (Rome, 1675), 599, 606, 636; F. Ughelli, *Italia Sacra*, 2nd ed. (Venice, 1720), 5: col. 321–22; *Bullarium Ordinis FF. Praedicatorum . . . opera reverendissimi patris F. Thomae Ripoll [et] . . . Antonino Bremond*, 8 vols. (Rome, 1729–40), 5:718, 727; 6:138; L. Cardella, *Memorie storiche de' cardinali della Santa Romana Chiesa* (Rome, 1793), 6:213–16; P. B. Gams, *Series Episcoporum*, 787, 896; G. Moroni, *Dizionario di erudizione*, 61:50–51; I. Taurisano, *Hierarchia Ordinis Praedicatorum* (Rome, 1916), 72 ff.; P. Gauchat, *Hierarchia Catholica Medii et Recentioris Aevi* (Munster, 1935), 4:238; L. von Pastor, *His-*

tory of the Popes (St. Louis, 1938), vols. 28, 29, passim. I wish to acknowledge my debt to Adriano Prosperi for generously bringing to my attention a letter from Scaglia to the inquisitor of Florence, thanking him for having sent the works of Vasari (costing eight *scudi*) and inquiring what further sum he owed for the shipment. The document is preserved in the Archivio della Curia Arcivescovile, Florence, S. Uffizio, b. 7, fol. 63 and is dated "Dalla S. Congr. del S. Offizio," 26 February 1618.

47. On Scaglia's contacts with Campanella during the latter's Roman confinement, including the examination of Campanella's witings, see L. Firpo, "Appunti campanelliani," *Giornale critico della filosofia italiana* 29 (1950): 84; 30 (1951): 510.

48. A summary of the proceedings of the Holy Office against De Dominis, in which Scaglia played a key role, is preserved in Paris, Bibliothèque de l'Arsenal, MS. 4111, 63–73. I am grateful to W. Brown Patterson of the University of the South for this reference. See also A. Zanelli, "Di alcune controversie," 196–97; V. M. Fontana, *Monumenta*, 606.

49. A. Favaro, *Galileo e l'Inquisizione*, 146.

50. On Scaglia *"papabile"* at the conclave that resulted in the election of Urban VIII, see Pastor, *History of the Popes*, 28:5. On Scaglia's worldliness, see the contemporary sketch sent back by the agent of the Spanish Inquisition in Rome to his superiors in Madrid, cited in P. H. Criado, "Los agentes de la Inquisición española," 254: ". . . es hombre muy docto y estadista pero codicioso de bienes temporales y también lo son sus deudos, sirve a los embajadores en lo que puede, no hace daño a los franceses ni a los venecianos, ha procurado con su maña estar bien con todos los potentados de Italia. . . ."

51. BA, MS. B–1863, fol. 81: "Reverendo padre. Per ordine di questi miei Illustrissimi Signori Cardinali Colleghi fo sapere a V. R. ch'ella faccia cercare nell'archivio del convento di San Domenico costì il processo altre volte formato contro Fra Desiderio Scaglia da Brescia, al presente Inquisitore di Pavia e la sentenza data contro di lui, e ne mandi quantoprima copia." On the envelope an official had penned the reminder: "Da trovare e mandare il processo del P. Desiderio da Brescia." This would not be the only case of an inquisitor undergoing a trial and yet rising to a high position. Paolo Constabile, accused of having assisted the flight of a prisoner, later became inquisitor of Milan and Master of the Sacred Palace (1573). See D.-A. Mortier, *Histoire des Maitres Généraux de l'Ordre des Frères Prêcheurs*, 8 vols. (Paris, 1911), 5:590. In another instance, a Venetian inquisitor, suspected of harboring Protestant sympathies, was himself tried in 1551, but eventually rehabilitated through the process of canonical purgation. See A. J. Schutte, "Un inquisitore al lavoro: Fra Marino da Venezia," in *I Francescani in Europa tra Riforma e Controriforma* (Perugia, 1987), 165–96.

52. A. Rovetta, *Bibliotheca Chronologica Illustrium Virorum Provinciae Lombardiae Sacri Ord. Praedicatorum* (Bologna, 1691), 172–73. Rovetta's principal source was Vincentius Rivelius's unpublished "Catalogue" of Dominican writers of the Lombard province.

53. R. Creytens, "L'oeuvre bibliographique d'Echard, ses sources et leur valeur," *AFP* 14 (1944): 43–71, at pp. 63–64 for his evaluation of Rovetta.

54. J. Quétif and J. Echard, *Scriptores Ordinis Praedicatorum* 2, pt. 1:501. Curiously, they do not list Scaglia in the index under those who have written "Contra magos, necromanticos, sagas, stryges, maleficas & similes fascinarias" (2, pt. 2: 959). He does appear, however, under those who have discussed "De Sacro Inquisitionis Tribunali" (2, pt. 2: 964).

55. Bodl. MS. Add. C 31; MS. Add. C 30. The second Bodleian copy is a working draft with interlinear and marginal notes, corrections, identifications of sources, and an index. The writing also circulated as a "Prattica" without attribution to Desiderio. See "The Question of Magic and Witchcraft," p. 230 in this volume.

56. "In questi casi, come che siano per se stessi difficili a penetrarne giuridicamente il nesso per essere la radice occulta et la materia incerta, il Sant'Officio procede con gran conspettione et lentezza, così in credere come in processare, et puochi o niun processo si trovano ben formati in questa materia . . . E però si ricerca in giudicio la fede del medico che quella infirmità non sia naturale, o almeno ne dubiti, et anco la fede d'un esperto et prudente essorcista che venga veramente da maleficio. Dico prudente essorcista perchè molti ve ne sono che ogni infirmità giudicano maleficii, o per poca pratica, o per farvi sopra mercantia . . ." (I cite from the copy of the "Prattica" in the miscellaneous volume BAV, Borg. lat., 660, pp. 37–38).

57. We know of at least one occasion when Eliseo Masini's popular and widely diffused manual, the *Sacro Arsenale*, which, as we saw (n. 16), embodied from the second edition forward the essential teachings of the *Instructio* in regard to witches, actually was in the hands of secular judges and might have influenced their procedures. Unfortunately, in this instance, it did not. We learn of this episode from L. De Biasio ("Esecuzioni capitali contro streghe nel Friuli orientale alla metà del secolo XVII," *Memorie storiche forogiuliesi* 58 [1978]: 147–58, esp. pp. 152, 157), who has published an extremely interesting letter from the vicar of Cormons (Friuli) to the inquisitor of Aquileia and Concordia (17 April 1647) reporting the trial and execution of two witches by lay authorities. Despite the fact, wrote the vicar, that these officials had borrowed the *Sacro Arsenale* (and now were being negligent about returning it), they had not followed its teachings. For example, the trial had been based on accusations stemming from what a witch claimed to have seen at the sabbat, "et non sopra il corpo del delitto, cioè del maleficio." Moreover, the women's hair had been shaved off "et pur il libro dice che non si faccia." Cf. R. Mandrou (*Magistrats et sorciers*, 428), who speculates that the *Instructio* might have encouraged "des magistrats scrupuleux, soucieux des intérêts de Dieu et de la religion." For its possible influence on Rhaetian secular authorities, see n. 14.

58. See above nn. 8, 9, 11.

59. C. Ginzburg, *The Night Battles*, 126; R. Brown, "Examination of an Interesting Roman Document: *Instructio Pro Formandis Processibus in Causis Strigum*," *The Jurist* 24 (1964): 169–91. Brown would have many long-standing features of inquisitorial theory and practice commence with the *Instructio*, including the provisions for defense: "From now onwards it was conceded that the accused might legitimately deny the charges against her. . ." (p. 184). On the contrary, see "Preliminary Observations," at p. 20 in this volume. G. Bonomo ("Nuove ricerche sulla stregoner-

ia," in *La strega, il teologo, lo scienziato*. Atti del Convegno "Magia, stregoneria e superstizione in Europa e nella zona alpina," Borgosesia, 1983, ed. M. Cuccu and P. A. Rossi [Genoa, 1986], 60) accepts Ginzburg's thesis of the caesura marked by the *Instructio*.

60. G. T. Castaldi, *De Potestate Angelica* 2:242. Cf. n. 21.

61. C. Carena, *Tractatus*, 537 (of the 1655 edition): "Ortum habent huiusmodi errores, ex eo quod iudices ex immanitate criminis, arbitrantur posse procedi non ordinarie, & iuris ordine servato, sed velo ut aiunt levato, & sine ulla iuris regula. . . ." On the departures from accepted procedures permitted to a judge in excepted crimes, see M. Del Rio, *Disquisitionum magicarum libri sex* (Lyons, 1612), 369.

62. TCD MS. 1227, fol. 139, sentence dated 31 May 1582 (promulgated 2 August) against Joannes Pilutius de Castro Julianelli, who was committed to the galleys for seven years, convicted of the unjust prosecution of four women "sub praetextu quod essent striges." See also BRB, MS. II 290, vol. 2, fols. 6r–9r, a letter from the cardinal of Santa Severina to the inquisitor of Florence (dated 18 November 1589) ordering him to take personal charge of a case which had been conducted with a number of judicial abuses in the episcopal court of Pistoia against a group of women suspected of occult practices. The trial had departed from proper procedure in two principal ways: testimony from ineligible witnesses had been accepted, and torture had been resorted to without prior opportunity for the suspects to defend themselves. Consequently, the confessions obtained were declared null and void.

63. B. da Como, "Tractatus de Strigibus," in *Lucerna Inquisitorum Haereticae Pravitatis* (Rome, 1584), 153: "Ita dicimus, quod ubi medici periti ex aliquibus coniecturis vel circumstantiis iudicant illam infirmitatem non ex defectu naturae, neque ex aliqua causa naturali intrinseca, sed ab extrinseco accidisse, & ab extrinseco, ubi non fit ex venenosa infectione, quia sic sanguis vel stomachus malis humoribus esset repletus, tunc ex sufficienti divisione iudicant effectum esse maleficialem"; I. Simancas, *De Catholicis Institutionibus*, Tit. 37, no. 18, p. 283: "Nec facile de infanticidiis fides lamiis est adhibenda, nisi prius constiterit infantes ipsos eodem tempore occisos esse." Cf. Cardinal Albizzi's remark (*De Inconstantia in Fide*, 344) that it was difficult to get physicians to testify in the Holy Office that illnesses had unnatural causes: "Medici difficiliter inducuntur ad testificandum in S. Officio morbos esse ex maleficio. . . ."

64. B. da Como, "Tractatus de Strigibus," 151: "Advertas insuper, & sis bene cautus, ne de facili facias aliquam detineri propter inculpationes talium strigiarum tantum, quia posset contingere quod demon assumeret personam alicuius, & se sub forma illius praesentarent in ipso ludo, ut illam personam infamet, & tamen illa persona erit innocens, & de tali crimine nullo modo culpabilis: quare cautius securiusque procedes, si ex solis inculpationibus seu manifestationibus sociarum non facies aliquam personam detineri. . . ." The same opinion was expressed by I. Simancas, *De Catholicis Institutionibus*, Tit. 37, nos. 14, 15, pp. 281–82. The prohibition against accepting the testimony of a witch against persons whom she named as fellow participants at sabbats was one of the factors sparing Italy the bloody persecutions that ravaged northern Europe. For an instance of this doctrine in practice, see the letter

from Cardinal Camillo Borghese of the Holy Office to the inquisitor of Florence (16 October 1604), BRB, MS. II 290, vol. 2, fol. 4: "In oltre, le dico, che nelle cose che la detta donna depone di haver visto ne' giuochi diabolici non se le crede contra di altre persone. . . ."

65. Sixteenth-century inquisitorial manuals are firm in their insistence that suggestive questioning was to be shunned in the interrogation of suspects. See, among others, B. da Como, "Tractatus de Strigibus," 150; F. Peña, commentary in N. Eymeric, *Directorium Inquisitorum* (Rome, 1587), 422 and the discussion in "Inquisitorial Sources," pp. 48–49 in this volume.

66. Decree of the Roman Congregation of the Holy Office, 5 June 1591: "Ill.mi et rev.mi domini cardinales generales inquisitores mandarunt moneri inquisitores ut de caetero abstineant a rasura capillorum mulierum inquisitarum et hominum, quia potest fieri inquisitio absque tali abrasione." See L. von Pastor, *Allgemeine Dekrete der Römischen Inquisition aus den Jahren 1555–1597* (Freiburg i. Br., 1912), 48.

67. See the Bologna case, below.

68. M. Battistini, "Una lettera," (cited in full at n. 1). The document speaks of verifying the *corpus delicti* through consultation with physicians, denies the validity of witches' testimony against other witches, warns against suggestive questioning, etc.

69. C. Ginzburg, *The Night Battles*, 127.

70. Ibid., 126. See also above at n. 5.

71. BA, MS. B–1861, fol. 133: letter of the cardinal of Santa Severina to the inquisitor of Bologna, 18 May 1592: "Et se ben' Antonia principale denuntiante era indisposta, e travagliata per la morte del figliuolo, et per questo non fu essaminata, nondimeno è stato ordinato, che si ricordi a V.R.tia che per l'avvenire essamini i denuntianti principali col giuramento loro avanti che carceri alcuno per reo, et proceda conforme alla dispositione de'sacri canoni."

72. Ibid.: ". . . le sue [Maria de' Gentili's] confessioni quanto all'homicidio sono parse assai inverisimili per molte circonstanze che si raccogliono dal suo processo." At least so far as the practice in Rome is concerned, this letter clearly disproves Brown's assertion: "Previously [i.e., before the *Instructio*] small inconsistencies and even manifestly incorrect facts contained in the confession of the accused had been disregarded by the witchtrial courts" ("Examination of an Interesting Roman Document," 183).

~

SEVEN

The Question of Magic and Witchcraft
in Two Inquisitorial Manuals
of the Seventeenth Century

I t is now well accepted that surviving inquisitorial records constitute
an important source for the reconstruction of many aspects of life in
the early modern period, including that shadowy world populated by
witches and magicians. But scholars intent on studying occult life through
documents of this type face a special obstacle. In addition to the destruction and dispersal of large numbers of inquisitorial trials at the time of
the suppression of monasteries in the eighteenth century and during the
Napoleonic occupation of Spain and Italy in the first decade of the nineteenth
century,[1] and the closed door policies that still bar access to certain
repositories (principally the Archive of the Holy Office in Rome), witchcraft materials were the object of a special fury. They were suppressed
and burned by inquisitors themselves, according to evidence found in various decrees. For example, one pronounced in Rome on 11 February 1573
stated: ". . . all written incantations existing in the Holy Office should
be burned; and if the trials have been terminated, mention should be made
of the combustion."[2] There are also numerous letters from the officials
of the Congregation of the Inquisition in Rome to those in the field, such
as the communication from Cardinal Pompeo Arrigoni to the inquisitor
of Bologna, dated 18 February 1612, which warns: "in preparing the sentence do not mention the sortileges and magical practices, abuses of sacraments, of sacred and sacramental things, that are contained in their trials

and confessions, so that people present at their abjurations will not have the opportunity to learn them."[3] In this chapter I wish to draw attention to some neglected materials that may help to fill a gap left by just such documents and data which perished centuries ago.

I am referring to two inquisitorial "Prattiche" or handbooks containing a wealth of information on popular superstition, witchcraft and the world of the occult, as well as on the practices and attitudes of the Holy Office toward them. Interestingly, they were written by members of the same family. Neither text has received the attention that it deserves, despite the extracts from one published several decades ago in Henry Charles Lea's *Materials Toward a History of Witchcraft*.[4]

The first of the two texts (the one that came to Lea's attention) circulated in manuscript in numerous copies in the seventeenth century under two main titles, "Prattica per procedere nelle cause del S. Offizio" ("Handbook on how to proceed in cases before the Holy Office") and "Relatione copiosa di tutte le materie spettanti al tribunale del S. Officio" ("Copious relation about all matters regarding the tribunal of the Holy Office"). The vast majority of copies are anonymous; a handful are ascribed in the title to a Cardinal Scaglia who is to be identified with Desiderio Scaglia, a native of Brescia, who studied theology at the Dominican faculty in Bologna; served as inquisitor successively at Pavia, Cremona, and Milan; was promoted to be *Commissario* of the Holy Office in Rome by Paul V; and finally became a cardinal in 1621.[5]

The attribution of the "Prattica" to Scaglia is strengthened by two particulars. First, the early bio-bibliographers of the Dominican order credit him with just such a work,[6] and, second, Cardinal Francesco Albizzi, a younger colleague of Scaglia's on the Congregation of the Holy Office, who would have been in a position to know, also specifically mentioned in his *De Inconstantia in Fide* that the cardinal was the author of a "Prattica," chapter eight of which dealt with "De Sortilegi."[7] This is precisely the text which will occupy us here. The distinguishing characteristic of the writing is its informal, almost chatty, tone, reflecting the author's great experience and familiarity with the subject, exactly what we might expect from a person who had held Scaglia's high positions in the Holy Office. Copies of it are widely dispersed in both Italian and foreign repositories, attesting to its popularity and widespread circulation in the seventeenth century.[8]

The importance and special interest of this work rest on a number of considerations: it is one of only a handful of manuals issued in the vernacular by the Roman Inquisition;[9] it raises the question of why (like the *Instructio* examined in the previous chapter, which it resembles)[10] it was not printed despite the great authority it enjoyed (the wide diffusion it received attests to this); the several surviving copies present dramatic textual variants which will require a special study to resolve;[11] and, finally, having been written sometime in the first two decades of the seventeenth century, it is one of the first attempts to articulate the cautious and moderate attitudes toward the phenomenon of witchcraft that had come to dominate Holy Office circles.[12]

The second inquisitorial treatise under discussion here is known to me in only one copy preserved in the Vatican Library: "La Prattica di procedere con forma giudiciale nelle cause appartenenti alla Santa Fede di Deodato Scaglia, vescovo di Melfi"[13] ("Handbook on How to Proceed in a Judicial Manner in Cases Pertaining to the Holy Faith by Deodato Scaglia, Bishop of Melfi"). It is dedicated to Cardinal Francesco Barberini and dated 10 January 1637. Deodato was Desiderio's nephew, himself a Dominican, and as had his uncle before him, served as bishop of Melfi, ending his career as bishop of Alessandria at his death in 1659.[14] Unlike Desiderio's "Prattica," which circulated widely in manuscript, Deodato's seems to have been lost to history. Surviving in this one known copy, it was never cited in the contemporary literature and went unrecorded in all the bio-bibliographies of the Dominican order. Nor is it mentioned in any of the sources that Deodato ever had any formal connections with the Holy Office, although as the occupant of an episcopal see he should have been familiar with inquisitorial procedure, especially in the Viceroyalty of Naples where the functions of the Holy Office devolved to the episcopal courts.[15]

Deodato states that he had written his treatise in the vernacular, "imitating certain great predecessors of mine [*miei maggiori*], not only of our Italian nation, but also of the Spanish."[16] Who were these authorities who had preceded him in expounding inquisitorial doctrine in the Italian language? I know of only two, Eliseo Masini's *Sacro Arsenale* (first ed., 1621) and Desiderio Scaglia's unpublished but widely circulated "Prattica," which, though undated, certainly preceded the effort by Deodato. But, curiously, these two authors are precisely the two who are not listed in the long bibliography with which Deodato opens his work: "Auctores ex quibus excerpta sunt ea, quae in hoc opere continentur."[17] With good reason, perhaps, because he plunders the writings of these two "maggiori," sometimes reproducing entire passages almost verbatim, without once acknowledging his debt and naming his sources.[18]

It should be mentioned that the present chapter is the first occasion, as far as I can ascertain, where the two "Prattiche" have been distinguished one from the other and treated as separate entities. From the early cataloguers of the Bodleian Library and the Casanatense, who could not make up their minds and alternately penciled in and canceled out the names of Desiderio and Deodato on the flyleaves of their copies of Desiderio's "Prattica,"[19] to a recent listing of inquisitorial texts which mistakenly lumped together the known copies of both writings under one name, that of Deodato, it has been assumed that only one such work existed, attributed sometimes to uncle, sometimes to nephew.[20]

The explanation is really quite simple. Vatican codex *Barb. lat.* 4615, the only known manuscript of Deodato's "Prattica," had never been compared with the surviving copies of the work which bore an almost identical title. It was not until I had the opportunity of seeing a photocopy of it that I realized I had before me not merely another copy of the more famous and widely circulated "Prattica" by Cardinal Scaglia, but a distinct and separate text.

But why the occasional attempt to assign this work to Deodato if his "Prattica" has apparently survived in one totally ignored copy buried in the Vatican's Barberini collection? Again, there is an explanation. The source of the mistaken attribution is a statement in Deodato's "La Theorica."[21] Here he claims: "After the 'Prattica' which I composed to demonstrate the manner in which one should proceed in general in cases pertaining to the Holy Faith. . . ."[22] The fact that the few known copies of the "Theorica," where this assertion is made, are generally encountered in codices containing a number of inquisitorial materials, occasionally including Desiderio's in many cases unsigned "Prattica," led some authorities to waver, as I mentioned above, and assume that it was in fact Deodato's. Now we know that two distinct and separate handbooks exist.

Let us turn, briefly, to the subject matter of the "Prattiche." The most systematic exposition of our topic, magic and witchcraft, is contained in chapter eight, "De Sortileghi," in Desiderio's work. The discussion opens with a wide-ranging and traditional definition of the crime, encompassing those who used magical practices, incantations, abuse of sacraments, and invocation of the Devil to obtain desired ends, "either to conserve money, so that even after it has been spent it returns to one's pocket, or for position, or knowledge, or for other things."[23] The suspicion of heresy arose in these cases from the abuse of sacraments or sacred objects or from acts which smacked of apostasy, such as the pacts with the Devil which frequently accompanied these abuses. The text then proceeds to a long discussion of the different grades of apostasy, explicit and implicit, the former involving actual direct invocation of the Devil, the latter simply the use of superstitious words and symbols and the abuse of sacred things. Invocation of devils, the author of the "Prattica" reminded his readers, was permitted in one set of circumstances: "... Christ left this power only to the Church so that they might be expelled as enemies and not harm us,"[24] in other words through the art of exorcism.

The denunciation of suspects of sortilege, when accompanied by legitimate evidence, was followed by the search of their domiciles, "because ordinarily they possess writings about magical signs and experiments, virgin paper, clavicles,[25] Almadel,[26] Centum Regum,[27] Arte Notoria Paolina,[28] Cornelius Agrippa,[29] Peter d'Abano,[30] L'opus mathematicum,[31] magical instruments such as inscribed swords, mirrors, rings, pentacles, fingernails, lodestones, which they are accustomed to baptize, and other things."[32] These constituted the *corpus delicti* and led to the interrogation of the suspect concerning his beliefs and intentions: did he really hold in his heart that it was permissible to practice magic, avail one's self of the Devil, make a pact with him, honor him, and apostatize from the true God?[33] Heresy, in the eyes of the Church, was a sin of the intellect, while possession of forbidden objects in itself merely created the suspicion of it. Thus, for example, where the sortilege had been committed in order to conquer someone's love, defendants were interrogated as to whether they really believed or had believed that the Devil could coerce the will.[34] According to the Church, the powers of the Devil over human destiny were limited: "... He can indeed stir human fantasy, either by way of dreams, or by inflaming the blood and the humours, imparting impulses, and exciting the spirits especially at the moment when the person who desires a woman's love appears before her."[35] This in no way was to be confused with the actual coercion of a victim's will.

Convicted offenders who believed the Devil possessed this power had to perform abjurations, the gravity of which depended on the quality of the person and the particulars of the crime. The ignorant and the uneducated, those "blinded by passion" abjured *de levi*; but if the sorcerer could not claim such extenuating circumstances, admitted believing that the human will could be coerced, and had possessed magical instruments over a long period, he or she might be liable to abjure as a formal heretic, *de vehementi*. In this category the implications were serious in the event of a second fall, because only in the instance of a previous formal abjuration might the extreme penalties reserved for the *relapsus* be subsequently invoked. The two forms of abjuration were also different in that the first could be performed privately, thus avoiding greater shame for the offender, while the second always had to be made in public.[36]

Witches proper were distinguished by the harmful effects of their occult practices, such as damage to crops and injury to domestic animals and even humans. They obtained their ends by devices similar to those employed in simple magic, "that is, with circles, symbols and by throwing salt or blessed beans into a fire, abusing the words of consecration by writing them on slips of paper, making powder out of certain herbs, blessed or not . . . invoking the Devil by these means explicitly."[37] But even more, they deal with foodstuffs: "they perform malefices with edible things, writing occult words and characters on fruits, mixing powders into foods, molding wax statuettes, piercing them with needles and having them dissolve, little by little on the fire. . . ."[38]

Many identical devices were often employed by these same practitioners to achieve beneficial ends, especially healings. In fact, so rampant was this phenomenon that healers, or *segnaresse* as they were called, from the signs they made over their patients, were robbing the medical profession of its livelihood. The Roman physician, Scipione Mercurio, in his book *De gli errori popolari d'Italia* (1645) complained:

> This plague is so widespread here where I am writing, that without any consideration or fear, almost everyone for a headache, or other infirmity, first goes to visit the *malefica* or witch to be signed by her, and for childbirth ailments, for tertiary or quartan fevers, for wounds or dislocations, and even for syphilis they go to be signed by these really witches, who, however, with less infamous name are called *segnaresse*.[39]

Interestingly, one of the largest professional or social groups which practiced magic under the mistaken assumption that the human will could be coerced were the prostitutes, because to make men come to their dwellings they perform many sortileges. They sweep the hearth, they cast salt on the fire, they bless beans, they tie ribbons into knots while they are at Mass. And while making these knots they pronounce unknown words, but lascivious and most indecent against this holy sacrifice, which [words] they frequently utter in the very moment of consecration or elevation of the host, or while the priest turns to intone "Dominus vobiscum."[40]

Such practices, many of which are also described in older treatises, and which were used especially for the discovery of secrets or the recovery of stolen objects, offer a rich harvest for the folklorist. They involve prayers to Saint Daniel and Saint Helen, and the use of such living props as little children, virgin girls, and pregnant women gazing into a phial by candlelight and made to recite, as the case might be, "Holy angel, white angel, through your sanctity and my purity," or "For the virginity that I carry in myself. . .," a reference to the foetus in the womb.[41]

In this hothouse of exotic practices the Holy Office moved cautiously. In prescribing correct judicial procedures, the "Prattica," echoing a handful of other contemporary documents, emphasized that: "In these cases, where it is so difficult to penetrate judicially to the cause, since the root is obscure and the subject dubious, the Holy Office proceeds with great circumspection and prudence, both in believing as well as in proceeding, and very few and perhaps no trials have been properly instituted in these cases."[42] The evidence, the writer acknowledges, was frequently deficient and often based on nothing more than a threat heard uttered by the accused against the victim: "I'll make you regret it, you'll pay for that"; or on dubious charges, such as illness ensuing from the consumption of food.[43] Verification of the *corpus delicti* figures prominently in the work: "And therefore we should seek the testimony of the physician that a certain infirmity does not have natural causes, or at least that he doubts it,[44] and also the opinion of an expert exorcist because there are many who judge any infirmity malefice, either because of their small experience, or to make profit from it."[45]

We can deduce what might have been intended by the words "expert exorcist" by leafing through the most celebrated manual of the day, Girolamo Menghi's *Flagellum Daemonum*. Exorcists, for example, were to refrain, whenever possible, from practicing their office in private homes, so as not to frighten the young or risk encounters with the women of the household, whose company exorcists were at all costs to avoid. Churches and other holy places were ideal sites for their work. Moreover, they should consult closely with physicians before initiating their labors, for example, never introducing oil or other potable remedies into afflicted parties without first seeking medical opinion.[46] From another source, the inquisitorial "Instruction" on the proper conduct of witchcraft trials, we learn that the Roman Congregation of the Holy Office vehemently rebuked the practice, admitted in other courts, of accepting in evidence testimony derived from the interrogation of demons residing in possessed people.[47]

Scaglia's "Prattica" drives home still another crucial procedural point, the prohibition against receiving in a witchcraft trial depositions against persons named by the accused as fellow participants at sabbats, since she might be misled in her identifications by reason of illusions planted by the Devil.[48] This important provision, so enlightened from a judicial viewpoint, even while giving full credence to all the superstitions, spared Italy the epidemics of bloody persecutions that ravaged many parts of northern Europe, inspired by procedures which went so far as to permit children to bear witness against their own mothers.[49]

Unlike secular courts which routinely administered the death penalty when the offender confessed participation in the sabbat, apostasy to the Devil, and perpetration of a *maleficium*, the Inquisition treated witchcraft as any other heresy and dealt relatively mildly with the first-time offender who expressed a desire to repent and be rejoined to the Church:[50]

> We have them stand on the door of the cathedral on feast days with a lighted candle in their hands; we banish them; we incarcerate them formally *ad tempum*, or assign them to their own homes, depending on the nature of their crime. And when we leave them at large we have them observed, requiring them to present themselves once a month to the local inquisitors or bishops. . . . Sometimes also they are whipped, but it's true that when they have a husband, or nubile girls, the Holy Office, in its mercy, abstains from this form of punishment since it casts shame on the daughters who because of it fail to find husbands, and husbands lose their love for the wives they have seen whipped.[51]

The actual administration of the punishment, of course, was in the hands of the secular court, the civil magistrates of the city, not of the Inquisition itself. But in smaller centers a *ministro di giustizia* was not always available when needed and other penalties had to be devised, as occurred in Imola in 1580 to a Jew, a certain Gioseffo Hebreo, convicted of passing secrets of necromancy to Christians. In the absence of the appropriate "minister of justice" to perform the whipping, six hours in the stocks, during which the penitential mitre would be worn on the head, could be substituted.[52] Johann Weyer, in his *De Praestigiis Daemonum*, has left us a vivid description of the act of applying ceremonial whipping in Bologna:

> The Bolognese are accustomed to punish witches, regardless of the sex, when their spells have not harmed either man or beast (Italians call these women in the vernacular *le strige*) in the following way. They are stripped naked to the waist and are led out from the city hall mounted backward on an ass, with their hands tied to the animal's tail, and are thus conducted slowly around the town by the minister of justice. On their heads they wear miters made out of paper in which are depicted frightful demons, stirring up the infernal fires with their pitchforks. While they are thus being solemnly paraded the official who accompanies them lets his whip fall first on their chests, then on their backs, until they leave the public streets and arrive at the cemetery in the house of the Dominicans, in the place where the nobility of the German race is buried. There the witches are made to dismount and are led to an upstairs chamber which has a projection screened off by an iron grille from which one looks down on the cemetery. This chamber is reserved for heretics by the brothers of the convent who are inquisitors of the faith. Here the witches, their heads encased in helmets, are thrice rolled up and down the length of this gallery, seated on a small four-wheeled cart, and prominently displayed to the populace below. They remain here for the space of a quarter of an hour during which the people below mock and cry at them and throw rocks, but in vain, because of the bars that protect them. At the end of this time they are released, having been punished befitting the quality of their crime, and banished.[53]

Weyer is quick to contrast what he terms Italian "moderation" to the "holocausts" occurring in other parts of Europe.[54] The relatively lenient practices of the inquisitorial courts did not find support in popular sentiment. Indeed, so deeply embedded and widespread was the fear and hatred of witches, that the Roman Congregation of the Holy Office continually had to remind its provincial officials to protect persons convicted of this crime. The need to issue these warnings persisted well into the seventeenth century. Despite these efforts, cases still occurred where suspected or convicted witches were killed extrajudicially by a frenzied populace ("a furor di popolo").[55]

The theme of magic and witchcraft is also touched upon in chapter twenty-five of Desiderio Scaglia's "Prattica," entitled "Delle Monache." Here he describes the disturbances which frequently occurred in convents among nuns as a result of mistreatment (real or imagined) received at the hands of their superiors, or because they might have been forced at an early age to take monastic vows against their will. Some of these women became desperate and claimed to have been bewitched by one of the less well loved members of the house, thereby throwing their entire establishment into predictable confusion.

The usual practice of superiors in these cases is to summon an exorcist, with the result, more often than not, that even if the alleged victim had not been obsessed, she quickly became so. The best course in these cases, according to our authority, "is to attempt to eradicate from the nuns the notion that they are bewitched, and exhort them not to be so credulous."[56] Despite Scaglia's supercilious opinion that "female rivalries and petty intrigues" ran rampant in these religious establishments, the chapter offers insights pertinent to the study of that sealed off and difficult to penetrate world of the cloister. It is interesting to note that Scaglia's skepticism influenced a contemporary detector of affected sanctity, Giorgio Polacco, who was confessor in the Augustinian convent of Santa Lucia and "vicario delle monache" for the patriarch of Venice, Federico Corner, in the years 1631–1644. When Polacco was reprimanded by his superiors for not calling in exorcists to deal with a case of diabolical possession in a convent, he attempted to exculpate himself by pointing to the teachings of the "Prattica."[57]

I can only begin to suggest the precious information concerning the subjects of magic and witchcraft contained in the second of the two handbooks we are examining, Deodato Scaglia's "La Prattica di procedere," dated 1637 and dedicated to Cardinal Francesco Barberini. Although here, as in the first writing, references to witchcraft are scattered throughout, two chapters are of special interest. Chapter eleven, devoted to the *corpus delicti*, is principally concerned with the verification of occult crimes, in cases where a confession on the part of the accused was not deemed sufficient for conviction and had to be proved.[58] Deodato's "Prattica" impresses us with the same mixture of judicial probity and rank credulity that we encountered in his uncle's work:

> We do not rush headlong, especially in the matter of these nocturnal games, to believe and proceed as if the crime were fully established; but, rather, the prudent judge weighs various questions: is the confession plausible or does it contain features that are impossible and contrary to nature, as is the case, for example, where a woman confesses that she has been in person at night participating in one of these covens and yet had not left her husband's bed; or when she asserts that she physically left her house without passing through any door or window.[59]

The chapter also contains a long and interesting description of the various forms which the notorious Devil's mark could take on the suspected witch, some resembling astrological symbols or the indelible colors tattooed on the foreheads of Turkish slaves to identify them as the property of specific owners. The text also describes the elaborate ceremony required to ascertain the authenticity of these stigmata, although Deodato talks of these rituals as outdated and urges great caution in applying them.[60] The only contemporary occurrence of this phenomenon in an inquisitorial court about which he had heard concerned the case of a famous witch tried in Vicenza in 1616.[61] In contrast, in many of the civil courts of the time the discovery of the presumed Devil's mark was considered sufficient proof to condemn the suspect.[62]

Chapter twenty-nine, entitled "De i maleficii di taciturnità in tortura" ("Concerning Spells to Induce Silence During Torture"),[63] discusses

> those who placed under torture, even when they are severely racked, do not confess or evince signs of pain, but remain firm just as if they did not feel discomfort of any kind. And the reason is that they had steeled themselves for the ordeal with secret remedies which are said to have such power, and by concealing on their persons certain malefices designed for that purpose, such things as tablets filled with various ingredients, powders from the hearts of roasted animals, the blood of birds, etc.[64]

These offenders also copied in hidden places superstitious words and prayers, and verses torn from the Psalms and elsewhere in Holy Scripture or the Mass: "And then using them as antidotes and preservatives, they either eat them or hold them under their tongues, or sewn in their clothing, or hidden in their hair, even in the most private parts of the body, and with these diabolical means called malefices of silence they resist torture without confessing."[65]

Deodato claims that occurrences of this particular superstitious practice were confined to the secular courts. The Inquisition had been spared since the Devil had no power against it, a holy tribunal, and thanks to God's providence neither witches nor necromancers had ever succeeded in thus prevailing over it.[66] Deodato admits that he has taken his facts from the writings of ancient doctors, rather than from actual experience. In my own work with inquisitorial records, although I have never encountered a single episode involving the so-called Devil's mark, I have come upon numerous cases where inquisitors suspected or actually discovered that victims sentenced to receive the *rigoroso esamine*, interrogation under torture, had steeled themselves for the ordeal through recourse precisely to devices such as those described by our author.[67] Cesare Carena, a high official of the Holy Office in Cremona, in his famous *Tractatus de Officio Sanctissimae Inquisitionis* referred to "magic for the purpose of concealing the truth against the torture of the rack and other devices" as a virtual "quaestione quotidiana."[68] It was to discover these remedies secreted in private parts of the body that courts routinely shaved the bodies of their victims until a succession of Holy Office decrees in the closing decades of the sixteenth century directed that it was possible to carry out interrogations "without such violence" ("absque tali abrasione").[69] We know that many unfortunates who were subjected to the strappado succeeded in resisting it. Alfred Soman's ongoing investigations in the criminal records of the *Parlement* of Paris for the late sixteenth and early seventeenth centuries suggests that torture produced a confession rate of only one percent.[70] We have no way of knowing what role was played, if any, by these so-called "maleficii di taciturnità" ("magical remedies for silence") in dulling pain, either because they possessed narcotic-like properties or, even when innocuous, for their psychological effects as placebos.

The concern of the two Scaglias in their respective "Prattiche" with the question of witchcraft and sorcery was not an academic matter. A recent statistical study reveals that the pursuit of the magical arts had become the overwhelming preoccupation of Italian inquisitors from the mid–1580s on. Whereas the prosecution of Protestants dominated Holy Office activity in the mid-sixteenth century, accounting for approximately 80 percent of the cases in Venice and 75 percent in the Friuli, a sharp reversal set in toward the end of the century. The figures for magic soared to over 40 percent of the total activity not only in these northern areas of the peninsula but even in the south, in Naples. This trend continued throughout the seventeenth century until by the decade 1700–1710 magic accounted for close to 70 percent of all Venetian inquisitorial cases and 60 percent of the Neapolitan.[71]

It is possible to venture some tentative explanations for this sudden shift. The flagging of the missionary impulse from such Protestant centers as Geneva in the latter sixteenth century obviously would have tended to reduce the number of cases to be tried for religious heresy. Moreover, after the Council of Trent the Inquisition began to claim for its exclusive jurisdiction cases of witchcraft and magic, even when heresy was not "manifest," which previously had been considered "mixti fori," i.e., which could be prosecuted by secular and episcopal as well as inquisitorial authorities. The pretensions of the Holy Office in these matters clearly would swell its figures for witchcraft prosecution, at least in the papal states where it had freer rein.[72] Elsewhere civil courts continued to insist on their former prerogatives and oppose inquisitorial encroachments, especially because they were not satisfied that the ecclesiastical judges treated the crime with appropriate severity. Indeed, more study needs to be devoted to secular trials for witchcraft in Italy in states where the jurisdiction of the Inquisition was curbed. No statistics for Spanish and Italian witchcraft will be complete until even the trials performed by civil courts are studied and counted—how many were held, what procedures did they follow, with what consequences, and over what period of time? Only then will we know that the two Catholic countries did indeed escape "the madness prevailing elsewhere," to quote H. C. Lea's benign assessment.[73]

The evidence adduced in the course of this chapter is drawn from theory and (to a lesser extent) from practice—from the legal manuals prepared for the use of inquisitors and from the actual records produced by the Inquisition at work. But it must be pointed out that most of this documentation is relatively late, primarily from the last quarter of the sixteenth century onward.[74] Because there are so few surviving records for the early years of the century, the comparison of witchcraft trials at the two poles of the *Cinquecento* will be difficult to accomplish, but ought to be a crucial area of future research. There are compelling questions to be answered connected with the reported mass persecutions of witches occurring in the early decades of the century.[75] A related issue, the precise teachings and influence of the notorious *Malleus Maleficarum* on witchcraft proceedings south of the Alps, secular and ecclesiastical alike, also needs to be investigated.[76]

The largest number of cases that came before the inquisitorial tribunals did not involve the perpetration of a *maleficium* with harmful effects, but rather magical arts to accomplish desired ends, such as healing, the recovery of lost treasures, the conquest of a loved one's favors. And the practitioners were by no means exclusively old women in rural surroundings. Among them were many city dwellers, and ecclesiastics in large numbers employing and abusing sacramental objects and liturgical rites and prayers,[77] sometimes with, but often without, formal apostasy to the Devil.

Clearly, our two "Prattiche" reflect the new concern with occult crimes that came to preoccupy the Holy Office toward the end of the sixteenth century. Alongside a handful of other contemporary documents, they were an attempt to guide its officials—especially provincial inquisitors among whom they were circulated in manuscript—through the maze of beliefs and procedural problems that came to the forefront with the large-scale prosecution of occult crimes.

It would be interesting to speculate why the two writings that we have been examining were not published in their day.[78] I have already mentioned and given examples of the informal tone of the first, presented almost as an outline or sketch of the subject, and I have also alluded to the derivative aspect of the second. Another possible explanation may lie in the hesitation on the part of the Holy Office to exacerbate its conflict with secular authorities—who were already vehemently claiming that the Inquisition lacked the severe remedies required to deal with witches—by bringing out to the light of day through the printed page, texts which placed heavy emphasis on careful judicial procedures.[79] But the answer simply may be that the two "Prattiche" revealed too many secrets about that exotic world which, as we saw at the beginning of this chapter, the Holy Office did not wish the faithful to enter.

Appendix

Provisional list of institutional copies of Cardinal Desiderio Scaglia's "Prattica per procedere nelle cause del Sant' Officio." I have not examined all the copies personally (see also n. 8).

Austin, University of Texas, Humanities Research Center, Ranuzzi Manuscripts, Ph. 12868 (vol. 62, no. 71)
Bergamo, Biblioteca Civica, MS. a 813, fols. 72r–81r
Bologna, Biblioteca Comunale dell'Archiginnasio, Fondo Inquisizione, vol. B 1000
Florence, Biblioteca Nazionale, Fondo Nazionale II. IV. 459
Madrid, Biblioteca Nacional, MS. 760
Milan, Archivio di Stato, *Decreta quaedam*, c. 41.21–50; FC, p.a. 2105, fols. 19 ff.
Milan, Biblioteca Ambrosiana, O 169, sup.
Modena, Archivio di Stato, manoscritti biblioteca, no. 166.
Oxford University, Bodleian Library: MS. Mendham 36; MS. Add. C. 30; MS. Add. C. 31
Paris, Bibliothèque Nationale, fonds ital. MS. 139
Perugia, Biblioteca Comunale: MS. 263 (E 10); MS. 1288
Philadelphia, University of Pennsylvania Library: MS. Lea 115; MS. Lea 184
Rome, Archivio di Stato (see n. 8)
Rome, Archivio Segreto Vaticano, fondo Borghese, ser. IV, 98
Rome, BAV, Barb. lat.: MS. 4544; MS. 5317
Rome, BAV, Chigi, MS. N III 84
Rome, BAV, Borg. lat.: MS. 571; MS. 660
Rome, BAV, Ferraioli, MS. 155
Rome, BAV, Ott. lat. MS. 788
Rome, BAV, Vat. lat.: MS. 8843; MS. 10408; MS. 12724; MS. 13292; MS. 13467
Rome, Biblioteca Casanatense: MS. 2889; MS. 2905
Rome, Biblioteca Vallicelliana, MS. G. 62
Venice, Archivio di Stato, Sant' Uffizio, Processi, B. 153

Notes

1. See J. Tedeschi, "The Dispersed Archives of the Roman Inquisition," pp. 23 ff. in this volume.

2. L. von Pastor, *Allgemeine Dekrete der römischen Inquisition aus den Jahren 1555–1597: Nach dem Notariatsprotokoll des S. Uffizio zum erstenmale veröffentlicht* (Freiburg i. Br., 1912), 32: "... quod omnia scripta incantationum existentia in S.to Officio comburantur; et si processus fuerint finiti, fiat mentio de huiusmodi combustione." See also the decree of 25 July 1590: "... quod libri superstitiosi reperti penes diversas personas inquisitas in S.to Officio et eorum processibus colligati, comburantur a rev.do patre domino commissario et annotetur eorum combustio in ipsis processibus," ibid., 47.

3. BA, MS. B–1864, fol. 48: "... nel formare la sentenza di non riferire i modi sortileghi et magici, abusi di sacramenti, cose sacre et sacramentali, come si contiene nei processi et confessioni loro, acciochè quelli che saranno presenti all'abiuratione non habbiano occasione d'impararli." These words seem to have been a formula used regularly in instructions for preparing sentences in occult crimes. See the letter from Cardinal Camillo Borghese to the inquisitor of Florence (1604): "Di più nella sentenza [against a presumed witch Lucrezia] non esprima i fatti particolari commessi ne' giuochi diabolici, nemmeno ne' sortileggi, ma stia su la generalità, acciò che quelli che saranno presenti alla publicatione della sentenza non habbiano occasione d'imparare gli eccessi commessi ..." (BRB, MS. II 290, vol. 2, fol. 4). It was also inquisitorial practice to suggest the private reading of sentences in cases where the recitation of crimes risked embarrassing the Church, as in the case of priests convicted of soliciting sexual favors in the confessional. See "Inquisitorial Sources and Their Uses" at n. 16.

4. H. C. Lea, *Materials Toward a History of Witchcraft*, arranged and edited by Arthur C. Howland, 3 vols. (Philadelphia, 1939; reprint New York, 1957), 2:963–66.

5. Since I wrote the original version of this essay I discovered that Desiderio Scaglia's "Prattica" was translated into Latin and published in disguised form toward the end of the seventeenth century (see "Literary Piracy" at pp. 259–72 in this volume), and recently in its original language: A. Mirto, "Un inedito del Seicento sull'Inquisizione," *Nouvelles de la Republique des Lettres* 1 (1986): 99–138. Unfortunately, Mirto's edition is based on a single manuscript (preserved in the Biblioteca Nazionale, Florence), an unacceptable procedure for a text which exists in many variant contemporary copies. Mirto treats the writing as anonymous despite the attribution to Cardinal Desiderio Scaglia discussed in my "The Roman Inquisition and Witchcraft," *Revue de l'Histoire des Religions* 200 (1983): 181 (reprinted in this volume in a revised version) and in my "La questione dei 'Sortileghi' in due 'Pratiche' inquisitoriali inedite del '600," in *La città dei segreti: Magia, astrologia e cultura esoterica a Roma (XV–XVIII)*, ed. Fabio Troncarelli (Milan, 1985), 78–95. The Florentine copy of the "Prattica" was cited by S. Mastellone ("Antonio Magliabechi: Un libertino fiorentino?," *Il Pensiero Politico* 8 [1975]: 33–53 at p. 46) and by Mirto (*Stam-*

patori, editori, librai nella seconda metà del Seicento [Florence, 1974], 48 ff.) for its chap. 10 dealing with the question of prohibited books.

For a fuller biographical sketch on Scaglia and the pertinent bibliography, see "The Roman Inquisition and Witchcraft," esp. pp. 211 ff. in this volume.

6. See A. Rovetta, *Bibliotheca Chronologica Illustrium Virorum Provinciae Lombardiae Sacri Ord. Praedicatorum* (Bologna, 1691), 172–73; J. Quétif and J. Echard, *Scriptores Ordinis Praedicatorum Recensiti*, 4 vols. (Paris, 1719–23), 2, pt. 1:501.

7. F. Albizzi, *De Inconstantia in Iure Admittenda vel non* (Amsterdam, 1683), 358: "Sed adhibendae sunt considerationes, quae ab eruditissimo ac eminentiss. Cardinali Scaglia in sua Praxi numerantur in tit. de Sortileg. cap. 8." The *De Inconstantia in Fide* is published in the *De Inconstantia in Iure*. The imprint Amsterdam is doubtful.

8. For a provisional list, see the Appendix. One of the Bodleian copies (MS. Add. C. 30) appears to be a working draft with interlinear and marginal notes, corrections, identifications of sources and an index. I am extremely grateful to Dr. Robert Evans for bringing the Bodleian material to my attention. Copies are cited in the following works: Bergamo, Biblioteca Civica (see S. Abbiati, "Intorno ad una possibile valutazione giuridico-diplomatica del documento inquisitorio," *Studi di storia medioevale e di diplomatica* 3 [1978]: 170); Bologna, Biblioteca Comunale dell'Archiginnasio (see M. Brugnoli, "Superstizione e repressione: Il tribunale della Santa Inquisizione a Bologna e contado nell'ultimo quarto del XVII secolo," 206, a *tesi di laurea* defended in the 1981–82 academic year at the University of Bologna, Faculty of Political Science); Florence (see n. 5); Milan, Archivio di Stato, copy 1 (see L. Fumi, "L'Inquisizione romana e lo stato di Milano," *ASL*, ser. 4, 13 [1910]: 24); copy 2 (see G. Signorotto, *Inquisitori e mistici nel Seicento italiano: L'eresia di Santa Pelagia* [Bologna, 1989], 32); Milan, Ambrosiana (see C. Molinier, "Rapport à M. le Ministre de l'Instruction Publique sur une mission executée en Italie de février à avril 1885," *Archives des missions scientifiques et litteraires*, ser. 3, 14 [1888]: 302); Modena, Archivio di Stato (see G. Biondi, "Le lettere della Sacra Congregazione romana del Santo Uffizio all'Inquisizione di Modena: Note in margine a un regesto," *Schifanoia* 4 [1989] 97 ff.); Perugia (see G. M. Monti, *Studi sulla Riforma cattolica e sul papato nei secoli XVI–XVII* [Trani, 1941], 174 ff.); Philadelphia (see *Catalogue of Manuscripts in the Libraries of the University of Pennsylvania*, compiled by N. P. Zacour and R. Hirsch, assisted by J. F. Benton and W. E. Miller [Philadelphia, 1965], 171, 185); Rome, Archivio di Stato (see L. von Pastor, *Allgemeine Dekrete*, 6, without indication of shelf number); Rome, Vat. lat. 10408, Vat. lat. 13292 (see G. M. Monti, *Studi sulla Riforma*, 174 ff.); Madrid (see *Inventario General de Manuscritos de la Biblioteca Nacional* [Madrid, 1956], 2:268, copy belonging to Philip V). Other copies of the "Prattica" with incomplete references are cited in H. C. Lea, *A History of the Inquisition of Spain*, 4 vols. (New York, 1906–7), 4:43; A. Lauro, *Il giurisdizionalismo pregiannoniano nel regno di Napoli: Problema e bibliografia (1563–1723)* (Rome, 1974), 179.

Allusion to the manuscript circulation of the "Prattica" among the provincial tribunals of the Inquisition is made by C. Carena, *Tractatus de Officio Sanctissimae*

Inquisitionis (Bologna, 1668), 438: "Praxis Sancti Officii quae circumfertur manuscripta in Inquisitionibus Italiae. . . ." Reference to it is made also by S. Salelles, *De materiis Tribunalium S. Inquisitionis* (Rome, 1651), 1:70: ". . . verum adducamus iam probationem pro solo privilegio spontaneae comparitionis ex Praxi illa MS. elaborata Italico idiomate per eminentissimus cardinalem N. Sacrae ac Supremae Inquisitionis Urbis ex iudicibus praecipuum . . ." (further evidence to strengthen attribution of the document to Cardinal Scaglia).

9. The vernacular manuals known to me are Eliseo Masini's *Sacro Arsenale* (Genoa, 1621); the "Prattica" and "Theorica" by Deodato Scaglia discussed below; Tomaso Menghini's, *Regole del Tribunale del S. Officio praticate in alcuni casi imaginarii* (Milan, 1689); and, of course, Desiderio Scaglia's "Prattica" being discussed here.

10. See "The Roman Inquisition and Witchcraft," pp. 205–27 in this volume.

11. The most obvious difficulties concern additions and interpolations of facts and dates, some clearly impossible to attribute to the presumed author because of their lateness; other problems are related to discrepancies in the contents and numbering of the chapters. For example, in several copies of the "Prattica," the *Instructio* cited at n. 10 above appears as chap. 26 of the "Prattica," (for example, Biblioteca Comunale, Perugia, MS. 1288).

12. For a fuller discussion of this point, see "The Roman Inquisition and Witchcraft," pp. 205–27 in this volume.

13. BAV, Barb. lat., 4615.

14. Deodato obtained his master's degree in theology from Bologna, and served as bishop of Melfi (1626–44) and Alessandria (1644–59); he was a distinguished preacher and diocesan reformer and published the *decreta* of his synods. See F. Ughelli, *Italia Sacra*, 2nd ed. (Venice, 1720), 1:941; P. B. Gams, *Series Episcoporum Ecclesiae Catholicae*, 2nd ed. (Leipzig, 1931), 811, 896; P. Gauchat, *Hierarchia Catholica Medii et Recentioris Aevi* (Münster, 1935), 4:77.

Deodato also wrote "La Theorica di Procedere tanto in generale, quanto in particolare ne'casi appartenenti alla Santa Fede," dedicated to Cardinal Francesco Barberini, a member of the Holy Office, and dated 10 October 1639. The presumed original is preserved in BAV, Barb. lat. 4616. Other copies are in the Archivio Segreto Vaticano, Carpegna, 166, fols. 80–361; BAV, Barb. lat. 4544, 5317; Biblioteca Casanatense, MS. 2905; Bodl. MS. Add. C. 31.

15. On this phenomenon, see A. Borromeo, "Contributo allo studio dell'Inquisizione e dei suoi rapporti con il potere episcopale nell'Italia Spagnola del Cinquecento," *Annuario dell' Istituto storico italiano per l'età moderna e contemporanea* 29–30 (1977–78): 219–76, and the bibliography cited at pp. 331–32 in this volume. For one piece of evidence that Deodato had access to the correspondence of the Congregation of the Holy Office, see his "Theorica" (cited in the note above) where he alludes to a letter dated 14 December 1618 of Cardinal Millino, a member of the Holy Office. (See Bodl. MS. Add. C. 31, fol. 77v).

16. BAV, Barb. lat. 4615, p. [6]: ". . . imitando altri miei maggiori non solo della nostra natione italiana, ma anco della spagnola."

17. Ibid., [12–13]. The list is an eclectic one, containing authors of several nationalities, medieval as well as modern, often holding opposed positions in the witchcraft debate, from the rigorous advocates Kramer and Sprenger to the skeptic Francesco Ponzinibio.

18. Among many passages from which one could choose, compare the following from Deodato's "Prattica" with Desiderio's text cited below (note 42): "Sebene (per dir il vero) pochi o quasi niuno processo si trovano ben formati in questa materia per la difficoltà delle prove, essendo per lo più fondate o sopra inditii remoti, come di qualche minaccia, 'Ti farò ben pentire, farò che tu mi ami e mi corri adietro,' o sopra inditii indifferenti come di cose mangiative, dopo le quali passa che la persona si sia infermata . . ." (BAV, Barb. lat. 4615, p. 75).

19. See Bodleian Library, MS. Add. C. 30 and MS. Add. C. 31. The Casanatense Library in Rome possesses two copies of the text. The first, MS. 2889, "Relazione copiosa" is assigned to Cardinal Desiderio Scaglia. But the second, MS. 2905, "Prattica per procedere" is catalogued under Deodato's name.

20. See A. Lauro, *Il giurisdizionalismo pregiannoniano*, 179.

21. First cited above at n. 14. In the "Theorica" Deodato heavily plagiarized his uncle's writing, just as he had in his "Prattica." See, as an example, Desiderio Scaglia, "Prattica," chap. 3 (Bodl. MS. Mendham 36): "Trattano de delitti heretical li tutti li autori che scrivono di questa materia, ma il più frequente che si prattica hoggi di è il Pegna nel *Direttorio* . . ."; and Deodato's "Theorica," chap. 13 (BAV, Borg. lat. 571): "Trattano diffusamente di questa materia tutti gli autori che scrivono de i delitti hereticali ma li più frequenti che hoggi di si pratticano sono il Pegna et il Farinaccio. . . ."

22. "Dopo la Prattica composta da me per dimostrar il modo di procedere in generale nelle cause spettanti alla Santa Fede . . ." (I cite from the copy of the "Theorica" in Bodleian MS. Add. C. 31, fol. 24r).

23. ". . . o per conservare monete, acciò spese [MS. spesse] tornino in borsa, o per dignità, o per scienza, o per altre cose." Here and following I cite from the copy of Desiderio's "Prattica" in the Humanities Research Center, the University of Texas at Austin, Ranuzzi MS. Ph. 12868 (vol. 62, no. 7), fol. [14]. On this important historical manuscript collection of Bolognese provenance, see the exhibition catalogue by M. X. Welles, *The Ranuzzi Manuscripts* (Austin, 1980).

24. Ranuzzi MS. Ph. 12868, fol. [15]: ". . . Christo non lasciò questa potestà nella Chiesa per altro, che per espulsione loro, in quanto nemici, acciò non ci [MS. si] nocino."

25. For illustrations and descriptions of these and the following objects, see E. A. Grillot de Givry, *Le musée des sorciers, mages et alchimistes* (Paris, 1929), passim (unfortunately lacking an index), and, in English translation, *Witchcraft, Magic and Alchemy*, trans. J. C. Locke (London, 1931; reprint New York, 1971). For the meaning of "virgin paper" see *Clavicula Salomonis Filii David* [n.p., 1600?], 39: "In multis experimentis necessaria est charta Virginea nominata & novata, 'Charta Virginea' novata est illa quae est de bestia quae neque concubitus habuit sive masculus, sive

faemina nominata charta est illa quae ex ventre bestiae mortuae nascitur, vel quae taliter ex ventre matris mortuae extrahitur . . ." (I cite from the copy of this booklet in the Duveen Collection of the University of Wisconsin-Madison Library). On the *Clavicula* itself, see K. Gesner, *Bibliotheca Instituta et Collecta* (Zürich, 1583), 741: ". . . circumfertur etiam magicus libellus titulo Clavis Salomonis"; L. Thorndike, *A History of Magic and Experimental Science* (New York, 1934), 4:632–33; P. Rossi, *Clavis Universalis: Arti mnemoniche e logica combinatoria da Lullo a Leibniz* (Milan, 1960). For a fuller identification, bibliography, and a history of the *Clavicula*'s prohibition, see J. M. De Bujanda, ed., *Index de l'Inquisition espagnole, 1551, 1554, 1559*, Index des Livres Interdits, 5 (Sherbrooke, 1984), 243.

26. K. Gesner, *Bibliotheca Instituta et Collecta*, 30: "Almadel, inter naturalis magiae scriptores numeratur, à quo forsan Almadel ars denominata est, ad theurgiam magiae partem pertinens." Thorndike (*History of Magic*, 4:343) describes "books called Almadel and Semafora on the divine work of angels and the notory art of Solomon by which knowledge is suddenly acquired." See also, by the same author, "Alfodhol and Almadel: Hitherto Unnoted Medieval Books of Magic in Florentine Manuscripts," *Speculum* 2 (1927): 326–31.

27. Not identified.

28. On this well-known occult art employed for the acquisition of knowledge, see Thorndike, *History of Magic*, vol. 2, chap. 49, "Solomon and the Ars Notoria," and p. 282 for the Pauline art "discovered by the Apostle Paul after he had been snatched up to the third heaven, and delivered by him at Corinth." Cf. D. P. Walker, *Spiritual and Demonic Magic* (London, 1958), 37, 80, 99, 105, 151. The Pauline art is not to be confused with Fabio Paolini, writer on demonological subjects and professor of Greek in Venice, who in 1584 published his book *Hebdomades*.

29. Henricus Cornelius Agrippa von Nettesheim (d. 1535), student of magic and esoteric knowledge, author of a treatise *De Occulta Philosophia* (1st complete ed., Cologne, 1533). See C. G. Nauert, *Agrippa and the Crisis of Renaissance Thought* (Urbana, 1965), and now the sketch by T. B. Deutscher, in *Contemporaries of Erasmus: A Biographical Register of the Renaissance and Reformation*, ed. P. G. Bietenholz and T. B. Deutscher, 3 vols. (Toronto, 1985), 1:17–19.

30. Peter d'Abano (1257–c. 1315) was one of the most influential medical writers of the Middle Ages, whose principal work was the *Conciliator differentiarum philosophorum et precipue medicorum* (Venice, 1476). Peter's astrological dabbling led him to affirm heterodox propositions. He contributed also to the introduction of Averroist thought at the University of Padua. See L. Thorndike, *History of Magic*, vol. 4, ad indicem.

31. The reference, possibly, is to the work by Agostino Ricci, *De motu octavae sphaerae: Opus mathematica atque philosophia plenum* (Paris, 1521). Ricci, who served as physician to Pope Paul III, was considered an important influence on the Kabbalistic thought of Agrippa. See Thorndike, *History of Magic*, 5:264, 284.

32. Ranuzzi, MS. Ph. 12868, fol. [15]: ". . . perchè ordinariamente hanno scritture di caratteri e esperimenti magici, carte vergini, clavicole, Alma del Centum

Regum, Arte Notoria Paolina, Cornelio Agrippa, Pietro d'Abbano, L'opus mathemati-cum, instrumenti magici, come spade caratterizzate, specchi, anelli, pentacoli [MS. pontaroli], ongie, calamita che sogliono battezzare, e altre cose." It should be noted that in examining the house of the witch the notary was obliged to list not only items which would serve the prosecution but also such things as religious icons, devotional books, etc. which would be to the advantage of the defendant. If such ambiguous objects as powders and ointments were discovered, they were to be exa-mined by experts to determine if they could have been used for ends other than sorcery. See E. Masini, *Sacro Arsenale*, 2nd ed. (Genoa, 1625), 175–82. On these devices, see Grillot de Givry, *Les musées des sorciers*, passim.

33. Ranuzzi, MS. Ph. 12868, fol. [15].

34. Ibid., fols. [15–16].

35. Ibid., fol. [16]: ". . . puol bene perturbare la fantasia, o per via di sogni, o commovendo il sangue e gli humori [MS. huomini], dando incentivo, et eccitan-do i spiriti, massime in quel punto che la persona che desidera l'amore della donna si fa presente a lei."

36. For the different grades of abjuration and their consequences see the com-mentary of F. Peña to N. Eymeric, *Directorium Inquisitorum* (Rome, 1587), 488; C. Carena, *Tractatus de Officio Sanctissimae Inquisitionis* (Bologna, 1668), 317; and the discussion at p. 152 in this volume.

37. Ranuzzi, MS. Ph. 12868, fol. [17]: ". . . circoli, caratteri et gettare il sale nel fuoco, e fave benedette, abusando delle parole della consecratione, scrivendole sopra bolettini, facendo [MS. facendola] polvere di certe herbe benedette che siano . . . invocando in questi modi il demonio espressamente. . . ." See also the bibliogra-phy cited at n. 77.

38. Ibid., ". . . maleficiano in cose commestibili, scrivendo parole incognite e carat-teri sopra frutti, mischiando polvere tra cibi, faciendo statue di cera, trafigendole con aghi e facendole a poco a poco dileguare al fuoco. . . ."

39. S. Mercurio, *De gli errori popolari d'Italia libri sette* (Verona, 1645; 1st ed., 1603), 310: "Questa peste è così commune in questa terra dove io scrivo questa opera, che senza alcun rispetto, o timore, quasi ciascuno per ogni mal di testa, e per qualunque altra infermità, prima va a ritrovar la malefica, o strega, che la segni, e poi il medi-co, e per mal di madre, per febri terzane, o quartane, per piaghe, e sluogamenti, e insino per il mal Francese si fanno segnar da queste veramente streghe, quali però con nome manco infame chiamano segnaresse." Cf. C. Bondi, *Strix: Medichesse, streghe e fattucchiere nell'Italia del Rinascimento* (Rome, 1989).

40. Ranuzzi, MS. Ph. 12868, fol. [19]: ". . . perchè per far venire huomini alle case loro attendono assai a sortilegii. Spazzano il camino, gettano sale nel fuoco, benedicono fave, ingroppano fettuccie mentre stanno alla messa, con certo numero di nodi. E nell'ingroppare dicono parole incognite, ma lascive e indecentissime a quel S. Sacrificio. Queste molte volte proferiscono nell'atto istesso della consecra-tione o elevatione dell'hostia, o mentre il sacerdote si volta a dir il 'Dominus Vobiscum.'"

41. Ibid., fols. [19–20]. These are common ritual formulae contained in other, earlier, inquisitorial manuals. See, for example, U. Locati, *Opus quod iudiciale inquisitorum dicitur* (Rome, 1570), 85: "Et nota quod divinatio ad inveniendum furta, vel ad sciendum aliqua secreta, quae fit cum candela benedicta, & aqua similiter benedicta, ac puero, vel puella in phiala aspiciente, & dicente haec vel similia verba, videlicet, 'Angelo bianco, angelo santo, per la tua santità e per la mia verginità etc.' sapit haeresim manifesta. . . ."

42. Ranuzzi, MS. Ph. 12868, fol. [18]: "In questi casi, come che siano per se stessi molto difficili a penetrarne giuridicamente il nesso, per essere la radice occulta e la materia incerta, il S. Officio procede con gran' circonspettione, così in credere, come in processare, e pochi o nesun processo si trovano formati bene in questa materia." These words virtually echo what one reads in another important contemporary writing issued and circulated in manuscript by the Congregation of the Holy Office, namely the *Instructio*, possibly also from the pen of Desiderio Scaglia, discussed at pp. 205–27 in this volume.

43. Ranuzzi, MS. Ph. 12868, fol. [18], "Ti farò pentire, me la pagherai. . . ."

44. On the verification of the *corpus delicti*, see Bernardo da Como, "Tractatus de strigibus," in *Lucerna inquisitorum haereticae pravitatis* (Rome, 1596), 153: "Ita dicimus, quod ubi medici periti ex aliquibus coniecturis vel circumstantiis iudicant illam infirmitatem non ex defectu naturae, neque ex aliqua causa naturali intrinseca, sed ab extrinseco accidisse, & ab extrinseco, ubi non fit ex venenosa infectione, quia sic sanguis vel stomachus malis humoribus esset repletus, tunc ex sufficienti divisione iudicant effectum esse maleficialem"; I. Simancas, *De Catholicis Institutionibus Liber, ad praecavendas & extirpandas haereses* (Rome, 1575), Tit. 37, no. 18, p. 283: "Ne facile de infanticidiis fides lamiis est adhibenda, nisi prius constiterit infantes ipsos eodem tempore occisos esse." See also the observation of Cardinal Francesco Albizzi, *De Inconstantia in iure*, 344: "Medici difficiliter inducuntur ad testificandum in S. Officio morbos esse ex maleficio," and the discussion at p. 214 in this volume. The standard early treatment on forensic medicine is by the Roman jurist P. Zacchia (1584–1659), *Quaestiones medico-legales in quibus omnes eae materiae medicae, quae ad legales facultates pertinere videntur, pertractantur et resolvuntur* (Lyons, 1630), several times reprinted and enlarged. I have used the Nuremberg 1726 edition prepared by J. D. Horstius, *Quaestionum medico-legalium tomi tres*. See T. 3, Consilium 49, pp. 70 ff., which suggests that natural origins and natural cures exist even for *morbi* thought traceable to demoniacal intervention: rubric 10) "Mulieres daemoniacae existimate naturalibus remediis aliquando perfecte sanatae"; 11) "Tam naturalis, quam daemoniacus morbus ab iisdem causis naturalibus dependet."

45. Ranuzzi, MS. Ph. 12868, fol. [18]: ". . . e anco la fede d'un esperto essorcista, perchè molti ve ne sono che ogn' infermità giudicano per malefitii, o per poca prattica, o per farvi sopra mercantia." On exorcism and the apposite bibliography, see the still useful older work by M. Petrocchi, *Esorcismi e magia nell'Italia del Cinquecento e Seicento* (Naples, 1951), and more recently: H. Weber, "L'exorcisme à la fin du XVI siècle, instrument de la Contre Reforme et spectacle Baroque," *Nou-*

velle revue du seizième siècle 1 (1983): 79–101; M. O'Neil, *"Sacerdote ovvero strione*: Ecclesiastical and Superstitious Remedies in 16th-Century Italy," in S. Kaplan, ed., *Understanding Popular Culture* (Berlin, 1984), pp. 53–83; B. Nischan, "The Exorcism Controversy and Baptism in the Late Reformation," *Sixteenth Century Journal* 18 (1987): 31–51. The classic study remains D. P. Walker's, *Unclean Spirits: Possession and Exorcism in France and England in the Late Sixteenth and Early Seventeenth Centuries* (Philadelphia, 1981), especially the introduction for general methodological considerations and the Italian ramifications of the question ("there are indications that exorcisms were one of the regular tourist attractions of Rome," p. 3). For an excellent inventory of the primary literature on exorcism, see J.-B. Molin and A. Aussedat-Minvielle, *Répertoire des rituels et processionaux imprimés conservés en France* (Paris, 1984), pt. 4, "Recueils d'Exorcismes et de Benedictions" (134 items).

46. G. Menghi, *Flagellum Daemonum: Exorcismos terribiles, potentissimos, et efficaces . . . accessit postremo pars secunda, quae fustis daemonum inscribitur* (Bologna, 1589), 44: "Exorcista debet praecavere, quantum potest, ne absque gravi necessitate exerceat hoc officium adiurandi daemones in domibus privatis, ne detur occasio scandali pusillis; sed debet exorcizare in ecclesia, vel in alio loco Deo dicato, vel alicui sancto, tum quia in domibus privatis, ut in pluribus, adsunt mulieres, quarum consortium debet summopere ab exorcistis vitari, ne incidant in laqueum diaboli . . ."; "Advertere debet exorcista, ne ullo pacto praebeat hoc oleum, vel aliquod aliud remedium potabili alicui infirmo sine consilio, & iudicio medicorum" (*Fustis daemonum*, 21).

47. I am referring to the *Instructio* cited above at n. 42 and discussed at pp. 205–27. "Hinc diversis vicibus observatum fuit, aliquos iudices formare processus contra praetensos maleficos nominatos a daemone ut supra, tanquam si ex dicto daemonis probentur praemissa. Unde super huiusmodi processibus nulla vis facta fuit ab hac sacra Congregatione, imo semper reprehensi fuerunt exorcistae, daemonem ut supra interrogantes, & iudices, qui super daemonis responsione processum formarunt. Et utinam non reperirentur aliqui exorcistae, qui parum fideliter officium tam pium exercentes multas imposturas confingant. Hinc est ut quandoque plures fuerint privati munere exorcizandi." I cite from the first printed edition of the *Instructio*, appearing in the *De Potestate Angelica sive de Potentia Motrice* of the Dominican Tommaso Castaldi, 3 vols. (Rome, 1650–52), 2:244. Menghi himself was reproved for advocating this practice by Deodato Scaglia in his "Prattica" discussed below: "E per questo non fanno bene gli essorcisti far tali quesiti al demonio, ancorche l'insegni quel loro libro chiamato *Flagellum Daemonum*, la cui prattica in questo punto non è accetta, & più volte non solo questi essorcisti sono stati ripresi dalla Sacra Congregatione, ma anco ammoniti i giudici . . . che hanno voluto ricevere in processo queste risposte del demonio, mostrando farci fondamento, e de i processi loro non si è fatta alcuna stima . . ." (BAV, Barb. lat. 4615, p. 72). Menghi's works on exorcism were, in fact, condemned by the Congregation of the Index by decree of 4 March 1709. See *Index Librorum Prohibitorum SS.mi D.D. pontificis maximi jussu recognitus, atque editus* (Rome, 1758), 179; F. H. Reusch, *Der Index der verbotenen Bücher*, 2 vols. (Bonn,

1885), 2:219. J. Hilgers (*Der Index der verbotenen Bücher* [Freiburg, i.Br., 1904], 439), however, cites a condemnation dated 7 July 1704.

48. Ranuzzi, MS. Ph. 12868, fol. [19]. See, among various authorities, Bernardo da Como, "Tractatus de Strigibus," 151: "Advertas insuper, & sis bene cautus, ne de facili facias aliquam detineri propter inculpationes talium strigiarum tantum, quia posset contingere quod daemon assumeret personam alicuius, & se sub forma illius praesentarent in ipso ludo, ut illam personam infamet, & tamen illa persona erit innocens, & de tali crimine nullo modo culpabilis: quare cautius securiusque procedes, si ex solis inculpationibus seu manifestationibus sociarum, non facies aliquam personam detineri. . . ." For an example of this doctrine being put into practice, see the letter of Cardinal Camillo Borghese of the Congregation of the Holy Office to the inquisitor of Florence (16 October 1604): "Inoltre le dico, che nelle cose che la detta donna depone di haver visto ne' giuochi diabolici non se le crede contra di altre persone . . ." (BRB, MS. II 290, vol. 2, fol. 4). On the concept of the sabbat, see now C. Ginzburg, *Storia notturna, una decifrazione del sabba* (Turin, 1989).

49. J. Bodin, *De la demonomanie des sorciers* (Paris, 1580), fol. 169r: "Car le plus souvent il c'est trouvé, qu'elles estoient instruites par leurs mères, & menées aux assemblées, & ce qu'on y faict." For late seventeenth-century evidence that coparticipants at sabbats continued to be accused in civil courts, see O. Aureggi, "La stregoneria nelle Alpi Centrali: Ricerche di diritto e procedura penale," *Bollettino della Società Storica Valtellinese*, no. 15 (1961): 114–58, at p. 132 f. and the trial of Maria la Pillona (1614) in the Val di Nona (Trentino) who took revenge on her accusers by implicating them as partners in the sabbat. See *La confessione di una strega, un frammento di storia della Controriforma*, introduzione e note di L. Sambenazzi, presentazione di A. Foa (Rome, 1989), p. 137.

50. On this point, among many other authorities, see P. Farinacci, *Tractatus de Haeresi, editio novissima* (Lyons, 1650), q. 181, no. 48, p. 61: "Bene verum est, quod si lamiae poenitentes veniam petunt, et ad Ecclesiam ex corde redire volunt, sunt admittendae ad poenitentiam, ac etiam reconciliandae, nec ullo pacto curiae saeculari tradendae; etiam quod infantes occiderint, seu alia atrociora et nefanda crima perpetraverint"; I. Simancas, *De Catholicis Institutionibus*, Tit. 37, no. 16, p. 282: "Posthaec, de poenis lamiarum videndum est, quas si constiterit haereticas fuisse, punire debent inquisitores, perinde atque alios quoscunque haereticos . . . si veram poenitentiam agere voluerint, recipiendae sunt benigne iuxta canonicas sanctiones. . . ." "Striges et sortilegi quomodo puniri possint" is the subject extracted from a group of letters written by officials of the Holy Office in the last two decades of the sixteenth century (BAV, Barb. lat. 1370, fols. 377–80). See also the sentences for the years 1579–80 in TCD, MS. 1225, fols. 61, 282.

51. Ranuzzi, MS. Ph. 12868, fol. [20]: "Si fanno stare su le porte della chiesa un giorno di festa con la candela accesa in mano; si esiliano, si tengono in carcere formale *ad tempus*, o in casa, secondo la qualità del delitto. Et quando si lasciano fuora si fanno osservare, et se l'impone che se presentino al Sant' Offitio dei luoghi, o a gl'Ordinarii una volta il mese. . . . Talvolta anco si frustano, ma è però vero

che quando hanno marito, o figlie nubili [MS. nobili] il Sant' Offitio per benignità si astiene da questa condanna, perchè ridonda in ignominia delle figlie che per questo rispetto non trovano mariti, e i mariti perdono l'amore alle mogli [MS. moglie] frustate [havendole vedute così infamate appresso il popolo]." The bracketed clause, which does not appear in the Ranuzzi manuscript, occurs in the majority of other texts of the "Prattica" that I have consulted.

52. See TCD, MS. 1225, fol. 351, sentence dated 3 September 1580 against Gioseffo Hebreo, son of Bonavito Hebreo "da Orlino," twenty-three years of age, residing in Massa de' Lombardi. It reads: "Te bandiamo o diamo bando dal stato temporale ecclesiastico per anni tre, sotto pena della galea per sette anni e in essa habbi a servir per remigante. Et te condemniamo che in Imola un Sabbato al hora del mercato sii frustato dal Vescovato sino a San Domenico et da San Domenico sino al Palazzo; et in caso non si trovasse ministro di giustizia che te frustasse, in vece della frusta te condemniamo a star col ferro al collo alla berlina nella piazza di detta città di Imola all'hora del mercato con la mitra in capo per spacio d'hore sei, cioè dalle quindici sino alle vent'uno, voltato con la faccia verso il popolo, di maniera che te possino vedere et conoscere."

53. J. Weyer, *De praestigiis daemonum, et incantationibus, ac veneficiis libri V. Tertia editione* (Basel, 1566), 681, "Poena, qua lamias afficere solent Bononienses." The first edition is from 1563 and does not seem to contain the quoted passage. We can only guess at the source of Weyer's account. There is no evidence that he visited Italy in J. J. Cobben, *Jan Wier, Devils, Witches and Magic*, trans. S. A. Prins (Philadelphia, 1976). (The original Dutch edition appeared in 1960.)

54. Weyer, *De praestigiis daemonum*, 682 : "Infinitis certe modis praeferri decet hanc moderationem magistratus Bononiensis, quae nonnihil adhuc vetustatis Italicae prudentiam sapere videtur, prae aliorum quorundam tyrannide, qui ad igneum illud holocaustum praecipites nimis feruntur: eoque non minus affici, quam innocentis sanguinis effusi fumo daemones, apparet: 'O caecas hominum mentes, o pectora caeca.'"

55. See n. 41 in "The Roman Inquisition and Witchcraft," p. 223 in this volume.

56. Ranuzzi, MS. Ph. 12868, fol. [45]. See the unpublished paper by A. Biondi, "Il controllo della devozione femminile nella 'Prattica' del cardinale Scaglia (ca. 1635) e nelle lettere della S. Congregazione del S. Ufficio," presented at the symposium "Santità 'Vera' e Santità 'Simulata': Per una storia sociale e religiosa tra XV e XVIII secolo," Udine, 25–28 October 1989. A classic case is studied by A. Silvestri, "I costituti per l'abiura di suor Eleonora de Ruggiero: Un episodio di possessione diabolica nel monastero di S. Maria Donnaregina in Napoli nell'età della Controriforma," *Rivista di letteratura e di storia ecclesiastica* 10 (1978), nos. 1–2: 3–32.

57. The source for this episode is Polacco's *Breve raccontamento di quanto gli è occorso nel corso di trenta sei anni continui mentre è stato confessor delle venerande monache di Santa Lucia di Venezia* (Venice, 1643), 30. He defends himself by saying that he had read in the "Partica [sic] de procedere nelle cause del S. Uffizio, che si serva in Roma e nell'Arcivescovato da Milano, che alcune monache se tengano maleficiate alle volte & obsesse, e come che tra loro facilmente nascono garre & rivalità don-

nesche . . .," and that for many reasons attacking the problem by exorcism only makes it worse. I am indebted to the courtesy of Anne J. Schutte for this interesting piece of evidence that the "Prattica's" skeptical attitude towards witchcraft was making converts, but also meeting resistance in more conservative circles.

58. Sentences emitted by provincial tribunals were ordinarily reviewed in Rome before they could take effect. The circumstances surrounding confessions obtained during torture, especially if they were subsequently retracted, received special scrutiny. For the case of a confession deemed implausible and unacceptable by the Congregation of the Inquisition, see n. 72 of "The Roman Inquisition and Witchcraft" in this volume.

59. BAV, Barb. lat. 4615, p. 63: "Con tutto ciò non si corre in furia particolarmente in materia di questi giuochi notturni a credere e procedere come se pienamente certasse il delitto, ma il prudente giudice va considerando dalle condizioni: se quella confessione habbia del verisimile, o pur contenga circostanze impossibili e ripugnanti all'istessa natura, come quando una donna confessa d'esser stata personalmente in tempo di notte a detti tripudii senza essersi partita dal letto del marito; o quando dice d'esser uscita corporalmente dalla sua casa senza passar per le porte, ne per le finestre."

60. Ibid., p. 68. Scaglia warned judges not to assume automatically that such marks alone constituted the *corpus delicti*, "potendo esser fatti o dalla natura nel modo ch'ella produce i nei, o da accidenti diversi, onde quando simili caratteri non siano accompagnati da altri indicii gravi nel processo pertinenti a simil fatto . . . non se doverà fare molto fondamento. . . ."

61. Ibid., p. 67, the case "di una strega famosa detta Montagna di Valdagno." All the other evidence cited by Deodato comes from such early Fathers as Irenaeus and Tertullian, or from the *Malleus maleficarum* (Speier, c. 1487) by the two German Dominicans, Heinrich Kramer and Jakob Sprenger.

62. See, for example, the trials studied by O. Aureggi, "La stregoneria nelle Alpi Centrali," 147, which speak of a "ravetta," an official specialized in detecting witches' marks; and for a trial conducted in the Trentino, 1612–15, similarly before a secular magistrate, see *La confessione di una strega*, esp. pp. 63 f. Additional evidence from these Alpine regions is furnished by L. Muraro, *La signora del gioco, episodi della caccia alle streghe* (Milan, 1976). For other contemporary evidence, see N. Remy (*Daemonolatreiae libri tres* [Lyons, 1595], 48), who describes the best known characteristic of the Devil's mark, its bloodlessness: "Et quod magis mirum videri possit, totus ille locus ita exanguis est, ac sensu labefactatus, ut ne admissa quidem acus altissime aut dolorem faciat, aut sanguinis minimum eliciat." The mark, as with baptism, sealed the adherence of the witch to a higher authority. This is explained, among others, by F. Perreaud, *Demonologie, ou traitté des demons et sorciers* (Geneva, 1653), 28: "Tous les sorciers confessent qu'après que le Diable leur a fait renoncer à leur baptisme, & fait promettre qu'ils seront ennemis de Dieu & de toute pieté, & que de là en autant ils serviront à lui seul, & autres choses; qu'il leur imprime une marque en une partie de leur corps . . . en la quelle on pourroit fourrer une grande aiguille

ou une alesne, sans qu'ils en sentent rien, affin de les obliger de plus en plus par ce moyen, comme par un sacrement"; Joost Damhouder, *Praxis rerum criminalium* (Antwerp, 1570), 146: "Mulieres autem maleficae, quae iam voluntate depravata, et consensu in consortium daemonum per pacta transierunt, notas quasdam et signa symbolica ab ipsis recipiunt, quibus exciti daemones mox prosiliunt." The author was a doctor of both laws. See also the standard treatise by J. Fontaine, *Des marques des sorciers et de la réelle possession que le diable prend sur les corps des hommes* (Lyons, 1611).

63. On judicial torture, see the bibliography cited at n. 95 in "The Organization and Procedures," p. 179 in this volume.

64. BAV, Barb. lat. 4615, p. 268: ". . . quelli che posti alla tortura, quantunque acremente tormentati, non però confessano mai, ne si dolgono, ma stanno anzi costantissimi come se non sentissero alcun dolore, e questo per essersi a ciò preparati con segreti, che dicono haver tal virtù, e per tener sopra la persona alcuni maleficii fatti a tal fine, le quali cose consistono per ordinario in pastelle di varii ingredienti, polveri di cuore d'un certo animale abbrusciato, sangue d'uccelli e simili."

65. Ibid., p. 270: "E questi poi come antidoti e preservativi o li mangiano, o li tengono sotto la lingua, o cuciti ne i panni, o se gli nascondano fra i capelli, et anco nelle parti più segreti del corpo, e con questi mezzi diabolici chiamati maleficii di taciturnità resistono ai tormenti senza confessare."

66. Ibid. For contemporary discussions of the phenomenon of *maleficium taciturnitatis* in the secular courts of Europe, see N. Remy, *Daemonolatreiae libri tres*, chaps. 8 and 9; J. Bodin, *Demonomanie*, fol. 170v: "Et si on voit que les sorciers ne confessent rien, il faut leur faire changer d'habits & leur faire razer tout le poil, & alors les interroger. . . . Car tous sont d'accord, que les sorciers portent des drogues de taciturnité, combien que c'est le diable qui les conforte et les assure. . . ." The distinguished jurist of Antwerp, Joost Damhouder (*Praxis Rerum Criminalium*, 88) provides a long eyewitness description of a Bruges witch who did not confess during prolonged tortures, but who admitted everything after her body was shaved and the malefice discovered in an orifice of her body: "Verum priusquam scamno imponeretur totius corporis pilos & crines abradi curavimus, postea scamno imponitur, acerrime torquetur, nihil tamen fateri voluit. Tandem quibusdam astantibus succurit eam non esse tonsam in pudendis, sub axillis, & culo ubi per tonsitrices illi quoque crine abrasi fuerunt, & inter radendum reperta fuit pergamena culo cunnoque inserta, cui inscripta fuerunt aliquot peregrina vocabula daemonum, crucibus aliquod inter se distincta." For an early skeptical view of these judicial practices and beliefs, see J. Weyer, *De praestigiis daemonum*, chap. 10.

67. See, as an example, the sentence promulgated at Mantua on 24 February 1581 against Nicolò Zani (TCD, MS. 1226, fol. 57): ". . . mentre ch'eri qui carcerato doppo la confessione delle sopradette cose fosti deposto avanti di noi qualmente havevi scritte con le tue proprie mani sopra tre bolettini la forma del Santissimo Sacramento della Eucarestia e che n'havessi dato duoi de quelli a un tuo compagno mentre eri prigione e, ritenuto l'altro per te stesso, et ch'havevi insegnato a detto compagno che ingiotessi uno de quelli bolettini quando era condotto ai tormenti perchè per

virtù di quello non haveria confessato cosa alcuna." See also MS. 3638 of the Biblioteca Casanatense, Rome, a miscellany of medical texts which describes "anestetici particolarmente temuti dai Domenicani, perchè servivano a resistere alla tortura" (*Roma ermetica: Cultura esoterica e società a Roma tra XV e XVIII secolo: Manoscritti ed immagini* [Rome, 1983], 16, 74).

68. (Bologna, 1668), 176: ". . . sortilegia contra tormenta funis & alias quaestiones ad reticendum veritatem. . . ."

69. Decree of the Roman Congregation of the Inquisition, 5 June 1591: "Ill.mi et rev.mi domini cardinales generales inquisitores mandarunt moneri inquisitores ut de caetero abstineant a rasura capillorum mulierum inquisitarum et hominum, quia potest fieri inquisitio absque tali abrasione" (L. von Pastor, *Allgemeine Dekrete*, 48).

70. A. Soman, "The Parlement of Paris and the Great Witch Hunt (1565–1640)," *The Sixteenth Century Journal* 9 (1978), no. 2: 31–44, at p. 41; "Deviance and Criminal Justice in Western Europe, 1300–1800: An Essay in Structure," *Criminal Justice History* 1 (1980): 1–28, at p. 24. See the Bibliography to this volume for the several other excellent studies by Soman on this and related questions in early modern French criminal law. On the physical characteristics which strengthened resistance to torture, see P. Fiorelli, *La tortura giudiziaria nel diritto comune*, 2 vols. (Milan, 1953), 1:215, and G. B. Scanaroli, *De Visitatione Carceratorum Libri Tres* (Rome, 1655), 292, where Scanaroli, who was the bishop of Modena, declares that women succeeded in resisting pain more easily than men "quia habent maiorem pectoris latitudinem" and because "carent certis partibus quae maxime dolorem augent."

71. See "Toward a Statistical Profile of the Italian Inquisitions" at pp. 94 f. in this volume.

72. A. De Sousa, *Aphorismi inquisitorum* (Turnoni, 1639), 137: "Cum sortilegorum crimina sint mixti fori, tam ab ecclesiastico, quam a seculari iudice possunt sortilegi puniri, ut a propriis iudicibus. Secundum ius commune inquisitores cognoscere non possunt, nec procedere contra sortilegos, nisi sortilegia haeresim sapiant manifeste. De iure novo inquirunt et procedunt inquisitores etiamsi sortilegia haeresim non sapiant manifeste." See also C. Carena, *Tractatus de Officio Sanctissimae Inquisitionis*, 176 (of the Bologna 1668 ed.): "Secundum hodierna iura iudex, tam sortilegiorum haereticalium, quam non haereticalium, est inquisitor" as decreed in Sixtus V's Bull "Creator Coeli." For evidence of a contrary trend within the Roman Congregation of the Inquisition, manifested in a reluctance to involve itself in cases of simple magic and superstition, see C. Ginzburg, *The Night Battles: Witchcraft and Agrarian Cults in the Sixteenth and Seventeenth Centuries*, trans. J. and A. Tedeschi (Baltimore, 1983), 178.

73. See H. C. Lea, *Minor Historical Writings*, ed. A. C. Howland (Philadelphia, 1942), 3. For the seventeenth century a start has been made by A. Gari Lacruz, "Variedad de competencias en el delito de brujería (1600–1650) en Aragon," in J. Pérez Villanueva, *La Inquisición española*, pp. 319–28.

74. For a preliminary calendar of witch trials through 1499 (not restricted to

Italy), see R. Kieckhefer, *European Witch Trials: Their Foundations in Popular and Learned Culture, 1300–1500* (London and Henley, 1976), 106–47.

75. For one such outbreak, critically evaluated, see A. Biondi, "Gianfrancesco Pico e la repressione della stregoneria: Qualche novità sui processi mirandolesi del 1522–23," *Deputazione di Storia Patria per le Antiche Provincie Modenesi: Biblioteca*, n.s., 76 (1984): 331–49, esp. pp. 335–39; between sixty and seventy arraigned (although not all tried), of whom ten were executed.

76. Cf. "Preliminary Observations," p. 20, n. 72 in this volume. I think the essays published here disprove the notion that the *Malleus* was "the text-book of the Inquisition," as recently asserted again, this time by N. Ben-Yehuda, "Problems Inherent in Socio-Historical Approaches to the European Witch Craze," *Journal of the Scientific Study of Religion* 20 (1981): 326–38, at p. 328. The influence of the *Malleus* earlier in the sixteenth century, even on Italian writers, is a definite possibility—witness the many references made to it by B. Spina in his *Questio de Strigibus* (1523)—but one which needs to be verified. At any rate, the *Malleus* did not serve as the unswerving guide in inquisitorial proceedings throughout the era of witchcraft trials. Among the few modern studies on this controversial manual, see G. Marta, "Il 'Malleus maleficarum' e il 'De pytonicis mulieribus.' Due modi d'intendere la stregoneria sul finire del XV secolo," in *Studi offerti a R. Morghen*, a cura dell'Istituto storico italiano per il medio evo (Rome, 1974), 1:407–26; S. Anglo, "Evident Authority and Authoritative Evidence: The *Malleus Maleficarum*," in S. Anglo, ed., *The Damned Art: Essays in the Literature of Witchcraft* (London, 1977), 1–31; and E. Camerlynck, "Feminité et sorcellerie chez les théoriciens de la démonologie à la fin du Moyen Age: Étude du *Malleus Maleficarum*," *Renaissance and Reformation* 19 (1983): 13–25; *Der Hexenhammer: Enstehung und Umfeld des "Malleus maleficarum" von 1487*, hrsg. P. Segl (Cologne, 1988). A survey of the demonological literature produced in the first half of the sixteenth century finds scarce echo of the *Malleus*. See S. Leutenbauer, *Hexerei- und Zaubereidelikt in der Literatur von 1450 bis 1550: Mit Hinweisen auf die Praxis im Herzogtum Bayern* (Berlin, 1972), 69–70.

77. Roman witchcraft trials conducted before a civil court, the *Tribunale del Governatore*, the majority before 1570, have been studied in two recent articles: I. Polverini Fosi, "Un processo per 'streghe e furfanterie' nella Roma di Paolo IV," *Ricerche per la storia religiosa di Roma* 4 (1980): 215–36, and A. Adorisio, "Stregoneria e vita religiosa tra città e campagna nel Cinquecento romano," *Sociologia: Rivista di scienze sociali dell'Istituto Luigi Sturzo* 17 (1983): 167–212. These impressive studies document the common practice of using sacramental objects for magical ends: "Importante è notare la forma di sincretismo magico-religioso che si determina nella messa in opere del sortilegio in questione. Mentre si invocano i misteriosi spiriti delle tenebre per conoscere il futuro . . . si recitano in ginocchio preghiere quali il Padre Nostro e l'Ave Maria tenendo in mano candele benedette. Una magia quindi che non si oppone alla religione ufficiale, ma anzi dei suoi stessi riti si serve per raggiungere i propri scopi. I protagonisti della vicenda non sono perfettamente coscienti di compiere atti che vanno contro i precetti cristiani, per loro è del tutto naturale invocare

lo spirito dello specchio recitando orazioni a carattere religioso" (Adorisio, pp. 196–97). The same conclusion that the large majority of trials concerned non-diabolical magic also emerges from the systematic surveys recently conducted on inquisitorial documents preserved in Modenese and Bolognese repositories: See M. O'Neil, "*Sacerdote ovvero strione*" (cited in full at n. 45) and "Magical Healing, Love Magic, and the Inquisition in Late Sixteenth-Century Modena," in *Inquisition and Society in Early Modern Europe*, ed. and trans. S. Haliczer (London and Sydney, 1987), 88–114. O'Neil's extensive research will appear shortly as a comprehensive monograph tentatively entitled "Healing and Harm: Inquisition Trials for Magical and Superstitious Offenses in 16th–17th Century Modena." See also the unpublished *Tesi di laurea* submitted in the academic year 1981–82 at the University of Bologna by Milena Brugnoli, "Superstizione e repressione: Il Tribunale della Santa Inquisizione a Bologna e contado nell'ultimo quarto del XVII secolo," based on a thorough examination of late seventeenth-century Bolognese trials. Among the many other recent studies that could be cited, see the suggestive comments by P. Burke in the chapter "Rituals of Healing in Early Modern Italy," in his *The Historical Anthropology of Early Modern Italy: Essays on Perception and Communication* (Cambridge, 1987), 207–20. The pertinent literature is listed in the Bibliography to this volume.

78. See above at n. 5.

79. This was the fate of still another reforming inquisitorial document, the *Instructio* (cited above at n. 10 and discussed in detail at pp. 205–27 in this volume), which circulated in manuscript for more than three decades before it was eventually printed—and then anonymously and under somewhat clouded circumstances, possibly to forestall the hostility of secular authorities.

EIGHT

☙

Literary Piracy
in Seventeenth-Century Florence:
Giovanni Battista Neri's
De iudice S. Inquisitionis opusculum

In the course of researching criminal law treatises of the sixteenth and
seventeenth centuries at the Huntington Library, I was specifically concerned to compare secular proceedings with those of the courts of the Italian
inquisitions and to learn more about how the questions of magic and witchcraft were handled.[1] At the time, I was studying two unpublished and
previously unexplored vernacular inquisitorial manuals — "Prattiche" or legal
handbooks — both compiled in the early decades of the seventeenth century by highly placed ecclesiastics, Desiderio and Deodato Scaglia, uncle and
nephew.[2] As I flipped through the Huntington's chronological catalogue,
a volume entitled *De iudice S. Inquisitionis opusculum*, written by a certain
Giovanni Battista Neri and printed in Florence in 1685, caught my attention. Despite well over a decade of research on the Inquisition, both the
title and author were new to me. The title page identified Neri as a Reader in Sacred Theology, professor of canon law, and former provincial for
Tuscany of his order, the Minorite friars of St. Francis of Paula. The title
page also gave note that the book was dedicated from the heart (ex corde)
to Cosimo III, sixth grand duke of Tuscany.[3] The actual text of the
dedication, with fitting modesty, invited the sovereign to accept the "crude"
opuscle, not for the sake of Neri's own glory, which was as fleeting as
a shadow, but for the public good.[4]

The author's greeting to the reader explained why he had set himself to the task of describing the duties of a judge of the Holy Office even though many before him had discoursed at length on the subject. From such a mass of diffuse material, our writer stated, one could deduce only with great difficulty how properly to conduct inquisitorial trials. So he had resolved to accept the challenge, treating the subject with brevity, clarity, and sure doctrine.[5] The fortunate reader could now easily peruse "hilari vultu" (with a smile on his face), the work Neri had produced by the sweat of his own brow ("quae ego sudore conscripsi").

The back of the book contained the information that the manuscript had been duly approved for publication, as ecclesiastical censorship law prescribed, by two expert theologians assigned to the task by the general and provincial of Neri's order, and, of course, by a consultor of the Holy Office in Florence.[6] The latter's imprimatur attested that the work had been accurately compiled and "contained nothing contrary to our Catholic faith and the honesty of morals."[7]

But it was the text which provided the surprises, starting at the brief prologue with which it opened: "Cases before the tribunal of the Holy Office either are for heresy or for the suspicion of heresy...."[8] These were very familiar words: they were, in fact, identical to the prologue of Desiderio Scaglia's "Prattica."[9] What a fantastic coincidence that a Florentine author writing well over half a century after Scaglia should have coined, except for the different language, an absolutely identical *prooemium* to his piece. The rest of this brief section followed the same pattern. My consternation grew when I began to find that the chapter titles also corresponded closely, too closely, to the arrangement in Scaglia's work.

It soon became obvious to me that Giovanni Battista Neri had simply plundered another man's labors.[10] In a Florentine archive he must have stumbled upon one of the many dispersed manuscript copies of Scaglia's "Prattica," which we know circulated widely in the 1620s.[11] He had dusted it off, translated it, given it a totally different title, embellished it, as we shall soon see, and passed it off, after many bows to his audience, as the fruit of his own honest efforts. And he had got away with it for three hundred years.

The text, marred by numerous misprints,[12] follows the basic chapter order of the model and generally produces a faithful Latin rendering of the original Italian. Neri occasionally expands the discussion of the "Prattica" and adds references to modern authorities, including several in a flattering vein to members of his own order.[13] Among his other innovations, he introduces section numbers within each chapter and occasionally continues the discussion begun in one chapter to the next, thus altering the total number of chapters. For example, whereas chapter eight in all the copies of Desiderio's "Prattica" deals with magic and witchcraft, "De Sortilegii," in Neri's work, is dedicated to solicitation of sexual favors by priests in the confessional, a continuation of the discussion from the previous chapter. Chapter twenty-five, which in the "Prattica" is entitled "Delle monache" and concerns itself with presumed spells afflicting nuns in their convents, is given over by Neri to an inquisitorial "Instruction" in witchcraft cases, an anonymous text which circulated independently and had no direct connection to the work at hand.[14]

But the biggest surprise of all was that Neri had introduced a totally new chapter, which he numbered twenty-six, dealing with "aliqua curiosa et necessaria." Curious it certainly was. My eyes immediately fell on the word tobacco, a subject not obviously connected with the previous long discussion on the duties of an inquisitor. Our author was attempting to answer what to us may seem to be a preposterous question, but one which, as I later discovered, was of some urgency in the seventeenth century—namely, whether it was sinful for priests to consume tobacco in a church or its immediate confines in whatever form: ". . . that is either solid, or chewed in small pieces, or taken as a powder through the mouth or nose, or inhaled as smoke by means of tubelets. . . ."[15]

This was the first of many questions raised by Neri dealing with the permissibility of the use of tobacco, questions prompted principally by Urban VIII's prohibition, *Cum Ecclesia,* dated 30 January 1642, directed against the wholesale consumption of tobacco in churches under the jurisdiction of the archbishopric of Seville. This was an abuse which had apparently been committed even during the performance of divine services by parishioners of both sexes blowing out acrid fumes to every corner of the holy edifices, while priests themselves performed their liturgical duties before the altar in vestments befouled by tobacco juice and spittle.[16] Neri's "curious" chapter merits brief discussion, both because it opens a small window on a forgotten episode in church history and because it constitutes an unrecorded item in the vast bibliography consecrated to tobacco.[17]

If, Neri concluded, Pope Urban's condemnation extended to tobacco consumption in all its forms and in all churches, not only the Spanish, what boundaries existed? Was the sacristy also off limits? After consultation with "non pauci gravissimi theologi," Neri decided it was, because it was there that priests prepared themselves for the celebration of the holy sacrament both spiritually and by donning their liturgical garments. The same prohibition, in Neri's estimation, extended to the choir, an area "deputatus ad divinas laudes decantandas, & non ad excitanda corporis excrementa."[18]

Neri opposed the position of certain Spanish priests who had argued that they would not be committing a mortal sin smoking secretly and unseen in church. Smoking had been forbidden for two reasons, they insisted: first, not to create any scandal and second, not to disturb the divine services. But when churches were empty and the doors had closed behind the faithful, the prohibitions, so ran their thought, lost their force. Neri disagreed with this position, warning mere mortals not to introduce distinctions where the law had not. Urban's Bull had not differentiated between a closed and open church, etc.[19]

The discussion moves on to the permissibility of smoking in the rectory, where priests reside, and asks whether, when the habitation was not physically attached to the church, it must still be considered, in the words of Urban's pronouncement, "in ambitu," or within its confines. Neri's opinion was that smoking in these premises would seriously disturb and distract priests preparing to celebrate the Mass. Tobacco taken by mouth necessarily stimulated the stomach to eject the foreign substance, with the consequent terrible danger that the host might be expelled along with it.[20]

Neri then attempts to place the problem in a larger context by asserting that tobacco could be taken in two ways, moderately and immoderately. Following the first course would be reasonable and would even safeguard bodily health. The second, on the other hand, would be harmful, and raised a moral question, since man was obliged, under pain of excommunication, to cultivate a sound mind and body. The ensuing sin would thus be venial or mortal, depending on the extent of the immoderation.[21]

In the opinion of our author, there are a number of issues to be pondered in regard to the consumption of tobacco in church by the laity. It might tempt others to indulge, and thus break their silence, waver in their attention to the sacred mysteries being celebrated at the altar, and run the risk of breaking out in sneezing fits, of having to blow their noses, or of provoking a lot of spitting and accompanying laughter—leading many to curse tobacco and its users, its inventors and vendors, and even the prince, for not having outlawed its use, or at least for not having taxed it heavily, which might have curbed its popularity. This commotion, of course, would be scandalous and an offense to the sacred rites.[22] The moderate use of tobacco, on the other hand, would not produce these depraved consequences, that is, if it were taken through the nostrils or chewed, rather than inhaled through a tube *(tubulum)*.[23] It was what we may presume to have been a primitive form of cigar smoking that was scandalous, provoking laughter on the part of the beholder and leading to noisy murmuring because of the noxious odor that it sent wafting through the place of worship.[24]

If there was agreement that tobacco was not a fitting accouterment to the divine service, should its consumption by the faithful before the Mass, in any form, be interpreted as a break in the fast every Catholic was obliged to observe before partaking of the Eucharist? On this point, Neri regretfully reported that authorities could not agree.[25] One school of thought peremptorily asserted that it did indeed represent an abrogation of the fast.[26] A second, less doctrinaire position allowed that it was an indecent practice and should be avoided especially by the clergy because of the special reverence they owed to the sacrament. At any rate, clergy and laity alike should abstain from chewing the leaf in the mouth, since there was the danger that a fragment or juice from it might inadvertently slip through to the stomach, and this would indeed constitute breaking the fast.[27] A third school, the realist, pointed out that tobacco was universally taken before the Mass, especially by Spaniards, and that this practice should not be considered an interruption of fasting and therefore was not a mortal sin.[28]

Neri, along with a majority of authorities, leaned toward this more lenient point of view. Tobacco did not break the fast unless it was somehow transmitted to the stomach. And although tobacco smoke was inhaled by mouth in the case of cigars, it was by no means intentionally taken into the stomach in the same way as food and drink. Moreover, it was plain for all to see that it was blown out through the nose, and even if a little smoke should inadvertently reach the stomach, this would be through a breathing process, not through consumption.[29] The moderate and orderly use of tobacco an hour or even a half hour before Mass had nothing indecent about it; on the contrary, there was much to recommend it, since it contributed to bodily cleanliness. After the nostrils were freed from obstruction, for example, speech became clearer, and a priest could preach or read more distinctly after he had sneezed a few times.[30]

It was the inordinate, immoderate consumption of tobacco before the Mass, especially when indulged in by a priest who was inexperienced in its use, that Neri found reprehensible and incompatible with the reverence due to the holy sacrament. And he paints an unedifying picture of a priest who has been indulging to excess, jittery, sneezing, expectorating, and blowing his nose, tears streaming from his eyes, staggering in a semi-stupor to the altar.[31]

How can we place Neri's chapter twenty-six, his disquisition on tobacco, in some sort of historical context? Clearly, it should be seen as part of the program of the Counter-Reformation church to introduce a heightened decorum into religious services.[32] The fact appears to be that the consumption of tobacco by clergy and laity alike during the celebration of the Mass had become widespread on both sides of the Atlantic from the late sixteenth century on. A series of provincial synods in Mexico and Peru beginning in the mid–1570s forbade the use of tobacco by priests about to celebrate Mass or by the faithful who were intent on receiving the holy sacrament.[33] But these prohibitions seemed to have served little purpose. The Dominican Tomás Ramon (d. 1634), in his *Nueva prematica de reformacion* published in 1635, describes clerical indulgence in tobacco that knew no limits, and was especially prevalent in Spain.[34]

The situation had reached a desperate point in Seville, where the dean and the chapter of the Metropolitan Church had beseeched Urban VIII to intervene when it had become obvious, as a contemporary account relates, ". . . that there was not a canon, chaplain, or cleric, in fact no lay person of either sex who, either while they were performing their services in the choir and at the altar, or while they were listening to the Mass and the divine offices, were not at the same time, and with great irreverence, taking tobacco; and with fetid excrements sullying the altar, holy places and pavements of the churches of that diocese."[35]

But the nuisance had reached the seat of Catholicism itself. Eight years after Urban had to take action against Seville, his successor, Innocent X, had to issue a similar sweeping prohibition for St. Peter's, to preserve unsullied from the expectorating of the faithful the beautiful new marble floors with which the church had been adorned.[36]

While a series of papal and episcopal pronouncements for the rest of the century attempted to suppress the clerical consumption of tobacco during or immediately preceding divine services,[37] theologians debated, as we have seen, what one authority described as "one of the most celebrated questions of our day": whether the use of tobacco before divine services constituted abrogation of ecclesiastical fasting and voided participation in the sacrament of the Eucharist.[38]

The march toward the restoration of proper decorum in religious services experienced its setbacks. On 10 January 1725, Benedict XIII removed the threat of excommunication which had been issued by Innocent X to preserve the pavements of St. Peter's. Benedict was compelled to act to prevent a different sort of nuisance, the disturbance caused by the constant coming and going of parishioners who could not forgo their tobacco habits for the duration of a single Mass. In his missive to Cardinal Annibale Albani, archpriest of the Vatican basilica, he claimed that he wanted

> to provide for the needs of everybody's conscience, and especially for the good order of the basilica, which is seriously compromised by the frequent walking out of those who cannot abstain from the use of tobacco which is so widespread today, partly due to the opinion of the physicians who recommend it as a remedy against many infirmities, especially for those people who are obliged to frequent cold and humid places in the early morning hours. Thus, we have resolved to permit the use of tobacco in the aforementioned basilica, its choir, chapels, sacristy, portals and atrium. . . .[39]

If such a decision seems farfetched, it should be remembered that tobacco had originally been introduced in Italy under the highest ecclesiastical sponsorship. Cardinal Prospero di Santa Croce is said to have returned in 1561 from a tour as nuncio in Portugal with a sample of the tobacco plant, which in his honor was dubbed the "Herba Santa Croce"; and it was another eminent churchman, toward the end of the sixteenth century, a Cardinal Crescenzio, who is credited with spreading the fashion of smoking tobacco for pleasure, a habit he acquired from Prince Virginio Orsini, who had learned it in England.[40]

The tobacco leaf, moreover, as we saw in Benedict's letter, was considered to have beneficial properties, from stimulating the secretion of gastric juices and acting as a laxative[41] to serving as a defense against the plague and other contagious diseases.[42] But for ecclesiastics there could be no greater encouragement to the consumption of tobacco than its alleged qualities in the repression of sensual impulses. As an early student of the subject declared,

> I say . . . that the use of tobacco, taken moderately, not only is useful, but even necessary for priests, monks, friars and other religious who must and desire to lead a chaste life, and repress those sensual urges that sometimes assail them. The natural cause of lust is heat and humidity. When this is dried out through the use of tobacco, these libidinous surges are not felt so powerfully. . . .[43]

Evidence of its use for this purpose by at least one saintly person emerged at the beatification trial of the Franciscan Joseph Desa of Cupertino (d. 1663). Witnesses declared that the good father, a heavy smoker, consumed tobacco so that he might keep awake during the long vigils of the night, but also to resist the temptations of the flesh. Other witnesses, such as Cardinal Giulio Spinola, testified that Cupertino resorted to tobacco as an act of humility to conceal the odor of sanctity that filled his cell, a sweet scent caused by the angels who kept him company during his arduous spiritual exercises.[44] Whatever the reasons, whether because of the pleasure it gave or the benefits it was thought to impart to body and spirit, recourse to tobacco had become a quasi-universal addiction, as Benedict XIII, himself an ardent snuff-taker, recognized when he opened the portals of St. Peter's to this habit. Other popes, Pius VII and Gregory XVI, were also heavy users, and the former was often noted with his white vestments stained by tobacco. An anecdote circulated about Benedict XIV who, in the course of a conversation opened an elegant case and offered his companion tobacco. The ungrateful person replied, "Thank you, Holy Father, but I don't have these vices." To which the pontiff promptly rejoined, "It is not a vice and if it were, you'd have this one too."[45]

Neri's chapter twenty-six, and its discussion of tobacco, may help to shed a little light on the persisting problems connected with the purification of rites and liturgy faced by the Counter-Reformation church, problems which the bishops assembled at Trent could scarcely have imagined, but which still retained all their immediacy in the closing years of the seventeenth century, since G. B. Neri felt compelled to make them an item of inquisitorial business in the *De iudice S. Inquisitionis opusculum.*

Notes

1. For example, the Huntington possesses six editions of the infamous *Malleus maleficarum* published between 1487 and 1496. Among the continental demonologists are Jean Bodin, Johann Wier, François Perreaud, Jacques d'Autun, Giovan Francesco Pico della Mirandola, Girolamo Mengo, François Placet, Sebastien Michaelis, G. B. Della Porta, Nicholas Remy, Giovanni Lorenzo d'Anania, Giuseppe Passi, etc. Under the rubric "Witches" in H. A. White's Index of the Huntington English STC imprints I counted over 130 items, including some translations of continental writers.

2. See my "The Question of Magic and Witchcraft," at pp. 229–58 in this volume. (Desiderio Scaglia's "Prattica" was published subsequent to my Huntington researches and after the first version of this article was written. See n. 11 below.)

3. *De Iudice S. Inquisitionis Opusculum A.R.A.P.F. Ioanne Baptista Neri Ordinis Minimorum, S. Francisci de Paula, S. Theologiae Lectore Iubilato, ac Iuris Canonici Professore Compilatum, & Sereniss. Cosmo III Magno Etruriae Duci Ex Corde Dicatum.* Florentiae, 1685. 4o; [6], 180, [14] pp. (Henceforth cited as *Opusculum*).

4. *Opusculum*, [4]: "Bonitas igitur Sereniss. Celsitudinis tuae suscipiat obsecro, non pro gloria mea cui velut umbra fugere est, & pro qua nunquam laborare constitui, sed pro, quae permanet, & pro qua sudasse decorum est, publica utilitate."

5. *Opusculum*, [5]: "De Iudice S. Inquisitionis ad scribendum me composui quia etiam si multi; multa in hac materia dixere diffuse, tamen ita scripsere; ut non sine magno labore ab eis certus modus in causis procedendi, inveniri possit. Ego [i.e., Ergo] in re ista peragenda, cordi praesertim fuit cum brevitate claritates, certaque doctrina."

6. Ibid., 177.

7. Ibid., 180.

8. Ibid., 1: "Causae quae accidunt in Tribunali Sanctae Inquisitionis, aut sunt haeresiae, aut suspicionis eiusdem, quare delinquentes, aut sunt haeretici, aut de haeresia suspecti; duobus modis considerantur; nempe, primo ut praeventi [sic] in iudicio, ex sufficientibus indiciis, secundo ut sponte comparentes [qua propter, sive de primis, sive de secundis, quomodo contra eos procedendum sit in hoc trattatulo breviter, agam]." The bracketed section has been added in Neri's text.

9. Rome, Biblioteca Casanatense, MS. 2889, f. 1r: "Le cause del S.to Offitio, o sono di heresia o di sospettione di essa. I delinquenti o sono heretici, o sospetti, si considerano in doi modi, primo come prevenuti in giuditio da inditii sofficienti, secondo, come sponte comparenti."

10. I have not attempted any in-depth research on Neri. The work is listed under his name, without allusion to its indebtedness to Desiderio Scaglia's "Prattica," in E. Van der Vekene's *Bibliotheca Bibliographica Historiae Sanctae Inquisitionis*, 2 vols. (Vaduz, 1982–83), 1:62. Similarly, H. C. Lea (*Materials Toward a History of Witchcraft*, arranged and edited by A. C. Howland, 3 vols. [Philadelphia, 1939; reprinted New York, 1957], 2:1035) did not question Neri's authorship but observed that

"Cardinal Scaglia's humane prescription not to scourge matrons and women with marriageable daughters on account of the humiliation is duly preserved." E. Cochrane (*Florence in the Forgotten Centuries, 1527–1800* [Chicago, 1973], 534–46) cites the *Opusculum* as a source for his chapters on contemporary religion. It is doubtful that our author is to be identified with the Giovanni Neri, an apologist for the Dominican Savonarola, listed in G. Negri, *Istoria degli scrittori fiorentini* (Florence, 1722), 290. At p. 5 of the *Opusculum* Neri claims to have written a commentary on canon law: ". . . ut dixi cum de matrimonio, in meo commentario secundi libri iuris canonicae institutionis. . . ." This information is confirmed by an epigram at the back of the volume signed L.N.M: "Ad eundem qui librum nuper de Philosophicis distiplinis [sic], Iurisque Institutiones, novissime tandem Sacrae Inquisitionis Praxim edidit."

11. For a preliminary inventory, see "A Question of Magic and Witchcraft," p. 243 in this volume. A copy of the "Prattica" preserved in the Biblioteca Nazionale, Florence was recently published by A. Mirto, "Un inedito del Seicento sull'Inquisizione," *Nouvelles de la Republique des Lettres* 1 (1986): 99–138. This may be the text which originally fell into Neri's hands. Mirto treats the document as an anonymous work.

12. For example, on p. 67, read "cartam" for "castam," "Agrippam" for "Agnippam," chapters are misnumbered, etc.

13. See, for example, chap. 9, "De Sortilegiis," which has a new first paragraph providing a definition of the crime according to Jean Bodin, Prospero Farinacci, and Paolo Grillando, and an added last paragraph with references to Martinus Del Rio and Cesare Carena. In chap. 6 (p. 23), Neri cites P. Ioannis des Bois of his order on the question of polygamy.

14. On this document, see my "The Roman Inquisition and Witchcraft," pp. 205–27 in this volume.

15. *Opusculum*, 144: ". . . hoc est sive solidum, sive concisum in frustra [i.e., frusta] illud masticando, vel in pulverem redactum ore, aut naso, vel in fumo per tubulos illud hauriendo. . ." (based on the text cited in the next note).

16. The Bull is published in C. Cocquelines, ed., *Bullarum, Privilegiorum ac Diplomatum Romanorum Pontificum Amplissima Collectio* (Rome, 1760), 6, pt. 2: 311–12. The prohibition reads: "Nobis nuper expositum fuit, pravus in illis partibus sumendi ore, vel naribus tabaccum vulgo nuncupatum usus adeo invaluerit, ut utriusque sexus personae, ac etiam sacerdotes, & clerici tam seculares, quam regulares clericalis honestatis immemores, illud passim in civitatis, & dioecesis Hispalen. ecclesiis, ac quod referre pudet, etiam sacrosanctum Missae sacrificium celebrando sumere, linteaque sacra foedis, quae tabbaccum hujusmodi proiicit, excrementis conspurcare, ecclesiasque praedictas tetro odore inficere magno cum proborum scandalo, rerumque sacrarum irreverentia non reformident . . . ne de caetero in quibusvis civitatis, & diaecesis praedictarum ecclesiis, earumque atriis, & ambitu tabaccum, sive solidum, vel in frusta concisum, aut in pulverem redactum ore, vel naribus, aut fumo per tubulos, & alias quomodolibet sumere audeant, vel praesumant sub excommunicationibus latae sententiae. . . ." The Archivo Santa Iglesia Catedral, Seville (Legajo 120, no. 6) preserves a contemporary

manuscript copy of Urban's Bull signed by Joan. Iacobo Pancirolo, papal nuncio in Spain. I owe this information to the kindness of Duncan Kinkead. I have not been able to consult P. Rubio Merino, "El archivo de la santa iglesia catedral de Sevilla," in *La Catedral de Sevilla*, ed. D. Angulo Iñiguez et al. (Seville, 1984), 749–75.

17. It is not recorded in *Tobacco, Its History Illustrated by the Books, Manuscripts and Engravings in the Library of George Arents, Jr., Together with an Introductory Essay, a Glossary and Bibliographic Notes by Jerome E. Brooks*, 5 vols. (New York, 1937–52), plus supplements (henceforth cited as *Arents Library*).

18. *Opusculum*, 146 f.

19. Ibid., 148: ". . . ubi lex non distinguit, nec non distinguere debemus." Urban's Bull "nullam fecit distinctionem de ecclesia clausa, vel aperta, praesente, vel non praesente alia persona, ergo neque nos possumus facere aliquam distinctionem."

20. Ibid., 151: "Ego autem dicerem quod si in tali sacristia fumentes tabaccum graviter perturbarent sacerdotes celebraturos, vel gratias Deo referentes, in hoc casu per accidens peccarent mortaliter ratio est, quia ex illa gravi perturbatione posset oriri grave aliud incommodum. . . . Perturbatio mentis esset causa gravis distractionis, vel alterius commissionis peccati saltem in deliberatione, vel possent excitari ad sumendum tabaccum, & per consequens posset excitari stomacus ad eijcienda excrementa, & ita etiam caput ad sua eijcienda, quod in celebraturis, vel Deo gratias agentibus esset grave periculum eijciendi Sacramentum."

21. Ibid., 157: "Praemitto, quod usus tabacci dupliciter spectari potest: primo, quatenus talis usus est ordinatus, & moderatus, secundo prout est inordinatus, & immoderatus: primo modo consideratus plures affert utentibus utilitates, & gravia commoda, ut sanitas corporalis conservari possit . . . secundo modo consideratus continet malitiam physicam, cum multa secum afferat incommoda, & quidem gravia sanitati corporali utentium, & per consequens continet gravitatem moralem, quia homo tenetur sub culpa providere saluti suae. Quae gravitas moralis dicetur esse capitalis, vel venialis iuxta gravitatem inordinati, & immoderati tabacchi usus. . . ."

22. Ibid., 158: "Siquidem etiam alii concitantur ad utendum tabacco, & ita non silent, non attendunt sacris ministeriis, non parum sternutari solent, eijciunt excrementa per nares, & multum expuere solent, non pauci rident, alii maledicunt, & ipsum tabaccum, & illo utentes, & illius inventores, & illius etiam delatores, & tandem illius venditores: alii proclamant contra principes, qui non prohibent tabaccum, vel saltem non apponunt grossam, ut ipsorum vocabulis utar, gabellam; & haec pravitas accidentalis est contra reverentiam rebus sacris debitam, & interdum solet esse scandalosa."

23. Ibid., 158: "Dicerem I. quod usus moderatus, & ordinatus tabacchi in ecclesiis extra limites Archiepiscopatus Hyspalensis existentibus non est peccatum, si tabaccum per nares sumatur, vel per os illud masticando; non autem si sumatur in fumo, illum hauriendo per tubulum."

24. Ibid., 159: ". . . quia usus tabacchi in fumo hausti per tubulum est scandalosus in ecclesiis; posset enim causare risum in aliis, & murmur sequi posset ex illo pravo, & tetro odore, quo ecclesia inficiatur."

25. Ibid., 161: "An usus tabacchi ante Missam solvat ieiunium naturale? Et quaesitum procedit de omni tabacco tam in pulvere per nares, quam conciso per masticationem, & in fumo per tubulos hausto. Circa hoc quaesitum non una est DD. theologorum sententia."

26. Ibid.: ". . . quarum prima docet solvere ieiunium naturale, ita Lezana in summa 99 regul. tom. 3 Verbo Eucharistia quoad Regulares, n. 18 & alii. . . ."

27. Ibid., ". . . secunda opinio docet, esse indecens multum, & quod hic usus sumendi tabaccum ante Missam esset plane ablegandus a sacerdotibus, & ministris altaris, tanquam corruptela: ita Marchantius in resolut. Pastor. tract. 4 in Append. ad c. 2. Immo Diana p. 8 resol. mor. tract. 7. miscell. resol. 3 consulit propter reverentiam tanto sacramento debitam, ut a sumptione tabacchi abstineatur, maxime in folio per os, ob periculum illud traijciendi in stomachum."

28. Ibid., 162: "Utuntur omnes communiter, & dicunt non esse illicitum, & praecipue Hyspanis . . . Tertia sententia docet, usum tabacchi ante missam non frangere ieiunium naturale, ac per consequens non esse peccatum mortale. . . ."

29. Ibid.: "Ego autem dicerem quod absolute loquendo usus tabacchi quocumque modo sumatur tabaccus non frangit ieiunium naturale . . . nam nequaquam violat ieiunium naturale tabacchi usus nisi cum per os accipitur, ac in stomachum transmittitur, nam in isto eventu videtur esse sumptio per modum cibi: et quamvis fumus tabacchi per os ex tubulo hauriatur, nihilominus nequaquam accipitur per modum cibi, vel potus, nam non propterea accipitur, ut per se, ac ex intento, & voluntate traijciatur ad stomachum manducando, aut bibendo, quod est proprium sub formalitate cibi, aut potus accipere; quin potius e naso videtur egredi. At licet concedatur, ut nonnulli volunt, quod aliquid fumi traijciatur in stomacum, nihilominus magis hoc effici videtur per modum respirationis, seu a virtute respirativa quam per aliquam actionem, que dicatur esse manducatio, aut potus."

30. Ibid., 164: "Dicerem quod usus tabacchi moderatus, & ordinatus per horam, vel dimidium horae saltem ante missam nullam secum affert indecentiam, imo multum decens, nam multum confert ad munditiam corporis, ex eo quod post purgationem narium magis districte [i.e., distincte] loquitur, & legit sacerdos illa, quae legere debet, item post aliquas sternuta, & capitis purgationem, maiorem habet attentionem celebrans ad illa, quae debet attendere."

31. Ibid., 166: "Quod sumere tabaccum inordinate, ac immoderate ante missam est multum indecens, & contra reverentiam debitam tanto sacramento, nam sacerdos esset in continuo corporis motu, vel sternutando, vel expuendo, vel eijciendo excrementa narium, vel lacrimando, & quasi stolidus accederet ad altare. . . ."

32. The attitude of the Catholic Church toward tobacco is surveyed by G. Moroni, *Dizionario di erudizione storico-ecclesiastica* (Venice, 1855), 72:168–97. Moroni himself admitted having used tobacco in powder form for about twenty years, a habit that he said comforted him and kept him good company during the compilation of his endless *Dictionary* (p. 184). See also *Arents Library* in the index under such headings as "Mass," "Churches," "Papal and Ecclesiastical Prohibitions against Use," etc.

33. See G. Moroni, *Dizionario* 72:176; S. A. Dickson (*Panacea or Precious Bane:*

Tobacco in Sixteenth-Century Literature [New York, 1954], 149 ff.) publishes excerpts from these conciliar edicts: "It is forbidden under penalty of eternal damnation for priests, about to administer the sacraments, either to take the smoke of *sayri*, or tobacco, into the mouth, or the powder of tobacco in the nose, even under the guise of medicine, before the service of the Mass" (1583 Synod at Lima, Peru).

34. T. Ramon, *Nueva prematica de reformacion* (Saragossa, 1635), 354: "Destas dos maneras se usa ya en España, y con tanta frequencia, que no ay casi momento que no le aplique à las narizes, ò boca, a todas horas y tiempo, ayuno, y comidos, estudiando, predicando; ye en el Coro cantando, inquietando a los demas, y divirtiendolos. . . ."

35. B. Stella, *Il tabacco, opera . . . nella quale si tratta dell'origine, historia, coltura, preparatione, qualità, natura, virtù, & uso in fumo, in polvere, in foglia, in lambitivo, et in medicina della pianta volgarmente detta tabacco* (Rome, 1669), 347: ". . . non v'era canonico, cappellano, o clerico, anzi ne meno persona secolare dell'uno, e l'altro sesso, che mentre quelli stavano attualmente al servitio di Dio in choro, e nell'altare, e questi ad ascoltar le messe, & i divini officii, che nel medemo tempo non prendessero, con grande irreverentia il tabacco, e con quelli fetidi escrementi non isporcassero gli altari, i luoghi sacri, ed i pavimenti delle chiese di detta diocesi." A later authority suggests that the papal prohibition generally went unheeded. J. Brunet (*Le bon usage du tabac en poudre* [Paris, 1700]), declares that Spanish priests continued to place their snuff boxes on the very altars (cited from *Arents Library*, 3:16).

36. Innocent's decree is dated 8 January 1650. See B. Stella, *Il tabacco*, 352 f. and G. Moroni, *Dizionario* 2:266, article on "Chiesa di S. Pietro in Vaticano."

37. G. Moroni, *Dizionario* 72:177, cites decrees of Innocent XI dated 1 April 1678 and 10 October 1681. The first ordered all bishops "ut sub poena suspensionis ipso facto incurrenda prohibere valeant sacerdotibus, ne mane antequam Missam celebrent ullatenus tabacum sumant"; the second imposed penalties of suspension "a divinis ipso facto incurrenda" and a fine of twenty-five *scudi* for priests who took tobacco in Roman sacristies.

38. B. Stella, *Il tabacco*, 333: "È questa una delle più celebri questioni che siano agitate à nostri tempi, ed à dottori, che l'una, e l'altra parte costantemente defendono. . . ."

39. G. Moroni, *Dizionario* 72:178: ". . . e volendo però provvedere all'indennità delle coscienze di tutti, ed in ispecie al buon servizio di detta basilica, il quale rimane molto pregiudicato dal frequente uscire dal coro, che fanno quelli che non possono astenersi dall'uso del tabacco oggidì avanzato, anco per parere dei medici, che lo consigliano per rimedio di molte infermità, massimamente per quelli, che sono obbligati a frequentare luoghi freddi ed umidi nelle ore della mattina, ci siamo determinati di permettere nella suddetta basilica ancora, suo coro, cappelle, sagrestia, portico ed atrio l'uso del detto tabacco. . . ."

40. *Arents Library* 1:227–29, account based on P. A. Mattioli, *Commentarii in sex libros . . . de medica materia* (Venice, 1565). There is no mention of the subject

in J. Lestocquoy and L. Duval-Arnould, "Le Cardinal Santa Croce et le Sacré Collège en 1565," *Archivum Historiae Pontificiae* 18 (1980): 263–96.

41. G. Moroni, *Dizionario* 72:181: "Il fumare parimenti con moderazione puo accrescere la secrezione della saliva e de' succhi gastrici, in quelli che ne difettano: puo in qualche caso risolvere le leggere ostruzioni de' visceri addominali, che concorrono collo stomaco alle funzioni digestive: puo rimuovere l'abituale stitichezza di ventre, e non è raro aver veduto arrestarsi o ritardarsi la carie de' denti."

42. A. Lavedan, *Tratado de los usos, abusos, propriedades y virtudes del tabaco, cafe, té, y chocolate* (Madrid, 1796), 61 f.: "Murray tambien dice que un cura parroco que asistió y administró los sacramentos á muchos apestados, se libertó de la peste fumando á menudo tabaco. Este autor asegura que es muy conducente el fumar en las enfermedades contagiosas, porque por su medio se expele la saliva y moco en que suele pegarse el contagio, los que tragados con facilidad comunican la infeccion pestilente. Esto es bastante para que se sepa que es un medicamento de mucha importancia para conservar la salud."

43. B. Stella, *Il tabacco*, 109: "Dico . . . che l'uso del tabacco, moderatamente preso non solo è utile, ma posso dire anche necessario a' preti, monaci, frati, ed altri religiosi che devono, e desiderano menar vita casta, e reprimere que' moti sensuali, che cotanto infastidiscono . . . perchè la causa naturale della libidine è il calore, ed humidità, quando questa venga con l'uso del tabacco diseccato, non si sentono quelli moti libidinosi così vehementi. . . ."

44. *Arents Library* 3:110 f., translating and summarizing Antonio Vitagliani, *De abusu tabacchi* (Rome, 1650): "The assiduous use of tobacco restrains lust as I myself have heard concerning Father Joseph of Cupertino who belonged to the order of St. Francis of Assisi, and the fame of whose sanctity is resplendent. Daily he is caught up in ecstatic rapture like a bird. He uses tobacco not only to keep awake at night for vigils, but also to resist the temptation of the flesh and to overcome the danger of yielding to human frailty." According to B. Stella (*Il tabacco*, 109), Vitagliani, a medical doctor, personally interrogated Cupertino on his heavy consumption of tobacco. The holy man replied, ". . . experientia didicit assiduum tabaci usum venerem a suo munere retrahere." I have not been able to consult *Sac. Rituum . . . Beatificationis Josephi a Cupertino* (Rome, 1718).

45. G. Moroni, *Dizionario* 72:173.

NINE

༄

Florentine Documents for a History of the Index of Prohibited Books*

From the documents which once must have formed a part of the archive of the Florentine Inquisition, I have selected for publication twenty-eight letters[1] addressed to the inquisitor of Florence by cardinals of the Congregations of the Index and Inquisition.[2] A number of these documents take the form of circulars and were addressed to more than one tribunal.[3] Spanning a short period of little more than a decade, from March 1592 to September 1606, the letters confirm the impression which recent studies have revealed of the devastating effects of Roman censorship practice on Italian culture.[4] They illustrate both the plight of the intellectual and the enormous difficulties encountered by the Catholic Church in its ambitious and unrealistic program of controlling what could be written, printed, and read in that part of Europe which remained under its jurisdiction.[5] The result was unmitigated confusion. Authors suffered interminable delays in the often vain hope that overworked censors (*revisori*) would approve the publication of their writings;[6] university professors were cut off from new developments in their disciplines;[7] and booksellers and printers were ruined financially as a result of prohibitions which ranged from Ariosto to Zasius.[8]

The Florentine documents illustrate both the reigning confusion and the efforts to correct it. The first letter, for example, attempts to settle the question whether provincial inquisitors could issue permits to read prohibited literature;[9] another, the uncertain status of the writings of Jean Bodin.[10] Several of the letters are concerned with the complications and embarrassments ensuing from the premature helter-skelter publication of the Index of Clement VIII, which had to be suspended so that some last-minute additions and revisions could be made.[11]

The letters also reflect the increasing severity of Roman censorship. Writers or specific classes of writing which had been partially tolerated in the Tridentine Index of Pius IV became totally prohibited. This was the fate of the Talmud and of vernacular Scriptures.[12] The printed catalogue of the Oxford and Cambridge University libraries was proscribed,[13] as was a seemingly innocuous work of historiography (see letter 15, below). A request by a Florentine literary academy for permission to possess copies of works by Boccaccio, Machiavelli, and Lodovico Castelvetro for the purpose of preparing expurgated editions was peremptorily refused,[14] while a decade or two earlier similar efforts had been tolerated by the Church.[15]

The topic of several letters is the projected _Index Expurgatorius_,[16] which, if successfully completed, would have permitted great numbers of prohibited books to circulate, though subject to the prescribed expurgations. The cardinals of the Index hoped to enlist the services, as correctors and censors, of trusted men of letters and theologians. The Florentine inquisitor was repeatedly asked to assist in their recruitment. Eventually, one solitary _Index Expurgatorius_ appeared,[17] containing corrections for a mere fifty books. A reason for the failure of the plan may lie in the uncooperative attitude of Italian scholars who would not participate in the required mutilations. Such a state of affairs seems to be reflected in a brief note hastily scribbled by the Florentine inquisitor at the foot of a letter (no. 22, dated 23 March 1602), enjoining him to constant vigilance in the control of the city's presses and to be more zealous in the matter of forwarding to Rome expurgations of prohibited books: "On 13 April I replied that as far as [the question of] printing was concerned we would not be found lacking. As for censorship, we would await it from Rome, since no one here wanted such an [assignment]."[18]

The Congregation of the Index regularly communicated to the provincial officials the titles of recently banned works toward which they should exercise special vigilance. On 2 July 1600 the Florentine inquisitor was warned that a copy of Philipp Camerarius's _Operae Horarum Succisivarum sive Meditationes Historicae_ (Nuremberg, 1599) had been confiscated in

Rome.[19] The book had been condemned "per esser pernitioso." Ordinarily we would be left to guess what might have been found objectionable in a book of historical meditations, but, in this instance, we know the reasons for the prohibition. I have been able to consult the manuscript *Correctio* or list of expurgations compiled for Camerarius's book by an unknown censor.[20] Works by arch-heretics dealing with religious topics were prohibited forthwith and could not be owned or read under any circumstances. Lists of expurgations were only prepared for a less dangerous class of literature. Though Camerarius was a Protestant, he was not as notorious as Calvin or Luther, all of whose works were prohibited, and he had written on a non-controversial subject. His book should have been temporarily suspended until authorities could examine it and recommend what expurgations, if any, were required.[21] This was the theory. In practice, because of reluctance on the part of Rome and the cumbersome censorship machinery, very few suspended books were permitted to circulate.[22]

The Camerarius expurgations might be imposed in the brutal form of ink erasures on the text, or they might be incorporated into a new printed edition, in the unlikely eventuality that one should be undertaken in Italy. It seems to have been the customary procedure for the local inquisitor to round up all available copies, introduce the expurgations and then restore them to their owners.[23] There is no certain way to determine whether the Camerarius *Correctio* was prepared in Rome by an official attached to the Congregation of the Index, or by one of the provincial Inquisitions. We know that expurgations drawn up in Rome were copied and circulated to the outlying tribunals,[24] and we also know that the latter possessed the authority to carry out the corrections themselves.[25] In light of the extreme rarity today of documents of this kind (the archive of the Inquisition in Rome which houses the papers of the defunct Congregation of the Index remains closed to scholars), the contents of the Camerarius *Correctio* deserve to be discussed.

The most frequently recommended deletions for the *Meditationes* concern laudatory references to heretics: to Calvin's successor in Geneva, Theodore Beza; to Zwingli's in Zürich, Heinrich Bullinger; to one of the leaders of the Italian Protestant emigration, Peter Martyr Vermigli, among many others; or they might apply to older prohibited writers, Machiavelli and Erasmus. Another expurgation slices off a quotation from the German historian Johannes Aventinus attacking the practice of begging, and especially its nefarious consequences in the hands of the mendicant orders. Also to be excised are Robert Gaguin's insinuation that in France the public good had invariably suffered when clergy became embroiled in affairs of state; a reflection by the historian of the early church, Eusebius of Caesarea, that the persecutions suffered by Christians under Diocletian were the result of strife and jealousy among bishops; an allegation of papal avarice attributed to a distant patriarch of Constantinople; and the ancient tale that a hairy monster had been born to the mistress of Pope Nicholas III. The four pages that are to be deleted at the end of chapter 58 are an eloquent plea for religious toleration, containing a reminder that men of different faiths have successfully co-existed, as well as Augustine's pronouncement that only God is lord over the consciences of men. Several pages in which the history of the exposure of the false "donation of Constantine" is related with fairness and objectivity come under the pen of the censor, as well as a reference to priests possessed by the Devil. The remark that Roman Catholics in Transylvania in the not-too-far-distant past had been idolatrous in their worship of sacred images was equally unacceptable. In a passage where Ariosto is said to have attributed the invention of printing to a monk, the word "monachus" is to be inked out. A derisive reference to a priest as "sacrifico cuidam" is to be replaced by the more respectful "presbitero vel sacerdote." Finally, a lament that human superstitions had frequently been exploited by priests ("a sacrificulis") for their own ends and for personal enrichment is to be erased.

How carefully did Camerarius's censor carry out his task? In spite of these expurgations, it is obvious that the list of changes was compiled in great haste, which is not surprising in view of the mountains of books for which this process had to be repeated, and the scarcity of personnel. The *revisore* did not trouble himself to identify the mysterious initials "I.B.B.M.O." appended to a long prefatory letter of commendation addressed to Camerarius. They belong to Giovanni Bernardino Bonifacio, Marchese d'Oria, a patron of many men of letters, one of the few Italian noblemen to apostatize from the Catholic Church in the sixteenth century. Names of countless other Protestants overlooked by the expurgator include those of the Venetian physician and religious martyr Girolamo Donzellini, the Calvinist historian Philippe de Mornay, and Thomas Erastus. A long disquisition on Lorenzo Valla and his research into the "donation of Constantine" is left intact although, as we have noted, a discussion of this subject occurring elsewhere was marked for deletion.

A cursory comparison of the method employed by the Italian censor with the corrections made to the *Meditationes* in a Spanish *Index Expurgatorius* (Madrid, 1667), yields this tentative conclusion.[26] Although the latter is clearly more severe and wide-ranging in its mutilations, it is also more consistent and, in some way, more intelligent. The Italian document is content simply to cancel out obnoxious names: it prescribes the deletion of Theodore Beza's but allows the accompanying epigram by him to stand. The Spanish Index seems to recognize that the threat to the faith is not in the name of a man but in his words. It removes both. Or, in numerous other instances (where the Italian document merely follows its name-erasing policy), it adopts a more sophisticated procedure: it leaves both a quotation and its heretical author's name, deleting only such complimentary attributes as "elegantissimus" and "praestantissimus."

Fragments from the dispersed archives of the Inquisition are all that we have available at present for studying certain aspects of the culture and institutions of the Counter-Reformation. I have thought it appropriate to publish them here because they help to detail the closing of that freer period to which Hans Baron has devoted a lifetime of study. With the outlawing of Boccaccio and Machiavelli, the Renaissance had ended in Italy.

The Florentine Letters

1. (T. 2, fol. 163)

Reverendo Padre. Questi miei Ill.mi et R.mi SS.ri Cardinali Generali Inquisitori Colleghi hanno ordinato che si scriva a tutti li reverendi inquisitori et se gli commandi espressamente, come con la presente si fa alla R. V., che non ardiscano ne presumano in modo alcuno dare licentia di tenere o leggere libbri prohibiti, perchè essi inquisitori non hanno auttorità di dare simili licentie, ne la trovaranno nelle patente loro, et per ciò V. R. doverà senz'altro astenersene per l'avvenire, et rivocare quelle c'havesse forse concesse per il passato.

Con questa occasione si fa intendere a V. R. come sin dell'anno 1591 per ordine della felice memoria di Gregorio XIIII fu prohibita la *Republica* di Giovanni Bodino in qualsivoglia lingua che si trovasse, o fusse stata tradotta, come opera ripiena di errori et impietà, ancorachè si dicesse di essere stata corretta et emendata. Per il che V. R. farrà diligentia et ordine espresso che non se ne legga, ne se ne tenghi alcuna, e trovandosene le facci tutte brugiare. Et appresso sono state prohibite tutte le altre opere sue sino che siano reviste o espurgate dalla Sacra Congregatione sopra l'Indice de' Libbri Prohibiti, et anco la *Demonomania*.[27] Per il che ella le sospenda tutte sino ad altro ordine, ne permetta che si vendano o concedano. Ne questa essendo per altro, la saluto ed il Signore la conservi nella Sua santa gratia.

Di Roma a XI di Marzo 1592.

Di V. R. come fratello,

Il Cardinale di Santa Severina[28]

2. (T. 2, fol. 164)

Reverendo Padre. Da questi Ill.mi et R.mi SS.ri Cardinali Generali Inquisitori miei Colleghi è stato ordinato che V. R. non ardisca in modo alcuno di conceder licenza a qualsivoglia persona di leggere libri prohibiti, non havendo gl'inquisitori particolari questa autorità; et che faccia conservar la presente negli atti di cotesto Santo Ufficio, acciochè in ogni evento

The Florentine Letters

1. (T. 2, fol. 163)

Reverend Father. My colleagues, these most illustrious and most reverend cardinal inquisitors have ordered that all inquisitors should be written to, commanding them expressly, as I do now to your reverence with the present letter, not to dare or presume in any way to grant licenses either to keep or read prohibited books. Inquisitors in themselves do not have the authority to issue these licenses, nor will they find it in their patents. Consequently, your reverence will unfailingly refrain from doing so in the future, and revoke any that you may have granted in the past.

I seize this occasion to remind your reverence that from the year 1591, by order of Gregory XIIII of blessed memory, the *Republic* of Jean Bodin was prohibited in whatever language it might be found or translated, since it is a work full of errors and impieties, even though it is said to have been corrected and emended. Therefore, your reverence will show diligence and give express orders that it be neither read nor possessed and that any [copies] found should be burned. In addition, all his other works, including the *Demonomania*, have been prohibited until they can be reviewed and expurgated by the Sacred Congregation of the Index of Prohibited Books. Therefore you will suspend them all until you receive new orders, and not permit any to be sold or given. Since I have nothing more to add for the moment, I bid you farewell and may Our Lord preserve you. Rome, 11 March 1592.

Of your reverence, fraternally,

The Cardinal of Santa Severina

2. (T. 2, fol. 164)

Reverend Father. It has been ordered by my colleagues, these most illustrious and most reverend cardinal inquisitors, that your reverence not presume in any way to grant a license to whatever person to read prohibited books. Individual inquisitors lack this authority. You should preserve the present instructions in the archive of your Holy Office so

quest'ordine possa esser noto ai successori di lei. Con che la saluto, et alle sue orationi mi raccomando.

Di Roma a VIII di Agosto MDXCII. Di V. R. come fratello,

Il Cardinale di Santa Severina

3. (T. 2, fol. 154)

Molto Reverendo Padre come fratello. In Fiorenza è stato stampato hora da Filippo Giunta un volume di diverse sorti di Versi latini d'un Giovanni Battista Pinello Genovese. Et perchè senza mia notitia et saputa me l'ha dedicato con un'Epistola latina, et altri versi sussequenti, et mandatomelo dopo ch'è stato stampato, et havendo visto in quei versi molte adulationi lontane et contrarie all'animo mio, et essendo anco l'opera cosa da giovane come la P. V. potrà vedere, però alla ricevuta di questa, la Paternità Vostra senza perderci tempo farà subito precetto a quel libraro che non la divulghi, ne ne dia fuori copia veruna, et così avvertirà che si faccia, ch'intanto ho scritto al Giovanni Battista auttore dell'opera che se ne venga a Fiorenza, et faccia levare l'Epistola et versi dedicati a me, et indrizzi poi l'opera, a chi li parve, ch'io resto sodisfatto della sua buona volontà.[29] Per il quale mando la lettera a V. P. che ce la potrà far tenere quanto prima con darmi avviso del seguito. Et la gratia di Dio sia con lei.

Di Roma li XXX di Ottobre 1593.

Di V. P. M. R. come fratello affettuosissimo,

Cardinale Pinello[30]

4. (T. 2, fol. 115)

Molto Reverendo Padre. La Santità di N. S. dopo molte consultationi della S. Congregatione dell'Indice, havendo tenuto molti giorni appresso di se l'Indice[31] che si manda a V. R., dopo haverlo Sua Beatitudine in tante occupationi voluto rilegere, et considerare con la sua pastoral diligenza tutte le cose che potessero impedire la debbita essecutione, l'ha rimandato alla Congregatione, commettendo che si publichi, et così in essecutione dell'ordine di Sua Santità si è publicato in Roma, et lo mandiamo col medesimo ordine a V. R. che lo facci publicare et esseguire ove s'estende la sua

that if the need arises this order will be known to your successors. With this I bid you farewell and recommend myself to your prayers.
Rome, 7 August 1592.
Of your reverence, fraternally,

The Cardinal of Santa Severina

3. (T. 2, fol. 154)

Very reverend Father, my brother. Filippo Giunta has printed in Florence a volume of various Latin verses by a Gio. Battista Pinello, a Genoese. Without my knowledge he dedicated it to me with a Latin Epistle and other verses, and sent it to me after its publication. Since I have recognized in these verses a great deal of flattery alien and contrary to my spirit, and since the work is a youthful effort, as your paternity will be able to see, at the receipt of this letter you will forthwith instruct that bookseller not to distribute it or make any copies available, and you will see that this is done. Meanwhile, I have written to Giovanni Battista, the author of the work, to come to Florence and remove the Epistle and verses dedicated to me. After he has done this he can offer the work to anyone he wishes, and I shall be satisfied with his good intentions. I am enclosing the letter so that your paternity will be able to forward it as soon as possible, and inform me of the result. May the grace of God be with you.
Rome, 30 October 1593.
Of your most reverend paternity, your affectionate brother,

Cardinal Pinello

4. (T. 2, fol. 115)

Very reverend Father. His Holiness, after many meetings of the Congregation of the Index, and after having kept the Index for many days which we are sending to your reverence, and after His Beatitude reread it, despite his many preoccupations, and considered with his pastoral diligence all the things which could prevent its proper execution, returned it to the Congregation. He has commissioned it to be published and this has been done in Rome in compliance with the orders of His Holiness. We now send it to your reverence with similar instructions to publish

giurisditione, come ricerca l'importanza del negotio, con partecipazione
di Monsignore Nuntio, facendo mandar ad essecutione quanto è scritto
nell'Instruttione[32] et nelle Regole[33] che si danno per l'espurgatione de'
libri per tener lontana, come conviene all'officio suo in tutti i modi, la
pestifera contagione dell'heresia, et essendo molto nota a Sua Santità et
alla Congregatione la pietà et il zelo dell'honor del Signore Iddio di V.
R. non se le scrive con più parole, tenendo per fermo che userà la solita
sua diligenza in questo negotio di servitio di Nostro Signore Dio, dal quale
le pregamo il colmo della sua santa gratia.
Di Roma il dì 27 di Marzo 1596.
Di V. P. M. R. come fratelli,

Il Cardinale di Verona[34]
Il Cardinale di Terranova[35]
[Two illegible signatures]

5. (T. 2, fol. 137)

Reverendo Padre. Perchè il Segretario della Congregatione sopra l'Indice de' Libri Prohibiti si trova haver mandato a V. R. l'Indice stampato
senza haverne fatta parola in questa Sacra Congregatione della Santa Romana
et Universale Inquisitione, non si sono messi in esso Indice alcune particolari dichiarationi che concernono l'Indice di Papa Pio quarto di felice
memoria, fatti da Papi successivi e dalla detta Sacra Congregatione dell'
Inquisitione. Perilchè Sua Santità mi ha espressamente commandato ch'io
debba scrivere a V. R. come fo con la presente, che non havendo publicato il detto Indice sino adesso, sopra seda a publicarlo insino a nuovo ordine; et havendolo publicato avverta, che Sua Santità non ha inteso, ne
intende di derogar ne innovar per il detto nuovo Indice cosa alcuna de'
decreti et regole contro di questa Santa Inquisitione, e della Beatitudine
sua, ne de'suoi predecessori, ma che si osservino inviolabilmente; et se bene
la quarta regola del detto Indice di Pio quarto concede che gli ordinarii
et inquisitori possano dar licenza di tener Biblie volgari, Evangelii et altri
libbri della Sacra Scrittura,[36] nondimeno dal tempo di Pio quarto istesso
in qua questa Santa Inquisitione ha prohibiti tali libri, et la lettione o riten-
tione loro, et così anco i Compendii, et Sommarii della Biblia, et Sacra

it and put it into force as far as your jurisdiction extends, as the importance of the matter requires, with the assistance of Monsignor, the nuncio. Execute what is written in the Instruction and in the Rules which have been promulgated for the expurgation of books so as to keep at a distance the pestiferous plague of heresy, as is required by your office. And since your reverence's piety and ardor for the honor of Our Lord God is well known to His Holiness and to the Congregation, we do not need to say anything more. We are convinced that you will apply your customary diligence in this matter in the service of Our Lord God, of whom we beseech for you the fullness of his holy grace.
Rome, 27 March, 1596.
Of your most reverend paternity, fraternally,

> The Cardinal of Verona
> The Cardinal of Terranova
> [Two illegible signatures]

5. (T. 2, fol. 137)

Reverend Father. The Secretary of the Congregation of the Index of Prohibited Books finds that he has sent the Index to your reverence without discussing it in advance in this Sacred Congregation of the Holy Roman and Universal Inquisition. Consequently, the Index does not contain certain statements which concern the Index of Pope Pius IV of blessed memory made by later popes and by the aforesaid Holy Congregation of the Inquisition. His Holiness has expressly commanded me to write to your reverence, as I am now doing, that if you have not already issued the Index, do not do so until you receive new instructions. If you have already promulgated it, you should be aware that His Holiness did not and does not, through the new Index, intend either to derogate from or innovate to the detriment of any decrees and rules of the Holy Inquisition, of his Beatitude, or of his predecessors. They are to be observed absolutely. And even if rule 4 of Pius IV's Index permits bishops and inquisitors to license the possession of vernacular Bibles, Gospels, and other books of Sacred Scripture, nevertheless from the time of Pius himself this Holy Inquisition has prohibited these books, their reading or possession. This includes compends and summaries of the Bible and of Sacred Scripture,

Scrittura, o sia del Testamento vecchio, o nuovo in lingua volgar. Per
questo V. R. non dia tale licenza, et, se per avventura l'ha data, la revochi.

Et perchè nel sopradetto Indice di Pio quarto, si concedeva la espurgatione de'libri del Thalmud,[37] per questo nuovo Indice [non è] mente di
Sua Santità di approbar tal cosa, ma che restino dannati questi et altri libri
di Ebrei secondo la sua Bolla et Constitutione "Contra libros et impia
scripta Hebraeorum,"[38] che sia inviolabilmente osservata, non ostante
altra carta in contrario.

Et se bene in questo Indice nuovo si trova per errore sospesa *La Republica* di Giovanni Bodino in sino che sia espurgata, nondimeno non si ha
da espurgare altrimenti; ma si debba tenere per condannata, come fu da
Papa Gregorio XIIII in qualsiasi lingua e stampa, si come ancora la sua
Demonomania è stata condannata dalla Santità del Nostro Signore.[39] Onde
l'una et l'altra opera si hanno da tenere per dannate. Per le [word obliter-
ated] et le dette cose, et altri particolari s' informaranno [?], et poi se darà
avviso a V. R. Intanto la saluto, et alle sue orationi mi raccomando.
Di Roma a XXVII di Aprile 1596.
Di V. R. come fratello,

Il Cardinale di Santa Severina

6. (T. 2, fol. 116)

Molto Reverendo Padre. Con l'occasione del novo Indice mandato di
ordine di Nostro Signore dalla nostra Congregatione a publicarsi in tutto
il Christianesmo son state mosse certe difficultà d'alcuni vescovi et inquisitori
per l'osservatione d'alcune Constitutioni Pontificie et Decreti delli Ill.mi
Sig.ri Cardinali della Congregatione del Santo Officio fatti per il passato
in materia dei libri, perilchè volendo dar a tutti compita sodisfatione Nostro Signore ha ordinato alla nostra Congregatione dell'Indice, che si mandino l'incluse osservationi et dichiarationi[40] conforme alle quali si publichi
et osservi l'Indice da tutti, et nella nova impressione che si farà in Roma
il tutto se inserisca nell'Indice. Sichè V. P. con il suo santo zelo et prudentia
attenda a far osservar l'Indice, et alla giornata occorrendo nove difficultà
conforme alla Constitutione di Sua Santità posta nell'Indice, si darà piena
sodisfatione dalla Congregatione nostra a tutti di quanto sarà ricercata in

whether of the Old Testament or New in the vernacular. Therefore, your reverence should not issue such a license, and if you have done so, revoke it.

And although in the aforesaid Index of Pius IV the expurgation of the books of the Talmud was permitted, in this new Index it is not the intention of His Holiness to approve it. These and other books of the Jews are damned according to his Bull and Constitution *Contra libros et impia scripta Hebraeorum*, which should be inviolably observed in spite of any other documents to the contrary.

And even if in this new Index the *Republic* of Jean Bodin is suspended until it can be expurgated, it actually does not qualify for expurgation, but should be treated as condemned in whatever language and edition, as was decreed by Pope Gregory XIV, along with his *Demonomania* condemned by his Holiness. Therefore, both works are to be considered proscribed. We shall notify your reverence about the [word obliterated] and the aforesaid things and other details as we are informed. Meanwhile, I bid you farewell, and commend myself to your prayers.
Rome, 27 April 1596.
Of your reverence, fraternally,

The Cardinal of Santa Severina

6. (T. 2, fol. 116)

Most reverend Father. On the occasion of the new Index sent out by order of His Holiness by our Congregation to be promulgated in all Christianity, certain difficulties have been raised by some bishops and inquisitors over the observance of a number of pontifical Constitutions and Decrees issued in the past in the matter of books by the illustrious Cardinals of the Congregation of the Holy Office. Since His Holiness desires to give full satisfaction to all, he has ordered our Congregation of the Index to send out the enclosed observations and declarations, in conformity with which the Index is intended to be published and observed by all; this material in its entirety will be included in the new printing which will take place in Rome. So that your paternity with your holy zeal and prudence may be able to enforce observance of the Index, if new difficulties should arise, in conformity with the Constitution of His Holiness placed in the Index, our Congregation will give full satisfaction to anyone who shall

servitio di Nostro Signore Iddio, dal quale li prego il colmo della Sua santa gratia.
Di Roma a li II di Maggio 1596.
Di V. P. M. R. come fratello,

Il Cardinale di Verona

7. (T. 2, fol. 138)

Reverendo Padre. Dopo che ho scritto a V. R. quel che occorreva intorno al nuovo Indice de' libbri prohibiti già stampato, la Santità di Nostro Signore ha fatto rimediare a quel mancamento che vi era con una osservatione di due fogli sopra alcuni capi che si mandano qui alligati.[41] Et si hanno da porre ne' volumi già stampati dopo le Regole dell'Indice di Pio Quarto di felice memoria et avanti la nuova instruttione per quei che hanno da espurgare o prohibire i libbri. Perchè per quei che si hanno da stampar di nuovo, si provederà meglio ne' luoghi proprii. Et in questo modo, conforme alla mente di Sua Beatitudine, V. R. potrà fare publicare et osservare il predetto Indice. Intanto la saluto, et alle sue orationi mi raccomando.
Di Roma ai X di Maggio MDXCVI.
Di V. R. come fratello,

Il Cardinale di Santa Severina

8. (T. 2, fol. 139)

Reverendo Padre. Dopo che ho scritto a V. R. quel che occorreva intorno al nuovo Indice de' libbri prohibiti già stampato, la Santità di Nostro Signore, quanto a i volumi già stampati e mandati di quà, ha fatto rimediare a quel mancamento che vi era con una osservatione di due fogli o carte sopra alcuni capi che si mandano qui alligati; et si hanno da porre ne' detti volumi già stampati dopo le Regole dell'Indice di Pio Quarto di felice memoria, et avanti la Instruttione fatta di nuovo per quei che hanno da espurgare, o prohibire i libbri. Et di più ha fatto mutare, o aggiugnere ancora alcune altre parole nella seconda pagina o faccia della detta Instruttione, et per questo ha fatto ristampare tutto il primo foglio di

seek it in the service of our Lord God, of whom I beseech for you the utmost of his holy grace.

Rome, 2 May 1596.

Of your reverence, fraternally,

The Cardinal of Verona

7. (T. 2, fol. 138)

Reverend Father. After I wrote to your reverence about what was needed in regard to the new, recently printed Index of Prohibited Books, His Holiness has caused that deficiency to be remedied with a two-page observation, dealing with certain points, which we enclose in the present letter. It is to be placed in the already published volumes after the Rules in the Index of Pius IV of blessed memory and ahead of the new instruction prepared for persons assigned to the expurgation or prohibition of books. When those [Indices] are printed afresh, a better arrangement will be made in the appropriate places. Following this arrangement, which conforms to the will of His Holiness, your reverence can proceed to have the aforesaid Index promulgated and observed. Meanwhile, I bid you farewell and recommend myself to your prayers.

Rome, 10 May 1596.

Of your reverence, fraternally,

The Cardinal of Santa Severina

8. (T. 2, fol. 139)

Reverend Father. After I wrote to your reverence about what was required in regard to the newly printed Index of Prohibited Books, His Holiness has remedied the deficiency in those copies that have already been printed and sent out from here with an observation on certain points in two pages or leaves which we enclose here. These sheets are to be inserted in the Index of Pius IV of blessed memory after the Rules and ahead of the Instruction newly prepared for persons who have the responsibility for the expurgation or prohibition of books. In addition he has had a few other words changed or added in the second page or leaf of the aforesaid Instruction; and because of this he has had the entire first page of the

essa Instruttione, e lo pur si manda alligato con questa a ciò che si levi quel primo che era nell'Indice mandato, et in luogo di esso si ripona quest'altro ristampato di nuovo, et che poi il predetto Indice si possa far publicare et osservare in questa maniera.[42] Perch'quanto a quei che si hanno da stampar di nuovo si provederà appresso ne' luoghi proprii. Con che la saluto, et alle sue orationi mi raccomando.

Di Roma, a XII di Maggio MDXCVI.

DI V. R. come fratello,

Il Cardinale di Santa Severina

9. (T. 2, fol. 117)

Molto Reverendo Padre come fratello. Hanno preso grande amiratione questi Ill.mi SS. miei Colleghi che sia stampato in Firenze doppo la publicatione dell'Indice, la *Diffesa di Silvestro Facio intorno lo sputo di sangue*,[43] senza osservarsi quello che ordina l'Indice nel S. V. *de librorum impressione*,[44] non si specificando la licentia de' superiori, che hanno permesso il libro, come altre volte in Firenze solevano fare gl'inquisitori, et non apparendo l'approvatione di chi habbi rivisto quel libretto, con osservare quanto nel S. 2[45] si comanda. Et se tutte queste cose da Nostro Signore ordinate nell' Indice si fussero osservate, non haverebbe causato qualche disordine questo libretto. Et da qui avanti sarete più cauto in dar' le licentie, e deputare li correttori de' libri, con esprimere sempre la licentia dell'Ordinario [e] dell'Inquisitore, e la fede del revisore, uno o più che siano stati, conservandosi l'essemplare authentico nell'Archivio da tutti sottoscritto. Con che fine mi raccomando alle sue orationi.

Di Roma li 27 di Gennaio 1597.

Di V. P. M. R. come fratello,

Il Cardinale [illegibile]

10. (T. 2, fol. 118)

Molto Reverendo Padre come fratello. Hanno distribuito questi Illustrissimi Signori miei Colleghi in varie Religioni et Università gran quantità di libri da espurgare per poter quantoprima publicare l'Indice

Instruction reprinted. We enclose it with this letter, requesting that you remove the one already placed in the Index, and substitute this one newly printed. When this is done the Index can be published and observed in this form. As for those which will be printed in the future, we will make the insertions in the appropriate places. I bid you farewell, and commend myself to your prayers.

Rome, 12 May 1596.

Of your reverence, fraternally,

The Cardinal of Santa Severina

9. (T. 2, fol. 117)

Very reverend Father, my brother. These illustrious colleagues of mine have expressed great amazement that the *Diffesa di Silvestro Facio intorno lo sputo di Sangue* should have been printed in Florence after the promulgation of the Index without observance of what it commands in section 5, "On the Printing of Books." The work appeared without mention of any permission granted by the superiors, a function which inquisitors used to exercise in Florence, and without indication of approval by the authority which examined the book, in conformity with what section 2 commands.

If all those things which had been ordered by His Holiness in the Index had been observed, this book would not have caused the disorder that it did. Henceforth, you will be more careful about issuing permissions and assigning expurgations, always including the approval of the bishop and inquisitor, and the sworn statement of the censor, however many there are, preserving the original copy in the archive, signed by all concerned. With this I close by commending myself to your prayers.

Rome, 27 January 1597

Of your reverence, fraternally,

Cardinal [illegible name]

10. (T. 2, fol. 118)

Very reverend Father, my brother. These illustrious colleagues of mine have distributed among various religious orders and universities a large quantity of books for expurgation so as to be able to publish as soon as

Espurgatorio[46] tanto universalmente desiderato. Et essendo una delle principali Inquisitioni la vostra, aspettano haver notitia di molti libri dannati e sospesi, che per prima fussero in cotesta Inquisitione, overo nell'essecutione dell'Indice si fussero scoperti, o alla giornata se n'havesse cognitione, con mandar' anco nota delle espurgationi altre volte fatte che costì si trovano, et di quelle che attualmente si van' facendo conforme al novo Indice. Con che fine alle vostre orationi mi raccomando.
Di Roma li 10 di Marzo 1597.
Di V. P. M. R. come fratello,

Il Cardinale di Verona

11. (T. 2, fol. 119)

Molto Reverendo Padre. Desiderano questi miei Ill.mi Sig.ri della Congregatione dell'Indice, che con diligentia attenda all'essecutione di quello, con dare aviso dell'espurgatione dei libri, qual con l'aiuto di varii consultori va facendo, mandandone copia autentica, et nota dei libri sospetti che alla giornata va scoprendo, con essar molto vigilante nei libri che si stampano, et avisar tutte le dificultà che occorrono. Con che fine alle vostre orationi mi raccomando.
Di Roma il dì 22 di Febbraio 1598.
Di V. P. M. R. amorevole,

Il Cardinale di Verona

12. (T. 2, fol. 120)

Reverendo Padre. Desiderano questi miei Ill.mi Sig. ri della Congregatione dell'Indice che mandi nota de' libri prohibiti e sospesi che si ritrovano nell'Offitio et appresso li Vicarii in diversi luoghi della sua giurisdittione, e che seguiti nel censurare libri con l'aiuto de' varii consultori, con mandar copia autentica conforme all'Indice delle censure. Con che fine alle sue orationi mi raccomando.
Di Roma ai 6 d'Agosto 1599.
Di V. R. amorevole,

Il Cardinale di Terranova

possible the *Index Expurgatorius* so greatly desired by all. And since yours is one of the principal Inquisitions, they await information on many condemned and suspended books which were first in your Inquisition, or were discovered in the course of executing the Index, or have come to light subsequently. In addition send along any old expurgations you can find, as well as those being prepared in compliance with the new Index. And I close by commending myself to your prayers.

Rome, 10 March 1597

Of your reverence, fraternally,

The Cardinal of Verona

11. (T. 2, fol. 119)

Very reverend Father. The illustrious members of the Congregation of the Index desire that you communicate diligently the book expurgations which you are performing with the assistance of various consultants, and forward authenticated copies, as well as a list of the suspected books which have come to light. Be extremely vigilant in regard to books that are being printed, and notify us about any difficulties that arise. I close by commending myself to your prayers.

Rome, 22 February 1598.

Of your reverence, benevolently,

The Cardinal of Verona

12. (T. 2, fol. 120)

Reverend Father. These illustrious members of the Congregation of the Index desire that you send a list of the prohibited and suspended books that are in your Holy Office and in the vicariates in the various places under your jurisdiction. They also want you to continue censoring books with the assistance of consultants, and send authenticated copies in conformity with the Index of Expurgations. I close by commending myself to your prayers.

Rome, 6 August 1599.

Of your reverence, benevolently,

The Cardinal of Terranova

13. (T. 2, fol. 121)

Reverendo Padre. Quantoprima mandarete nota alfabetica de tutti libri sospesi, o prohibiti, che si ritrovano nella vostra Inquisitione, overo appresso librari, et anco di tutti quelli che si ritrovaranno appresso tutti li vostri Vicarii in altre città, e quanto al censurar libri si darà rimedio per effettuar quanto si desidera. Con che fine alle vostre orationi mi raccomando.
Di Roma a 22 di Settembre 1599.
Di V. R. amorevole,
                                              Il Cardinale di Terranova

14. (T. 2, fol. 122)

Reverendo Padre. Aspettano questi miei Ill.mi SS.ri la nota de'libri prohibiti, o sospesi, che si trovano appresso li suoi Vicarii, et anco copia delle censure, che si ritrova, con la nota delle licenze, che ha dato di legger libri, et attenda a far eseguir l'Indice come si conviene, et alle sue orationi mi raccomando.
Di Roma li 3 di Dicembre 1599
Di V. R. amorevole,
                                              Il Cardinale di Verona

15. (T. 2, fol. 123)

Reverendo Padre. Sapendo quanto sia il suo valore, et quanto habbi zelo del servitio d'Iddio, non mi stenderò in ricordarli, che attenda all'essecutione dell'Indice, havendo particolar cura nella stampa, e scoprendo alla giornata libri pernitiosi, ne dia aviso, confidando che sarà vigilante, e darà conto del tutto a questi miei Ill.mi SS.ri della Congregatione dell'Indice, a quali sempre sarà grato ogni suo aviso, et hauran gusto di veder alcuna censura de' libri sospesi. Et capitando costì un libro intitolato, *Opere succisive seu meditationes historicae Philippi Camerarii*, stampato in Norimberga,[47] sappiate che per esser pernitioso, è stato dannato. Con che fine alle sue orationi mi raccomando.
Di Roma li II di luglio 1600.
Di V. R. amorevole,
                                              Il Cardinale di Verona

13. (T. 2, fol. 121)

Reverend Father. As soon as possible send a list in alphabetical order of all the suspended and prohibited books in your Inquisition, or in the bookshops, as well as those that are in your vicariates in other cities. As for the censorship of books we shall take measures to effect what is needed. I close by commending myself to your prayers.
Rome, 22 September 1599.
Of your reverence, benevolently,

The Cardinal of Terranova

14. (T. 2, fol. 122)

Reverend Father. These illustrious lordships await the list of prohibited or suspended books which exist in your vicariates, and also copies of the expurgations, together with a list of the licenses which you have granted to read books. Attend to the proper execution of the Index, and I commend myself to your prayers.
Rome, 3 December 1599
Of your reverence, benevolently,

The Cardinal of Verona

15. (T. 2, fol. 123)

Reverend Father. Well aware of your worth and your great zeal in the service of God, I do not need to remind you to oversee the execution of the Index, taking particular care in regard to what is printed, and to alert us if you should discover pernicious books. We are confident that you will be vigilant, and will make a full accounting to these illustrious members of the Congregation of the Index, who will always be grateful for any information you pass on and who desire to see some of your expurgations of suspended books. And if a volume should come your way entitled *Opere succisive seu meditationes historicae Philippi Camerarii*, printed in Nuremberg, know that it has been condemned as a pernicious work. I close by commending myself to your prayers.
Rome, 2 July 1600
Of your reverence, benevolently,

The Cardinal of Verona

16. (T. 2, fol. 149)

Reverendo Padre. È venuto fuora un libro in ottavo intitolato *Rerum memorabilium iam olim deperditarum et contra recens, atque ingeniose inventarum libri duo a Guidone Pancirolo juris consulto clarissimo italice primum conscripti, nec unquam hactenus editi, nunc vero, et latinitate donati, et notis quamplurimis ex jurisconsultis, historicis, poetis, et philologis illustrati per Henricum Salmuth*, Ambergae typis Forsterianis MDIC. Et perchè si è osservato che nelle note del detto Henrico si contengono molte heresie et errori gravissimi, sebene Guido Pancirolo autore del libro fu cattolico, come è il testo del libro, questi miei Ill.mi et R.mi SS. Cardinali Generali Inquisitori Colleghi hanno prohibite le note fatte dal sopradetto Henrico heretico, con ordine che per l'avvenire non si possano tenere, ne leggere, e hanno ordinato che V. R. publichi et notifichi la prohibitione delle sudette note non solamente in cotesta città, ma anco la faccia publicare negli altri luoghi de' suoi Vicarii in modo tale che per la prohibitione non venga notato il Pancirolo, persona Cattolica, ma solamente le note del sudetto Henrico Salmuth heretico.[48] Et non comporti che per l'avvenire alcuno ardisca di tenere et leggere il libro con le sudette note, ma usi in ciò ogni diligenza necessaria. Ne questa essendo per altro la saluto, et il Signore la conservi nella Sua santa gratia.

Di Roma a IX di Maggio MDCI.
Di V. R. come fratello,

Il Cardinale di Santa Severina

[On the verso, the subscriptions of Florentine booksellers]

Noi Filippo Giunti habbiamo ricevuto la sopra detta intimatione dal Molto R.do P. Inquisitore di Fiorenza questo dì 16 di Maggio 1601.

Io Giovanni [name illegible] ho ricevuto la detta intimatione per Cosimo Giunti dal Molto R.do P. Inquisitore di Fiorenza questo dì 16 di Maggio 1601.

Io Salvestro di Domenico Magliani ho ricevuto la detta intimatione dal Molto R.do P. Inquisitore e prometto osservarla. E in fede ho scritto di mia propria mano questo dì 16 Maggio 1601.

Io Filippo di Lionardo Mondicelli libraro ho ricevuto la detta intimatione dal Molto R.do P. Inquisitore di Fiorenza questo dì 16 di Maggio 1601.

Io Bartolomeo Ruoti libraro ho ricevuto la detta intimatione dal Molto

16. (T. 2, fol. 149)

Reverend Father. A book in octavo has been printed entitled *Rerum memorabilium iam olim deperditarum et contra recens, atque ingeniose inventarum libri duo a Guidone Pancirolo juris consulto clarissimo italice primum conscripti, nec unquan hactenus editi, nunc vero, et latinitate donati, et notis quamplurimis ex jurisconsultis, historicis, poetis, et philologis illustrati per Henricum Salmuth*, Ambergae typis Forsterianis MDIC. Since it was noted that the notes by the above mentioned Henry contain many heresies and grievous errors, although Guido Pancirolo, the author of the book, was a Catholic as is the text of the work, my illustrious colleagues the cardinal inquisitors have prohibited the notes by the above mentioned heretical Henry, enjoining that they be neither possessed nor read in the future. They ask your reverence to promulgate and announce the prohibition of these notes, not only in your city, but also in the other places occupied by your vicars, but done in such a way that Pancirolo, a Catholic person, is not named in the prohibition, but only the notes of the aforementioned Henry Salmuth heretic. In the future do not permit anyone to possess or read the book with these notes, and employ all necessary diligence in this matter. Since I have nothing more to add, I bid you farewell and may the Lord preserve you in His holy grace.
Rome, 9 May 1601

The Cardinal of Santa Severina

[On the verso, the subscriptions of Florentine booksellers]

I, Filippo Giunti, have received the above notification from the most reverend father inquisitor of Florence on this 16th day of May, 1601.
I, Giovanni [name illegible], have received the aforesaid notification on behalf of Cosimo Giunti from the most reverend father inquisitor of Florence on this 16th day of May, 1601.
I, Salvestro di Domenico Magliani, have received the aforesaid notification from the most reverend father inquisitor and promise to obey it. And in faith I have signed with my own hand on this 16th day of May, 1601.
I, Filippo di Lionardo Mondicelli, bookseller, have received the aforesaid notification from the most reverend father inquisitor of Florence on this 16th day of May, 1601.
I, Bartolomeo Ruoti, bookseller, have received the aforesaid notification

R.do P. Inquisitore e prometto osservarla, e in fede ho scritto il dì sopradetto.

E io Girolamo di Jacopo Franceschi [h]o ricevuto la presente intimatione questo 16 sopradetto di propria mano.

Io Bartolomeo [name illegible] [h]o ricevuto dal R.do P. Inquisitore la sopradetta intimatione questo dì sopradetto.

Io Alessandro di Zanobi Camerino libraro ho ricevuto la detta intimatione questo dì sopradetto.

Io Bartolomeo Francesco ho ricevuto dal R.do P. Inquisitore la sopradetta intimatione questo dì sopradetto.

Io Piero di Ventura Bassini ho riscevuto la medesima intimatione.

17. (T. 2, fol. 150)

Reverendo Padre. Da questa Sacra Congregatione della Inquisitione è stato prohibito il libro intitolato *Ecloga Oxonio Cantabrigensis distributa in libros duos, quorum prior continet catalogum confusum librorum manuscriptorum in illustrissimis bibliothecis florentissimarum Academiarum Oxoni et Cantabrig., posterior catalogum eorundem distinctum et dispositum in quatuor facultates. Omnia haec opera et studio T.J. novi Collegii in Academia Oxoniensi socii et utriusque Academiae in artibus magistri.* Londini impensis Georg. Bishop et Jo. Narson [i.e., Norton], 1600.[49] Et in subscriptione epistolae legitur nomen auctoris per extensum, Thomas James. Però ne do avviso a V. R. a fine ch'ella faccia publicare la prohibitione con ordinare ai librari et a ciascuno che haverà il detto libro che lo debbano consegnare sotto quelle pene che a lei pareranno convenienti. Et non essendo la presente per altro, stia sana et il Signore la conservi nella Sua santa gratia.

Di Roma a gli VIII di Giugno MDCI.

Di V. R. come fratello,

Il Cardinale di Santa Severina

[On the verso, signatures of Florentine booksellers as above]

18. (T. 2, fol. 151)

Reverendo Padre. Essendo venuto a notitia della Santità di N.S. che in un libro del Padre Tomaso Saiglio Gesuita, intitolato *Thesaurus Litaniarum,*[50] si contengono 365 sorti di litanie, et che in un'altro libro intitolato

from the most reverend father inquisitor and promise to obey it, and in faith I have written the above date.

And I, Girolamo di Jacopo Franceschi, have received the present notification the 16th of this month with my own hand.

I, Bartolomeo [name illegible], have received from the reverend father inquisitor the aforesaid notification on this date.

I, Alessandro di Zanobi Camerini, have received the aforesaid notification on this date.

I, Bartolomeo Francesco, have received from the reverend father inquisitor the aforesaid notification on this date.

I, Piero di Ventura Bassini, have received the same notification.

17. (T. 2, fol. 150)

Reverend Father. This Sacred Congregation of the Inquisition has prohibited a book entitled *Ecloga Oxonio Cantabrigensis distributa in libros duos, quorum prior continet catalogum confusum librorum manuscriptorum in illustrissimis bibliothecis florentissimarum Academiarum Oxoni et Cantabrig. posterior catalogum eorundem distinctum et dispositum in quatuor facultates. Omnia haec opera et studio T.J. novi Collegii in Academia Oxoniensi socii et utriusque Academiae in artibus magistri.* Londini impensis Georg. Bishop et Jo. Narson [i.e., Norton], 1600. At the foot of the letter the name of the author, Thomas James, can be read in full. I am informing your reverence so that you will have the prohibition published, ordering the booksellers and anyone who possesses the book to surrender it subject to whatever penalties you deem appropriate. Since I have nothing more to add for the moment, stay well and may the Lord preserve you in His holy grace. Rome, 8 June 1601. Of your reverence, fraternally,

The Cardinal of Santa Severina

[On the verso, the subscriptions of Florentine booksellers as above]

18. (T. 2, fol. 151)

Reverend Father. Since it has come to the attention of His Holiness that a book by Father Tomaso Saiglio, a Jesuit, entitled *Thesaurus Litaniarum*, contains 365 different litanies, and that a book entitled *Thesaurus*

Thesaurus Sacrarum pretium sive litaniae variae,[51] come in altri libretti si contengono diversi modi di litanie, la Santità Sua ha sospesi per hora i sudetti libri, & l'uso delle sopradette litanie, et solo ha eccettuate le ordinarie che sono nel Messale et nel Breviario, et le litanie in honore della Madonna Santissima di Loreto, volendo Sua Beatitudine appresso fare quella deliberatione, et risolutione, che conviene sopra la diversità et numero delle sudette litanie.[52] Però V. R. non manchi di notificare la sospensione a tutti i librari, Vicarii Episcopali, et suoi particolari ne'luoghi sottoposti alla sua giurisdittione, et a tutti quelli che sarà di bisogno, et faccia in maniera che si osservi la mente et volontà di Sua Beatitudine, dando avviso di quanto haverà poi esseguito. Ne questa essendo per altro, stia sana, et il Signore la conservi nella Sua santa gratia.

Di Roma a XVI di Giugno MDCI.

Di V. R. come fratello,

Il Cardinale di Santa Severina

[On the verso, signatures of Florentine booksellers as above]

19. (T. 2, fol. 152)

Reverendo Padre. La Santità di Nostro Signore ha prohibito il trattato del Dottor Pietro Antonio Pietra Piacentino intitolato *De iure quaesito per Principem non tollendo, seu de potestate Principis*, Venetiis apud Damianum Zenarum 1599[53] perchè in esso si contengono espressamente molte propositioni heretical. Però lo fo sapere a V. R. a ciò che ella publichi Editto sopra la prohibitione di tal libro, con farsi consegnare da librari, et anco dalle persone particolari li volumi che ne havessero appresso di se, con prohibire espressamente, che per l'avvenire niuno possa tenere, ne leggere il detto libro sotto le pene statuite contra quelli che tengono libri prohibiti. Onde ella alla ricevuta di questa esseguisca il presente ordine ne' luoghi soggetti alla sua giurisdittione, et lo notifichi dove, et a chi sarà di bisogno. Et dia avviso della essecutione. Intanto la saluto, et alle sue orationi mi raccomando.

Di Roma a VII di Luglio MDCI.

Di V. R. come fratello,

Il Cardinale di Santa Severina

[On the verso, signatures of Florentine booksellers as above][54]

Sacrarum pretium sive litaniae variae, and other pamphlets as well also contain various forms of litanies, His Holiness has for the time being suspended these books and the use of the above mentioned litanies. He has excepted only the usual ones in the Missal and the Breviary, as well as the litanies in honor of the Most Holy Madonna of Loreto, wanting to make subsequently that decision and resolution needed in regard to the diversity and number of the above mentioned litanies. Your reverence must not fail to communicate this suspension to all the booksellers, episcopal vicars, and your own [vicars] in those places that are under your jurisdiction, and anyone else who should know. Do it in a way so that the intention and will of His Holiness is observed, and then notify us of what has been done. Since I have nothing more, stay well, and may the Lord preserve you in His holy grace.

Rome, 16 June 1601.

Of your reverence, fraternally,

The Cardinal of Santa Severina

[On the verso, the subscriptions of Florentine booksellers, as above]

19. (T. 2, fol. 152)

Reverend Father. His Holiness has prohibited the treatise by Dr. Pietro Antonio Pietra of Piacenza entitled *De iure quaesito per Principem non tollendo, seu de potestate Principis*, Venice, apud Damianum Zenarum, 1599 because it contains many heretical propositions. Therefore I am informing your reverence so that you may promulgate an edict prohibiting the book, ordering booksellers and even private individuals to surrender whatever copies they might possess, expressly forbidding anyone in the future to possess or read the above mentioned book, in accordance with the penalties established against those who keep prohibited books. Upon receipt of this, execute the present order in the places under your jurisdiction, and notify wherever and whomever is necessary. And inform us when this shall have been done. Meanwhile, I bid you farewell, and commend myself to your prayers.

Rome, 7 July 1601.

Of your reverence, fraternally,

The Cardinal of Santa Severina

[On the verso, the subscriptions of Florentine booksellers, as above]

20. (T. 2, fol. 153)

Reverendo Padre. Havendo la Santità di Nostro Signore fatto un Decreto da osservarsi in materia delle Litanie,[55] ne mando a V. R. l'alligata copia in stampa, acciochè ella lo faccia publicare in cotesta città, & per maggiore commodità ne faccia stampare ancora alcuni essemplari conformi, et gli distribuisca tra gli Ordinarii, et Preti delle Chiese Cathedrali Collegiate et Parochiali, et tra i Conventi, Monasterii di Regolari, et Oratorii di Compagnie, et altri a chi sarà bisogno, a ciò che ne habbiano notitia, et osservino quanto è mente et ordine di Sua Beatitudine. Et non essendo la presente per altro, la saluto et alle sue orationi mi raccomando.

Di Roma a XX di Ottobre MDCI.

Di V. R. come fratello,

Il Cardinale di Santa Severina

21. (T. 2, fol. 155)

Reverendo Padre. Si è inteso che alcuni Ginevrini, o de' paesi convicini hanno portato in Italia Bibbie stampate in Ginevra, che contengono molte parole, et note d'heretici, et le hanno distribuite fra i librari et persone particolari, ancorchè in esse Bibbie falsamente sia notato che siano stampate in Lione.[56] E potendo di ciò succedere gravissimi danni et pregiuditii alla Santa fede Cattolica, la Santità di Nostro Signore ha ordinato che V. R. usi ogni essatta et possibile diligenza per ritrovare se fin hora siano state portate et distribuite simili Bibbie costì et da chi; et che per l'avvenire ella invigili, come ricerca la gravità del fatto, et dia in ciò gli ordini necessarii acciochè non vi siano portati tali libri, et trovando che ve ne siano proceda contro i transgressori con ogni rigore et secondo sarà di giustitia, confidandosi ch'ella per la parte sua non mancarà di esseguire quanto sarà di bisogno per corrispondere con gli effetti alla mente et ordine espresso di Sua Beatitudine. Ne questa essendo per altro, saluto V. R. et alle sue orationi mi raccomando.

Di Roma a XXIII di Febraro MDCII.

Di V. R. come fratello,

Il Cardinale di Santa Severina

20. (T. 2, fol. 153)

Reverend Father. Since His Holiness has issued a decree that needs to be observed in the matter of Litanies, I enclose a printed copy so that you may publish it in your city. For greater convenience you may have additional copies of it printed and distributed among the bishops and priests of the cathedral and parish churches, among the convents and monasteries of the orders, and among the oratories of the confraternities, and among others who will need it, so that they will be familiar with it and obey the intention and order of His Holiness. And since I have nothing more to add, I bid you farewell and commend myself to your prayers. Rome, 20 October 1601.
Of your reverence, fraternally,

The Cardinal of Santa Severina

21. (T. 2, fol. 155)

Reverend Father. We have learned that certain Genevans, or some of their neighbors, have brought to Italy Bibles printed in Geneva, which contain many words and commentaries written by heretics. They have distributed them among booksellers and private persons, although it is falsely stated in these Bibles that they were printed in Lyons. Since great harm and disservice to the holy Catholic Church can ensue from this, His Holiness orders your reverence to expend every diligence possible to discover if any of the Bibles have been distributed there and by whom. And in the future be watchful as the gravity of the matter requires, and issue the necessary orders so that such books will not be brought in again. If you find that some are circulating, proceed against the transgressors with the utmost rigor and as justice requires, with the assurance that for your part you will be fulfilling that which is required to satisfy the intention and express order of His Holiness. Since I have nothing more to add, I bid your reverence farewell and commend myself to your prayers. Rome, 23 February 1602.
Of your reverence, fraternally,

The Cardinal of Santa Severina

22. (T. 2, fol. 124)

Molto Reverendo Padre. Aspettano questi miei Ill.mi Sig.ri haver relatione del progresso che si è fatto in osservanza dell'Indice con l'aiuto dell' Ordinario et di varii Consultori circa la censura de' libri. Et sia vigilante circa la stampa de' libri in non admettere cosa, se ben frivola, che sia contro le Regole dell'Indice, et habbi particolar cura in ciò alle cose di menantarie. Con che fine alle sue orationi mi raccomando.
Di Roma a dì 23 di Marzo 1602.
Di V. R. amorevolmente,

Il Cardinale di Verona

23. (T. 2, fol. 125)

Molto Reverendo Padre. Restano questi miei Ill.mi Sig.ri della Congregatione dell'Indice molto maravigliati in veder la negligentia che si usa circa le stampe, e tanto maggiore quanto che più volte è stato scritto che si usi ogni diligentia et si stia vigilante, et con tutto ciò è comparso un *Giardino de Madrigali* stampato in Rimini di Mauritio Moro,[57] quale si è prohibito di espresso ordine di Nostro Signore per contenere molte obscenità, et una *Praxi Episcopale* di Monsignore Thomasso Zerola,[58] Vescovo di Minori, stampata in Venetia, nella quale essendo alcuni gravi errori, e perciò si prohibisce, che non si venda, o legga, sinchè non sia publicata la Censura. Però V. R. non mancarà di publicare la prohibitione dell'uno, e dell'altro libro, e con maggior diligenza invigilare circa la stampa, e' libri novi, et che vengono di fora, con dare aviso di quanto alla giornata andrà scoprendo di errore ne i libri. Con che fine alle sue orationi mi raccomando.
Di Roma a 20 di Dicembre 1602.
Di V. P. M. R. amorevole,

Il Cardinale di Terranova[59]

24. (T. 1, fol. 157)

Reverendo Padre. In risposta alla lettera di V. R. delli 4 di Dicembre le dico, che questi Ill.mi e R.mi Sig.ri Cardinali miei Colleghi non hanno

22. (T. 2, fol. 124)

Most reverend Father. These illustrious lordships desire a progress report in regard to the enforcement of the Index with the help of the bishops and the various consultants assigned to the censorship of books. Watch over the printing of books carefully, not permitting anything, however trivial, which goes against the Rules of the Index, paying special attention to matters of transcription [*menantarie*]. And I close commending myself to your prayers.
Rome, 23 March 1602.
Of your reverence, benevolently,

The Cardinal of Verona

23. (T. 2, fol. 125)

Most Reverend Father. These illustrious lordships of the Congregation of the Index are astounded to see the negligence being shown in regard to the printing of books, especially since they have written on so many occasions to employ every diligence and to keep vigilant. In spite of this, a *Giardino de Madrigali* by Mauritio Moro, printed in Rimini has appeared, which has been prohibited by express order of His Holiness because it contains many obscenities; and also a *Praxi Episcopale* by Monsignor Thomasso Zerola, Bishop of Minori, printed in Venice. Since it contains some grievous errors, it is prohibited and is not to be sold or read until its expurgations have been published. Therefore your reverence shall not fail to promulgate the prohibitions of both books, exert greater vigilance over the printing of new books as well as those which come from outside, and communicate what errors you discover in them. I close by commending myself to your prayers.
Rome, 20 December 1602.
Of your most reverend paternity, benevolently,

The Cardinal of Terranova

24. (T. 1, fol. 157)

Reverend Father. In reply to the letter of your reverence of 4 December, I want to say that these most illustrious and reverend cardinals, my

voluto conceder licenza al Regente dell'Accademia de' Spensierati[60] di tenere e leggere l'opere del Machiavello, Boccaccio e Castelvetro ad effetto di correggerle, e farle ristampare di nuovo. . . .[61]
Di Roma li 12 di Febraro 1605.

Il Cardinale Borghese[62]

25. (T. 2, fol. 140)

Reverendo Padre. Questi Ill.mi et R.mi SS.ri Cardinali Generali Inquisitori miei Colleghi stimando necessaria ogni diligenza che si possa fare in materia delle stampe, per quel che tutto dì si prova per esperienza, mi hanno commesso, ch'io avvisi V. R. a dovere stare vigilante, et usare ogni diligenza possibile per se stessa, et per mezzo di persone dotte, zelanti, et pie nel rivedere li libri, et altre operette, o historiette, che alla giornata si stampano costì, acciochè non contengano cose prohibite conforme alle Regole dell'Indice, nè conceda licenza di stamparsi, che prima non siano reviste con ogni accuratezza. Non manchi ella dunque di sodisfare in ciò al debito suo, et notifichi la presente a' suoi Officiali ne' luoghi dove si stampa, facendo anco sopra tutto conservare gli originali, che si approvano, et danno alla stampa acciochè si veda se in essi viene commessa alteratione alcuna, et sempre apparisca da chi siano stati revisti et approvati i libri et opere che si stampano. In questa maniera con l'osservanza inviolabile del presente ordine verrà a provedere al beneficio pubblico, et ella non potrà essere notata di trascuraggine o negligenza, dove al contrario, oltra la mala sodisfattione, potrebbe ancora dar occasione di farsene risentimento con suo poco honore. Et il Signore la conservi.
Di Roma a XXIX di Aprile MDCV.
Di V. R. come fratello,

Il Cardinale Borghese

26. (T. 2, fol. 165)

Reverendo Padre. Sebene altre volte è stato ordinato, et prohibito a gl'Inquisitori che non diano licenze di tenere et leggere libri prohibiti,

colleagues, have not seen fit to grant a license to the Regent of the Academy of the Spensierati to possess and read the works of Machiavelli, Boccaccio, and Castelvetro for the purpose of correcting them so that new editions can be published. . . .
Rome, 12 February 1605

The Cardinal Borghese

25. (T. 2, fol. 140)

Reverend Father. These most illustrious and most reverend cardinal general inquisitors, my colleagues, deeming essential any diligence that can be exerted over printed material, as we learn from our experience every day, have commissioned me to communicate this to your reverence. Be vigilant and apply every possible care, yourself and through learned, zealous, and pious persons, in the censorship of books, booklets, and the small histories which from day to day are printed there, so that they will not contain prohibited things in line with the Rules of the Index. And do not issue permits to print them before they are examined with all possible accuracy. Do not fail, then, to perform your duty and to pass on this communication to your officials in the towns where printing takes place, asking them to preserve the originals which have been examined and passed on to the printers. This will permit us to determine if any changes at all were made. It should also be clearly stated who examined and gave his approval to the works printed. By your unswerving observance of the present order you will be providing for the public good, and no sort of indifference or neglect will be imputed to you. In case of the opposite, in addition to great dissatisfaction, there would also be the occasion for resentment to the detriment of your honor.
Rome, 29 April 1605.
Of your reverence, fraternally.

The Cardinal Borghese

26. (T. 2, fol. 165)

Reverend Father. Although on other occasions inquisitors have been prohibited to grant licenses to keep and read prohibited books, neverthe-

tuttavia alcuno Inquisitore non ostante tal prohibitione s'è ingerito in dar tal licenze. Però questi Ill.mi SS.ri Cardinali miei Colleghi hanno ordinato che di nuovo si faccia sapere a ciascuno Inquisitore che per l'avenire non ardisca in modo alcuno dar licenza a qualsivoglia persona di tenere et leggere libri prohibiti. Il che serve a V. R. acciochè a suo tempo ella così osservi et faccia osservare da suoi Vicarii, registrando la presente ne' libri di cotesta Inquisitione per informatione de soccessore. Et stia sana. Di Roma li 15 di Aprile 1606.
Di V. R. come fratello,

Il Cardinale Arigoni[63]

27. (T. 2, fol. 141)

Reverendo Padre. Mando a V. R. un'essemplare dell'Editto fatto da questa Sacra Congregatione in materia de' libri e scritture, si stampate, come manoscritte sopra l'interdetto et potestà del Papa,[64] acciò lo faccia publicare in latino et volgare in tutti li luoghi che conoscerà necessarii della sua giurisdittione potendoli far ristampare anco bisognando. E stia sano.
Di Roma li 30 di Giugno 1606.
Di V. R. come fratello,

Il Cardinale Arigoni

28. (T. 2, fol. 142)

Reverendo Padre. Sebene per l'Editto publicato a' mesi passati sono prohibiti li libri e trattati circa le censure et interdetto di Nostro Signore con la Republica di Venetia,[65] ne' quali si contengono propositioni scandalose, scismatiche, erronee, et heretiche respettive, con tutto ciò sono stati prohibiti alcuni altri libri venuti a luce, o che si publicaranno per l'avenire sopra l'istessa materia, purchè meritano le sopradette note e censure come vedrà dall'allegato Editto[66] V. R., acciò lo faccia publicare in cotesta città, et ove conoscerà essere di bisogno ne' luoghi della sua giurisdittione. E stia sana.
Da Roma li 23 di Settembre 1606.
Di V. R. come fratello,

Il Cardinale Arigoni

less, some inquisitors, despite the prohibition, permit themselves to do so. Therefore these most illustrious cardinals, my colleagues, have ordered that every inquisitor be once again instructed never to presume in the future to give permission to whatsoever person to keep and read prohibited books. Let this serve your reverence as a guide of what you should observe and have your vicars observe; and record the present communication in the books of your Inquisition for the information of your successor. And stay well.

Rome, 15 April 1606.

Of your reverence, fraternally,

The Cardinal Arigoni

27. (T. 2, fol. 141)

Reverend Father. I am sending to your reverence a copy of the Edict decreed by this Holy Congregation in regard to books and writings, whether printed or in manuscript, on the interdict and authority of the pope, so that you may have it published in both Latin and the vernacular in all the appropriate places within your jurisdiction, with permission to reprint them as needed. And stay well.

Rome, 30 June 1606.

Of your reverence, fraternally,

The Cardinal Arigoni

28. (T. 2, fol. 142)

Reverend Father. Through the Edict published a few months ago a prohibition has already been issued against books and treatises on the censures and interdict of His Holiness with the Republic of Venice, which contain scandalous, schismatic, erroneous, and heretical propositions. Nevertheless, a new prohibition has been published against other books which have since seen the light of day or may appear in the future on the same subject, provided they qualify for the above mentioned censures as your reverence will see from the attached Edict. We ask that you have it published in your city, and wherever you will perceive there is a need in the places under your jurisdiction. Stay well.

Rome, 23 September 1606.

Of your reverence, fraternally,

The Cardinal Arigoni

Notes

*The inspiration and model for this article are provided by Antonio Rotondò's valuable edition of inquisitorial correspondence preserved in the Biblioteca dell'Archiginnasio, Bologna and the Archivio di Stato, Modena: "Nuovi documenti per la storia dell' 'Indice dei Libri Proibiti' (1572–1638)," *Rinascimento*, ser. 2, 3 (1963): 145–211. In the transcription of the letters I have not broken up common abbreviations (see the Table of Abbreviations at the front of the volume), and I have attempted to keep my intervention in the text to a minimum.

    1. Four volumes from the archive of the Florentine Inquisition were purchased by the Royal Library in Brussels in 1878. They are preserved in MS. II 290 summarily described by J. Van Den Gheyn, *Catalogue des Manuscripts de la Bibliothèque Royale de Belgique* (Brussels, 1903), 4:84–86. The letters are contained in vols. 1 and 2. The collection has been transferred in very recent times to the State Archives. For the pertinent literature, see "The Dispersed Archives of the Roman Inquisition," pp. 39–40.

    2. For a general discussion of the work of the Congregation of the Index, see A. Rotondò's comprehensive essay, "La censura ecclesiastica e la cultura," *Storia d'Italia: I documenti* (Turin: Einaudi, 1973), 5, pt. 2: 1399–1492 and P. Simoncelli, "Documenti interni alla Congregazione dell'Indice, 1571–1590: Logica e ideologia dell'intervento censorio," *Annuario dell'Istituto storico italiano per l'età moderna e contemporanea* 35–36 (1983–84): 188–215. This rich study is based on a Vatican Library codex (Vat. lat. 6207) consisting of opinions and questions raised in regard to the censorship of a broad range of books. Simoncelli's work permits the reconstruction of the motives underlying the censures. I refer the reader to these two model studies and to the ongoing series, *Index des Livres Interdits*, ed. J. M. De Bujanda for the general bibliography on the subject. H. H. Schwendt's brief survey ("Der römische Index der verbotenen Bücher," *Historisches Jahrbuch* 107 [1987]: 296–314) carries the account to the twentieth century. It is important to remember that the religious orders also censored works by their members destined for publication, an activity that predated the founding of the Congregation of the Index. U. Baldini ("Una fonte poco utilizzata per la storia intellettuale: Le *censurae librorum* e *opinionum* nell'antica Compagnia di Gesù," *Annali dell'Istituto storico italo-germanico in Trento* 11 [1985]: 19–67) focuses on Jesuit expurgations. I am grateful to James M. Lattis for bringing this article to my attention.

    For studies dealing specifically with the censorship and the application of the Index in Tuscany, see A. Panella, "La censura sulla stampa e una questione giurisdizionale fra stato e chiesa in Firenze alla fine del secolo XVI," *Archivio storico italiano*, ser. 5, 43 (1909): 140–51; idem, "L'introduzione a Firenze dell'Indice di Paolo IV," *Rivista storica degli archivi toscani* 1 (1929): 11–25; M. Plaisance, "Littérature et censure à Florence à la fin du XVIe siècle: Le retour du censuré," in *Le pouvoir et la plume: Incitation, contrôle et répression dans l'Italie du XVIe siècle* (Paris, 1982), 233–52. On the operation of the Florentine Inquisition itself, see now the excellent studies by Adriano Prosperi, the first modern investigations based on its documents in the Archivio della Curia Arcivescovile (cited in "Toward a Statistical Profile of the Italian Inquisitions" at n. 5). I refer the reader to these articles for the older bibliography on the subject.

3. See, for example, letters 7, 18, 21, 23, which are virtually identical to communications addressed to the inquisitor of Aquileia and Concordia (see ACAU, Epistolae S. Officii, 1588–1613 [unpaginated] under date). See also letter 1, which mentions that it is being sent to all the provincial inquisitions, and letter 19, which also turns up among the Modenese correspondence. See below at n. 53.

4. See P. Prodi's description of its effects on Bolognese university life and on the career of the historian Carlo Sigonio in Prodi's *Il Cardinale Paleotti (1522–1597)*, 2 vols. (Rome, 1959–67), vol. 2, chap. 12, "Riforma religiosa e cultura"; idem, "Storia sacra e controriforma. Nota sulla censura al commento di Carlo Sigonio a Sulpicio Severo," *Annali dell'Istituto storico italo-germanico di Trento* 3 (1977): 75–104. Cf. W. McCuaig, *Carlo Sigonio: The Changing World of the Late Renaissance* (Princeton, 1989), esp. chap. 4, "Sigonio Versus the Censors." See also R. De Maio, "I modelli culturali della Controriforma: Le biblioteche dei conventi italiani alla fine del Cinquecento," in his *Riforme e miti nella Chiesa del Cinquecento* (Naples, 1973), 365–81, at p. 372 where he speaks "della morte culturale che l'Indice arrecava." Cf. the nuanced panorama sketched by G. Benzoni, "Intellettuali e Controriforma," *La Cultura* 22 (1984): 128–71.

5. See, for example, A. Rotondò, "Cultura umanistica e difficoltà di censori: Censura ecclesiastica e discussioni cinquecentesche sul Platonismo," in *Le pouvoir et la plume*, 15–50. The article focuses on the difficulties confronted by censors attempting to ferret out erroneous propositions deeply rooted in complex theoretical systems such as Platonism.

6. Fra Damiano Rubeo, in the service of the Master of the Sacred Palace, once confidentially urged a theologian who had just written on the sensitive topic of predestination to have his treatise published in Venice. There was no chance that it could appear in Rome where there was an enormous backlog of material to examine. See A. Rotondò, "Nuovi documenti," 157 (letter of 25 April 1576).

7. Shortly after the publication of the sweeping, draconian Index of Paul IV (January, 1559), the city of Bologna sought for its university a blanket permission to use prohibited books which were not directly concerned with religion. The request was eventually refused. The best that could be obtained was the occasional license granted to individual professors to consult specific books. See P. Prodi, *Il Cardinale Paleotti* 2:237. The Pauline Index is reprinted in F. H. Reusch, *Die Indices Librorum Prohibitorum des sechzehnten Jahrhunderts* (Tübingen, 1886; reprint, Nieuwkoop, 1961), 176–208.

8. See J. Tedeschi, "The Cultural Contributions of Italian Protestant Reformers in the Late Renaissance," in *Libri, idee, e sentimenti religiosi nel Cinquecento italiano* (Ferrara and Modena, 1987), p. 82 and n. 20.

9. The provincial inquisitors' own rights in the matter had not been easy to

determine. See, for example, the letter sent to the Bolognese Inquisition by the Holy Office in Rome (24 November 1572): "Quanto a quello poi che Vostra Reverentia domanda, se uno inquisitore ha licentia di legere libri prohibiti, li dico che molte volte se n'è raggionato tra questi Signori in Congregatione, et sempre si è detto di sì, ch'hanno licentia, però quando importa il bisogno dello officio et non altramente" (BA, MS. B–1860, fol. 101).

    10. See letters 1 and 5.

    11. See letters 5–8.

    12. See letter 5.

    13. See letter 17.

    14. See letter 24. Since the Index of Paul IV, Machiavelli had been one of those authors "quorum scripta omnino prohibentur." By the end of the sixteenth century permission to read him was extremely difficult to obtain and was refused even to individuals of high rank: in 1610, for example, to Baron de Fucariis, the imperial ambassador in Venice. In the same year a certain Cesare di Pisa, alias Astrologhino, was arrested, tortured, and convicted because copies of Machiavelli and Bodin had been found in his possession. See G. Procacci, *Studi sulla fortuna del Machiavelli* (Rome, 1965), 317 ff., 327. A decree of the Roman Inquisition, dated 4 October 1600, denied permission to Baccio Valori to place a copy of the *Discorsi* in the Medici library. See A. Sorrentino, *Storia dell' antimachiavellismo europeo* (Naples, 1936), 117, and, in general, A. Gerber, *Niccolò Machiavelli: Die Handschriften, Ausgaben und Übersetzungen seiner Werke im 16. und 17. Jahrhundert* (Gotha, 1912), chap. 6, "Der Index von 1559 und seine Wirkungen." See now H. Lutz, "Antimachiavellismus im Italien des 16. Jahrhunderts," *Mitteilungen des oberösterreichischen Landesarchivs* 14 (1984): 5–12.

    The literary critic, Lodovico Castelvetro, rightfully suspected as the translator of Melanchthon, was condemned as a contumacious heretic by the Roman Inquisition on 20 November 1560. Castelvetro's writings were proscribed first by the Index of Pius IV. See F. H. Reusch, *Der Index der verbotenen Bücher*, 2 vols. (Bonn, 1883–85), 1:153. On his Melanchthon translations see "Northern Books and Counter-Reformation Italy," at n. 12. A. Sorrentino, "Il Petrarca e il Sant'Uffizio," *Giornale storico della letteratura italiana* 101 (1933): 259–76 concentrates on Castelvetro's editions and commentaries of the *Rime*.

    On the prohibition of Boccaccio, see F. H. Reusch, *Der Index* 1:383–92; A. Sorrentino, *La letteratura italiana e il Sant'Uffizio* (Naples, 1935), chap. 5, "Il Boccaccio"; and the following note.

    15. A commission under Vincenzo Borghini was established in Florence in 1571 to correct the *Decameron*. The project was undertaken with papal blessing. The Master of the Sacred Palace, Tommaso Manriques, and the confessor of Pius V, Eustachio Locatelli, selected the passages requiring expurgation. As they were completed, chapters were sent to Rome for approval. The new authorized edition was published by the Giunta in Florence in 1573, but meanwhile popes had changed, and in June of the same year a new Master of the Sacred Palace, Fra Paolo Costabili, ordered that it be removed from circulation—a fine example of confusion in Roman censorship prac-

tice. See A. Rotondò, "Nuovi documenti," 152 n. 5. Other expurgated editions followed, Lionardo Salviati's in 1582 and Luigi Groto's in 1588. On the entire question, in addition to Sorrentino, *La letteratura italiana e il Sant'Uffizio*, chap. 5, see now P. M. Brown, *Lionardo Salviati: A Critical Biography* (Oxford, 1974), 160–82 (for the 1582 expurgated edition); R. Mordenti, "Le due censure: La collazione dei testi del 'Decameron' 'rassettati' da Vincenzo Borghini e Lionardo Salviati," in *Le pouvoir et la plume*, 253–73; G. Chiecchi and L. Troisio, *Il Decameron sequestrato: Le tre edizioni censurate nel Cinquecento* (Milan, 1984). On censorship of Italian literature in general in this period, see P. Paschini, "Letterati ed Indice nella Riforma Cattolica in Italia," in *Cinquecento romano e riforma cattolica* (Rome, 1958), 237–373; N. Longo, "Prolegomeni per una storia della letteratura italiana censurata," *La rassegna della letteratura italiana*, ser. 7, 78 (1974): 402–19; idem, "Fenomeni di censura nella letteratura italiana del Cinquecento," in *Le pouvoir et la plume*, 275–84.

As for Machiavelli, an expurgated version of his works was prepared by two of his grandsons during the pontificate of Gregory XIII. They would not publish it, however, with Rome's condition that it should appear without the author's name, or with that of a substitute. See G. Procacci, *Studi sulla fortuna del Machiavelli*, 317 ff. C. De Job (*De l'influence du Concile de Trente sur la littérature et les beaux arts chez les peuples catholiques* [Paris, 1884; reprint, Geneva, 1969], 393–97) publishes two letters from Pier Vettori in Florence to Cardinal Guglielmo Sirleto of the Congregation of the Index supporting respectively the Boccaccio and Machiavelli expurgation projects. The letters are dated 6 February 1573 and 17 May 1578.

16. Letters 10–13.

17. See letter 10, note.

18. "Adì 13 di Aprile si risposa che in quanto alla stampa, non si mancava. In quanto alla censura, che s'aspettava da Roma, non essendo qui chi voglia tal con[pito?]."

19. Letter 15. The *Opere* were specifically prohibited by an edict issued 29 July 1600, a little over three weeks after the present letter announcing its confiscation. See J. Hilgers, *Der Index der verbotenen Bücher* (Freiburg i. Br., 1904), 418. Philipp Camerarius, jurist, philologist, and man of letters, was the son of Joachim Camerarius, many of whose writings he edited. During a student journey to Italy the younger Camerarius was briefly imprisoned by the Roman Inquisition. The episode and Camerarius's account of it are the subject of J. G. Schelhorn's "Relatio vera et solida de captivitate romana, ex falsa delatione orta, et liberatione fere miraculosa Philippi Camerarii et Petri Rieteri," in Schelhorn's *De vita, fatis ac meritis Philippi Camerarii* (Nuremberg, 1740). The text of Camerarius's biographical statement has now appeared in a Polish edition, with new historical information, prepared by L. Szczucki, *Philippus Camerarius: Prawdziwa i wierna relacja o uwiezieniu w Rzymie* (Warsaw, 1984). The Camerarius captivity received passing attention in P. Paschini, "Episodi dell'Inquisizione a Roma nei suoi primi decenni," *Studi romani* 5 (1957): 285–301. See also H. Jantz, "The Renaissance Essays of Philipp Camerarius," in *Virtus et Fortuna: Zur deutschen Literatur zwischen 1400 und 1720*, Festschrift für Hans-Gert Roloff

zu seinem 50. Geburtstag, ed.. J. P. Strelka and J. Jungmayr (Bern, Frankfort a. M., New York, 1983), 315–27 devoted to the *Living Librarie* (1625), the English translation of the *Meditationes*; and G. Becker (*Deutsche Juristen und ihre Schriften auf den römischen Indices des 16. Jahrhunderts* [Berlin, 1970]) for earlier condemnations of German jurists.

The *Meditationes* grew from one "centuria" to three in subsequent editions. It was translated into French by Simon Goulart as *Les meditations historiques* (Lyons, 1610) and into English by John Molle, entitled first *The Walking Librarie* (London, 1621) and, in later printings, *The Living Librarie*.

20. The *Correctio* was acquired by Antonio Rotondò from a Modenese book-seller and presented to me in December 1968. This document in four leaves begins: "Correctio libri, cuius tit. est, Operae Horarum Succisivarum, sive Meditationes Historicae, per Philippo Camerario auctore, Norimberga, 1599, in 4o." Then follows the list of prescribed expurgations with precise page references. A sample entry reads: "In cap. 62 p. 288 deleantur verba ista qua sunt circa medium, 'Quoniam autem de hac donatione,' slz. Constantini usque ad fin. capitis; totum n. tendit ad ostendendum donationem Constantini Imper. factam D. Sylvestro, fabulam esse." Presumably the Archive of the Inquisition in Rome, which houses the papers of the defunct Congregation of the Index, contains many similar documents. R. De Maio (*Riforme e miti*, 366 n. 3) states that the Index collection totals 491 volumes. P. Simoncelli in his "Documenti interni" (cited at n. 2) analyzes a codex containing suggested corrections which is now in the Vatican Library.

21. See the clarification issued by the Congregation of the Index to certain doubts which had been raised by the Bolognese inquisitor (1583): "I libri sospesi con questa ragione si sospesero, acciò che, venendone per le mani, non si permettessero se non corretti, sendoli trovati dentro errori; però quelli non sono tali assolutamente proibiti. Ogni inquisitore però debbe fare in quelli la sua diligenza et revisti et ispurgati darli, né permettere in quel mentre che i librai li vendano, se non dopo fatta la censura; ispurgati, sì." See A. Rotondò, "Nuovi documenti," 163.

22. P. Prodi, *Il Cardinale Paleotti* 2:237: "Ma questa regola rimase in realtà lettera morta perché gli esami e le correzioni da parte degli inquisitori e delle facoltà teologiche procedevano con estrema lentezza o non erano permesse da Roma, spesso con il deliberato proposito di ritardare la diffusione di quei libri."

23. See, for example, the letter (2 October 1603) from Cardinal Borghese to the inquisitor of Modena communicating the corrections prescribed by the Congregation of the Index for the recently published study of St. Thomas by the Jesuit Francisco Suarez: "Pertanto V.R. farà diligenza di raccogliere o da' librari o da altri, tutti i volumi del detto 4o tomo che in cotesta sua giurisditione si trovassero et gli corregga secondo la sopradetta forma et così corretti poi gli restituisca a' padroni, ordinando a gli stampatori et librari che, in caso si facesse di nuovo stampare, si debbono regolarsi secondo l'istessa correttione prescritta di sopra." See A. Rotondò, "Nuovi documenti," 179.

24. See the document cited in n. 21. Rome's answer to the Bolognese query

("Se si può havere tutte le correttioni fatte in Roma particolarmente di queste opere infrascritte . . .") is "Le correttioni de i libri fatte fin qui in Roma si daranno. Ben è vero che essendovene alcune longhe et bisognando tempo assai a ricavarle, saria bisogno di uno che non havesse altro da fare che rescriverle. . . ." See A. Rotondò, "Nuovi documenti," 164.

25. In several letters, as we have noted, the Florentine inquisitor is asked to send to Rome expurgations compiled in Florence.

26. See J. M. De Bujanda, "Censure romaine et censure espagnole au XVIe siècle: Les Index Romain et Espagnol de 1559," *Annuario dell'Istituto storico italiano per l'età moderna e contemporanea* 35–36 [1983–84]: 167–86. For a fuller bibliography on the subject of Spanish censorship, see by the same author, *Index de l'Inquisition Espagnole, 1551, 1554, 1559*, Index des Livres Interdits, 5 (Sherbrooke and Geneva, 1984). Cf. also A. Borromeo ("Inquisizione spagnola e libri proibiti in Sicilia ed in Sardegna durante il XVI secolo," *Annuario dell'Istituto storico italiano per l'età moderna e contemporanea* 35–36 [1983–84]: 219–71) who compares the direction and findings of recent research on the Spanish and Roman censorship machinery.

27. On the prohibition of Bodin's writings, see F. H. Reusch, *Der Index* 1:417, 537 and J. Hilgers, *Der Index*, 422, 521, 536 ff. More recently, see R. Crahay, "Jean Bodin devant la censure: La condamnation de la *République*," *Il pensiero politico* 14 (1981): 154–70; idem, *D'Erasme à Campanella* (Brussels, 1985), 132–55, "Controverses et censures religieuses à propos de la *République* de Jean Bodin"; L. Firpo, "Ancora sulla condanna di Bodin," ibid., 173–86. M. D'Addio (" 'Les six livres de la République' e il pensiero cattolico del Cinquecento in una lettera del Mons. Minuccio Minucci al Possevino," in *Medioevo e Rinascimento: Studi in onore di Bruno Nardi*, 2 vols. [Florence, 1955], 1:127–44) explains Bodin's condemnation in terms of affinities perceived between his thought and Machiavelli's. See also letter 5 and note.

28. Giulio Antonio Santorio (1532–1602), cardinal of Santa Severina, a senior member of the Congregation of the Inquisition in this period. He left us, among other writings, an autobiography cited in "Inquisitorial Sources and Their Uses" at n. 118.

29. There is no more than a passing reference to G. B. Pinelli in M. Giustiniani, *Gli scrittori liguri* (Rome, 1667), 340–42 and G. Tiraboschi, *Storia della letteratura italiana*, 8 vols. in 16 (Modena, 1787–94), 7, pt. 4: 1438. A. Oldoino (*Athenaeum Ligusticum, seu Syllabus Scriptorum Ligurum* [Perugia, 1680], 331) rates Pinelli's talents rather cautiously: ". . . quare inter aetatis nostrae summos poetas non ultimum obtinuit locum." And, similarly, C. Jannaco, *Il Seicento* (Milan, 1963), 377, includes him in a long string of "commediografi che si ricordano a titolo di documentazione."

The work which had aroused the ire of the cardinal is the *J. B. Pinelli Carminum liber primus (-tertius)* (Florence: Giunta, 1594). According to the *Short-Title Catalogue of Books Printed in Italy and of Italian Books Printed in Other Countries from 1465 to 1600 now in the British Museum* (London, 1958), 520, the colophon is dated 1593. Pinelli recalls this sorry episode in a later edition of his poetry, *Carminum Libri IIII ad Illustrissimum D.D. Iacobum Auriam* (Genoa, 1605), p. [3] of the dedication: "Tibi

haec nostra, Iacobe, prodeunt. O ne ingrata quae in vestibulo potissimum. Porto minima damus, verum tua. Tua arbos, tui fructus, in hisce quae potiora, tibi, aut tuis scripta. Florentino prelo superioribus annis expressa, ut reconcinnata, quae postmodo tui patris in laudes typis in patria commisimus, adnexa. Iam tibi coniunctim omnia quicquid hinc ablegatum, nostrum haud esto."

30. A note, probably in the Florentine inquisitor's hand, at the bottom of the page states (in my interpretation) that he has communicated the order to Giunta, the printer, who has promised to keep him informed of developments: "Et così esseguirà et me ne darà avviso."

Domenico Pinelli (1540–1611), a Genoese, was elected cardinal in 1586. He held the title of archbishop of Fermo and on several occasions served as legate to papal states.

31. The Index of Clement VIII is discussed in detail by F. H. Reusch, *Der Index* 1:532–49 and J. Hilgers, *Der Index*, 536–38. The full text of the Index is reprinted in Reusch, *Die Indices*, 524–78. The critical edition of the Clementine Index is scheduled for the series *Index des Livres Interdits*, vol. 10. The best modern account of the circumstances leading up to the revocation of the preceding Index is V. Frajese's "La revoca dell' 'Index' Sistino e la Curia romana (1588–1596)," *Nouvelles de la Republique des Lettres* 1 (1986): 15–49. See also U. Rozzo, "Dieci anni di censura libraria (1596–1605)," *Libri e documenti* 9 (1983): 43–61.

32. An important addition to the Clementine Index are the Instructions prepared for the use of persons responsible for the prohibition, expurgation, and printing of books: "Instructio eorum, qui libris tum prohibendis, tum expurgandis, tum etiam imprimendis diligentem ac fidelem, ut par est, operam sunt daturi." The text is published in Reusch, *Die Indices*, 529–35. An abridged English version of these Instructions is in H. Brown, *The Venetian Printing Press* (London, 1891), 144–47.

33. The ten "Regulae" drawn up by the Tridentine fathers and first published in the Index of Pius IV (1564) set down the guidelines for Roman policy in the control of printing and the prohibition of books. They are reprinted in Reusch, *Die Indices*, 247–51.

34. Agostino Valerio (d. 1606), Bishop of Verona, elevated to the cardinalate by Gregory XIII in 1583. See P. B. Gams, *Series Episcoporum Ecclesiae Catholicae*, 2nd ed. (Leipzig, 1931), 806; *Hierarchia Catholica Medii et Recentioris Aevi*, ed. G. van Gulik and C. Eubel (Munster, 1923), 3:331.

35. Simone Tagliavia d'Aragona (d. 1604), elected cardinal in 1584.

36. *Regula* 4 in Reusch, *Die Indices*, 248.

37. The Index of Pius IV prohibited the Talmud ("Thalmud Hebraeorum ejusque glossae, annotationes, interpretationes et expositiones omnes"), permitting it, however, if the name was deleted ("si tamen prodierint sine nomine Thalmud et sine injuriis et calumniis in religionem Christianam, tolerabuntur"). See Reusch, *Die Indices*, 279.

38. A special separate section in the Index of Clement VIII provides for the absolute prohibition "De Thalmud et aliis libris Hebraeorum." See Reusch, *Die Indices*, 536. See also n. 40 below. Clement VIII's Bull had been issued on 28 February

1593 "Contra Haebreos, tenentes legentesque libros Thalmudi, & alios hactenus damnatos, aut blasphemias, & contumelias in Deum, & Sanctos continentes," in C. Cocquelines, ed., *Bullarum, Privilegiorum ac Diplomatum Romanorum Pontificum Amplissima Collectio* (Rome, 1751), 5, pt.1: 428–29. See also W. Popper, *The Censorship of Hebrew Books* (New York, 1899; reprint, New York, 1968), 90 ff., and the apposite pages in P. F. Grendler, *The Roman Inquisition and the Venetian Press, 1540–1605* (Princeton, 1977). The reader is referred to this work for the recent bibliography.

39. See also n. 27 above. The original intention of Clement VIII's Index was to prohibit Bodin's *Daemonomania* wholly and the *De Republica* and *Methodus* until such time as they could be properly expurgated. See F. H. Reusch, *Die Indices*, 559. This conditional prohibition was made absolute for all of Bodin's works by a late addition to the Index (ibid., p. 537 and n. 40 below). The interdiction was later relaxed in the case of the *Methodus*. An expurgated version was authorized in the *Indicis Librorum Expurgandorum* issued at Rome in 1607 by the Master of the Sacred Palace, Giammaria Guanzelli of Brisighella. In the Bergamo 1608 edition, the expurgations to be applied to the *Methodus* occur at pp. 499–501. On this Index, see below at n. 46.

40. The last-minute corrections and revisions to the Index sent out with the present letter provided for the revision of Rules 4 and 9 in the Index of Pius IV, and the total prohibition of the Talmud, the writings of Bodin, and the Book of Magazor. These changes were included in subsequent editions of the Clementine Index as an *Observatio*. See F. H. Reusch, *Die Indices*, 536–37.

41. See n. 40.

42. These late revisions are explained in J. Hilgers, *Der Index*, 536–38.

43. S. De Renzi, *Storia della medicina in Italia* (Naples, 1845), 3:577. Cf. G. Veneroso, *Risposta alla querela sotto nome di 'Difesa intorno allo sputo di sangue'* (Ferrara, 1597).

44. The responsibility of bishop and inquisitor in the proper licensing of a book for the press is the subject of paragraph 5 under the rubric "De impressione librorum" in the *Instructio* introduced in the Clementine Index. See F. H. Reusch, *Die Indices*, 535.

45. Paragraph 2 under the rubric "De impressione librorum" of the *Instructio*. See F. H. Reusch, *Die Indices*, 534.

46. The Roman Church finally brought out one volume of this Index: *Indicis Librorum Expurgandorum in studiosorum gratiam confecti: Tomus primus in quo quinquaginta auctorum libri prae ceteris desiderati emendantur. Per Fr. Jo. Mariam Brasichellen. Sacri Palatii Apostolici Magistrum in unum corpus redactus, et publicae commoditati aeditus* (Rome, 1607). It was reprinted in Bergamo the following year, twice in the eighteenth and once in the nineteenth century. Nothing, beyond the first volume, was published. Bodin, as we have seen (n. 39), was among the expurgated authors. See Reusch, *Der Index* 1:549–59. The Spanish Inquisition was more successful in issuing Indices with expurgations. See, for example, *Tres Indices Expurgatorios de la Inquisición Española en el Siglo XVI* (Madrid, 1952).

47. See above pp. 311 f.

48. Guido Panciroli (b. Reggio Emilia, 1523- d. Padua or Venice, 1599) was a distinguished jurist who taught successively at Bologna, Padua, and Turin. The *Rerum Memorabilium*, an encyclopedia of technology from antiquity to modern times, was first condemned by an edict issued at Rome by the Master of the Sacred Palace on 2 May 1601. See J. Hilgers, *Der Index*, 418.

The editor, Heinrich Salmuth, was a jurist and syndic of Amberg, son of the homonymous Lutheran theologian. See C. G. Jöcher, *Allgemeines Gelehrtenlexicon* (Leipzig, 1751), 4: col. 70. Salmuth's commentary occupies a much larger part of the *Rerum Memorabilium* than Panciroli's text. It would have been found objectionable by the censors for numerous complimentary references to such heretics and condemned authors as Melanchthon, Bodin, Joachim and Philipp Camerarius; and for quoting such a statement as Melanchthon's that printing could be considered a divine gift, coming as it did at a time "ut renascentis in Ecclesia sincerioris doctrinae" (p. 591). I have consulted the second edition (Amberg, 1608).

49. The condemnation of the *Ecloga* was contained in the edict published at Rome on 1 June 1601. See J. Hilgers, *Der Index*, 418. Thomas James (1573?–1629) was the Bodleian's first librarian, and the present work is nothing more dangerous than a listing of the books and manuscripts at Oxford and Cambridge. One wonders whether Rome knew that earlier James had brought out a translation into English of *La Cantica di Salomò* by the suspected heretic Antonio Brucioli (*Commentary upon the Canticle of Canticles* [London, 1598]). James went on to publish several anti-Catholic works, including a counterfeit edition of the Roman Index. His purpose was to draw attention to books which deserved special consideration because their survival was threatened by censorship: *Index Generalis Librorum Prohibitorum a Pontificiis, una cum editionibus expurgatis vel expurgandis . . . in usum Bibliothecae Bodleianae . . . designatus per Tho. Iames . . .* (Oxford, 1627). The work is not listed in G. Bonnant, "Les Index Prohibitifs et Expurgatoires contrefaits par des protestants au XVIe et au XVIIe siècle," *Bibliothèque d'Humanisme et Renaissance* 31 (1969): 611–40. See *Dictionary of National Biography* 10:658–60.

50. The writings of the Belgian Jesuit, Thomas Sailly (b. 1558) are listed in C. Sommervogel, *Bibliothèque de la Compagnie de Jésus . . . nouvelle édition* (Brussels and Paris, 1896), 7: cols. 403–7. The *Thesaurus Litaniarum ac Orationum Sacer. Cum suis adversus Sectarios Apologiis Opera P. Thomae Sailly Presbyteri Societatis Jesu editus* (Brussels, 1598) is no. 7 in his catalogue. Sommervogel notes: "Cet ouvrage a été mis à l'Index, le 7 août 1603, à cause de certaines litanies non approuvées." Cf. A. de Backer, *Bibliothèque des écrivains de la Compagnie de Jesus: Supplément* (Louvain and Lyons, 1876), 3: cols. 469–72, esp. 470: ". . . c'est qu'on a jugé à propos de s'en tenir aux litanies anciennes, qui se trouvent dans le Bréviaire, et autres livres qui servent à l'office de l'Eglise." In his *Thesaurus Precum et Exercitiorum Spiritualium* (Antwerp, 1609), p. [4] of preface, Sailly explains that the objectionable litanies in the earlier version had been inserted without his knowledge.

51. It is unlikely that this is also by Sailly. Neither de Backer nor Sommervogel attributes to him a work with this title. And the decree issued at Rome, 7 August

1603, prohibiting the *Thesaurus Sacrarum Pretium* lists it as an anonymous writing. This and similar decrees are published as an appendix to the *Index Librorum Prohibitorum Alexandri VII . . . iussu editus* (Rome, 1664), 295.

52. Clement VIII's *Breve, Cum in Ecclesia*, introducing the revised Roman Breviary was issued on 10 May 1602. See J. Hilgers, *Die Bücherverbote in Papstbriefen* (Freiburg i. Br., 1907), 20.

53. A portion of an identical letter sent to the inquisitor of Modena is published by A. Rotondò, "Nuovi documenti," 173. According to L. Cerri (*Memorie per la storia letteraria di Piacenza in continuazione al Poggiali* [Piacenza, 1895], 176 f.), Pietra was compelled to appear personally before the Roman Inquisition to answer charges arising from his book, which was burned in his presence. Due to his advanced age (in 1599 he would have been 87 years old according to Cerri) he was condemned only to salutary penances. Without having seen a copy of Pietra's treatise, it is impossible to identify the "propositioni hereticali" which led to its condemnation. Cerri merely informs us that Pietra had addressed himself to the problem of the relationship of a prince to the private property of his subjects. Rome did not attempt to enforce the prohibition in Venice. See P. F. Grendler, *The Roman Inquisition*, 275. For the printer, Damiano Zenaro, this was not the first time that one of his books was confiscated and burned. See G. Pesenti, "Libri censurati a Venezia nei secoli XVI-XVII," *La Bibliofilia* 58 (1956): 27, and Grendler, op. cit., 167.

54. One of them subscribed with these words: "Io Cosimo Giunti ho ricevuto la retroscritta notificatione sotto pena del Arbitrio questo dì detto [11 July 1601]. In botega ce ne uno quale si è consegniato al Padre Inquisitore."

55. See F. H. Reusch, *Der Index* 2:73.

56. The forgery of Lyons on the titlepages of books actually published in Geneva was a practice which infuriated French printers and resulted in a number of royal proclamations intended to check this illicit practice. By the substitution of imprints, Geneva's printers obviously hoped to obtain a freer circulation for their merchandise in Catholic Europe. Antoine Blanc, formerly of Lyons, who was received as *Bourgeois* of Geneva in 1585, frequently employed this device, as when, for example, he printed the *Catalogus Testium Veritatis, qui ante nostram aetatem Pontifici Romano atque papismi erroribus reclamarunt . . .* MDXCVII Ex typographia Antonii Candidi, Lugdun. See, on this whole subject, J. Baudrier, *Bibliographie Lyonnaise* (Lyons and Paris, 1921), 12:468–500. Some of the Bibles mentioned in the present letter may have been Italian translations. The question of vernacular Scriptures is discussed by A. Del Col, "Appunti per una indagine sulle traduzioni in volgare della Bibbia nel Cinquecento italiano," in *Libri, idee, e sentimenti religiosi* (Modena and Ferrara, 1987), 165–88 and F. Barberi, "Le edizioni della Bibbia in Italia nei secoli XV e XVI," *Bergomum* 78 (1984), nos. 1–2: 3–20. On the production of books in Geneva for an Italian market, see G. Bonnant, "La librairie genevoise en Italie, jusqu'à la fin du XVIIIe siècle," *Genava* 15 (1967): 117–60; Enea Balmas, "L'activité des imprimeurs italiens réfugiés à Genève dans la deuxième moitié du XVI siècle," in J.-D. Candaux and B. Lescaze, eds., *Cinq siècles d'imprimerie genevoise: Actes du Colloque inter-*

national sur l'histoire de l'imprimerie et du livre à Genève, 27–30 avril 1978, 2 vols. (Geneva, 1980), 1:109–31; T. Bozza, "Italia calvinista. Traduzioni italiane di Calvino nel secolo XVI," in *Miscellanea in onore di Ruggero Moscati* (Naples, 1985), 237–51, and the bibliography cited in "Northern Books," esp. n. 12.

57. The edict of condemnation was issued in Rome on 14 December 1602. See J. Hilgers, *Der Index*, 418. The *Catalogue* of printed books in the British Museum (164: col. 646) lists *I tre giardini de' Madrigali del Costante, Academico Cospirante, M. Moro vinetiano* (Venice, 1602). That Moro was in sacred orders results from the title of another book, *Rappresentatione del figliuolo prodigo del Rev. P. D. Mauritio Moro, novamente dal detto in ottava rima composta* (Venice, 1585). There is only a passing reference to our author in L. Ughi, *Dizionario storico degli uomini illustri ferraresi* (Ferrara, 1804), 2:80.

58. The *Praxi Episcopale* was condemned by an edict issued on 14 December 1602. See J. Hilgers, *Der Index*, 418. The two parts which comprise the book originally appeared separately, in 1595 and 1598, and subsequently as one work in 1599 and 1602. See G. Sbaraglia, *Supplementum et castigatio ad scriptores trium ordinum S. Francisci, A. Waddingo aliisve descriptos* (Rome, 1936), 3:140. Zerola served as Bishop of Minori from 1597 until his death in 1603. See P. B. Gams, *Series Episcoporum Ecclesiae Catholicae*, 898.

59. There is a note at the bottom of the letter, presumably in the hand of the Florentine inquisitor, which reads: "Alli 3 di Gennaio 1603 si pubblicorno gli editti della prohibitione delli 2 sopradetti libri per la città, et per lo stato alli Vicarii del S.to Offitio."

60. See also nn. 14 and 15 above. This certainly is one of the more obscure Florentine academies. Its existence is not recorded in E. Cochrane, *Tradition and Enlightenment in the Tuscan Academies* (Chicago, 1961); idem, *Florence in the Forgotten Centuries, 1527–1800* (Chicago, 1973); or by G. Prezziner, *Storia del pubblico Studio e delle società scientifiche e letterarie di Firenze*, 2 vols. (Florence, 1810). M. Maylender (*Storia delle Accademie d'Italia* [Bologna, 1930], 5:237–38) cites a document "I Capitoli riformati degli Accademici Spensierati col parere dell'Accademia delli Conservadori, l'anno 1607," preserved in the Biblioteca Nazionale, Florence (Cod. Cl. VI, no. 163); and he furnishes the names of three Spensierati: the poet Pier Girolamo Gentile (1563–1640), the jurist Fabbrizio Mattei of Forlì, and P. A. Canonieri. E. Benvenuti published "Un curioso manifesto satira degli Accademici Spensierati," *Rivista delle biblioteche e degli archivi* 22 (1911): 15–17 and describes the academy as "il prodotto più genuino di quello scetticismo e di quell'umorismo che nacque, si puo dire, con gli spiriti bizzarri fiorentini" (p. 15). One wonders what part, if any, was played by Pietro Andrea Canonieri, a leading exponent of "Tacitism" and the *Ragion di Stato*, in the Spensierati's proposal to prepare an expurgated edition of Machiavelli's writings. *Tacitismo* has been defined succinctly as "uno sforzo di controriformizzare il pensiero di Machiavelli." See G. Toffanin, *Machiavelli e il Tacitismo* (Padua, 1921), 6.

61. The present letter is not part of the "Index" group and is preserved in a different volume. I omit the remaining paragraph because it is off the subject.

62. Camillo Borghese (1552–1621), elected Pope Paul V in 1605. Curiously, there is no entry for him in the *DBI*, which does take into consideration, however, his cousin, also a cardinal, similarly named Camillo Borghese (d. 1612).

63. Pompeo Arrigoni (1552–1616), elevated to the College of Cardinals in June 1596. See *DBI* 4:320–21.

64. The edict against Venice was issued on 27 June. Its contents are summarized in a second proclamation of 20 September ("fuerint expresse prohibiti nonnulli libelli, & scripturae typis mandatae, & evulgatae, occasione censurarum, & interdicti S.D.N in Rempublicam Venetam") published as an appendix to the *Index* of Alexander VII (p. 299; cited in full at n. 51). A. Rotondò ("Nuovi documenti," 183) mentions the existence of two copies of the rare 27 June edict in the Archivio di Stato, Modena.

65. The edict of 27 June.

66. The edict of 20 September (see n. 64 above) prohibited books hostile to the papacy and siding with Venice which had appeared since the publication of the decree of 27 June.

INDEX
Librorū Prohibitor.
BENEDICTI XIV P.O.M.
jussu editus

Gioan Fabri Inc.

Multi eorum, qui fuerant curiosa
sectati, contulerunt Libros, et
combuserunt coram omnibus.
Act. Cap. XIX. V. 19.

The 1758 *Index* of Benedict XIV. [From the author's collection.]

TEN

❧

A Sixteenth-Century Italian Erasmian and the Index

The text which is published below is intended as a footnote to the rapidly unfolding account of one of the more controversial aspects of Roman policy in the second half of the sixteenth century: the censorship of the book. In modern times the broad outlines of the story have been dealt with magisterially by Antonio Rotondò.[1] Paul Grendler and Pasquale Lopez have probed the question in detail within the circumscribed and probably atypical contexts of the Venetian Republic and the *Vicereg-no* respectively.[2] J. M. De Bujanda and his Sherbrooke team, in preparing critical editions of all sixteenth-century Indices of Prohibited Books, are engaged in a historico-bibliographical project of Herculean proportions that is advancing the state of our knowledge profoundly.[3] Nevertheless, much work remains to be done; the impact of ecclesiastical censorship on Italian culture and learning is difficult to measure and remains a hotly contested question. A partial answer to this and related problems is offered by the surviving records of the disciplinary bodies entrusted with the tasks of molding and implementing the censorship policy, namely the Congregations of the Index and of the Holy Office.

The official decrees and other records of the deliberations of the Index were transferred to the palace of the Holy Office in 1917 and, consequently, are inaccessible.[4] Pertinent material, however, is available elsewhere, among the "dispersed archives" of the Roman and outlying inquisitions now in foreign as well as in Italian libraries and archives.[5]

The document which I publish here is the sentence pronounced on 31 July 1580[6] by the bishop of Campagna and Satriano, Geronimo Scarampo,[7] against an obscure schoolmaster of Campagna, a certain Angelo Mazza,[8] convicted of possessing prohibited books.[9] Campagna, situated about twenty miles to the east of Salerno and an even shorter distance from Eboli, a name that has become associated with what is God-forsaken on earth, was not a wholly isolated provincial backwater in the sixteenth century. It was the site of several monasteries and convents, including San Bartolomeo, a Dominican house. It was here, early in 1572, that Giordano Bruno, then twenty-four years of age, celebrated his first Mass after being ordained to the priesthood by Bishop Scarampo. A *Monte*, a hospital, a printing establishment or two, and some minuscule academies, which replaced as centers of organized intellectual life a short-lived *Studio*, also flourished in the town. Several noble families had ancestral roots there; and it was the birthplace of such literary figures as Giulio Cesare Capaccio and Marco Fileto Filioli. Census and tax records for the year 1561 reveal the existence of seven hundred eighty-five hearths (*fuochi*).[10]

Ordinarily, the case against Mazza, involving as it did the suspicion of heresy, would have been heard before an inquisitorial tribunal. But the Holy Office was barred from publicly exercising its functions in Neapolitan territory. In those instances where the extradition to Rome of a suspect could not be arranged or was not deemed necessary, the preservation of the faith rested in the hands of the episcopal courts. The Congregation of the Inquisition in Rome would be kept informed of developments and, invariably, directed each step of the investigation and of the subsequent judicial proceedings. Occasionally, a bishop's vicar might serve as the disguised representative of the Inquisition in an episcopal curia, a role for which Jesuits were deemed well-suited.[11] These practices are confirmed by the present document, which is a copy of the sentence pronounced in Campagna prepared for the use of the Holy Office in Rome.[12] It is now preserved at Trinity College, Dublin among the hundreds of other sentences issued by inquisitorial tribunals.

Angelo Mazza was tried on three separate charges: first, of having dictated obscene and lascivious Latin passages to his students;[13] second, of having possessed pedagogical and lexical works by such forbidden authors as Erasmus, Melanchthon, Robert Estienne, Celio Secondo Curione, and

Johann Rivius; third, of having prepared a sacrilegious and superstitious composition in the company of a converted Jew.

The penalties imposed by the court can also be subsumed under three categories: the obscene passages were to be publicly burned in the cathedral square in the presence of the populace and with a bare-headed and penitent Mazza in attendance; the books had to be surrendered to the custody of the court; and, in addition to the usual salutary penances prescribing the strict observance of a rigorous schedule of religious devotions, he was ordered to receive each year, for as long as he remained in Campagna, three of the poorest children in the town for free instruction in his school; and he was to attend to them with the same diligence that he would employ in behalf of any tuition-paying student. What the bishop took away from the cause of learning with one hand, he was attempting to restore with the other.

The confiscated books were of two general categories. Curione's edition of Mario Nizolio's *Observationes omnia M.T. Ciceronis verba*[14] and Robert Estienne's *Thesaurus linguae latinae*[15] were to be censored in accordance with the provisions of the Tridentine Index of Prohibited Books published by Pius IV in 1564, and then restored to their owner. The ten *Regulae* which made their first appearance in this compilation established the possibility for the circulation of literature on non-religious subjects by heretical authors after its expurgation.[16] Censorship would entail the inking out of the heretical editors' names wherever they appeared in the volumes and the deletion of any questionable words or phrases from the prefatory and dedicatory material. Both Curione and Estienne were listed in the Index as "auctores primae classis." This was the designation for authors whose *opera omnia* were forbidden,[17] although lexicons and books on non-controversial subjects by them could be permitted after expurgation.[18]

As for the remaining books, the court proposed a more cautious course. They were to be consigned to the place "where the other unexpurgated suspected books are kept" until a proper decision about them could be reached. The titles in question—such famous schoolbooks as Erasmus's *De duplici copia rerum*[19] and *De conscribendis epistolis*,[20] Melanchthon's edition of Cicero's *Offices*,[21] among others—were not really less innocuous in subject matter than the two great Latin dictionaries restored to their owner. But the names of Melanchthon and Erasmus were anathema in Italy. Because the former was designated as a heresiarch, all of his books, even those furthest from religious concerns, would be forbidden.[22] The Tridentine Index had retreated a step from the total prohibition of the writings of Erasmus decreed by Paul IV.[23] The name of the great humanist now appeared in the second class of forbidden authors, "certorum auctorum libri prohibiti," signifying that the prohibition was reserved for only certain of his books, among them the *Colloquia* and the *Moriae encomium*.[24] In theory a title that was not expressly banned might be retained after proper expurgation. In actual practice it is doubtful, in the face of

[Sentence Against Angelo Mazza]

Copia

Noi Geronimo Scarampo, per gratia di Iddio et della S.ta Sede Apostolica vescovo di Campagna et Satriano, per questa nostra diffinitiva sententia, overo che ha forza di diffinitiva nella causa et cause tra il Reverendo Promotore et Fiscale della nostra corte vescovale, et nostra corte attrice da una parte; et Angelo Mazza della città di Campagna, mastro di scola publico accusato, diffirito, et imputato et reo convento sopra la sporcità et oscenità et dishonestà di alcuni latini, o frasi o dittati, dati a suoi scolari, et dettentione di alcuni libri di humanità con apostile, prohemii, prefationi, notationi di Erasmo, di Philippo Malantone, di Celio Secondo [Curione] et di Roberto Stefano rispettivamente, et di havere cercato per instructione da uno Hebreo fatto Cristiano capitato qui in Campagna di fare per secreto qualche arte una sacrilega et superstitiosa compositione, da l'altra parte.

In prima instantia che vertano, et sono versate di consiglio di periti, invocato il nome santissimo di Cristo et sedendo per tribunali, et havendo solo Iddio innanzi alli occhi, dicemo, dicernemo, dichiaramo et sententiamo: quanto al capo di Latini sporchi che quelli innanzi alla chiesa Catedrale in presentia dil popolo et in conspetto di esso presente, senza barretta humilmente tacito et penitente, ditto Angelo Mazza vidente et patiente, si debbano abrusciare talmente che da tutti gli circumspectanti si vedano combusti, et ditto Angelo diversi obligare publicamente et palesemente ancho in foglio sotto scritto di sua mano et penis alla Curia di mai incorrere in simili errori, ma astinersene in perpetuo. Anzi, sempre dare Latini

the ecclesiastical hostility reserved for Erasmus,[25] the continuing confusion about his acceptability,[26] and, especially, the enormous task of reviewing the ever-growing number of suspended books, that many Erasmian items would be permitted to circulate.[27]

In transcribing the manuscript, I have retained the original spelling but have modernized the punctuation slightly and have introduced accents. Doubtful readings are followed by question marks enclosed within square brackets. Ellipses indicate illegible words.

Copy

I Geronimo Scarampo, by the grace of God and of the Holy Apostolic see bishop of Campagna and Satriano, by this our conclusive sentence, which has definitive force in the case and cases between the Reverend Prosecutor and Fiscal of our episcopal court, and our court acting as one party; and, as the other, Angelo Mazza of the city of Campagna, public school teacher, accused, arraigned, and convicted over the filth, obscenity, and dishonesty of some Latin phrases and dictations given to his students, and also accused of possessing certain books in the humanities with commentaries, preambles, prefaces and notes by Erasmus, Philipp Melanchthon, Celio Secondo [Curione], and Robert Stephanus, respectively; and also of having attempted, instructed by a Jew turned Christian who appeared here in Campagna, to compose a sacrilegious and superstitious writing through some secret art.

In the first instance which is a matter of controversy and has occupied the opinion of the experts, after invoking the most holy name of Christ, constituted as a tribunal, and with God alone before our eyes, we say, make clear, declare, and sentence, as follows: in regard to the charge of the dirty Latin verses, they are to be burned in the sight of all those assembled in front of the Cathedral church in the presence of all the people and in the sight of Angelo Mazza, hatless, humbly silent and penitent. And the above named Angelo must oblige himself publicly and openly, even in a document subscribed to in his own hand and in the possession of the court, never to fall into similar errors, but to refrain *in perpetuo*.

epistole et exercitationi di lingua Latina ad suoi scolari, dittare, scrivere et componere cose honeste et approbate dalla Cristiana religione et lontane da ogni oscenità et lascivia sotto le pene infrascritte. Et di più per penitentia salutare legere ogni sexta feria mentre starà mastro di scola in questa nostra città o diocese la dottrina Cristiana nella sua scola publicamente a suoi scolari, et explicarla ad loro fidelmente et cattolicamente secondo la capacità di essi et insegnarla come si deve con ogni diligentia. Et di più per uno anno continuo nelli istessi giorni di sexta feria digionare conforme al rito et costume di digiunarsi secondo la forma di S.ta Chiesa, et in quelli istessi giorni dire li sette salmi penitentiali devotamente come conviene, *flexis genibus*, et andare sempre che si predica in detta città ad odire le prediche, et quando serà in esso costrengere anco li suoi scolari andarci.

Quanto al capo de' libri per hora dichiaramo sin' a nuova dispositione che si restituiscano a ditto Angelo, Mario Nizolio sopra Cicerone che chiamano le *Osservationi*, cassato prima il nome di Celio Secondo che fa la Epistola prohemiale, et quella revista che non vi sia cosa prohibita; et anco il *Thesoro della lingua latina* con l'Epistola a' lettori di Roberto Stefano, parimente scancellato il nome e revista non esservi cosa che non si debbia permettere. Et li altri libri, cioè la *Parafrasi* di Erasmo sopra le *Eleganze* di Laurenso Valla,[28] la *Sphera* di Sacro Busco con la prefatione di Malantone,[29] uno libretto delle Interpretationi di Erasmo sopra li versi di Catone,[30] Erasmo *De copia verborum* dupplicato, et *De conscribendis epistolis*, Marco Tullio *De Officiis* con la addicione di Philippo Malantone et di altri, et le *Epistole famigliari* del medesmo con le annotationi di Erasmo et di Giovanni Rivio Attendoriense,[31] dichiaramo et decernimo che si debano consignare dove si tengano li altri suspetti libri non expurgati sino che da noi si delibererà quello che se ne haverà da fare.

Et per penitentia salutare ordiniamo che ditto Angelo sia tenuto ogni anno nel giorno della festività della S.ma Natività della gloriosa Vergine titulo della chiesa nostra Catedrale di Campagna comparire innanzi ad noi o ad nostro vicario mentre ditto Angelo starà in Campagna et dare [?] la lista di tutti li suoi libri; et equalmente [?] si debia obligare et così sia obligato non comparare, non tenere, ne legere libri suspetti, ne lascivi, ne osceni, nonche hereticali. Et di più havere appresso di se l'Indice delli Libri Prohibiti acciò non si possa excusare di ignoranza. Et di più che sia

On the contrary, always to give Latin epistles and exercises in the Latin language to his pupils, dictate, write, and compose things that are honest and approved by the Christian religion and far removed from all obscenity and lasciviousness, subject to the penalties below. And, in addition, as a salutary penance, to read every Friday as long as he shall be schoolmaster in this city or diocese of ours, the Christian doctrine publicly to his pupils in his school, and explicate it to them faithfully and in the Catholic way on a level with their capacity, and teach it with utmost diligence as one ought. In addition, for a year continuously on the same Fridays he must fast in accordance with the rites and customs of fasting observed by the Holy Church, and in those days recite the seven penitential psalms devoutly, as is proper, on his knees, and go whenever a preacher visits the city to hear his sermons, and also compell his students to attend.

As for the charge concerning the books, we declare until we dispose differently that the following should be returned to the aforenamed Angelo: Mario Nizolio on Cicero entitled the *Osservationi*, after expunging the name of Celio Secondo who wrote the prefatory Epistle, and reviewing it to see that it contains nothing prohibited; and also the *Thesoro della lingua latina* with the Epistle to readers by Robert Stephanus, with the name similarly erased, and reread to see that it contains nothing that cannot be permitted. And as for the other books, namely the *Parafrasi* of Erasmus on the *Eleganze* of Lorenzo Valla, the *Sphera* of Sacrobosco with the preface by Melanchthon, a booklet of interpretations by Erasmus on the poetry of Cato, Erasmus's *De copia verborum* duplicated and *De conscribendis epistolis*, Marcus Tully, *De officiis* with additions by Philipp Melanchthon and others, and the *Epistole famigliari* by the same person with the annotations of Erasmus and of Giovanni Rivius Attendoriensis, we declare and decree that they must be consigned to the place where the other unexpurgated suspected books are kept until such a time as we decide what shall be done with them.

As for a salutary penance, we order that the aforesaid Angelo be obliged each year on the day of the celebration of the Most Holy Nativity of the glorious Virgin protectress of our Cathedral of Campagna to appear before us or our vicar as long as the aforenamed Angelo shall remain in Campagna and present the list of all his books; and, equally, he must agree to and be obliged not to purchase, possess, or read books that are suspect, lascivious, obscene, or heretical. And, moreover, to keep the Index of Prohibited Books so that he will not be able to plead ignorance

obligato ad insegnare a tre delli più poveri della città di Campagna, scolari da deputarsi o elegersi o confirmarsi ogni anno dalli Magnifici Signori loro, et eletti *per tempore servando* mentre ditto Angelo tenerà scola in la ditta città di Campagna gratis et *Amor Dei* senza premio alcuno. Et ad quelli attenderà con la diligenza che fa ad qualsivoglia altro scolaro che paghi pene. Et questa penitentia anchora serà in proposito di sodisfactione dil primo capo. Circa al terzo capo di quella mistura abominevole et diabolica inventione et soprastitione ... decernemo et dichiaramo non costare sufficientemente da quello sin'hora dedutto innanzi. Et però ditto Angelo sia tenuto ad obligarsi et si oblighi di se representando ad ogni monito nostro et di nostra corte sotto pena et con pena dil delitto confessato, privatione perpetua di scola, et perpetua infamia et scommonica, senza altra dichiaratione ipso fatto di incorrersi et ducati ducento applicarsi allo S.to Officio della Inquisitione di Roma, di qual debia oltra sua obligatione dare idonea plegiaria parimente da incorersi senza altra nova dichiaratione. Et così fatta questa obligatione et data detta sicurità permanente lo licentiamo dalle carceri assignate che possa questi [?] tenere scola insegnando como li conviene, abstenendosi dalle cose supra scritte. Et così li diamo licentia et ordinamento che non sia molestato non obstante li nostri ordinamenti [?] et di nostra corte et moniti [?] passati, et così dicemo, sententiamo, decernemo et dichiaramo con questo et ogni altro meglior modo.[32]

as an excuse. In addition, he will be obliged to teach three of the poorest in the city of Campagna, pupils to be chosen, elected, or confirmed each year by the Magnificent Governors, and selected *per tempore servando* as long as the above named Angelo keeps his school in the city of Campagna, free and for the love of God without charges of any kind; and he will attend to them with the same diligence he would show to any other tuition-paying student. This penance will be applied also toward the satisfaction of the first charge. As for the third count, which concerns that abominable medley and diabolical invention and superstition . . . we decree and declare that we are not sufficiently informed from the evidence that is before us. In conclusion, the aforenamed Angelo is obligated and must oblige himself to present himself at any summons of ours and of our court under penalty and with the penalty of the crime confessed, perpetual deprivation of his school, and perpetual infamy and excommunication, without further proceedings required and a fine of two hundred ducats to be paid to the Holy Office of the Inquisition in Rome, of which [sum] he must in addition to his obligation furnish a suitable surety equally to be forfeited without further new proceedings. And after he has fulfilled this obligation and given this permanent security we release him from the prison assigned to him so that he can run his school, teaching as is proper, and abstaining from the things described above. Thus we give license and order that he not be disturbed further despite past injunctions of ours and of our court, and thus we state, sentence, decree and declare with this and any other suitable device.

Notes

1. "La censura ecclesiastica e la cultura," in *Storia d'Italia* (Turin: Einaudi, 1973), 5, pt. 2: 1399–1492. For the pertinent bibliography I refer the reader to this study and to "Florentine Documents" at pp. 273-319 in this volume.

2. P. F. Grendler, *The Roman Inquisition and the Venetian Press, 1540–1605* (Princeton, 1977); P. Lopez, *Inquisizione, stampa, e censura nel Regno di Napoli tra '500 e '600* (Naples, 1974).

3. The publication of eleven volumes is contemplated in the series *Index des Livres Interdits*, including Indices from the Low Countries, France, Germany, Italy, Portugal, and Spain.

4. An indication of the contents is furnished by L. Firpo, "Filosofia italiana e Controriforma," *Rivista di filosofia* 41 (1950): 150–73, 390–401; 42 (1951): 30–47 and by S. M. Pagano, *I documenti del processo di Galileo Galilei* (Vatican City, 1984). Both scholars were permitted entrance to the Archive of the Holy Office.

5. See "The Dispersed Archives of the Roman Inquisition," pp. 23–45 in this volume.

6. The sentence is preserved at Trinity College, Dublin: MS. 1225, fols. 253–57. On the provenance and contents of the Trinity collection of inquisitorial documents, see "The Dispersed Archives of the Roman Inquisition," esp. pp. 25–26.

7. Scarampo (d. 1584) reigned over the see of Campagna and Satriano, 1571–83. He was a doctor in both branches of the law. See P. B. Gams, *Series Episcoporum Ecclesiae Catholicae*, 2nd ed. (Leipzig, 1931), 865; G. Moroni, *Dizionario di erudizione storico-ecclesiastica* (Venice, 1853), 61: 289; F. Ughelli, *Italia Sacra*, 2nd ed. (Venice, 1721), 7:458.

8. I have not found him mentioned in the literature cited at n. 10 below or in such bio-bibliographies of the region as N. Toppi's *Biblioteca napoletana et apparato a gli huomini illustri in lettere di Napoli e del Regno* (Naples, 1678), where several names of *literati* who resided in Campagna are encountered.

9. The evidence presented here should be integrated with similar data in C. De Frede, "Roghi di libri ereticali nell'Italia del Cinquecento," in *Ricerche storiche ed economiche in memoria di Corrado Barbagallo* (Naples, 1970), 2:315–28. See at p. 325: "Anche nei centri minori d'Italia e nelle lontane province del Regno di Napoli furono attuati sequestri e imposti roghi per distruggere il materiale eretico." De Frede's earlier articles on the circulation of the heretical book in Italy (with special emphasis on Naples) are cited in his "Roghi." A list of books compiled for the use of the Inquisition (12 January 1565) possessed by the Neapolitan bookseller Battista Cappello contained many pedagogical works by Erasmus, including several copies of the *De conscribendis epistolis* and the *De copia verborum*, writings owned by Mazza. See S. Bongi, *Annali di Gabriel Giolito de' Ferrari da Trino di Monferrato stampatore in Venezia* (Rome, 1890), 1:lxxxv–cix. For the bibliography on Erasmus in Italy, see nn. 25 ff. below.

10. E. Bacco, *Breve descrittione del Regno di Napoli diviso in dodeci provincie* (Naples,

1644), 154–57; G. Fumagalli, *Lexicon Typographicum Italiae* (Florence, 1905; reprint with supplements 1966), 60–61; L. Giustiniani, *Saggio storico-critico sulla tipografia del Regno di Napoli* (Naples, 1793), 152–53; idem, *La biblioteca storica e topografica del Regno di Napoli* (Naples, 1793), 26–27; idem, *Dizionario geografico-ragionato del Regno di Napoli* (Naples, 1797), 3:49–54; M. Maylender, *Storia delle Accademie d'Italia*, 5 vols. (Bologna, 1927–30), 2:206, 244; 5:290; V. Spampanato, *Documenti della vita di Giordano Bruno* (Florence, 1933), 80; G. Aquilecchia, *Giordano Bruno* (Rome, 1971), 7. Unfortunately, I have not been able to consult the following: A. Sanfelice, *Campania* (Naples, 1562); N. de Nigris, *Campagna antica e moderna, sacra e profana, overo compendiosa istoria della città di Campagna* (Naples, 1691); A. Rivelli, *Memorie storiche della città di Campagna* (Salerno, 1894); G. Lamattina, *Manoscritti inediti e relazioni ad limina della diocesi di Satriano-Campagna (sec. XVI–XVII)* (Pompeii, 1988).

11. Indiscreet talk by the vicar of the archbishop of Naples concerning his role as agent of the Inquisition brought remonstrances from the viceroy and embarrassment to Rome. See the letter from the nuncio in Naples, Antonio Sauli, to Tolomei Galli, the Cardinal Secretary of State, in P. Villani, ed., *Nunziature di Napoli* (Rome, 1962), 1:188: "Hier mattina mons. ill.mo Granvela viceré mi fece una gagliarda querela del vicario di mons. arcivescovo di Napoli et mi fece più volte instanza che lo dovessi far sapere a S.S.tà. Lamentasi S.S. Ill.ma, dicendo che di ciò glie ne siano state fatte querele da più parte, che detto vicario s'habbia lasciato uscir di bocca più volte, che esso è stato posto in questo loco dal Santo Officio della Inquisitione di Roma, dalle qual parole ne potria un giorno succedere qualche gran scandolo essendo in questa città et regno tanto abhorrito questo nome d'Inquisitione, come ben sa ognuno per li rumori passati." M. Scaduto ("Tra inquisitori e riformati, le missioni dei Gesuiti tra Valdesi della Calabria e delle Puglie, con un carteggio inedito del Card. Alessandrino [S.Pio V] [1561–1566]," *Archivum Historicum Societatis Iesu* 15 [1946]: 1–76, at p. 54) publishes the instructions of the cardinal inquisitor Ghislieri to the Jesuit Christophoro Rodriguez, about to embark on a mission to the south (19 April 1564): "Le patenti [confirming Rodriguez as a commissioner of the Roman Inquisition] non si mandano, perché il signore viceré non vuole che noi mandiamo comisario alcuno, ma che li ordinarii siano aiutati da qualche persona da bene, che habbi qualche cognitione et zelo della religione catholica; et per questo, tutto quello che V.R. haverà da fare, lo farà sotto ombra e nome delli ordinarii, osservandosi però le regole sudette che li furono date per la Voltorara." On the problems connected with studying the operations of the Holy Office in Neapolitan territory, see G. Romeo, "Per la storia del Sant'Ufficio a Napoli tra '500 e '600: Documenti e problemi," *Campania sacra* 7 (1976): 5–109 and "Una città, due Inquisizioni: L'anomalia del Sant'Ufficio a Napoli nel tardo '500," *Rivista di storia e letteratura religiosa* 24 (1988): 42–67. The question of episcopal and inquisitorial jurisdictions is treated in A. Borromeo, "Contributo allo studio dell'Inquisizione e dei suoi rapporti con il potere episcopale nell'Italia Spagnola del Cinquecento," *Annuario dell'Istituto storico italiano per l'età moderna e contemporanea* 29–30 (1977–78): 219–76. See also "Toward

a Statistical Profile of the Italian Inquisitions," p. 116 in this volume for additional bibliography.

12. "Copia" appears on the first and last leaves of the document.

13. These are not identified. The reference may be to classical writers.

14. *Marii Nizolii Brixellensis Observationes, omnia M.T. Ciceronis verba, universamque dictionem complectentes . . . nunc tandem Caelii Secundi Curionis opera, vigiliis, labore, et industria . . . auctus* (Basel, 1548). Markus Kutter (*Celio Secondo Curione, sein Leben und sein Werk [1503–1569]* [Basel and Stuttgart, 1955], 288) lists seven editions or reprintings of Curione's version published between 1548 and 1595, all Basel imprints. A number of editions missed by Kutter are scattered in the British Library, Biblioteca Nazionale, Florence, The Newberry Library, etc. Nizolio's *Observationes* were first published at Brescia in 1535.

15. *Dictionarium seu Thesaurus linguae Latinae*, 1st ed. (Paris, 1531), the standard Latin dictionary for much of the sixteenth century. Estienne emigrated to Geneva about 1550. See E. Armstrong, *Robert Estienne Royal Printer, an Historical Study of the Elder Stephanus* (Cambridge, 1954; revised ed., Abingdon, 1986).

16. The Index was reprinted by F. H. Reusch, *Die Indices Librorum Prohibitorum des sechzehnten Jahrhunderts* (Tübingen, 1886; reprint, Nieuwkoop, 1961), 243–81. Cf. Rotondò, "Censura ecclesiastica," 1452. Jesuit agitation had some influence in moderating the severity of the Index of Paul IV and establishing the exemptions from prohibition contained in the *Regulae*: M. Scaduto, "Lainez e l'Indice del 1559," *Archivum Historicum Societatis Iesu* 24 (1955): 3–32, esp. pp. 28–29.

17. The Index of Paul IV issued in 1559 also established two other classes of forbidden writers: "Certorum auctorum libri prohibiti" ("authors only some of whose books were banned") and "Libri prohibiti ab incerti nominis auctoribus compositi" (anonymous and pseudonymous works). The Pauline Index was reprinted in Reusch, *Indices*, 176–208. The tripartite division endured until the Index of Alexander VII published in 1664 which introduced a purely alphabetical listing. For the prohibitions of Curione and of Estienne, see Reusch, *Indices*, 255, 277.

18. This proviso was contained in *Regula* 5 of the Tridentine Index. See Reusch, *Indices*, 248.

19. *De duplici copia rerum ac verborum commentarii duo* (Paris, 1512). This textbook of rhetoric was greatly expanded in subsequent editions. It was intended as an aid to the beginner in Latin composition, providing him with a variety of words and phrases. H. D. Rix, "The Editions of Erasmus' De Copia," *Studies in Philology* 43 (1946): 595–618 corrects many of the entries in the *Bibliotheca Erasmiana* (Gand, 1893), ser. 1, 65–70, and adds about 50 new editions. See now the excellent English translation by B. I. Knott in *The Collected Works of Erasmus*, vol. 24 edited by C. R. Thompson (Toronto, 1978). On Erasmian schoolbooks, including those cited in Mazza's sentence, see the encyclopedic work by J. Chomarat, *Grammaire et Rhetorique chez Erasme*, 2 vols. (Paris, 1981).

20. *Libellus de conscribendis epistolis* (Cambridge, 1521). See *Bibliotheca Erasmiana*, ser. 1, 55–59. It has been critically edited by J.-C. Margolin in the *Opera Omnia*

Desiderii Erasmi Roterodami (Amsterdam, 1971), vol. 1, pt. 2: 153–579 (and in modern English translation by J. K. Sowards in *The Collected Works of Erasmus*, vol. 25 (Toronto, 1985). E. von Richthofen ("A Spanish Inquisitor's Objections to Erasmus," *Erasmus in English*, no. 7 [1975]: 4–6) examines manuscript expurgations made to a copy of the *De conscribendis epistolis*.

21. *Ciceronis Officia cum scholiis Melanchthonis, item in Aristotelis Ethica commentarius doctissimus eodem authore* (Hagenau, 1530). Cf. K. Hartfelder, *Philipp Melanchthon als Praeceptor Germaniae* (Berlin, 1889), 589.

22. For Melanchthon's appearance in the Index of Pius IV, see Reusch, *Indices*, 276, and 247 for *Regula* 2 proscribing any book by a heresiarch, regardless of content.

23. For the Pauline condemnation, see Reusch, *Indices*, 183: "Desiderius Erasmus Roterodamus cum universis commentarii, annotationibus, scholiis, dialogis, epistolis, censuris, versionibus, libris et scriptis suis, etiam si nil penitus contra religionem vel de religione contineant."

24. Reusch, *Indices*, 259.

25. D. Cantimori, "Note su Erasmo e la vita morale e religiosa italiana nel secolo XVI," now in A. Saitta, *Antologia di critica storica* (Bari, 1959), 2:473–93, at p. 480: ". . . il suo nome [of Erasmus] era divenuto in Italia come un segnacolo di ribellione, di eresia." On the whole question, see now the definitive study, based on a thorough examination of the apposite printed and manuscript evidence, by S. Seidel Menchi, *Erasmo in Italia, 1520–1580* (Turin, 1987). I refer the reader to this extraordinary work for the bibliography on the Italian reception of Erasmus. For a positive, critical evaluation of this important contribution, see the remarks by A. Del Col, S. Cavazza, and A. Prosperi, "Erasmo in Italia," *Quaderni storici*, a. 24, no. 70 (1989): 269–96.

26. The provision in the Tridentine Index suggesting that the non-religious works of Erasmus were free to circulate after expurgation (Reusch, *Indices*, 259) seems not to have been observed in practice. See the letter (Rome, 25 April 1576) from Fra Damiano Rubeo, an official on the Congregation of the Index, to the inquisitor of Bologna: "Delli *Apophtegmi* d'Erasmo non si parla d'espurgatione, ma si levano tutti perchè niun'opra d'Erasmo, sia qualsivoglia, si concede in Roma." It is cited in A. Rotondò, "Nuovi documenti per la storia dell' 'Indice dei Libri Proibiti' (1572–1638)," *Rinascimento*, ser. 2, 3 (1963): 145–211, at p. 157. R. Crahay has noted the contradiction in the Tridentine Index itself where under the letter *D* "Desideriii Erasmi Roterodami" is entered as author of the second class (Reusch, *Indices*, 259), while under the letter *E* ("Erasmus Roterodamus") he is an author of the first class, all of whose works must be prohibited (ibid., 260): "Les censeurs Louvanistes d'Erasme," in J. Coppens, ed., *Scrinium Erasmianum*, 2 vols. (Leiden, 1969), 1:221–49. The ambiguity continued in the Index of Sixtus V (1590) where "Desiderius Erasmus Roterodamus" is listed as an author of both the first and second classes, with only his *Adagia* in the thoroughly expurgated edition by Paolo Manuzio being permitted. See Reusch *Indices*, 474–75 and G. Van Calster, "La censure Louvaniste du Nouveau Testament et la rédaction de l'Index Erasmien expur-

gatoire de 1571," in *Scrinium Erasmianum* 2:379–436. Van Calster traces the encounter of Erasmus's works with censorship from the Sorbonne condemnations of 1527 through 1571, and he analyzes the expurgated passages of his New Testament editions with a view to identifying what were considered to be the objectionable elements. The entire question of "Erasmus im Index" is treated by Reusch in his *Der Index der verbotenen Bücher*, 2 vols. (Bonn, 1883–85), 1:347–55. For critical editions of the Paris and Louvain Indices, see now *Index des Livres Interdits*, ed. J. M. De Bujanda, vols. 1, 2.

27. See P. Prodi, *Il Cardinale Paleotti (1522–1597)*, 2 vols. (Rome, 1959–67), 2:237: ". . . gli esami e le correzioni da parte degli inquisitori e delle facoltà teologiche procedevano con estrema lentezza o non erano permesse da Roma, spesso con il deliberato proposito di ritardare la diffusione di quei libri."

28. *Paraphrasis seu potius epitome inscripta D. Erasmo Rotero. luculenta, iuxta ac brevis in elegantiarum libros Laurentii Vallae, ab ipso iam recognita* (Freiburg, 1531). An earlier, unauthorized edition had appeared at Cologne in 1529. See *Bibliotheca Erasmiana*, ser. 1, 152–53. The work has been critically edited by C. L. Heesakkers and J. H. Waszink in the Erasmus *Opera* (cited in full at n. 20), vol. 1, pt. 4, 187–351.

29. *Libellus de Sphaera, accedit ejusdem autoris de anni ratione sive computus ecclesiasticus, cum praefatione P. Melanthonis* [Wittenberg, 1531]. Twenty-five Melanchthon editions of the *Sphaera* published between 1531 and 1601 are recorded by J. C. Houzeau and A. Lancaster, *Bibliographie générale de l'Astronomie* (Brussels, 1887), vol. 1, pt. 1, 508.

30. The reference plausibly can be to either of two works: *Cato pro pueris*, 1st ed. (London, 1513) or *Catonis disticha moralia, cum scholiis Erasmi* (Cologne, 1514). See *Bibliotheca Erasmiana*, ser. 1, 28 and ser. 2, 14–18.

31. *Familiarium epistolarum libri XVI, cum annotationibus [Erasmi, etc.]* (Paris, 1549). See *Bibliotheca Erasmiana*, ser. 2, p. 21. On Rivius, the great humanist educator of Attendorn, see K. Schottenloher, *Bibliographie zur deutschen Geschichte im Zeitalter der Glaubensspaltung, 1517–1585* (Leipzig, 1935), 2:184. Rivius was a forbidden author of the first class, all of whose writings were forbidden. See Reusch, *Indices*, 191.

32. The sentence concludes with the signatures of the attending officials, all of which are illegible to me with the exception of "Hieronimo Vescovo di Campagna et Satriano" and the bishop of the nearby town of Acerno, who is only identified by his title. At this date he would have been Laelius Jordani. See P. B. Gams, *Series Episcoporum*, 844. A notary's entry declares the sentence to be a duly authenticated copy.

INDEX
AVCTORES PRIMAE CLASSIS.
F.

Fabritius Capito Vuolphangus.
Fabritius Montanus.
Firmianus Chlorus, qui & Viretus.
Foelicianus de Ciuitella.
Foelix Malleolus, Tigurinus.
Foelix Manfius.
Francifcus Bertus.
Francifcus Burgardi.
Francifcus Cotta, Lemburgius.
Francifcus Enzinas.
Francifcus Kolbius.
Francifcus Lambertus.
Francifcus Lamperti.
Francifcus Lifmaninus.
Francifcus Niger Baffianenfis.
Francifcus Portus, Græcus.
Francifcus Stancarus.
Fridericus a Dinhein.
Fridericus Iacob.
Fridericus Myconius.
Fridericus a Than.
Fridolinus Brombach.
Fridolinus Lindouerus.

Certorum auctorum libri prohibiti.
Fabulæ Lauretii Abftemii, & Gilberti Cognati.
Francifci Balduini I.C. Conftantinus Magnus, fiue

fiue de Conftantini Imperatoris legibus Ec-
clefiafticis atque ciuilibus comment.
Francifci Franchini liber poematum.
Francifci Trachelæi Statii Propedeumata ora-
toria.
Francifci Zabarellæ liber de Schifmate, atque
eiufdem libri præfationes Argetinæ impref-
fæ, quamdiu non prodierit expurgatus.
Friderici Fregofi tractatus de Oratione, de Iu-
ftificatione, de Fide & operibus, & Præfatio
in Epiftolam D. Pauli ad Romanos: qui tamen falfo illi creditur adfcriptus.
Friderici Furii Ceriolani Valentini Bononia,
fiue de libris facris in uernaculam linguam
conuertendis.

Auctorum incerti nominis libri
prohibiti.

Farrago concordantiarum infignium totius
Bibliæ.
Fafciculus rerum expetendarum, & fugienda-
rum.
Forma delle Orationi Ecclefiaftiche, & il modo
di amminiftrare i facramenti, & di celebrare
il fanto matrimonio . auctor creditur effe
Caluinus.
Francifci nocturna apparitio .
Fundamentum malorum , & bonorū operum .
AV-

An entry from the Tridentine *Index* showing the three classes of prohibited literature.
[Courtesy of the University of Wisconsin-Madison Library.]

DECRETVM

Sacrę Congregationis Indicis Illuftriſſimorum S.R.E.Cardinalium à S.D.N. VRBANO
PAPA VIII. Sanctaq; Sede Apoſtolica ad Indicem Librorum, eorumdemq;
permiſſionem, prohibitionem, expurgationem, & impreſſionem, in vni-
uerſa Republica Chriſtiana deputatorum vbique publicandum.

 ACRA Indicis Congregatio Infraſcriptos libros præſenti Decreto damnat, & prohibet: Omnibus, ac ſingu-
lis cuiuſcunque gradus, & conditionis ſub pœnis in Indice librorum prohibitorum contentis mandans; ne
eos in poſterū imprimere, legere, vel quomodocumque apud ſe detinere quis audeat, ſed à præſentis Decreti
notitia illos omnes locorum Ordinarijs, ſeu Inquiſitoribus ſtatim, qui eos habuerint, exhibere teneantur.

Libri autem ſunt Videlicet.

Antidoto contra le calunnie de' Capuccini, compoſto per li Fedeli Confeſſori della verità nelle leghe di Grigioni.
Apologeticus eorum, qui Hollandiæ, VVeſtfriſiæq; & vicinis quibuſdam Nationibus ex legibus præfuerunt ante mutationem, quæ euenit
anno M DC XVIII. ſcriptus ab Hugone Grotio; cum refutatione eorum, quæ aduerſos ipſum, atque alios acta, ac iudicata ſunt.
Editio noua Axiomatum œconomicorum, acceſſione multarum nouarum Regularum, multarumq; ſententjarum, & exemplorum aucta &
locupletata à Gregorio Richtero Gorlicio. Eiuſdemq; etiam Axiomata Eccleſiaſtica.
Caſpar. Hofmanni Commentarij in Galeni de vſu partium corporis humani. lib. xvij.
Chronica Slauorum, ſeu Annales Helmoldi, opera Reineri Reineccij. Francofurti apud VVechelum ann. 1581. Cui addita eſt etiam
Hiſtoria de vita Henrici IV. & Gregorij VII.
Ciſta Medica ad prælum elaborata à Ioanne Hornungo Rotenburgo Tuberano. Amoueatur ab eo epiſtola eius dedicatoria.
Folium Idiomate Gallico conſcriptum, de comparatione Euangelij Papæ, & Chriſti, circa remiſſionem peccatorum, & conſecutionem vitæ æternæ.
Gerardi de Meynard Collectio controuerſiarum forenſium Senatus Toloſani, ac collatio cum alijs Franciæ Arreſtis. Cum additionibus Hieronymi
Bruchner. In qua collectione multa falſa dictus Gerardus; ſicut & in additionibus quoque Bruchnerus, ex propria ſententia addunt, & aſſerunt.
Guerharti Elmenhorſtij Notæ ad Gennadium Presbyterum Maſſilienſem de Eccleſiaſticis Dogmatibus ; Ad Veteris cuiuſdam Theologi
Homiliam ſacram ; & ad Epiſtolas Martialis Epiſcopi Lemouicenſis.
Hieronymi Treutleri à Kroſchvvitz, necnon Andreæ Schopſij Conſiliorum ; ſiue Reſponſorum volumina duo.
Eiuſdem Hieronymi Treutleri, Selectarum Diſputationum ad Ius Ciuile Iuſtinianeum, volumina duo.
Noua quædam editio Hiſtoriæ Guicciardini in duobus voluminibus facta apud Iacobum Stoer de anno 1621. abſque impreſſion loci, &
ſcripta. La Hiſtoria d'Italia di M. Franceſco Guicciardini Gentilhuomo Fiorentino ; con le poſſibile in margine delle coſe notabili, in-
ſieme la tauola per ordine d'Alfabeto, con la vita dell' Autore, di nuouo riueduta & corretta per Franceſco Sanſouino, con l'aggiun-
ta di quattro vltimi libri laſciati indietro dall' Autore; appreſſo Iacobo Stoer M. DC. XXI.
Hiſtoria Pontificiæ Iuriſdictionis, Auctore Michaele Rouſſel, Pariſijs 1625, apud Ioannem & Stephanum Richerū.
Hugonis Grotij Poemata collecta, & edita à Fratre Guilielmo Grotio.
Eiuſdem de Iure Belli, ac pacis.
Inſtructione fodamentale, Se vna ſetta duri più, ò meno di cent' anni. Similmente, qual' ſia l' antica, e noua' ſede, e doue auanti la Rifor-
matione eſſa ſia ſtata, data in luce dal Signor Gio. Giacomo Breitingero.
Io. Baptiſtæ Marini Poema inſcriptum l' Adone.
Eiuſdem Gli amori Notturni.
Ioannis Franciſci Spinæ. De Mundi Cataſtrophe, hoc eſt, de maxima rerum Mundanarum reuolutione poſtannum 1625.
De Legatione Euangelica ad Indos Compeſcenda Admonitio. Iuſti Heurnij.
Duo libelli famoſi, quorum primus inſcribitur; Supplica alla Santità di N. Sig. Papa Paolo Quinto, per varij Cittadini Bologneſi. Impreſ-
ſus Bononiæ apud Hæredes Io. Roſſi 1619. Et alter inſcribitur, Replica d' vna ſupplica diretta à N. Sig. Paolo Quinto, da Creditori,
in difeſa della verità d' eſſa, & dell' honor de Creditori, & altri nominati in vna tal riſpoſta, vſcita contro detta Supplica. Francfurti 1620.
La lucerna di Eureta Miſoſcolo Academico Filarmonico.
Mythologiæ Chriſtianæ, ſiue virtutum & vitiorum vitæ humanæ Imaginum, libri tres.
Nota Anonymi cuiuſdam Heretici ad quaſdam Epiſtolas, & Carmina Iuſti Lypſij. Editæ Hardeuici.
Nouiſſima Polianthea in libros viginti diſtributa Ioſephi Lang,j Cæfaremontani. Venetijs apud Ioannem Guerilıı̃. 1626. Suſpenſa donec corrigatur.
Paritla in tres priores libros Codicis. Authore Henrico Scotano.
Perſ de Vrnies, liber inſcriptus : Æſtilium otium ad repetitionem ritus 535. Magnæ Curiæ Vicariæ Neapolitanæ. & de-
ciſionibus auctum, & locupletius redditum, opera, & ſtudio Ioachimi Scheplith.
Relatione dello ſtato della Religione del Caualier Edoino Sandio: tradotto dall' ingleſe in linguaggio Italiano.
Roberti Flud Vtriuſque Coſmi, maioris ſcilicet, & minoris, metaphyſica, phyſica, atque technica Hiſtoria.
Inſuper etiam declaratur, ac notiſcatur omnibus, qualiter liber Thomæ Sanchez diſputationum de Sacramento Matrimonij in multis impreſſioni-
bus mutilati ſunt Tomo Tertio, libro Octauo, Diſputatione Septima, numero 4. in quibus totus dictus numerus quartus adimptus eſt.
Et ideo omnes libri prædicti ſic mutilati prohibentur : donec prædictus locus ademptus (cuius initium eſt . At frequentiſſima, ac ve-
rior ſententia habet id poſſe. Finis verò . Et his diebus in hoc prætorio Granatenſi ſent. pars hæc definita eſt.) non ſubrogetur.
In quorum fidem manu , & ſigillo Illuſtriſſimi & Reuerendiſſimi D. Cardinalis Pij præſens Decretum ſignatum , & munitum iuſt .
Romæ die 4. Februarij 1627.

Carolus Card. Pius.   *Loco ✠ ſigilli.*   Fr. Franciſcus Magdalenæ Capiferreus Ord. Præd. Secret.

E Nos Fra Franceſco Galaſſini dell Ord.de' Præd. Maeſtro della Sac. Theol. Generale Inquiſitore di Perugia, dell' Vmbria, e dell' anneſſi Città, co-
mandiamo ſotto l'iſſeſe pene a tutti i ſedeli Chriſtiani di qualſuoghi grado, ſtato, e conditione, che tutti i ſopradetti libri ſiano quanto prima
preſentati al Sant' Offitio come prohibiti , e dannati , eſſortando tutti paternamente ad obedire per euitar gl' emergenti danni , che ſeco apportano.

FR. FRANCISCVS GALASSINVS Ord. Præd. Sac. Theol. Mag. Peruſiæ, annexarumq; Ciuitatū Generalis Inquiſitor.

ROMÆ, & iterum PERVSIÆ Apud Petrum Tomaſium. 1627.

ELEVEN

◁∿▷

Northern Books
and Counter-Reformation Italy

There are at least two sides to a discussion of northern books and
Counter-Reformation Italy. The first is concerned with the role
played in the northern diffusion of the thought and literature of the Italian
Renaissance by Italian religious émigrés working through the printing
presses of Basel, Zürich, Lyons, Antwerp, Frankfort, and London. These
humanist scholars were responsible for a truly breathtaking outpouring
of editions and translations, ranging from such modern authors as Guicciardini, Machiavelli, Pomponazzi, Bembo, Giovio, Giannotti, and Tasso
to such classics as Dante's *Monarchia* which received its *editio princeps* at
Basel in 1559. The exiles not only contributed to the diffusion in Protestant lands of Italian culture through their Latin translations of Machiavelli's
Prince, Guicciardini's *History of Italy*, Paolo Giovio's *Turkish Commentaries*,
and portions of Boccaccio's *Decameron*, but they were doing so at a time
when a curtain of censorship had descended over Italy itself. Many works
by these authors were now forbidden in their own country and succeeded
in seeing the light of day only after lengthy delays in broken and mutilated editions.[1]

The other side of this topic concerns the reverse process, the penetration of northern books into Counter-Reformation Italy, and it is this aspect
of the question that I shall touch upon briefly in this paper. The clandestine circulation of books in the sixteenth century is a fascinating story,

one that still remains to be written—and one that I recommend enthusiasti-
cally to anyone in search of a lively subject. There have been several valuable chapters written in that story in recent years. In general, they have
been regional in focus and have relied primarily on local records.[2]

A full history of the Italian clandestine book trade would require an
examination of a broad array of sources scattered in the libraries and archives of Europe—the correspondence of reformers, of printers, and of
patrons;[3] such institutional records, in Geneva for example, as the documents connected with the church of the Italian exiles in that city, the
registers of the Venerable Company of Pastors, permissions for publication, and, of course, the books themselves.[4] Precious insights can also be
gleaned, as a recent study on the diffusion of Erasmian thought in Italy
has demonstrated convincingly, from the records of the Inquisition and
Index, the two Congregations of the Roman Church which served as
the chief bulwarks against the circulation of suspect literature.[5]

Even at the present incomplete stage of research we catch tantalizing
and surprising glimpses of how the clandestine book trade functioned and
how some of it was financed. We know that the cost of the famous Olivétan Bible, the first French Protestant translation of the Scriptures, published in 1535, was defrayed by the rustic Waldensians who inhabited
the remote French-speaking mountain villages of Piedmont.[6] From his
feudal domains in the distant kingdom of Naples, the wealthy nobleman
Bernardino Bonifacio, Marchese d'Oria, is thought to have provided the
subsidy for the publication at Basel in 1554 of one of the first and most
influential toleration manifestoes produced in the Reformation era, the
De haereticis, compiled by the Savoyard Sebastian Castellio to protest the
burning of Michael Servetus in Geneva the previous year.[7] Francesco
Rustici, a physician from Lucca, personally paid for the printing of an
Italian Bible published in Geneva in 1562;[8] and Pietro Paolo Vergerio,
apostate bishop of Capodistria and incomparable Protestant pamphleteer,
dreamed of being able "to war on the Devil" with the financial support
of Edward VI of England.[9]

We know also that the exiles had embarked on an ambitious program
to translate into Italian the writings of northern reformers for distribution in the peninsula;[10] and at least one of these theologians, Heinrich
Bullinger, minister of Zürich, might well have entertained doubts about
the veracity of one of Vergerio's translations. The Swiss reformer did not
know Italian and could not have checked the final result. This was proba-

bly just as well since Vergerio himself confided to a colleague that he had translated Bullinger's booklet "not literally, but embellishing it."[11] Despite such risks, by the end of the century a large corpus of writings by Luther, Melanchthon, Brenz, Bucer, Bullinger, Calvin, and Beza, and a host of minor reformers, could all be read in Italian translation.[12]

Behind many of the ingenious means for the surreptitious introduction of prohibited books into Italy stood the tireless and imaginative Vergerio. On one occasion he might hire the services of a traveling salesman, a "merciaio vagante," who would retain a third or half of the profits;[13] on another, he would take advantage of the immunity enjoyed by a special envoy to Venice of the duke of Württemberg, stuffing his diplomatic pouch with literary contraband;[14] and Vergerio himself, marked man as he was, casting himself as an ambassador of King Maximilian, brazenly reentered the Friuli during Lent in 1558, in a carriage drawn by six swift horses, leaving a trail of little books in his wake.[15]

The heretical book trade was not a compact, homogeneous movement, nor one about which it is easy to generalize. Vergerio's fellow reformers, for example, found him almost as obnoxious as did Rome.[16] They felt that his vulgarity, as expressed in his scurrilous illustrated pamphlet depicting "pope Joan" giving birth in the midst of a procession of cardinals,[17] or his libelous invention of a romantic liaison between Pier Luigi Farnese and the young bishop of Fano were discrediting the entire community of exiles.[18]

Anomalies abound. Calvin's *Institutes* were laboriously translated into Italian and finally published in Geneva in 1557 by Giulio Cesare Pascale, a poet from Messina. It must be one of history's small ironies that this monumental translation, which served as an introduction to Calvin's theology for so many Italians, was actually prepared by a man, Pascale, who would shortly be excommunicated by the Genevan church for not partaking of the Lord's Supper; who would be accused of plotting to flee to more tolerant Basel at the head of a contingent of other Italians in 1559—only two years after the publication of his *magnum opus*; and who finally would be pronounced an incorrigible sinner by Genevan authorities when he was discovered in 1572 with his head covered during a singing of the Psalms.[19] We are taken aback also to discover that an Italian translation of Luther's *Small Catechism*, published at Tübingen in 1585, was prepared not for the purpose of making religious conversions on the peninsula but rather to comfort Christian slaves of the Turks in Constantinople.[20]

As for Rome's reaction to this output and to its circulation in Italy, there are fewer surprises. Suspected books were classed into two main categories, prohibited or suspended. The first category, "prohibited," is obvious and included the religious writings of the Protestant reformers and the *opera omnia* of such archheretics as Luther, Calvin, and Melanchthon, the type of book that has been discussed above. The category "suspended" was used for books on non-religious or uncontroversial subjects by forbidden authors or issuing from forbidden northern presses, such works, for example, as editions of the classics, dictionaries, histories, scientific treatises, and so forth. One of the chief features of the Tridentine Index of Pius IV published in 1564 was to permit the circulation of this seemingly innocuous literature after proper expurgation.[21] In the earlier draconian Index of Paul IV promulgated in 1559 even these books had been totally prohibited.[22]

In my opinion, one of the more interesting questions connected with the circulation of northern books in Italy remains unresolved. What was the effect of ecclesiastical censorship on Italian culture and learning and to what extent did it remain possible to maintain intellectual contact between Protestant north and Catholic south during the sixteenth century? In other words, what was the fate of the "suspended" category of books? What was the possibility that northern scholarship, if it was of an uncontroversial nature, might find its way to the shelves of Italian libraries, public and private alike? Modern authorities seem to have responded to this question with one voice. Romeo De Maio in his admirable study of monastic libraries, has spoken of the "cultural death" resulting from the Index;[23] Paolo Prodi, in his model biography of Cardinal Paleotti, archbishop of Bologna, has described an iron curtain shutting Italy off not only from the cultural advances of northern Europe but also from constructive new Catholic religious currents;[24] and Antonio Rotondò, in his magisterial survey of the relationship between culture and censorship over several centuries, has lamented that Italy became enclosed within a narrow isolation.[25] All these writers have emphasized the repressive measures, the prohibitions, the disruptions and delays in publication, distribution, and circulation of books.

On the other side, Paul Grendler has argued, at least as far as Venice is concerned, that in an earlier period when bookmen operated virtually at will, such a compromised author as Melanchthon could be published in Italy into the late 1530s; and that by the end of the century, with some sacrifice and ingenuity, it was still possible to obtain prohibited literature even after the Congregations of the Inquisition and Index were in full operation.[26]

I should like briefly to supplement the data presented by Grendler with fragments of new evidence drawn from Venice and elsewhere, and suggestions for further work. Recently, more out of idle curiosity than anything else, I tried a small experiment which, if repeated more systematically and on a larger scale, could cast some new light on the question of the cultural interaction surviving between Protestants and Catholics in the so-called Reformation era. My experiment consisted in examining about a hundred sixteenth-century editions of Erasmus, Curione, and other northern humanists in The Newberry Library, Chicago. My aim was to see in how many cases it might be possible to establish Catholic ownership. I realized even before beginning that this might be a forlorn hope since it would be unlikely that a person would compromise himself by needlessly advertising the possession of books of doubtful orthodoxy. Quite to my surprise, in numerous instances, I encountered names or other marks, such as marginal comments, that clearly identified the owner as Italian. Although accompanying dates were infrequent, the hands helped to identify many of the inscriptions as being of the sixteenth or early seventeenth century. A further unmistakable indication of Catholic ownership was the tell-tale trace of the censor's labors, the designation "libro proibito" scrawled on the title page or, more frequently, the inking out of the author's name, or other visible forms of censorship. A number of the Erasmian editions had been owned by Catholic religious establishments, such as Jesuit schools, a monastery in Vercelli, and so forth.[27]

In view of the inaccessibility of the records of the Congregation of the Index, insight into censorship policy is provided by the comparison of deleted portions against the original texts in unexpurgated copies. For that matter, even the many names and passages of a compromising nature which escaped the censor's scissors or erasures have something to teach us about the care (or lack of it) with which the work was carried out. The censor's intervention is extensive, coherent, and easy to reconstruct in a Basel, 1542 edition of Erasmus's *Adagia*, with the majority of deletions directed against passages which describe the decline of the Church.[28] More frequently, censorship was erratic, superficial, and hasty. The title page of a Basel, 1551 edition of Curione's version of Nizolius's Ciceronian Latin lexicon, the *Observationes*, formerly "In usum Societatis

Iesu" (from a MS inscription), had suffered the following mutilations: Curione's name, which appears three times in the preliminary matter, has been inked out, but ineffectively, since it remains quite legible. A slip of paper has been pasted over the mark of the printer Hervagius and a feeble attempt has been made to obliterate the place of publication, Basel. The same procedure was repeated with the colophon. Curiously, Curione's preface, the only possibly controversial feature of the book, was left intact.[29]

In a copy of a 1539 edition of the *Comedies* of Terence which contains the printed annotations of several classical and modern commentators, all of whose names appear on the title pages, the censor stooped to some thinly disguised trickery. The names of two of them, Erasmus and Melanchthon, were cut out and replaced with a hand-written label, "praedictorum auctorum," supposedly referring the reader to Donatus, Servius, Badius Ascensius, etc., who had been mentioned ahead of Erasmus and Melanchthon. An attentive reader could not have been deceived. Within the volume itself both their names and the texts of their commentaries were left intact.[30]

Needless to say, a really systematic survey of this sort should be conducted with the holdings of Italian libraries, many of which are extraordinarily rich in sixteenth-century northern imprints. An opportunity to conduct just such a survey is now presented by a project launched recently in Bologna to catalogue separately all foreign sixteenth-century imprints preserved in one of its richest repositories. A very preliminary inventory reveals the presence of such northern writers as Theodore Beza, Jean Bodin, Otto Brunfels, George Buchanan, and Guillaume Budé, and of such printing centers as Basel, Geneva, Heidelberg, London, Tübingen, and Zürich.[31] Identical results are yielded by the modern catalogue of a seminary library in one of Italy's most northeasterly provinces,[32] as well as by a number of aristocratic sixteenth-century collections. The library of the nobleman Gian Vincenzo Pinelli included at least ninety prohibited titles by about forty-four different banned authors;[33] the Medici grand dukes possessed works of Erasmus and Machiavelli, numerous Basel imprints, and, according to an inventory drawn up in 1610, over a hundred books and manuscripts designated by the letter *P[rohibitus]*.[34] The library of Prospero Podiani (d. 1615), who turned over his rich collection numbering c. seven hundred books and manuscripts to the city of Perugia, contained works by Agrippa of Nettesheim, Erasmus, Melanchthon, and other controversial northern authors.[35] Even more remarkable, perhaps, the library established in 1566 at the convent of Bosco Marengo by Pius V, the founder a few years later of the Congregation of the Index, contained editions by Erasmus, Matteo Gribaldi, C. S. Curione, and Savonarola, produced by such northern Protestant printers as Isingrin, Oporinus, Petri, Hervagius, etc. individually condemned in the Index of 1559.[36]

There is other evidence of continuing exchanges and contacts. The presence of hundreds of students every year from northern and eastern Europe in such famous universities as Padua, Bologna, and Siena is well known.[37] When the so-called Marian exiles, Protestant to a man, had to abandon England precipitously, a goodly number could not imagine a safer haven than Catholic Padua and Venice.[38] The famous Paduan jurist Matteo Gribaldi Mofa regularly vacationed at his summer home in Farges in Bernese territory, a mere thirty kilometers as the crow flies from Geneva, and was accustomed to pay his respects to Calvin before returning to his classes in the fall.[39] Some years later Gribaldi's colleague on the medical faculty, Girolamo Mercuriale, conducted a decade-long correspondence with the rector of the University of Basel, Theodor Zwinger, who had himself obtained a Paduan medical degree in 1559. When Mercuriale developed an urgent need to consult Zwinger's *Theatrum vitae humanae*, the exile printer and bookseller Pietro Perna obtained it for him, in 1572.[40] And when Perna himself applied for Basel citizenship in 1555 he first had to return to his native Lucca to obtain a notarized copy of a document attesting to his legitimate birth.[41]

Many are the academics active in Italian universities who found publishing outlets for their works through the presses of Basel printers, especially Perna's. Perna was responsible for the publication from his new home in Basel of some of the most virulent anti-Roman propaganda to issue from the pens of his fellow-émigrés. Yet, in 1553, he was chosen as agent for the import-export of books by Lorenzo Torrentino, printer to the Medici grand dukes. Writing in January 1560 to the jurist Marco Mantova, a leading member of the Padua law faculty, Perna spoke casually of paying him a visit in the near future to clinch the contract for the publication of Mantova's writings.[42] Matteo Gribaldi published at Basel in 1545 his repertory of ancient jurists, the *Catalogus jureconsultorum veterum*, through the presses of Johannes Oporinus, who also brought out in 1551 Cornelio Donzellini's Greek grammar, *Methodus linguae graecae*, dedicated to Giovanni and Francesco de' Medici. The *De historia liber* by the humanist

Antonio Riccoboni likewise appeared in Basel, in 1579, and Francesco Patrizi's *Discussiones peripateticae* in the same city two years later. Several editions of works by the poet and classical scholar Aonio Paleario, teacher of rhetoric in several Italian cities, were brought out by the Basel establishments of Thomas Guarin and Oporinus.[43] We know that for many of these authors an important incentive in seeing their works published abroad was the clear superiority as craftsmen that northern printers enjoyed over their Italian colleagues. The philosopher Patrizi undoubtedly echoed the sentiments of many when he wrote to Mercuriale in July 1580 that he had just received the unbound sheets of a book which Perna had printed for him: "I am very pleased with the type, format and paper."[44] Andrea Alciato, Girolamo Cardano, Lilio Gregorio Giraldi, Paolo Giovio are only a few of the sixteenth-century Italian authors whose works were published abroad without licenses and thus in defiance of inquisitorial regulations.[45]

More surprising, perhaps, is the evidence of a reverse process, namely of works by well-known Italian heretics living abroad whose writings managed to be published in Italy proper. The *Varia opuscula* by the émigré historian and publicist Pietro Bizzarri, which appeared in Venice in 1565, are dedicated to Queen Elizabeth of England, Francis Russell, duke of Bedford, Lord William Cecil, and other Protestant notables.[46] The writings of the literary critic Lodovico Castelvetro appeared in several Italian editions published in Modena, Parma, and Venice despite the fact that he had been condemned *in absentia* as a contumacious heretic after he fled from the custody of the Roman Holy Office in 1560, and found haven in Swiss exile. The single concession to his status seems to have been the omission of his name from the title pages.[47] When the treatise *Difesa contra la peste* by the former physician of Piombino Marcello Squarcialupi was reprinted in Milan in 1576, he had already been in exile for a number of years achieving notoriety as a leader of anti-trinitarian dissent in Moravia and Transylvania.[48] There are several contemporary Italian editions of Tasso's *Gerusalemme* which prominently announce that they contain the "Annotations" of Scipione Gentili, who had fled persecution with his family in the mid–1570s and eventually succeeded Hugo Donellus as professor of law at the University of Altdorf.[49] The *Italicae grammatices praecepta*, the Italian grammar composed by Scipione Lentolo, ardent Calvinist and minister of the evangelical church at Chiavenna in the Valtellina, a work based on his earlier tutoring activities in Geneva, received numerous Italian editions.[50] Venice saw the publication in 1563 of the style manual, *De ratione consequendi styli*, by C. A. Curione, followed some decades later by the *Ieroglifici* of Giovanni Piero Valeriani, published in 1602 "enlarged with two books by Celio Augustino Curione." The latter's contribution was dated "Basel, 17 July 1567" and dedicated to Basil Amerbach. Curione was the son of the notorious heretic Celio Secondo Curione.[51] Even more surprising, perhaps, is evidence of Italian publication of works by northern authors, from editions of Terence in 1539 and 1545 glossed by Philipp Melanchthon,[52] to medical treatises by the Tübingen scholar and physician, Leonhard Fuchs, whose *opera omnia* were destined to be banned by the Indices of Paul IV and Sixtus V.[53]

I should like to draw attention also to still another literary attempt to bridge the cultural chasm caused by the schism in Christendom. It fits neither of the categories briefly alluded to above. It is not a book published in Protestant lands by an Italian scholar active in the academic life of his country, nor is it a work by an evangelical published in Italy proper. The item in question is the Italian translation of Georgius Agricola's *De re metallica*. The translator of this famous treatise on mining was the minister of the tiny village of Soglio in the Valtellina. Michelangelo Florio was not an ordinary small town pastor. Born into a family of Tuscan conversos at the beginning of the century, he had joined the Franciscan order and later suffered an imprisonment of twenty-seven months at Rome after his evangelical leanings became known. He managed to escape and eventually made his way to England, where in 1550 he founded a church for the Italian exiles, wrote an Italian grammar, and became a tutor to Lady Jane Grey, a cousin of Edward VI, who ruled for nine days after his death until she was supplanted and executed by Mary Tudor. Early in 1554 Florio returned to the continent in the great wave of Marian exiles and eventually entered the Valtellina. He was accompanied by his young son, John, who one day would return to England and become that country's leading advocate of Italian studies.[54]

In 1563 Michelangelo published through Froben at Basel his Italian translation of the *De re metallica*, which, as I mentioned above, is considered the first systematic modern study of mining techniques and technology. In his dedication to Queen Elizabeth of England Florio parried the anticipated criticism of those who might challenge the concept of vernacular translation. He expressed the hope that his labors would serve to spur similar efforts, especially in the fields of Scripture and religious literature.[55] In a similar apologetic vein, in his preface to the reader, Florio defended himself from those partisans of the Tuscan language who he foresaw would accuse his translation of not employing all those rules of reading and writing they had learned from Pietro Bembo and his school. Florio explained that he was not writing for "literati" alone; the language had changed since the days of Boccaccio, and, moreover, he wanted his book read outside Florence. This is the point of interest for us. Despite the fact that this expensively produced, richly illustrated folio volume reeked of heresy—it made no attempt to conceal the suspect imprint Basel and the Frobens (the publishers of the outlawed Erasmus), nor the contumacious, apostate translator's name, nor the long adulatory dedication to Elizabeth, and the espousal of the forbidden notion of the vernacular translation of Scripture—it was clearly intended for an Italian market. Florio makes this point explicit: ". . . if I had only given the terms current in Florence to the instruments named in this book, the honored Frobens, for whom I translated it, could most justly have reproached me, saying that they had not asked me to translate it so that it could be sold in Florence alone, but in every other part of Italy as well." That the translation actually was conceived for an Italian market is corroborated by the fact that it survives in a very few copies and, with a handful of exceptions, in a mutilated state, lacking the dedication to the heretical queen of England.[56]

Scattered pieces of evidence testify to the possibility of continuing literary contacts into the seventeenth century. It is amusing to reflect that a Dutchman visiting Padua might be able to purchase there an edition of a classical author by a northern heretic. The Newberry Library copy of the 1545 Terence mentioned above has this MS note on the title page: "Ex libris Fr. H. Van Bergen Amstelae. Bat. emptus Patavii 26 Novemb. A. 1653." The earliest catalogue published by an English antiquarian bookseller, Henry Fetherstone's in 1628, consisted exclusively of books purchased in Italy. In fact, in the opinion of Dennis Rhodes, one of our leading authorities on printing history, "Italy was the easiest and most fruitful market for the London booksellers to explore."[57] Later in the same century Italian scholars were reviewing the latest works by their English colleagues, usually within six months of a book's first appearance in England. A perusal of the pages of the Roman *Giornale de' Letterati* betrays no mention of such contemporary literary giants as Milton, Bunyan, and Dryden. The interest is primarily in works of science—medicine, mathematics, astronomy—

with Robert Boyle holding a prominent place.[58] And there is further evidence from both the sixteenth and the seventeenth centuries that scholars who were insistent enough and had the right connections could obtain special dispensations or licenses to read prohibited literature.[59] This was a privilege which previously had been granted only to a few ecclesiastics, usually for the purpose of refuting the works of northern heretics.

If there is one overarching explanation for the continuing exchanges and contacts that I have touched upon, it must be sought, partly, in the inability of the censorship machinery to accomplish its task. The surviving documents are full of laments that the ambitious and unrealistic policies of the Roman Curia only provoked confusion and were unenforceable to the letter. It could not be otherwise when a broad range of authors from Andrea Alciato to Ulrich Zasius were considered suspect in one or another of their writings. The correspondence of the inquisitors and of members of the Congregation of the Index is full of reproaches for the failure to exert proper vigilance; for the assignment of the task of expurgating a particular work to a close friend of the author; for confusing two homonymous writers with the name Pietro Paolo Vergerio, even though one lived in the fifteenth century and wrote humanistic treatises and the other in the sixteenth, and was a notorious Protestant pamphleteer; for careless expurgations (of which we have seen samples earlier in this essay), and a thousand other faults.[60]

Needless to say, the findings presented here suggesting a presence, perhaps larger than commonly imagined, of northern books in Counter-Reformation Italy are of an extremely fragmentary and provisional nature. Of themselves they prove nothing. They have been gathered at random and are offered now in the hope of stimulating a more systematic examination of library collections, censuses of sixteenth-century imprints, booksellers and publishers lists, especially those connected to the great international book fairs, lists of books confiscated by the Holy Office, inventories of private libraries, and other appropriate sources. The Counter-Reformation will not emerge from such a process as an age of free cultural exchange. No end of facts and figures could accomplish such a miracle. I merely wish to suggest that the images of "cultural death" and of an "iron curtain" may be similarly inappropriate and overly harsh representations of the age.

Notes

1. I have touched upon the literary activity of the exiles in "The Cultural Contributions of Italian Protestant Reformers in the Late Renaissance," in *Libri, idee e sentimenti religiosi nel Cinquecento italiano* (Ferrara and Modena, 1987), 81–108, also in Italian translation in *Italica* 64 (1987): 19–61.

2. I am thinking, for example, of such studies as C. De Frede, "Roghi di libri ereticali nell'Italia del Cinquecento," in *Ricerche storiche ed economiche in memoria di Corrado Barbagallo* (Naples, 1970), 2:315–28; P. Lopez, *Inquisizione, stampa e censura nel Regno di Napoli tra '500 e '600* (Naples, 1974); P. F. Grendler, *The Roman Inquisition and the Venetian Press, 1540–1605* (Princeton, 1977); idem, "The Circulation of Protestant Books in Italy," in J. C. McLelland, ed., *Peter Martyr Vermigli and Italian Reform* (Waterloo, 1980), 5–16; S. Cavazza, "Libri in volgare e propaganda eterodossa: Venezia, 1543–1547," in *Libri, idee e sentimenti religiosi*, 9–28; the many contributions of A. Del Col, such as his "Il Nuovo Testamento tradotto da Massimo Teofilo e altre opere stampate a Lione nel 1551," *Critica storica* 15 (1978): 642–75. Cf. also n. 26 and the studies by C. Fahy and U. Rozzo cited elsewhere in this volume and in the Bibliography.

3. For the correspondence of a family of Swiss patrons and men of letters with extensive Italian connections, see A. Hartmann and B. R. Jenny, eds., *Die Amerbachkorrespondenz* (Basel, 1942–). For the activities of the Italians in exile and for news of attempts to introduce the Reformation in Italy, the correspondence of Heinrich Bullinger, the minister of Zürich, is one of our richest sources: T. Schiess, ed., *Bullingers Korrespondenz mit den Graubündnern*, 3 vols. (Basel, 1904–6).

4. For the history of book publishing in Geneva, and the pertinent bibliography, see P. Chaix, *Recherches sur l'imprimerie à Genève de 1550 à 1564* (Geneva, 1954; reprint 1978); H. J. Bremme, *Buchdrucker und Buchhändler zur Zeit der Glaubenskämpfe: Studien zur Genfer Druckgeschichte, 1565–1580* (Geneva, 1969); P. Chaix, A. Dufour, and G. Moeckli, *Les livres imprimés à Genève de 1550 à 1600: Nouvelle édition, revue et augmentée par G. Moeckli* (Geneva, 1966). The *Registres de la Compagnie des Pasteurs de Genève* are being published in Geneva by the Librairie Droz, under various editors. The documentation begins with the year 1546. Photocopies of records dealing with the Italians in Geneva extracted from the registers of the city councils are at The Newberry Library, Chicago in seven volumes (6A 367). As for the books themselves, the largest collection of Italian Reformation imprints is the collection gathered by Count Piero Guicciardini in the nineteenth century and now housed in the Biblioteca Nazionale, Florence. The publication of a critical catalogue of the collection is now underway, beginning with the nineteenth-century books: *Il fondo Guicciardini nella Biblioteca Nazionale Centrale di Firenze*, catalogo a cura di Lia Invernizi (Florence, 1984–). The recent commemorative volume, *Piero Guicciardini (1808–86): Un riformatore religioso nell' Europa dell' Ottocento: Atti del convegno di studi, Firenze, 11–12 aprile 1986* (Florence, 1988), contains a number of contributions devoted to the Guicciardini collection.

5. S. Seidel Menchi, *Erasmo in Italia, 1520–1580* (Turin, 1987), which now replaces her numerous earlier articles on the subject.

6. See, most recently, G. Audisio, "Les Vaudois et le livre (XVe–XVIe siècles)," in *Les Réformes: Enracinement socio-culturel: XXV colloque international d'études humanistes, Tours, 1er–13 Juillet 1982,* études réunies par B. Chevalier et R. Sauzet (Paris, 1985), 183–89, and J.-F. Gilmont, "La fabrication et la vente de la Bible d'Olivétan," *Musée neuchâtelois* (1985): 213–24. For a fuller bibliography, see J. Tedeschi, "The Cultural Contributions," n. 27.

7. M. Welti, "La contribution de Giovanni Bernardino Bonifacio, Marquis d'Oria, à l'édition princeps du *De haereticis an sint persequendi*," *BSSV*, a. 90, no. 125 (1969): 45–49. Welti's several contributions, illuminating Bonifacio's career as a whole, are cited in my "The Cultural Contributions," n. 26 and, more fully, in the version published in *Italica* 64 (1987): 44 n. 26. The old tradition that assigned to Lelio Sozzini a role in the preparation of the *De haereticis* has been overturned convincingly by A. Rotondò in his edition of Sozzini's *Opere* (Florence, 1986), 308–10.

8. J. B. G. Galiffe, *Le refuge italien de Genève aux XVIme et XVIIme siècles* (Geneva, 1881), 35n.

9. On Vergerio's career as pamphleteer, see F. Hubert, *Vergerio's publizistische Thätigkeit nebst einer bibliographischen Übersicht* (Göttingen, 1893). On the efforts of the Italians in general, see E. Droz, "Propagande italienne (1551–1565)," in Droz's *Chemins de l'hérésie*, 4 vols. (Geneva, 1970–76), 2:229–93. The best study of Vergerio before his apostasy, is A. J. Schutte, *Pier Paolo Vergerio: The Making of an Italian Reformer* (Geneva, 1977), now in an unrevised Italian translation, but with a new preface, updated bibliography, and illustrations: *Pier Paolo Vergerio e la Riforma a Venezia, 1498–1549* (Rome, 1988). The reformer's entire tumultuous career has been reconstructed in F. Tomizza's *Il male viene dal nord: Il romanzo del vescovo Vergerio* (Milan, 1984). On Vergerio's hopes of obtaining English support, see his letter to R. Gwalther, dated Vicosoprano, 8 March 1551, published in P. D. R. da Porta, *Historia Reformationis Ecclesiarum Raeticarum* (Chur, 1772), T. 1, Lib. 2, p. 150.

10. *Bullingers Korrespondenz mit den Graubündnern, passim.* See also n. 12 below.

11. Vergerio to R. Gwalther, letter written from "Samadeno in Agnedina," 24 April 1551, and published in da Porta, *Historia Reformationis*, T. 1, Lib. 2, p. 251.

12. See, from the vast literature on the subject, S. Seidel Menchi, "Le traduzioni italiane di Lutero nella prima metà del Cinquecento," *Rinascimento* 17 (1977): 31–108; S. Caponetto, "Due opere di Melantone tradotte da Lodovico Castelvetro: 'I principii della theologia di Ippophilo da Terra Negra' e 'Dell'autorità della Chiesa e degli scritti degli antichi,' " *NRS* 70 (1986): 253–74; D. Perocco, "Lodovico Castelvetro traduttore di Melantone (Vat. Lat. 7755)," *Giornale storico della letteratura italiana* 156 (1979): 541–47; J. Tedeschi and E. D. Willis, "Two Italian Translations of Beza and Calvin," *Archiv für Reformationsgeschichte* 55 (1964): 70–74; J. Tedeschi, "Genevan Books of the Sixteenth Century," *Bibliothèque d'Humanisme et Renaissance* 31 (1969): 173–80. The largest single collection of this type of material is the Guicciardini in the Biblioteca Nazionale, Florence. Cf. nn. 19 and 20.

13. P. Paschini, *Eresia e riforma cattolica al confine orientale d'Italia* (Rome, 1951), 58; for other surreptitious means to introduce heretical literature into Italy, see E. Pommier, "Notes sur la propagande protestante dans la république de Venise au milieu du XVI siècle," in *Aspects de la propagande religieuse* (Geneva, 1957), 240–46.

14. Vergerio himself described this episode in one of his pamphlets: *Del Cardinal Durante, che ha posto in prigione un ambasciador di uno di maggiori principi dell'Imperio* (N.p., 1553). Hubert, no. 81.

15. Paschini, *Eresia e riforma*, 59.

16. See, for example, C. S. Curione writing to A. Musculus from Basel, 1 August 1550, letter published in *Museum Helveticum* 7, Particula 28, p. 561. Calvin shared this opinion. See his letter to G. Farel and P. Viret, dated 15 August 1549: *Corpus Reformatorum* (Braunschweig, 1874), 41: col. 359.

17. *Historia di Papa Giovanni VIII che fu femmina* (N.p., 1556). Hubert, no. 112.

18. R. Massignan, "Pier Luigi Farnese e il vescovo di Fano," *Atti e memorie della R. Deputazione di storia patria per le province delle Marche*, n.s., 2 (1905): 249–304; B. Croce, *Poeti e scrittori del primo e del tardo Rinascimento*, 3 vols. (Bari, 1945–52), 3:158; G. B. Parks, "The Pier Luigi Farnese Scandal: An English Report," *Renaissance News* 15 (1962): 193–200.

19. *Institutione della Religione Christiana di Messer Giovanni Calvino* (Geneva, 1557). My information on Pascale's transgressions is taken from E. W. Monter's manuscript notes on Genevan Consistory records now in my possession. Cf. T. R. Castiglione, "Un poeta siciliano riformato, Giulio Cesare Pascali: Contributo alla storia dell'emigrazione protestante nel sec. XVI," *Religio* 12 (1936): 29–61; M. Richter, "Giulio Cesare Paschali: Attività e problemi di un poeta italiano nella Ginevra di Calvino e di Beza," *Rivista di storia e letteratura religiosa* 1 (1965): 228–57.

20. L. Santini, "A proposito di una traduzione del *Piccolo Catechismo di M. Lutero*," *NRS* 49 (1965): 627–35.

21. These censorship procedures are spelled out in the ten *regulae* introduced in the Tridentine Index and reprinted in F. Reusch, *Die Indices Librorum Prohibitorum des sechzehnten Jahrhunderts* (Tübingen, 1886); reprint Nieuwkoop, 1961), pp. 247–51.

22. Reprinted in F. Reusch, *Die Indices*, 176–208.

23. R. De Maio, "I modelli culturali della Controriforma: Le biblioteche dei conventi italiani," in the author's *Riforme e miti nella Chiesa del Cinquecento* (Naples, 1973), 372.

24. P. Prodi, *Il Cardinale Paleotti (1522–1597)*, 2 vols. (Rome, 1959–67), 2:262.

25. A. Rotondò, "La censura ecclesiastica e la cultura italiana dal XVI al XVIII secolo," in *Storia d'Italia* (Turin, 1973), 5, pt. 2: 1404.

26. *The Roman Inquisition*, passim. For a cogent critique of this view, generally unpopular among Italian scholars, see G. Cozzi, "Books and Society," *Journal of Modern History* 51 (1979): 86–98, esp. pp. 90–97. Cozzi objects to Grendler's tendency to downplay the impact of Inquisition and Index. Cf. A. Del Col, "Il controllo della stampa a Venezia e i processi di Antonio Brucioli (1548–1559)," *Critica storica* 17 (1980): 457–510. This article corrects Grendler in a number of instances

and adds much new relevant information. See also Del Col's criticism of Grendler's historical introduction to the *Index de Venise, 1549, et de Venise et Milan, 1554*, ed. J. M. De Bujanda, Index des Livres Interdits, 3 (Sherbrooke and Geneva, 1987), in the *Sixteenth Century Journal* 20 (1989): 152–53 and the exchange of letters between Grendler and Del Col (ibid, pp. 479–80) prompted by the latter's review.

27. Italian owners of Erasmian books were Octavius Peregrinus (Case Y 6785. 85); Antonio Galluzzi (Case B 835. 798); Domenico Meoni da San Casciano, 1625 (Case 3A 1115); Faustini Zenoni, Venetian (Case 3A 1596); P. Onviato Bambrini of Prato (Case fY 672. L 504); "Ex libris Monasterii Beatissimae Mariae S. Victorii Vercellarum. Ad usum R.mi D. Gasparii Antonii Petrinae Abbatis" (Case 6A 261). A partially illegible date, either 1625 or 1628, accompanies this inscription.

28. The Newberry Library, Case 6A 209, an edition produced by the Frobens.

29. Idem, Case Y 672. C 73578.

30. Idem, Wing f ZP 535. R 85.

31. See D. Bufalini, R. Landi, G. Zannoni, "Catalogo delle cinquecentine straniere conservate nella Biblioteca Comunale dell'Archiginnasio (lettera B)," *L'Archiginnasio* 81 (1986): 185–319. The list is described as helping to illuminate the "patrimonio antico" of the library (p. 185). See also G. Mazzetti, *Le prime edizioni di Lutero (1518–1546) nelle biblioteche italiane* (Florence, 1984); M. and P. Grendler, "The Erasmus Holdings of Roman and Vatican Libraries," *Erasmus in English* 13 (1984): 2–29; S. Adorni Braccesi, "Libri e lettori a Lucca tra Riforma e Controriforma: Un' indagine in corso," in *Libri, idee e sentimenti religiosi*, 39–46, a solid study, based on the large collections of sixteenth-century books in the public libraries of Lucca, which attempts to match the books to their owners. It concludes that about a third of the volumes were acquired contemporaneously.

32. *Catalogo del fondo antico della Biblioteca del Seminario di Gorizia*, ed. S. Cavazza (Florence, 1975). The volume records the presence of works by Calvin, S. Castellio, Erasmus, Melanchthon, S. Münster, etc. On their possible provenance, see pp. xxx ff.

33. M. Grendler, "Book Collecting in Counter-Reformation Italy: The Library of Gian Vincenzo Pinelli (1535–1601)," *Journal of Library History* 16 (1981): 143–51; P. F. Grendler, *The Roman Inquisition*, 321–24.

34. See L. Perini, "Editori e potere in Italia dalla fine del secolo XV all' Unità," in *Storia d'Italia: Annali 4. Intellettuali e potere*, ed. C. Vivanti (Turin, 1981), 765–853, at p. 807; idem, "Contributo alla ricostruzione della biblioteca privata dei Granduchi di Toscana nel XVI secolo," in *Studi di storia medievale e moderna per Ernesto Sestan* (Florence, 1980), 571–667.

35. C. Black, "Perugia and Post-Tridentine Church Reform," *Journal of Ecclesiastical History* 35 (1984): 429–51.

36. See the excellent analysis of the library by U. Rozzo, "Pio V e la biblioteca di Bosco Marengo," in *Pio V e Santa Croce di Bosco: Aspetti di una committenza papale* (Alessandria, 1985), 315–40. Rozzo concludes that books ended up in ecclesiastical libraries "che non avrebbero dovuto trovarsi in quegli scaffali" (p. 335).

37. B. Brugi, "Gli scolari tedeschi e la S. Inquisizione a Padova nella seconda metà del secolo XVI," in *Per la storia della giurisprudenza e delle università italiane: Saggi* (Turin, 1915), 11:154–69. Six thousand German students were enrolled at the University of Padua from 1550 to 1599.

38. On this curious and fascinating episode, see K. Bartlett, "Worshipful Gentlemen of England: The Studio of Padua and the Education of the English Gentry in the Sixteenth Century," *Renaissance and Reformation*, n.s., 6 (1982): 235–48 and "Dangers and Delights: English Protestants in Italy in the Sixteenth Century," in *Forestieri e stranieri nelle città basso-medievali,* Atti del Seminario internazionale di studio, Bagno a Ripoli (Firenze), 4–8 giugno 1984 (Florence, 1988), 215–22. One of the important contributions of these essays, extracts from the author's doctoral dissertation at the University of Toronto, is to show that the Reformation did not interrupt the ancient English tradition of study in Padua.

39. See F. Ruffini, *Studi sui riformatori italiani*, ed. A. Bertola, L. Firpo, E. Ruffini (Turin, 1955), 52 ff. As a subject of Berne, Gribaldi had to obtain the permission of its Senate before he could accept his Paduan university appointment in 1548 (ibid., 53).

40. See A. Rotondò, *Studi e ricerche di storia ereticale italiana del Cinquecento* (Turin, 1974), 287, 400; idem, "La censura ecclesiastica e la cultura," pp. 1450 and 1453 for other frustrated scholarly attempts to obtain the book in the course of the century. The manuscript account book (BAV, Vat. lat. 6604, fol. 47r), principally covering the years 1589–95, of the jurist and curialist Francisco Peña records the purchase of the *Theatrum*. I owe this reference to the kindness of Patricia H. Jobe.

41. L. Perini, "Note e documenti su Pietro Perna libraio-tipografo a Basilea," *NRS* 50 (1966): 145–200, at p. 150. Cf. the following note.

42. See, in general, for the production of Italian books in Basel and for the role of publishers and booksellers of that city in filling requests for northern books desired by Italian scholars: P. Bietenholz, *Der italienische Humanismus und die Blütezeit des Buchdrucks in Basel: Die Basler Drucke italienischer Autoren von 1530 bis zum Ende des 16. Jahrhunderts* (Basel and Stuttgart, 1959); L. Perini (in addition to the article cited in the preceding note), "Ancora sul libraio-tipografo Pietro Perna e su alcune figure di eretici italiani in rapporto con lui negli anni 1549–1555," *NRS* 51 (1967): 363–404; idem, "Note sulla famiglia di Pietro Perna e sul suo apprendistato tipografico," in *Magia, astrologia e religione nel Rinascimento, Convegno polacco-italiano (Varsavia: 25–27 settembre 1972)* (Wroclaw, Warsaw, etc., 1974), 163–209; A. Rotondò, "Pietro Perna e la vita culturale e religiosa di Basilea fra il 1570 e il 1580," in Rotondò's *Studi e ricerche*, 273–391; M. Welti, "Le grand animateur de la Renaissance tardive à Bale: Pierre Perna, éditeur, imprimeur et libraire," in *L'humanisme allemand (1480–1540): Colloque international de Tours* (Munich and Paris, 1979), 131–39. See also D. M. Manni, *Vita di Pietro Perna* (Lucca, 1763) for a listing of books produced by Perna.

43. For Paleario, see A. R. Salem, "The Badly Printed Book of an Unfortunate Author: The *Epistolae* of Aonio Paleario," *Harvard Library Bulletin* 2 (1948): 249–52

and the general treatment by A. Caponetto, *Aonio Paleario (1503–1570) e la Riforma protestante in Toscana* (Turin, 1979).

44. A. Rotondò, *Studi e ricerche*, 546. But see the note above for one highly dissatisfied author.

45. See *Regula* 10 in the Index of Pius IV (1564), reprinted in Reusch, *Die Indices*, 250.

46. The work ends with a series of verses by various writers in praise of Elizabeth. On the prolific author, see M. Firpo, *Pietro Bizzarri, esule italiano del Cinquecento* (Turin, 1971).

47. For example, *Giunta fatta al ragionamento degli articoli et de verbi di Messer Pietro Bembo* (Modena: Heredi di Cornelio Gadaldino, 1563), "Con licentia del reverendo padre Inquisitore di Modona"; *Ragione d'alcune cose segnate nella canzone d'Annibal Caro, 'Venite a l'ombra de gran gigli d'oro'* (Parma: Seth Viotto, 1573). On Castelvetro, see the excellent entry by V. Marchetti and G. Patrizi in the *DBI* 22 (Rome, 1979): 8–21. On his Melanchthon translations, see n. 12 above.

48. Published in Milan by Pietro and Francesco Tini and dedicated by them to Pietro Antonio Lonato "Cavalier d'Alcantera, e Regio, e Ducal Senatore di Milano." The first edition had appeared in Milan in 1565. On Squarcialupi as a religious radical, see D. Caccamo, *Eretici italiani in Moravia, Polonia, Transilvania (1558–1611)*, Biblioteca del Corpus Reformatorum Italicorum (Florence and Chicago, 1970), esp. p. 128.

49. *La Gierusalemme Liberata di Torquato Tasso . . . e le Annotationi di Scipio Gentili* (Genova, 1590). See *La Raccolta Tassiana della Biblioteca Civica 'A. Mai' di Bergamo* (Bergamo, 1960), 61 and passim.

50. *Italice Grammatices Praecepta ac Ratio* (Padua: apud A. et P. Meiettos, 1569; reissued 1585). The work had its first edition in Geneva in 1567 and was reprinted there the following year. Numerous editions appeared before 1650, including further Italian imprints: Venice, 1578; Vicenza, 1620; Padua, 1641; Rome, 1647. On the work, which obtained great success in England, see P. Buzzoni, ed., *I 'Praecepta' di Scipione Lentulo e l'adattamento inglese di Henry Grantham* (Florence, 1979). In the preface to the original edition Lentolo informs the reader that the grammar was a by-product of instruction in the Italian language which he had been giving to two Frenchmen and an Englishman in Geneva in 1559. In the unsigned prefatory note to the Italian editions, the scene of the instruction had been changed prudently from Geneva to Paris. I have consulted the Venice, 1578 edition of the *Italicae grammatices institutio* (Newberry Library, X 714. 51) unrecorded by Buzzoni.

51. Grendler (*The Roman Inquisition*, 190) mentions "a work of logic" by Celio Agostino published in Venice by Giordano Ziletti in 1563. This is the *De ratione consequendi styli*. For the publishing history of the *De ratione* and of the *Ieroglifici*, see M. Kutter, *Celio Secondo Curione, sein Leben und sein Werk (1503–1569)* (Basel and Stuttgart, 1955), 293 f.

52. Editions of 1539 and 1545. Cf. at n. 30. See also A. Kurcz, "Ismeretlen velencei Melanchton kiadás: Egy töredékes ars moriendi meghatározasa" ("An Unknown

Venetian Edition of Melanchthon: The Identification of a Fragmentary *Ars Morien-di*"), in *Országos Széchényi Könyvtár Évkönyve* (1973): 67–72. I have been unable to consult this work. For other Italian Melanchthon imprints, see n. 12.

53. *Methodus seu Ratio compendiaria perveniendi ad veram solidamque medicinam, mirifice ad Galeni libros recte intelligendos utilis* (Venice: Per Io. Ant. et Petrum fratres de Nicolinis de Sabio, 1543); for the prohibitions, see Reusch, *Die Indices*, 193, 497. Grendler (*The Roman Inquisition*, 119n.) cites a permission to read Fuchs's *De Historia Stirpium Commentarii* granted to the bishop of Spalato in 1559, while Rotondò ("La censura ecclesiastica," 1453) discusses expurgation of Fuchs's works.

54. *Opera di Giorgio Agricola de l'Arte de Metalli partita in XII Libri . . . Aggiugnesi il libro del medesimo autore, che tratta de gl'animali di sottoterra, da lui stesso corretto, e riveduto: Tradotti in lingua toscana da M. Michelangelo Florio fiorentino* (Basel: Per Hieronimo Frobenio et Nicolao Episcopio, 1563). I have used the facsimile edition by Luigi Firpo (Turin, 1969). For the pertinent biographical information on Florio, see the preface.

55. Ibid., [4].

56. Ibid., [11]: "Se a gli stromenti nominati in questo libro io havessi dato solamente i nomi usati a Firenze, gl'honorati Frobenii, per li quali l'ho tradotto, si sarebbeno potuti giustissimamente dolere di me, con dirmi che essi non me l'hanno fatto tradurre per venderlo solamente a Firenze, ma in ogni altra parte d'Italia." The *Primo catalogo collettivo delle biblioteche italiane* (Rome, 1963), 2:113, based on a census of eleven major Italian libraries, records four copies of the *Opera*. The fact that the dedication to Queen Elizabeth is usually missing from the surviving copies is stated by Zeitlin and Ver Brugge, Booksellers, catalogue 253, p. 3. For the prohibition of the Frobens, see the list of banned printers in the Index of Paul IV, reprinted in Reusch, *Die Indices*, 206.

57. D. E. Rhodes, "Some Notes on the Import of Books from Italy into England, 1628–1650," in Rhodes's *Studies in Early Printing* (London, 1982), 319–26, at p. 326. The catalogues of Venetian booksellers roughly from the turn of the century advertised works by such Italian Protestant exiles as Alberico Gentili, Matteo Gribaldi, Scipione Lentolo, and Giulio Pace: *Catalogus eorum librorum omnium, qui in ultramontanis regionibus impressi apud Io. Baptistam Ciottum prostant* (Venice, 1602); *Catalogus eorum librorum omnium, qui in ultramontanis regionibus impressi apud Robertum Meiettum prostant* (Venice, 1602). P. F. Grendler focuses on Meietti's activity in "Books for Sarpi: The Smuggling of Prohibited Books into Venice during the Interdict of 1606–1607," in S. Bertelli and G. Ramakus, eds., *Essays Presented to Myron P. Gilmore*, 2 vols. (Florence, 1978), 1:105–14.

58. D. E. Rhodes, "Libri inglesi recensiti a Roma, 1668–1681," in Rhodes's *Studies*, 79–88. See at p. 80: "Fra l'Inghilterra e l'Italia c'è nel Seicento un grande scambio di libri." S. Mastellone has given us a richly documented study of a principal figure in these continuing contacts and exchanges: "Antonio Magliabechi: Un libertino fiorentino?" *Il pensiero politico* 8 (1975): 33–53. For further information on Magliabechi, librarian to the Medici grand dukes, and the methods practiced

to circumvent restrictions on the book trade, which included cultivating the friendship of the local inquisitor, see also A. Mirto, *Stampatori, editori, librai nella seconda metà del Seicento* (Florence, 1984), chap. 3, "L'Inquisizione e la censura."

59. See the letter from the physician Francesco Redi to Cardinal Colonna, dated Ferrara, 9 July 1686: "È terminato il tempo, senza che io me ne sia accorto, della mia licenza dei libri proibiti, della quale restai graziato per la protezione dell'Eminenza Vostra: onde ricorro di nuovo con ogni più profonda umiltà alle sue grazie, per la conferma della medesima. Se sono importuno, ne incolpi V. Eminenza se medesima, che con tanti e così continuati favori mi ha cagionato l'ardire. . . ." F. Redi, *Opere*, 9 vols. (Milan, 1809–11), 8:312 f. For an instance from mid-sixteenth century, see n. 53 above. Consultors of the Holy Office regularly sought permission to read prohibited literature as compensation for the otherwise free service that they were rendering. See at n. 103 in "The Organization and Procedures of the Roman Inquisition." And inquisitors, early in the seventeenth century, were besieged by similar requests which they passed on to their superiors in Rome. See, as an example, ACAU, Epistolae S. Officii, 1588–1613 (unpaginated), letter to the inquisitor in Udine from Cardinal Arrigoni, dated 2 June 1612: "Per risposta di quanto V. R. scrisse con lettera di 29 di Aprile circa l'instanza, che spesso li vien fatta di concedere licenza di leggere libri prohibiti o sospesi, le dico per ordine di questi miei Ill.mi Sig.ri colleghi ch'ella mandi la nota de i libri, de' quali le vien chiesta licenza, et anco delle persone, che la dimandano alla giornata, perchè se li darà risoluzione, se debbia concedere o negare tali licenze. . . ."

60. A good many are recounted in A. Rotondò, "Nuovi documenti per la storia dell' 'Indice dei Libri Proibiti,' (1572–1638)," *Rinascimento*, n.s., 3 (1963): 145–211.

Select Bibliography

Manuscripts Consulted

Austin, University of Texas, Humanities Research Center
    Ranuzzi MS. Ph. 12868, contains Desiderio Scaglia's "Prattica per procedere. . . ."
Berkeley, University of California, Institute of Medieval Canon Law
    MS. 121, "Compendio di varie abiure."
Bologna, Biblioteca Comunale dell'Archiginnasio
    MS. B–1859, "Consilia et Vota in Materia S. Officii" (15th and 16th centuries).
    MS. B–1860–MS. B–1867, correspondence of Congregation of Inquisition with inquisitor of Bologna, January 1571–December 1634.
    Fondo Ospedali, MS. 53, "Libro de' Morti," 1540–1567; MS. 54, "Libro de' Morti," 1568–1588.
Brussels, Bibliothèque Royale
    MS. II 290, four volumes of decrees, correspondence, and trials, 16th–18th centuries, concerned with Inquisition of Florence.
Chicago, The Newberry Library
    Case 5A 107, A. Caracciolo's "Vita del Sommo Pontefice Paolo IIII."
    MS. Case 6A, Giulio Antonio Santorio, "Autobiography."
Dublin, Trinity College
    MS. 1224, sentences, 16 December 1564–January 1568.
    MS. 1225, sentences, 1580.
    MS. 1226, sentences, 1581–82.
    MS. 1227, sentences, 1582.

MS. 1228, sentences, 1603.

MS. 3216, Documents connected with the acquisition of the Inquisition materials.

Florence, Archivio della Curia Arcivescovile

S. *Uffizio*, b. 7, letter of Desiderio Scaglia to inquisitor of Florence.

S. *Uffizio*, b. 2–3, no. 163, "Instructio pro formandis processibus. . . ."

Florence, Archivio di Stato, I, XI, vols. 1271–1278, financial documents of Florentine Inquisition, 16th–18th centuries.

Oxford, Bodleian Library

MS. Add. C. 30, heavily annotated draft of Desiderio Scaglia's "Relatione copiosa. . . ."

MS. Add. C. 31, first three chapters of Desiderio Scaglia's "Relatione copiosa . . ." and Deodato Scaglia's "Theorica di procedere. . . ."

MS. Mendham 36, miscellaneous inquisitorial materials, including Desiderio Scaglia's "Pratica di procedere. . . ."

Paris, Bibliothèque Nationale

Cod. lat. 8994, miscellaneous volume concerned with French subjects before the Inquisition.

Philadelphia, University of Pennsylvania Library

MS. Lea 115, Desiderio Scaglia's "Pratica del modo di procedere. . . ."

MS. Lea 137, collection of Roman Holy Office decrees, 16–17th centuries.

MS. Lea 184, Desiderio Scaglia's "Prattica per le cause del Sant' Offitio. . . ."

Rome, Biblioteca Apostolica Vaticana

Barb. lat. 1370, inquisitorial handbook compiled from correspondence.

Barb. lat. 6334, letters of the Congregation of the Inquisition for the year 1626.

Barb. lat. 4615, autograph of Deodato Scaglia's "La Prattica di procedere. . . ."

Barb. lat. 4616, contains Deodato Scaglia's "La Theorica di procedere. . . ."

Barb. lat. 5205, account of affairs of Venetian Inquisition from reign of Clement VIII to July 1625.

Borg. lat. 548, inquisitorial handbook compiled from correspondence.

Borg. lat. 558, idem.

Borg. lat. 660, miscellaneous inquisitorial materials.

Borg. lat. 571, contains Deodato Scaglia's "La Theorica di procedere. . . ."

Vat. lat. 8193, miscellaneous codex which includes a copy of the "Instructio pro formandis processibus. . . ."

Vat. lat. 12728, expurgations of prohibited books compiled by a Fra Gregorio Capuccino (late 16th century).

Rome, Biblioteca Casanatense

MS. 2889, Desiderio Scaglia's "Relazione copiosa. . . ."

MS. 2905, Desiderio Scaglia's "Prattica per procedere. . . ."

MS. 3825, decrees of the Congregation of the Inquisition for the years 1600–1602.

Udine, Archivio della Curia Arcivescovile

Sant'Uffizio, vol. 59, letters of the Congregation of the Inquisition to the inquisitor in Udine, 1588-1613.
Sant'Uffizio, vol. 60, idem, 1614-46.
Venice, Archivio di Stato
    Santo Uffizio, Index 303, inventory of trials of Venetian Inquisition, c. 1541-c. 1794.

Printed Works

Abbiati, S. "A proposito di taluni processi inquisitori modenesi del primo Cinquecento." *BSSV*, no. 146 (1979): 101-18.

————. "Intorno ad una possibile valutazione giuridico-diplomatica del documento inquisitorio." *Studi di storia medioevale e di diplomatica* 3 (1978): 167-79.

Abbott, T. K. *Catalogue of the Manuscripts in the Library of Trinity College, Dublin.* Dublin and London, 1900. Reprint 1980.

Accati, L. "Lo spirito della fornicazione: Virtù dell'anima e virtù del corpo in Friuli fra '600 e '700." *Quaderni storici*, a. 14, no. 41 (1979): 644-72.

Acta Capitulorum Generalium Ordinis Praedicatorum. Ed. B. M. Reichert. Rome and Stuttgart, 1901-2. The pertinent volumes, chronologically, are 4, 1501-53; 5, 1558-1600; 6, 1601-28; 7, 1629-56. They appear as vols. 8-12 of the *Monumenta Ordinis Fratrum Praedicatorum Historica.*

Acta nuntiaturae Gallicae. Publiés par la Faculté d'Histoire Ecclésiastique de l'Université Pontificale Grégorienne et l'École française de Rome. Rome, 1961-.

Ademollo, A. "Le giustizie a Roma dal 1674 al 1739 e dal 1796 al 1840." *ASRSP* 4 (1880-81): 429-534.

Adorisio, A. "Stregoneria e vita religiosa tra città e campagna nel Cinquecento romano." *Sociologia: Rivista di scienze sociali dell'Istituto Luigi Sturzo* 17 (1983): 167-212.

Adorni Braccesi, S. "Il dissenso religioso nel contesto urbano lucchese della Controriforma." In *Città italiane del '500*, 225-39.

————. "Giuliano da Dezza, caciaiuolo: Nuove prospettive sull'eresia a Lucca nel XVI secolo." *Actum Luce: Rivista di studi lucchesi* 9 (1980), nos. 1-2: 89-138.

————. "Libri e lettori a Lucca tra Riforma e Controriforma: Un' indagine in corso." In *Libri, idee e sentimenti religiosi*, 39-46.

Alberghini, Giovanni. *Manuale Qualificatorum Sanctae Inquisitionis.* Palermo, 1642.

Albèri, E., ed. *Le relazioni degli ambasciatori veneti al Senato durante il secolo decimosesto.* 15 vols. Florence, 1839-63.

Alberigo, G. "Diplomazia e vita della Chiesa nel XVI secolo (a proposito di recenti edizioni di nunziature)." *Critica storica* 1 (1962): 49-69.

————. "Problemi e indirizzi di storia religiosa lombarda, secoli XV-XVII." In *Problemi di storia religiosa lombarda*, 111-27. Como, 1972.

Albizzi, Francesco. *De Inconstantia in Iure Admittenda vel non.* Amsterdam, 1683.

――――. *Risposta all' Historia della Sacra Inquisizione, composta già dal R.P. Paolo Servi-ta*. ... N.p., n.d., but c. 1670.

Alcalá, A., ed. *Inquisición española y mentalidad inquisitorial*. Ponencias del Simposio Internacional sobre Inquisición, Nueva York, abril de 1983. Barcelona, 1984. Also in English as *The Spanish Inquisition and the Inquisitorial Mind*. Atlantic Studies on Society in Change, 49. Boulder, 1987.

Alce, V., and D'Amato, A. *La biblioteca di S. Domenico in Bologna*. Florence, 1961.

Alessi Palazzolo, G. "Pene e 'remieri' a Napoli tra Cinque e Seicento: Un' aspetto singolare dell'illegalismo d'ancien régime." *Archivio storico per le province napole-tane*, ser. 3, 15 (1976): 235–51.

――――. *Prova legale e pena: La crisi del sistema tra evo medio e moderno*. Naples, 1979.

Amabile, L. *Fra Tommaso Campanella: La sua congiura, i suoi processi e la sua pazzia*. 3 vols. Naples, 1882.

――――. *Il Santo Officio della Inquisizione in Napoli. Narrazione con molti documenti inediti*. 2 vols. Città di Castello, 1892. Reprint 1987.

Amiel, C. "The Archives of the Portuguese Inquisition: A Brief Survey." In *The Inquisition in Early Modern Europe*, 79–99.

Anglo, S. "Evident Authority and Authoritative Evidence: The *Malleus Malefica-rum*." In *The Damned Art: Essays in the Literature of Witchcraft*, ed. S. Anglo, 1–31. London, 1977.

Antoniazzi Villa, A. "Per la storia degli Ebrei a Venezia: Pier Cesare Ioly Zorattini ed i 'Processi del Sant'Uffizio di Venezia contro ebrei e giudaizzanti.'" *NRS* 67 (1983): 138–43.

Antonovics, A. V. "Counter-Reformation Cardinals: 1534–90." *European Studies Review* 2 (1972): 301–28.

Aquarone, B. *Vita di Fra Jeronimo Savonarola*, 2 vols. Alessandria, 1857–58.

Aquilecchia, G. *Giordano Bruno*. Rome, 1971.

Arens, A., ed. *Friedrich Spee von Langenfeld, zur Wiederauffindung seines Grabes im Jahre 1980*. Trier, 1981.

Armstrong, E. *Robert Estienne Royal Printer, an Historical Study of the Elder Stepha-nus*. Cambridge, 1954. Revised ed. Abingdon, 1986.

Aubert, A. "Alle origini della Controriforma: Studi e problemi su Paolo IV." *Rivis-ta di storia e letteratura religiosa* 22 (1986): 303–55.

Audisio, G. "Les Vaudois et le livre (XVe–XVIe siècles)." In *Les Réformes: Enracinement socio-culturel: XXV colloque international d'études humanistes, Tours, 1er–13 Juillet 1982*. Études réunies par B. Chevalier & R. Sauzet, 183–89. Paris, 1985.

Aureggi, O. "La stregoneria nelle Alpi centrali: Ricerche di diritto e procedura penale." *Bollettino della società storica valtellinese*, no. 15 (1961): 114–60.

――――. "Stregoneria retica e tortura giudiziaria." *Bollettino della società storica valtel-linese*, no. 17 (1963–64): 46–90.

Aventures (Les) de Joseph Pignata echappé des prisons de l'Inquisition de Rome. Cologne, 1725.

Avventure di Giuseppe Pignata, fuggito dalle carceri dell'Inquisizione di Roma, ed. O. Guerrini. Città di Castello, 1887.

Aymard, M. "Chiourmes et galères dans la Méditerranée du XVIe siècle." In *Histoire économique du monde méditerranéen, 1450–1650*. Melanges en l'Honneur de Fernand Braudel, 1: 49–64. Toulouse, 1973.

Backer, A. de. *Bibliothèque des écrivains de la Compagnie de Jesus: Supplement*. 3 vols. Louvain and Lyons, 1869–76.

Bainton, R. H., and Gibbons, L. O., eds. *George Lincoln Burr, His Life . . . Selections from His Writings*. Ithaca, 1943.

Baldini, U. "Una fonte poco utilizzata per la storia intellettuale: Le *censurae librorum* e *opinionum* nell'antica Compagnia di Gesù." *Annali dell'Istituto storico italo-germanico in Trento* 11 (1985): 19–67.

Balestracci, D. "Le confraternite romane fra tardo medioevo ed età moderna nei contributi della recente storiografia." *Archivio storico italiano* 146 (1988): 321–30.

Balmas, E. "L'activité des imprimeurs italiens réfugiés à Genève dans la deuxième moitié du XVI siècle." In *Cinq siècles d'imprimerie genevoise: Actes du Colloque international sur l'histoire de l'imprimerie et du livre à Genève, 27–30 avril 1978*, ed. J.-D. Candaux and B. Lescaze, 2 vols., 1: 109–31. Geneva, 1980.

Balzani, U. "Di alcuni documenti dell'archivio del Santo Uffizio di Roma relativi al ritrovamento del cadavere di Paolo Sarpi." *Rendiconti della reale Accademia dei Lincei, classe di scienze morali, storiche e filologiche*, ser. 5, 4 (1895): 595–617.

Bamford, P. W. *Fighting Ships and Prisons: The Mediterranean Galleys of France in the Age of Louis XIV*. Minneapolis, 1973.

Barberi, F. "Le edizioni della Bibbia in Italia nei secoli XV e XVI." *Bergomum* 78 (1984), nos. 1–2: 3–20.

Baron, S. W. *A Social and Religious History of the Jews*. Vol. 13, *Inquisition, Renaissance and Reformation*. 2nd rev. and enl. ed. New York and London, 1969.

Barrera, P., ed. *Una fuga dalle prigioni del Sant'Uffizio (1693)*. Milan, 1934.

Bartlett, K. "Dangers and Delights: English Protestants in Italy in the Sixteenth Century." In *Forestieri e stranieri nelle città basso-medievali*, Atti del Seminario internazionale di studio, Bagno a Ripoli (Firenze), 4–8 giugno 1984, 215–22. Florence, 1988.

———. "Worshipful Gentlemen of England: The Studio of Padua and the Education of the English Gentry in the Sixteenth Century." *Renaissance and Reformation*, n.s., 6 (1982): 235–48.

Battafarano, I. M., ed. *Friedrich von Spee: Dichter, Theologe und Bekaempfer der Hexenprozesse*. Apollo: Studi e testi di Germanistica e Comparatistica, 1. Gardolo di Trento, 1988.

Battistella, A. "Alcuni documenti sul S. Officio in Lombardia nei secoli XVI e XVII." *ASL*, ser. 3, 3, a. 22 (1895): 116–32.

———. "Brevi note sul S. Offizio e la Riforma religiosa in Friuli." *Atti dell'Accademia di Udine*, ser. 3, no. 10 (1902–3): 265–85.

————. "Notizie sparse sul Sant'Officio in Lombardia durante i secoli XVI e XVII." *ASL*, ser. 3, 17, a. 29 (1902): 121–38.

————. *Processi d'eresia nel Collegio di Spagna (1533–1554): Episodio di storia della Riforma in Bologna.* Bologna, 1901.

————. *Il S. Officio e la Riforma religiosa in Bologna.* Bologna, 1905.

————. *Il S. Officio e la Riforma religiosa in Friuli.* Udine, 1895.

Battistini, M. "Una lettera del Cardinale Mellini riguardo un processo di stregoneria." *RSCI* 10 (1956): 269–70.

————. "Per la storia dell'Inquisizione fiorentina (documenti inediti della Biblioteca reale di Bruxelles." *Bilychnis* 18 (1929): 425–48.

Baudrier, J. *Bibliographie Lyonnaise.* 12 vols. Lyons and Paris, 1895–1921. Plus 2 vols. of Indices, and Supplement, 1967–.

Becker, G. *Deutsche Juristen und ihre Schriften auf den römischen Indices des 16. Jahrhunderts.* Berlin, 1970.

Beinart, H. *Conversos on Trial: The Inquisition in Ciudad Real.* Jerusalem, 1981.

Bell, H. F. "Research in Progress in Legal History." *American Journal of Legal History* 17 (1973): 66–84.

Ben-Yehuda, N. "Problems Inherent in Socio-Historical Approaches to the European Witch Craze." *Journal of the Scientific Study of Religion* 20 (1981): 326–38.

Bendiscioli, M. "Penetrazione protestante e repressione controriformistica in Lombardia all'epoca di Carlo e Federico Borromeo." In *Festgabe Joseph Lortz*, ed. E. Iserloh and P. Manns, 2 vols., 1: 369–404. Baden-Baden, 1958.

Bennassar, B. *Les Chretiens d'Allah: L'histoire extraordinaire des renégats, XVe–XVIIe siècles.* Paris, 1989.

————. "Conversion ou reniement? Modalités d'une adhésion ambiguë des chretiens à l'Islam (XVIe–XVIIe s.)." *Annales: E.S.C.*, 43 (1988): 1349–66.

————. *L'Inquisition espagnole, XVe–XIXe siècle.* Paris, 1979.

————. "Un phénomène historiographique: L'accélération des recherches sur l'Inquisition espagnole; enjeux et débats." *Histoire, economie et société* 2 (1983): 367–72.

Benrath, K. "Akten aus römischen Archiven in Trinity College Library, Dublin." *Historische Zeitschrift* 41 (1879): 249–62.

————. "Atti degli archivi romani della Biblioteca del Collegio della Trinità in Dublino." *La rivista cristiana* 7 (1879): 457–72, 497–505; 8 (1880): 10–13, 55–58, 94–97, 137–43.

————. *Über die Quellen der italienischen Reformationsgeschichte.* Bonn, 1876.

Benvenuti, E. "Un curioso manifesto satira degli Accademici Spensierati." *Rivista delle biblioteche e degli archivi* 22 (1911): 15–17.

Benvenuti, M. "Come facevasi giustizia nello stato di Milano dall'anno 1471 al 1763." *ASL* 9 (1882): 442–82.

Benzoni, G. "Intellettuali e Controriforma." *La Cultura* 22 (1984): 128–71.

Berengo, M. *Nobili e mercanti nella Lucca del Cinquecento.* Biblioteca di Cultura Storica, 82. Turin, 1965.

Bernardini, R. "Un convegno sulla vita a bordo delle navi nel Mediterraneo nel

Cinquecento e nel Seicento." *Archivio storico italiano*, a. 145, no. 534 (1987): 677–86 (the papers from this symposium have been published in *Quaderni stefaniani* 6 [1987]: 1–198).

Bernardo da Como. *Lucerna Inquisitorum Haereticae Pravitatis*. [Ed. F. Peña]. Rome, 1584. New ed. Venice, 1596.

Bertolotti, A. *Martiri del libero pensiero e vittime della Santa Inquisizione nei secoli XVI, XVII e XVIII*. Rome, 1902.

———. *Le prigioni di Roma nei secoli XVI, XVII e XVIII*. Rome, 1890.

———. "La schiavitù in Roma dal secolo XVI al XIX." *Rivista di discipline carcerarie* 17 (1887): 3–41.

Bertora, G. "Il tribunale inquisitorio di Genova e l'Inquisizione romana nel '500 (alla luce di documenti inediti)." *La Civiltà cattolica*, vol. 104, t. 2 (1953): 173–87.

Bévenot, M. "The Inquisition and Its Antecedents." *The Heythrop Journal* 7 (1966): 257–68, 381–93; 8 (1967): 52–69, 152–68.

Biagi, G. "Le carte dell'Inquisizione fiorentina a Bruxelles." *Rivista delle biblioteche e degli archivi* 19 (1908): 161–68.

Bianco, C. "La comunità di 'fratelli' nel movimento ereticale modenese del '500." *RSI* 92 (1980): 621–79.

Bietenholz, P. *Der italienische Humanismus und die Blütezeit des Buchdrucks in Basel: Die Basler Drucke italienischer Autoren von 1530 bis zum Ende des 16. Jahrhunderts*. Basler Beiträge zur Geschichtswissenschaft, 73. Basel and Stuttgart, 1959.

Biffi, S. *Sulle antiche carceri di Milano e del ducato milanese e sui sodalizi che vi assistevano i prigionieri ed i condannati a morte*. Milan, 1884.

Biondi, A. "Gianfrancesco Pico e la repressione della stregoneria: Qualche novità sui processi mirandolesi del 1522–23." *Deputazione di Storia Patria per le Antiche Provincie Modenesi: Biblioteca*, n.s., 76 (1984): 331–49.

———. "Lunga durata e microarticolazione nel territorio di un ufficio dell' Inquisizione: Il 'Sacro Tribunale' a Modena (1292–1785)." *Annali dell'Istituto storico italo-germanico in Trento* 8 (1982): 73–90.

———. "La 'Nuova Inquisizione' a Modena: Tre inquisitori (1589–1607)." In *Città italiane del '500*, 61–76.

———, and Prosperi, A., eds. *Il processo al medico Basilio Albrisio, Reggio 1559*. Contributi, Biblioteca Municipale "A. Panizzi." Reggio Emilia, 1978.

Biondi, G. "Le lettere della Sacra Congregazione romana del Santo Ufficio all'Inquisizione di Modena: Note in margine a un regesto." *Schifanoia* 4 (1989): 93–108.

Black, C. "Perugia and Post-Tridentine Church Reform." *Journal of Ecclesiastical History* 35 (1984): 429–51.

———. *Italian Confraternities in the Sixteenth Century*. Cambridge, 1989.

Blázquez, J. Miguel. *Inquisición e criptojudaismo*. Madrid, 1988.

Boccato, C. "Processi ad Ebrei nell' archivio degli Ufficiali al Cattaver a Venezia." *Rassegna mensile di Israel* 41 (1975): 164–80.

———. "Un processo contro Ebrei di Verona alla fine del Cinquecento." *Rassegna mensile di Israel* 40 (1974): 345–70.

Bodin, Jean. *De la demonomanie des sorciers*. Paris, 1580.

Bonazzoli, V. "Gli Ebrei del Regno di Napoli all'epoca della loro espulsione." *Archivio storico italiano* 137 (1979): 495–559; 139 (1981): 179–287.

Bondì, C. *Strix: Medichesse, streghe e fattucchiere nell'Italia del Rinascimento*. Rome, 1989.

Bongi, S. *Annali di Gabriel Giolito de' Ferrari da Trino di Monferrato stampatore in Venezia*. 2 vols. Rome, 1890.

———. "Le prime gazzette in Italia." *Nuova antologia* 11 (1869): 311–46.

Bonnant, G. "Les Index Prohibitifs et Expurgatoires contrefaits par des protestants au XVIe et au XVIIe siècle." *Bibliothèque d'Humanisme et Renaissance* 31 (1969): 611–40.

———. "La librairie genevoise en Italie, jusqu'à la fin du XVIIIe siècle." *Genava* 15 (1967): 117–60.

Bono, S. *I corsari barbareschi*. Turin, 1964.

Bonomo, G. *Caccia alle streghe: La credenza nelle streghe dal sec. XIII al XIX con particolare riferimento all'Italia*. Palermo, 1971.

———. "Nuove ricerche sulla stregoneria." In *La strega, il teologo, lo scienziato*, Atti del Convegno "Magia, stregoneria e superstizione in Europa e nella zona alpina," Borgosesia, 1983, ed. M. Cuccu and P. A. Rossi. Genoa, 1986.

Bordier, H. *Les archives de la France, ou histoire des archives de l'empire*. Paris, 1855.

Bordoni, Francesco. *Manuale consultorum in causis S. Officii contra haereticam pravitatem refertum, quamplurimis dubiis novis, & veteribus resolutis*. Parma, 1693.

Borromeo, A. "A proposito del 'Directorium Inquisitorum' di Nicolas Eymerich e delle sue edizioni cinquecentesche." *Critica storica* 20 (1983): 499–547.

———. "Contributo allo studio dell'Inquisizione e dei suoi rapporti con il potere episcopale nell'Italia Spagnola del Cinquecento." *Annuario dell'Istituto storico italiano per l'età moderna e contemporanea* 29–30 (1977–78): 219–76.

———. "Le controversie giurisdizionali tra potere laico e potere ecclesiastico nella Milano spagnola sul finire del Cinquecento." *Atti dell'Accademia di San Carlo: Inaugurazione del IV Anno Accademico*, 43–89. Milan, 1981.

———. "The Inquisition and Inquisitorial Censorship." In J. W. O'Malley, ed., *Catholicism in Early Modern History: A Guide to Research*, 253–72. St. Louis, 1988.

———. "Inquisizione spagnola e libri proibiti in Sicilia ed in Sardegna durante il XVI secolo." *Annuario dell'Istituto storico italiano per l'età moderna e contemporanea* 35–36 (1983–84): 219–71.

Bourdet-Pléville, M. *Justice in Chains: From the Galleys to Devil's Island*. Trans. from the French by A. Rippon. London, 1960.

Bourgin, G. "Les archives pontificales et l'histoire moderne de la France." *Bibliographe moderne* 9 (1905): 251–362.

———. "Fonti per la storia dei Dipartimenti romani negli Archivi Nazionali di Parigi." *ASRSP* 29 (1906): 97–144.

Boyle, L. E. *A Survey of the Vatican Archives and Its Medieval Holdings*, 145–48. Toronto, 1972.

Bozza, T. "Introduzione al processo del Carnesecchi." *Annuario dell'Istituto storico italiano per l'età moderna e contemporanea* 35–36 (1983–84): 81–94.

———. "Italia calvinista: Traduzioni italiane di Calvino nel secolo XVI." In *Miscellanea in onore di Ruggero Moscati*, 237–51. Naples, 1985.

Braudel, F. *La Méditerranée et le monde méditerranéen à l'époque de Philippe II*. 2nd ed. 2 vols. Paris, 1966.

Bremme, H. J. *Buchdrucker und Buchhändler zur Zeit der Glaubenskämpfe: Studien zur Genfer Druckgeschichte, 1565–1580*. Geneva, 1969.

Brown, H. *The Venetian Printing Press 1469–1800*. London, 1891. Reprint Amsterdam, 1969.

Brown, P. M. *Lionardo Salviati: A Critical Biography*. Oxford, 1974.

Brown, R. "Examination of an Interesting Roman Document: *Instructio Pro Formandis Processibus in Causis Strigum*." *The Jurist* 24 (1964): 169–91.

Brugi, B. "Gli scolari tedeschi e la S. Inquisizione a Padova nella seconda metà del secolo XVI." In *Per la storia della giurisprudenza e delle università italiane: Saggi*, 11: 154–69. Turin, 1915.

Brugnoli, M. "Superstizione e repressione: Il tribunale della Santa Inquisizione a Bologna e contado nell'ultimo quarto del XVII secolo." *Tesi di Laurea*, Faculty of Political Science, University of Bologna, academic year 1981–82.

Bufalini, D., Landi, D. R., Zannoni, G. "Catalogo delle cinquecentine straniere conservate nella Biblioteca Comunale dell'Archiginnasio (lettera B)." *L'Archiginnasio* 81 (1986): 185–319.

Bulgarella, P. "Fonti d'Archivio sull'Inquisizione spagnola in Sicilia." *Annuario dell'Istituto storico italiano per l'età moderna e contemporanea* 37–38 (1985–86): 143–60.

———. "I registri contabili del Sant'Uffizio di Sicilia nell'Archivio di Stato di Palermo." *Rassegna degli Archivi di Stato* 31 (1971): 677–89.

Bulgarelli, T. *Gli avvisi a stampa in Roma nel Cinquecento*. Rome, 1967.

Bullarium Ordinis FF. Praedicatorum . . . opera reverendissimi patris F. Thomae Ripoll (et) . . . Antonino Bremond. 8 vols. Rome, 1729–40.

Burke, P. *The Historical Anthropology of Early Modern Italy: Essays on Perception and Communication*. Cambridge, 1987.

———. "Witchcraft and Magic in Renaissance Italy: Gianfrancesco Pico and His Strix." In *The Damned Art: Essays in the Literature of Witchcraft*, ed. S. Anglo, 32–52. London, 1977.

Burr, G. L. "The Literature of Witchcraft." *Papers of the American Historical Association* 4, pt. 3 (1890): 37–66.

Buzzoni, P., ed. *I 'Praecepta' di Scipione Lentulo e l'adattamento inglese di Henry Grantham*. Florence, 1979.

Caccamo, D. *Eretici italiani in Moravia, Polonia, Transilvania (1558–1611)*. Biblioteca del Corpus Reformatorum Italicorum. Florence and Chicago, 1970.

Caiazza, P. "Nunziatura di Napoli e problemi religiosi nel Viceregno post-tridentino." *RSCI* 42 (1988): 24–69.

Cairns, C. *Domenico Bollani, Bishop of Brescia: Devotion to Church and State in the Republic of Venice in the Sixteenth Century.* Nieuwkoop, 1976.

Cairoli, A., and Chiaberto, G. "La strega, i corpi, la terra: Lettura di processi per stregoneria nel baliaggio di Mendrisio (1536–1615)." *Archivio storico ticinese* 20 (1979): 183–248.

Calbetti, Arcangelo. *Sommaria instruttione a' suoi RR. vicarii nella Inquisitione sodetta intorno alla maniera di trattar alla giornata i negotii del Sant' Ufficio per quello che a loro s'appartiene.* Modena, 1604.

Calzolai, C. C. "L'Archivio arcivescovile fiorentino." *Rassegna storica toscana* 3 (1957): 127–81.

Camerarius, Philipp. *Operae Horarum Succisivarum sive Meditationes Historicae.* Nuremberg, 1599.

Camerlynck, E. "Féminité et sorcellerie chez les théoriciens de la démonologie à la fin du Moyen Age: Étude du *Malleus Maleficarum.*" *Renaissance and Reformation* 19 (1983): 13–25.

Campeggi, Ridolfo. *Racconto degli heretici iconomiasti giustiziati in Bologna a gloria di Dio, della B. Vergine et per honore della patria....* Bologna, 1623.

Canale, Cristoforo da. *Della milizia marittima.* Ed. M. N. Mocenigo. Rome, 1930.

Canosa, R. *Storia dell'Inquisizione in Italia dalla metà del Cinquecento alla fine del Settecento.* 5 vols. to date. Rome, 1986–. I. Modena; II. Venezia; III. Torino e Genova; IV. Milano e Firenze; V. Napoli e Bologna.

————, and Colonnello, I. *Storia dell'Inquisizione in Sicilia dal 1600 al 1720.* Biblioteca Siciliana di Storia e Letteratura. Quaderni, 45. Palermo, 1989.

Cantimori, D. *Eretici italiani del Cinquecento: Ricerche storiche.* Biblioteca storica Sansoni, n.s., 1. Florence, 1939. Reprint, 1967. And in a slightly revised German translation, *Italienische Haeretiker der Spätrenaissance: Deutsch von W. Kaegi.* Basel, 1949.

————. "Note su Erasmo e la vita morale e religiosa italiana nel secolo XVI." In *Antologia di critica storica*, ed. A. Saitta, 2:473–93. Bari, 1959.

————. *Prospettive di storia ereticale italiana del Cinquecento.* Biblioteca di cultura moderna, 550. Bari, 1960.

Caponetto, A. *Aonio Paleario (1503–1570) e la Riforma protestante in Toscana.* Turin, 1979.

————. "Dell'Agostiniano Ambrogio Bolognesi e del suo processo di eresia a Palermo (1552–1554)." *BSSV* 76, no. 102 (1957): 39–49. Reprinted with notes and the text of the trial in the *Bibliothèque d'Humanisme et Renaissance* 20 (1958): 310–43.

————. "Due opere di Melantone tradotte da Lodovico Castelvetro: 'I principii della theologia di Ippophilo da Terra Negra' e 'Dell'autorità della Chiesa e degli scritti degli antichi.'" *NRS* 70 (1986): 253–74.

————. "Ginevra e la Riforma in Sicilia." In *Ginevra e l'Italia*, 287–306. Florence, 1959.

————. "Origini e caratteri della Riforma in Sicilia." *Rinascimento* 7 (1956): 219–341.

————. *Studi sulla Riforma in Italia* (collected essays). Università degli Studi di Firenze, Dipartimento di Storia. Florence, 1987.

Carcereri, L. "Agostino Centurione mercante genovese processato per eresia e assolto dal Concilio di Trento (1563)." *Archivio trentino* 21 (1906): 65–99.

Cardella, L. *Memorie storiche de' cardinali della Santa Romana Chiesa.* Rome, 1793.

Carena, Cesare. *Tractatus de Officio Sanctissimae Inquisitionis et Modo Procedendi in Causis Fidei.* Cremona, 1642. New eds. Cremona, 1655 and Bologna, 1668.

Carpzov, Benedict. *Practica Rerum Criminalium.* Wittenberg, 1670.

Carratori, L. *Inventario dell' Archivio Arcivescovile di Pisa: I. (Secoli VIII–XV).* Pisa, 1986.

Carte (Le) strozziane del R. Archivio di Stato di Firenze. Ser. 1, vol. 2. Florence, 1891.

Carusi, E. "Nuovi documenti del processo di Giordano Bruno." *Giornale critico della filosofia italiana* 6 (1925): 121–39.

————. "Nuovi documenti sui processi di Tommaso Campanella." *Giornale critico della filosofia italiana* 8 (1927): 321–59.

Castaldi, Giovanni Tommaso. *De Potestate Angelica, sive de potentia motrice, ac mirandis operibus angelorum atque daemonum.* 3 vols. Rome, 1650–52.

Castiglione, T. R. "Un poeta siciliano riformato, Giulio Cesare Pascali: Contributo alla storia dell'emigrazione protestante nel sec. XVI." *Religio* 12 (1936): 29–61.

Catalogo de' capi d'opera di pittura, scultura, antichità, libri, storia naturale ed altre curiosità trasportati dall'Italia in Francia. Seconda edizione, fatta su quella di Venezia del 1799. Milan, n.d.

Catalogue (A) of Canon and Roman Law Manuscripts in the Vatican Library, I: Codices Vaticani latini 541–2299. Compiled under the direction of S. Kuttner and R. Elze. Studi e Testi, 322. Vatican City, 1986.

Catalogue of Manuscripts in the Libraries of the University of Pennsylvania. Compiled by N. P. Zacour and R. Hirsch. Assisted by J. F. Benton and W. E. Miller. Philadelphia, 1965.

Catalogus eorum librorum omnium, qui in ultramontanis regionibus impressi apud Robertum Meiettum prostant. Venice, 1602.

Catalogus eorum librorum omnium, qui in ultramontanis regionibus impressi apud Io. Baptistam Ciottum prostant. Venice, 1602.

Cavazza, S. *Catalogo del fondo antico della Biblioteca del Seminario di Gorizia.* Florence, 1975.

————. "Inquisizione e libri proibiti in Friuli e a Gorizia tra Cinquecento e Seicento." *Studi goriziani* 43 (1976): 29–80.

————. "Libri in volgare e propaganda eterodossa: Venezia, 1543–1547." In *Libri, idee e sentimenti religiosi,* 9–28.

Celani, E. "Processi di Fr. Tommaso Campanella: Note sommarie inedite." *Archivio storico per le province napoletane* 25 (1900): 462–66.

Ceyssens, L. *Le cardinal François Albizzi (1593–1684): Un cas important dans l'histoire du jansénisme.* Rome, 1977.

Chadwick, O. *Catholicism and History: The Opening of the Vatican Archives.* Cambridge, 1978.

Chaix, P., Dufour, A., and Moeckli, G. *Les livres imprimés à Genève de 1550 à 1600*. Nouvelle édition, revue et augmentée par G. Moeckli. Travaux d'Humanisme et Renaissance, 86. Geneva, 1966.

————. *Recherches sur l'imprimerie à Genève de 1550 à 1564: Étude bibliographique, économique et littéraire*. Travaux d'Humanisme et Renaissance, 16. Geneva, 1954. Reprint 1978.

Chamson, A. *La Superbe*. Paris, 1967.

Chevailler, L. "Torture." In *Dictionnaire de droit canonique*, 7: cols. 1293–1314. Paris, 1965.

Chevaillier, L. "Les origines et les premières années de fonctionnement de la 'Nonciature de Savoie' à Turin (1560–1573)." In *Études d'Histoire du Droit Canonique dediées à Gabriel Le Bras*, 1:489–512. Paris, 1965.

Chiecchi, G., and Troisio, L. *Il Decameron sequestrato: Le tre edizioni censurate nel Cinquecento*. Milan, 1984.

Ciaconius, A., and Oldoino, A. *Vitae et res gestae Pontificum Romanorum et S.R.E. cardinalium....* 4 vols. Rome, 1677.

Cioni, M. *I documenti galileiani del S. Uffizio di Firenze*. Florence, 1908.

Cirillo da Leguigno. "Giambattista Scanaroli (1579–1665) apostolo modenese nelle carceri romane." *Italia francescana* 45 (1970): 318–40.

Città italiane del '500 tra Riforma e Controriforma: Atti del convegno internazionale di studi, Lucca, 13–15 ottobre 1983. Lucca, 1988.

Clavicula Salomonis Filii David. N.p., 1600 (?).

Cobben, J. J. *Jan Wier, Devils, Witches and Magic*. Trans. S. A. Prins. Philadelphia, 1976.

Cochrane, E. *Florence in the Forgotten Centuries, 1527–1800*. Chicago, 1973.

————. "New Light on Post-Tridentine Italy: A Note on Recent Counter-Reformation Scholarship." *Catholic Historical Review* 56 (1970): 291–319.

————. *Tradition and Enlightenment in the Tuscan Academies*. Chicago, 1961.

Cocquelines, Carolus. *Bullarum, Privilegiorum ac Diplomatum Romanorum Pontificum Amplissima Collectio*. 14 vols. in 28. Rome, 1733–62.

Comba, E. "Elenco generale degli accusati di eresia dinanzi il Sant'Ufficio della Inquisizione di Venezia an. 1541–1600." *Rivista cristiana* 3 (1875): 28–34, 71, 100–101, 158, 207, 235, 297, 326, 366–67, 411–12, 447; 4 (1876): 14, 57, 93, 136, 178.

Confessione (La) di una strega, un frammento di storia della Controriforma. Introduzione e note di L. Sambenazzi. Presentazione di A. Foa. Rome, 1989.

Coniglio, G. "Società e Inquisizione nel Viceregno di Napoli." *Annuario dell' Istituto storico italiano per l'età moderna e contemporanea* 37–38 (1985–86): 127–39.

Conlon, P. M. *Jean-François Bion et sa relation des torments soufferts par les forçats protestants*. Geneva, 1966.

Contemporaries of Erasmus: A Biographical Register of the Renaissance and Reformation. Ed. P. G. Bietenholz and T. B. Deutscher. 3 vols. Toronto, 1985.

Contreras, J. "Algunas consideraciones sobre las relaciones de causas de Sicilia y Cerdeña." *Annuario dell' Istituto storico italiano per l'età moderna e contemporanea* 37–38 (1985–86): 181–99.

————. "Las causas de fe de la Inquisición de Galicia: 1560–1700." In *La Inquisición española*, ed. J. Pérez Villanueva, 355–70.

————. *El Santo Oficio de la Inquisición en Galicia, 1560–1700: Poder, sociedad y cultura*. Madrid, 1982.

————, and Henningsen, G. "Forty-four Thousand Cases of the Spanish Inquisition (1540–1700): Analysis of a Historical Data Bank." In *The Inquisition in Early Modern Europe*, 100–129.

Corradini, N. "I processi delle streghe a Modena nella prima metà del sec. XVI." In *Folklore modenese*, Atti e Memorie del I Congresso del Folklore modenese, 1–2 Nov. 1958, 44 ff. Modena, 1959.

Corvisieri, C. "Compendio dei processi del Santo Uffizio di Roma (da Paolo III a Paolo IV)." *ASRSP* 3 (1880): 261–90, 449–71.

Coulton, G. G. *The Death Penalty for Heresy*. Medieval Studies 18. London, 1924.

Cox, E. *A Reference Guide to the Literature of Travel*. 2 vols. Seattle, 1935.

Cozzi, G. "Books and Society." *Journal of Modern History* 51 (1979): 86–98.

————. "La difesa degli imputati nei processi celebrati col rito del Consiglio dei X." In *La 'Leopoldina': Criminalità e giustizia criminale nelle riforme del '700 europeo*, ed. L. Berlinguer. Milan, 1989.

————. "Note su tribunali e procedure penali a Venezia nel '700." *RSI* 77 (1965): 931–52.

————. *Religione, moralità e giustizia a Venezia: Vicende della magistratura degli Esecutori contro la bestemmia*. Padua, 1969.

————. *Stato, società e giustizia nella repubblica veneta (sec. XV–XVIII)*. Rome, 1980.

Crahay, R. "Les censeurs Louvanistes d'Erasme." In *Scrinium Erasmianum*, ed. J. Coppens, 2 vols., 1:221–49. Leiden, 1969.

————. "Controverses et censures religieuses à propos de la *République* de Jean Bodin." In *D' Erasme à Campanella*, 132–55. Brussels, 1985.

————. "Jean Bodin devant la censure: La condamnation de la *République*." *Il pensiero politico* 14 (1981): 154–70.

Creytens, R. "L'oeuvre bibliographique d'Echard, ses sources et leur valeur." *AFP* 14 (1944): 43–71.

————. "Il Registro dei maestri degli studenti di Bologna (1576–1604)." *AFP* 46 (1976): 25–114.

Cristiani, L. *L'Église à l'époque du Concile de Trente*. Paris, 1948.

Croce, B. *Poeti e scrittori del primo e del tardo Rinascimento*. 3 vols. Bari, 1945–52.

————. "La vita infernale delle galere." *Quaderni della critica* 3 (1948), no. 10: 84–91.

Cugnoni, G. "Vita del Card. Giulio Antonio Santori, detto il Card. di S. Severina composta e scritta da lui medesimo." *ASRSP* 12 (1889): 329–72; 13 (1890): 151–205.

D'Addario, A. *Aspetti della Controriforma a Firenze*. Ministero dell' Interno. Pubblicazioni degli Archivi di Stato, 77. Rome, 1972.

D'Addio, M. " 'Les six livres de la République' e il pensiero cattolico del Cinquecento in una lettera del Mons. Minuccio Minucci al Possevino." In *Medioevo e Rinascimento: Studi in onore di Bruno Nardi*. 2 vols., 1:127–44. Florence, 1955.

Damaska, M. "The Death of Legal Torture." *Yale Law Journal* 87 (1978): 860–84.

Damhouder, Joost. *Praxis rerum criminalium.* Antwerp, 1570.

Darwin, F. "The Holy Inquisition: Suppression of Witnesses' Names." *Church Quarterly Review* 125 (1938): 226–46; 126 (1938): 19–43.

Davari, S. "Cenni storici intorno al tribunale della Inquisizione in Mantova." *ASL* 6 (1879): 547–65, 773–800.

Davidson, N. "Chiesa di Roma ed Inquisizione veneziana." In *Città italiane del '500,* 283–92.

―――. "Rome and the Venetian Inquisition in the Sixteenth Century." *Journal of Ecclesiastical History* 39 (1988): 16–36.

Davis, N. Z. *The Return of Martin Guerre.* Cambridge, MA, 1983.

De Antoni, D. "Processi per stregoneria e magia a Chioggia nel XVI secolo." *Ricerche di storia sociale e religiosa* 4 (1973): 187–228.

De Biasio, L. "L'eresia protestante in Friuli nella seconda metà del secolo XVI." *Memorie storiche forogiuliesi* 52 (1972): 71–154.

―――. "Esecuzioni capitali contro streghe nel Friuli orientale alla metà del secolo XVII." *Memorie storiche forogiuliesi* 58 (1978): 147–58.

―――. "Fermenti ereticali in Friuli nella seconda metà del sec. XVI." In *La filosofia friulana e giuliana nel contesto della cultura italiana: Atti del primo convegno regionale di filosofia friulana e giuliana . . . Cividale del Friuli, 6–8 dicembre 1970,* 145–53. Udine, 1972.

―――, and Facile, M. R. *1000 Processi dell'Inquisizione in Friuli (1551–1647).* Udine, 1976.

―――. *I Processi dell'Inquisizione in Friuli dal 1648 al 1798.* Udine, 1978.

De Bujanda, J. M. "Censure romaine et censure espagnole au XVIe siècle: Les Index Romain et Espagnol de 1559." *Annuario dell'Istituto storico italiano per l'età moderna e contemporanea* 35–36 (1983–84): 167–86.

―――, ed. *Index de l'Inquisition Espagnole, 1551, 1554, 1559.* Index des Livres Interdits, 5. Sherbrooke and Geneva, 1984.

―――, ed. *Index de Venise, 1549, et de Venise et Milan, 1554.* Index des Livres Interdits, 3. Sherbrooke and Geneva, 1987.

Dedieu, J.-P. "The Archives of the Holy Office of Toledo as a Source for Historical Ethnology." In *The Inquisition in Early Modern Europe,* 158–89.

―――. "Les causes de foi de l'Inquisition de Tolède: Essai statistique." *Melanges de la Casa de Velázquez* 14 (1978): 143–71.

―――. *L'Inquisition.* Paris, 1987.

―――. "L'Inquisition et le droit: Analyse formelle de la procedure inquisitoriale en cause de foi." *Melanges de la Casa de Velázquez* 23 (1987): 227–51.

―――. "Le refus de la Réforme et le contrôle de la pensée." In *L'Inquisition espagnole,* ed. B. Bennassar, 269–311.

―――, and Demonet, M. "L'activité de l'Inquisition de Tolède: Étude statistique, méthodes et premiers résultats." *Annuario dell' Istituto storico italiano per l'età moderna e contemporanea* 37–38 (1985–86): 11–39.

De Frede, C. "Per la storia della stampa nel Cinquecento in rapporto con la diffusione della Riforma in Italia." *Gutenberg Jahrbuch* 39 (1964): 175–84.

———. *La prima traduzione italiana del Corano sullo sfondo dei rapporti tra Cristianità e Islam nel Cinquecento.* Naples, 1967.

———. "Roghi di libri ereticali nell'Italia del Cinquecento." In *Ricerche storiche ed economiche in memoria di Corrado Barbagallo*, 2:315–28. Naples, 1970.

———. "La stampa nel Cinquecento e la diffusione della Riforma in Italia." *Atti della Accademia Pontaniana*, n.s., 13 (1963/64): 87–91.

———. "Tipografi, editori, librai italiani del Cinquecento coinvolti in processi di eresia." *RSCI* 23 (1969): 21–53.

De Gregorio, V. "Gli 'Indici' della libreria privata del cardinale Girolamo Casanate." *Accademie e biblioteche d'Italia* 52 (1984): 199–211.

De Job, C. *De l'influence du Concile de Trente sur la littérature et les beaux arts chez les peuples catholiques.* Paris, 1884. Reprint Geneva, 1969.

Del Bene, Tommaso. *De Officio S. Inquisitionis circa Haeresim.* Lyons, 1666.

Del Col, A. "L'abiura trasformata in propaganda ereticale nel duomo di Udine (15 Aprile 1544)." *Metodi e ricerche* 2 (1981): 57–73.

———. "Appunti per una indagine sulle traduzioni in volgare della Bibbia nel Cinquecento italiano." In *Libri, idee, e sentimenti religiosi*, 165–88.

———. "Il controllo della stampa a Venezia e i processi di Antonio Brucioli (1548–1559)." *Critica storica* 17 (1980): 457–510.

———. *Domenico Scandella, detto Menocchio: I processi dell'Inquisizione (1583–1599)*, ed. A. Del Col. Pordenone, 1990.

———. "Fermenti di novità religiose in alcuni cicli pittorici del Pordenone e dell'Amalteo." In *Società e cultura del Cinquecento nel Friuli occidentale: Studi*, ed. A. Del Col, 229–54. Pordenone, 1984.

———. "L'Inquisizione romana e il potere politico nella Repubblica di Venezia (1540–1560)." In press in the volume *La Inquisición y los poderes políticos.* Actas del Congreso de Madrid-Alcalá-Sigüenza, Septiembre 1984.

———. "Il Nuovo Testamento tradotto da Massimo Teofilo e altre opere stampate a Lione nel 1551." *Critica storica* 15 (1978): 642–75.

———. "Organizzazione, composizione e giurisdizione dei tribunali dell'Inquisizione romana nella repubblica di Venezia (1500–1550)." *Critica storica* 25 (1988): 244–94.

———. "Problemi per la catalogazione e repertoriazione unificata degli atti processuali dell'Inquisizione romana." *Critica storica* 25 (1988): 155–67.

———. "I processi dell'Inquisizione come fonte: Considerazioni diplomatiche e storiche." *Annuario dell'Istituto storico italiano per l'età moderna e contemporanea* 35–36 (1983–84): 29–49.

———. "La riforma cattolica nel Friuli vista da Paschini." In *Atti del convegno di studio su Pio Paschini nel centenario della nascita, 1878–1978: Pubblicazioni della Deputazione di Storia Patria per il Friuli*, 10: 123–41.

———. "Il secondo processo veneziano di Antonio Brucioli." *BSSV*, no. 146 (1979): 85–100.

————. "La storia religiosa del Friuli nel Cinquecento: Orientamenti e fonti." *Metodi e ricerche*, n.s., 1 (1982): 69–87.

————. "Il Tribunale del Sant'Ufficio del patriarcato e diocesi di Aquileia nei primi anni di attività (1557–1562)." Unpublished dissertation, University of Trieste, Facoltà di Lettere, 1970–1971.

————, and Paolin, G., ed. *L'Inquisizione romana in Italia nell'età moderna: Archivi, problemi di metodo e nuove ricerche* (in press).

Delisle, L. *Le Cabinet des Manuscrits de la Bibliothèque Nationale*, 2:33–36. Paris, 1874.

————. *Manuscrits latins et français ajoutés aux fonds des nouvelles acquisitions pendant les années 1875–1891*. Paris, 1891.

————. Review of "Memorie storiche," by M. Marini. *Journal des Savants* (1892): 429–41, 489–501.

Dell'Acqua, M. "Una benandante friuliana in un processo di stregoneria a Parma nel 1611." *Archivio storico per le provincie parmensi*, ser. 4, no. 28 (1976): 353–81.

Del Re, N. *La Curia romana: Lineamenti storico-giuridici*. 3rd. ed. Rome, 1970.

————. "Prospero Farinacci giureconsulto romano (1544–1618)." *ASRSP*, ser. 3, 29 (1975): 135–220.

Del Rio, Martinus. *Disquisitionum Magicarum Libri Sex*. Lyons, 1612.

Delumeau, J. "Les progrès de la centralisation dans l'état pontifical au XVIe siècle." *Revue historique* 226 (1961): 399–410.

De Maio, R. "I modelli culturali della Controriforma: Le biblioteche dei conventi italiani alla fine del Cinquecento." In his *Riforme e miti nella Chiesa del Cinquecento*, 365–81. Naples, 1973.

De Rosa, G. "Magismo e pietà nel Mezzogiorno d'Italia." In *Società, chiesa e vita religiosa nell'Ancien Regime*, ed. C. Russo, 443–98. Naples, 1976.

Derosas, R. "Moralità e giustizia a Venezia nel '500-'600: Gli Esecutori contro la bestemmia." In *Stato, società e giustizia*, ed. G. Cozzi, 431–528.

De Sousa, Antonino de. *Aphorismi Inquisitorum in quatuor libros distributi*. Turnoni, 1639.

Dettling, A. *Die Hexenprozesse im Kanton Schwyz*. Schwyz, 1907.

Diana, Antonino. *Coordinati, seu omnium resolutionum moralium . . . editio novissima*. Venice, 1698.

Dickens, A. G. *The Counter Reformation*. London, 1968.

Di Molfetta, G. "Superstizione e magia a Bisceglie nei Sinodi e nelle visite pastorali dei secc. XVI e XVII." In *Momenti e figure di storia pugliese: Studi in memoria di Michele Viterbo (Peucezio)*, ed. M. Lanera and M. Paone, Biblioteca di Cultura Pugliese, 21–22, 1:273–93. Galatina, 1981.

Di Napoli, G. "L'eresia e i processi campanelliani." In *Tommaso Campanella (1568–1639): Miscellanea di studi nel 4o centenario della sua nascita*. Naples, 1969.

Ditchfield, S. "Alla ricerca di un genere: Come leggere la 'cronica dell'origine di Piacenza' dell'inquisitore piacentino Umberto Locati (1503–1587)." *Bollettino storico piacentino* 82 (1987): 145–67.

Dondaine, A. "Le manuel de l'inquisiteur (1230–1330)." *AFP* 17 (1947): 85–194.

Döpler, J. *Theatrum poenarum, suppliciorum et executionum criminalium.* Sondershausen, 1693.

Dressendörffer, P. *Islam unter der Inquisition: Die Morisco-Prozesse in Toledo, 1575–1610.* Veröffentlichungen der orientalischen Kommission der Akademie der Wissenschaften und der Literatur, 26. Wiesbaden, 1971.

Droz, E. "Propagande italienne (1551–1565)." In *Chemins de l'hérésie,* 4 vols., 2:229–93. Geneva, 1970–76.

Duhr, B. *Die Stellung der Jesuiten in den deutschen Hexenprozessen.* Cologne, 1900.

Dykmans, M. "Les bibliothèques des religieux d'Italie en l'an 1600." *Archivum historiae pontificiae* 24 (1986): 385–404.

Edgerton, S. Y. *Pictures and Punishment: Art and Criminal Prosecution during the Florentine Renaissance.* Ithaca, 1985.

Editto del Maest.[ro] F. Francesco Galassini Generale Inquisitore di Perugia, Umbria, e dell'altre città annesse. Perugia, 1626.

"Erasmo in Italia." *Quaderni storici,* a. 24, no. 70 (1989): 269–96 (contributions by A. Del Col, S. Cavazza, and A. Prosperi).

Escamilla-Colin, M. "L'Inquisition espagnole et ses archives secrètes." *Histoire, Economie et Société* 4 (1985): 443–77.

Evans, A. P. "Hunting Subversion in the Middle Ages." *Speculum* 33 (1958): 1–22.

Evennett, H. O. *The Spirit of the Counter-Reformation. . . . Edited with a postscript by J. Bossy.* Cambridge, 1968.

Eymeric, Nicolau. *Directorium Inquisitorum . . . cum commentariis Francisci Pegnae . . . in hac postrema editione iterum emendatum et auctum, et multis litteris apostolicis locupletatum.* Rome, 1587.

Fahy, C. "The *Index Librorum Prohibitorum* and the Venetian Printing Industry in the Sixteenth Century." *Italian Studies* 35 (1980): 52–61.

Farinacci, Prospero. *Tractatus de Haeresi, editio novissima.* Lyons, 1650.

Favaro, A. *Galileo e l'Inquisizione: Documenti del processo Galileiano esistenti nell' Archivio del S. Uffizio e nell' Archivio Segreto Vaticano per la prima volta integralmente pubblicati.* Florence, 1907.

———. Review of *I documenti galileiani del S. Uffizio di Firenze,* by M. Cioni. *Archivio storico italiano,* ser. 5, 42 (1908): 451–69.

Ferlin Malavasi, S. "Intorno alla figura e all'opera di Domenico Mazzarelli, eterodosso rodigino del Cinquecento." *BSSV* 94 (1973), no. 134: 28–33.

———. "Il processo per eresia di Alfonso Ariano." *Archivio veneto,* ser. 5, 114 (1980): 112–19.

———. "Sulla diffusione delle teorie ereticali nel Veneto durante il '500: Anabattisti rodigini e polesani." *Archivio veneto,* a. 103 (1972): 5–24.

Ferrai, L. A. "Il processo di Pier Paolo Vergerio." *ASI,* ser. 4, 15 (1885): 201–20, 333–44; 16 (1885): 25–46, 153–69.

Ferraironi, P. F. *Le streghe e l'Inquisizione.* Rome, 1955.

Ferrone, V., and Firpo, M. "Galileo tra inquisitori e microstorici." *RSI* 97 (1985): 177–238.

Festa, P. M. *Breve informatione del modo di trattare le cause del S. Officio per li molto R.R. vicarii della Santa Inquisitione istituiti nella diocesi di Bologna.* Bologna, 1604.

Finlay, R. "The Foundation of the Ghetto: Venice, the Jews and the War of the League of Cambrai." *Proceedings of the American Philosophical Society* 126 (1982): 14–54.

Fiorani, L., ed. *Le confraternite romane: Esperienza religiosa, società, commitenza artistica.* Ricerche per la storia religiosa di Roma, 5. Rome, 1984.

————, ed. *Storiografia e archivi delle confraternite romane.* Ricerche per la storia religiosa di Roma, 6. Rome, 1985.

Fiorelli, P. *La tortura giudiziaria nel diritto comune.* 2 vols. Milan, 1953.

Firpo, L. "Ancora sulla condanna di Bodin." In *D' Erasme à Campanella*, 173–86. Brussels, 1985.

————. "Appunti campanelliani." *Giornale critico della filosofia italiana* 29 (1950): 68–95; 30 (1951): 509–24.

————. "Esecuzioni capitali in Roma, 1567–1671." In *Eresia e Riforma nell'Italia del Cinquecento*, Biblioteca del Corpus Reformatorum Italicorum, 309–42. De Kalb and Chicago, 1974.

————. "Filosofia italiana e Controriforma." *Rivista di filosofia* 41 (1950): 150–73, 390–401; 42 (1951): 30–47.

————. "In margine al processo di Giordano Bruno: Francesco Maria Vialardi." *RSI* 68 (1956): 325–64.

————. "I primi processi Campanelliani in una ricostruzione unitaria." *Giornale critico della filosofia italiana* 20 (1939): 5–43.

————. "Il processo di Galileo." In *Nel quarto centenario della nascita di Galileo Galilei.* Milan, 1966.

————. "Il processo di Giordano Bruno." *RSI* 60 (1948): 542–97; 61 (1949): 5–59. Reprinted separately Naples, 1949 in *Quaderni della Rivista storica italiana*, 1.

————. "Una relazione inedita su l'Inquisizione romana." *Rinascimento* 9 (1958): 97–102.

————. *Il supplizio di Tommaso Campanella: Narrazioni, documenti, verbali delle torture.* Rome, 1985.

Firpo, M. "La fase [difensiva] del processo inquisitoriale del cardinal Morone: Documenti e problemi." *Critica storica* 33 (1986): 121–48.

————. "Juan de Valdés e l'evangelismo: Appunti e problemi di una ricerca in corso." *Studi storici*, no. 4 (1985): 733–54.

————. *Pietro Bizzarri, esule italiano del Cinquecento.* Turin, 1971.

————. "Gli 'Spirituali,' l'Accademia di Modena e il formulario di fede del 1542: Controllo del dissenso religioso e Nicodemismo." *Rivista di storia e letteratura religiosa* 30 (1984): 40–111.

————. "Valdesianesimo ed evangelismo alle origini dell' *Ecclesia Viterbiensis* (1541)." In *Libri, idee e sentimenti religiosi*, 53–71 and the "Intervento" by G. Fragnito, 73–76.

————, and Marcatto, D. *Il processo inquisitoriale del Cardinal Giovanni Morone: Edizione critica*. 5 vols. to date. Rome: Istituto storico italiano per l'età moderna e contemporanea, 1981–. (Vol. 1 was edited by Firpo alone.)

Fondo (Il) Guicciardini nella Biblioteca Nazionale Centrale di Firenze. Catalogo, ed. L. Invernizi. Florence, 1984–.

Fontaine, Jacques. *Des marques des sorciers et de la réelle possession que le diable prend sur les corps des hommes*. Lyons, 1611.

Fontana, B. "Documenti vaticani contro l'eresia luterana in Italia." *ASRSP* 15 (1892): 71–165, 365–474.

Fontana, Vincenzo Maria. *Monumenta dominicana breviter in synopsim collecta*. Rome, 1675.

———. *Sacrum Theatrum Dominicanum*. Rome, 1666.

Formazione (La) storica nel diritto moderno in Europa. Atti del Terzo Congresso Internazionale della Società Italiana di Storia del Diritto. Florence, 1977.

Forte, S. L. *The Cardinal-Protector of the Dominican Order*. Rome, 1959.

———. "I Domenicani nel carteggio del card. Scipione Borghese, protettore dell'Ordine (1606–1633)." *AFP* 30 (1960): 351–416.

———. "Le province domenicane in Italia nel 1650, conventi e religiosi." *AFP* 39 (1969): 425–585; 41 (1971): 325–458; 42 (1972): 137–66.

Fowler, L. "Recusatio iudicis in Civilian and Canonist Thought." *Studia Gratiana* 15 (1972): 719–85.

Frajese, V. "La revoca dell'"Index' Sistino e la Curia romana (1588–1596)." *Nouvelles de la Republique des Lettres* 1 (1986): 15–49.

Friedberg E. A. *Corpus iuris canonici*. 2nd ed. 2 vols. Graz, 1955.

Friedman, E. G. "Christian Captives at 'Hard Labor' in Algiers, 16th–18th Centuries." *International Journal of African Historical Studies* 13 (1980): 616–32.

———. "The Exercise of Religion by Spanish Captives in North Africa." *The Sixteenth Century Journal* 6 (1975), fasc. 1: 19–34.

———. *Spanish Captives in North Africa in the Early Modern Age*. Madison, 1983.

Fumagalli, G. *Lexicon Typographicum Italiae: Dictionnaire géographique d'Italie pour servir à l'histoire de l'imprimerie dans ce pays*. Florence, 1905. Reprint with supplements and indices 1966.

Fumi, L. "L'Inquisizione romana e lo stato di Milano." *ASL*, ser. 4, 13 (1910): 5–124, 285–414; 14 (1910): 145–220.

Gaeta, F. "Documenti da codici vaticani per la storia della Riforma in Venezia." *Annuario dell'Istituto storico italiano per l'età moderna e contemporanea* 7 (1955): 5–53.

Gaidoz, H. "De quelques registres de l'Inquisition soustraits aux archives romains." *Revue de l'instruction publique* (May 1867), nos. 16 and 23: 102–4, 114–17.

Galasso, G., and Russo, C., eds. *L'Archivio storico diocesano di Napoli*. 2 vols. 2: 627–914: "Sant'Ufficio," ed. L. Osbat and collaborators. Naples, 1978.

Galiffe, J. B. G. *Le refuge italien de Genève aux XVIme et XVIIme siècles*. Geneva, 1881.

Gams, P. B. *Series Episcoporum Ecclesiae Catholicae*. 2nd ed. Leipzig, 1931.

Garcia Carcel, R. "El modelo mediterraneo de brujeria." *Annuario dell'Istituto storico italiano per l'età moderna e contemporanea* 37–38 (1985–86): 245–57.

Gari Lacruz, A. "Variedad de competencias en el delito de brujería (1600–1650) en Aragon." In *La Inquisición española*, ed. J. Pérez Villanueva, 319–28.

Garufi, C. A. *Fatti e personaggi dell'Inquisizione in Sicilia.* Palermo, 1978 (originally published in installments in the *Archivio storico siciliano*, 1914–17).

———. *Graffiti e disegni dei prigionieri dell'Inquisizione.* Palermo, 1978.

———. "Secundo proceso de Jacopo Bruto reconciliado por la Inquisizion del Reyno de Sicilia y relaxado en Palermo al brazo seglar con sentencia de 10 Julio 1590." *Bulletin de la société d'histoire vaudoise*, no. 36 (1916): 68–96.

Garzoni, Tommaso. *La piazza universale di tutte le professioni del mondo. Discorso 63*, "De gli Heretici et de gl'Inquisitori." Venice, 1585.

Georgiades Arnakis, G. "The Greek Church of Constantinople and the Ottoman Empire." *Journal of Modern History* 24 (1952): 235–50.

Gerber, A. *Niccolò Machiavelli: Die Handschriften, Ausgaben und Übersetzungen seiner Werke im 16. und 17. Jahrhundert.* Gotha, 1912.

Gesner, Konrad. *Bibliotheca Instituta et Collecta.* Zürich, 1583.

Gherardi, Pierantonio. *Breve istruzione. . .per i novelli vicari foranei del S. Uffizio.* Rome, 1752.

Gherardi, S. "Il processo Galileo riveduto sopra documenti di nuova fonte." *Rivista europea*, a. 1, vol. 3 (1870): 3–37, 398–419.

Gibbings, R. *Records of the Roman Inquisition: Case of a Minorite friar, who was sentenced by St. Charles Borromeo to be walled up, and who having escaped was burned in effigy, edited with an English translation and notes.* Dublin, 1853.

———. *Report of the trial and martyrdom of Pietro Carnesecchi, sometime secretary to Pope Clement VII and apostolic protonotary, transcribed from the original manuscript.* London, 1856.

———. *Were "Heretics" ever burned alive in Rome? A report of the proceedings in the Roman Inquisition against Fulgentio Manfredi; taken from the original manuscript brought from Italy by a French officer, and edited, with a parallel English version, and illustrative additions.* London, 1852.

Gigli, G. *Diario romano, 1608–1670.* Rome, 1958.

Gilbert, C. "When Did a Man in the Renaissance Grow Old?" *Studies in the Renaissance* 14 (1967): 7–32.

Gilissen, J. "La preuve en Europe du XVIe au debut du XIX siècle." In *Recueils de la société Jean Bodin pour l'histoire comparative des institutions. XVII. La preuve. Deuxième partie. Moyen age et temps modernes*, 755–833. Brussels, 1965.

Gilly, C. "Juan de Valdés, traductor y adaptador de escritos de Lutero en su *Diálogo de Doctrina Christiana.*" In *Miscelánea de Estudios Hispánicos: Homenaje de los Hispanistas de Suiza, a Ramon Sugranyes de Franch (Se publica al cuidado de Luiz López Molina)*, 85–106. Montserrat, 1982. Reprinted in an amplified German translation in the *Archive for Reformation History* 74 (1983): 257–305.

Gilmont, J.-F., "La fabrication et la vente de la Bible d'Olivétan," *Musée neuchâtelois* (1985): 213–24.

Ginzburg, C. *The Cheese and the Worms: The Cosmos of a Sixteenth-Century Miller.* Trans. J. and A. Tedeschi. Baltimore, 1980.

————. "The Dovecote Has Opened Its Eyes: Popular Conspiracy in Seventeenth-Century Italy." In *The Inquisition in Early Modern Europe*, 190–98.

————. "Folklore, magia, religione." In *Storia d'Italia* [Einaudi], 1:603–76. Turin, 1972.

————. *The Night Battles: Witchcraft and Agrarian Cults in the Sixteenth and Seventeenth Centuries*. Trans. J. and A. Tedeschi. Baltimore, 1983.

————. *Storia notturna, una decifrazione del sabba*. Turin, 1989.

————. "Una testimonianza inedita su Ludovico Zuccolo." *RSI* 79 (1967): 1122–28.

————. "Witchcraft and Popular Piety: Notes on a Modenese Trial of 1519." In Ginzburg's *Clues, Myths and the Historical Method*. Trans. J. and A. C. Tedeschi, 1–16, 165–70. Baltimore, 1989.

————. "The Witches Sabbat: Popular Cult or Inquisitorial Stereotype?" In *Understanding Popular Culture: Europe from the Middle Ages to the Nineteenth Century*, ed. S. Kaplan, 39–51. Berlin, etc. 1984.

Giura, V. "Gli Ebrei nel Regno di Napoli tra Aragona e Spagna," In *Gli Ebrei e Venezia, secoli XIV–XVIII: Atti del Convegno internazionale organizzato dall'Istituto di storia della società e dello stato veneziano della Fondazione Giorgio Cini, Venezia, Isola di San Giorgio Maggiore, 5–10 giugno 1983*, ed. G. Cozzi, 771–80. Milan, 1987.

Giusti, M. "Materiale documentario d'archivio degli archivi papali rimasto nell'Archivio Nazionale di Parigi dopo il loro ritorno a Roma negli anni 1814–1817." In *Roemische Kurie, Kirchliche Finanzen, Vatikanisches Archiv: Studien zu Ehren von Hermann Hoberg*, ed. E. Gatz, 2 vols., 1:263–74. Rome, 1979.

————. *Studi sui registri di bolle papali*. Collectanea Archivi Vaticani, 1. Vatican City, 1968.

Given, J. "The Inquisitors of Languedoc and the Medieval Technology of Power." *American Historical Review* 94 (1989): 336–59.

Gonnet, G. "Le Protestantisme dans l'Italie meridionale à l'epoque moderne." In *Religion et culture dans la cité italienne de l'antiquité à nos jours: Actes du colloque du Centre Interdisciplinaire de Recherches sur l'Italie des 8–9–10 Novembre 1979: Bulletin du CIRI*, ser. 2, 117–27. Université de Strasbourg, 1981.

————. "Recent European Historiography on the Medieval Inquisition." In *The Inquisition in Early Modern Europe*, 199–223.

González de Caldas, M. V. "La correspondencia inquisitorial como fuente de estudio del Santo Oficio: Las relaciones de causas." In *Jornadas (II) de metodología y didactica de la historia. Historia moderna: Letras*. Presentación de Angel Rodríguez Sánchez, 443–49. Cáceres, 1983.

————. "Nuevas Imagenes del Santo Oficio en Sevilla: El auto de fe." In *Inquisición española y mentalidad inquisitorial*, ed. A. Alcalá, 237–65. And in English, "New Images of the Holy Office in Seville: The Auto de Fe." In *The Spanish Inquisition and the Inquisitorial Mind*, ed. A. Alcalá, 265–300.

González Novalín, J. L. "L'Inquisizione spagnola: Correnti storiografiche da Llorente (1817) ai nostri giorni." *RSCI* 39 (1985): 139–59.

————. "Luteranismo e Inquisición en España (1519–1561): Bases para la periodización del tema en el siglo de la Reforma." *Annuario dell'Istituto storico italiano per l'età moderna e contemporanea* 37–38 (1985–86): 43–73.

Grand, R. "La prison et la notion d'emprisonement dans l'ancien droit." *Revue de l'histoire du droit français et étranger* 19–20 (1940–41): 58–87.

Greenleaf, R. E. *The Mexican Inquisition of the Sixteenth Century.* Albuquerque, 1969.

Grégoire, R. "Le confraternite romane: Esperienza religiosa, società, commitenza artistica." *Studium* 81 (1985): 367–70.

Grendler, M. "Book Collecting in Counter-Reformation Italy: The Library of Gian Vincenzo Pinelli (1535–1601)." *Journal of Library History* 16 (1981): 143–51.

———, and P. F. Grendler. "The Erasmus Holdings of Roman and Vatican Libraries." *Erasmus in English* 13 (1984): 2–29.

Grendler, P. F. "Books for Sarpi: The Smuggling of Prohibited Books into Venice during the Interdict of 1606–1607." In *Essays Presented to Myron P. Gilmore,* ed. S. Bertelli and G. Ramakus, 2 vols., 1: 105–14. Florence, 1978.

———. "The Circulation of Protestant Books in Italy." In *Peter Martyr Vermigli and Italian Reform,* ed. J. C. McLelland, 5–16. Waterloo, 1980.

———. *Culture and Censorship in Late Renaissance Italy and France.* London: Variorum Reprints, 1981.

———. *The Roman Inquisition and the Venetian Press, 1540–1605.* Princeton, 1977.

———. "The *Tre Savii sopra Eresia*: A Prosopographical Study." *Studi veneziani,* n.s., 3 (1979): 283–340.

Grigulevic, J. R. *Ketzer-Hexen-Inquisitoren. Geschichte der Inquisition (13.–20 Jahrhundert).* 2nd ed., 2 vols. Berlin, 1987.

Grillando, Paolo. "Tractatus de sortilegiis." In *Tractatus illustrium,* ed. F. Peña, fols. 381v–398r.

Grillot de Givry, E. A. *Le musée des sorciers, mages et alchimistes.* Paris, 1929. And in English as *Witchcraft, Magic and Alchemy,* trans. J. C. Locke. London, 1931. Reprint New York, 1971.

Gualandi, M., *Un auto-da-fé in Bologna il 5 Novembre 1618: Documento originale pubblicato con commentario e note.* Bologna, 1860.

Guazzini, Sebastiano. *Tractatus ad defensam inquisitorum, carceratorum, reorum et condemnatorum super quocunque crimine.* 2 vols. Rome, 1614.

Guglielmotti, A. *Storia della marina pontificia.* 10 vols. Rome, 1886.

Hale, J. R. *England and the Italian Renaissance.* London, 1954.

Hansen, J. *Quellen und Untersuchungen zur Geschichte des Hexenwahns und der Hexenverfolgung im Mittelalter.* Bonn, 1901. Reprint Hildesheim, 1963.

Hartmann, A., and Jenny, B. R., eds. *Die Amerbachkorrespondenz. Im Auftrag der Kommission für die Öffentliche Bibliothek der Universität Basel.* 9 vols to date. Basel, 1942–.

Hauptsinstruktionen (Die) Clemens VIII für die Nuntien und Legaten an den europäischen Fürstenhöfen, 1592–1605. 2 vols. Tübingen, 1984.

Heimbucher, M. *Die Orden und Kongregationen der katholischen Kirche.* 3 vols. Paderborn, 1907–8.

Helbing, F. *Die Tortur: Geschichte der Folter im Kriminalverfahren aller Zeiten und Völker.* Aalen, 1983. Reprint of 2nd, 1926 ed.

Helmholz, R. "Canonists and Standards of Impartiality for Papal Judges Delegate." *Traditio* 25 (1969): 386–404.

Henner, C. *Beiträge zur Organisation und Competenz der päpstlichen Ketzergerichte.* Leipzig, 1890.

Henningsen, G. "El 'Banco de datos' del Santo Oficio: Las relaciones de causas de la Inquisición española (1550–1700)." *Boletín de la Real Academia de la Historia* 174 (1977): 547–70.

———. "La coleccion de Moldenhawer en Copenhague: Una aportacion a la archivologia de la Inquisición española." *Revista de Archivos, Bibliotecas y Museos* 80 (1977): 209–70.

———. "La elocuencia de los números: Promesas de las 'relaciones de causas' inquisitoriales para la nueva historia social." In *Inquisición española y mentalidad inquisitorial,* ed. A. Alcalá, 207–25. And in English, with revised calculations, as "The Eloquence of Figures: Statistics of the Spanish and Portuguese Inquisitions and Prospects for Social History." In *The Spanish Inquisition and the Inquisitorial Mind,* ed. A. Alcalá, 217–35.

———. *The European Witch-Persecution.* DFS-Translations, 1. Copenhagen, 1973.

———. "The Papers of Alonso de Salazar Frias: A Spanish Witchcraft Polemic, 1610–1614." *Temenos* 5 (1969): 85–106.

———. " 'The Ladies from Outside': An Archaic Pattern of the Witches' Sabbath." In *Early Modern European Witchcraft: Centres and Peripheries,* ed. B. Ankarloo and G. Henningsen, 191–215. Oxford, 1990. The volume, the proceedings of a 1984 Stockholm conference, first appeared in Swedish as *Häxornas Europa, 1400–1700.* Lund, 1987.

———. *The Witches Advocate: Basque Witchcraft and the Spanish Inquisition (1609–1614).* Reno, 1980.

Hess, A. G. "Hunting Witches: A Survey of Some Recent Literature." *Criminal Justice History* 3 (1982): 47–79.

Hierarchia catholica medii [et recentioris] aevi, sive summorum pontificum, S.R. E. cardinalium, ecclesiarum antistitum series ab anno 1198 usque ad annum [1605] perducta. . . . 8 vols. Munster, 1898-.

Hilgers, J. *Die Bücherverbote in Papstbriefen.* Freiburg i. Br., 1907.

———. *Der Index der verbotenen Bücher.* Freiburg i. Br., 1904.

Hinschius, P. *System des katholischen Kirchenrechts, mit besonderer Rücksicht auf Deutschland.* 6 vols. Berlin, 1869–97.

Horst, G. *Zauberbibliothek.* 6 vols. Mainz, 1821–26.

Hroch, M., and Skybová, A. *Ecclesia Militans: Inquisition im Zeitalter der Gegen-Reformation.* Übersetzung aus dem Tschechischen von W. B. Oerter. Leipzig, 1985.

Hubert, F. *Vergerio's publizistische Thätigkeit nebst einer bibliographischen Übersicht.* Göttingen, 1893.

Huerga Criado, P. "Los Agentes de la Inquisición española en Roma durante el siglo XVII." In *La Inquisición española*, ed. J. P. Villanueva, 243–56.

Ilardi, V., and Shay, M. L. "Italy." In *The New Guide to the Diplomatic Archives of Western Europe*, ed. D. H. Thomas and L. M. Case, 165–211. Philadelphia, 1975.

Index des Livres Interdits. Ed. J. M. De Bujanda. 5 vols. to date. Sherbrooke and Geneva, 1984–. See also De Bujanda.

Index Generalis Librorum Prohibitorum a Pontificiis, una cum editionibus expurgatis vel expurgandis . . . in usum Bibliothecae Bodleianae . . . designatus per Tho. Iames. . . . Oxford, 1627.

Indicis Librorum Expurgandorum in studiosorum gratiam confecti: Tomus primus in quo quinquaginta auctorum libri prae ceteris desiderati emendantur: Per Fr. Jo. Mariam Brasichellen. Sacri Palatii Apostolici Magistrum in unum corpus redactus, et publicae commoditati aeditus. Rome, 1607.

Index Librorum Prohibitorum SS.mi D.D. pontificis maximi jussu recognitus, atque editus. Rome, 1758.

Inquisition [The] in Early Modern Europe: Studies on Sources and Methods. Ed. G. Henningsen and J. Tedeschi in Association with C. Amiel. De Kalb, 1986.

Instructio circa Judicia Sagarum. Cracow, 1670.

Instructio particularis circa conficiendos processus inquisitionis . . . Iussu D.N. Urbani PP. VIII. Rome, 1627.

Instructio pro formandis processibus in causis strigum, sortilegiorum, & maleficiorum. Rome, 1657.

Instruttione per consolar i poveri afflitti condannati a morte. Bergamo, 1586.

Ioly Zorattini, P. C. "Aspetti e problemi dei nuclei ebraici in Friuli durante la dominazione veneziana." In *Atti del Convegno Venezia e la Terraferma attraverso le Relazioni dei Rettori, 23–24 ottobre 1980*, 227–36. Milan, 1981.

————. *Battesimi di fanciulli ebrei a Venezia nel Settecento.* Udine, 1984.

————. "Battesimi 'invitis parentibus' nella Repubblica di Venezia durante l'età moderna: I casi padovani." In *Ebrei e Cristiani nell'Italia medievale e moderna: Conversioni, scambi, contrasti.* Atti del VI Congresso internazionale dell'AISG, S. Miniato, 4–6 novembre 1986, 171–82. Rome, 1988.

————. "I cimiteri ebraici del Friuli veneto." *Studi veneziani*, n.s., 8 (1984): 375–90.

————. "Il diavolo del Sant'Uffizio e le tradizioni popolari friulane." *Rassegna di pedagogia* 26 (1968), nos. 2–3: 84–130.

————. "Gli Ebrei a Udine dal Trecento ai giorni nostri." *Atti dell'Accademia di scienze, lettere e arti di Udine* 74 (1981): 45–58.

————. "Gli Ebrei a Venezia, Padova e Verona." In *Storia della cultura veneta*, vol. 3, pt. 1: 537–76. Vicenza, 1980.

————. "Gli Ebrei nel Veneto durante il Settecento." In *Storia della cultura veneta*, vol. 5, pt. 2: 459–86. Vicenza, 1980.

————. "Ebrei sefarditi e marrani a Ferrara dalla fine del Quattrocento alla devoluzione del Ducato estense." In *Libri, idee e sentimenti religiosi*, 117–30.

————. "L'emigrazione degli Ebrei dai territori della Repubblica di Venezia verso le contee di Gorizia e Gradisca nel Settecento." In *Gli Ebrei a Gorizia e a Trieste tra 'Ancien Regime' ed Emancipazione*. Atti del Convegno Gorizia, 13 giugno 1983, ed. Ioly Zorattini, 111–18. Udine, 1984.

———. "Un giudaizzante cividalese del Cinquecento: Gioanbattista Cividin." *Studi storici e geografici* 1 (1977): 193–208.

———. "The Inquisition and the Jews in Sixteenth-Century Venice." In *Proceedings of the Seventh World Congress of Jewish Studies: History of the Jews in Europe*, 83–92. Jerusalem, 1981 (an Italian version appeared earlier in *RSCI* 33 [1979]: 500–508).

———. "Gli insediamenti ebraici nel Friuli veneto." In *Gli Ebrei a Venezia, secoli XIV–XVIII: Atti del Convegno internazionale organizzato dall'Istituto di storia della società e dello stato veneziano della Fondazione Giorgio Cini, Venezia, Isola di San Giorgio Maggiore, 5–10 giugno 1983*, ed. G. Cozzi, 261–80. Milan, 1987.

———. "The Jews and the Inquisition of Aquileia and Concordia." In *Jews and Conversos: Studies in Society and the Inquisition*. Proceedings of the Eighth World Congress of Jewish Studies, Hebrew University of Jerusalem, August 16–21, 1981, ed. Y. Kaplan, 225–36. Jerusalem, 1985.

———. *Leandro Tisanio un giudaizzante sanvitese del Seicento: Tra i nuclei ebraici del Friuli e la diaspora marrana*. Florence, 1984.

———. "Il 'Mif'aloth Elohim' di Isaac Abravanel e il Sant'Offizio di Venezia." *Italia: Studi e ricerche sulla cultura e sulla letteratura degli Ebrei d'Italia* 1 (1976): 54–69.

———. "Note e documenti per la storia dei marrani e giudaizzanti nel Veneto del Seicento." In *Michael: On the History of the Jews of the Diaspora*, ed. S. Simonsohn, 326–41. Tel-Aviv, 1972.

———. "Per lo studio della stregoneria in Italia nell'età moderna." *RSCI* 25 (1971): 231–37.

———. "'Preenti' contro il lupo negli atti del S. Uffizio di Aquileia e Concordia." *Ce fastu?* 52 (1976): 131–46.

———. "Un 'Preento' contro il lupo in un procedimento seicentesco del S. Uffizio di Aquileia e Concordia." *Memorie storiche forogiuliesi* 59 (1979): 163–68.

———. "Il prestito ebraico nella fortezza di Palma nel secolo XVII." *Studi storici Luigi Simeoni* 33 (1983): 271–76.

———. "Processi contro ebrei e giudaizzanti nell'Archivio del S. Uffizio di Aquileia e Concordia." *Memorie storiche forogiuliesi* 58 (1978): 133–45.

———. "Processi del S. Uffizio di Aquileia e Concordia contro 'Lapsi' nell'Islamismo tra Sei e Settecento." *Memorie storiche forogiuliesi* 60 (1980): 117–28.

———. *Processi del S. Uffizio di Venezia contro Ebrei e giudaizzanti*. 7 vols. to date. Florence, 1980-.

———. "The Trials of the Holy Office of Adria (Rovigo) against Jews and Judaizers." In *Ninth World Congress of Jewish Studies: Division B, vol. 1, The History of the Jewish People (from the Second Temple Period until the Middle Ages)*, 167–74. Jerusalem, 1986.

Iserloh, E., and Repgen, K., eds. *Reformata Reformanda: Festgabe für Hubert Jedin zum 17. Juni 1965.* 2 vols. Münster, 1965.

Istruzioni ed atti relativi ad un procedimento inquisitoriale di stregoneria nella terra di Sermoneta, l'anno 1575: Lettere delli cardinali di Pisa e Sermoneta al vicario Gio. Francesco Bonamici Commissario dell' Inquisitione di Roma a Sermoneta. Florence, 1920.

Jantz, H. "The Renaissance Essays of Philipp Camerarius." In *Virtus et Fortuna: Zur deutschen Literatur zwischen 1400 und 1720.* Festschrift für Hans-Gert Roloff zu seinem 50. Geburtstag, ed. J. P. Strelka and J. Jungmayr, 315–27. Bern, Frankfort a. M., New York, 1983.

Jedin, H. *Die Autobiographie des Kardinals Giulio Antonio Santorio.* Akademie der Wissenschaften und der Literatur. Abhandlungen der Geistes-und Sozialwissenschaftlichen Klasse. Jhrg. 1969, no. 2. Mainz, Wiesbaden, 1969.

————, ed. *Handbuch der Kirchengeschichte: IV. Reformation, Katholische Reform und Gegenreformation.* Freiburg, Basel, Vienna, 1967.

————. "Osservazioni sulla pubblicazione delle 'Nunziature d'Italia.'" *RSI* 75 (1963): 327–43.

Jobe, P. H. "Inquisitorial Manuscripts in the Biblioteca Apostolica Vaticana: A Preliminary Handlist." In *The Inquisition in Early Modern Europe,* 33–53.

Johnston, N. *The Human Cage: A Brief History of Prison Architecture.* New York, 1973.

Kaeppeli, T. "Antiche biblioteche domenicane in Italia." *AFP* 36 (1966): 5–80.

Kamen, H. "Confiscation in the Economy of the Spanish Inquisition." *Economic History Review* 18 (1965): 511–25.

————. *Inquisition and Society in Spain in the Sixteenth and Seventeenth Centuries.* London, 1985. A revised version of *The Spanish Inquisition.* London, 1965.

Kellenbenz, H. "I rapporti tedeschi con l'Italia nel XVI e all'inizio del XVII secolo e la questione religiosa." In *Città italiane del '500,* 111–25.

Kelly, H. A. "Inquisition and the Prosecution of Heresy: Misconceptions and Abuses." *Church History* 58 (1989): 439–51.

Kidd, B. J. *The Counter-Reformation, 1550–1600.* London, 1933. Reprinted 1937, 1958.

Kieckhefer, R. *European Witch Trials: Their Foundations in Popular and Learned Culture, 1300–1500.* London and Henley, 1976.

Kingholz, O. *Die Kulturarbeit des Stiften Einsiedeln.* Munich, 1909.

Kristeller, P. O. "Francesco Patrizi da Cherso, 'Emendatio in libros suos Novae Philosophiae.'" *Rinascimento,* ser. 2, 10 (1970): 215–18.

Kurcz, A. "Ismeretlen velencei Melanchton kiadás: Egy töredékes ars moriendi meghatározasa" (An unknown Venetian edition of Melanchthon: The identification of a fragmentary *Ars Moriendi*). *Országos Széchényi Könyvtár Évkönyve* (1973): 67–72.

Kutter, M. *Celio Secondo Curione, sein Leben und sein Werk (1503–1569).* Basler Beiträge zur Geschichtswissenschaft, 54. Basel and Stuttgart, 1955.

La Mantia, V. "Origine e vicende dell'Inquisizione in Sicilia." *RSI* 3 (1886): 481–598. Reprinted separately Rome, Turin, Florence, 1886. And in a new edition Palermo, 1977.

Lamattina, G. *Manoscritti inediti e relazioni ad limina della diocesi di Satriano-Campagna (sec. XVI–XVII).* Pompeii, 1988.

Landi, A. "Sfogliando le carte di un tribunale ecclesiastico del Cinquecento." In *Da Dante a Cosimo I. Ricerche di storia religiosa e culturale toscana nei secoli XIV–XVI,* ed. D. Maselli, 254–88. Pistoia, n.d.

Lane, F. C. "Wages and Recruitment of Venetian galeotti, 1470–1580." *Studi veneziani,* n.s., 6 (1982): 15–44.

Langbein, J. "The Historical Origins of the Sanction of Imprisonment for Serious Crime." *Journal of Legal Studies* 5 (1976): 35–60.

———. *Prosecuting Crime in the Renaissance: England, Germany, France.* Cambridge, MA, 1974.

———. *Torture and the Law of Proof: Europe and England in the Ancien Régime.* Chicago and London, 1977.

Lanzoni, F. *La controriforma nella città e diocesi di Faenza.* Faenza, 1925.

Larquié, C. "Le Protestantisme en Espagne au XVI siècle." *Bulletin de la Société de l'Histoire du Protestantisme français* 129 (1983): 155–82.

Laurent, M.-H. *Fabio Vigili et les bibliothèques de Bologne au début du XVIe siècle d'après le ms. Barb. lat. 3185.* Studi e Testi, 105. Vatican City, 1943.

Lauro, A. *Il giurisdizionalismo pregiannoniano nel regno di Napoli: Problema e bibliografia (1563–1723).* Rome, 1974.

Lea, H. C. *A History of the Inquisition of the Middle Ages.* 3 vols. New York, 1888. Reprint, 1955.

———. *A History of the Inquisition of Spain.* 4 vols. New York, 1906–7.

———. *The Inquisition in the Spanish Dependencies.* New York, 1908.

———. *The Inquisition of the Middle Ages, Its Organization and Operation.* With an historical introduction by Walter Ullmann. London, 1963.

———. *Materials Toward a History of Witchcraft.* Arranged and edited by A. C. Howland. 3 vols. Philadelphia, 1939. Reprint New York, 1957.

———. *Minor Historical Writings.* Ed. Arthur C. Howland. Philadelphia, 1942.

———. *Torture, with Original Documentary Sources in Translation.* Introduction by E. Peters. Philadelphia, 1973 (first published in 1866 as pt. 4 of Lea's *Superstition and Force*).

Lenci, M. "Riscatti di schiavi cristiani dal Maghreb: La Compagnia della SS. Pietà di Lucca (secoli XVII–XIX)." *Società e storia* 9 (1986): 53–80.

Léonard, E. G. "Il principe di Scalea Giovanni Battista Spinelli processato per libertinaggio dall'Inquisizione." *Archivio storico per le province napoletane,* n.s., 19 (1933): 397–400.

———. "Protestants français poursuivis par l'Inquisition dans l'Italie meridionale au XVIe siècle." *Bulletin de la Société de l'histoire du protestantisme français* 83 (1934): 470–74.

Lerri, Michelangelo. *Breve informatione del modo di trattare le cause del S. Officio per li molto reverendi vicarii della Sancta Inquisitione, instituiti nelle diocesi di Modena, di Carpi, di Nonantola e della Garfagnana.* Modena, 1608.

Leutenbauer, S. *Hexerei-und Zaubereidelikt in der Literatur von 1450 bis 1550: Mit Hinweisen auf die Praxis im Herzogtum Bayern*. Berlin, 1972.

Levy, L. W. "Accusatorial and Inquisitorial Systems of Criminal Justice: The Beginnings." In *Freedom and Reform: Essays in Honor of Henry Steele Commager*, ed. H. M. Hyman and L. W. Levy, 16–54. New York, 1967.

————. *Treason against God: A History of the Offense of Blasphemy*. New York, 1981.

Libri, idee, e sentimenti religiosi nel Cinquecento italiano, 3–5 aprile 1986, ed. A. Prosperi and A. Biondi. Istituto di Studi Rinascimentali, Ferrara, Saggi. Ferrara and Modena, 1987.

Lilienthal, J. A. *Die Hexenprozesse der beiden Städte Braunsberg*. Königsberg, 1861.

Locati, Umberto. *Opus quod iudiciale inquisitorum dicitur . . . Cum additione nonnullarum quaestiuncularum, & decisionum quorundam notabilium casuum tam in Urbe, quam Placentiae discussorum, ac formulis agendorum in fine positis*. Rome, 1568. New eds. Rome, 1570 and Venice, 1583.

Longo, N. "Fenomeni di censura nella letteratura italiana del Cinquecento." In *Le pouvoir et la plume*, 275–84.

————. "Prolegomeni per una storia della letteratura italiana censurata." *La rassegna della letteratura italiana*, ser. 7, 78 (1974): 402–19.

Lopez, P. *Inquisizione, stampa e censura nel Regno di Napoli tra '500 e '600*. Naples, 1974.

————. *Il movimento valdesiano a Napoli, Mario Galeota e le sue vicende col Sant'Uffizio*. Naples, 1976.

Lowell, A. Lawrence. "The Judicial Use of Torture." *Harvard Law Review* 11 (1897–98): 220–33; 290–300.

Lucchesi, C. "L'antica libreria dei padri domenicani di Bologna alla luce del suo inventario." *Atti e memorie della R. Deputazione di storia patria per l'Emilia e la Romagna* 5 (1940): 205–51.

Lutz, G. "Le ricerche internazionali sulle nunziature e l'edizione delle istruzioni generali di Clemente VIII (1592–1605)." In *L'Archivio Segreto Vaticano e le ricerche storiche*. Città del Vaticano, 4–5 giugno 1981, ed. P. Vian, 167–80. Rome, 1983.

Lutz, H. "Antimachiavellismus im Italien des 16. Jahrhunderts." *Mitteilungen des oberösterreichischen Landesarchivs* 14 (1984): 5–12.

————. "Nuntiaturberichte aus Deutschland: Vergangenheit und Zukunft einer 'klassischen' Editionsreihe." *Quellen und Forschungen aus italienischen Archiven und Bibliotheken* 45 (1965): 274–324.

Maffani, G. *Operetta la qual contiene lordine & il modo hanno a tenere quelli de la Compagnia di Giustizia di Perugia quando haveranno a confortare li condannati alla morte*. Perugia, 1545.

Maisonneuve, H. *Études sur les origines de l'inquisition*. 2nd ed. Paris, 1960.

Mandrou, R. *Magistrats et sorciers en France au XVIIe siècle: Une analyse de psychologie historique*. Paris, 1968.

Manni, D. M. *Vita di Pietro Perna*. Lucca, 1763.

Mansio, M. *Documenti per confortare i condannati a morte*. Rome, 1625.

Manzoni, G., ed. "Estratto del processo di Pietro Carnesecchi." *Miscellanea di storia italiana* 10 (1870): 187–573.

Marchetti, V. "L'Archivio dell'Inquisizione senese." *BSSV*, a. 93, no. 132 (1972): 77–83.

———. *Gruppi ereticali senesi del Cinquecento*. Florence, 1975.

Marchi, G. *La riforma tridentina in diocesi di Adria nel secolo XVI, descritta con il sussidio di fonti inedite*. Cittadella, 1969. 1st ed. 1946.

Marini, M. "Memorie storiche." In *Regestum Clementis Papae V*, 1:ccxxviii–cccxxv. Rome, 1885.

Márquez, A. "Estado actual de los estudios sobre la Inquisición." *Arbor* 101 (1978): 85–96.

Marta, G. "Il 'Malleus maleficarum' e il 'De pytonicis mulieribus.' Due modi d'intendere la stregoneria sul finire del XV secolo." In *Studi offerti a R. Morghen*. A cura dell'Istituto storico italiano per il medio evo, 1:407–26. Rome, 1974.

Martin, J. "L'Inquisizione romana e la criminalizzazione del dissenso religioso a Venezia all'inizio dell'età moderna." *Quaderni storici*, a. 22, no. 66 (1987): 777–802.

Martinez Diez, G. *Valoración historico-Cristiana de la tortura judicial*. Cornillas, 1964.

Maselli, D. *Saggi di storia ereticale lombarda al tempo di S. Carlo*. Naples, 1979.

Masini, Eliseo. *Sacro Arsenale, overo prattica dell'officio della Santa Inquisitione*. Genoa, 1621. New eds. Genoa, 1625, Bologna, 1665, etc.

Massarius, Hieronymus. *Eusebius captivus, sive modus procedendi in Curia Romana contra Lutheranos*. Basel, 1553.

Massignan, R. "Pier Luigi Farnese e il vescovo di Fano." *Atti e memorie della R. Deputazione di storia patria per le province delle Marche*, n.s., 2 (1905): 249–304.

Mastellone, S. "Antonio Magliabechi: Un libertino fiorentino?" *Il pensiero politico* 8 (1975): 33–53.

Mathieux, J. "Trafic et prix de l'homme en Méditerranée aux XVIIe et XVIIIe siècles." *Annales: ESC* 9 (1954): 157–64.

Maylender, M. *Storia delle Accademie d'Italia*. 5 vols. Bologna, 1927–30.

Mazzatinti, G., and Sorbelli, A. *Inventari dei manoscritti delle biblioteche d'Italia: 79. Bologna, Biblioteca Comunale dell'Archiginnasio*. Florence, 1954.

Mazzetti, G. *Le prime edizioni di Lutero (1518–1546) nelle biblioteche italiane*. Florence, 1984.

Mazzolini da Prierio, Silvestro. *Modus solennis et authenticus, ad inquirendum & inveniendum & convincendum Luteranos. . . .* Rome, 1553.

McDowell, R. B., and Webb, D. A. *Trinity College Dublin, 1592–1952: An Academic History*. Cambridge, 1982.

Medici, G. C. "Cesare Carena, giurista cremonese del secolo XVII." *ASL*, ser. 6, a. 57 (1930): 297–330.

Meersseman, G. "La bibliothèque des Frères Prêcheurs de la Minerve à la fin du XVIe siècle." *Melanges Auguste Pelzer, Université de Louvain, Recueil de travaux d'histoire et de philologie*, ser. 3, 26 (1947): 605–31.

Melinkoff, D. "Right to Counsel: The Message from America." In *First Images of America*, ed. F. Chiappelli, 2 vols., 1:405–13. Berkeley and Los Angeles, 1976.

Mellor, A. *La torture: Son histoire, son abolition, sa réapparition au XXe siècle.* Paris, 1949.

Menghi, Girolamo. *Flagellum Daemonum: Exorcismos terribiles, potentissimos, et efficaces . . . accessit postremo pars secunda, quae fustis daemonum inscribitur.* Bologna, 1589.

Menghini, Tomaso. *Regole del Tribunale del S. Officio praticate in alcuni casi imaginarii.* Milan, 1689.

Mercati, A. *I costituti di Niccolò Franco (1568–1570) dinanzi l'Inquisizione di Roma esistenti nell' Archivio Segreto Vaticano.* Studi e Testi, 178. Vatican City, 1955.

———. *Il sommario del processo di Giordano Bruno: Con appendice di documenti sull'eresia e l'Inquisizione a Modena nel secolo XVI.* Studi e Testi, 101. Vatican City, 1942. Reprint 1961.

Mercurio, Scipione. *De gli errori popolari d'Italia libri sette.* Verona, 1645. 1st ed. 1603.

Merlo, G. G. "I registri inquisitoriali come fonti per la storia dei gruppi ereticali clandestini: Il caso del Piemonte basso medievale." In *Histoire et clandestinité du Moyen-Age à la première guerre mondiale: Colloque de Privas (Mai 1977).* Actes recueillis par M. Tilloy, G. Audisio et J. Chiffoleau, 59–74. Albi, 1979.

Midelfort, H. C. Erik. "Recent Witch Hunting Research, or Where Do We Go from Here?" *Papers of the Bibliographical Society of America* 62 (1968): 373–420.

———. *Witchhunting in Southwestern Germany, 1562–1684: The Social and Intellectual Foundations.* Stanford, 1972.

Miele, M. "Malattie magiche di origine diabolica e loro terapia secondo il medico beneventano Pietro Piperno (m. 1642)," *Campania Sacra* 6 (1975): 166–223.

Miesen, K.-J. *Friedrich Spee: Pater, Dichter, Hexen-Anwalt.* Düsseldorf, 1987.

Milano, A. *Bibliotheca historica italo-judaica.* Florence, 1954. And *Supplemento 1954–1963.* Florence, 1964.

Milva, L. "Violenza, guerra, pena di morte: Le proposte degli eretici medievali." *RSCI* 43 (1989): 123–44.

Mirto, A. "Un inedito del Seicento sull'Inquisizione." *Nouvelles de la Republique des Lettres* 1 (1986): 99–138.

———. *Stampatori, editori, librai nella seconda metà del Seicento.* Florence, 1984.

Moeller, C. "Les bûchers et les auto-da-fé de l'Inquisition depuis le moyen âge." *Revue d'histoire ecclésiastique* 14 (1913): 720–51; 15 (1914): 50–60.

Molin, J.-B., and Aussedat-Minvielle, A. *Répertoire des rituels et processionaux imprimés conservés en France.* Pt. 4, "Recueils d'Exorcismes et de Benedictions." Paris, 1984.

Molinier, C. "Rapport à M. le Ministre de l'Instruction Publique sur une mission executée en Italie de fevrier à avril 1885." *Archives des missions scientifiques et litteraires*, ser. 3, 14 (1888): 133–336.

Monter, E. W. *Enforcing Morality in Early Modern Europe.* London (Variorum Reprints), 1987.

———. "European Witchcraft: A Moment of Synthesis?" *The Historical Journal* 31 (1988): 183–85.

————. *Frontiers of Heresy: The Spanish Inquisition from the Basque Lands to Sicily.* Cambridge, 1990.

————. "The Historiography of European Witchcraft: Progress and Prospects." *Journal of Interdisciplinary History* 2 (1972): 435–51.

————. "The Italians in Geneva, 1550–1600: A New Look." In *Genève et l'Italie*, ed. L. Monnier, 53–77. Geneva, 1969.

————. "The New Social History and the Spanish Inquisition." *Journal of Social History* 17 (1984): 705–13.

————. *Ritual, Myth and Magic in Early Modern Europe.* Athens, OH, 1984.

————. *Witchcraft in France and Switzerland: The Borderlands during the Reformation.* Ithaca, 1976.

————. "Women and the Italian Inquisitions." In *Women in the Middle Ages and the Renaissance, Literary and Historical Perspectives*, edited with an introduction by M. B. Rose, 73–87. Syracuse, 1986.

Monti, G. M. *Studi sulla Riforma cattolica e sul papato nei secoli XVI–XVII.* Trani, 1941.

Mordenti, R. "Le due censure: La collazione dei testi del 'Decameron' 'rassettati' da Vincenzo Borghini e Lionardo Salviati." In *Le pouvoir et la plume*, 253–73.

Moroni, G. *Dizionario di erudizione storico-ecclesiastica da S. Pietro sino ai nostri giorni.* 108 vols. Venice, 1840–61.

Mortier, A. *Histoire des Maitres Généraux de l'Ordre des Frères Prêcheurs.* 8 vols. Paris, 1903–30.

Moryson, Fynes. *An Itinerary.* 4 vols. Glasgow, 1907.

Muraro, L. *La signora del gioco: Episodi della caccia alle streghe.* Milan, 1976.

N[iccoli], [M.] "Inquisizione." *Enciclopedia italiana* 19:335–39.

Naselli, C. A. *La soppressione napoleonica delle corporazioni religiose: Contributo alla storia religiosa del primo Ottocento italiano, 1808–1814.* Miscellanea Historiae Pontificiae, 52. Rome, 1986.

Nauert, C. G. *Agrippa and the Crisis of Renaissance Thought.* Urbana, 1965.

Neri, Giovanni Battista. *De Iudice S. Inquisitionis Opusculum A.R.A.P.F. Ioanne Baptista Neri Ordinis Minimorum, S. Francisci de Paula, S. Theologiae Lectore Iubilato, ac Iuris Canonici Professore Compilatum, & Sereniss. Cosmo III Magno Etruriae Duci Ex Corde Dicatum.* Florence, 1685.

Nischan, B. "The Exorcism Controversy and Baptism in the Late Reformation." *Sixteenth Century Journal* 18 (1987): 31–51.

Nuntiaturberichte aus Deutschland nebst ergänzenden Actenstücken. . . . Hrsg. durch das K. Preussische Historische Institut in Rom. Gotha, etc. 1892–.

Nunziature d'Italia. Fonti per la storia d'Italia. Published by the Istituto storico italiano per l'età moderna e contemporanea. Rome, 1958–.

O'Brien, J. A. *The Inquisition.* New York, 1973.

O'Connell, M. R. *The Counter-Reformation, 1559–1610.* New York, 1974.

Olivari, M. "A proposito di Inquisizione spagnola." *Rivista di storia e letteratura religiosa* 24 (1988): 331–46.

Olivieri, A. "Un 'modello' Mediterraneo: La città nave in Cristoforo da Canal." *Il Veltro* 23 (1979): 229–40.

————. "Ordine e fortuna: Lo spazio della galea veneziana del '500." *Il Veltro* 27 (1983): 469–76.

————. "Permanenze nella storiografia religiosa italiana: Il XV Convegno di studi sulla Riforma e i movimenti religiosi in Italia (Torre Pellice, 1–3 settembre 1975)." *BSSV*, a. 96, no. 138 (1975): 131–48.

Olivieri Baldissarri, M. *I "poveri prigioni": La confraternità della Santa Croce e della Pietà dei carcerati a Milano nei secc. XVI–XVIII.* Milan, 1985.

O'Neil, M. "Magical Healing, Love Magic, and the Inquisition in Late Sixteenth-Century Modena." In *Inquisition and Society in Early Modern Europe*, ed. and trans. S. Haliczer, 88–114. London and Sydney, 1987.

————. "Sacerdote ovvero strione. Ecclesiastical and Superstitious Remedies in 16th-Century Italy." In *Understanding Popular Culture*, ed. S. Kaplan, 53–83. Berlin, 1984.

Orano, D. *Liberi pensatori bruciati in Roma dal XVI al XVIII secolo.* Rome, 1904. Reprint Livorno, 1971.

Ordini da osservarsi da gl'Inquisitori, per decreto della Sacra Congregatione del Sant'Officio di Roma. Rome, 1611.

Orlandi, G. *La fede al vaglio: Quietismo, satanismo e massoneria nel ducato di Modena tra Sette e Ottocento.* Modena, 1988.

Ortolani, O. *Per la storia della vita religiosa italiana nel Cinquecento: Pietro Carnesecchi. Con estratti dagli atti del processo del Santo Officio.* Florence, 1963.

Osbat, L. "Un importante centro di documentazione per la storia del Mezzogiorno d'Italia nell'età moderna: L'archivio storico diocesano di Napoli." *Melanges de l'École Française de Rome* 85 (1973): 311–59.

————. *L'Inquisizione a Napoli: Il processo agli ateisti, 1688–1697.* Rome, 1974.

————. "I processi del Sant'Ufficio a Napoli: Alcuni problemi di metodo." In *La società religiosa nell'età moderna*, 941–61. Naples, 1973.

————. "La sezione 'denunce' del fondo 'Sant'Ufficio' nell'archivio storico diocesano di Napoli." In *Atti del Congresso internazionale di studi sull'età del Viceregno*, 2:403–33. Bari, 1977.

————. "Sulle fonti per la storia del Sant' Ufficio a Napoli alla fine del Seicento." *Ricerche di storia sociale e religiosa* 1 (1972): 419–27.

Ossola, C. "Lutero e Juan de Valdés: Intorno alla formula 'Beneficio di Cristo.'" In *Lutero e la Riforma, Vicenza, 27/28 Novembre 1983.* Vicenza, n.d. (I have consulted the offprint).

Pagano, S. M., ed. *I documenti del processo di Galileo Galilei . . . collaborazione di Antonio G. Luciani.* Pontificiae Academiae Scientiarum Scripta Varia, 53. Vatican City, 1984.

————. "L'edizione delle istruzioni generali di Clemente VIII." *Benedictina* 33 (1986): 183–90.

————, and Ranieri, C. *Nuovi documenti su Vittoria Colonna e Reginald Pole*, Collectanea Archivi Vaticani, 24. Vatican City, 1989.

Paglia, V. *La morte confortata: Riti della paura e mentalità religiosa a Roma nell'età moderna.* Rome, 1982.

――――. *"La pietà dei carcerati": Confraternite e società a Roma nei secoli XVI–XVIII.* Rome, 1980.

Palese, S. "Pratiche magiche e religiosità popolare in terra di Bari durante l'epoca moderna." In *Scritti demolinguistici, Studi e ricerche,* 1:221–42. Bari, 1978.

Panella, A. *Gli archivi fiorentini durante il dominio francese, 1808–1814.* Florence, 1911.

――――. "La censura sulla stampa e una questione giurisdizionale fra stato e chiesa in Firenze alla fine del secolo XVI." *Archivio storico italiano,* ser. 5, 43 (1909): 140–51.

――――. "L'introduzione a Firenze dell'Indice di Paolo IV." *Rivista storica degli archivi toscani* 1 (1929): 11–25.

Panetta, M. *La "libraria" di Mattia Casanate.* Rome, 1988.

Panetta, R. *Pirati e corsari turchi e barbareschi nel mare nostrum, XVI secolo.* Milan, 1981.

Panizza, A. "I processi contro le streghe nel Trentino." *Archivio trentino* 7 (1888): 1–95.

Paolin, G. "Dell'ultimo tentativo compiuto in Friuli di formare una comunità Anabattista: Note e documenti." *NRS* 62 (1978): 3–28.

――――. "L'eterodossia nel monastero delle clarisse di Udine nella seconda metà del '500." *Collectanea franciscana* 50 (1980): 107–67.

Paolini, L., ed. *Il "De Officio Inquisitionis": La procedura inquisitoriale a Bologna e a Ferrara nel Trecento.* Bologna, 1976.

――――. "Le origini della 'Societas Crucis.'" *Rivista di storia e letteratura religiosa* 15 (1979): 173–229.

Parker, G. "Some Recent Work on the Inquisition in Spain and Italy." *Journal of Modern History* 54 (1982): 519–32.

Parnisetti, C. "La pena capitale in Alessandria e la confraternità di S. Giovanni Decollato." *Bollettino storico-bibliografico subalpino* 29 (1927): 353–463.

Paschini, P. "Episodi dell'Inquisizione a Roma nei suoi primi decenni." *Studi romani* 5 (1957): 285–301.

――――. *Eresia e riforma cattolica al confine orientale d'Italia.* Lateranum, n.s., 17, nos. 1–4. Rome, 1951.

――――. "Letterati ed Indice nella Riforma Cattolica in Italia." In *Cinquecento romano e riforma cattolica,* 237–373. Rome, 1958.

Pastor, Ludwig von. *Allgemeine Dekrete der römischen Inquisition aus den Jahren 1555–1597. Nach dem Notariatsprotokoll des S. Uffizio zum ersten Male veröffentlicht.* Freiburg i. Br., 1912 (originally published in the *Historisches Jahrbuch der Görres-Gesellschaft* 33 [1912]: 479–549).

――――. *The History of the Popes from the Close of the Middle Ages.* 40 vols. St. Louis, 1898–1953.

Pasztor, L. "La Curia romana e i registri di bolle papali." *Studi romani* 17 (1969): 319–23.

――――. *Guida delle fonti per la storia dell'America latina negli archivi della Santa Sede e negli archivi ecclesiastici d'Italia.* Collectanea Archivi Vaticani, 2. Vatican City, 1970.

Patschovsky, A. *Die Anfänge einer ständigen Inquisition in Böhmen: Ein Prager Inquisitoren-Handbuch aus der ersten Hälfte des 14. Jahrhunderts.* Berlin, 1975.

Paulus, N. *Hexenwahn und Hexenprozess vornehmlich im 16. Jahrhundert.* Freiburg i. Br., 1910.

Peña, Francisco. *Instructio seu Praxis Inquisitorum.* In Cesare Carena, *Tractatus de Officio Sanctissimae Inquisitionis,* 348–434. Bologna, 1668.

————, ed. *Tractatus illustrium in utraque tum pontificii, tum Caesarei iuris facultate iurisconsultorum de iudiciis criminalibus S. Inquisitionis . . . Tomi XI, Pars II.* Venice, 1584.

Perini, L. "Ancora sul libraio-tipografo Pietro Perna e su alcune figure di eretici italiani in rapporto con lui negli anni 1549–1555." *NRS* 51 (1967): 363–404.

————. "Contributo alla ricostruzione della biblioteca privata dei Granduchi di Toscana nel XVI secolo." In *Studi di storia medievale e moderna per Ernesto Sestan,* 571–667. Florence, 1980.

————. "Editori e potere in Italia dalla fine del secolo XV all' Unità." In *Storia d'Italia: Annali 4. Intellettuali e potere,* ed. C. Vivanti, 765–853. Turin, 1981.

————. "Note e documenti su Pietro Perna libraio-tipografo a Basilea." *NRS* 50 (1966): 145–200.

————. "Note sulla famiglia di Pietro Perna e sul suo apprendistato tipografico." In *Magia, astrologia e religione nel Rinascimento, Convegno polacco-italiano (Varsavia: 25–27 settembre 1972),* 163–209. Wroclaw, Warsaw, etc., 1974.

Perocco, D. "Lodovico Castelvetro traduttore di Melantone (Vat. Lat. 7755)." *Giornale storico della letteratura italiana* 156 (1979): 541–47.

Perreaud, François. *Demonologie, ou traitté des demons et sorciers.* Geneva, 1653.

Pesenti, G. "Libri censurati a Venezia nei secoli XVI–XVII." *La Bibliofilia* 58 (1956): 15–30.

Peters, E. "Editing Inquisitors' Manuals in the Sixteenth Century: Francisco Peña and the *Directorium Inquisitorum* of Nicholas Eymeric." *The Library Chronicle* 40 (1974): 95–107.

————. *Inquisition.* New York and London, 1988.

————. "*Res fragilis*: Torture in Early European Law." In Peters' *The Magician, the Witch and the Law,* 183–95. Philadelphia, 1978.

————. *Torture.* Oxford and New York, 1985.

Petrocchi, M. *Esorcismi e magia nell'Italia del Cinquecento e Seicento.* Naples, 1951.

Peyronel Rambaldi, S. *Speranze e crisi nel Cinquecento modenese: Tensioni religiose e vita cittadina ai tempi di Giovanni Morone.* Milan, 1979.

Piazza, Hieronimo. *A Short and True Account of the Inquisition and Its Proceedings . . . in Italy. . . .* London, 1722.

Piccolomini, P. "Corrispondenza tra la corte di Roma e l'inquisitore di Malta durante la guerra di Candia (1645–69)." *Archivio storico italiano,* ser. 5, 41 (1908): 45–127.

————. "Documenti del R. Archivio di Stato in Siena sull'eresia in questa città durante il secolo XVI." *Bullettino senese di storia patria* 17 (1910): 3–35.

————. "Documenti fiorentini sull'eresia in Siena durante il secolo XVI (1559–1570)." *Bulletino senese di storia patria* 17 (1910): 159–99.

Pico, Giovanni Francesco. *Dialogus in tres libros divisus: Titulus est Strix, sive de Lu-dificatione Daemonum.* Bologna, 1523, etc.

Piero Guicciardini (1808–86): Un riformatore religioso nell' Europa dell'Ottocento: Atti del convegno di studi, Firenze, 11–12 aprile 1986. Florence, 1988.

Pignatelli, Giacopo. *Novissimae Consultationes Canonicae, praecipuas controversias . . . praesertimque illas quae circa S. Inquisitionis tribunal versantur,* 2 vols. Cosmopoli, 1711. New ed. Venice, 1736.

Pike, R. "Penal Servitude in Early Modern Spain: The Galleys." *Journal of European Economic History* 2 (1982): 197–217.

———. *Penal Servitude in Early Modern Spain.* Madison, 1983.

Pitré, G. *Del Sant'Uffizio a Palermo e di un carcere di esso.* Rome, 1940.

Plaisance, M. "Littérature et censure à Florence à la fin du XVIe siècle: Le retour du censuré." *Le pouvoir et la plume,* 233–52.

Polacco, Giorgio. *Breve raccontamento di quanto gli è occorso nel corso di trenta sei anni continui mentre è stato confessor delle venerande monache di Santa Lucia di Venezia.* Venice, 1643.

Polverini Fosi, I. "Un processo per 'streghe e furfanterie' nella Roma di Paolo IV." *Ricerche per la storia religiosa di Roma* 4 (1980): 215–36.

Pommier, E. "Notes sur la propagande protestante dans la République de Venise au milieu du XVIe siècle." In *Aspects de la propagande religieuse,* Travaux d'Humanisme et Renaissance, 28. Geneva, 1957, pp. 240–46.

Popper, W. *The Censorship of Hebrew Books.* New York, 1899. Reprint New York, 1968.

Porta, P. D. R. da. *Historia Reformationis Ecclesiarum Raeticarum.* 2 vols. Chur, 1771–77.

Porteau-Bitker, A. "L'emprisonnement dans le droit laïque du Moyen-âge." *Revue historique de droit français et étranger* 46 (1968): 211–45, 389–428.

Pouvoir (Le) et la plume: Incitation, contrôle et répression dans l'Italie du XVIe siècle. Actes du Colloque international organisé par le Centre Interuniversitaire de Recherche sur la Renaissance italienne et l'Institut Culturel Italien de Marseille: Aix-en-Provence, Marseille, 14–16 mai 1981. Paris, 1982.

Prete, S. "Le 'Difese' del Capitano Paolino Paolini da Offida al Santo Ufficio (1627)." *RSCI* 15 (1961): 491–97.

Problemi di vita religiosa in Italia nel Cinquecento. Atti del Convegno di storia della Chiesa in Italia (Bologna, 2–6 Sett. 1958). Italia Sacra, 2. Padua, 1960.

Procacci, G. *Studi sulla fortuna del Machiavelli.* Rome, 1965.

Prodi, P. *Il Cardinale Paleotti (1522–1597).* Uomini e Dottrine, 7, 12. 2 vols. Rome, 1959–67.

———. *La crisi religiosa del XVI secolo.* Bologna, 1964.

———. *Il sovrano pontefice.* Bologna, 1982. Translated as *The Papal Prince, One Body and Two Souls: The Papal Monarchy in Early Modern Europe,* trans. S. Haskins. Cambridge, 1987.

———. "Storia sacra e controriforma: Nota sulla censura al commento di Carlo

Sigonio a Sulpicio Severo." *Annali dell'Istituto storico italo-germanico di Trento* 3 (1977): 75–104.

———. *Lo sviluppo dell'assolutismo nello stato pontificio, secoli XV–XVI. 1. La monarchia papale e gli organi centrali di governo.* Bologna, 1968.

Prosperi, A. "Il 'budget' di un inquisitore: Ferrara, 1567–1572." *Schifanoia* 2 (1987): 31–40.

———. "Inquisitori e streghe nel Seicento fiorentino" in *Gostanza, la strega di San Miniato, processo a una guaritrice nella Toscana medicea*, ed. F. Cardini, 217–50. Rome and Bari, 1989.

———. "L'Inquisizione fiorentina al tempo di Galileo." In *Novità celesti e crisi del sapere: Atti del convegno internazionale di studi galileiani.* Supplement to the *Annali dell' Istituto e Museo di Storia della Scienza*, Anno 1983, fasc. 2: 315–25.

———. "L'Inquisizione fiorentina dopo il Concilio di Trento." *Annuario dell' Istituto storico italiano per l'età moderna e contemporanea* 37–38 (1985–86): 97–124.

———. "L'Inquisizione romana e la morte dell'eretico." In *Glaubensprozesse-Prozesse des Glaubens? Religiöse Minderheiten zwischen Toleranz und Inquisition*, ed. T. Heydenreich and P. Blumenthal, 43–52. Stuttgart, 1989.

———. "Mediatori di emozioni: La compagnia ferrarese di giustizia e l'uso delle immagini." In *L'impresa di Alfonso II: Saggi e documenti sulla produzione artistica a Ferrara nel secondo Cinquecento.* Bologna, 1987.

———. "Il sangue e l'anima: Ricerche sulle compagnie di giustizia in Italia." *Quaderni storici* 17 (1982): 959–99.

———. "Vicari dell' Inquisizione fiorentina alla metà del Seicento: Note d'Archivio." *Annali dell'Istituto storico italo-germanico in Trento* 8 (1982): 275–304.

Pullan, B. *The Jews of Europe and the Inquisition of Venice, 1550–1670.* Oxford, 1983. Translated as *Gli Ebrei d'Europa e l'Inquisizione a Venezia dal 1550 al 1670.* Rome, 1985.

———. "'A Ship with Two Rudders': 'Righetto Marrano' and the Inquisition in Venice." *The Historical Journal* 20 (1977): 25–58.

Quétif, Jacobus, and Echard, Jacobus *Scriptores Ordinis Praedicatorum.* 4 vols. Paris, 1719–23. Reprint New York, 1959.

[Rastrelli, Modesto]. *Fatti attenenti all'Inquisizione e sua istoria generale e particolare di Toscana.* Venice, 1782. Reprint Florence, 1783.

Razzi, Serafino. *Istoria degli Huomini illustri, così nelle prelature come nelle dottrine, del Sacro Ordine degli Predicatori.* Lucca, 1596.

Recensio manuscriptorum codicum qui ex universa Bibliotheca Vaticana selecti iussu Dni Nri. Pii VI . . . procuratoribus Gallorum jure belli . . . et initiae pacis traditi fuere. Leipzig, 1803.

Regesti di bandi, editti, notificazioni e provvedimenti diversi relativi alla città di Roma ed allo stato pontificio. 7 vols. Rome, 1920–28.

Registres de la Compagnie des Pasteurs de Genève au temps de Calvin. Geneva, 1964–.

Reinhard, J. R. "Burning at the Stake in Medieval Law and Literature." *Speculum* 16 (1941): 186–209.

Relazioni dei rettori veneti in Terraferma. Milan, 1973–.

Potestà civile e autorità spirituale in Italia nei secoli della Riforma e Controriforma, ed. G. Catalano and F. Martino. Milan, 1984.

Remy, Nicholas. *Daemonolatreiae libri tres.* Lyons, 1595.

Repertorium Inquisitorum Pravitatis Haereticae. In quo omnia, quae ad haeresum cognitionem, ac S. Inquisitionis forum pertinent, continentur: Correctionibus, & annotationibus praestantissimorum Iurisconsultorum Quintilliani Mandosii, ac Petri Vendrameni decoratum & auctum. Venice, 1588.

Represa Rodríguez, A. "Documentos sobre Inquisición en el Archivo de Simancas." In *La Inquisición española*, ed. J. P. Villanueva, 845–54.

Reusch, F. H. *Der Index der verbotenen Bücher.* 2 vols. Bonn, 1883–85.

———. *Die Indices Librorum Prohibitorum des sechzehnten Jahrhunderts.* Tübingen, 1886. Reprint Nieuwkoop, 1961.

Reviglio della Veneria, C. *L'Inquisizione medioevale ed il processo inquisitorio.* 2nd ed. Turin, 1951.

Reyes, A. "La confesión y la tortura en la historia de la iglesia." *Revista española del derecho canonico* 24 (1968): 595–624.

Rhodes, D. E. "Libri inglesi recensiti a Roma, 1668–1681." In Rhodes's *Studies in Early Printing*, 79–88. London, 1982.

———. "Some Notes on the Import of Books from Italy into England, 1628–1650." In Rhodes's *Studies in Early Printing*, 319–26. London, 1982.

Richter, M. "Giulio Cesare Paschali: Attività e problemi di un poeta italiano nella Ginevra di Calvino e di Beza." *Rivista di storia e letteratura religiosa* 1 (1965): 228–57.

Richthofen, E. "A Spanish Inquisitor's Objections to Erasmus." *Erasmus in English*, no. 7 (1975): 4–6.

Riggio, A. "Schiavi calabresi in Tunisia barbaresca (1583–1701)." *Archivio storico per la Calabria e la Lucania* 5 (1935): 131–77.

Righi, A. "Eretici a Verona nella seconda metà del secolo XVI." *Nuovo archivio veneto*, ser. 3, 20 (1910): 305–13.

Righi, C. "L'Inquisizione ecclesiastica a Modena nel Settecento." In *Formazione e controllo della opinione pubblica a Modena nel Settecento*, ed. A. Biondi, 53–95. Modena, 1986.

Ritter, J. F. *Friedrich von Spee, 1591–1635: Ein Edelmann, Mahner und Dichter.* Trier, 1977.

Ritzler, R. "Die Verschleppung der paepstlichen Archive nach Paris unter Napoleon I und deren Rückführung nach Rom in den Jahren 1815 bis 1817." *Römische Historische Mitteilungen* 6–7 (1962–64): 144–90.

Robbins, R. H. *Encyclopedia of Witchcraft and Demonology.* New York, 1974.

———. Introduction to *Catalogue of the Witchcraft Collection in Cornell University Library.* Millwood, 1977.

Robinson, J. M. *Cardinal Consalvi, 1757–1824.* New York, 1987.

Roda, M. "Processi per stregoneria in Val Levantina." *NRS* 63 (1979): 331–48.

Rodolico, N. *Stato e chiesa in Toscana durante la reggenza lorenese (1737–1765)*. Florence, 1910.

Rojas, Juan de. *Singularis iuris in favorem fidei, haeresisque detestationem, Tractatus de haereticis*, ed. F. Peña. Venice, 1583.

Roma ermetica: Cultura esoterica e società a Roma tra XV e XVIII secolo: Manoscritti ed immagini. Rome, 1983.

Romanello, M. "Culti magici e stregoneria del clero friulano." *Lares* 36 (1970): 341–72.

Romeo, G. "Una città, due inquisizioni: L'anomalia del Sant'Ufficio a Napoli nel tardo '500." *Rivista di storia e letteratura religiosa* 24 (1988): 42–67.

———. *Inquisitori, esorcisti e streghe nell'Italia della Controriforma*. Florence, 1990.

———. "Per la storia del Sant'Ufficio a Napoli tra '500 e '600: Documenti e problemi." *Campania sacra* 7 (1976): 5–109.

Rosi, M. "La Riforma religiosa in Liguria e l'eretico umbro Bartolomeo Bartoccio." *Atti della società ligure di storia patria* 24 (1892): 555–726.

Rossi, P. *Clavis Universalis: Arti mnemoniche e logica combinatoria da Lullo a Leibniz*. Milan, 1960.

Rostagno, L. "Apostasia all'Islam e Santo Ufficio in un processo dell' Inquisizione veneziana." *Il Veltro* 23 (1979): 293–313.

———. *Mi faccio Turco: Esperienze ed immagini dell'Islam nell'Italia moderna*. Studi e materiali sulla conoscenza dell'Oriente in Italia. Rome, 1983.

Rotelli, E. "Il XVI convegno di studi sulla Riforma ed i movimenti religiosi in Italia." *BSSV*, a. 97, no. 140 (1976): 129–37.

Roth, C. "The Inquisitional Archives as a Source of English History." *Transactions of the Royal Historical Society*, ser. 4, 18 (1935): 107–22.

———. *The Jews in Venice*. Philadelphia, 1930.

Rotondò, A., ed. *Camillo Renato, opere, documenti e testimonianze*. Corpus Reformatorum Italicorum. Florence and Chicago, 1968.

———. "La censura ecclesiastica e la cultura." In *Storia d'Italia: I documenti*, 5, pt. 2: 1399–1492. Turin: Einaudi, 1973.

———. "Cultura umanistica e difficoltà di censori: Censura ecclesiastica e discussioni cinquecentesche sul Platonismo." In *Le pouvoir et la plume*, 15–50.

———. *Lelio Sozzini, Opere*. Edizione critica. Studi e testi per la storia religiosa del Cinquecento, 1. Florence, 1986.

———. "Nuovi documenti per la storia dell' 'Indice dei Libri Proibiti' (1572–1638)." *Rinascimento*, ser. 2, 3 (1963): 145–211.

———. "Per la storia dell'eresia a Bologna nel secolo XVI." *Rinascimento*, ser. 2, 2 (1962): 107–54.

———. *Studi e ricerche di storia ereticale italiana del Cinquecento*. Pubblicazioni dell'Istituto di Scienze Politiche dell'Università di Torino, 31. Turin, 1974.

Rovetta, A. *Bibliotheca Chronologica Illustrium Virorum Provinciae Lombardiae Sacri Ord. Praedicatorum*. Bologna, 1691.

Rozzo, U. "Dieci anni di censura libraria (1596–1605)." *Libri e documenti* 9 (1983): 43–61.

————. "Pio V e la biblioteca di Bosco Marengo." In *Pio V e Santa Croce di Bosco: Aspetti di una committenza papale*, 315–40. Alessandria, 1985.

————. "Il rogo dei libri: Appunti per una iconologia." *Libri e documenti* 12 (1986): 7–32.

Rudt de Collenberg, W. H. *Esclavage et rançons des chrétiens en Méditerranée (1570–1600), d'après les "Litterae Hortatoriae" de l'Archivio Segreto Vaticano.* Paris, 1987.

Ruffini, F. *Studi sui riformatori italiani*, ed. A. Bertola, L. Firpo, E. Ruffini. Pubblicazioni dell'Istituto di Scienze Politiche dell'Università di Torino, 3. Turin, 1955.

Ruffino, O. "Ricerche sulla condizione giuridica degli eretici nel pensiero dei glossatori." *Rivista di storia del diritto italiano* 46 (1973): 30–190.

Ruiz, T. R. "La Inquisición medieval y la moderna: Paralelos y contrastes." In *Inquisición española y mentalidad inquisitorial*, ed. A. Alcalá, 45–66. Translated as "The Holy Office in Medieval France and in Late Medieval Castile: Origins and Contrasts." In *The Spanish Inquisition and the Inquisitorial Mind*, ed. A. Alcalá, 33–51.

Russell, J. B. *Witchcraft in the Middle Ages*. Ithaca, 1972.

Sala-Molins, L. *Le dictionnaire des inquisiteurs: Valence 1494*. Paris, 1981. A modern version and translation of the *Repertorium Inquisitorum*.

————. *Le manuel des Inquisiteurs*. Paris, 1973. A modern version and translation of Eymeric's *Directorium Inquisitorum*.

————. "Utilisation d'Aristote en droit inquisitorial." In *XVI Colloque International de Tours: Platon et Aristote à la Renaissance*, 191–99. Paris, 1976.

Salazar, L. "Documenti del Santo Officio nella Biblioteca del Trinity College." *Archivio storico per le province napoletane* 33 (1908): 466–73.

Salelles, Sébastian. *De materiis Tribunalium S. Inquisitionis, seu de Regulis multiplicibus pro formando quovis eorum ministro, praesertim consultore. . .* 3 vols. Rome, 1651–56.

Salem, A. R. "The Badly Printed Book of an Unfortunate Author: The *Epistolae* of Aonio Paleario." *Harvard Library Bulletin* 2 (1948): 249–52.

Salimbeni, F., ed. *Le lettere di Paolo Bisanti, vicario generale del Patriarca di Aquileia (1577–1587).* Rome, 1977.

————. "La stregoneria nel tardo Rinascimento." *NRS* 60 (1976): 269–334.

Sallmann, J. M. *Chercheurs de trésors et jeteuses de sorts: La quête du surnaturel à Naples au XVIe s.* Paris, 1986.

Sambuc, J. "Le procès de Jean de Roma, inquisiteur, Apt 1532." *BSSV*, a. 97, no. 139 (1976): 45–55.

S.mi D.N.D. Gregorii Papae XV. Constitutio adversus Maleficia, seu Sortilegia Committentes. Rome, 1623.

Sandonnini, T. *Lodovico Castelvetro e la sua famiglia: Note biografiche.* Bologna, 1882.

Santini, L. "A proposito di una traduzione del *Piccolo Catechismo di M. Lutero*." *NRS* 49 (1965): 627–35.

Santosuosso, A. "The Moderate Inquisitor: Giovanni Della Casa's Venetian Nunciature, 1544–1549." *Studi veneziani*, n.s., 2 (1978): 119–210.

Sarpi, Paolo. *Historia della Sacra Inquisitione: Composta già dal R.P. Paolo Servita ed hora la prima volta posta in luce.* Serravalle, 1638.

Sarra, M. "Distribuzione statistica dei dati processuali dell'inquisizione in Friuli dal 1557 al 1786: Tecniche di ricerca e risultati." *Metodi e ricerche*, n.s., 7 (1988): 5–31.

Sarti, N. "Appunti su carcere-custodia e carcere-pena nella dottrina civilistica dei secoli XII–XVI." *Rivista di storia del diritto italiano* 53–54 (1980–81): 67–110.

Sbaraglia, G. G. *Supplementum et castigatio ad scriptores trium ordinum S. Francisci, A. Waddingo aliisve descriptos*. 3 vols. Rome, 1908–36.

Scaduto, M. "Le carceri della Vicaria di Napoli agli inizi del Seicento." *Redenzione umana* 6 (1968): 393–412.

――――. "Lainez e l'Indice del 1559." *Archivum Historicum Societatis Iesu* 24 (1955): 3–32.

――――. "Tra inquisitori e riformati: Le missioni dei Gesuiti tra Valdesi della Calabria e delle Puglie, con un carteggio inedito del card. Alessandrino (S. Pio V), 1561–1566." *Archivum Historicum Societatis Iesu* 15 (1946): 1–76.

Scanaroli, Giovanni Battista. *De Visitatione Carceratorum Libri Tres*. Rome, 1655.

Scarabello, G. *Carcerati e carceri a Venezia nell' età moderna*. Rome, 1979.

――――. "Figure del popolo veneziano in un processo degli Esecutori contro la bestemmia alla fine del' 700." *Studi veneziani* 17–18 (1975–76): 321–98.

――――. "La pena del carcere: Aspetti della condizione carceraria a Venezia nei secoli XVI-XVIII." In *Stato, società e giustizia nella repubblica veneta (sec. XV–XVIII)*, ed. G. Cozzi, 317–76. Rome, 1980.

Schatzmiller, J. "Processi del Sant'Uffizio di Venezia contro ebrei e giudaizzanti." *Studi storici* 28 (1987): 531–35.

Schelhorn, J. G. *De vita, fatis ac meritis Philippi Camerarii*. Nuremberg, 1740.

Schiess, T., ed. *Bullingers Korrespondenz mit den Graubündnern*. Quellen zur Schweizer Geschichte, 23–25. 3 vols. Basel, 1904–6.

Schottenloher, K. *Bibliographie zur deutschen Geschichte im Zeitalter der Glaubensspaltung, 1517–1585*. 7 vols. Leipzig, 1933–66.

Schulte, J. F. von. *Die Geschichte der Quellen und Literatur des Canonischen Rechts*. 3 vols. Stuttgart, 1875. Reprint Graz, 1956.

Schutte, Anne J. "Un inquisitore al lavoro: Fra Marino da Venezia e l'Inquisizione veneziana." In *I Francescani in Europa tra Riforma e Controriforma: Atti del XIII Convegno internazionale, Assisi, 17–18–19 ottobre 1985*, 165–96. Perugia, 1987.

――――. "Periodization of Sixteenth-Century Italian Religious History: The Post-Cantimori Paradigm Shift." *Journal of Modern History* 61 (1989): 269–84.

――――. *Pier Paolo Vergerio: The Making of an Italian Reformer*. Travaux d'Humanisme et Renaissance, 160. Geneva, 1977. Translated as *Pier Paolo Vergerio e la Riforma a Venezia, 1498–1549*. Rome, 1988.

Schwendt, H. H. "Der römische Index der verbotenen Bücher." *Historisches Jahrbuch* 107 (1987): 296–314.

Segatti, E. "La *Cautio Criminalis* di Friedrich von Spee fra precedenti e contemporanei." In *Studi di letteratura religiosa tedesca in memoria di Sergio Lupi*, 375–441. Florence, 1972.

Segl, P., ed., *Der Hexenhammer: Enstehung und Umfeld des "Malleus maleficarum" von 1487*. Cologne, 1988.

Segre, R. "Il mondo ebraico nei cardinali della Controriforma." In *Italia Judaica: "Gli Ebrei in Italia tra Rinascimento ed Età barocca": Atti del II Convegno internazionale, Genova 10–15 giugno 1984.* Ministero per i Beni Culturali e Ambientali, 119–38. Rome, 1986.

————. "Neophytes during the Italian Counter-Reformation: Identities and Bibliographies." In *Proceedings of the Sixth World Congress of Jewish Studies, Held at the Hebrew University of Jerusalem, 13–19 August 1973.* 2 vols., 2:131–42. Jerusalem, 1975–77.

Seidel Menchi, S. *Erasmo in Italia, 1520–1580.* Turin, 1987.

————. "Humanismus und Reformation im Spiegel der italienischen Inquisitionsprozessakten." In *Renaissance-Reformation: Gegensätze und Gemeinsamkeiten,* ed. A. Buck, 47–64. Wiesbaden, 1984.

————. "Inquisizione come repressione o Inquisizione come mediazione? Una proposta di periodizzazione." *Annuario dell'Istituto storico italiano per l'età moderna e contemporanea* 35–36 (1983–84): 53–77.

————. "Lo stato degli studi sulla Riforma in Italia." *Wolfenbütteler Renaissance-Mitteilungen* 5 (1981): 35–42, 89–92.

————. "Le traduzioni italiane di Lutero nella prima metà del Cinquecento." *Rinascimento* 17 (1977): 31–108.

Selge, K.-V., ed. *Texte zur Inquisition.* Gütersloh, 1967.

Shannon, A. C. "The Secrecy of Witnesses in Inquisitorial Tribunals and in Contemporary Secular Trials." In *Essays in Medieval Life and Thought Presented in Honor of Austin Patterson Evans,* ed. J. Mundy, 59–69. New York, 1955.

Signorotto, G. *Inquisitori e mistici nel Seicento italiano: L'eresia di Santa Pelagia.* Annali dell'Istituto storico italo-germanico in Trento. Monografia, 11. Bologna, 1989.

Silvestri, A. "I costituti per l'abiura di suor Eleonora de Ruggiero: Un episodio di possessione diabolica nel monastero di S. Maria Donnaregina in Napoli nell'età della Controriforma." *Rivista di letteratura e di storia ecclesiastica* 10 (1978), nos. 1–2: 3–32.

Simancas, Iacobo de. *De Catholicis Institutionibus Liber, ad praecavendas & extirpandas haereses admodum necessarius.* Rome, 1575.

————. *Enchiridion Iudicum Violatae Religionis, ad extirpandas haereses, theoricen & praxim summa brevitate complectens.* Antwerp, 1573.

Simoncelli, P. *Il caso Reginald Pole: Eresia e santità nelle polemiche religiose del Cinquecento.* Rome, 1977.

————. "Clemente VIII e alcuni provvedimenti del Sant'Uffizio ('De Italis habitantibus in partibus haereticorum')." *Critica storica* 13 (1976): 129–72.

————. "Documenti interni alla Congregazione dell'Indice, 1571–1590: Logica e ideologia dell'intervento censorio." *Annuario dell'Istituto storico italiano per l'età moderna e contemporanea* 35–36 (1983–84): 188–215.

————. "Inquisizione romana e Riforma in Italia." *RSI* 100 (1988): 5–125.

Società e cultura del Cinquecento nel Friuli occidentale. Catalogo della mostra, ed. P. Goi. Chap. 5, "Inquisizione." Pordenone, 1985.

396

Select Bibliography

Soman, A. "La decriminalisation de la sorcellerie en France." Histoire, économie et
société 4 (1985), no. 4: 179–203.

———. "Deviance and Criminal Justice in Western Europe, 1300–1800: An Essay
in Structure." Criminal Justice History 1 (1980): 1–28.

———. "La justice criminelle aux XVIe-XVIIe siècles: Le Parlement de Paris et
les sièges subalternes." In Actes du 107e Congrès national des Sociétés savantes, Brest,
1982, Section de Philologie et d'Histoire jusqu'à 1610: 1. La faute, la répression et le
pardon, 15–52. Paris, 1984.

———. "The Parlement of Paris and the Great Witch Hunt (1565–1640)." The
Sixteenth Century Journal 9 (1978), no. 2: 31–44.

Sommervogel, C. Bibliothèque de la Compagnie de Jésus ... nouvelle édition. 12 vols.
Brussels, Paris, and Toulouse, 1890–1911. Reprint 1960.

Sorrentino, A. La letteratura italiana e il Sant'Uffizio. Naples, 1935.

———. "Il Petrarca e il Sant'Uffizio." Giornale storico della letteratura italiana 101
(1933): 259–76.

———. Storia dell' antimachiavellismo europeo. Naples, 1936.

Spaccini, G. B. Cronaca di Modena dal 1588 al 1636, ed. P. E. Vicini, T. Sandonnini,
G. Bertoni. Modena, 1911–1919.

Spampanato, V. Documenti della vita di Giordano Bruno. Florence, 1933.

Spee, F. von. Cautio criminalis, ovvero dei processi contro le streghe. Edizione italiana
a cura di A. Foa. Traduzione di N. Timi. Rome, 1986.

Stella, A. Anabattismo e antitrinitarismo in Italia nel XVI secolo. Padua, 1969.

———. Chiesa e stato nelle relazioni dei nunzi pontifici a Venezia. Ricerche sul giurisdizionalismo veneziano dal XVI al XVIII secolo. Studi e Testi, 239. Vatican City,
1964.

———. Dall'Anabattismo al Socinianesimo nel Cinquecento veneto. Padua, 1967.

———. "L'Inquisizione romana e i movimenti eretici al tempo di San Pio V."
In San Pio V e la problematica del suo tempo, 65–82. Alessandria, 1972.

———. "Il processo veneziano di Guglielmo Postel." RSCI 22 (1968): 425–66.

———. "Ricerche sul Socinianesimo: Il processo di Cornelio Sozzini e Claudio
Textor (Banière)." Bollettino dell'Istituto di Storia della Società e dello Stato veneziano
3 (1961): 77–120.

———. "Tentativi controriformistici nell'Università di Padova e il rettorato di Andrea
Gostynski." In Relazioni tra Padova e la Polonia, 75–87. Padua, 1964.

Stow, K. R. Catholic Thought and Papal Jewry Policy, 1555–1593. New York,
1977.

———. "Zorattini's 'Processi del S. Uffizio di Venezia.'" Jewish Quarterly Review
74 (1983/84): 88–90.

Stoye, J. English Travellers Abroad, 1604–1667. London, 1952.

Stregoneria (La): Diavoli, streghe, inquisitori dal Trecento al Settecento, ed. S. Abbiati,
A. Agnoletto, M. Rosario Lazzati. Milan, 1984.

Strumenti di tortura, 1400–1800 / Torture Instruments, 1400–1800, nella Casermetta di
Forte Belvedere, Firenze, May–September, 1983. Florence, 1983.

Stutz, J. "Eine kirchliche Instruktion über die Führung von Hexenprocessen." *Katholische Schweizerblätter für Wissenschaft, Kunst und Leben* (1888): 601–25.

Summers, M. *The Geography of Witchcraft.* New Hyde Park, 1965.

Szczucki, L. *Philippus Camerarius: Prawdziwa i wierna relacja o uwiezieniu w Rzymie.* Warsaw, 1984.

Taurisano, I. *Hierarchia Ordinis Praedicatorum.* Rome, 1916.

———. "Series Chronologica Commissariorum S. Romanae Inquisitionis ab Anno 1542 ad annum 1916." *Analecta Sacri Ordinis Fratrum Praedicatorum* (1916): 495–506.

Tedeschi, J. "The Cultural Contributions of Italian Protestant Reformers in the Late Renaissance." In *Libri, idee, e sentimenti religiosi nel Cinquecento italiano*, 81–108.

———. "Genevan Books of the Sixteenth Century." *Bibliothèque d'Humanisme et Renaissance* 31 (1969): 173–80.

———. "A 'Queer Story': The Inquisitorial Manuscripts." In *Treasures of the Library, Trinity College, Dublin*, ed. P. Fox, 67–74. Dublin, 1986.

———, and von Henneberg, J. "Contra Petrum Antonium a Cervia relapsum et Bononiae concrematum." In *Italian Reformation Studies in Honor of Laelius Socinus*, ed. J. Tedeschi, 243–68. Florence, 1965.

———, and Willis, E. D. "Two Italian Translations of Beza and Calvin." *Archiv für Reformationsgeschichte* 55 (1964): 70–74.

Tenenti, A. *Cristoforo da Canal: La marine vénitienne avant Lépante.* Paris, 1972.

———. *Piracy and the Decline of Venice.* London, 1967.

———. "Gli schiavi di Venezia alla fine del Cinquecento." *RSI* 67 (1955): 52–69.

Thomas, A. H. "La profession religieuse des Dominicains: Formule, cérémonies, histoire." *AFP* 39 (1969): 5–52.

Thorndike, L. "Alfodhol and Almadel: Hitherto Unnoted Medieval Books of Magic in Florentine Manuscripts." *Speculum* 2 (1927): 326–31.

———. *A History of Magic and Experimental Science.* 8 vols. New York, 1923–58.

Toffanin, G. *Machiavelli e il Tacitismo.* Padua, 1921.

Tomas y Valiente, F. *El derecho penal de la monarquía absoluta (siglos XVI–XVII–XVIII).* Chap. 3, "El proceso penal." Madrid, 1969.

———. "La tortura judicial y sus posibles supervivencias." In the author's *La tortura en España, estudios historicos*, 209–46. Barcelona, 1973.

Tomizza, F. *Il male viene dal nord: Il romanzo del vescovo Vergerio.* Milan, 1984.

Tori, G. "I rapporti tra lo stato e la chiesa a Lucca nei secoli XVI–XVIII: Le istituzioni." *Rassegna degli archivi di stato* 36 (1976): 37–81.

Tosti, S. "Descriptio codicum Franciscanorum Bibliothecae Riccardianae Florentinae." *Archivum Franciscanum Historicum* 8 (1915): 618–57.

Tractatus illustrium. See Peña, F.

Tres Indices Expurgatorios de la Inquisición Española en el Siglo XVI. Madrid, 1952.

Tresoldi, L. *Viaggiatori tedeschi in Italia, 1452–1870: Saggio bibliografico.* 2 vols. Rome, 1975–77.

Troncarelli, F., ed. *La città dei segreti: Magia, astrologia e cultura esoterica a Roma (XV–XVIII).* Milan, 1985.

Trusen, W. "Der Inquisitionsprozess: Seine historischen Grundlagen und frühen Formen." *Zeitschrift der Savigny-Stiftung für Rechtsgeschichte: Kanonistische Abteilung* 105 (1988): 168–230.

Ughelli, Ferdinando. *Italia Sacra.* 2nd ed. 10 vols. Venice, 1717–22.

Ugolini, Zanchino. "Tractatus de Haereticis." In *Tractatus illustrium*, ed. F. Peña, fols. 234r–271r.

Ullmann, W. "The Defense of the Accused in the Medieval Inquisition." *The Irish Ecclesiastical Record*, ser. 5, 73 (1950): 481–89.

————. "Reflections on Medieval Torture." *Juridical Review* 56 (1944): 123–37.

————. "Some Medieval Principles of Criminal Procedure." *Juridical Review* 59 (1947): 1–28.

Valenti, F. "Il carteggio di padre Girolamo Papino informatore estense dal Concilio di Trento durante il periodo bolognese." *Archivio storico italiano* 124, T. 451 (1966): 303–417.

Van Caenegem, R. "La preuve dans le droit du Moyen Age occidental." In *Recueils de la société Jean Bodin pour l'histoire comparative des institutions. XVII. La preuve. Deuxième partie. Moyen age et temps modernes*, 691–753. Brussels, 1965.

Van Calster, G. "La censure Louvaniste du Nouveau Testament et la rédaction de l'Index Erasmien expurgatoire de 1571." *Scrinium Erasmianum* 2: 379–436.

Van Den Gheyn, J. *Catalogue des Manuscrits de la Bibliothèque Royale de Belgique.* Vol. 4. Brussels, 1903.

Van der Vekene, E. *Bibliotheca Bibliographica Historiae Sanctae Inquisitionis.* 2 vols. Vaduz, 1982–83.

————. "Die gedruckten Ausgaben des *Directorium Inquisitorum* des Nicolaus Eymerich." *Gutenberg Jahrbuch* (1973): 286–97.

————. *Zur Bibliographie des Directorium Inquisitorum des Nicolaus Eymerich.* Luxembourg, 1961.

Vecchi, A. "Le memorie di un uomo da remo (1565–1576)." *Rivista marittima* 16 (1884): 51–80, 209–58.

Vella, A. P. *The Tribunal of the Inquisition in Malta.* Malta, 1964.

Verga, E. "Il municipio di Milano e l'Inquisizione di Spagna, 1563." *ASL*, ser. 3, 8 (1897): 86–127.

Vergara Doncel, M. "Breves notas sobre la Sección de Inquisición del Archivo Histórico Nacional." In *La Inquisición española*, ed. J. P. Villanueva, 839–43.

Vergerio, Pietro Paolo. *A gl'Inquisitori che sono per l'Italia: Del catalogo di libri eretici, stampati in Roma nell'anno presente MDLIX.* N.p., 1559.

Viario, A. "I forzati sulle galere veneziane (1760–1797)." *Studi veneziani*, n.s., 2 (1978): 225–50.

————. "La pena della galera." In *Stato, società e giustizia*, ed. G. Cozzi, 377–480.

Villani, P. "Origine e carattere della nunziatura di Napoli (1523–1569)." *Annuario dell' Istituto storico italiano per l'età moderna e contemporanea* 9–10 (1957–58): 283–539.

————, ed. *Nunziature di Napoli. I. 26 Luglio 1570–24 Maggio 1577.* Rome, 1962.

Villanueva, J. Pérez, ed. *La Inquisición española: Nueva visión, nuevos horizontes.* Madrid, 1980.

————, and Escandell Bonet, B., eds., *Historia de la Inquisición en España y America.* Madrid, 1984–.

Villien, A. "Le Sainte-Office et la suppression de la Congregation de l'Index." *Le canoniste contemporain* 40 (1917): 98–111.

Viscardi, G. M. "Magia, stregoneria e superstizioni nei sinodi lucani del Seicento." *Ricerche di storia sociale e religiosa* 27 (1985): 144–87.

Wadding, Lucas. *Annales Minorum, seu trium Ordinum a S. Francisco institutorum....* 3rd ed. 31 vols. Ad Claras Aquas, 1931–56.

Wakefield, W. L. "Inquisition." In *Dictionary of the Middle Ages,* ed. J. R. Strayer, 6:483–89. New York, 1985.

Walker, D. P. *Spiritual and Demonic Magic.* London, 1958.

————. *Unclean Spirits: Possession and Exorcism in France and England in the Late Sixteenth and Early Seventeenth Centuries.* Philadelphia, 1981.

Warhafftige Newe Zeittung, was sich für Empörung nach des Bapsts Pauli des IIII Todt, welcher den 18 Augusti dises 1559 Jars verschiden, zu Rom zugetragen hat ... Von Rom geschriben an einen guten Freundt in Deudtschlandt. N.p., n.d.

Weber, H. "L'exorcisme à la fin du XVI siècle, instrument de la Contre Reforme et spectacle Baroque." *Nouvelle revue du seizième siècle* 1 (1983): 79–101.

Weisz, J. S. *Pittura e Misericordia: The Oratory of S. Giovanni Decollato in Rome.* Ann Arbor, 1984.

Welles, M. X. *The Ranuzzi Manuscripts.* Austin, 1980.

Welti, M. "La contribution de Giovanni Bernardino Bonifacio, Marquis d'Oria, à l'édition princeps du *De haereticis an sint persequendi.*" *BSSV,* a. 90, no. 125 (1969): 45–49.

————. "Le grand animateur de la Renaissance tardive à Bale: Pierre Perna, éditeur, imprimeur et libraire." In *L'humanisme allemand (1480–1540): Colloque international de Tours,* 131–39. Munich and Paris, 1979.

————. *Kleine Geschichte der italienischen Reformation.* Gütersloh, 1985. Also in translation as *Breve storia della Riforma italiana.* Casale Monferrato, 1985.

Weyer, Johann. *De Praestigiis Daemonum, et Incantationibus, ac Veneficiis Libri V. Tertia editione.* Basel, 1566.

Willaert, L. *Après le Concile de Trente: La Restauration Catholique, 1563–1648.* Paris, 1960.

Witchcraft in Europe, 1100–1700: A Documentary History. Ed. with an introduction by A. C. Kors and E. Peters. Philadelphia, 1972.

Zaccagnini, G. "Le scuole e la libreria del convento di S. Domenico in Bologna dalle origini al secolo XVI." *Atti e Memorie della R. Deputazione di Storia Patria per le Provincie di Romagna,* ser. 4, 17 (1927): 228–37.

Zacchia, Paolo. *Quaestiones medico-legales in quibus omnes eae materiae medicae, quae ad legales facultates pertinere videntur, pertractantur et resolvuntur.* Lyons, 1630. New ed. Nuremberg, 1726.

Zanelli, A. "Di alcune controversie tra la Repubblica di Venezia e il Sant'Officio nei primi anni del pontificato di Urbano VIII (1624–1626)." *Archivio veneto*, ser. 5, 6 (1929): 186–235.

Zanier, G. "La nobiltà castellana e l'Inquisizione aquileiese." In *Castelli del Friuli. La vita nei castelli friulani*, ed. T. Miotti, 93–124. Udine, 1981.

Zarri, G. "Aspetti dello sviluppo degli ordini religiosi in Italia tra Quattro e Cinquecento: Studi e problemi." In *Strutture ecclesiastiche in Italia e in Germania prima della Riforma*, ed. P. Prodi and P. Johanek, 207–57. Bologna, 1983.

Zucchini, G. *Le librerie del convento di S. Domenico a Bologna*. Pistoia, 1937 (originally published in *Memorie domenicane*, 1936–37).

Index of Names

Hinschius, P. 155, 216
Hirsch, R. 40, 245
Horst, G. 220
Horstius, J. D. 250
Hotman, François 71
Houzeau, J. C. 334
Howland, A. C. 16, 19, 70, 124, 191, 216, 244, 256, 267
Hubert, F. 347, 348
Huerga Criado, P. 217, 224
Hunger, Konrad 210
Hyman, H. M. 16

Ilardi, V. 77
Innocent III 82, 137
Innocent IV 141, 175
Innocent IX 14. See also Facchinetti, Giovanni Antonio.
Innocent X 264, 265
Innocent XI 271
Invernizi, Lia 346
Ioly Zorattini, P. C. xiv, 41, 109, 111, 112, 120, 121, 216
Irenaeus 254
Isengrin, Michael 341
Iserloh, E. 12, 125, 162, 222

James, Thomas 296, 316
Jannaco, C. 313
Jansen, Cornelis 221
Jantz, H. 311
Jean de Roma 184
Jedin, H. 4, 76, 85
Jenny, B. R. 346
Jobe, P. H. xiv, 75, 83, 163, 350
Jöcher, C. G. 316
Johanek, P. 77
John Paul II 34
John XXIII 34
Johnston, N. 88
Jordani, Laelius 334
Jungmayr, J. 312

Kaeppeli, T. 80
Kamen, H. xiv, 16, 72
Kaplan, S. 251
Kaplan, Y. 120
Kellenbenz, H. 43
Kelly, H. A. xv
Kidd, B. J. 12, 156
Kieckhefer, R. 257
Kingdon, R. M. xiv
Kingholz, O. 221
Kinkead, D. 269
Knott, B. I. 332
Kors, A. C. 71
Kramer, Heinrich 247, 254
Kristeller, P. O. 35
Kurcz, A. 351
Kutter, M. 332, 351
Kuttner, S. 71

La Mantia, V. 116
Lainez, Diego 332
Lamattina, G. 331
Lancaster, A. 334
Landi, A. 110
Landi, R. 349
Lane, F. C. 196
Langbein, J. H. 8, 17, 18, 180, 189, 194, 202
Lanzoni, F. 157
Lanzoni, Silvio 85
Larquié, C. 118
Lattis, J. M. 308
Laurent, M.-H. 80
Lauro, A. 245, 247
Lavedan, Antonio 272
Laymann, Paul 218
Lea, H. C. 3, 7, 9, 15, 16, 52, 70, 103, 116, 124, 179, 180, 191, 201, 216, 217, 220, 221, 223, 230, 241, 244, 245, 256, 267
Lenci, M. 42
Lentolo, Scipione 342, 351, 352
Leo XIII 34

The Prosecution of Heresy consists of essays written over almost two decades on the theme of the pursuit of heresy in early modern Italy. It concentrates on the activities of the two bodies—the Congregations of the Inquisition and Index—established by the Catholic Church in the sixteenth century to counter the Protestant challenge in that country, and later the widespread phenomenon of witchcraft and the occult arts.

These essays, thoroughly revised and updated bibliographically for this volume, represent a pioneering effort to understand objectively the judicial processes and theories which constituted Inquisitorial law through a critical, firsthand examination of a broad range of primary sources. They overturn traditional platitudes and stereotypes which have long been associated with the work of the Holy Office, and persuasively argue that in legal terms the Inquisition provided one of the most modern and progressive forms of criminal justice available to the times.

John Tedeschi is an Honorary Member of the Department of History and Curator of Rare Books and Special Collections at Memorial Library at the University of Wisconsin, Madison. He has edited numerous volumes, including *Italian Reformation Studies* (1965), *Renaissance Studies in Honor of Hans Baron* (with Anthony Molho; 1971), and *The Inquisition in Early Modern Europe: Studies on Sources and Methods* (with Gustav Henningsen and Charles Amiel; 1986). In addition, he has translated with Anne C. Tedeschi three books by Carlo Ginzburg: *The Cheese and the Worms* (1980), *The Night Battles* (1983), and *Clues, Myths and the Historical Method* (1989).

mrts

medieval & renaissance texts & studies
is the publishing program of the
Center for Medieval and Early Renaissance Studies
at the State University of New York at Binghamton.

mrts emphasizes books that are needed —
texts, translations, and major research tools.

mrts aims to publish the highest quality scholarship
in attractive and durable format at modest cost.

DATE DUE

HIGHSMITH   # 45220